The Diary of
CALVIN FLETCHER

Volume I
1817-1838

*Published by the Indiana Historical Society
as a contribution to the observance of the
Sesquicentennial of Indianapolis, 1971*

Dedicated to
ELI LILLY
*whose appreciation
of the historical value
of the diary
has made possible its publication*

INDIANA HISTORICAL SOCIETY

Calvin Fletcher
by Jacob Cox, c.1833

The Diary of
CALVIN FLETCHER

Volume I
1817-1838

Including Letters of
CALVIN FLETCHER
and Diaries and Letters of His Wife
SARAH HILL FLETCHER

Edited by
GAYLE THORNBROUGH

INDIANA HISTORICAL SOCIETY
Indianapolis
1972

Contents

Illustrations

Introduction

The Diary of CALVIN FLETCHER extends from 1817 to 1866 and is contained in one unnumbered volume, 10 by 8¼ inches, and twelve numbered volumes, 13½ by 8½ inches. Into the former are bound the several diaries kept by Calvin Fletcher which cover intermittently the years between 1817 and 1834 and the diary of his wife Sarah Hill Fletcher, 1821–24, and two brief journals or diaries which she kept in 1830 and in December, 1837, and January, 1838. Also bound in this volume are miscellaneous papers including Fletcher's commission as prosecuting attorney and his licenses to practice law in Ohio and Indiana, some poems written by him, early family financial accounts, printed funeral notices (reflecting a custom of the day), clippings, and broadsides. On the flyleaf of this volume is written "Calvin Fletcher. Journals of Calvin and Sarah Fletcher Arranged by Miles J. Fletcher, Brown University, Providence, R.I. June 9, 1851." Miles J. was the Fletcher's fourth child. The twelve numbered volumes contain the Diary from 1835 to 1866.

The earliest of Calvin Fletcher's diary entries, May 1–20, 1817, were set down at the time he left his native Vermont, and there are also fragments dated between July and December, 1817. All these were written on folded sheets, 3¼ by 8 inches and 2¾ by 4¾ inches, and are so broken and often illegible that they have not been reproduced here. Instead letters written to his parents and one to his brother Stephen have been included to cover the period from the time he set out until in Urbana, Ohio, on November 9, 1820, he begins a more formal diary. Letters of both Calvin and his wife Sarah and the important diary kept by Sarah covering the first years in Indianapolis, 1821–24, and the two brief journals kept by her have been used to supplement Calvin's diaries down to 1835 when he began keeping a systematic daily record which continues with only a few breaks until just before his death on May 26, 1866.

The letters that are included are from the Fletcher Papers unless otherwise indicated. The Papers consist primarily of family correspondence extending from 1817 to 1866 plus clippings, broadsides, and miscellaneous items, totaling some three thousand pieces.

The Diary and Papers descended to Laura Fletcher Hodges, granddaughter of Calvin Fletcher, daughter of his son Stoughton Alonzo, and wife of Dr. Edward F. Hodges. After her death in 1923 the Diary and Papers were placed in the custody of the Indiana Historical Society by her son Dr. Fletcher Hodges.

There seems to be a continuing desire on the part of mankind to learn more about his ancestors, to see them as they really were, to be able to visualize how they lived day by day, how they met the manifold problems that confronted them, to know what constituted their daily business and their pleasures. We want to "feel the reality of the past." The Diary of Calvin Fletcher affords us this opportunity.

Calvin Fletcher was not a great public figure. The only political office for which he ever ran was that of state senator to which he was elected in 1826 and from which he resigned in 1833. His Diary, therefore, is not important as a record of political struggles and public affairs. It is important rather as a record of the daily life of one who was a successful professional man (a lawyer), a prosperous farmer and landowner, and a businessman (banker), with a growing family and large responsibilities, who became deeply religious and was intellectually curious, and who had a strong concern for the educational and civic development of the community in which he lived. Calvin and Sarah Hill Fletcher were married May 1, 1821, at Urbana, Ohio, and came to Indianapolis the following September before the first land sales, and their lives were interwoven with the growth and development of the tiny settlement of 1821 into a city and state capital. Calvin arrived in Indianapolis virtually penniless. In 1865 he was the highest income taxpayer in the city.

As a lawyer Calvin Fletcher developed a large practice in Indianapolis and for some twenty years, twice a year, traveled over the fifth judicial circuit which then included as many as ten central Indiana counties. His practice ranged from the justice of the peace courts to the Supreme Court and included both civil and criminal cases and he also conducted a lucrative collecting business. He and his partners, notably Ovid Butler and Simon Yandes, composed one of the leading law firms in the city and state in the thirties and forties.

Fletcher bought land to farm and for speculation, and gradually his farming interests superseded his law practice, and in the latter part of his life he was dividing his time between banking and farming. The Diary therefore is a valuable source of information on various aspects of agriculture from cultivation of the soil, crops grown, planting and harvesting, and stock breeding and raising, to farm prices and farm labor. Fletcher's land ventures are revealed and the record of his service as director of the State Bank and as president of the Indianapolis branch of the State Bank and his later private banking career form an important source of business and economic history. While effort has been made in the footnotes to document some of the land transactions he mentions specifically in the Diary, no attempt has been made to locate all of his very extensive holdings over the state.

Calvin Fletcher "read law" with a successful lawyer in Urbana, Ohio, then began his practice there and continued in Indianapolis. He kept up his legal studies, and one of the interesting facets of the diary is the noting down of the law books he read and acquired. His reading extended beyond his professional interest. He had deep respect for learning and a genuine intellectual curiosity. He read widely and encouraged his wife and family to read. He perused the local press and subscribed to other newspapers and periodicals. He read the Bible and Plutarch throughout his life, but he also enjoyed history and novels, lectures and sermons, and travel books about such faraway places as Africa and the North

Pole. His interests included astronomy (he was always fascinated by eclipses) and the migration of birds (in later years he noted the arrival of various birds in the spring and their nesting and eating habits), and in 1863 he rejoiced in the acquisition of a seven-volume set of Audubon's *Birds of America.* The Diary becomes a valuable record of the books that were available to him and of what was being read in Indianapolis during these years.

Calvin Fletcher always regretted that his own formal schooling had been limited. He believed strongly in the importance of education, was an advocate of free public schools, and was unstinting of the time and effort he devoted to the development of a free public school system for Indianapolis. The education of his own children was always a primary concern. Thus the Diary forms an important source for the schools of the time and the history of Indianapolis schools from the beginning to the 1860s.

Calvin joined the Methodist Church in 1829 and was a regular attendant at services. Never strongly sectarian, he gave financial aid to the building of churches by other denominations and was also active in the Indianapolis Sabbath School. He was antislavery and joined in the support of the colonization movement. A promoter of scientific agriculture, he participated in organizing the first agricultural fairs in the county and state. He worked diligently for the local Benevolent Society which cared for the community's poor and he played a very active role in the Temperance Movement. His diary records the Civil War years and his and his family's contribution to and participation in the war effort.

However, despite this strong sense of community responsibility and participation—which is reflected throughout the Diary—Calvin Fletcher was primarily a family man, a private rather than a public person. His life centered around his home and his wife and children. The Fletchers had eleven children—nine sons and two daughters—all of whom lived to adulthood. Besides the immediate family there were usually one or two bound boys and girls living as members of the family and helping with the domestic chores, and frequently relatives or others who were making their home for a time with the Fletchers. From the day-to-day recordings emerges a detailed picture of family life at the time, its economy—food, clothing, cost of living—its chores and its pleasures, its hardships and its illnesses, its birthday parties and the observance of the Fourth of July and other holidays.

Besides riding the circuit, Fletcher traveled over the state in connection with his land speculations, and his private business and duties with the State Bank took him frequently to Cincinnati and sometimes to Louisville. He made several trips East—to Philadelphia, Washington, New York, Boston, and to the family home in Vermont and to visit his brother Elijah in Virginia. He traveled on foot, on horseback, by canoe and skiff, by stagecoach and canal boat, and finally by rail. The Diary not only affords information on the methods, conditions, and hazards of travel but also on the accommodations afforded the traveler. Fletcher regarded travel as an educational and broadening experience and took members of his family with him whenever possible.

Simon Yandes, who studied law in Fletcher's office and was associated with him in practice, attributed Fletcher's success in part to the "remarkable physical and nervous force which he enjoyed to a high degree." This he maintained until a few weeks before his death. Life demanded a strong constitution then. The Diary records the death toll of friends and neighbors—the fast decline of apparently healthy men; deaths in the "sickly season" from fevers and ague; deaths of infants and children and of mothers in childbirth; deaths when the cholera raged. While Calvin suffered a few bouts with the fever and from various afflictions, he enjoyed good health to an unusual degree and rode horseback and worked in the fields until shortly before his death which was due to complications resulting from a fall from his horse. In build he was a stocky man, not tall, and as the years passed he was concerned about gaining weight.

Those associated with Fletcher remembered his remarkable memory. They also recalled his strong sense of humor and his talent as a storyteller and player of practical jokes. Interestingly, the sense of humor is not evident in the Diary which is consistently a sober record. He refers now and then to his quick temper and his efforts to control it.

Sarah Hill Fletcher is almost as important a figure in the Diary as Calvin Fletcher himself, emerging as the prototype of the pioneer mother. She describes herself as slender and not tall. She must have had both physical strength and great inner strength. While she may not have had the intellectual interest that Calvin had, he recorded that a phrenologist rated her intellectual faculties higher than his own. He mentions that she "lacked hope," which might mean that she was more resigned and stoical than he. She bore him eleven children, all of whom lived to adulthood, and being left alone with the growing family for days and weeks at a time when Calvin was riding the circuit, she assumed much of the responsibility of raising them. She took charge of the operation of a household which included not only the immediate family, the hired hands, and domestic help, but usually a relative or two and widows and orphans who were making their home with the family. Then there was what seems to the reader to be an almost constant stream of overnight guests, itinerant preachers and travelers who were always welcome to receive what hospitality the overcrowded home could afford. She also took charge of sugar making, helped with the corn planting, the butchering and preservation of the family's meat supply, spun and sewed, and cared for the sick. Her responsibilities did not seem to lessen as Calvin prospered financially.

While the immediate Fletcher family escaped the dreaded cholera, they suffered from the prevailing fevers and agues, measles, and other diseases and afflictions. Their recoveries probably were due not to the prescriptions of the local physicians but to the mother's innate sense of what to do. Sarah Fletcher was remembered by her children as a wonderful nurse, tireless in ministering not only to her own family in times of illness but to other members of the large household and would always answer the call of neighbors for a nurse or midwife.

Sarah Fletcher died on September 27, 1854. On November 4, 1855, Calvin married Mrs. Keziah Price Lister of Hallowell, Maine, a schoolteacher, who survived him. Calvin Fletcher dominated the family until his death. Even after his sons were grown and married he tended to keep them dependent. Sarah Hill Fletcher was no doubt responsible in large measure for the strong family ties, and after her death there were some breaks in the family circle. However, all the children with the exception of the eldest, James Cooley, who became a Presbyterian minister and foreign missionary, settled in and around Indianapolis.

Introduction to Volume I

This first published volume includes the diaries and letters of Calvin Fletcher, April 10, 1817, to February 4, 1838, and the diary of Sarah Hill Fletcher, June 20, 1821, to August 2, 1824, which covers the first years in Indianapolis—a unique and invaluable document—some letters of hers, and two brief journals which she kept in June, 1830, and from December 23, 1837, to February 14, 1838.

The first letter was written by Calvin to his parents as he was preparing to leave Westford, Massachusetts, where he had been attending school and working, to go South or West to make his own way in the world. In May, 1852, Calvin wrote the following sketch of his life down to this time, which he copied at the back of the sixth numbered volume of the Diary.

> My father, Jesse Fletcher, was born in Westford Mass., the 8 of Nov. 1763 [1762].[1] His mothers name was Richardson who I think was born in Chelmsford. . . . Of his father I know but little

1. Jesse Fletcher belonged to the sixth generation of Fletchers in America, being descended from Robert who settled at Concord, Massachusetts, in 1630. The name was originally "Fledger" which was the name of the trade of one who was responsible for the fletching or feathering of arrows. The Fletchers were of English or Welsh stock and Yorkshire was probably the county from which they emigrated to America. Edward H. Fletcher (comp.), *Fletcher Genealogy: An Account of the Descendants of Robert Fletcher, of Concord, Mass.* (Privately printed, 1871), p. 9.

that is my grandfather but I have supposed from all accounts he was limited in enterprise but saving & perhaps parsimonious. Name Timothy.

My father was the youngest of 4 children.[2] Elijah, the eldest, had been at Cambridge or Harvard College. He was designed for the ministry. Settled in Hopkinton N.H. The next son was Josiah, who was a man of good education & acted as Major during some part of the Revolution & my father was attached to his command. . . .[3]

The 3d was Bridget the only sister of my father who married Isaac Parker. She was 13 years older than my father. Indeed he was the child of the old age of my grandfather and grandmother. It was designed he should have a liberal education & he was once sent to my uncle E. to Hopkinton to read law and did commence & made some progress but the Revolution broke up the design. My father however got a good education for that time. . . .

The town of Westford was some 8 or 10 miles from Lexington where the first blood of the Revolution fell after hostilities actually broke out, but [he] was then only 13 years of age. But during the last 3 [?] years of the contest was stationed at Rhode-island & served two terms under my uncle Josiah.

He [was] married to Lucy Keyes at the age of 19 that is during the year 1781. In 1782 with several emigrants visited Black River Vermont now Ludlow Windsor County & settled on the little stream that runs from the base of Green mountain East to the Connecticut River. . . .

Here my father & mother came quite young & inexperienced. He had not quite attained his majority, & she only 17 with one child. This was no small undertaking for those so young—to contend with inexperience with uncongenial soil,

2. According to the *Fletcher Genealogy* (pp. 72–73) Jesse was the youngest of six, Elijah (b. 1747), Josiah (b. 1749), Bridget (b. 1751, died young), Lucy (b. 1754, died young), and Bridget (b. 1760), having been born before him. There is a discrepancy between this record and Calvin's sketch. According to the *Genealogy* it was the second Bridget (b. 1760) who married Isaac Parker.

3. Elijah Fletcher (1747–1786) was the second Congregational minister of Hopkinton, being ordained there in 1773. His daughter Grace was the first wife of Daniel Webster. According to family records Josiah Fletcher (1749–1825) fought at Bunker Hill, White Plains, Bennington, and Ticonderoga, and was in the Rhode Island campaign where he served as adjutant. The rank of major is not confirmed. Like Jesse Fletcher he settled in Ludlow, Vermont. *Fletcher Genealogy*, pp. 72–73.

with rugged rocks and giant Hemlocks, spruce pine, birch & elm & with long winters & early frosts. He [my father] inherited only enough to pay something less than a dollar on an acre for something near 100 acres, laying along the little valley of Black river & running up the precitpious hills that come down to the little rivalet. Here he made a small improvement & then moved my mother to it.[4] They came in an ox cart to the place over the most rugged road. The means of subsistence were scarce and difficult to obtain. . . . My father had no money had to rely on his own energy. He was not skilful in expidients or a very good contriver. No trader nor very skilful in husbandry, & having thus to overcome these obsticles before him, he labored hard & lived poor. My eldest sister Charlotte lived to be 12 & died. My eldest brother Stephen was run over by a Slay & killed when 3 or 4 years of age. . . .

There was born before me Charlotte, Stephen, Michael, Fanny, Jesse, Elijah, Timothy, Lucy, Stephen the 2d, and Laura. I was the 12 [11] child.[5] After me were born Miles, Dexter (who died at 2 or 3), Louisa, & Stoughton. In all 15 childrin. The first childrin received more personal attention in their education from my father than the middle & last. He had a better education than most of his neighbors. Was made the 1st town clerk & recorded all the deeds of the town of Ludlow—all births deaths & marriages & kept the records some 30 years. . . . He was also the 2d Representative and went to the Vermont legislature that set at Vergennes & was Justice of the peace for near 30 years.[6] He was a real Puritan in many things. He was uncommonly rigid in relation to the Sabbath. . . . He was studious. Read much. A very good historian, & always took a newspaper & the Bible

4. In 1784 Jesse Fletcher built a log cabin where the family lived for eight years. He then built a small frame house that became the ell of the two-story farmhouse, erected about 1805, which stands today. Martha von Briesen (ed.), *The Letters of Elijah Fletcher* (Charlottesville, Va.: University Press of Virginia, 1965), p. [xv].

5. C.F. was born February 4, 1798.

6. According to a local history Jesse Fletcher was elected the first town clerk of Ludlow in 1792 and served one year and was elected again in 1795, serving until 1809. He served as Ludlow's selectman from 1792 to 1801 and from 1803 to 1808. He also represented Ludlow in the state legislature, 1798–99, being the second representative for the town, his brother Josiah having been the first. Joseph N. Harris, *The History of Ludlow, Vermont* (Charlestown, N.H., c. 1949), pp. 16, 82, 85, 87.

was read & reviewed. He supported the Congregational church under the care of the Reverend Peter Reed who came from Connecticut at the close of the Revolution & preached for 50 years in my native town. . . . His church was some 2 miles from my father's, & summer & winter I was made to attend from my earliest recollection. . . .

I was sent to a school for a few days to Mr. Reeds, a farmer nearby. I was very small & went only to gratify my desire for a few days with my sisters. It was before any school house was erected in the district & the school was kept by a woman on the barn floor, which was swept & kept clean. Soon after [I] was sent to a Miss Parker a mile or 2 to Mr. Levi Ives then at about 6 I went to a Miss Saloma Fletcher, daughter of Dr. Aseph Fletcher of Cavendish some 2 miles east of my father's. . . .[7]

In June 1805 or 1806 there was a famous eclipse of the sun between 10 & 12 in the A.M.[8] It was almost total. I was at school, in a new school house just built some ½ mile west of my father's. . . . It was a solemn occasion to me. The birds went to roost. It seemed to me as dark as the last twilight & when the eclipse began to pass off, the chickens crowed & the birds began to sing as at early dawn.

The school district I lived in was rather poor, and did not afford but a short two months in the winter & summer. . . . I usually attended the winter schools till 16 years of age, and the summer schools till 12 or 13. The former were kept by men, I think of not much education. Could read write & cipher to the Golden Rule, certain & often were more advanced. But they were usually tyrannical & knew very little about the philosophy of teaching. The school house was over a half mile west of my fathers under a high hill that ran back to the north.

7. Asaph Fletcher (1746–1839) was born in Westford, Massachusetts. A devout Baptist and a physician, he was a member of the Massachusetts convention that drafted the commonwealth's constitution in 1780. In 1787 he moved to Cavendish, Vermont, and there served in the convention which applied for Vermont's admission to the Union. He also served in the state legislature and held other public offices besides continuing the practice of medicine. Salome Fletcher married Dr. Luther Fletcher in 1806 and lived for a while in Grantville, New York, returning to Cavendish where she died in 1867. Edward Fletcher, *Fletcher Genealogy*, pp. 167–68, 172.

8. This is probably the eclipse of the sun that occurred June 16, 1806. It was most apparent in New England and had a duration of totality of 4.6 minutes. *Encyclopædia Britannica* (11th ed., 1910), VIII, 892.

Each man in the district furnished his part of the wood & the boys of the family would cut it up. I had some of this labor to perform.

I had a great thirst for knowledge & treasured up all I heard read before I could read. Yet I was extremely hard to learn to read or attain figures with ease and I had labored so hard at 10 that my hand was as stiff & hard as an old man's hand. Indeed I had no mechanical ingenuity which makes a writer.

From about 11 to 13 we had no schools in consequence of the house being burned & the district not able or were unwilling to build. One of these winters I went to a Mr. Johnson to Proctorsville or what was then known as Proctor's store. . . . This intermission of schools was of great injury to me. . . .

From 1808 to the time I left my father's in 1815, there were what may be truly denominated hard times. Our troubles with Great Britain. . . . brought on nonintercourse embargo. . . . There was no circulating medium, no money. My father lived very poorly with a large family. From 1806 to 1810 he tried to educate my brother Elijah who first went to Westford, Mass., then to Hanover, N.H. & at last entered Middlebury College, Vermont. Kept school.[9] My mother & sisters spun and wove and made his clothes & all was done that could be to give him a college education. In the meantime my sister Lucy & brother Stephen were sent from home to give them a better education.

My oldest brother Michael was sent to Massachusetts to work to earn money to aid my father. This he did one or 2 years & then with my brother Timothy in 1810 or 1811 went to Albany N.Y. to live. . . . Stephen Elijah Timothy & Michael were absent from home leaving Jesse the 2d [living] son myself and Miles to help my father. Jesse was speculative proude & destitute of much calculation and forsight. He had entered into a long courtship & finally married a woman more vain & proude than himself, into a family not remarkable for their honesty. His influence over my father was great & his vanity was equal to that influence. He bo't things on credit without Judgment & involved my father so that the annual income did not meet the outgoes.

My father at 50 was somewhat corpulent and not able to perform much labor. His corpulence was somewhat promoted

9. For a sketch of Elijah Fletcher, C.F.'s brother, see below, Pt. I, note 11.

by the custom then of drinking regular drams. This dram seems to have been common in N[ew] E[ngland]. The army and navy had their regular rations of spirits. . . . My father's activity mental or physical was not promoted by this practise & public opinion did not rebuke it. With a profligate son, the habit before mentioned & the "embargo times" (from 1810 to 1812) & war declared against great Britain in June 1812 all tended to depress commerce and the agriculture of N.E. & my father suffered pecuniarily thereby.

During the years 1813 and 1814 my brother Jesse who lived with my father undertook to carry on the farm in part and I with my father the other part. We worked together but the separate or partially separate interest did not work well & pecuniarily my father fell behind. In the spring of 1815 I informed my father that I did not think we could thus get along & on the 11th of April that year he in a rather pettish moode I think, gave me permission to leave him at 17 years 2 months and 7 days old. He so informed about 7½ in the morning & by 9 I had borrowed $2.50 from my sister Lucy was encouraged by her & my good mother, & I took leave of my home with a small bundle of clothes. . . .

I went to Windsor our county town on the Connecticut River. I stayed over night & in the morning met with a Squire Jabez Delano of West Windsor who was on his road home from Boston where he had been with fat cattle. He hired me on condition that a certain man did not come to work for him. I went back to Weathersfield where I had left my clothes the day before to get them & by sundown reached Delano's. The snow was on the ground. I worked some days for him. The man he had partially hired came on & he got a place for me at old Esquire Cummins near West Windsor meeting house. I worked for him for a few days & on Sunday returned to Esquire D.'s who was to help me to get a good place. Esquire Cummins was looking out for a full grown man that could chop & do field work. I was not able to perform such work quite equal to a man. Esquire D. Sunday as it was took me to a Mr. Phineas Hemanway living right in the corner of Windsor Reading Hartford & Woodstock. His farm in the first named town. Here I got imploy for 6 months at $10. per month. I began the 24th day of April Snow on the ground in places. I here worked for 6 months in 1815 & never lost a day, but gained 2 or 3 days by taking tasks. . . . I began my services on the 24th of April, and the 24th of October I left with a portion of my earnings for home, where my sister Lucy & mother had prepared some cloth made in the house to make my winter clothes. The family of Mr. Hemanway parted with me with great regret urged me to continue my services another year & flattered me with being one of the *best laborers* they had ever had. . . . I had earned some $60 or 70 by my labor. . . .

In the early part of November 1815 I repaired to Royalton, on White River Vermont some 60 miles from home to an academy kept by one Chamberlain; a man of no great ability, a sort of dandy.[10] I boarded with one Deacon Safford who has had a very intellectual descendant a remarkable boy, a great methematician.[11] I stayed with him (the Deacon) from November till February & went home. Stayed a short time and then returned in March to Royalton. There I continued a short time, became disgusted with my teacher & place of boarding, & left for Randolph some 20 miles North West. At Randolph they had a very reputable academy and Mr. Rufus Nutting a very reputable teacher.[12] I began to study English Grammar and lattin. I soon found my course at Royalton was far from being thoro' & that all I had gone over was only calculated to make a superficial & a blunder. Mr. Nutting I thought exhibited me to his pupils as a specimen of a poorly taught boy at a rival school. I was excessively dull & much discouraged & came near leaving but Nutting thro another pupil gave me to understand that I should no longer be made a subject of exhibition on account of want of knowledge in what I had supposed I had learned at Royalton.

The sketch breaks off at this point. In the Diary under date of April 11, 1845, Calvin recalled that he stayed at Randolph from February to December, 1816, going to school about half the time

10. Remembrance Chamberlain was principal of Royalton Academy for about a year, beginning in August, 1815. Evelyn M. Wood Lovejoy, *History of Royalton, Vermont* . . . (Royalton and Royalton's Woman's Club, 1911), p. 20.

11. Nathan Safford whose grandson was the mathematician and astronomer Trueman Henry Safford (1836–1901). *Dictionary of American Biography* (20 volumes. New York: Charles Scribner's Sons, 1928–37), XVI, 287.

12. Randolph Academy (or Orange County Grammar School) was established in 1806 by William Nutting. Rufus Nutting served as principal from 1814 to 1818. The *Vermont Historical Gazetteer*, II, edited by Abby Maria Hemenway (Bennington, Vt., 1871), p. 995; *Illlustrated Historical Souvenir of Randolph, Vermont* (Randolph, Vt., 1895), pp. 42, 43.

and working the other half. He returned again to Ludlow where he studied under Horace Fletcher, a son of Asaph Fletcher, until February, 1817, then repaired to Westford, Massachusetts, living with the Joseph Fletcher family and going to school. The letters and diaries constituting Volume I start at this point and continue the story of his life.

Editorial Note

In rendering the text of the Diary and letters the intent of the editor has been to seek a "median ground between pedantic fidelity and readability," to use the words of Lyman H. Butterfield, editor of *The Adams Papers*. All superscript letters have been lowered and contractions written out and mere slips of the pen have been corrected. In all instances of doubt the writer has been assumed to have spelled correctly. Punctuation and capitalization have been preserved generally as in the original manuscript, but for the sake of clarity and readability periods have been supplied at the end of sentences and all sentences begin with a capital letter. Periods follow all abbreviations and initial letters. Superfluous dashes have been omitted. An effort has been made to make the dates of the daily entries uniform, and to set them off from the text they have been italicized. Words that are missing or illegible are indicated by square brackets with a conjectural reading inserted within the brackets or by suspension points [. . .] if no meaning can be conjectured. A missing number or part of a number is indicated by brackets [ ] separated by blank space.

Effort has been made within reason to identify persons in the footnotes the first time that their names appear. It was, of course, impracticable and often impossible to identify every person mentioned. In some instances first names are supplied in the Index for persons who are mentioned by the last name only and for whom a footnote identification is not given. In order to avoid writing the name in full the initials C.F. are used throughout the notes for Calvin Fletcher. Footnotes also explain, clarify, document, or describe places and events alluded to in the text.

Complete bibliographical citations are given when a published work is cited for the first time and a short citation is used for it thereafter.

Acknowledgments

It would be impossible to list, for the editor cannot be aware, of all the persons who have made possible the publication of the Calvin Fletcher Diary. One would have to go back to Calvin himself and to his sons who had the volumes collected and bound and carefully preserved, and to Laura Fletcher Hodges and her son the late Dr. Fletcher Hodges. And the family interest in the Diary has been sustained by Dr. Hodges' widow, Mrs. Rebecca Hodges, of Indianapolis, and their children, Fletcher Hodges, Jr., of Pittsburgh, Bradford H. Hodges, of Hazel Crest, Illinois, and Dr. Anne C. Garrison, of East Lansing, Michigan.

At the time the Diary and the papers which accompanied it were placed in the custody of the Indiana Historical Society by Dr. Hodges, the late Dr. Christopher B. Coleman was serving as secretary of the Society. He and other members of the Society's Board of Trustees, notably the late Lee Burns, and Mr. Eli Lilly and Mr. John G. Rauch, Sr., both of whom are still serving on the Board, were aware of the unique historical value of the Diary and the desirability of its being published. At the Annual Meeting of the Society on December 12, 1930, a motion by Mr. Burns that the executive committee of the Society be authorized to investigate the possibility of publication was adopted unanimously. Arrangements were made to have the complete Diary transcribed by Miss Helen Lee Baldwin, her fee being paid out of the Society's Delavan Smith

Fund. Miss Baldwin with the help of Mrs. Cleta F. Robinson accomplished this tremendous task between 1931 and 1936, producing a typewritten transcript of over six thousand pages. The editor has collated the transcript with the original diary and is deeply appreciative of the excellent job that was performed. The transcript has served as the copy for editing.

It was estimated that the published Diary would run to several volumes and the magnitude of the project as well as other concerns delayed publication until 1968, when the Board of Trustees authorized the editing and publication of the Diary.

The editor wishes to express thanks to Fletcher Hodges, Jr., for permission to reproduce the portraits of Calvin Fletcher and Sarah Hill Fletcher by T. C. Steele and the sampler made by Louisa Fletcher Miller;

to Martha von Briesen, public relations director of Sweet Briar College, who was instrumental in the college giving to the Indiana Historical Society the portrait of Calvin Fletcher by Jacob Cox which is reproduced as the frontispiece, and who also supplied copies of several letters of Calvin Fletcher from the Sweet Briar collection and was helpful in many other ways;

to Carl Weinhardt, director, and Jeffrey R. Brown, curator, Art Association of Indianapolis, for the cleaning and restoration of the Cox portrait of Fletcher;

to Charles T. Morrissey, director of the Vermont Historical Society, and his staff for answering questions relating to Vermont;

to Richard W. Haupt, director, and Frances Forman of the Cincinnati Historical Society for information relating to Cincinnati persons and places;

to Miss Alameda McCollough of the Tippecanoe County Historical Society, Lafayette, Indiana, for information relating to Andrew Ingram;

to Scott Clifford of Indianapolis for turning over to the Indiana Historical Society Library papers of Ovid Butler, law partner of Calvin Fletcher;

to Donald Johnson of the Pioneer National Title Insurance Company of Indianapolis, for his assistance in regard to Calvin Fletcher's land holdings in Indianapolis and Marion County;

to John W. Fletcher, Woodside, California, Mrs. Robert Hollingsworth, of Indianapolis, and Mrs. Charlton B. Rogers, of St. Louis, Missouri, for the interest they have shown in the publication of the Diary;

to Hubert H. Hawkins, executive secretary of the Indiana Historical Society;

to Miss Caroline Dunn, librarian of the Indiana Historical Society, who searched out material in the Society's collection relating to the Fletcher family and made many valuable suggestions, and to the staff of the Society's library;

to Mrs. Hazel Hopper, chief of the Indiana Division of the Indiana State Library and members of her staff and to the staff of the Archives Division of the State Library;

to Mrs. Terry Joan Dean, formerly editorial assistant for the Indiana Historical Society who organized and indexed the Fletcher Papers and helped in the early stages of the editorial work, and to Mrs. Paula Jean Corpuz who succeeded Mrs. Dean and has aided in completing the editorial work;

and to James H. Olin of Typoservice Corporation, Indianapolis, for designing a suitable and attractive format for the Diary.

A special word of thanks goes to Miss Dorothy Riker, formerly editor of the Indiana Historical Bureau and presently with the Indiana Historical Society, who read the edited manuscript, researched land and deed records for Fletcher's land holdings, and has assisted in seeing the first volume through the press.

Calvin Fletcher Chronology, 1798-1838

February 4, 1798	Born on farm at Ludlow, Vermont, the eleventh child of Jesse and Lucy Keyes Fletcher
c. 1804–1815	Attends local schools intermittently and helps with work on family farm
April 11, 1815	Leaves home and works for six months as farm laborer
November, 1815–December, 1816	Attends schools at Royalton and Randolph, Vermont
February–May, 1817	Attends school at Westford, Massachusetts
May 1, 1817	Starts out to seek his fortune in the South or West
June, 1817	Settles in Urbana, Ohio, and begins teaching school the following month
November 17, 1817	Begins to read law with James Cooley in Urbana while continuing to teach
May–November(?), 1820	With his brother Elijah at Lynchburg, Virginia
November, 1820	Returns to Urbana, Ohio, resumes law study, and is admitted to practice *ex gratia*

January 18, 1821	Admitted to practice by Supreme Court of Ohio
May 1, 1821	Marriage to Sarah Hill, daughter of Joseph Hill of near Urbana, and Margaret Oliver Hill
August 2–9, 1821	Visits Indianapolis, the new capital of the State of Indiana
October 1, 1821	Arrives with Sarah in Indianapolis and settles in cabin on square bordered by Missouri, Washington, West, and Maryland streets
October 9, 1821	Granted license to practice law in circuit and inferior courts in Indiana
March 1, 1822	Starts on first circuit court ride (He would ride the circuit for some twenty years.)
April, 1822	Appointed overseer of poor for Center-Warren townships, Marion County
May 28, 1822	Moves to house owned by James Blake on the lot on the point formed by Washington Street and Kentucky Avenue
September 26, 1822	Admitted to practice by Marion County Circuit Court and appointed prosecuting attorney
April 15, 1823	Birth of first child, James Cooley
May 19–August 8, 1824	Journeys to Vermont to visit parents
August 21, 1824	Birth of second child, Elijah Timothy Fletcher
November 9, 1824	Makes first land purchase, six acres northwest of Indianapolis in the southwest quarter of section 10, T16N, R3E
c. 1825	Moves to Dr. Kenneth Scudder's house on the southeast side of Kentucky Avenue just below Illinois Street
August 9, 1825	Appointed prosecuting attorney for fifth judicial circuit, serving one year
August 7, 1826	Elected to Indiana Senate for two-year term

September 30, 1826	Birth of third child, Calvin, Jr.
1826–1830	Acquires 450 acres of land comprising farm some five miles northeast of town's limits in sections 21 and 22, T16N, R4E
June 15, 1828	Birth of fourth child, Miles Johnson
August 4, 1828	Re-elected to Indiana Senate for full three-year term
January 4, 1829	Joins Methodist Church
May 25–July(?), 1829	Journeys to Vermont and Virginia
November 4, 1829	Elected manager of newly organized Indiana Colonization Society
June 8–29, 1830	Journeys to Ohio with Sarah
February 14, 1831	Death of father, Jesse Fletcher
Spring of 1831	Moves from Kentucky Avenue to house purchased December 29, 1830, located on the south side of East Ohio Street between Alabama and New Jersey streets, lot 12, square 42
August 1, 1831	Re-elected to Indiana Senate
October, 1831	Stoughton, C.F.'s youngest brother, comes to Indianapolis
October 25, 1831	Birth of fifth child, Stoughton Alonzo
January 26, 1833	Resigns from Indiana Senate
June 25–July 1(?), 1833	Journeys to Cincinnati and Louisville on business while the cholera is raging
October 29, 1833	Birth of sixth child and first daughter, Maria Antoinette Crawford
January, 1834	Purchases 1,200 acres of land in La Porte County, the beginning of his speculation in land
February 1, 1834	Elected a director of the State Bank by the General Assembly

August 30, 1834	Acquires first land at the Bluffs in Morgan County
January 6–15, 1835	Journeys to Cincinnati on business of State Bank and other matters
February, 1835	Appointed attorney for Indianapolis branch of State Bank
March 23, 1835	Enters into law partnership with Ovid Butler
June 22, 1835	Birth of seventh child, Ingram
June 27, 1835	Elected treasurer of Marion County Agricultural Society upon its organization
June 30–July 7, 1835	Journeys to Fort Wayne to attend ceremonies on the opening of the Wabash and Erie Canal between Fort Wayne and Huntington
July 24–August 1, 1835	Journeys to Cincinnati on business, accompanied by James Cooley and Elijah
September 3–17, 1835	Journeys north to attend land sales at La Porte and to purchase Michigan Road lands including an interest in the Potawatomi mills
October 30–31, 1835	Serves as treasurer of first Marion County Fair
November 11, 1835	Attends first meeting of board of trustees of Marion County Seminary
December 4, 1835	Joins with Nicholas McCarty in purchase of Wood Lawn estate from Dr. John H. Sanders
February 9, 1836	In partnership with Nicholas McCarty buys first Shelbyville property
March 28, 1836	Michael, C.F.'s eldest brother, and wife arrive in Indianapolis which will become their home
May 23–June 17, 1836	Goes north to lay out town as possible county seat of Porter County (rejected by commissioners) and to attend sales of lots at Michigan City
July 8, 1836	Lays off lots on his land adjoining town of Anderson

September 6–21, 1836	Goes north to Michigan City and elsewhere to sell land
October 8, 1836	Delivers address at second Marion County Agricultural Fair
November 2–14, 1836	Journeys to inspect branch banks at New Albany, Madison, and Lawrenceburg
December, 1836	Considers running for Congress to succeed George L. Kinnard (deceased), but decides against it
December 14, 1836	Re-elected a director of the State Bank by the General Assembly
January 1, 1837	Estimates that he and Nicholas McCarty are indebted jointly $16,577 for some 14,000 acres of land; estimates his private debts at $6,900
May 13, 1837	Instrumental in calling meeting of merchants of Indianapolis to consider their financial interests (Panic of 1837)
May 17–19, 1837	Participates in steps taken by State Bank in face of nationwide financial crisis
May 29, 1837	Offers for sale in partnership with Nicholas McCarty 98 lots laid out on the Wood Lawn property
June 19–21, 1837	Goes to Greencastle with sons Elijah and Cooley to attend cornerstone laying for Indiana Asbury University where he makes a short address
August 18, 1837	Birth of eighth child, William Baldwin
December 23, 1837–February 14 (?), 1838	Journeys to Washington, D.C., Philadelphia, Boston, Ludlow, Vermont, back to Washington, and home

The Diary of
CALVIN FLETCHER

Volume I
1817-1838

I

Letters and Diary of CALVIN FLETCHER *April 10, 1817-October 1, 1821*

C.F., Westford, Mass., to his parents, Ludlow, Vermont, April 10, 1817

. . . I have boarded at Uncle F[letcher's][1] as it was agreede on by you and Uncle P[atten].[2] The six weeks that I told you that I should spend here at school have about expired but I have to stay two weeks longer which will make it about the 28th before I shall be ready to leave Westford which I calculate to do if nothing unseen prevents. I have no particular place of destination determined as yet but think I then shall go to the Southward. I shall be under the necessity to starte with but very little money; the thought of it gives me a very disagreeable sensation and it picturs much hardship to me in the journey I have proposed to myself.

This undertaking I am fered will not meete your approbation. I should be happy to consult your opinion about it; I feel to want a Fathers advise. . . . There is my close and trunk which I hope w[MS torn] got home from Randolph but if not I wish they might be; th[MS torn] there for tuition and board is only $6.50 and the

1. Joseph Fletcher, a relative but not a true uncle. *Fletcher Genealogy: an Account of the Descendants of Robert Fletcher of Concord, Mass.*, compiled by Edward H. Fletcher (Boston: Privately printed, 1871), p. 75. In a diary fragment in the Fletcher Papers, Indiana Historical Society Library, C.F. wrote: "This may certify that Calvin Fletcher began to board with Mr. Joseph Fletcher March the 13th 1817."

2. Isaac Patten, husband of Lydia Keyes, twin sister of C.F.'s mother.

close [MS torn] books that are there are worth $10.00. If Jesse[3] will go an[d] get them for me the first money that I ever earn shall pay him for all the trouble he is at. I have not vis[i]ted any of my Relations since [I] began to go to school but expect to pay them one visit before I leave. . . . I think I shal visit Michael[4] on my way to South. I shall go through the State of Connecticut.[5]

C.F., Urbana, Ohio, to his parents, Ludlow, Vermont, June 27, 1817

I at length find an opportunity to fu[l]fill an engaguement, which [you] undoutedly have long expected, but I must tell you, I have been Traveling ever since I wrote you at Westford; at which you may be astonished for it excedes all premeditated calculatins of my own; and I look with amazement on the distance I have conveyed my self from my Parents and Friends. . . . I prepared to leave W[estford] soon after I wrote you which was about the last of May [April]. I was destitute of mo[n]ey and in debt three dollars. I made application to Uncle P[atten]. He willingly gave me $7.50 as much as I expected from him. I then had 14.50. I thought that woud not cary me through to Michael where I intended to go. I sold my Trunk, Virgil and dixonary for 5.00 took my pay in Small things out of a Store such as nedles, pins, Thimbles Cotten balls &c.[6]

Wednesday April 30th I left Uncle Jo. Fletchers where I had passed eight weeks of my life, with agility, and I did not part with Shagrin. . . . I went to Uncle Deaco[n]s[7] and staid over night. The

3. C.F.'s brother who was living on his father's farm.

4. C.F.'s brother, who at this time was living in Staatsburgh, New York.

5. In another autobiographical sketch C.F. wrote: "In 1817, I determined on a seaman's life, and in April of the same year went to Boston, a total stranger, and tried my best to obtain a berth on board an East-Indiaman; but failed." Quoted in *Memoir of the Hon. Calvin Fletcher, of Indianapolis, Ind.*, by William B. Trask (Reprinted from the *New-England Historical and Genealogical Register*, October, 1869. Boston: David Clapp & Son, 1869), p. 5. This is confirmed by an entry in the fragmentary diary for 1817: "April 14, 1817. I started for Boston with Joseph Fletcher. Stayed over night at Charleston went into Boston the 15. Expences 0.20."

6. In a fragmentary record that C.F. kept of his journey, which is in the Fletcher Papers, he noted under date of May 2, that he procured some bread and milk in exchange for "a skain of silk and four needles." The next day for a breakfast of bread and milk he gave two skeins of silk.

7. Samuel Fletcher of Westford, a church deacon, a relative but not a true uncle of C.F. Edward H. Fletcher (comp.), *Fletcher Genealogy*, p. 185.

next mor[ning] May the 1st I gave Horatio my mittings he gave me a Knapsack to cary my cloaths in. Maryan and Betsey[8] took me into the Chais and carried me to Harverd (about 6 miles). I travled on to Wocester that day (about 35 miles). This is a very handsome place. May 2d I fell in company with a yong man from Mane. We went into Connecticit. The third day I arrived in Hartford 4 oclock in P.M. I calculated to go from there acrossed to Stattsburgh which was 80 miles; but my feet were very much swolen and blistered so that I was not able to walk. So I thought I would give up the idea of going to Michael and go to Pensylvania if I could get a chance to go by water. I staid over Sunday and found a chance to go in a Sloop to N.Y. for 1.50 which was going to sail Monday. About sundown I understood that it would not sail till Tusday. I knew [it] would not do for me to stay upon expence. I concluded to go to New haven where I could get an opportunity to go to New York any day. So I paid my bill wich was 1.25 then I had but 7.25 remaining. I left my buget [baggage] to be brought in the Stage. I travled out about 4 mils put up (Sunday night). Monday I [s]tarted early. I this day went through Meridon and Walingsford. I arrived in New [Haven] 5 oclock P.M. There was a packet just ready to sail for N.Y. The Capt. said he woud carry me for two dollars .50 cents. I was at a stand whether to go or not. At length I concluded to go. We sat sail about 10 oclock in the evening. I under went a great fear that I should be seasick. In the morning I got up and found to my surprise we had not got out of the Harbour; could see the town plain, but soon there sprung up a breeze and we left the harbour. We had good wind all day. We passed along by Long island. I saw the most butiful farms that ever I beheld befor. Wedensday morn at 8 oclock we cast anchor in N.Y. harbour. I left the ship soon with only 75 cents (25 I spent before I le[f]t the city).

. . . I walked a round the City with a young man from Connecticut, who came in the Packet with me and we calculated to go to Philadelphia togeather. We left City at 11 oclock passed into Newjursey. We travld 18 m. and he was taken unwell and could not travel. I felt the best for travling that I had since I set out. I left him and went on. I had the good luck to by a fifty Cent bill for a

8. Horatio, Mary Ann, and Betsey were children of Samuel Fletcher. *Ibid.*

trifle on a Philadelphia bank which was not current there but was the next day as good as silver to me. I travld 28 miles this day after 11 oclock; put up at Dutch Tavern; in the morn (Thursday 8th) it rained. The yong man I left behind went on in the stage. I started at 9. It was very mudy, it being all level clay land. I arrived at Brunswick at noon 14 miles from where I started. That is very flourishing place and a handsome Colledge. I went a mil beyond there and I saw the stage coming. It got [MS torn] me and stoped and one of the gentleman called to me. I went up to [the] stage he said that they had agreed to cary me on a peace. They were two French gentlman and two that belonged to southward; they asked [MS torn] many questions which I answered; we went 6 miles from the place where I got in and stopt. They wanted to know what I would drink. I refused to take any thing told them I did not drink any liquor. They went [and] got a mug of Cider. I drank as much as I coud of it. I went on with them. We passed through Princetown. I saw the Coledges which are very handsome built of stone; this town stands upon a very high hill about the bigness of Chester South St. They stopt 10 miles from Trentown to chang horses. I went on. Travled two miles and it overtook me again. The stage stopt and the gentlman told me to get in agin. I endeavored to express my grattitude to them & they told me only to remembe[r] and do as I would be done by. I told them I hoped that I brought that maxim from home with me. I left them at Trentown. The next day I arrived in Philadelphia (the 9th day). I had about two shillings in money.

. . . I intended to go on to the South west part of Pensilvania. Here you will perhaps wonder what should induce me to go there: I met with two yong men in Connecticut returning from there. They had been teaching schools there and gave me great encouragements to go there, togeather with some recommendations to a gentleman. I put up to a Tavern and changed my cloths and went out in pursuit of the two mentioned. I first enquired for Mr. Hall. I found he had gone to the South. I then with difficulty found Patten.[9] I gave him an invitation [to] call on me at the tavern in the evening as he was in Something of a hurry just entering in

9. Perhaps a relative of C.F.'s uncle Isaac Patten.

trad[e] agin in English goods store. I went back to the tavern. There I become acquainted with a quaker gentleman a man whom nothing but the loss of reason will ever obliterate from my mind. I waited till 1 oclock before I retired. Patten did not come. I in the meantime rose early and walked with the quaker who tried to make my happiness as great as possible. We returned and I found that Patten had been in and left a note for me, that he would call upon me Sunday morning at 9 (this Saturday). This day I spent viewing the City in company with the quaker. He told me it was a very bad Tavern that I had quit[?] at, very dear and did not keep good company &c. He sayd "If thou will go with me to a Tavern (and the Landlord of which is a friend of mine) thou shall be well-come to stay one or two weeks and rest thy self and if thou art in want of any thing, ask me." I complyed with his proposition and went. I was paid great atten[tion] to by all the house for they all reverenced my Benefactor. Sunday morn I went to meet P. at the Tavern. I understood he had just been there but did not wait a moment. Judge What my feelings were when I had anticipated an interview with him. I thought I would call on him Monday morn, and I felt pervoked enough to show a resentment. Monday morn I called upon him. He took me acide for to talk. He said that he had recieved a letter from Joh[n][10] that Elijah[11] would be in Philadelphia in four or five days. He asked me some questions relative

10. John Patten, a cousin, who had moved to Virginia, first to New Glasgow and then to Lynchburg. A merchant, he married Sarah Crawford, sister of Maria Crawford, wife of C.F.'s brother Elijah. Martha von Briesen (ed.), *The Letters of Elijah Fletcher* (Charlottesville, Va.: University Press of Virginia, 1965), pp. 84, 97, 121.

11. C.F.'s brother Elijah. Having studied at Middlebury College and Dartmouth, he received a bachelor of arts degree from the University of Vermont in 1810. He taught school in Alexandria, Virginia, and served as principal of an academy in New Glasgow. He married Maria Antoinette Crawford, daughter of William Sidney Crawford, a highly respected and well-known plantation owner. Upon Crawford's death in 1815 Elijah became administrator of his estate and manager of his plantations. In 1818 he moved to Lynchburg where he engaged in various enterprises and prospered. He participated in community affairs, helped to found the first Episcopal church in the town, and served as mayor for one term, 1831–32. In 1841 he retired from business to his plantation known as Sweetbrier and became a full-time farmer. He died in 1858. Elijah had four children who grew to maturity, Sidney (b. 1821), Lucian (b. 1824), Indiana (b. 1828), and Elizabeth (b. 1831). Martha von Briesen, "Elijah Fletcher, Citizen of Lynchburg," in Lynchburg Historical Society Museum, VII, No. 2, 1970.

to business & he wanted to know when I was going out. I told him I did not know—asked me if I would call agin I told him if I could make it convenient I would. I left him and have not seen him since. I staid in the City 15 days.

I found Mr. Steward the one who married Col. Wimans daughter. He is considered as a gentleman there. He used me very handsomely and gave me a recommendation and got it Signed by Dr. Flagger, M.D. and several other gentleman.[12] I told my quaker friend I must leave him. He thought I had better stay another week. I told him I could not. . . . He told me to get all my things washed, boots and shoes fixed &c.[13]

I left the City May 22d. I took southwest course. The 26th in the morn I arrived in Abbotstown 100 from Philadelphia and 40 from Baltimore. Here I calculated to stay a week or two and work in a brickyard. (I was drove to this by Poverty) but before I went to work I meet with a yong man from Connecticutt who was to work at [MS torn] and he said he was going in a week on to the Ohio and goin[g] through Wheeling in Virginia. . . . I went to work the rest of the week and earned 2.25 (in 4 days). Saturday night I called agin upon the yong man who was going on to the Ohio. He was anxious for me to go on and I was glad to get away from high

12. This letter of recommendation, signed by Stephen Steward and dated Philadelphia, May 21, 1817, is in the Fletcher Papers. It reads: "The bearer Mr. Calvin Fletcher is a young man with whom I am acquainted and particularly with his parents and near connections, and from such acquaintance have no hesitation in recommending him to the public as a moral, industrious worthy young man, and deserving the patronage and encouragement of his country men. His business is teaching the various branches of literature, and from his untarnished Reputation believe him well qualified to give the utmost satisfaction as a Teacher." It was endorsed by Gilbert Flagler, M.D., and John Moulson.

13. Elijah Fletcher wrote to his father from Philadelphia, July 24, 1817: ". . . I arrived the 9th instant. I . . . could get no particular information of Calvins situation. I saw one or two persons that had become acquainted with him, particularly a Mr Stewart who married one of Col. Wyman's daughters & formerly lived in Walpole [N.H.]. He told me that Calvin while there was in good heart and good spirits, that Calvin was introduced to him by a Quaker gentleman who seemed to be particularly attached to him, and had made up a small school for Calvin, but Calvin thought it not an object sufficient for him to stay for. . . . Mr Stewart said he seemed to have money and not to be in any want. He said Calvin had a happy faculty of forming acquaintances and making friends and everyone [who?] became acquainted with him was much pleased & seemed to take an interest in his welfare." Von Briesen (ed.), *Letters of Elijah Fletcher*, p. 86.

Dutch. They could not talk a word English where I worked and lived worse than Canibals of New Zealand. This yong man (whose name was Foot) was going to buy land. He had considerable money and was a fraid of being robed, for such things had just hapened in the Alleganey Montains which we were to cross. We started June 2d. There Sir I could picture a Catelogue of Disagreeable scenes we went through in travling 250 miles among a most inhumane set of beings. We crossed the Blue ridge Laural hill North-mountain Alleganey. I got out of money and told Foot I shoud not go on any further. He said if I would go on he [would] let me have what I wanted by paying him when I could earn it. We arrived in Wheeling June 10th. . . . Wednesday morn I got up walked out and viewed the butiful river, Ohio. Mr. Foot thought we had better get passage in boat and [go] down to Cincenati 550 from Wheeling. . . .[14]

C.F., Urbana, Ohio, to his brother Stephen, Cincinnati, Ohio, January 13, 1818[15]

. . . I fear you will not get business in cincinnati and to start

14. Unfortunately the last part of this letter has not been found. In it C.F. may have explained why after reaching Cincinnati he went on to Urbana, county seat of Champaign County, Ohio. In his diary entry for October 22, 1860, he recalled: "At Cincinnati O. I undertook with him [Mr. Foote] to go to Dayton but Providentially was taken to Urbana Ohio." A note in the Fletcher Papers indicates that he began boarding with a Mr. Hunter in Urbana on June 25. On July 4, he was "living at a little dirty tavern" in Urbana, perhaps Mr. Hunter's. See entry for July 4, 1837, below. Then on July 14 he began teaching in a school for a term of three months and boarding with the Joseph Hill family, who lived five miles out of the town. Diary fragment in the Fletcher Papers.

Joseph Hill, who would become C.F.'s father-in-law, was born in Berkeley County, Virginia, in 1779, and came with his parents to Mason County, Kentucky, in 1789. On February 19, 1801, he married Margaret Oliver, daughter of a Yankee, Peter Oliver, and Mildred Randolph Oliver, a Virginian. The young couple migrated to Ohio. Their oldest child, Sarah, born in Kentucky, November 21, 1801, became the wife of C.F. She was a pupil in C.F.'s school. Margaret Hill died in 1816, and Joseph Hill married Mary Purcell on September 25, 1817. He died October 28, 1836. See diary entries for October 19, 1837, and June 1, 1855, and genealogical chart, below.

15. This letter is addressed to Cincinnati. It was unclaimed and was returned to Urbana, February 27, 1818. In the Fletcher Papers there is a letter from Stephen to C.F. dated Baltimore, November 24, 1817, and another dated Pittsburgh, December 28, 1817, indicating his intention to come to the West. Stephen

for New orleans at this time of year looks despicable. I must agan intreat you to come to Urbana[16] if nothing more favourable offers. I have made some inqureies relative to getting business here as a clerk. I think you would suceed but wages are small and cash is call'd scarce. I am now teaching a school[17]—have been ingag'd in it about six weeks. I spend my time with Mr. Cooley[18] an attorney at Law mornings and evinings. I have lived [with] Mr. C. about 3 months....

C.F., Urbana, Ohio, to his father, Ludlow, Vermont, January 24, 1818

. . . Soon after I wrote you I commenced with Mr. Cooley. I continu'd about two months. There being a vacancy for a school and knowing that my clothing would want repairing and a great many necessaries would be want'd before next spring (a time when I had calculated to again commence school-keeping) I engaged & have been at this employment about 1 month. I lodge and spend all my time with Mr. Cooley except the 6 hours in school. I have 30 scholars about one ½ of them are men grown. School-keeping you men[tion]ed in your other letter to be an honorable employment. I think it so but it is the most fatiguing and wearing to the con-st[it]ution of those who dislike it of any employment whatever. I

---

died in New Orleans, August 17, 1818. Edward H. Fletcher (comp.), *Fletcher Genealogy*, p. 74.

16. Urbana in 1818 had a population of between five and six hundred persons. Laid out in 1805 it became the county seat in 1807. During the war years, from the summer of 1812 until the fall of 1814, it was virtually a military camp. The war gave impetus to its growth both financially and in population and it was incorporated in 1816. Evan P. Middleton, *History of Champaign County Ohio* . . . (2 volumes. Indianapolis, Ind.: B.F. Bowen & Co., 1917), I, 948–61, 978.

17. This was probably a different school from the one mentioned in note 14, and located in the town of Urbana.

18. James Cooley, a leading lawyer of Urbana. He was serving as prosecuting attorney for Champaign and Logan counties in 1826 when he was appointed chargé d'affaires in Peru by President John Quincy Adams. He died in Peru in 1828. *Ibid.*, I, 1093–96.

In a brief diary fragment in the Fletcher Papers, under date of November 17, 1817, C.F. wrote: "I began the study of law with Mr. Cooley . . . my feelings respecting my commencing the study of Law I can not express, but I consider I have undertook a hard and almost insurmountable job. . . ."

have not meet with any difficulty as yet nor fear none, except they complain I am too riged and strict. I have 2.50 per quarter for which term I engag'd.

. . . I have stipulat'd no time to stay with Mr. Cooley no fa[r]ther than this till I am prepar'd to [. . .]. He uses me like [a] frend and confident. He uses no bad Language nor descends to no small Intreagues. I have no desire to return to Vt. though I frequently draw involuntary sighs when I think of home!

C.F., Urbana, Ohio, to his father, Ludlow, Vermont, July 25, 1818

. . . Our crops of small grain . . . are very good. We began to harvest about the 1st of July. The Farmers all join togeather—men women & children collect at some one of the neighbours finish his harvesting & so around. At these meetings they drink a great deal of whiskey & it is not uncommon for them to fight. The Kentuckyans & Virginians frequently have a piched Battle between each other. Dueling is strictly prohibited in this state. The penalty is between [ ] & seven years imprisonement. But this does not entirly prevent it—there was [one] fought this summer near cincinati. There was one fought in this place about 5 years since.

We have some corn fit to roast. But generally our corn is not ripe so soon as yours: it grows very tall. I think about as high as the top of our old shed (between the Barns).

I commenced my 3d Quarter of school the 21 of June. I have become so familiar with this business I prosecute it with as much pleasure as I did the 1st term (& that was not great). I proceed with more deliberacy for when I first began here my movements were all cautious & studied. But now I have a particular channel to move in. During the vacation of my last quarter I formed a constitution for my school which I read to every new scholar that is initiated. This place supports 2 schools. When I began here I took the place of a man who had taught here 2 years. He was from Baltimore. He was a merchant there but during the late war he moved to this place & for the sake of educating his children he took a school. But this business did not suit him, his employers were dissatisfyed & he disagre'd with the other teacher, who being a Methodist was very much beloved & had a very full school. I felt timid myself on account of him. But before I began I visited him told my intentions &c & requested a visit at my school which I received & ever after this we have been on the best of terms. I always avoided speaking a word against him though the scholars who have left him & come to me would frequently tell me of his partiality negligence &c. But to these I have always turned a Deaf Ear. Others have told me he was mad because I pretend to teach Latin. It is not my disposition to have unprofitable controversies & people must try some more noble means to hurt my feelings, than to report a thing about me that I am not guilty of. I have a very full school & it daily increases—43—signed. I am happy to tell you the young men who went to me last winter & spring (my school was made up mostly of great ones) are very cordial friends of mine. They meet me with smiles in their faces & appear to be happy in my company.

I board with a man from N. Jersey. I give 2.00 per week. I have studyed some by candle light most all summer. Mr. Cooley has been appointed the prosecuting attorney (or states att.) in Logan county, a newly organized Court during the last Supreme Court held here. . . .

C.F., Urbana, Ohio, to his father, Ludlow, Vermont, November 21, 1818

. . . We have had an election here, for Governor Representatives to Congress States senator and two Representatives for the Legislator. The political parties are about alike here in number. You are acquainted with the manner of holding elections in the Southern States so I need not mention the intreague and stratigeues used here. They began to hold nocturnal meetings or caucuses 2 months before the elections. Every person wishing to represent his Destrict or county Declares himself a candidate in the Public print or Hand Bills & have to descend to the turpitude of self praise, so much, as to declare "that he thinks himself amply qualified to represent his constituents & can do it better than any other man." Political animostity arrose to such a pitch that circles would be formed and some hot headed fellows dispute all night. Men of the most unexceptionable characters were not exempt from slander. All the principal characters went armed day or two before the election. There were several mobs in Urbana which were repelled by the civil orthority. One man got his thomb bit off and another his eye much damaged (when two men fight as ever they clinch they fall to biting and goueging. I have witness'd several of these scenes of human depravity which at first made my blood freeze in my veins)....

I had a vacation of near a month in Sept. and began my school about the 1st of Oct. I have obligated myself to teach 6 months which will be out the 1st of April. I hope to earn 28 dollars per month. I shall pass those tedious days in school hoping I shall be able to rest a long time from this unpleasant employment.

You may want to know what proficency I make in the study of Law. Sir, I bend my mind to it as much as possible. I am much pleased with which was dull and unpleasant at first. I make a division of my time. I keep school 7 hours in a day. I study 1 hour at noon 4 at night & 3 in the morning. I have made it my rule for 2 months past to go to bead at 11 and get up at 5 but I often get up at 4. I feel very avaritious of my time. I find myself extremely ignorant. I shudder at recollecting how I left home. I was but a mere helpless infant! I mourn that it was not my fortune to have got a liberal education. I think it would have made me a man. . . .

I have made some attempts at the study [of] chymestry this summer & was highly delighted with it. I have got my three choice Books viz. Paley's Moral Philosophy, Mosses Geography and Duncans Logic.[19] Logic I have been studying 2 weeks. I shall spend 1 more upon it & then return to Blackstone. I have a desire to talk [with] you upon Religion. This has been a theme of but [MS torn] in mind for a year till since I read Logic and Moral Philosophy which have caused me to look with more scrutiny upon the objects around me and contemplate [the] author that gave them the functions they perform. I do not hardly ever tend church, for which I feel justified, as the ministers are uncooth low bread Methodist whom I despise. I generally retire to the office where I spend the day in solitude. . . .

19. William Paley, 1743–1805 *(The Principles of Moral and Political Philosophy)*; Jedidiah Morse, 1761–1826, the "Father of American Geography" *(The American Geography, Elements of Geography*, etc.); and William Duncan, 1717–1760 *(The Elements of Logic)*.

C.F., London, Ohio, to his father, Ludlow, Vermont, June 18, 1819

. . . I last March Finish'd my school in Urbana which I taught 18 month. I quit feeling conscious that I had acquitted my self of the important Trust committed with propriety to my charge. I earn'd the last 12 weeks clear from all expense $125.00. I was urged to continue a year. I could have had $575.00 & find myself. But this would not answer—money is no temptation tho I never spent a cent, as I know of, needlessly. I do not value it in comparison with my Time no more than the sods I walk on. I must tell you one thing that is—I schoold the widows sons and Daughters—orphans—and all such as were not able to pay (and who would have staid at home had I not told them their tuition should be gratis if they could not pay) without exacting the demands which I had against them.

After setling my business in Urbana I in company with a woman (Mother to the cashier of one [of] the Cincinnati Banks) went to Cincinnati. We were 3 days on the road; this was the first of April and trees were in the bloom at Cincinnati where I staid a week.

. . . Cincinnati is growing very fast. The river is lined with Steam boats, flatt Bottoms &c. When I enterd Cincinnati I felt very different from the time I left it in 1817 at which time I was pennyless and without friends or acquaintance. . . . I attended the auction—bought myself $30.00 worth of books that I have since had brought on. I left April the 11 and rode my pos[t]ing steed to Urbana in 2 days. This journey never was performed in less time. I soon settled all my affairs (and for the first time had to sue a man) and repaird to London Madison County. I live 2 miles from the city in the family of Mr. Gwynne.[20] He was from Maryland—about 33 years of age. Has been six voyages to the East Indies as a sea captain. He has one store in Urbana and one in London. One of his

20. Thomas Gwynne. He and his brothers John E., William, Eli W., David, and Horatio, came to the vicinity of London, Ohio, as early as 1810, and engaged in trade. Thomas Gwynne also conducted a tavern. In 1820 he opened a store in Urbana and moved there. He served as mayor of Urbana, 1820–22. *History of Madison County, Ohio . . .* (Chicago: W. H. Beers & Co., 1883), pp. 540–41; Middleton (ed.), *History of Champaign County Ohio*, I, 962.

tenants keeps the dairy which consists of 40 cows. The[re are] six beautiful children—five of them are confin'd with me six hours in a day—those are all I have to be plauged with the rest of my time I devote to study. I have a horse to ride when I please. I visit Urbana once in 4 weeks to recite. Mr. Cooley when I left him for this place evinced his satisfaction as to my conduct while with him by telling me I was heartily wellcome for all favors I had received. Our agreement was at first that I should give him $1.00 for the use of Books and all other privileges if I staid with him till—but he said he should make no charges & should be happy in considering me his student. I am not certain how long I shall stay here but expect to return to Urbana ere long. . . .

DIARY

Urbana Nove. the 9 [*–30, 1820*].[21] I arrived her from Va. Made the same night a proposition to Mr. Cooley to enter into the prac-

21. There are no letters or diary entries between June 18, 1819, and November 9, 1820. On June 11, 1820, Elijah Fletcher wrote to his father from Lynchburg, "I have the pleasure of informing you that Calvin is now with us. He left Ohio about three weeks ago and arrived here last Wednesday. He introduced himself to me, for I should have no more known him than the greatest stranger in the world. . . . I wrote for him to quit his school, come here and finish his study of Law. I thought he was sacrifising precious time and that he ought to have an opportunity better than he could get in Ohio. . . . He had been sick, for some time confined, & his physicians thought a ride would help him. . . .

"Calvin resembles none of our Family but Miche. He is the very picture of Michael—low, stout-built, broad-shouldered, but rather thin at present, tho he has perfectly recovered his health. . . . He has disciplined his mind to a good code of morality. He has the most tender and delicate feelings. . . . He is like a sensative plant. Take Calvin all in all I think him a son you may be proud of." Von Briesen (ed.), *Letters of Elijah Fletcher*, pp. 89–90.

According to a biographical sketch C.F. was admitted to the Virginia bar, and Elijah wrote his father on August 31, 1820, that C.F. was thinking "of returning to the Western Country some time first of Nov. next. He will get Licence to practice Law first." Trask, *Memoir of The Hon. Calvin Fletcher of Indianapolis, Ind.*; Von Briesen (ed.), *Letters of Elijah Fletcher*, p. 91. No mention of his being admitted to the bar in Virginia has been found in C.F.'s diary, letters, or autobiographical notes and sketches. It has been said that he left Virginia and returned to Ohio because of his opposition to slavery, and his consistently strong antislavery stand would support this. It is interesting to note in this connection a sentence in a letter from Elijah to C.F., March 19, 1830: "Lucian [Elijah's younger son] says

tice of law with him which he in part excepted and intirely concluded the next day. I found myself very deficient in the practicle part of the law. The second week that is from the 18 to the 26 Mr. Cooley was at Springfield. I commenced an action of slander for Mr. Hains. On the 27 of Nove. our court commenced. I strictly attended and found myself extremely ignorant in the practice. Mr. Cooley appears to repose confidence in me. I therefore feel extremely anxious not to disappoint him. The import case of the Rectors came in to be tried and they were cleared of the horrid crime of perjury. On Friday the 30 Mr. Cooley made application to Judge Crane[22] for my admittance to practice *ex gratia* this winter which he admitted. I shall go to Logan County where I shall help Bacon[23] in Mr. Cooley's Business. I expect I shall have many combats with my ignorance. The lawyers do not appear to manifest the least degree of friendship towards the young and rising.

Sunday December the 2d [*3d*]. I started after making some preparations for Logan in company with Moses B. Corwin[24] and Jos. Law. It rained all the way to Logan (a little snow which disap-

---

he does not exactly like his uncle Calvin, for he told him he ought to black his own shoes, and he says he is no negro to do such work." Although Elijah was a slaveholder, he wrote to his brother on March 29, 1831, "You may feel very happy that you are not in a slave state with your fine Boys, for it is a wretched country to destroy the morals of youth." And Elijah, like C.F., supported the idea of colonization of blacks in Africa. Von Briesen (ed.), *Letters of Elijah Fletcher*, pp. xvi–xvii, 111, 122.

22. Joseph Halsey Crane (1782–1851), state legislator, prosecuting attorney for Montgomery County, Ohio, member of Congress (1829–37), and associate judge of the Ohio Supreme Court. At this time he was serving as president judge of the court of common pleas. *Biographical Directory of the American Congress, 1774–1949* (Washington: U.S. Government Printing Office, 1950), p. 1030.

23. Henry Bacon, lawyer and earlier prosecuting attorney for Champaign County. Middleton (ed.), *History of Champaign County Ohio*, I, 406.

24. Born in Kentucky, Moses Bledso Corwin (1790–1872) was admitted to the Ohio bar in 1812. A Whig, he served as state representative in 1838 and 1839 and as representative in Congress, 1849–51 and 1853–55. He was a brother of Thomas Corwin, Ohio governor, United States senator, secretary of the treasury, and minister to Mexico. *Biographical Directory of the American Congress*, p. 1021.

First page of Calvin Fletcher's earliest formal diary, November 9, 1820

Urbana Since the 9 Jan I do now from the
made the same night a proposition to Mr Cooley to enter
into the practice of law with him which he in part excepted
and interely complied the next day. I found myself very
deficient in the practicle part of the law— The second
week that is from the 18 to the 26 Mr Cooley was at
Springfield I commenced an action of Slander for the
Plaintiff— on the 27 of June our court commenced I strictly
attended and found myself extremely ignorant in the
practice Mr Cooley appears to repose confidence in me
I therefore feel extremely anxious not to disappoint him
The import cases of the Rectors came on to be tried and they
were cleared of the horrid crime of perjury. on Friday
the 30 Mr Cooley made application to Judge Crane
for my admittance to practice ex gratia this winter
which he admitted. I shall go to Logan County where I
shall sell Bacon in Mr Cooleys Business— I expect
I shall have more contacts with my ignorance. The
Lawyers do not appear to manifest the least degree of
friendship towards the young and rising.

Tuesday Decem
the 2nd I started after making some preparations for Logan
in company with Moses B. Corwin and Lo. Powell. It snowed
all the way to Logan for little snow which disappeared very
fast— We arrived at Mr Fellas about sun down. We
found the Layers viz. Swan, C Parish and Henry Bacon and
Judge Crane who were all seated around a very good fire
reading a story in the Evenings at home. Judge Crane I much
admire for his wise and just sayings. C P made a very
singular expression— that he did not care what a man's
private character was if he was only a man of genius. this
expression J C censured very much in him I sat with
out making any observations till late when we were conversing about the false declamations of the Methodist

peared very fast). We arrived at Majr. Zellas about sun down. We found the La[w]yers viz. Swan,[25] O. Parish[26] and Henry Bacon and Judge Crane who were all seated around a very good fire reading a story in the Ev[en]ings at home. Judge Crane I much admired for his wise and just sayings. O. P. made a very singerlar expression—That he did not care what a man's private character was if he was only a man of genius. This expression Judge C. censured very much in him. I sat without making any observations till late when we were conversing about the false declamations of the Methodist Jewet come from Springfield whom I disliked very much for his dry aukey wit.

Monday the 3d [4] of Dec. After court was opened and minutes red it was adjourned till the 4. The evening was spent in talk and singing. Gen. Vance[27] was present. The inhabitants extremely rough. About 4 log cabins in Bellfoun[taine] the seat of justice for the county.

Tuesday [Dec. 5]. The Bill for perjury against Jno. Enoch was again found and the trial put off till next term. Mr. Bacon done the persecuting business for the fees—an order on Logan County of $40. I made my first speech this day in a dog-case. I was not prepared to say any thing of consequence. I was not so very much afrighted

25. Gustavus Swan (1787–1860), a native of New Hampshire, who emigrated to Ohio in 1810 and was admitted to the bar in that year. He served two terms as state representative from Franklin County, as judge of the court of common pleas, and as director and president of the state bank. *History of Franklin and Pickaway Counties, Ohio* . . . ([Cleveland, Ohio:] William Bros., 1880), pp. 64–65.

26. Orris Parish who came to Franklin County, Ohio, as a young lawyer from New York and settled in Columbus upon its being selected as the state capital. In 1816 he was elected president judge of the court of common pleas. He resigned his judgeship in 1819 after having been cleared of charges of bad conduct. He died in Columbus in 1837. *Ibid.*, p. 65.

27. Joseph Vance (1786–1852), who moved to Ohio from Pennsylvania in 1801. He served as the first clerk, recorder, and auditor of Champaign County and was among the first settlers in Urbana. Following military service in the War of 1812, he continued his career of public service as state representative for six sessions; representative to Congress, 1821–35, 1843–47; governor of Ohio, 1836–38; state senator, 1840–41; and member of the state constitutional convention in 1851. *Biographical Directory of the American Congress*, p. 1947; Middleton (ed.), *History of Champaign County Ohio*, II, 360–63.

as vacant—yet I fe[l]t a little intimidated with fear. In the evening we had a mock trial against Jno. Enoch for putting his horse and not serving as groom but trusting Mr. Corwin to officiate as such. I here made a speech more to my mind than before. All got rather high save myself. I slept with O. Parish. Vance Chaplin[28] Thompson and Walpers plaid cards. About midnight Parish called for something to eat. We had bread and cheese. [. . .] Boils Wm. and C[. . .] were at Belvill.

Wednesday the 5 [Dec. 6]. We all started after breakfast for Urbana—a little snow on the ground and froze hard. I rode some distance before I was overtaken by Chaplin and Parish who stumpt me to swop horses. I consented to swop even and we exchanged even. I rode to Urbana very well satisfied that I had made a good bargin, but was perswaded that I had got cheated and reexchanged by the solicitude of Mr. Parish.

I found myself very incapabl in my profession as a Lawyer. Much application must [be] given before I can expect to reap an agreeable and ful harvest. I find myself very ignorant of the world and destitute of that fund of book knowledge that is necessary for to acquit myself with honor and eclat at the bar. I have had some peculiar exercises of late respecting my native home and concluded that if I live I will surely visit my native state in two years from this time of which I will apprise my friend as soon as posible. I now begin to look with a more philosophic eye on my past misfortunes. I cant but desire once more to clasp the hand of my aged parents who will both soon yeild to the rude and corroding movements of time. I then with them can see the improvements made on my younger Brother and sister and I hope many new affections would arise I feel not.

Sunday December the 10th. I have received a letter from Mr. Cooley and the Govs.[29] message. I did talk of visiting Shelby county this week but gave out. I have commenced a laborious work—that

28. Jonathan Chaplin, schoolteacher and preacher who served as mayor of Urbana from 1822 to 1825. Middleton (ed.), *History of Champaign County Ohio*, I, 555, 926; *History of Champaign County, Ohio* . . . (Chicago: W. H. Beers & Co., 1881), p. 340.

29. The Ohio governor, Ethan Allen Brown.

is an alphabetical list of the laws of Ohio wrote on a large sheet. I last night attended a debating society which we have formed here. I injoyed myself very well. I saw in it much talk and but very little reason. In this society I cannot expect to make great improvements as there requires but a very trifling exertion. Mr. Fyffe[30] is our president, Mr. Whitford our secretary. I hope I shall make due improvement of my time this winter. I am now some little hindrd by company. I have had Mr. M. Williams call on me for advice this week. Am to defend a suit for him in Logan County. I am now intimate in several families in this place, viz Mr. [. . .], Hites, Gwynnes, Vances &c. I hope still to cultivate which ought to exist in families. Banes[31] has just commenced shop-keeping in D. Vance's office. I sincerely hope he will be successful in his undertaking and do not doubt but in five years he will be the most noted Physicion in the Miami Country. Maj. G. and lady are here from Detroit, and Mrs. Edmonds from Columbus. I shall now pursue my dige[s]t of the laws and keep them as a memento of my exertions of eighteen hundred and twenty. It is rather cold this day—no snow on the ground. I now injoy the very best of health—weigh about one hundred and forty five.

Thursday Dec. the 13d [*14th*]. I this day received several newspapers in which I found some considerable news. I received an invitation to ride with Dr. Carter to Wilkersons where I saw old Mrs. Stretch and so on. I returned and visited George Bells[32] school with which I felt very well pleased. I think him a man who uses his best endeavors to improve the rising. I was called upon by one or two clients this day respecting business. I am yet under some apprehensions that I shall not do right and shall neglect to do my duty. Chaplin has returned from Sydney court. Capt. Riley is in Town. I expect to have the pleasure of seeing him tomorrow.

Sunday Dec. the 17. I went to Buck Creek with Dr. Banes and

30. William H. Fyffe, a native of Virginia who settled in Urbana in 1805. He opened the first saddle shop and was elected a trustee of the town in 1816. Middleton (ed.), *History of Champaign County Ohio,* I, 950, 961, 1098.

31. Evan Banes (1797–1878), physician, mayor of Urbana, and newspaper editor and publisher. *Ibid.*, I, 363–64.

32. An Irishman who was reputed to be a good teacher and an extremely strict disciplinarian. *History of Champaign County, Ohio* (1881), pp. 339–40.

Baldwin[33] and suffered not a little from the cold—snow three inches deep. I was somewhat pleased with Bane's father's situation—likewise Baldwin's. We arrived at Urbana after dark. I soon repaired to the church where I heard a very good sermon preached and tolerable exortation from Mr. Shaw.

I returned home with a resolution to prosecute a certain project which I am *determined to commence as soon as posible and shall do it with as much dexterity as I posibly can. I may be defeated yet I know I am in truth able to bear such a defeat. I do not know the time I shall ever be more able to effect this or a like project. I shall commence next Sunday. I will see what progress I make in one month from this. I may say I was foolish—but I can say I have done greater feats within one year than what this would be if accomplished.*

Tuesday Dec. the 18 [*19*]. I went with Mr. Wilson from Clarksburg in Va. to James Thomas'es for the purpose of securing a debt in which we in part succeeded. He left his business with me to transact. I have for several days been writing in the clerks office for the purpose of gaining information &c.

Thursday [*Dec.*] *the 21st.* Very muddy disagreeabl moving. I feel very much depressed at this time on several accounts—I am rather uneasy—cannot but believe that if I were married I should be contented. Am perhaps reaching forward for a scorpean instead of a lamb. I am altering from my former inquisitive habits to those of remisness. I have not those fears to restrain me that I formerly had which perhaps was a very great inducement to my former attention and reflection. I this night found another theory—that is to educate H. S.[34] and then * * * * * * * * * * * *

33. William Baldwin. C.F. named his seventh son after him: ". . . my esteemed friend . . . in early life my friend & comforter. . . . while studying law at Urbana he was a clerk in a store with Messrs. Gwynnes now a merchant in the city of N.Y." Diary, August 18, 1837. Upon Baldwin's death in 1848 C.F. recalled that Baldwin "advanced to me 27 years ago all he had to commence housekeeping $33. Was then a clerk in a store at $15 per month. He rose to be one of the biggest merchants of Ohio then one of the biggest in N.Y. City & died worth from $50 to 200 thousand perhaps." Diary, August 4, 1848.

34. This is the first reference to Sarah Hill, daughter of Joseph Hill with whose family C.F. boarded when he taught his first school in Urbana. See note 14, above.

This plan perhaps would be noble within itself. It might cause me to be more attentive and anxious in preparing for future trials. By this plan I have thought I should be able [to] keep alive ambition cherish virtue and make myself known. I would be one or two years preparing whereas otherwise I shall like to be precipitate.

Christmas the 25 of December. I went to Mr. Hills for Sally whom I brought hither. I had some talk with her on the road upon the subject above mentioned. In the evening I attended the consert where I enjoyed myself extremely well. The next night I was at Mr. Gibbs'es. I did not stay late but slept with Dr. Carter. The eve of the 27th I was at P. Coldwell's and was pursuaded to dance. The remainder of the week I was walking up and down the streets.

Friday the 29. I in company of several others meet to regulate the Library. There was some difficulty attending our proceedings. I, from an ungarded expression, made several enemies I fear which will teach me always to be on my guard for I am too apt to make expressions of people which if they should hear would tend much to injure their feelings—and it is not my desire to wantonly injure any persons feelings.

The 30 of Dec. I read Bane's New-Years address. In the evening I went to church and returned home with Miss H——. I sat up with her at Mr. G.s. I again talked with her on the former subject. I am now about to make a decision on what I shall do—yet Pride has a very great influence Poverty some considerable and other objections I shall not mention.

Monday January the 1 1821. Mr. Corwin and McClaine[35] and myself set out for Columbus. Went by the way of London. Staid at Haine's. There was a party at Reeve's which I attended. Danced several times became acquainted with two ladies by the name of Hull from Montpelier Vt.

Jan. the 2d [–Feb. 4]. We started for Columbus—extremely cold and disagreeable riding. We got to Col. about 2 P.M.—got dinner—found Mr. Cooley well &c. I attended the U.S.A. Circuit court

35. John McLean (1785–1861), associate judge of the Supreme Court of Ohio. Upon Ohio's admission to the Union he was elected to Congress, serving from December, 1818, to March, 1819. He was commissioner of the United States General Land Office, 1822–23, postmaster general, 1823–29, and associate justice of the United States Supreme Court, 1829–61. *Biographical Directory of the American Congress,* p. 1546.

which commenced that day. Wednesday I spent in court and in the legislator. Thursday Night I was examined by Judge Parish, Mr. Corwin & McClane together with Mr. Chaplin.[36] I saw the agregate talants of Ohio collected at Col. viz—Hammond Wright Goodenno Harrison[37] &c and to crown all the worthy observations that I have made in that state of the human and brutal kingdom I had the pleasure [of] measuring in my noddle the height Breadth features jestures and politeness of the renowned Henry Clay—the Cicero—at least so pronounced by the wisdom of the U.S.A. of America. Yet for the want of taste and deser[n]ment and being destitute of the impartial scales by which we can rightly Judge of human greatness, I should have pronounced him only a common man. His manner of address is more indicative of politeness than good sense of which I think Hammond is possessed of far the greatest quantity. I left Columbus on Friday in company of Jo. Foley Capt. Tuner [Turner?] and Madox Fisher. Saterday morning it commenced snowing and continued so till I arrived in Urbana. I attended a debating school that eve &c. The next week past off imperceptibly. For some unknown reasons I at this time am rather discontented—yet I think it arrises from a fear that I shall not perform the functions prescribed for me [to] fulfill. On the subject of Divinity Toporgraphy or Natural Phil[osophy] I have no discoverie to mention. On the 28 of Jan. I was at the wedding of Mr. Comer and Mildred Fitch which took place at Mr. Gibbs. The Nuptials were celebrated by Mr. Samuel Hitt in very solemn and grave style. I never till then was impressed with the solemnity of the marriage contract. I here could pause and make comments on what my feelings are in respect to marriage—but it would avail nothing. Miss Hill was present at the celebration of these marriage rights. For her I have a very great esteem. I have good and sufficient proofs that our esteem for each other is reciprocal. She is poor and without Education. Is she not aimiable notwithstanding all those defects? Perhaps if I should make an answer it would proceede from my partiality. I know

36. C.F. was granted a license to practice law by the Supreme Court of Ohio on January 18, 1821. The document signed by Joseph N. Couch and John McLean, judges, and William Ward, clerk of the Supreme Court of Ohio, is in the Fletcher Papers.

37. Charles Hammond, John Crafts Wright, John Milton Goodenow, and William Henry Harrison.

"the world yet prevails and its dread laugh which scarce the firm philosopher can scorn." But I have thus far been successful in this life, and could I repay that maker and preserver of my existence in a more ample way than in doing good to all my fellow creatures and for instance where virtue is invelloped with life's common misfortune poverty and ignorance, would it not be amiable in me to rescue the victim from these two mal[a]di[e]s? I think [it] would. Then have I not my own [reasons] for doing as I have done or would do? I think I have. I waited upon Miss Hill home and promised to visit her in three weeks. I returned home and done some writing in the clerk's office the same and following week, and concluded from some new reflections on the proceedings I was going about that Instead of abandoning her as I had had some thought of I concluded I would make and fix my choice on *her* permenantly. That *she* and she only should be my companion if God willed in the early part of my life and coming to such a conclusion I altered my plan as to the mode and time of visiting her. So on the 2d day of February I mounted my horse and without much excitement I rode with carless steps and slow across the river thro' mud to be the herald of my own intentions. I arrived about dark. A room was prepared. I there had an interview with the object of my desire—and to her I disclosed my intentions I presume to her surprise and agreed to make my intentions known to her parents in the morning which I did without any fear &c. Their approbation I received without hesitation and agreed that I would be an adopted child as soon as preparations could be made which we thought could be done within two or three months.

The above written essay on my agreement to be married is wrote on the 4 day of *February in the Year of O'r Lord One Thousand Eight Hundred and Twenty One the Anniversary of my Twenty Third Year.*

I will here suggest my reasons for these ingagements that I am about to fulfil so that I shall be able here after to satisfy myself and if not myself others that may have an inspection of this Book, that I deliberately went into the marriage contract being sensible of all the disadvantages under which I labor—and firstly of all I shall make some general observations and then dwell on particulars. I know and have long been impressed with a belief that man was made with many latent principles of affection friendship &c—that those two affections exercised properly are the only things which make men respec[t]able, useful and happy. Therefore if there is wonderful powers of friendship and esteem in men wrapt up and there are certain applications which will bring them forth, we certainly ought so [to] do. For our general and continued happiness we ought to fix our affections to a certain spot to a few select friends who will estimate us for a long and continued acquaintance with the practice of virtue and constancy. Now what will stimulate us to those virtues? Is [it] not necessity? Yea. Then let us soon take to us that attraction which will bind us to the spot we choose, and this object is a *wife* an help meat for man. At what age is man generally capable of protecting the object for which he has a natural regard? As soon as the body becomes mature at which I have now arrived. I have seen something of the wor[l]d for my age—I have enjoyed the friendship of the friendly—I have by exertion placed myself in as happy a situation at present as I could wish. Yet to say I have those friends whom a happy weedlock could produce, would be expressing vanity. I am poor—can I take a person into poverty? can I find one that is willing to enter into poverty and run the risk of being delivered therefrom by my exertion? I think I have. I therefore have made a choice and if not disappointed shall rush perhaps into a state which will render me unhappy. God only knows. I can say that I have proceeded without any lucrative motives, or any mercenay views. May God in his i[n]finite wisdom counsel me in all my doings hereafter, as he has been abundent in his goodness to me. May I ever praise him. the *F*[o]*urth of February 1821.*

[*Feb.* 22–25]. On the 22d day of February it being the day appointed for a party at Hunters I attended after going over the river after the Miss Hill whom I brought to town. Extremely bad riding and rather cold. I must confess that I injoid myself very extremely—the partner I had perhaps was not the most beautiful yet she was the most modest. We rather imprudently sat up all night a thing I now very much disapprove of. The 23d it was very cold. I went over the river with the Miss Hill and returned the same night. Saturday the [24th] I filled a deed and completed a declaration. Sunday the 25 I wrote a caput to the school act which I want published. I am likewise [. . .].

Friday P.M. *the 2d of March.* I went to E. Petty's with a notice and from there to Jo Hills where I spent the eve in company with &c. I feel very much inspired with the idea of once being able to make the situation of S[arah] better. I rather at present dispair. I feel the disadvantages under which I labor. I am poor and ignorant of my profession, which are both obsticles to my marrying & it is said by my friends that I cannot obtain any eminance in my profession if I now marry. I cannot dispute this but hope with the aid of kind providence I may be able to attain a subsistance. I think I shall enter into a matrimoneal state let the consequences be what they [may]. The object I am to join in this union cannot be objected to only by those [who] are more fond of wealth than I am. I know that those temporal possessions are agreeable—yet I think I shall applaude myself hereafter should I bear one who is destitute thro' the ocean of troubles which beset us in this world. I find that I have much to do to attain any emenance in my profession. And to droop in the grades of mediocrity is painful to me. I moan that my feelings of honors are not more acute—that my resentment and pleasure are not more extreme. I am sensible that if I ever wish to attain any worthy honors in my profession they must come thro' the medium of application integrity and virtue. Let me pursue. Let me reach forward.

Sunday the [ ] *of March.* Warm and pleasant.

Sunday the 25 of March. I have for two weeks back been engaged in the study of evidence. I on the [ ] of this Inst. went to H—s. I did not feel so well satisfied as usual. I learned that I had given an affront &c. I about these times feel much anxiety about my improvement and future success which I know must and does depend much on the exertions I make of the few dull and unfruitful faculties I possess. Yet I cannot use those to the advantage that some might or would. I think that hope and anticipation the noblest inmate of the youthful heart has been expelled. I feel some fears when I consider the relation in which I stand with C[ooley]. I am often doubtful whether I do my duty which to neglect would be gross in me. I likewise am rather opposed in my project of marriage by one that I do not like to thwart in opinion. I fear this step will tend to my discredit and future sorrow but I believe I shall try it. There is one course I mean to pursue tho' it be much to my disadvantage that is to be virtuous in all my actions. If I get enimies let them be made without any fault on my side. I have [at]tended a debate in public last night (24). I was there unexpectedly out done by [. . .]. It rather grieves me yet I must suffer it. This is Sunday night about 9 o'clock. I am now going to bed as I have no candles. I have been to church today. I am getting rather remiss on such occasions. Rather blustry and squally weather.

Thursday March the 28 [29]. Cold sudden changes–at night warmer. Had Music in the eve. I went. A. Allen married to a Sargent girl. Mr. Cooley at Springfield at court. I feel rather diffident about the approach of our court. I have been rather unsuccessful in my public declamations. I know that for esteem of the attorneys it would be prudent for me to say but very little, but ignorance says a man must be measured according to his loquacity. I feel ambitious to acquit myself at least with decency in my first sally into the world as a public character. I have to lament an apathy that now pervades my mind and desposition in respect to scollastic acquisitions. This will I fear be an obsticle to my futur advancement.

I have laid my intentions before Mr. C[ooley] as to my getting married. He at first rather disaproved of it but I got his consent by rather insisting upon the necessity than otherwise of the case. He intimated to me the disadvantages that would arrise from my marrying a poor girl and one of low parantage. But this I am determined shall not be an obsticle. My expenses are great. I much fear of getting in debt and being unable to extricate myself. My Books have arrive[d] in Cincinnati. I think from my indigent circumstances, I shall have some difficulty in obtaining them. I yesterday received a letter from A. Ingram.[38] He has been at Cin[cinnati]. I

38. Andrew Ingram, who became one of C.F.'s closest friends. He was born in Philadelphia and came to Ohio as a youth. At the time of his death, August 1, 1865, C.F. wrote in his diary: "He came under my friendship and care when 16 years of age–in 1819 at London, Ohio. He got his education under my advise and some assistance. Went to Cincinnati & Athens College a year or two Kept School came to Indianapolis in the spring of 1824." From 1824 on, Ingram's name ap-

think he has performed wonders within a year and suppassed all my expectations.

Sunday night April the 1st one thousand eight hundred and twenty one. I this morning arose rather late—found it cloudy and unpleasant moving. I made some preparation to go out to Mr. Gibbs' but concluded that my Journey would be lost as the person whom I had a desire to see would not be there as I had before expected. I read some in Anarchusas [Anacharsis] travels in Greece. Did not feel any way disposed to attend church. I felt rather dispon[d]ancy than otherwise. I have formed a plan of a Journal that I intend to keep as soon as practible that is when I get to keep a house of my own &c. I feel very concerned[?] that I shall spend the remainder of my days rather in forgetfulness than otherwise. I think that some few of my Bosom friends are Jealous of me for some reason or other &c. But this time will fully disclose. My imagination does not run as high as it did formerly. I sleep without dreaming which is a sure indication of a tranquil mind which I think is no recommendation to a young man in asmuch as it is sure proof [of] his negligence and inattention to the most important events that are passing. Awake arise. Now is the time for mental exertions and acquisition. May I lay hold with the hand with dilligence and perseverance and press forward to the improvement of the understanding than which there is nothing more noble. If I fail in one point of view let me try another. Shall I die an ignorant man or not? This is query and a questionable thing indeed. I yet believe in works. Therefore I have no one to accuse but myself *If* [I] do not arrive at the Historical facts and moral truths that are prevelent among men.

April the 15th. My Books arrived. I was much pleased on the reception thereof. During court week I attentively paid my visits to the court. I made one speech only. Perhaps I was not as attentive as I should have been for some reasons. I had in contemplation of getting married.

---

pears regularly in the Diary until his death, and there are many letters from him in the Fletcher Papers. He moved to Lafayette in 1831, where he practiced law and served as prosecuting attorney and circuit judge. Lafayette *Daily Courier,* August 2, 1865.

April 18 [–*April 30*]. On the 18th of April Mrs. Oliver[39] returned from Ft. Meigs. It snowed and a disagreeable time a backward Spring. I visited Mr. Hills on the 24th. I told them of my intentions of having the solemn cerimony of marriage performed on the 1st of May. I returned and hasted to make preparations. On the 28th of April it rained. I again visited Mr. Hill's and I sincerely hoped it was the last expedition of the like I ever should make. I returned on Sunday the 29th. On Monday the 30th I worked in the Garden. I made some preparations for the first of May. I rode up to Mr. Hitts without much embarrassment and requested him to perform the ceremony which he consented to do with much cheerfulness.

April 30 at night. This scene which now lies before me make[s] not that impression on me that I should have expected. I once was impressed with the idea that as man felt an indescribable sensation [on] such an occasion—but I approach it not with those feelings of immoderate curiosity that I expected but with some degree of solemnity. I know it is one of the most momentous events in my life. I hope it is the only one of the kind that I shall pass thro'. I am now twenty three years old—commencing a life which requires the performance of all the functions of a real citizen. I have one thing to lament. I am poor. I commence rather on the goodness of one or two of my intimates than otherwise. Wm. Baldwin must not be forgotten in all my movements in life together with several other friends I have. The dark unfathomed waste lies before me—clouds and darkness rest upon it. I some times am ready to take the pinions of anticipation and soar into the regions of futurity and look around to see the path through which I shall pass. I thus stop and conclude that my life has been rather misterious and been thus pursued without any paticular series of calculation; therefore think that the remainder is only known to him who rules over the destinies of men—that I am to fill the circle marked by Heaven.

39. Probably Sarah Hill's maternal grandmother, Mildred (Mrs. Peter) Oliver. In the Diary entry for October 19, 1837, C.F. recalled her kindness to him when he arrived in Urbana in 1817. As mentioned above, note 14, she was a member of the Randolph family of Virginia and married a Yankee schoolteacher, Peter Oliver. They had several children, some of whom migrated to Ohio, and in 1811 or 1812 they, too, moved to that state.

I hope as a married man that I shall pursue the paths of rectitude and virtue that nothing shall be said of me that will be a reproach to my former life which I now declare has been upright in my intentions. I have chosen the companion of my heart. May it be my happy lot to sustain her through the mazes of a terestial world. May it be my fortune to bring to light hidden excellence of personal goodness. This night and tomorrow are two memorable days in my life. Four years from tomorrow I left my friends in New England. I started I think into the world then as I am now starting into the marriage state. I sincerely hope that same directing hand which has led me will still be a pillar of fier by night to direct me and may I ever be thankful for the manifold blessings I have received and always recollect that a proper dependance on that Being who sustains who gave life who is conversant in the ways of men, will ultimately terminate in something more valuable than temporal happiness. "May God the Soul of my soul sustain me for some good to my fellow creatures which is & has been the desire of my heart. *The Th[i]rtieth of April one thousand Eight Hundred and Twenty One 1821 1821 30th April.*

Tuesday May the 1st [–*May 8*] *1821.* I arose early in the morning and made preparations for to visit Miss Hill and consumate the marriage before-mentioned. About 10 A.M. I was prepared with Gig and horse without attendants the reason of which was, the friends and relatives of Sarah were not invited nor desired by me therefore I should have a good excuse in asmuch as I did not ask my own acquaintances. I arrived at Mr. Hills about 1 P.M. where I found a few country chaps collected for the purpose of being forward at the celebration of the marriage. At first I felt somewhat disconcerted at their appearance but when I came to take all things properly in to view I dissipated those feelings. I was received by smiles by the family. I did not see Sarah who was dressing herself in the Chamber. I waited till about 3 at which time Mr. S. Hitt had arrived whom I had a conference with and desired him to be formal in the marriage ceremony. I then had the household seated and went into the chamber to wait upon Sarah. [She came] down and [I] presented her at the alter of Himen. I found her rather disconcerted and affrighted. I took her by the hand with indifference and lead her into the room. Mr. Hitt proceeded to the celebration

&c first the marriage ceremony next an address very pertinent to the occasion and closed with a prayer. I after dinner had a conference with him and he returned home. I spent the evening not very pleasantly but I was uneasy. The next day we left and repaired to Town. I found Mr. G.s [Gwynne's] family in great readiness for our reception. A few choice friends were invited and we dined. After that we spent the P.M. pleasantly &c. From that time till the eighth I spent in making preparations for moving. Still boarded at Mr. G. where every mark of hospitality was exhibited towards me and wife—yea quite as much as I could have expected from a sister or a Brother.

On the 8th at night we arrived in our own house—Llewellyn David & Murdock G[wynne] came with us. We had a small fire built and I drew out my papers to write the above and some few resolutions by which I mean my house shall be guided. In viewing the things necessary for keeping house before we commenced, I thought of but few articles that we should want—but on commencing I found many things wanting.

May the 12th. I arose very early and read a few pages in Franklin's Philosophical Epistles in which is contained a translation of Cicero on old age. I have concluded to read this and select the best pasages for Llewellyn Gwynne. I have commenced writing several declarations some of which I had before wrote but had done them incorrect. I do not take that inquisitive delight in searching out moote points in law that I ought. I furthermore fear that I am losing that taste I once possessed for Philosophical researches. But let me banish far hence that sluggish forgetfulness which characterises a great part of my fellow beings. I find that two thirds of the human rase are held together and guided by a few characters, and why could I not be a profitable guide as long as it is the design of society that there should be a preferance in its members. I therefore say let me once more summon up the best of resolutions and commence my researches. Altho' I do it alone and unapplauded, it will certainly be of use to me hereafter to think I have spent the morning of my life profitably.

I have emploid a boy to live with me this summer so that I need not make a slave of myself and family for I know now is the time I ought to devote my hours to literary pursuits.

[May] 13 Sunday in the P.M. I wrote a declaration and helped Mr. Cooley to start for Cincinnati. Very warm and agreeable weather. I walked with Sarah to the woods and got some wood Bine. Went to A. R. Colwells and Miss [. . .] called on us. Took tea. We then went to D. Vance's. Retur[n]ed and went to bed.

Monday [May] the 14. I made some further improvement in the garden. Some frost in the morning and very cool. Trees in Bloom. In the P.M. an old gentleman called on me from Deleware County to see if a sum of money had been collected for him &c. Mr. Taber called to see if his father should proceede in a personal property [suit] as he would on real. I sowed some beets and spent the eve with G. in company of Dr. Banes who for the first time appeared to injoy himself in such a situation. We returned home and went to bed but got up very late the next morning.

[May] 16. I called on Mrs. Hunt. I this day am determined to commence writing in the clerks office &c. Some frost this morning. Still reading Cicero on old age.

The 17th of May. Cool & clear. I commenced writing in the clerks office. Kept rather close at home feeling desireous to improve a person in whose wellfare I take as great an interest as I do in my own.

Friday [May] the Eighteenth. I wrote some. Was to have had a boy come to live with me. When I arose I made an unpleasant discovery which had rather a bad effect on my feelings—I found that I must not be too inquisitive in things. I well know this was a subject relative to Geo. Percell. I this day was determined to secret a *Ring* given by [. . .] to [. . .] which I knew but never thought of the cause of the gift till a few days since.

May the 19. I arose early in the morning. I found some frost yet it had not injured our garden any of consequence. I wrote some in our office. It was quite cool. I took tea with Sarah at Mr. Colwells & returned home in the evening with several pictures which I got framed and a pair of shews. I had a fire made in the front room. I then went in quest of Mr. Eli G. who had called on me in the P.M. & I was out. I returned & found Sarah alone. I sat a few minutes with her & heard a grammar lesson she had committed for the first time. She complains of a bad memory which I think has never been cultivated & how can the prairie bring forth any thing but wild flowers till it [is] cultivatet by the careful hand of man and for a mind in a state of nature I never have seen one that I thought bid fairer for a fertile garden than hers. Yet she is discouraged and wishes to drag out the remainder of her too precious life to me in ignorance & obscurity which thought is a piercing goard to me which unless removed will ever be perplexing to me. I have been already tantalized by Mrs. [. . .] on the account of S[arah's] ignorance which I hope to disipate. I have not paid that strict devotion to my studies that I ought. I have been still making acquisitions to my household furnature. I now live in peace & in the bonds of fellow ship with all men. I have a competence for which to my God I hope to be thankful yet I fear I shall some day or other want. But God only knows.

May the 26. I must here relate a circumstance that has occured, one more painful than any in my life. Sometime the last of April I heard it reported that the girl that lives at Gwynne's was pregnant by me. I let the report pass without saying much. After I got married the report still continued to be current and was suggested as being the cause of my precipitate marriage. * * * * I let it pass till this morning—when to my surpprise L. G. told me that the girl had told his mother that I had been the instrument of her pregnancy ! ! ! ! ! I feel something agitated at present—I think the declaration of the girl will tend to injure me very much in the estimation of the family. If so I cannot help it.

May the 29. EXTRAORDINARY. On the 26th after the above was wrote I called on Mr. G. and had a conversation on the report of the girl. I hardly thought he credited it in as much as what she had stated respecting the time of her conception did not correspond with her looks on Sunday. I kept still—my friends as well as myself were a little agitated. On Monday I wrote some in the clerk's office but did not feel much like worke. I called on Mrs. G. in the P.M. I there saw the girl. She kept at a distance. In the evening I called on Tom G. and had a conversation with him and told [him] I had reasons to suspect Sam McCord as being an instrument for the propegation of the diabolical charge. He also told me I might make an experiment by fright to elicit the truth from her. I therupon started for home but had not got far before Mr. G. called me back —told me that Cresy had just packed up her cloths and & cleared out. He advised me to follow her. I did accordingly but could not find her. I returned—took Banes & Baldwin with me and we scoured every negro house in town. I broke into one where I was refused admittance. I at length found her at Simons. She utterly refused charging me with it but refused being with any person whatever. I took the Rattan from the hands of Banes & I chastised her in a very severe manner without any compassion for which, considering her forward state of pregnancy I may perhaps feel a degre of remorse and I already cannot but shed a tear of regret at the frailty of her own sex and am now of an opinion that but a very few women are the fit companion of a Philosopher. She at length confessed that Col. Flourny[?] of Columbus had been the villan who had put her up to make this report about me. I left her the[n].

May the 29. In the morning I had heard some reports about what had happened as coming from McCord. I felt determined to have some satisfaction. I thereupon asked him into the office and charged him with the baseness of his conduct. He gave me some insulting language. I according I attacked him and have full faith to believe that I should have whiped him if I had not been prevented. And now swear by him who gave me this power for natural vindication that I will fight when ever I am insulted.

June 7th [*–8*]. This month came in with rains and showers. I have wrote in the clerks office some of late but not much. I am rather negligent and inattentive to the improvement of my mind. I find that my profession is not studied much by the Lawyers in this place in as much as they are all taken up by domestic affairs. I know now it is not imposible to become as eminent in the profession as most of lawyers if I do not spend my life in dull forgetfulness. My wife has commenced the English grammar. I am fraid that I cannot induce her to get into habits of reflection & contemplation. I enjoy the company of Dr. Banes. We are appointed overseers of a Thespian society which has made rapid progress—far beyond our expectations. I have of late had some contemplation as to making myself amiable to my neighbours. I know it is my Duty to always conduct myself in all respects with modesty and affection not get above them in my feelings but always consider them as my equals.

N. P. Fletcher[40] wrote me a letter which I have answered. He gave me an invitation to correspond with him. I wrote him an independant letter as I thought—yet with a mutual invitation to write—and should he imbrace the invitation and write I think it may be of great advantage to me in some respects but I think from his haughty disposition he will trouble me but if he does I am determined to give him as good as his illiberality will be very likely to send; for [I] feel not in the least disposed to favor him or any of that family in their odities which they think have by perscription.

June 29th. Cool & agreeable. Corn in the garden tasling—had the first beans & scarcities [?] 2½ inches in diameter—cucumbers set for.

[June] 30. In the morning cloudy and warm. About 11 it began to rain and continued incessantly till 6½ P.M. in which time there fell more rain than there has at any other time since the fore part of April. There have since things began to vegitate been seasonable showers not too much nor to little.

July 1st 1821. In the morning cloudy and warm—very likely for rain in the morning—continued cloudy all day. Warm and growing.

July the second. Cold and c[l]oudy likewise July the 4th the anniversary of our former independance.

July the 5th. The sun rose clear but very cold—ve[g]itables will not grow much at this time.

Ju[ly] 6th. Cool but clear weather rather altering for the better. This day is a consert at which I shall not attend. Corn begins to silk.

[July] 7th. Warm in the P.M. Banes & Fisher had a quarrel.

Sunday July the 8th. Rode to Buck creek to meeting with Mr. [and] Mrs. Gwynne. I perceive that wheat crops are very poor both thin & smutty the latter of which was produced by the rains that have lately fallen.

40. Nathan P. Fletcher, C.F.'s first cousin, a son of his father's brother Josiah Fletcher. He was born in Ludlow, Vermont, in 1783, became a lawyer, and practiced in Ludlow until 1825. He then moved to Hadley, Massachusetts, and in 1830 to Ohio. He died in St. Clair, Michigan, in 1835. Edward H. Fletcher (comp.), *Fletcher Genealogy*, p. 83.

July 9th. Very warm. Mr. Cooley started for Union County. He commenced boarding with me on the 6th of July. I have taken him into my family hoping I shall be able to make him a home complete. This day the 9th I commenced again to teach Gwynnes Children. I think that it will not be in my power to do justice by them. But I shall endeavor to [do] the best I can for them. I do not take hold of latin with that taste of pleasure that I formerly did but I hope to regain it This day I got very tired. I retired to bed in good season and arose on the morning of the tenth at which time I saw the most beautiful rain-bow in the west. At 6 A.M. It began to rain and continued to rain very hard till 9. I wrote a piece for the Urbana Gazette for and by the request of Banes. I am rather indebted a little at this time.

10th of July. Cold and rather gloomy weather. I have this day made an addition to my family. I have made some discoveries of the mean disposition of my neighbors. I find that none of them are so willing to do right as I am myself.

[*July*] *11.* This is an extreme[ly] cold day for June [July]. Mrs. Gwynne Mrs. Britton & Miss Baldwin were here in the eve. Had music. My piece came out yesterday.[41] I do not know that it excited much attention. I wrote it perhaps with more ease than common.

[*July*] *12th* [–*15*]. Cool. The Judges of the Supreme Court were here and went to Logan but returned the same day. I felt for the first time a disposition to accompany them. The Eve of the 13 very cold & severe very much like the nights in September. I [k]now it must be an obstruction to the vegitable growth and it is my opinion there will be but slim crops both of corn & wheat. Cold but rather warmer than it has been for a few days past. I made a speech in favor of bringing Black & mulato persons to Justice in or by which I done myself perhaps a little credit. I cannot yet reason as I should like. I have not a sufficient acquaintanc with mankind in general to possess a reasonable degree of confidence (in as much as I am) conscious of my own ignorance.

July the 16. I this day have been setting in court. I am much pleased with the supreme Judges. They look venerable. At the bar at this time there appeared 16 attorneys—twenty oppose[?]. The

41. No copy of the Urbana *Gazette* for this date is known to be in existence.

day has been rather pleasant. I have felt sick. Mrs. Carter & Gwynne called on us.

I this day formed a new plan to go to the capital of Indiana.[42] I find it will be with much difficulty that I can get in to business here as it is ingrossed by many men who cannot get away. I cannot go away as well fixed as I should wish yet I can go perhaps better now than ever. I shall try & visit that place next week and see what the prospect is.

Mrs. Fletcher has a very painful finger so much so that she has not slept for two nights in succession. It is very cold for [the] time of year. What will be the result of corn crops I cannot tell. We have had roasting ears this day. I am recording some in the clerks office.

July the 25th. Cold & wet. I have not done much for this day I am rather in desperate circumstances & know not how to better

42. Upon the admission of Indiana into the Union in 1816 Congress provided for a donation of four sections of land for a capital. It was generally agreed that the site should be in the central part of the state and on the West Fork of White River, the main stream of that section. At that time the area was an unsettled wilderness still claimed by the Indians, but by the New Purchase treaty of 1818, made with the two tribes concerned, the Miami and Delawares, the United States gained possession of the land covering roughly the central third of the state, and the government surveys were begun. In January, 1820, the General Assembly of Indiana appointed a commission to locate the capital site, and by an act approved January 6, 1821, the Assembly approved the site selected by the commissioners located on the White River below the mouth of Fall Creek. The latter act also provided for the appointment of a commission to meet at the site on April 1 to lay out the town. The name of the new capital was to be Indianapolis. Since the state constitution provided that Corydon should be the seat of government of the state until 1825, the state offices could not be moved to Indianapolis before that year. *Laws of Indiana,* 1819–20, pp. 18–20; 1820–21, pp. 44–53.

In his diary entry for February 9, 1861, C.F. recalled that James Paxton (see below, Pt. II, Note 15), whom he knew in Urbana, had visited the area at the mouth of Fall Creek in the winter of 1819–20 and returned in the winter of 1820–21 to build a house. While he was there the site was selected for the location of the capital. "Col. P. got out the timber & raised a log cabin. . . . He returned to Urbana . . . & exhorted [?] to Mr. Cooley with whom I had studied & with whom I was then practising law. Mr. C. & I had a conversation on the subject & it was agreed I was to visit the new seat of Government of Ind. Last of July I came down. Returned determined to move here. In Sept., thereafter (1821) Col. P. & myself were to move together but he could not come with me & I brot his cow & proceeded him some 4 or 5 weeks."

them. I think I shall start for the west next week even if I go without money. Mrs. F.'s hand has been very bad for some time and so painful she could not sleep for several nights past.

Augt. 2d [–9]. I left Urbana for Indianapolis & went to Piqua the first night. The 2d day I staid at Winchester Ind.—3d at Anderson Town & the fourth at Indianapolis. The fifth I spent in viewing the New seat of government with which I was well satisfied and on the 6th I left (Sunday morn) and rode to Blue R[iver?] alone. The 7th I went [to] Salsbury and on the 8th to Dayton on the 9th I arrived at home. Found all well. During the 9 days of absence I had no rain. I continued in Urba[na] till the 19th of Sept. at which time I started for Indianapolis where we arrived on the first day of Oct.

Oct. 1. I got a small house to go into which stood on Block 70 Lot 2d.[43] I found the place very sickly.[44]

43. The cabin into which the Fletchers moved and which they occupied until the following May was situated in the square bounded by Missouri, West, Washington, and Maryland streets. Lot 2 was on Washington Street, the second lot west of Missouri. John H. B. Nowland recalled that his father, Matthias R. Nowland (see below, Pt. II, Note 7) advised C.F. to take possession of the deserted cabin since the man who had raised it had left because of the prevailing sickness. The cabin had no floor; there was a door and a place for a chimney had been cut out. *Early Reminiscences of Indianapolis* . . . (Indianapolis: Sentinel Book and Job Printing House, 1870), pp. 121–22. See also below, pp. 40, 42.

44. It was true that the summer of 1821 had brought a general sickness to the young community, attributed to unusually heavy rains. The "intermittent and remittent fevers" began in July and did not abate until October. About twenty-five persons died, mostly children, and few in the town escaped completely. Some newcomers were disheartened and left. Ignatius Brown, "History of Indianapolis from 1818 to 1868 . . . ," in *Logan's Indianapolis Directory* . . . , 1868 ([Indianapolis:] Logan & Co., 1868), pp. 5–6.

II

Letters and Diary of SARAH HILL FLETCHER *June 20, 1821–August 2, 1824*

Sarah Hill Fletcher, Urbana, Ohio, to Louisa Fletcher,[1] *Ludlow, Vermont, June 20, 1821*

Pardon me for this abrupt introduction to you as your sister by marriage. I was wedded to your Brother Calvin on the first of May last. I have since asked him why he did not keep up a correspondence with his friends in New-England and he tells me his long absence from you and his present ingagement in business, have rendered him incapable of making these agreeable communications that I could open a correspondence with his sister Louisa and carry it on at leisure. . . .

In addressing you, my Dear Louisa, It would undoubtedly be pleasing & proper for me to give you a short history of my connexion with Mr. Fletcher, of my Fathers family & my-self. I become acquainted with Mr. Fletcher four years this summer at which time I was a student of his. I was then in my fourteenth year[2] yet notwithstanding I had a strong attachment for him which originated mutch from the melancholy & studious habits he

1. C.F.'s younger sister. She married Joseph Miller of Newark, New York, December 21, 1823.

2. According to family records Sarah Hill Fletcher was born November 21, 1801. If this date is correct, she would have been more than fourteen in 1817. Calvin, too, says that she was but fourteen at the time. See below, p. 87.

then possess'd and I am pleased to state that our affection for each other was mutual and continued so till it was consumated in marriage.

My Father, Joseph Hill lives five miles from Urbana. He was formerly from Kentucky and my Grand-pa on his side was from Va. My grand-pa on my mother's side was, as I have been informed from Boston Mss. but went to Va. as an instructor of a literay institution before the revolutionary war.

Mr. Fletcher tells me I am rather taller than either of his sisters yet I am low in statue for this country and slim.

I have a very great anxiety to see you and your Dear mother whom Mr. Fletcher wants to see more than any of his relatives he says. He thinks if we are favored we shall visit you in a few years. My curiosity is much raised to see those mountains your country abounds in as I have never been blessed with the sight of touring hills and rugged rocks. I think you wold be much pleased with Ohio notwithstanding most N.E. people dislike it. We live in an agreeable part of the City. We have no family but a boy whom Mr. Fletcher has taken to keep me company as he is absent a great part of his time. I cant but wish you were contented to come and spend a few years in Ohio with us. I wish that you would now continue a correspondence with me. . . .

DIARY

Sunday August the 19 1821. I this day commenced reading the life of George Washington, commander in chief of the Armies of the United States of America, throughout the war which established their independence and first president of the United States, by David Ramsay, M.D. Author of the history of the American Revolution.

Sept. the Second 1821. Mrs. Gwynne set off for Cumberland. The fourth S. H. was weded to Mr. James Johnstone.

[*Sept.*] *19th.* We started to Indianapolis.

Oct. the 1. We arived and procured a house or rough cabin into which I entered with alacrity after enduring the fatigues of our Journey which lasted thirteen days.

Sarah Hill Fletcher, Indianapolis, to her father, Urbana, Ohio, October 2, 1821

After I left you on the 20th of last month we proceeded with much difficulty to this place. The fatigues were much greater than I could have imagined therefore would advise every body who have a good situation in Ohio, to be contented. We were eleven days after on the road. Our Waggoner caused Mr. Fletcher much trouble and unnecessary labor. We were travelling two days while it rained thro' the wilderness. The people all sick and distressed—many were moving into the old settlements from whence they came which caused me to wish myself back again yet I have courage and hope that we may escape sickness. Mr. Fletcher is not discouraged.

The second day after we left you our white cow run back from us. She had a calf at Gibbs' lease where she has gone. I want you should get her and keep till next spring at which time Mr. Bayles of Urbana will come with cattle and you can then send her. . . .

DIARY

October the 8th. The sale of lots commenced near our house—a large concourse of people were present.[3]

3. The first sale of lots in the newly platted town took place at the tavern of Matthias R. Nowland on Washington Street west of Missouri and continued for a week. The weather was raw and cold with a high wind. Three hundred and fourteen lots were sold, mostly in the central and northern parts of the plat for a total of $35,596.25, of which $7,119.25 was paid in cash. "The town was very much crowded. Strangers from various quarters had come to settle in the new place or to secure property. The three taverns kept by [John] Hawkins, [Thomas] Carter, and Nowland, were crowded, and in many cases the citizens were called upon to share their homes with the new-comers till they could erect cabins." It should be noted, however, that of the 314 lots sold, 161 were subsequently either forfeited or relinquished under a relief act of 1826. As speculation investments Indianapolis lots were not a success. Total cash receipts up to 1831 were less than $35,000. By 1844, when the agent of state for the sale of lots closed his books, the entire receipts were less than $100,000. Berry R. Sulgrove, *History of Indianapolis and Marion County* (Philadelphia: L. H. Everts & Co., 1884), pp. 27–28; Brown, "History of Indianapolis," in *Logan's Indianapolis Directory*, 1868, p. 4; Jacob P. Dunn, *Greater Indianapolis* . . . (2 volumes. Chicago: Lewis Publishing Co., 1910), I, 32–33. The sales of lots are recorded in the Agent of State,

Sarah Hill Fletcher, Indianapolis, to Miss Mariah Britten, Urbana, Ohio, October 15, 1821

After I parted with you on the 30th ult. I proceeded with many retrospective views of the place and few friends I was about leaving, to my fathers where I spent the night and took leave early the next morning. Parting from my young sisters in the care of a step mother was the most grievous trial I ever met with. It brought to mind the misfortune I had met with in loosing the best of Mothers. I overtook the waggon on Thursday 2 o'clock P.M. We were twelve days from Urbana to this place. I need not try to describe the fatigue of our Journey as you have some recollection of your father's moving to the State of Ohio which was then very similar to this part of the Country now. We met many families moving from White River into the State of Ohio on the account of sickness but not any from the seat of Goverment. Yet this place has been subject to agues but no malignant disorders but that the people could recover using proper caution. Camping out in the woods several nights prepared me excellently well to be contented with the modest cabin the place could afford yet we were fortunate in getting a very good one in which we shall live this winter. There are many very gentel families in this place. Some of them I have become acquainted with. The number of people here are about twelve hundred.[4] They are very polite and attentive to each other. Mr. Fletcher says there are many fine young men settled here from Kentucky who are somewhat more attentive to the ladies than those at Urbana.

DIARY

Tuesday October 23, 1821. I commensed Arithmetic.

Fryday Oct. 26. I commited the multiplication table.

Saturday [*Oct. 27*]. I red a few pages in the elements of Gesture &c. &c. and wrote a verse which was the last of essay on Man. This

---

Indianapolis Sale of Lots Day Book July 1820–May 1831 and subsequent volume and papers of the Agent of State in the Archives Division, Indiana State Library, Indianapolis.

4. This estimate of the population is interesting. Brown says that in the fall of 1821 there were between fifty or sixty resident families and that the total population was between four and five hundred. Brown, "History of Indianapolis," in *Logan's Indianapolis Directory*, 1868, p. 6.

day is very pleasant and reather smokey. It appears a little like indian summer. We have had but very little rain in the place for about three weakes back and has been very favorable for those who has mooved in and are building.

Thursday Nov. the first. I was spining wool at Mr. Mcvains.[5]

Fryday [*Nov.* 2]. Was cool and cleare.

Saturday [*Nov.* 3]. Was cold and cloudy & I had but little fire. Mr. F. went up the river about two milds.

Munday Nov. the 5 1821. I have been washing all day and Mr. F. has been helpin Mr. B.[6] husk corne.

Fryday Nov. the 9th. It snowed very fast. The ground froze at night.

Saturday [*Nov.* 10]. Was windy and freezeing and Mr. F. went to Mr. R. [?] to take breckfast.

Wednesday Nov. 14th. I finished Reading the Vicar of Wakefield which was wrote by Goldsmith and returned it home. Then I borowed a singing Book from Mr. B.

Thursday [*Nov.* 15]. A very pretty day & Mr. F. calculates on

5. James McIlvain, justice of the peace, elected at a special election on August 11, 1821. He later served as an associate judge. As justice he held court at the door of his little cabin, "pipe in mouth, with the jury in front on a fallen tree, and the first constable, [Jeremiah] Corbaley, standing guard over the culprits. . . ." *Executive Proceedings of the State of Indiana 1816–1836*, edited by Dorothy Riker (*Indiana Historical Collections*, XXIX, Indianapolis: Indiana Historical Bureau, 1947), p. 193n (cited hereinafter as *Indiana Executive Proceedings*); Brown, "History of Indianapolis," in *Logan's Indianapolis Directory*, 1868, p. 4. McIlvain's cabin was located at the southwest corner of Ohio and Meridian streets. Dunn, *Indianapolis*, I, 47n.

6. James Blake (1791–1870), who came to Indianapolis in July, 1821, and remained to become one of its most outstanding citizens, no one being more identified "with the rise and progress of the city and its philanthropic and benevolent institutions." He was a partner in the city's first steam mill, a director of the Indianapolis branch of the State Bank, a director of the Madison and Indianapolis Railroad and of the Indianapolis & Lafayette Railroad, but much of his fortune came from a wholesale dry goods business. He was the "unofficial host for Indianapolis," serving as leader or manager of such affairs as the observance of the Fourth of July, the reception for Kossuth, and the welcome of the returning Mexican War soldiers. Like C.F. he had little aspiration for political life and his only public office was that of county commissioner, 1855–58. Also like C.F. he was active in the Indianapolis Sabbath School, an ardent church worker (Presbyterian), a promoter of education, and a strong temperance man. He was also a collector of books. In 1831 he married Miss Eliza Sproule of Baltimore. Sulgrove, *History of Indianapolis*, pp. 86–87; Dunn, *Indianapolis, passim.*

finishing what he engaged to do for Mr. B. I commence the life of Washington again and I entend to read it through as soon as posible.

Fryday Nov. 16th 1821. I was spining at Mr. Noldins.[7]

Sat. [*Nov. 17*]. I was bakeing Pumpkin pys.

Sunday [*Nov. 18*]. I attended prayre meating at Mr. Stephens.[8]

Munday Nov. 19th 1821. This day I was shoping. I onely bought half a pound of cotten.

Thursday Nov. 22d 1821. I spun some candlewick.

Fryday [*Nov. 23*]. I washed.

Saturday [*Nov. 24*]. Mrs. Noldin[9] was makeing a bonnet. She came to me to know whether I could make it. I did not undertake it but I gave her all the instruction I posible could.

Sunday [*Nov.*] *25.* I attended at Mr. Hockinses[10] whareas I heard a verry good sermind delivered by an Newlight minister.[11] The text was thus see then that ye walk circumspectly not as fools but as wise Redeeming the time because the days are evle.

Fryday Nov. 30 1821. Dr. M.[12] took Bckfast at our house.

7. Matthias R. Nowland, tavernkeeper. He came to Indianapolis in November, 1820 and died November 11, 1822. Brown, "History of Indianapolis," in *Logan's Indianapolis Directory,* 1868, p. 7; Indianapolis *Gazette,* November 16, 1822.

8. Isaac Stevens (Stephens), a local merchant. In 1822 he was elected a justice of the peace for Pike and Wayne townships, Marion County. *Indiana Executive Proceedings,* p. 220.

9. Elizabeth (Betsey) Nowland, wife of Matthias R. Nowland. Upon her husband's death she opened a boardinghouse.

10. John Hawkins, whose Eagle Tavern was located in a double log house on the north side of Washington Street a little east of Meridian.

11. The "New Lights" were an early nineteenth-century offshoot of the Presbyterians in the West. They took a less orthodox view on election and predestination than did the staunch Calvinists and "preached God's love for the whole world and believed that sinners could accept the newer means of salvation." R. Carlyle Buley, *The Old Northwest: Pioneer Period, 1815–1840* (2 volumes. Indianapolis: Indiana Historical Society, 1950), II, 424–25.

12. Probably Dr. Samuel G. Mitchell, Indianapolis' first physician, who came from Kentucky in April, 1821. He had his office in his house, first at the southwest corner of Washington and Tennessee (Capitol Avenue) streets and then at the northwest corner of Washington and Meridian. He was president of the Central Medical Society organized at Indianapolis in 1823 to license physicians. Dr. Mitchell died in 1837. Dunn, *Indianapolis,* I, 542, 545.

Saturday Dec. the 1st 1821. Mrs. N[owland] & Mrs. Buckner[13] cawled to see me. I was made acquainted with Mrs. B. and she solicited me to pay her a visit.

Monday [Dec.] the 3d. Mr. Royalston[14] & Dr. M. to Coriden.

Fryday Dec. 7 1821. We killed a Beef Mr. Paxton[15] & Mr. Blake healped to butcher & Mr. B. took tea with us. Saturday I was very much ingaged in trying out my tallow.

Sunday Dec. 9th. I attended prayer meating at Mr. S[t]ephens's.

Thursday Decr. 13 1821. I wrote a letter to Mrs. Comer which was the 5 letter I wrote since I came here & never have recieved an answer.

13. Wife of George Buckner.

14. Alexander Ralston, a Scottish engineer and surveyor who assisted Pierre L'Enfant in laying out Washington, D.C. He was selected to survey and lay out the new capital of Indiana and he is generally credited with its plan of radiating avenues and broad streets similar to that of the nation's capital. Ralston had come West, first to Kentucky, then to Indiana. He had been employed as a surveyor by Aaron Burr and was caught up in the Burr Conspiracy. While he was indicted he never was tried, and his associations with Burr apparently did not tarnish his reputation. He settled in Indianapolis in 1822, building a little brick house on the north side of Maryland west of Tennessee Street (now Capitol Avenue). He died in 1827 at the age of fifty-six. A tall man, gentlemanly in dress and bearing, he was remembered as being hospitable, kindly, and generous. Emmett A. Rice, "A Forgotten Man of Indianapolis," in *Indiana Magazine of History,* XXXIV (1938), 283–97; Dunn, *Indianapolis,* I, 28–29.

15. James Paxton. He and his wife, Elizabeth Luse Paxton, came to Indianapolis from Urbana, Ohio. See above, Pt. I, note 42. Paxton was a carpenter by trade, and he and John E. Baker won the contract in September, 1822, for erecting the Marion County Courthouse, completed in the fall of 1824. This building also served as the state capitol when the state offices were moved from Corydon in 1825. The Paxtons, devout Methodists, lived on lot 13 in the southwest section of the Circle, and Paxton, by his will, left the adjoining lot (lot 12) for a parsonage for Wesley Chapel which was erected in 1829 on lot 11 on the southwest corner of the Circle and Meridian Street. He also left five hundred dollars toward the building of the parsonage. Paxton was a representative from Hamilton, Johnson, Madison, and Marion counties in the 1823–24 and 1825 sessions of the General Assembly and was colonel of the local militia. He died in 1829. See below, p. 165, and Dunn, *Indianapolis,* I, 46, 61–62, 134, 135, 593; Nowland, *Early Reminiscences of Indianapolis,* pp. 84–85; and Ernestine Bradford Rose, *The Circle "The Center of our Universe"* (Indiana Historical Society *Publications,* XVIII, No. 4, Indianapolis, 1957), pp. 385–86.

In the Fletcher Papers there is an appointment of C.F. as paymaster of the 40th Regiment of Indiana militia signed by Paxton as colonel and dated October 19, 1822.

Fryday [*Dec. 14*]. I diped candles & washed.

Saturday [*Dec. 15*]. Mr. Glover came.

Sunday [*Dec. 16*]. I recieved a letter from Miss Mariah Briton & a pattern with it.[16] The Idea of geting a letter was very pleasing but when I red it I began to reflect to think how much more esteem an acquaintance expressed by writing to me & not one of my relatives evin sent a complement.

Weddensday Decr. the 19 1821. I spent the evening very agreeable at Mr. Stephens's for they treated upon nothing but what was commendable.

Saturday Decr. the 22 1821. I recieved a letter from Sister Louisa F.[17] & Mr. F. recieved 7 which give us both great Satisfaction in peruseing them.

Sunday [*Dec. 23*]. I stayed at home all day & red my letter again & some nosepapers.

Monday [*Dec. 24*]. I did not dwo anything hard.

Tuesday [*Dec. 25*] *Christmas*. Mrs. Bradly[18] came to spend the day with me & Mrs. Paxton. She dined with us then we both went to Mr. P[axton] & took tea & set a while then I came home and went in to Mr. N[owland's]. I then came home again & red a chapter in the Bible &c.

Weddensday [*Dec. 26*]. I went to singing school & suffered very much with the cold. Thursday I washed & did not get done till late. I was setting by the fire nursing my hands for they ware very raw & inflamed by washing & Mr. F. was reading the History of

16. The letter, which was delivered by Mr. Glover, dated Urbana, November 29, 1821, is in the Fletcher Papers.

17. Louisa's letter, dated October 8, is in the Fletcher Papers. It comprises a short, friendly but rather formal note to Sarah and another to "Brother Calvin" which includes some family news and chides him for not writing.

18. Wife of Henry Bradley. The Bradleys moved to Indianapolis from Kentucky in the spring of 1820. Henry Bradley was described by Nowland as "an old line Whig" and "a hard-shell Baptist." He served as a justice of the peace from 1827 to 1838. A successful merchant, he formed a partnership with C.F.'s brother Stoughton in 1833. *Early Reminiscences of Indianapolis*, p. 79; Sulgrove, *History of Indianapolis*, p. 502.

Page from the diary of Sarah Hill Fletcher

again & some nosepapers Man
I did not diuo of anything har
tuseday Christmas Mrs Bradly
Came to spend the day with me
& Mrs Paxton she dined with us
then we both went to Mr P &
took tea & set a while then I cam
home and went in to Mr N
I then came home again &
red a chapter in the Bible &c
Weddensday I went to singing schoo
& suffered very much with the cold
thursday I washed & did not get don
till late I was seting by the fire
nursing my hands for they ware very
sore & inflamed by washing & Mr J
I was reading the History of Amer
ica when nose came that Mr B
had arived from Corydon Mr P
has gone to see him & [illegible] wen
I write a few more lines I'll go
my self all though I feel very
much fatieuged for it has been so
long since I have heard the fiddle
plaid that I think it wauld saun
very mealodious & I am jest goin
to start to hear it
Sunday Dec the 30 1821 I herd
a sermon delivered by an newly
Minister which I did not think

America when nose came that Mr. R.[19] had arived from Corydon. Mr. F. has gone to see him & wen I write a few more lines Ill go my self all though I feel very much fatieuged for it has been so long since I have heard the fiddle plaid that I think it would sound very malodious & I am jest going to s[t]art to hear it.

Sunday Decr. the 30 1821. I herd a sermon delivered by an newlight Minister which I did not think commendable but we must alowe for it has not been but about three months since he began to speak in public.

Munday [Dec. 31]. I did not doo much of anything.

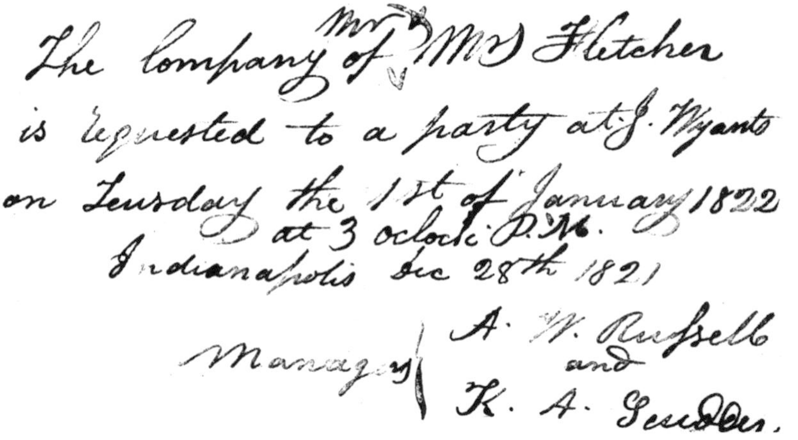
The Company of Mr & Mrs Fletcher
is requested to a party at J. Wyants
on Teusday the 1st of January 1822
at 3 oclock P.M.
Indianapolis Dec 28th 1821
Managers { A. W. Russell and K. A. Scudder.

FLETCHER PAPERS

Invitation to the New Year's party, January 1, 1822

Tuesday January the 1st. 1822. I attended a party at Mr. Wiants. I enjoyed my self very well.[20]

19. Col. Alexander W. Russell, who came to Indianapolis from Kentucky in May, 1821. A merchant, he served as Marion County sheriff, militia officer, and postmaster. He was also a fiddler of note and in great demand at all the early entertainments in the town. Dunn, *Indianapolis*, I, 84; Nowland, *Early Reminiscences of Indianapolis*, pp. 84–85.

20. A note inviting Mr. and Mrs. Fletcher to a party at J. Wyant's on Tuesday, January 1, 1822, at 3 o'clock, signed by A. W. Russell and K. A. Scudder, managers, is in the Fletcher Papers.

Kenneth A. Scudder was a young physician who came to Indianapolis from New Jersey in the summer of 1821. Dunn, *Indianapolis*, I, 542. The John Wyants lived in a log cabin on the east side of White River south of Washington Street. An account of the party, based on recollections of various persons present, is

Wedensday [*Jan.* 2]. Wm. Vance took tea with us & I visited Mrs. N[owland] & Mr. Russel plaid a few toons on the fidd[le] & we danced a few reels.

Thursday the 3 of Jan. I felt sore & sleepy.

Fryday [*Jan.* 4]. Was very cold. I think the coldes day we have had this winter.

Saturday Jan. the 4 [5] *1822.* At night. I now seat myself to commit a few things to paper that past through the day. This day has been remarkable cold & windy & Mr. & Mrs. Paxton came home from the Bluffs[21] which they visited about a week. Mr. F. is absen at this time & I have a sever headache & bad cold. This day I mended a pare of overalls for Mr. Foot[22] & a great coat for Mr. F.

Sunday [*Jan.* 6]. I staided at home all day with the same affliction I have hereto fore mention. Mr. & Mrs. Cu[. . .] called as they were going to prayr meeting. They said perhaps they woud call on theyr return. I preparde for them they did not stop. I had my tea ready to set upon the table when Mr. Foot & Mr. C.[23] both of

---

given in Dunn, *Indianapolis,* I, 82–84. Ample food was provided including biscuits, sweet bread, gingerbread, and pound cake, and there were gallons of coffee. The fiddle of Alexander W. Russell furnished the music for dancing, and, as decreed by the host, every man danced with his own wife, "those that had no wife could dance with the gals."

21. Previously named Port Royal by the French, these bluffs rise abruptly from the White River at a point about one and a half miles northwest of Waverly in Morgan County and about twenty miles southwest of Indianapolis. They were the terminal point of the trace which was cut through the wilderness by Jacob Whetzel from near Laurel in Franklin County in 1818, an important factor in the settlement of Morgan County. The Bluffs was one of the sites considered by the commissioners for the state capital.

22. Obed Foote, a native of Delaware and a lawyer, came to Indianapolis in 1821. He served as a justice of the peace for Marion County from 1822 until his death in 1833. Upon the incorporation of Indianapolis in 1832 he became town treasurer. He also served as librarian for the Indianapolis Library Society, privately organized in 1827. Foote generally outranked the other justices in his knowledge of the law and in ability but was inclined to be erratic and eccentric in administering his court. It was he who provoked C.F. sufficiently that he committed the assault and battery mentioned below, pp. 94–95n. *Indiana Executive Proceedings*, pp. 221, 515, 517n; Sulgrove, *History of Indianapolis*, p. 29; Dunn, *Indianapolis*, I, 557.

23. Perhaps Hiram M. Curry, who was admitted to practice before the newly organized Fifth Circuit which included Marion County in September,

them Atternys at Law came in. They drank tea with us & set till near sondown.

Monday Jan. 6 [7]. I cut out a Shirt for Mr. F. In the evening I visited Mrs. N[owland] where I got some little idea of playing Dominos.

Tuseday [*Jan. 8*]. I visited Mrs. B[radley]. Mrs. N. accompaned me. I spent the evening not so pleasant as I would wish for. She did not converse much upon any thing much. Mr. F. & Mr. N. came in after darke to escorte us home.

Fryday the 11 of Jan. 1822. In the Morn I washed. Mrs. N. came in jest as I commenced & Obsurved that Mr. [Dr.] Scudder would take us both to Mr. Woods[24] about 2 M. east of this place & when we about ready the Dr. was called off.

Sat. [*Jan.*] *12.* I did not doo much of anything.

Sun. [*Jan.*] *13.* I stayed at home all day and read a few pages in Earl of Chesterfields Letters to his Son.

Mond. [*Jan. 14*]. I took Tea at Mr. N. where I had an introduction to Miss W.[?] & Miss H.

Wed. the 16 of Jan. I & Mrs. N. spent the Eve at Mr. Carters[25] where we had plenty of cyder to drink.

Tuse. Jan. the 22 1822. Mr. Gates was wedded to Miss Patsy Chinn both of Indianapolis. I attended the wedding. It was a very disagreeable day but not with standing there was a great concourse of people.[26]

1822, at the same time that C.F. was admitted. He soon after took a position in the county clerk's office and in a few years moved West. Leander J. Monks *et al.* (eds.), *Courts and Lawyers of Indiana* (3 volumes. Indianapolis: Federal Publishing Co., 1916), III, 114.

24. Perhaps David Wood, who arrived in 1820 and entered 160 acres of land in July, 1821, in Center Township. Sulgrove, *History of Indianapolis*, pp. 28, 60.

25. Probably Maj. Thomas Carter, one of early Indianapolis' noted tavern-keepers. His first tavern was kept in a cabin which he built between Washington and Market streets just east of Illinois in 1821. Later he built the story-and-a-half Rosebush Tavern facing on Washington in front of the cabin. This burned in January, 1825. The following spring he moved the two-story Jacob R. Crumbaugh house from its location at Missouri and Market streets near the present canal to the site of the Rosebush and conducted his business in it. Nowland, *Early Reminiscences of Indianapolis*, pp. 64–65.

26. This wedding, said to be the second in the New Purchase, and its accompanying festivities are described in Nowland, *Early Reminiscences of In-*

Wed. [Jan.] the 23. I attened at Mr. Ragans[27] who gave them an infare whare we danced till a bout 1 o clock then we returned home.

Thurs. [Jan. 24]. I had an invitation to a quilting which I did not attenend. The reason was I had company & did not think it proper for me to go when I had been up 2 nights & felt very much fatigued.

Fryday [Jan.] the 25. Very cold & disagreea[b]le I did not do much of any thing.

Sat. the 26 of Jan. I did not do much in the morning. I calculated on washing but Mr. F. was called off to attend a trial before the Esq. whereas he gained the soot for his cliant. The same night Mrs. Bradley came & stayed with me till a bout 11 o clock & Mr. B. & Mr. F. was gone to a debateing school.

Sun. [Jan.] the 27. Mr. F. went a bout 5 ms. West of this place a cross the River. After he started I went to Mr. N[owland's]. I set a few minuts. I began to feel very sick. I came home and went to bed.

Monday [Jan.] the 28. I got better.

Tuseday [Jan.] the 29. I attened a quilting at Mrs. Buc[kner's]. There were several ladys who were formaly from Kentucky & I think in there descorse a mong the Females they use a gradeal of vulgarity.

Wed. [Jan.] the 30. This day is very muddy & disag[r]eeable & I have this day maid some candle wick for Mr. Foot. Mr. Morris[28]

---

dianapolis, pp. 128–30. The groom was Uriah Gates and the bride was the daughter of Thomas Chinn, whose farm was east of the town on the north side of Pogue's Run.

27. Wilkes Reagan, who came to Indianapolis in the summer of 1821. He was a butcher. His shop was on the northwest corner of Delaware and Washington streets and his slaughter house on Pogue's Run between New Jersey and East streets. Dunn, *Indianapolis,* I, 53. He served as justice of the peace for Marion County, 1822–26 and 1833–36. Sulgrove, *History of Indianapolis,* p. 502.

28. Morris Morris (1780–1864), a Virginian who moved to Kentucky in his youth and to Indianapolis in 1821. Although a successful lawyer, he had abandoned his practice before coming to Indiana, giving as his reason that "the pursuit of his profession interfered with the Christian life he wished to lead." He acquired large landholdings in and around the new capital. He was elected auditor of state by the General Assembly in 1828 and continued in that office for sixteen years. He also served as one of the commissioners to superintend the erection of the state capitol which was completed in 1835. Sulgrove, *History of Indianapolis,* pp. 216–17.

has wrote a pamphlet & had it put in print & Mr. F. is now gone to writ an answer to it & I am all a lone.[29]

Sat. the 2d of Febuary. Mrs. Buckner dined with us. Mr. Osborn[30] stayed hear the same night.

Sunday the 3 of Febuary 1822. The hand bills come out in oposition to one which Mr. Morris wrote.

Monday [Feb.] the 4th. Mr. Luse[31] arived at this place. He could not tell any thing of any account a bout Urbana.

Tuseday night [Feb. 5]. Mrs. Paxton & her Brother visited us & set till 11 o clock.

Fryday the 8th of Febr. I went to Mrs. B. & assisted her with her quilt. We finished.

Sat. [Feb. 9]. I went to singing school & very much against my will.

Sunday [Feb. 10]. I went to the Printing Office.

Monday [Feb.] the 11th. In the P.M. noon I took Tea at Mr. Stevens'.

Tuesday [Feb.] the 12. Mr. S. mooved out to the Country 2 mi. from Indianapolis. The same day I had very pressing invitations

29. Morris Morris was candidate for clerk of the circuit court at the April 1 election, the first election held in Marion County. (See below, p. 85.) He was supported by the so-called Kentucky faction and opposed by James M. Ray who was supported by the Whitewater faction. The latter faction was identified with Governor Jennings, Senator James Noble, and Congressman William Hendricks, and traced its beginnings back to the struggle against slavery in the territorial period. Morris' political pamphlet was the first item besides the newspaper to be printed by the Indianapolis *Gazette* press. The first issue of the *Gazette,* Indianapolis' first newspaper, was published January 28, 1822. C.F. supported the Whitewater faction and apparently was designated to answer Morris. This was the beginning of a battle of words that lasted until the election. Unfortunately none of the pamphlets, handbills, or broadsides that it produced have survived. Dunn, *Indianapolis,* I, 50.

30. John T. Osborn, a candidate for the office of county commissioner, supported by the Whitewater faction. In his diary entry for October 16, 1862, C.F. mentions encountering Osborn in Cincinnati. He then recalled that Osborn had supplied him with $6.00 in half dollars in February, 1822, which had permitted him to attend his first court in Lawrence County. Osborn went to New Orleans in 1823 and lived there until the Civil War. He returned to Indianapolis and C.F., in turn, let him have $200 to aid him over a difficult time.

31. Fleming T. Luse, a brother of Mrs. Paxton and a cabinetmaker. Dunn, *Indianapolis,* I, 95.

to go a visiting with Mrs. N. & Mrs. B. to Mr. Yandes's[32] but I did not feel disposed to go.

Wed. [Feb.] the 13th. In the Evening Mr. & Mrs. P[axton] took Tea at my table. Then Mr. P. & Mr. F. went out a hunting & stayed till a bout 11 o clock.

Thursday the 14th of Febr. 1822. I was solicited to attend a party at Mrs. Ragans. I had no anxiety to go therefore I staid at home. Mr. F. I suppose by this time is there but whether he will enjoy himself or not I cannot tell tho he appeard to antisipate a grateal of pleasure. I am all alone at this time & injoy myself very well. I use to think that I should be very lonesome when Mr. F. was abscent but it is quite to the revers if he dose not stay out till a late hour, for as soon as he starts & I get my domestic afares in order I then get my penn ink & paper & feel quiet Happy. I will this night endeavour to file Mr. F. scraps of writing while he is abscent. I have put the papers all in good order & Mr. F. has not come yet. I think that I have the easiest times since I have been maried of any girl that has entered in to the state of Matrimony with in a year. But I am afraid that I have spent my time so trifling (I may say) at the end of a few Year perhaps I may say if I had the same time to live over a gain I would Spende it quiet different tho I am confident that I have done my duty this night. I will now read a Chapter & go to repose for I know that I have satisfied Mr. F. request that he maid mention of when he started. I have wrote as much tonight as I have wrote with in 2 weaks & I hope he will not be displeased with my Composition.

Fryday the 15 of Febr. 1822. Mr. M. Morris's second hand bill came out. That day I washed & went to bed very early. Mr. F. was writeing an answer to the hand bill & did not go to bed that night.

Sat. [Feb. 16]. He wrote till [he] got very sleepy. He then layed

32. Daniel Yandes. Born in Fayette County, Pennsylvania, in 1793, he migrated to Fayette County, Indiana, then to Indianapolis in 1821. He served as Marion County treasurer from 1822 to 1829. His various successful enterprises included milling, manufacturing, and merchandizing. Dunn, *Indianapolis,* I, 50; II, 728–30; Annabelle Robinson *et al., Daniel Yandes and His Family, Pioneers from Pennsylvania to Indiana, 1818* (Crawfordsville: R. E. Banta, 1936). He was the father of Simon Yandes, who later worked and studied in C.F.'s law office and became a member of the firm of Fletcher, Butler, and Yandes.

down & took but a short nap & then was oblieged to attend a trial at Mc[Il]vains.

Sunday [Feb. 17]. I spent the day at Mr. Ys. Mr. F. went to bed in the P.M. noon & Slept till after 8 o clock in the Evening. I awakend him & we both went to the Printing Office & Stayd till 2 o clock in the morning.

Monday the 18th of Febr. 1822. In the morning the hand bill came out & great was the mistery to know who the Legal voter alluded to where he mentions Col. Puff Back Capt. Swellback & myself.

Tuseday the 19th of Febr. I helped Mrs. Paxton make a pair of overalls.

Wedensday [Feb.] the 20th. Very rainy.

Thursday the 21st of Febr. 1822. Mr. Paxton started to Urbana & cont[in]ues muddy & rainy.

Sat. [Feb.] 23. At night Mr. F. went to the Debaiting Scool.

Sunday [Feb.] the 24. I went up to Mr. Buckners lot[?].

Mon. the 25 of Febr. Warm & pleasant. I washed & Irond.

Tuseday [Feb. 26]. Continude warm and clear. I suffered more pain that day than ever I did before except one time with a felon.

Wedensday night the 27th of Febr. Mr. Osborn came here & set till 11 o clock.

Thursday the 28th of Febr. 1822. He come back & set till after 12 o clock & Mr. F. wrote a peas upon Slander.

Friday the 1st of Mrch. Mr. Fletcher Started on the circuit.[33] It is a very muddy & disagreeable day and I fear he will be very sick of his trip. Mrs. P[axton] stayed with me four nights then Mr. P. returned from Ohio. He brought 5 noose papers and three letters. I came home and broke the letters open & red 2 one from my Father & the other from Dr. Banes & one from Mr. Cooley which I could not read. I had very peculiar feelings. It seemed as if I was forsaken & Mrs. P. overjoyed. I did not envey her her happiness—for I know how I would of felt had it been Mr. F. returned.

33. This was the first of the circuit court rides which for many years would take C.F. twice annually over a large segment of central Indiana. At this time the Fifth Judicial Circuit included besides Marion County, Lawrence, Monroe, Morgan, Greene, Owen, Decatur, Bartholomew, Shelby, and Jennings counties. See Pt. III, note 2.

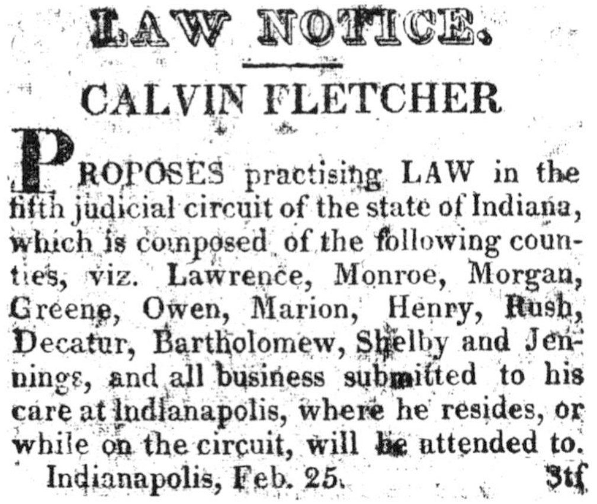

LAW NOTICE.

CALVIN FLETCHER

PROPOSES practising LAW in the fifth judicial circuit of the state of Indiana, which is composed of the following counties, viz. Lawrence, Monroe, Morgan, Greene, Owen, Marion, Henry, Rush, Decatur, Bartholomew, Shelby and Jennings, and all business submitted to his care at Indianapolis, where he resides, or while on the circuit, will be attended to.

Indianapolis, Feb. 25. 3tf

Calvin Fletcher's advertisement for practice in the Fifth Judicial Circuit, which ran in the Indianapolis *Gazette* from February 25, to September 28, 1822

Tuseday the 5 of March. The same day that Mr. P. came I visited Mrs. Wick.[34] I did not find evry [thing] in such print as I expected neither did I find such a polished Lady.

Wed. the 5 [6] *of March.* I began to make soap.

Friday [*March*] *8th.* I washed & recieved 2 letters one from Ingram & one from Britten.

Sat. [*March 9*]. I could not keepe any fire & I spent the fore part of the day with Mrs. Paxton & the after noon with Mrs. N[owland].

Sun. 9th [*10th*] *of March.* I visited Mr. S.

Mon. [*March*] *10th* [*11th*]. I began makeing shugar.

Friday [*March*] *15th.* Mr. Fletcher came home.

Sun. [*March*] *17th.* In the Evening I walked up to Judg Wicks. I returned with Mr. Fletcher & we both went to the River and called in to Mr. McGeorge's.[35]

34. Wife of William Watson Wick (1796–1868), president judge of the Fifth Judicial Circuit. A native of Washington County, Pennsylvania, Wick began his law practice in Connersville in 1820, then moved to Indianapolis. He had a long career of public service as president judge, 1822–25, 1834–39, 1849–52, 1852–53, and 1859; secretary of state, 1825–29; prosecuting attorney, 1829–31; Democratic representative in Congress, 1839–41 and 1845–49; and Indianapolis postmaster, 1853–57. Monks *et al.* (eds.), *Courts and Lawyers of Indiana,* I, 89, II, 848–49; *Biographical Directory of the American Congress,* p. 2009.

35. Samuel McGeorge, who came to Indianapolis shortly after it was

Tuseday 19th of March 1822. I washed with Mrs. Paxton. We got done & went to the Shoe makers shop.

Wedensday [March] 20th. Mrs. Hendison[36] was delivered of a Son.

Thursday [March] 21st. Mr. Mc[Il]Vain raised a house. Mr. McDoogle[37] called to see Mr. F. but he was not at home.

Friday 22d of March. Mr. Gluver mooved.

Sat. [March] 23d. Mr. Johnstone[38] came to this place with the intension of staying all Summer to improve his Farm.

Sunday 24th of March. Mr. F. started to Morgan County. After he started I went about one mild to a sugar camp. I returned & attended a Funeral & a burial. I did not see a single tear shed in the whole congegation except Mrs. Nowland when she shewd me w[h]ere her Child was buried.

Monday [March 25]. I dined at Mr. Paxtons.

Tuesday [March 26]. Mr. Fletcher came home.

Wednesday [March 27]. It rained.

Thursday the 28th of March. Was very win[d]y. Mr. Brown started from here the same day & I felt a little concerned about him traveling through the woods.

Sat. 30th of March 1822. I spent the day with Mrs. Bates[39] &

---

platted and kept a tavern on the bank of White River south of Washington Street. Sometime before 1828 he moved to a location on Wildcat Creek in Tippecanoe County and became an Indian trader. Nowland, *Early Reminiscences of Indianapolis*, pp. 173–74.

36. Wife of Samuel Henderson, Indianapolis' first postmaster. The town was made a post office in February, 1822. In 1824 Henderson joined with James Blake in erecting a new frame tavern on Washington Street which they labeled Washington Hall. He was elected trustee of the town upon its incorporation in 1832 and became the city's first mayor in 1847. He joined the gold rush to California and died there in 1883. Dunn, *Indianapolis*, I, 18, 46, 65, 71, 92, 112, 157, 160, 342.

37. Perhaps William C. McDougal, who had the first real estate agency in Indianapolis. Sulgrove, *History of Indianapolis*, p. 54. He is listed as a candidate for lieutenant colonel in the militia in the Indianapolis *Gazette*, August 24, 31, 1822. In July, 1822, he married Cynthia Reagan. *Ibid.*, July 20, 1822. He later moved to Natchez. Diary entry for March 17, 1836, below.

38. Probably James Johnson who came from Butler County, Ohio, in 1822, and settled in Wayne Township, Marion County. Nowland, *Early Reminiscences of Indianapolis*, pp. 98–99.

39. Sidney Sedgwick Bates, wife of Hervey Bates and cousin of Noah Noble, governor of Indiana, 1831–37, and Senator James Noble. The Bateses moved from

found her a very an agreeable Woman.

Sunday [March] the 31st. I spent the day very idol for there were so many Candidates coming in that I could neither read wright nor do anything else.

Monday [April 1]. The Election was held that was on the first of Aprile.[40]

Wednesday the 3d of Aprile 1822. Mrs. Wick Mrs. Paxton Miss C. & myself spente the P.M. noon at Mr. Nowlans.

Sunday 7th of Aprile 1822. It raind very hard & haild. Monday night & Tuesday morning continued raining.

Aprile 10th 1822. This day Mr. F. & Mr. B[lake] entered in to an agreement about a house & lot which we are to take posession of as soon as it is finished.[41]

Friday 12th of Aprile. Mrs. P[axton] & Sally Ann Nowland[42]

Connersville to Indianapolis upon Hervey Bates's appointment as the first sheriff of Marion County. He became a prosperous merchant, president of the Indianapolis branch of the State Bank, and was a promoter of many successful business enterprises. He built the Bates House, commenced in 1852, one of the finest hotels in the West at the time, located on the northwest corner of Illinois and Washington streets. Nowland, *Early Reminiscences of Indianapolis*, pp. 138–41.

40. There were 336 votes cast in the county, 224 of them in Indianapolis, for county offices. Those elected were James M. Ray, clerk; James McIlvain and Eliakim Harding, associate judges; Joseph C. Reed, recorder; and John McCormick, John T. Osborn, and William McCartney, county commissioners. It was a victory for the Whitewater faction. Indianapolis *Gazette*, April 3, 1822; Dunn, *Indianapolis*, I, 50.

The newly elected commissioners met on April 15, 16, and 17. Among business transacted was the appointment of Daniel Yandes as county treasurer, the dividing of the county into townships for administrative purposes, provision for the election of justices of the peace for the townships on May 11, the adoption of a county seal, and setting of rates of ferriage across White River and rates to be charged by taverns for food, lodging, and liquor. It was also at this first session of the commissioners that C.F. received his first appointment to public office. He and John Packer were appointed to serve as overseers of the poor for the combined Center and Warren townships. That this should be his first appointment was very appropriate for he had a strong sense of responsibility for the poor throughout his life and was active in such charitable organizations as the Indianapolis Benevolent Society. Marion County Commissioners Records, Book 1, April 1822–March 1827, records for April session, 1822; Dunn, *Indianapolis*, I, 50–53. The following October C.F. was commissioned a notary public by Governor Jonathan Jennings. *Indiana Executive Proceedings*, p. 241.

41. See below, note 55.

42. Daughter of Matthias R. Nowland, she became the wife of the Rev.

& myself spent the P.M. noon at Mr. Buckners where I got the sight of a young Lady Jest from Kentucky. At a distanc She looked very flashy & carried a very high head. I did not have the pleasure of geting acquainted with her. Perhaps if I had I would of found the lady as empty as myself.

Sat. [*Apr. 13*]. Mrs. P. & I set out some roots & made a begining at gardening. The waters are very high at this time & has been for a Week back.

April 13th 1822. Mr. Levington[43] and Some other Men has been 10 ms. up the River on the Public Land cuting saw logs for several weeks. They made a contract with Mr. Yanders to delive[r] him two Thousan at one dollar per piece[?] & since rain they have come down by water.

Sunday 14th of Aprile 1822. This day is very windy cold & snows a little & the people are runing continually to see the River. I have a g[r]eat curiosity to see it my self but it is such a disagreeable day that I shall not go.

Monday [*Apr.*] *15th.* This day is cool & beautiful Sun. The woods are very green at this time & furthermore I think that the Springs here are forwarder than what they are in the State of Ohio.

Tuesday 16th of Aprile. This day I dined with Mrs. Smith.[44]

Edwin Ray, Methodist minister who was assigned to the Indianapolis Circuit in 1826. Dunn, *Indianapolis,* I, 591–92.

43. Perhaps Noah Leverton. He was awarded the contract to build the first Marion County Jail ordered by the county commissioners at their meeting on May 15, 1822. The log structure, fourteen feet square and two stories high with a dungeon below, was erected for $312 on the northwest corner of the Courthouse Square. It was completed September 28. Dunn, *Indianapolis,* I, 57; Indianapolis *Gazette,* May 18, 25, 1822.

44. Nancy Bolton Smith, the wife of George Smith, bookbinder and printer who came to Indianapolis in August, 1821, and with his stepson Nathaniel Bolton began publication of the Indianapolis *Gazette,* January 28, 1822. (See note 29, above). Smith retired from the paper in August, 1822, when he was elected Marion County's first coroner. From 1825 to 1834 he served as associate judge. He then purchased a farm where the state Central Insane Hospital now is and named it Mount Jackson. He lived there until his death in 1836. Mrs. Smith died in 1844. Brown, "History of Indianapolis," in *Logan's Indianapolis Directory,* 1868, pp. 6, 7, 8, 10; Dunn, *Indianapolis,* I, 70–71; Nowland, *Early Reminiscences of Indianapolis,* pp. 91–92; diary entry, February 12, 1844.

Wednesday [Apr.] [1]7th. I went to Givens's Store[45] & bought one comb & on my return home I stoped to see Mrs. Wick likewise Mrs. Mitchel. I then came home & went to was[h]ing. Before I finished I was taken very sick. I did not stop till I got done then I was not able to set up but necessity compelled me to doo it.

Thursday [Apr.] 18th. I continued sick but did not go to bed for Mr. Curry was laboring with Mr. F. & in the P.M. noon Mrs. Buckner & Miss Hockings came and spent with me.

Friday [Apr.] 19th. I was very bad & oblige[d] to go to bed.

Sat. 20th of Aprile 1822. Mr. Robertson from Columbus stoped to see us in the morning as he was passing through. Mrs. McGeorge & her sister called to see me & in the P.M. noon I walked down to the River where I saw a g[r]eat many people crossing. It is now nine o clock at night & Mr. F. is not at home.

Sunday 21st of Aprile 1822. Mrs. Wick Miss Carter & myself went to the River & had the pleasure of rideing up to the mouth of Fall Creek & back a gain to the forde in the flat.

Monday [Apr.] 22d. Johnson mooved upon Market Street.

Tuesday [Apr.] 23d. I commenced makeing garden at Mr. B[lake's] house.

Wednesd. [Apr.] 24th. I was at the same business.

Thursday [Apr.] 25. I finished makeing garden except some few seeds in case there should bee frost. All three of the days that we were makeing garden were warm & dry.

Friday [Apr.] 26th. Mrs. N[owland] Mrs. Bradly & myself spent the P.M. noon with Mrs. Yanders.

Sat. 27th of Aprle. Very cloudy cool & rainy.

Sunday [Apr.] 28th. Very pleasant & Mr. Glover & Mr. Smith returned from Jefferson[ville] the same evening. Judg Wick & his Lady spent about two hours very agreeablely with us.

Monday 29th of Aprile. I washed.

45. James Givan and his son John were among Indianapolis' first merchants, opening a store near the river in 1821. The father helped organize the first Methodist society in Indianapolis. Nowland, *Early Reminiscences of Indianapolis*, pp. 118–20; Indianapolis *Indiana Democrat*, July 24, 1835; Fernandez C. Holliday, *Indiana Methodism* . . . (Cincinnati: Hitchcock and Walden, 1873), p. 198.

Tuesday 30th of April 1822. Mr. Osborn & Mr. Conner[46] brecfasted with us.

Wednesday 1st of May 1822. Was extremely warm. The woods are very beautiful at [this] time—And it appears that nature has been industrious. We have gentle showers evry day. The same day George Martin started to the State of Ohio near Fathers and about 9 o clock in the evening Mr. F. & I walked to Judg Wicks where we spent 1 hour. While we were there a whipperwill began to holow which reminded me of Urbana.

Thursday [May] 2d. This morning I planted some beanes. I was ingaged the balance of the day in Sowing.

Friday 3d of May. Very wrm and close not much air stiring. This day I had intro[d]uction to Mr. Homes who formerly lived in & about Dayton.

Sunday 5th of May. Mrs. N[owland] I & several others dined at Mr. Buckner's. They had a variety and an excellant dinner.

Monday [May] 6th. Mrs. Bradly & I took Tea at Mrs. Nowland's. Mrs. B. had been sick for a Week back and came out in order to gain her strength.

Tuesday 7th of May. Very cloudy & rainy but not withstanding all that Mrs. N[owland] & I started to Spend the P.M. with Mrs. Scudder.[47] Unfortunately she was not at home.

Wednesday [May] 8th. She Scent for us to go and take Tea with her. We did so. That night Mr. F. & I went to Mr. Paxtones and staid till 11 o clock. Mr. F. was writing for Mr. P.

Thursday [May] 9th. I finished a pair of panteloons for Mr. Hall. Mr. F. was out all day appraising Lots.

Friday [May] 10th. This morning I went to my garden planted

46. Probably John Conner, Indian agent and interpreter, scout and guide for William Henry Harrison, founder of Connersville, and state senator and representative. He was a member of the commission to locate the state capital. He purchased the Horseshoe Prairie site on White River south of Noblesville where he erected a grist mill and sawmill, and in June, 1823, opened a store in Indianapolis in partnership with Richard Tyner and Isaac N. Phipps. He died April 19, 1826. Charles N. Thompson, *Sons of the Wilderness, John and William Conner* (Indianapolis: Indiana Historical Society, 1937).

47. Wife of Caleb Scudder. See below, Pt. III, note 12.

some corn & beans. Tomorrow the Election is; which the people are to elect a magistrate.[48]

Sat. [*May*] *11.* I did not doo much of anything.

Sunday 12th of May 1822. I attened Preaching at the Governer's Circle; it was the first Sermon that ever was delivered at that place. He took his texts in the 3d Chapter of Proverbs 17th Verse & left the words upon record her ways are ways of pleasantness; & all her paths are peace. In the P.M. he delivered an other Sermon. He took his texts in the XV Chapter Luke 7th verse I say unto you, that likewise joy shall be in heaven over one Sinner that repenteth. He is a Presbyterian and a very good Orator. He will speak again on Tuesday in the P.M.[49]

Monday [*May*] *13th.* This day it rained all day, and it has continued now for about 24 hours.

Tuesday [*May*] *14th.* In the A.M. it rained & in the P.M. it was clear but mudy & Mr. F. & [I] attened Preaching at the School hous.[50] The Sermon was delivered by Mr. Proctor. He took his text in the forty second Psalm 1st verse As the heart panteth after the waterbrooks; so panteth my Soul after thee, O God.

48. At this county election the following were chosen as justices of the peace: William D. Rooker and Joel Wright for Washington and Lawrence townships; Abraham Hendricks and Isaac Stephens for Pike and Wayne townships; Peter Harmonson for Decatur, Perry, and Franklin townships; and Wilkes Reagan, Lismund Basye, and Obed Foote for Center and Warren townships. For the district outside the county proper William C. Blackmore and William Bush were chosen for White River and Delaware townships and Judah Leaming and Abel Ginney for Anderson and Fall Creek townships. Dunn, *Indianapolis,* I, 53; Indianapolis *Gazette,* June 1, 1822; *Indiana Executive Proceedings,* pp. 220–21.

49. This was the Rev. David C. Proctor, a Presbyterian missionary preacher who at this time was serving both Bloomington and Indianapolis. He visited Indianapolis for a week in May, 1822, under the direction of the Connecticut Missionary Society. He served briefly as the first pastor of the Presbyterian Church, organized in Indianapolis on July 5, 1823. Sulgrove, *History of Indianapolis,* p. 51; Dunn, *Indianapolis,* I, 86, 575; Indianapolis *Gazette,* March 1, 29, June 14 and 21, 1823. A resolution of the Presbyterian congregation expressing thanks to the Rev. Mr. Proctor for his services appeared in the Indianapolis *Gazette,* September 23, 1823.

50. In 1821 a log schoolhouse was erected at Illinois and Washington streets by volunteer labor to house a subscription school. The first teacher was Joseph C. Reed, who was elected county recorder the following year. Thereafter classes were held very irregularly and the school was shortly closed. Brown, "History of Indianapolis," in *Logan's Indianapolis Directory,* 1868, p. 7.

Wednesday [*May*] *15th.* Clear & very warm, in the A.M. I was at work in my garden & in the P.M. I took Tea at Mr. N[owland's] with Mrs. Buckner. The Commissioners have set for 3 or 4 days[51] & Mr. F. has been with them the most of the time. I suppose it is a greate advantage for him to doo so if not I know in reason he would not devote so much of his time from his study (not that I am accuesing him of being unstudious) to be with them & others for he is a man among an hundred that is one who knows his business as well.

Friday 16th [*17th*] *of May 1822.* In the A.M. I washed & read about 7 pages in Chester Fields letters to his Son which compleeted the Book; And in the P.M. I attended Preaching.

Sat. [*May*] *the 17th* [*18th*]. I ironed and piddled about.

Sunday [*May*] *18th* [*19th*]. I staid at home all day & Mr. F. attened two Sermonds. The same Evening Mr. F. & I walked up to Judg Wick's and set till about 9 o clock.

Monday the 20th of May 1822. Rainy and disagreeable, & Mr. Proctor, Dr. Cow,[52] Mr. Linton,[53] Mr. Fletcher, & myself, we all dined at Mr. Nowland's.

51. At this second regular session the county commissioners established the tax rate for items to be taxed for county purposes including horses and stallions, taverns, ferries, town lots, carriages, watches, and a poll tax. They also took up matters pertaining to the opening and maintenance of roads, listing of petit and grand jurors, and contracting for the erection of a jail. Dunn, *Indianapolis,* I, 54–56.

52. Dr. Isaac Coe. He came to Indianapolis in May, 1821, and was the one doctor who escaped falling victim to the ague the following summer and fall. He alone was able to attend patients, and was on the go night and day. He was the first president of the Fifth District Medical Society organized in 1826. A Presbyterian, he organized a Bible Class in February, 1822, and was the leader in obtaining the services of a missionary preacher. He was the chief promoter and secretary or clerk of the Indianapolis Sabbath School. Dr. Coe served as State Fund Commissioner from 1836 to 1839 when the mammoth internal improvement program threw the state's finances into chaos. He was accused of profiting personally from his transactions as agent for the state but was not found guilty. Dunn, *Indianapolis,* I, 9, 86, 542, 546; Nowland, *Early Reminiscences of Indianapolis,* pp. 104–105; Gayle Thornbrough (ed.), *Messages and Papers Relating to the Administration of Samuel Bigger Governor of Indiana 1840–1843* (*Indiana Historical Collections,* XLIV. Indianapolis: Indiana Historical Bureau, 1964), Index.

53. James Linton, a millwright who came to Indiana in the summer of 1821. He built and operated a sawmill on Fall Creek just above Indiana Avenue. Sulgrove, *History of Indianapolis,* p. 29; Dunn, *Indianapolis,* I, 72.

Tuesday the 21st. I rode out to the Country about two miles to Mr. Brinton's[54] with Mrs. N[owland] & Mrs. P[axton].

Wednesday [May] 22d. In the A.M. I transplanted Some Beets & Parsnip's And in the P.M. I took Tea at Mr. Ralston's.

Thursday Friday & Saturday [May 23, 24, 25]. I was makeing soap and in ill health all the time.

Sunday 26th of May 1822. This day Mr. Fletcher calculated to starte to Morgan County for the purpose of attending the sale of Lots but he was disapointed; it commensed raining early in the morning & continued on all day; I still remain sick.

Monday [May] 27th. I get no better but notwithstanding all that; I went to scrubing Mr. Blake's house in order that we might moove on Tuesday. I had several very pressing invitations to attend a Tea drinking at Mr. Nowlands but when I was done cleaning my hous I was not able to attend.

Tuesday 28th of May 1822. We come in to Mr. Blake's hous & took possession for one Year.[55]

Wednesday [May] 29th. I was ingagued in fixing my house & Mr. F. was helping Mr. Paxton to build fence.

Thursday [May] 30th. I washed & scrubed & done the greatest that ever I have done Since I have been here.

Friday [May] 31st. This day Mr. F. started on the circuit. This morning we got up very Early & it was quiet pleasing to hear the birds how cheerfully they Sung; their notes so mingled that a per-

54. Robert Brenton, one of the organizers of the Methodist Church in Indianapolis and a licensed exhorter. His farm lay on the south side of Pleasant Run in Section 23, T15N, R3E. He was a brother of the Rev. Henry Brenton who settled in Perry Township in 1822. Sulgrove, *History of Indianapolis,* pp. 60, 578, 580; Holliday, *Indiana Methodism,* p. 198.

55. The agreement made by Calvin Fletcher and James Blake on May 28, 1822, concerning Blake's house is in the Fletcher Papers. It gave Fletcher possession "of the framed house Standing on Block sixty seven, lot twelve . . . together with the said Lot which the said Fletcher is to have and injoy for the term of one year. . . .

"In consideration of the above premises he the said Fletcher is to board the said Blake during the year . . . and the said Blake is to give the said Fletcher ten Bushels of corn as a further consideration of Board and the said Blake is to have privileges of the east room of the said house in common with said Fletcher together with the stable on said Lot."

The lot was located on the point formed by Kentucky Avenue and Washington Street, and the house faced on Washington. Diary entry for August 19, 1837.

son could not distinguish one bird's note from another. This day Mr. Wrice a Presbyterian Preacher & Dr. Cow dined with Mr. B[lake] & myself. It is very growing weather at this time; this day we had a gentle shower & evrything in our garden appears to grow & flourish.

Sat. June the 1st. I visited Mrs. Wick.

Sunday [June] 2d. I Staid at home all day & Mr. B[lake] attended Preaching. In the P.M. a number of Ladys & Gentlemen Called on me. Mrs. W[ick] & Mrs. Buckner took Cofee with us; after sundown Mr. B. went with me to Judg Wick's & I staid with the Madam all night & got up early Monday Morn 3d & came home waken'd Mr. B. got breakfast & dinner & Set Mr. B. to geathe[r]ing bean Sticks & I visited Mrs. Wilson.[56] Got some eggs to set a hen.

Tuesday [June] 4th. Mrs. Scudder spent the P.M. with me.

Wednesday [June] 5th. Mrs. S. & myself Spent the P.M. with Mrs. Bates.

Thursday [June] 6th. I was[h]ed and scrubed in the Evening. Mrs. Wick came in and took Tea then I went home with her & Staid all night.

Friday [June] 7th. I irond & mended. The same day Mr. B[lake] bought a cow & calf from Mr. Johnstone & give 10 dollar's.

Sat. [June] 8th. I Spent the P.M. with Mrs. Wick.

Sunday [June] 9th. Mrs. Wick & I attended methodist Preaching; in the P.M. it rained & continued on all night without much intermission.

Monday [June] 10th. We had a very hard rain. It laid the corne & Potatoes flat to the ground, thundered before the rain.

Tuesday [June] 11th. I was altering a dress.

Wednesday 20th [12th] of June 1822. I took dinner with Mrs. Wick; she had her table spread with the fruits of her industry; such as beans & beets. I then came home & intended to Spend the P.M. at Mr. Nowland's; while I was makeing preparations to starte I received a Letter from Mr. F. which States he would not be at home

56. Perhaps the wife of Isaac Wilson who came to Indianapolis in the spring of 1820. He was a miller, and James Linton built for him the first gristmill in the town, located on Fall Creek at Walnut Street. Dunn, *Indianapolis*, I, 72; Nowland, *Early Reminiscences of Indianapolis*, pp. 25–26.

until Friday or Saturday; but notwithstanding all that I looked for him all the P.M. on Thursday neither was I disapointed.

Friday & Saturday which made the 15th of June I was washing.

Sunday [June] 16th. In the morning I feel quiet unwell; Mr. Blake & Mr. F. dressed themselves. Mr. B. went to Sabbath School[57] & Mr. F. went to Mr. Ray's[58] office, & left me all alone in which time I composed these few lines. In the Evening Mr. F. & I went to our lot.

Monday [June] 17th. I irond.

Tuesday [June] 18th. I finished a pair of pantaloons for Mr. B[lake].

Wednesday [June] 19th. In the A.M. it rained very hard. I hemed two hankerchief's for Mr. B. In the Eve I went to see Mrs. Wick.

Thursday [June] 20th. I went to Mr. Paxton's in order to get Mrs. P. to assist me in Sewing.

Friday [June] 21st. I washed & scrubed, there has been a greatdeal of talk about celebrating the fourth of July all this week.

Sat. [June] 22d. I irond & finished another pair of pantaloons.

Sunday [June] 23d. Mr. B[lake] rode to the country & Mr. F. & I staid at home all day.

Monday [June] 24th. I commensed a roundabout for Mr. B. but did not finish it till Wednesday on the account of being sick; it is very dry at this time, but our gardens flourish & grow.

Friday [June] 28. Mrs. Bates spent the P.M. with me like wise Mrs. Drake.[59]

57. Probably Dr. Coe's Bible class. Dunn, *Indianapolis*, I, 86.

58. James M. Ray (1800–1881), who was elected clerk of Marion County on April 1. He served as clerk until 1834 when he became cashier of the State Bank. A native of New Jersey, he came to Indianapolis from Kentucky in the fall of 1821. "Quiet, unobtrusive, vigilant, never idle, never careless," he was highly regarded and trusted. His services to the community included serving as secretary or business manager of a variety of organizations from town meetings to the fire company and missionary society. Sulgrove, *History of Indianapolis*, p. 105.

59. Mrs. Aaron Drake. At a meeting of citizens of the town held at Hawkins' tavern on January 30, 1822, Aaron Drake was chosen special postmaster for Indianapolis, and he carried the mail between Connersville and Indianapolis until the town became a regular United States post office in March. Brown, "History of Indianapolis," in *Logan's Indianapolis Directory*, 1868, p. 9; Indianapolis *Gazette*, February 11, 1822.

Sat. [*June*] *29th.* It rained.

Sunday [*June*] *30th.* Mr. Cutler[60] & his Son with us.

Monday July 1st 1822. I washed.

Tuesday [*July*] *2d.* Very Wet.

Wednesday [*July*] *3d.* This day Mr. F. is ingagued in writing toasts for the forth of July.[61]

Thursday the forth of July. This day there apered to be a great stir & livelaness among the people. The men had a barbacu & dined inder the green sugar trees at the West end of Washington St. The Evening of the same day Mr. Crumbaugh had a large party held at his dwelling.[62]

Friday [*July*] *5th.* Mr. B[lake] Started up Fallcreek.

Tuesday [*July*] *9th.* I getherd a large mess of young Corn & Mr. Foot dined with us. In the P.M. Mr. F. & I visited Mr. Johnson's a mild & a half in the Country. I was highly pleased with accommodation we met with.

Wednesday [*July*] *11th* [*10th*]. In the P.M. we had a ver[y] hard rain & Mr. McCarty[63] staid all night with us.

60. Jacob Cutler, associate judge of Morgan County, 1822–27. *Indiana Executive Proceedings*, pp. 210, 536.

61. In the Fletcher Papers, in C.F.'s hand, there are drafts of these toasts, dated July 3, 1822, and also what appears to be a draft for a speech for the occasion.

62. The program for the formal observance of the day was prepared by a committee headed by Dr. Coe. Following singing and prayers and the sermon by the Rev. John McClung, Judge William W. Wick read the Declaration of Independence and delivered an address, Obed Foote read Washington's First Inaugural Address and added his commentary, and John Hawkins read Washington's Farewell Address, accompanying it with an outline of the important events in Washington's administration. The program concluded with singing and prayers. A barbecue dinner prepared by Samuel McGeorge, Matthias R. Nowland, and a Mr. Davis followed. It was held in the middle of Washington Street near Missouri. Here Dr. Samuel G. Mitchell delivered a patriotic oration which was followed by appropriate toasts. The day concluded with a ball at Jacob R. Crumbaugh's tavern at the corner of Missouri and Market streets. Indianapolis *Gazette*, June 29, July 6, 1822; Nowland, *Early Reminiscences of Indianapolis*, pp. 130–32.

63. According to Nowland, Dunn, and Sulgrove, Nicholas McCarty did not settle in Indianapolis until the fall of 1823. Ignatius Brown says that he was among those arriving in the summer or fall of 1821. Born in Moorefield, Virginia (West Virginia), he learned merchandising in Newark, Ohio, and when he came to Indianapolis at the age of twenty-eight he was already a successful businessman. He opened a general store—the first of any considerable importance in the

Friday Eve [July 12]. I went down to Mr. P[axton's] & Set till 8 o clock.

Sat. [July] 13th. Mr. F. set off about 1 o clock for Columbus & I Staid all nigt with Mrs. Wick.

Sunday 12th [14th] of July 1822. This day Mr. Jones[64] departed his life about 8 o clock in the Morn. I have not the least doubt in my mind but what he was prepared to depart from this world of sin & folly. I fear it will be very sickly t[h]is Summer, it appears so at this time. This day I attended baptist Preaching at the School hous. Mr. Jones is to be buried this P.M. I think we have had as hard a rain this day as ever I saw & very high wind; I am all alone & very uneasy fearing that Mr. F. & the Judg are caught in the storm & perhaps crippled.

Monday [July] 15th. Last nigt Mrs. Wick staid with me & this morning Mr. Wick came & took Breakfast with us. Monday night I staied with Mrs. W. & we were both very much frighened.

Thursday [July] 18th. I spent the day with Mrs. N[owland] & Mrs. P[axton] & that night went to Mrs. Wickes. About 9 o clock Mr. F. returned from court & we staid with the madam all night.

Thursday [July] 25. I Spent the Eve with Mrs. Bates & after Sundown Mr. F. & I called on Mrs. Walpole[65] and the Eve f[o]llowing we took Tea with her.

---

town—on the southwest corner of Washington and Pennsylvania streets and soon established branches in other Indiana towns. He also prospered, in partnership with James Blake, in the collecting, drying, and shipping to Philadelphia, of ginseng for sale to the China market. He became an associate of C.F. in land speculation and was involved in various efforts to introduce new industries into Indianapolis. He served as state Fund Commissioner from 1832 to 1836, resigning the post upon the passage in 1836 of the act providing for the great internal improvement program which he predicted would be financially ruinous to the state. A Whig, he made unsuccessful bids for various political offices including representative in Congress and the governorship in 1852. He was elected to one term in the state Senate in 1849. He died in 1854. Nowland, *Early Reminiscences of Indianapolis*, pp. 158–59; Sulgrove, *History of Indianapolis*, pp. 99–100; Dunn, *Indianapolis*, II, 668–73; Brown, "History of Indianapolis," in *Logan's Indianapolis Directory*, 1868, p. 7; diary, May 17–21, 1854.

64. F. G. Jones. Indianapolis *Gazette*, July 20, 1822.

65. Wife of Luke Walpole, who moved to Indianapolis in 1822, arriving in a keelboat which carried his family of thirteen, a Negro servant girl, baggage and household furniture, and a general stock of merchandise for sale. Dunn, *Indianapolis*, I, 70. He advertised his business in the Indianapolis *Gazette* of June 1, 1822.

Sat. [July] 27th. Mr. F. started to Winchester. That day we had hard thunder & rain; Mr. F. was in it all.

Sund. [Aug.] 11th. I visited the Sick.

Wednesday [Aug.] 13 [14th]. Mrs. P. spent the day with me. About 9 o clock in the Eve Mr. F. had a chill purhaps an hour then the fever continued till 10 o clock the nexte day at which time I left him alone & rode out to Mr. Wood's but I left him with great r[e]luctanc[e] on the account of his illness.

Thursday 15th of August. Mr. F. still remains unwell.

Tuesday 27th August 1822. Mr. F. has just raised out of a very severe attact of the fever & I fear he will expos himself so much that he will be sick again. This day is cloudy & wet & Mr. F. has ventured out.

Sunday 1st of Sept. Very cludy & rainy. This day I wrote a letter to Father & Mother. The people are generaly healthy at this time.

Thursday the 5th of Sept. 1822. The three Miss Walpoles called on me for the first time.

(It has been considerable sickly this season)[66]

Thursday [Sept.] 12. They all took tea with me.

Wednesday 18th of Sept. I commensed drying grapes. Camp-meating commensed the 13th of Sept. and held four days.[67] Court commensed at this plaice Sept. 26th 1822 for the first [time]. Several strange lawyers attended it.[68]

66. The summer of 1822 was generally more healthy than that of the preceding year. Brown, "History of Indianapolis," in *Logan's Indianapolis Directory,* 1868, p. 11. The Indianapolis *Gazette,* on June 22, declared "that the inhabitants of this town and neighborhood enjoy, at the present time, a greater degree of health than is known in many towns of long standing—the reports to the contrary notwithstanding." It reiterated this in later issues. Five deaths due to "the fever" occurred between mid-July and mid-September in the town and nearby. Indianapolis *Gazette,* March 6, June 22, August 10, and September 14, 1822.

67. According to Brown and the Indianapolis *Gazette,* the Methodist camp meeting, the first in the town, began September 12 and lasted three days. It was under the charge of the Rev. James Scott. Brown, "History of Indianapolis," in *Logan's Indianapolis Directory,* 1868, pp. 11–12; Indianapolis *Gazette,* July 27, 1822.

68. The first circuit court in Marion County opened at John Carr's cabin on Washington Street just west of the present canal but moved to a more spacious room at Jacob R. Crumbaugh's at the southwest corner of Market and Missouri streets. William W. Wick was the president judge and associate judges

Sat. the 28th. The three miss Walpols give me a call.

Sunday 29th. Mr. F. and I walked a half a mild towards Mr. Lintons mill.

Oct. the 10th 1822. I resume once more to note down a few things, to wit, within one week Mr. F. has been at the expense of purchasing 6 yards of shirting and two pare of shoes. We have not had but 3 hard frosts this fall, people are still sickly.

Wednesday 16th of Oct. 1822. Mr. F. and I went a grapeing.

Oct. 20th 1822. I commensed reading Schultz's Travels.[69]

Sat. the 2d Nove. 1822. Mr. F. and I geathered our Beets carrots and Potatoes. In the Eve butchered a pig.

Monday [Nov.] *the 4th.* I was spining wool.

Tuesday [Nov.] *5.* In the morning Mr. F. & I bilt A corn crib. In the P.M. and all next day I was ingaged stewing pumping [pumpkin] out of dors. It rained all the P.M.

Friday [Nov.] *8th.* Mr. F. started to Winchester.

Saturday [Nov. *9*]. I went down to Mr. P[axton's] and called at Mr. N[owland's].

Sunday [Nov. *10*]. I staid at Mr. Col. [?] I finished my book.

Monday [Nov. *11*]. We had high winds from the South so much so that I could not keep any fire. About two oclock in the P.M. Mr. Nowland departed this life it was said very happy. He said he had maid his peace with God and was willing to go.

Tuesday [Nov. *12*]. Mr. Proctor delivered a very pathetick Seirmon, on the occation. His Text red thus It is better to go to the hous of mo[u]rning than the hous feasting.

Thursday [Nov.] *the 14th.* Mr. F. returned from Winchester.

Sunday [Nov.] *17th.* Mr. F. started to Martinsvill. I spent the day very idol, for my hous smoket so bad I could neither read write or doo anything els. In the night it rained very hard, next

---

were James McIlvain and Eliakim Harding. Local lawyers admitted to practice included Calvin Fletcher, Hiram M. Curry, Obed Foote, and Harvey Gregg. Nonresidents included Daniel B. Wick, Oliver H. Smith, James Noble, James Rariden, James Whitcomb, and Lot Bloomfield. Dunn, *Indianapolis*, I, 554; Brown, "History of Indianapolis," in *Logan's Indianapolis Directory*, 1868, p. 10. C.F. was appointed prosecuting attorney. See below, p. 92.

69. Probably Christian Schultz, *Travels on an Inland Voyage* . . . (New York, 1810).

morning there was snow to be seen. It was cold and disagreeable and I had to pick up all my wood.

Wednesday [*Nov.*] *20th*. Mr. F. returned home.

Thursday [*Nov.*] *the 21st*. We moved back into our hous—

Friday [*Nov. 22*]. I washed and fatiegued myself I believe more than ever I did before.

Sat. & Sunday [*Nov. 23 and 24*]. I spent very idle thou[g]h Sun. I commensed reading Thompson's treating upon Spring Summer Autumn & Winter.

Monday [*Nov. 25*]. I began sewing & have been ingagued evry day this week except this day Saturday and it has snowed all day.

Sunday [*Nov.*] *24th*. The snow was about 3 or 4 inches deep. Mr. F. did not return till in the night, He had suffered very much with the cold. Monday I washed & [did not] doo anything more of any consequence. The balance of the week I was sick.

Tuesday 17th of Decr. 1822. We butchered a beef.

Sat. [*Dec.*] *28th*. Mr. F. has this day spent about 6 dollars for my sake. In the Evening we went to Mr. B. [?] and spent till 10 o clock.

Monday [*Dec.*] *30th*. We butchered our hogs and I was in gagued in preserveing my lard and sausage's and worst every day till Fri. That day I diped candle'ss.

Sat. [*Jan.*] *the 4th 1823*. Very wet and thawing. I assisted in puting up an ash hopper and exposed myself very much.

Sunday [*Jan. 5*]. Cold and feezing.

Monday [*Jan.*] *6th*. Sarah ann Nowland helped me to wash.

Tuesday [*Jan.*] *7th*. I spent the day with Mrs. N[owland] and made a dress.

Wednesday [*Jan.*] *8th*. I visited Mrs. Wick and made a shimmee.

Thursday eve [*Jan. 9*]. Mrs. N. spent with me.

Friday [*Jan. 10*]. Mrs. Wick.

Sunday 12th of January 1823. Mr. Johnson dined with us.

Wednesday [*Jan.*] *15th*. Mr. Brackenridg[70] began bording with us.

70. John Adams Breckenridge, a lawyer who came to Indianapolis in October, 1822. He entered into a brief partnership with C.F., leaving for Florida in the spring of 1823. Advertisements in Indianapolis *Gazette*, October 12, 1822, and following issues, March 22, 1823, and following issues, and January 4, 1824, and

Thursday [Jan. 16]. Mrs. Buckner & Mrs. Linton spent the P.M. with me.

Monday January 20th 1823. Very muddy and snowing. I road to Mrs. P[axton's] and staid till the next day.

February the 1st 1823. Mr. F. was taken with the agu fever again. For one Weeak we have had as cold weather as I ever felt.

Sunday 9th of Febr. We can descover a little alteration, and I think the Winter will soon brake.

Wednesday [Feb.] 12th. I was sewing at Mrs. N[owland']s.

Thursday [Feb. 13]. I visited Mrs. Wilson.

Tuesday [Feb.] 18th. I was shopping & purchased the amount of five dollars.

Thursday 6th of March 1823. I was solicited to attend a Tea party at Mr. Walpole's. I did not attend on account of ill health.

Wednesday [March] 12. I commensed reading the horrors of Oakendale Abby a romance and finished Friday 14th 1823.

Sat. [March] 15. Mr. F. & I visited Col. Paxton.

Wednesday [March] 19th. I boiled my last pumking.

Tuesday 25th of March 1823. Miss Mc Doogle spent the P.M. with me. I thought her a very inteligent girl.

Aprile 4th 1823. Mr. F. started to Morgan county.

Sat. [Apr. 5]. I visited Mrs. P.

Sun. [Apr. 6]. Our school commensed which I hope will be of greate benefit to the children of our Town.[71]

---

following issues; below, pp. 89–90, 94. In his diary on May 23, 1859, C.F. wrote: "John Adams Breckenridge of Texas is here a lay delegate to the Presbyterian general assembly. He was in 1822 a partner in the practice of law. We went to Morgan court in spring of 1823 [on] foote & the fall before to Shelby having hired a horse (one horse) of Joshua Glover to ride and tie. He started before me and I was to overtake him. He took the wrong road (road to Rushville) & but for coming to some wagoners camped in the woods would have laid out. He is now a frail old man, a Texas planter of wealth."

71. The Indianapolis Sabbath School which opened in Caleb Scudder's cabinet shop. The school was conducted by the Indianapolis Sabbath School Union which included members of all denominations in the town and also non-church members. James M. Ray was superintendent. Teachers included Caleb Scudder, Douglass Maguire, Henry Bradley, Bethuel F. Morris, Livingston Dunlap, Miss Coe, Mrs. Morris, Miss McDougal, Mrs. Scudder, and Mrs. Paxton. The school was a great success. Its chief promoter was its secretary or clerk Dr. Coe. Dunn, *Indianapolis*, I, 87–88.

Mon. [*Apr.* 7]. Cloudy and rainy and Mr. B[lake] and Dr. D[unlap] fixed my bed stid.

Tues. [*Apr.*] *the 8.* I had a number of Lady's called upon me.

Thursday [*Apr.* 10]. Mrs. Dayly washed.

Friday [*Apr.* 11]. I fixt up a stand of curtans.

Saturday [*Apr.*] *12th.* Mr. F. returned home from M[a]rtins Ville.

Sun. Eve. [*Apr.* 13]. Walked down to Col. P.

Mon. [*Apr.* 14]. I was quiet unwell. Made some gardin.

Tues. [*Apr.*] *15th.* I was delvered of a son.[72] Dr. Mitchel was with me the rest of the copany was Mrs. Nowland Mrs. Mitchel Mrs. Bradly Mrs. Colup and Mrs. Paxton. Betsy Huggins staid with me 2 weekes then done my worke one weeke. Betsy Vanblaricum staid 2 days. Margret Hyet came on Wednesday the 7th day of May and staid two weekes. Scalded her foot on Thursday. Staid till Saturday the 24th.

Fri. 30th of May. I fraimed a quilt.

Sun. the 8th of June 1823. Mr. F. & myself wal[k]ed to the River.

Tuesday the 8th of July 1823. Miss Eliza Linton came to stay with us.

Sat. [*July*] *12th.* My finger began to get sore.

Tues. [*July*] *15th.* I took a quilt out of the fraim.

Sun. 17th of August 1823. We got a Girl by the name of Polly Crawford.

Friday 12th Sept. 1823. Mr. F. started to Columbus.

Wednesday 22d [*24th*] *of Sept.* I recieved a letter from him which gave me great satisfaction.[73] I had just come from Mrs. Wick's who was very sick with the fever and felt very much distressed for her situation, (asking myself whether I could bare things with as much fortitude or not. She certainly displais a g[r]eat [d]eal of philosophy). The letter relieved me.

Monday 29th of Sept. 1823. I visited Dr. Cow's Daughter's. I found them plain and neat but unsociable.

72. James Cooley Fletcher.

73. This letter, dated Bloomington, September 22, and the one mentioned below from Burlington in Greene County, dated September 30, are in the Fletcher Papers. Burlington was then the county seat of Greene County.

Oct. 3d. I recieved another letter from Mr. F. he was then at Burlington Green County.

Sunday 12th of Oct. 1823. I rode about two miles in to the country.

Sunday the 19th. I spent the P.M. at Mr. Willson's.

Tues. the 25th of Nove. 1823. Mr. Paxton started to coriden.[74] I staid with Mrs. P. all night.

Fri. 5th Decr. Mrs. Nowland had a quilting where I heard some talk of a party which is to take place at Washington hall on the 25th. I had an interdu[c]tion to Brown and think her a very ag[r]ee-able and inteligen Girl.

Fri. 12th inst. I spent the Eve with B. F. Moris[75] Lady. I found her a very sociable woman though I did not injoy myself in the least altho I might appea[r]ed to do so. Mr. F. was present a great part of the Eve which rendered me quiet unhappy & imbarast thinking he was mortified at my actions. I made no convercesion and trembleing fearing there mite be some question asked that would expose my ignernce. He's taken a greateal of pains with me. It seames as if my eyes are just opened and I view evry thing in its darkest dyes and some times make myself miserable again. I reflect I know it is my duty to be cheerful and make evrything appear in the best light.

Sun. Dece. 14th 1823. Cold and all nature is robed in a mantle of snow.

Wednesday 24th of Decr. 1823. Mr. F. and I attended a ball at Washington hall.

Thursday & Friday [Dec. 25 and 26]. I did not do much of anything.

74. To attend the session of the General Assembly.

75. Bethuel F. Morris, Franklin County recorder, was elected by the General Assembly agent of state to sell the public lots at Indianapolis on December 6, 1822. He succeeded James Milroy who had succeeded John Carr. Morris served until January 18, 1825, when he resigned to become president judge of the Fifth Judicial Circuit. He continued in that position until his resignation November 13, 1834, when he became cashier of the Indianapolis branch of the State Bank. *Indiana Executive Proceedings*, pp. 25, 245, 269, 275–76, 278, 309; Dunn, *Indianapolis*, I, 342. He advertised as a lawyer in the Indianapolis *Gazette* as early as March 29, 1823, and was briefly associated in a partnership with C.F. which was dissolved in March, 1825. Indianapolis *Gazette*, March 8, 1825, and following issues.

Sat. [*Dec.* 27]. I washed.

Sunday [*Dec.* 28]. Sliped off tolerable well. Mr. B[lake] dined with us for the first time cince he left off b[oa]rding.

Monday [*Dec.* 29]. I cut out a dress which I [blank].

Thursday 1st of January 1824. This day in the Eve I attended preaching at Col. Paxton's very much against my will.

Sunday [*Jan.*] *4th.* I had an introduction to Mrs. Johnson[76] from Kentucky.

Mon. [*Jan.*] *5th.* It rained all day. Tuesday I washed.

Wed. [*Jan.*] *7th.* I scrubed & ironed and spent the Eve at Dr. Dunlop's.

Thursday [*Jan.*] *8th.* Clear & pleasant, and I spent the Eve at Judg Wicks.

F[*r*]*i.* [*Jan.* 9]. Rained all day and I spent the Eve at Mr. Brown's.[77]

Sat. [*Jan.* 10]. Continued raining.

Sun. [*Jan.*] *11th.* Clear & windy. Mr. B[lake] dined with us. This Eve Mr. F. spent at home for the first in a great many weeks in writing a letter.

Wednesday 21st of January 1824. I visited Mr. Johnson.

Thursday [*Jan.* 22]. I called on Mr. & Mrs. [. . .].

Friday [*Jan.* 23]. I visited Mrs. P[axton] Staid till late.

Sat. [*Jan.* 24]. I am quiet unwell.

Sun. [*Jan.* 25]. I do not feel any better. This Eve. I recieved the 3d number of the Casket[78] which I read and considered the contents very good.

Sunday February 1st 1824. Clear and cold.

Wed. 4th of Feb. Mr. P. returned from Corydon.

Thursday [*Feb.* 5]. Continues cold.

76. Wife of Gabriel J. Johnston, partner of Harvey Gregg. See below, p. 100.

77. Perhaps Hiram Brown, who studied law with Thomas Corwin in Lebanon, Ohio, came to Indianapolis in November, 1823, was admitted to the bar the following year, and practiced with notable success until his death in 1853. He served as prosecuting attorney of the Fifth Circuit, 1831–32. Sulgrove, *History of Indianapolis*, pp. 171–74; *Indiana Executive Proceedings*, pp. 306–307.

78. The short-lived *Western Ladies Casket* was published at Connersville, Indiana, in 1823 and 1824, "edited by a lady." It has been described as a "poor little fortnightly affair" which consisted largely of extracts from English magazines, treatises on chemistry, etc. Buley, *The Old Northwest*, II, 524.

Friday [*Feb. 6*]. Little warmer and I visited Mrs. Willson. Found her all most helpless and very low spirited.

Sat. 7th. Quiet warm and clouday. I washed & scrubed & intended visiting Mrs. Osborn at her request but was disapointed. The lady went a visiting herself. It is 9 o clock at night. Mr. F. is at a debate. Polly & James are both asleep & I am just going to iron.

Tuesday 10th Fe[*b*]*uary 1824*. I visited Mrs. Willson staid all night & till 12 o clock Wednesday on account of a storme.

Friday 20th of Feb. 1824. Clear & warm a good sugar day. Mr. F. rode 5 milds in the Country to an infair. Col. Gregery[79] arives the same day. Mr. Ray sent for Mr. F. in the Eve.

Wed. 3d of March 1824. I went to eat shugar with Mr. Ralston.

Mon. [*March*] *8th* [–22]. We had a very agreeable party. Our Boy has been sick for several days but is geting better. Mr. F. started the 9th of March 1824 to Cort & returned Fri. the 19. That day I spent in runing about and the day before I spent the P.M. at Mr. Hendersons. Thursday 11th I was copying a letter. Mon. 22 I visited Mrs. Bradly with Mrs. W[ick] & Mrs. N[owland].

Sarah Hill Fletcher, Indianapolis, to C.F., Shelbyville, Indiana, March 16, 1824

. . . I have not seen Owen[80] since I wrote you. He sent for his close the Eve after he left. I sent him word he should not have them till you came home. He is I understand in the brick yard at Lanes, and Mr. Bradly says you must be put on your gard or else Isaac will teare you up for whipping Owen. I laught and told him he darenot speak on the subject where you was. Mr. Web halled a load of wood to day. [. . .] and Washington Colup cuts my wood. I make my fires with pleasure and injoy peas. I stay close at home and

79. Col. James Gregory, of Shelby County, who was elected to the state Senate in 1823 and 1825 from the district including Marion County. He was reelected in 1828 from the district comprising Decatur, Johnson, Morgan, and Shelby counties when C.F. was elected from the district comprising Carroll, Hamilton, Hancock, Hendricks, Madison, and Marion. *Indiana Election Returns 1816–1851*, compiled by Dorothy Riker and Gayle Thornbrough (*Indiana Historical Collections*, XL, Indianapolis: Indiana Historical Bureau, 1960), Index.

80. Owen Batman was a young boy whom C.F. apparently had taken into his household as a bound boy. See below, p. 103.

keep Polly at her book which will be conformable to your feeling and wishes. *Your Boy is just singing himself to sleep* in Polly's lap. She is noding.

. . . Mr. Morris came down yesterday Eve. I r[e]cieved one dollar from him which you sent. I hav not had an opportunity of geting sugar. Swet[81] has been here. He has got into some dificulty he says and wants to see you very bad. It is I suppose that slander case you mention. He says he 'il bring me sugar at six & a forth cents for what he owes you. It is to be good. . . .

DIARY

Sat. [Apr.] 3d. Warm. I received another letter wrote at Rushville. Wrote an answer but did [not] send it.

Sun. [Apr.] 4th. Very pleasant about 2 o clock I went home with Mrs. P. & staid till Monday morning. Then called on Mrs. Osborn to see her child that lay at the point of death. Came home raised my cabbage set out my stalks & turnip's & attended to a great many little things which I had long neglected.

Tuesday [Apr.] 5th [6th]. I staid with Mrs. O. all day & till after she buried her child.

Wed. [Apr.] 6th [7th]. I called on Mr. Morris, to know whether he was going to madison county, that I might send a letter to Mr. F. His wife was so ill he did not go. I then called on Judg Wick came home put a quilt in the frame.

Thurs. [Apr. 8]. I washed & quilted some.

Friday [Apr.] 9th. I visited Mrs. Scudder & took a pleasant ride in Com[pany] with Mr. Landes[82] Mrs. S. & Miss Mary in the deer-

81. Joseph Swett. It was from him that C.F. bought his first land. According to the Marion County deed records C.F. acquired from Joseph Swett on November 9, 1824, six acres of land, part of the northeast quarter of the southwest quarter of section 10, T16N, R3E. It lay northwest of Indianapolis, west of the present Lafayette Road, on the west side of White River. The price paid was $112. Apparently he was never on this land until August 1, 1856. See diary entry for that date.

82. Jacob Landis, who came to Indianapolis in the spring of 1822 and opened a grocery store on the south side of the State House square near Mississippi Street (now Senate Avenue). He served as sheriff of Marion County from 1828 to 1832. Nowland, *Early Reminiscences of Indianapolis*, pp. 144–46; *Indiana Executive Proceedings*, p. 515.

burn Waggon. The are was warme & pleasant. Betsey Willson staid with me all night.

Sat. [Apr.] 10th. Mr. F. came home all wet & muddy for it rained all day.

Sun. [Apr. 11]. Mr. B[lake] came down.

Mon. [Apr.] 12th. Cort commesed at this plaice which held 9 days. On the 21st Mr. F. started to Hamilton coun[ty]. I got my garden plowed the saim day.

Thurs. [Apr.] 22d. Put all my seeds in the ground & now trust to nature to do her part.

Sunday 2d of May. Mr. F. & myself walked to the River with Mr. C. & Wife. The 2d week in may I was ingaged at sewing & makeing preparations for Mr. F. to start to N.Y.

Wednesday [May] 19th. Mr. F. started to the North & will be abcent about 2 months—which time will seem long to me.[83]

Thursday [May] 20th. Mrs. Nowland started to Ky. Her children all stay with me till she returns. The same day I run in debt to Mr. I.N.P.[84] 10 dollars.

Friday [May] 21st. I maid a bedtick.

Sat. [May] 22d. I scrubed & cleaned out my seller.

Sun. [May] 23d. I attended preaching—heard a very good sermon deliverd by one Mr. Martin.

Mon. [May] 24th. This day commensed makeing a dress. Mrs. Johnson came & spent the P.M. with me.

Thursday 27th of May 1824. Mr. Ingram arived whom we had been looking for a long time. He will live with us. I think him a very find studious young man. I have been ingagued at sewing all this week. I do not get to read any onely on Sunday & not much then.

Thursday 10th of June. I have been quiet unwell for several days, but never stoped work. This day Mrs. Nowland came home from Ky.

Sat. 12th of June. Mr. Ingram planted potatoes.

Mon. [June the 14th]. I set with Mrs. Mitchel.

83. For C.F.'s diary of this journey to Vermont see below, pp. 104–29.

84. Isaac N. Phipps, who came to Indianapolis in 1823. He was a partner in the firm of (John) Conner, (Richard) Tyner and Company, which operated a successful general store in the town. Nowland, *Early Reminiscences of Indianapolis*, pp. 154–55.

Tues. [June] 15th. Mrs. M. & myself spent P.M. with Mrs. H.

Wednesday [June] 16th. I washed.

Thursday [June 17]. I scrubed.

Fri. [June] 18th. I commensed sewing for Mr. Blake.

Sunday [June] 20th. I went home with Mrs. Paxton as she returned from preaching. Last Eve I received a letter from Malinda with which I was not altogether satisfied.[85]

Wednesday 23d of June in the P.M. I spent at Mr. Hendersons helping her sew.

Thursday [June] 24th. The Festival of St. John—I spent the whole day there, and was much pleased with the appearence of the mason's & wished that I could see Mr. F. in C.O.[86]

Fri. [June] 25th. In the P.M. I had 8 visiters all unexpected.

Sat. 3d July. I received a letter from Mr. F. which was very gratifiing.

Friday 9th of July 1824. I went in company with an number of

85. Malinda Hill was Sarah's younger sister. The letter, written from Urbana, Ohio, June 1, 1824, is in the Fletcher Papers. Malinda had become an ardent convert to Methodism and her letter reproached Sarah and C.F. for such frivolity as attending a ball. "You must know," she wrote, "that bodily exercise of that kind has no tendency to qualify its votaries for its business of life, nor for the important duties of religion; & according to old Cicero neither is it very praiseworthy or honorable. I was secondly astonished that you could not discriminate between the atrocity of the crimes as you called them of dancing all night or shouting & jumping at a camp-meeting &c. . . . We have had a great Revival of religion in this region of late. . . . O My Bro. & Sister Fletcher 'seek the Lord while he may be found. . . .' " In a postscript she urged them to join the Methodists.

Malinda Hill married Alhannon Sweet, described by C.F. as a "backwoods preacher." The couple came to Indiana and lived on land owned by C.F. near Lafayette. Malinda died December 3, 1831 and C.F. looked out for the three children that she left. Diary, March 7, 1862, and genealogy of the Hill family, below.

86. The Grand Lodge of Indiana, Free and Accepted Masons, granted a dispensation to Center Lodge at Indianapolis on March 27, 1822, and a charter was granted October 7, 1823. Among the first officers were Harvey Gregg, Milo R. Davis, John T. Osborn, Samuel Henderson, James M. Ray, Obed Foote, and Samuel McGeorge. The program for St. John's day in 1823 included an address by the Rev. Mr. Proctor, music provided by Caleb Scudder, Daniel B. Wick, and Dr. J. W. B. Moore, and dinner prepared by John Hawkins. Dunn, *Indianapolis*, I, 371. C.F. became a member of Center Lodge in 1825. Will E. English, *A History of Early Indianapolis Masonry and of Center Lodge* (Indiana Historical Society *Publications*, III, No. 1, Indianapolis, 1895), p. 15.

others about 3 milds to gether raspburys. We took our provision with us, *and dined at Mr. Helvay's.*[87] It rained so hard I gethered but few buries.

Friday 23d of July 1824. Mrs. Foote died leveing a Husband & one child about 3 months old, to morn her loss. On Sunday 25 I heard her funeral sermon.

Sunday 1st of August. I attended the funeral sermon & Burial of Mr. Lorance[88]—evry thing was performed in magic order.

Monday [Aug.] 2d. This is the 4th Evening that I could hardly give up looking for Mr. F. without seeing him.

87. Robert Helvey, one of the first settlers in Wayne Township. His farm was situated in School Section 16 west of Eagle Creek, near the "big raspberry patch." Nowland, *Early Reminiscences of Indianapolis*, pp. 115–18; Sulgrove, *History of Indianapolis*, pp. 651–52.

88. Rice B. Lawrence. Indianapolis *Gazette*, August 3, 1824.

III

Diary and Letters of CALVIN FLETCHER *November 1, 1821–March 30, 1824* and Diary of a Tour from Indianapolis to Ludlow, Vermont *May 19–July 25, 1824*

[*Nov. 1, 1821*]. I continued till the first of Nove. without much of any thing occuring at which time I drew up some resolutions for purpose of sending a Loby member to the assembly. I was likewis chosen secretary of the meeting & elec[ted] a member of the Committee to draw a Petition which I assisted in doing.[1] This make [mark?] of distinction I very much appreciate and hoped my conduct was such that I may have yet further calls.

Nove. the 8th. I was applied to by Mr. Blak[e] to draw a Petition to the Govr. for the Shff. office.[2] I find there is much strife and

1. James Blake and Dr. Samuel G. Mitchell were selected at a meeting held at Hawkins' tavern to serve as lobbyists in Corydon to work for the organization of a new county which would include Indianapolis. By an act of the General Assembly of December 31, 1821, Marion County was created and Indianapolis designated the county seat. Hervey Bates of Connersville was appointed sheriff by Governor Jonathan Jennings, and he came on in February, 1822, to assume his duties. *Laws of Indiana*, 1821–22, pp. 135–39; Brown, "History of Indianapolis," in *Logan's Indianapolis Directory*, 1868, p. 5; *Indiana Executive Proceedings*, p. 203.

2. This is the earliest diary entry recording an application to C.F. for professional aid in Indianapolis. However, there is in the Fletcher Papers a crude record of fees due C.F. for legal services in 1821 which indicates he had done some prior business. His license to practice law in the circuit and inferior courts in Indiana, dated October 9, 1821, and signed by Davis Floyd and William W. Wick, president judges, is also in the Papers, as is his license to practice in all courts in the state, superior and inferior, dated November 5, 1824, and signed by Supreme Court Judges James Scott, Jesse L. Holman, and Isaac Blackford. When Judge

contention brewing among the citizens of this place yet I sincerely hope to escape all censure by asking no favors myself.

Nove. the 9th. It began to snow & continued so—wet and cold.

Sometime the first of Nove. I commenced reading a Novel calld Ema wrote by some person unknown.[3] Some of the characters were pleasing but the whole tenor of discription was tinged rather too deeply with high life to suit the tastes of all people. The Effects that it would produce on a young and inexperienced person particularly a girl I think would be good with mature explanations after this was read. Mrs. F. Read the Vicar of Wakefield.

The 20th of Nove. Commenced Duncans Logic which I have once before read. I think my mind is much better preprared to receive Philosophical instruction than ever but I must lament that my memory is not so well qualified to store up the quintescence of those principles as It formerly was. I am better pleased with Style of Duncan than I formerly was, but like Lock I think him too prolox. I mean to extract and distill what I can from him, and then read Parks travels.[4] I have commenced Solomon's Proverbs which I intend to read thro' in course and mark and make Brackets of those sayings which I think will be useful for a refferance thereto. The three foundations of human Judgment are first Intuition 2d Experience the Ground of our knowledge of powers & qualities of bodies 3d Testimony the ground of historical knowledge.

Decr. the 4th 1821. I commenced reading the travels of Mongo Park into the Interior of Affrica. He left Dr. Daily's residence upon the Gambese some time in the fall of 1795 and proceeded with much difficulty thro' many petty states of Negroes Easterly course till he struck the Niger whose source was the principle object of his mission by the African Society of London which had been disputed by several Geographical writiers &c. Park manifested in his travels a most persevering & intriped disposition. The fatigues he endured and the Dangers he encountered would seem to deter

---

Blackford died in January, 1860, C.F. recorded: "I knew the Judge in 1824—was examined and licensed before Scott Holeman & Blackford at Corydon." Diary, January 12, 1860.

3. Perhaps Jane Austen's *Emma*, published in 1816.

4. Mungo Park, the Scottish African explorer, whose *Travels in the Interior of Africa* was published in 1799.

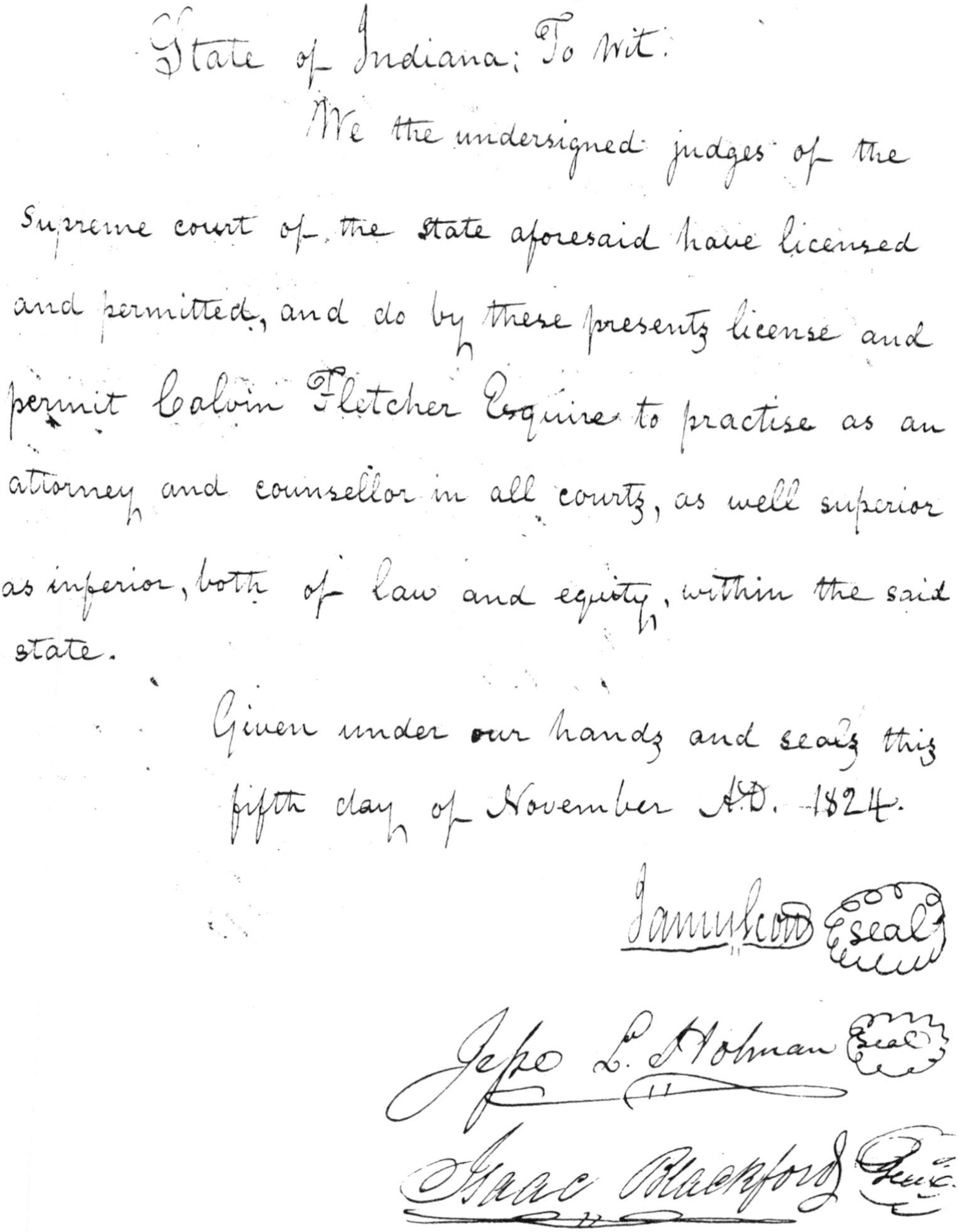
State of Indiana: To wit:

We the undersigned judges of the Supreme court of the state aforesaid have licensed and permitted, and do by these presents license and permit Calvin Fletcher Esquire to practise as an attorney and counsellor in all courts, as well superior as inferior, both of law and equity, within the said state.

Given under our hands and seals this fifth day of November A.D. 1824.

James Scott (Seal)

Jesse L. Holman (Seal)

Isaac Blackford (Seal)

FLETCHER PAPERS

Calvin Fletcher's license to practice in all the courts, superior and inferior, in Indiana, signed by the three judges of the Supreme Court, November 5, 1824

the most adventerous & daring unless accident placed them within the regions thro' which he passed. He in his travels was the sport of the most capricious & superstitious barbarians whose ignorance made them Jealous to the extreme. Among themselves there was no confidence. Assassinations and plundering was some part of their religion and intreague their study yet there were some exceptions and by the good treatment Park received from some of the africans I am more confirmed in the belief that there is something originally good in menkind. Park was absent about 18 months. The source of the Niger appeared to be that which the ancients discribe but disputed by modern writers. Majr. Horton set out on the same expedition a very few years previous to Parks engagment but he was murdered by the Moors before he had proceeded half the distance Park went before he reached the Joliba or Niger. Park deels the least in trifles of any traveler I ever have been acquainted with. He does not seem to make the superstition and belief of the Poor African that Bugbear that most of writers would have done. He does not seem to lament that there are no changes to be wrought in there condition & religion But thot their conveniences are not so despicable and more than most of writers upon the natural faculties & genius he does not consider them inferior to the Uropeans. In all I was highly Edefied Delighted & pleased with his whole naritive which is destitute of arragance Pedantry & self esteem. I perceive it is intimated that the Romans & Greecians had a knowledge of the Niger & the mysterious city of Tombucto. The Niger runs East the Senegal S.W. & the Gambia about a S. course.

Decr. The 25th 1821. Christmas Eve. Reading Robinsons History of America.[5] Cold. Poor house. Wife studying Joseph Olds Geography. I have done but very little this day. I got up about sunrise. I visited several of my neighbors who all appeared friendly. About 10 o'clock I went to the river & found at McGeorges a larg collection of men Principly the candidate[s] for the New county which is said to be just laid off.[6] McG. had the only barrel of cider

5. Probably *The History of America*, by William Robertson (1721–1793), Scottish historian, first published in 1777.

6. The act organizing Marion County (see note 1, above) was not approved until December 31, but there apparently was little doubt of its enactment. Officers to be chosen for the new county included two associate judges, a clerk, re-

in Town which I suppose to have cost about seven Dollars. In the liberality of the candidates the barrel was unheaded and all permiscussously drank & it being froze The dog Irons were put read hot into the barrel. After having drank hearty of the cider they took brandy which soon produced intoxication. A friend of mine having in some way made a mistake as to its inebriating qualities took too much, I therefore left the company and came home with him. I found a great degree of accommadation and courtesy used among all classes. The candidate[s] led the concourse from one place to another till sundown. I will here mention the names of some of the candidates for the offices of our new county—For associates Judges, James McIlvain Mr. Patterson—Clerks of the court, Mr. Ray M. Morris Milo Davis Mr. Hawkins &c.—For commissioners Mr. Stagden Osbern Morrow.[7]

I am now reading by a good fire in a cold cabin.

Decr. 31st 1821. A very agreeable day—no snow, thaughed a little. Reading Robinsons History of America A.M. P.M. repaired my chimeny visited Mr. Foot. Carried him some presents. Returned and vis[i]ted Mr. Nowland's where I found Mr. Graigg[8] a gentleman that is about to settle here from Kent[ucky]—a Lawyer by Profession about 34 good size well made full of Kentucky anecdotes. Great memory &c but not much reading. Rich and self-important. Has twenty-seven hundred volumes of Books. With all these quali-

---

corder, and three county commissioners. Political enthusiasm ran high. In fact, nearly half the male population had announced for some office by the time the election was held on April 1. For earlier references to the election and the results see above, Pt. II, Notes 29, 40; Brown, "History of Indianapolis," in *Logan's Indianapolis Directory*, 1868, p. 9.

7. For McIlvain see above, Pt. II, Note 5; Robert Patterson, who served as probate judge of Marion County from 1836 to 1850; James M. Ray (above, Pt. II, Note 58); Milo R. Davis, a painter by trade; John Hawkins, tavernkeeper; Robert Stockton, John T. Osborn (above, Pt. II, Note 30), and Samuel Morrow.

8. Harvey Gregg. He was admitted to the practice of law at the same time as C.F. (see above, Pt. II, note 68) and formed a partnership with Gabriel J. Johnston. He served as prosecuting attorney for the Fifth Judicial Circuit, 1824–25 and from 1832 until his death on April 3, 1833. He and Douglass Maguire, also from Kentucky, began publication of the second Indianapolis newspaper, the *Western Censor and Emigrant's Guide* on March 7, 1823. Gregg retired after a few months and the paper continued under Maguire and John Douglass, the name being changed to *The Indiana Journal* on January 11, 1825. Dunn, *Indianapolis*, II, 71, 554, 556.

fications I feel disposed to think he will cut a great swath & petty men will cower before him & hunt about for dishonorable graves. Nunc mei. I am now here situated on block 70 and lot No. 2 in a little cabin Sixteen feet by seventeen belonging to a Mr. Cap[9] of Cincinnati. I perhaps enjoy myself as well as ever I did in my life. I know not what I am to do next summer for a living and indeed I am totally ignorant of my future situation and have lear[n]ed from the precipitant and unpremeditated movements of my life that it is not best to be too anxious about the future events which may happen—but think it the best thing I can do is to prepare myself to meet any events that occur in this world. Of all fears that of poverty I most dread, yet it has been a companion thus far thro' life. Tomorrow I & Mrs. F. contemplate spending at a party. I am not able to tell the agregate of the happiness we shall enjoy.

Jany. 1st 1822. Rather wet but warm without being very muddy. I called at Friend Nowlands and had a Stein in company of Mr. Graigg Gen. Carr[10] Hall [?] Dunlop[11] Russel & Scudder.[12] I then

9. Jacob G. Capp. Three lots which he owned in Indianapolis were listed for sale for delinquent taxes in November 1823, including Lot 2, Square 70, on which he owed seventy-five cents. Indianapolis *Gazette*, October 14, 1823.

10. John Carr (1793–1841), of Clark County, Indiana. He joined the Tippecanoe expedition and served with the United States rangers on the frontier during the War of 1812. He held the rank of major general in the Indiana militia. Appointed the agent for the sale of lots in Indianapolis by the General Assembly, he conducted the first sale in October, 1821. He resigned as agent August 23, 1822. He later served four terms as representative in Congress, being elected in 1831, 1833, 1835, and 1839. Lewis C. Baird, *Baird's History of Clark County Indiana* (Indianapolis: B. F. Bowen & Co., 1909), pp. 97–98; Brown, "History of Indianapolis," in *Logan's Indianapolis Directory*, 1868, p. 4; *Indiana Executive Proceedings*, pp. 162, 234n–35n; *Indiana Election Returns*, pp. 85, 86, 91, 98.

11. Dr. Livingston Dunlap, who came from Cherry Valley, New York, to Indianapolis in July, 1821. He was the only surgeon in the town until 1830. He continued his medical studies while practicing and received his degree in medicine from Transylvania Medical College in 1830. He was secretary of the Central Medical Society organized at Indianapolis in 1823 and was elected secretary of the State Medical Society the same year. He became a professor in the Central Medical College of Asbury (De Pauw) University in 1849 and died in 1862. Dunn, *Indianapolis*, I, 542, 545, 546.

12. Caleb Scudder, Indianapolis' first cabinetmaker. Born in Trenton, New Jersey, he moved first to Ohio, then to Indiana, arriving in Indianapolis in February, 1820. He lived and worked in a log structure on the south side of Washington Street between Illinois Street and Capitol Avenue. The Indianapolis Sabbath School Union was organized in his shop. He served as a justice of the peace,

went to Mr. Bradley's where we had some apple tody. I returned home and spent the fore part of the day rather sluggishly. About 3 o' of the clock Mr. Stogden [Stockton] called with a carriage and carred Mrs. F. & myself to Mr. Wiants on the River where we met about 20 couple. We enjoyed ourselves very much and we returned home about 12 and not fatiged.

January the 2d 1822. Wm. Vance called on me who had been at the Salt works and was on his way home. He took tea with us and started on the 3rd for Urbana.

[*Jan.*]*3d.* I kept close. Wrote a letter to Mr. G. Visited the River where I find the people much agitated about the approaching Election. There is much canvassing the character of candidates and their Elegibility. There is hardly a man in town but that offers for some office either civic or military. I am now reading the History of America by Robinson. Cold.

C.F., Indianapolis, to his brother Michael, Staatsburgh, New York, February 23, 1823

. . . In my courtship and marriage there were some things rather novel. I was always determined to be the first courtier of my intended wife—to have the first requittals of her esteem and that she should not be one who was hackneyed in the ways of coquettry. The same year I came to Ohio I boarded in the house of my wive's father then a widower. She was then fourteen and rather small of her age but now of the middle size—remarkably bashful and possessed some other qualities of mind which it would be flattering in me to mention. She was very fraid of me for I was a tyrant in the capacity of a school-teacher. When fifteen (before which time I had left the house) I began to pay those little attentions common in our Juvenile days which I continued till I married. So you will perceive I had every opportunity to become acquainted with her.

. . . Now my country &c. We have had no snow to cover the ground this winter but have had some very cold wether. But the full

---

captain of the volunteer fire company, and was the city's third mayor, serving from 1851 to 1854. Dunn, *Indianapolis*, II, 1014–15; Sulgrove, *History of Indianapolis*, p. 486; *Indiana Executive Proceedings*, pp. 298, 339, 514, 516, 519.

rage of the Northern blast attendant on winter are over, people are now making sugar from the sugar tree (what we used to call the rock maple) which they manufactur in great abundance. From one hundred trees it is very common to make five hundred cwt. tho the tree is not near as large here as in Vt. They here have the sugar *water* (what we called sap) on slides—have the kettles set in a furnace. Sugar can be got for 6 & one fourth cents (6/4 cts, fourpence happenny is the least change that I ever saw here. It is too far from the mint to transport cent pieces).

Our land is very productive—around this vicinity, tho not common to the western country, the land is rather sandy after diging 2 feet—very productive. 75 bushels of corn is but an ordinary crop to the acre. Last year corn could be got for 20 cts. per bushel. The corn this year was literally destroyed, unless in the prairies by grey and black squirrel.[13] Sir, there was by one man killed round one corn field 248 in 3 days in about 4 miles of this place. Many people lost whole cornfields—12 were supposed to destroy as much corn as one hog. They only eat the heart or pit of the kernel. The squirrel appeared to be emigrating towards the S.W. instead of the E. as he has always done heretofore. The reason of his emigration this year was this—our woods or wilderness it scarce ever fails to produce a sufficient quantity of mast to support such vermin but this year they entirely fail'd—the word mast is used by the people here for the fruit and nuts that grow on forrest trees. I never saw the word used but once in composition that was in Homer's Oddessey (Mast). There are thousand of deer here. Last June a hunter would kill 4 or five in one night. The flies here in that month are insuportable by cattle. People build fires for them to stay by and musketoes & gnats in the night are equally bad—which drives the deer into the river in the night to eat moss and protect themselves from insects. The hunter goes in a canoe with a torch. He can approach very near them as the reflection of the light on the water blinds them. Hogs and hens grow almost spontaneous here. Our markets are, as I believe I told you before Cincinnati and New Orleans. There were some boats started from here last fall with hogs &

13. Both Brown and Sulgrove refer to this invasion by squirrels in 1822. Brown, "History of Indianapolis," in *Logan's Indianapolis Directory*, 1868, p. 11; Sulgrove, *History of Indianapolis*, p. 49.

cattle in flat bottomed boats and there are other boats about to start load with lumber—mostly cherry plank. These N. Orleans trips make many a poor widow here and leave many a mother to lament the loss of her son whose homes know them no more. . . .

The people here are vastly different from N.Y. or N.E. Most of them are emigrants—all have traveled more or less. They have not such or so much of that small knowledge which is instilled into the people with you. They are bold & independant in their sentiments as to public men or measures. The most ignorant man here knows who governs him & who administers justice. In N.E. the goverment are becoming arresticratical & the common people put all credence in great men. The language here among the common people has many provincial expressions and would be diverting to a New Englander.

. . . I often get vexed in my professional concerns and almost swear I will become one [a farmer] myself or at least I imagin I should be happy if I were digging my mother earth. I have not only my own concerns but that of a number of other persons. A lawyer here must become a good advocate or speaker in public. In your cou[n]try any man can be a good lawyer without saying a word. I was difident to the extreme when I first began to speak. I have got over this much and am said to be abundant in Irony & sarcasm when I aim therefore.[14] A Gent from Cherry valley N.Y.[15] tells me he has heard more able addresses here than ever he heard by their greatest attorneys in his country. In N.E. & N.Y. it is almost a crime to be a young *man* & of course they are diffident. The Western and Southern states will ever produce the greatest orator. I have a partner in my law business by the name of Breckenridge[16] whose father has been a former chaplin to congress. He is from W. City—a man

14. Simon Yandes in his "Recollections of Calvin Fletcher as a Lawyer," said that C.F. "viewed his cases dramatically. He realized them in actual life. Then the points and authority were examined, and the questions arising were settled, after cautious and labored deliberations. On the trial he was not what is called oratorical, but had a fine clear voice and was a shrewd and effective speaker. His most prominent talent was an insight into the motives of parties and witnesses; and he was especially strong in cross examining witnesses." MS in Fletcher Family Papers, Indiana Historical Society Library.

15. Probably Dr. Livingston Dunlap.

16. John A. Breckenridge. See above, Pt. II, Note 70.

of talants—educated at Princeton College. We do the best business that is done here.

. . . We have a paper printed here[17] the editorial department of which I have had the conducting since It was established tho' not in my name. I shall send you one in which the funeral notice of the printers father is given it being the last paper printed.[18] This notice I wrote. You will likewise observe an advertisement for the Indiana Justice or Farmers Scrivener for sale at this office with a recomendation by W. W. Wick our Judge of the Circuit Court. This book I with the aid of the Clerk of our Court,[19] wrote, yet it is not known here who the author is. Some of my enemies admired it not knowing the writer.[20]

You say your eldest son[21] is 6 years old—an age at which you ought to consider as essential to his education. I most fervantly hope my brothers and sisters will not neglect the Education of their

17. The Indianapolis *Gazette.*

18. The issue of February 22, 1823, contains the obituary of William Smith, father of George Smith, co-publisher of the *Gazette.*

19. James M. Ray.

20. The first issue of the Indianapolis *Gazette*, January 28, 1822, carried a notice by the publishers Smith & Bolton of a proposed publication to be entitled "The Indiana Justice, and Farmer's Scrivener: Containing, The Office and Duty of Justices of the Peace, Sheriffs, Clerks, Coroners, Constables, Township Officers, Jurymen and Jailors. Also, The most correct forms of *deeds, mortgages, leases, releases, discharges, powers of attorney, bonds, obligations, notes of hand, bills of exchanges,* &c &c and, indeed, the greater part of the written contracts which a Farmer, Mechanic or Trader will have occasion for in the management of their respective concerns," by "A Gentleman of the Bar." The book would comprise between 250 and 300 pages and "bound in boards" would sell for $1.50 or "stitched," for $1.12½. Any person procuring orders for twelve copies would be entitled to one copy free.

This advertisement ran through June 8. Then on October 26, the book was advertised as in press and to be published shortly. This notice continued until on January 4, 1823, the book was advertised as "Just Published . . . and for sale." Judge Wick's unqualified recommendation appeared for the first time with the advertisement in the *Gazette* of February 1.

Copies of *The Indiana Justice, and Farmer's Scrivener* are in the Indiana Historical Society Library, the Indiana State Library, and the Burton Historical Collection, Detroit Public Library. The imprint date is 1822.

21. Doubtless C.F. means youngest instead of eldest. Michael's eldest son, William, was born in 1809. The youngest was Timothy Richardson who would later come to Indianapolis. *Fletcher Genealogy*, compiled by Edward H. Fletcher, p. 83.

THE

INDIANA JUSTICE,

AND

FARMER'S SCRIVENER:

CONTAINING,

THE OFFICE AND DUTY OF JUSTICES OF THE PEACE, SHERIFFS, CLERKS, CORONERS, CONSTABLES, TOWNSHIP OFFICERS, JURYMEN AND JAILORS.

ALSO,

THE MOST CORRECT FORMS OF DEEDS, MORTGAGES, LEASES, RELEASES, DISCHARGES, POWERS OF ATTORNEY, BONDS, OBLIGATIONS, NOTES OF HAND, BILLS OF EXCHANGE, &C. &C.

TO WHICH IS ADDED,

THE CONSTITUTION

OF THE

State of Indiana.

BY A GENTLEMAN OF THE BAR.

INDIANAPOLIS:

PRINTED AND PUBLISHED BY SMITH AND BOLTON.

1822.

INDIANA HISTORICAL SOCIETY

Title page of *The Indiana Justice and Farmer's Scrivener,* compiled by Calvin Fletcher

children. . . . Sir I feel anxious that the family of Fletchers from which we sprang tho' now obscure should one day or other be able to trace a respectable lineage. In bestowing an education on our childrin, let us not break down the noblest traits nor subdue that natural boldness which every one possesses. It always was a victory in our father ever to enslave the mind & hamper the spirit of his childrin. Damned be that policy. Let it fo[re]ver be bloted out of my tablett & forsaken as a guide. . . .

DIARY

April the 20th 1823. I have deferred and omitted to continue my Journal for the space of sixteen months, much to my own regret and displeasure. Time in this interval has passed unnoticed and without record! yet were there a history of every transaction, I could not, with pleasure revert to the record thereof. These sixteen months have rolled away without much of importance transpireing —In my profession, be it said with shame, I have made no great progress. My opportunity for practical information therein has been poor. At the first court held for Marion County I was appointed prosecuting attorney for that and the succeeding term.[22] In February

22. See above, Pt. II, note 68. Indictments were brought at the first term, September, 1822, against John Wyant, Samuel McGeorge, Peter Haas, Moses Cox, Jeremiah Johnson, Jacob Landis, Robert Siddell, Jeremiah Collins, Henry Ogden, and Jacob B. Reid for selling liquor without a license. Prior to the organization of Marion County it would have required a trip to Connersville to obtain such a license, and apparently many tavernkeepers had neglected to comply with the law in this respect. Most of them showed proof they had obtained licenses after the organization of the county and were not prosecuted. Other indictments were against William Foster, John McCormick, Andrew Wilson, and Daniel Yandes for obstructing White River, and against Daniel Stevens, Daniel Lakin, Samuel Roberts, Abram Richardson, and James Croley for assault and battery. The state won the case against Stevens and he was fined $2.00. In another case, State vs Thomas Bradley for "gaming at a tavern with cards," the defendant pleaded guilty and was fined $10.00. O. H. Smith and James Rariden (see notes 23 and 24 below) were the attorneys for the defendants in practically all of the above cases. Fletcher was also the attorney in at least one private case during this term. Order Book of Marion County Circuit Court, Book 1, 1822-1828, pp. 1–26.

At the November 1822 session of the Marion County Commissioners C.F. was allowed $30.00 for his services as prosecuting attorney for the Marion County Circuit Court; at the May, 1823, session he was allowed $50.00; at the November,

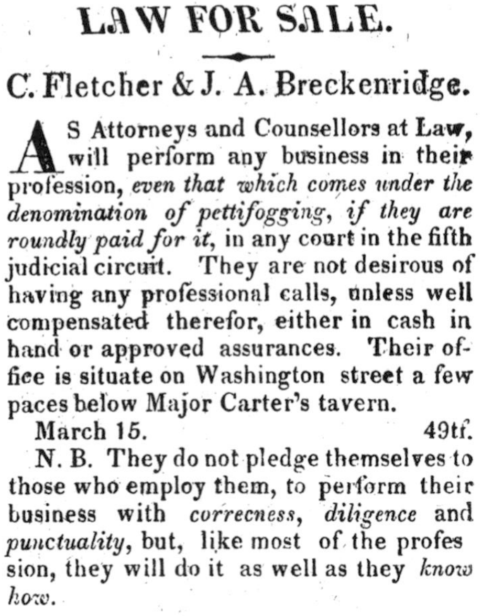

LAW FOR SALE.

C. Fletcher & J. A. Breckenridge.

AS Attorneys and Counsellors at Law, will perform any business in their profession, *even that which comes under the denomination of pettifogging, if they are roundly paid for it*, in any court in the fifth judicial circuit. They are not desirous of having any professional calls, unless well compensated therefor, either in cash in hand or approved assurances. Their office is situate on Washington street a few paces below Major Carter's tavern.

March 15. 49tf.

N. B. They do not pledge themselves to those who employ them, to perform their business with *correcness*, *diligence* and *punctuality*, but, like most of the profession, they will do it as well as they *know how*.

Advertisement of the law partnership of Fletcher & Breckenridge, which ran in the Indianapolis *Gazette*, from March 22 to May 17, 1822

the [. . .] I entered into partnership with Mr. J. A. Brackenridge. We never formed no paticular article of partnership—Tho' we have made some agreement so to do. We live in very good terms. He talks of going to West Florida. We have much business on hand of a small kind. My profession I am tolerable well pleased with. I have made a tolerable support thus far—am not much in debted—but am poor. I feel the stings of poverty as sharp as ever. On the fifteenth of April I had a son born by name of [James Cooley], Between the hours of eight and nine on Teusday. Had present Mrs. Nowland, Bradly, Mitchell, Paxton, and Collop—and Dr. S. G. Mitchell—Betsy Huggins Nurse. I have sowed part of my Garding. There has been a great portion of rain this spring. Trees are just putting forth. This is sunday. A number of persons have called—women. I have been rather drowsey—not read any thing but am about to take up Paleys Philosophy.

1823, session he was allowed $45.00; and at the May, 1824, session he was allowed $20.00 and his successor, Harvey Gregg, was allowed $30.00. Marion County Commissioners Record, Book 1, April 1822–March 1827, pp. 58, 88, 107, 128.

May 5. Court commenced. Lawyers Rarridon[23] Smith[24] Switzer[25] Test[26] Noble[27] (foreign) Foote, Curry, Wick, Gregg, Morris & Cox.[28] I commenced court under much depression of spirits. The week previous I had been sick with sever fits of fever and ague. I douted the friendship of —— and found the foreign Lawyers looked with suspeicion on every lawyer her[e] and more particularly at me. Much to my mortification Brackenridge appeared rather obstinate and many of my indictments were quashed with much triumph by Rarridon and Smith [who] were happy in rasing their own fame upon my ruin. I passed the whole week (to the 10) with much depression and fatigue—prepaired about 30 indictments for the grand jury.[29] I was indict[ed] and plead guilty to assault and battery

23. James Rariden of Centerville. The Indianapolis *Gazette* during March and April, 1825, carried a notice of the formation of a law partnership between C.F. and Rariden for practice in Marion County Circuit Court. This was apparently a short-lived association. Rariden was elected to the General Assembly as senator in 1823 and 1826 and as representative in 1829 and 1832. He was elected to two terms in Congress, serving from 1837 to 1841. *Indiana Election Returns*, Index; *Biographical Directory of the American Congress*, p. 1719.

24. The "prince of the circuit riders" and the author of *Early Indiana Trials and Sketches*, Oliver H. Smith (1794–1859) of Connersville was a leading lawyer, who also served as a representative from Fayette County (1822–23), as prosecuting attorney for the Second Judicial Circuit (1824–26), as Jacksonian representative in Congress (1827–29), and as Whig United States senator (1837–43). *Biographical Directory of the American Congress*, p. 1832.

25. Philip Sweetser of Columbus, elected as state representative from Bartholomew County in 1825, 1826, and 1828, and from Marion County in 1839 and 1840. He served as prosecuting attorney of the Fifth Judicial Circuit, 1830–31. *Indiana Election Returns*, Index, and *Indiana Executive Proceedings*, pp. 305, 306.

26. John Test of Brookville, eminent lawyer, member of the General Assembly of Indiana Territory, clerk of Franklin County, president judge of the Third Judicial Circuit, and member of Congress for three terms, serving from 1823 to 1827 and from 1829 to 1831. *Biographical Directory of the American Congress*, p. 1906.

27. James Noble, likewise of Brookville, one of Indiana's first two United States senators, serving from 1816 until his death in 1831. *Ibid.*, p. 1619.

28. Moses Cox who moved from Marion County to Madison County and became that county's first clerk and recorder, 1823–26. *Indiana Executive Proceedings*, pp. 261, 509.

29. Seven of the indictments at the May, 1823, term were for gaming, two for assault and battery, and one, against Robert Massey, for issuing a challenge to fight a duel. In the last case, the state won and Massey was fined one cent and sentenced to sixty days in jail. Order Book of the Marion County Circuit Court, Book 1, 1822–1828, pp. 27–58.

—fined 2$.[30] My allowance for state services was $50. and ten convictions. Since court I have lamented much my deficiency in practice as a lawyer and am therefore determined to loose no opportunity in gaining information as to the practice. I have learnt much to my chagrin that the lawyers who triumphed at my unsuccessful attempts have indeavered to spread such impressions as are calculated [to] injure my reputation and standing as a lawyer. My brief success here has likewise ca[u]sed me many internal or domestic enemies. I mean to remedy these obstacles by an unyielding perserverance. I mean to dispense with every species of business unless well paid for (of law). Breckenridge has left for Florida. I purchased some law books of him (to wit) Sanders Reports, Roberts on Frauds and Woods Conveyancing &c.[31]

C.F., Indianapolis, to his father and mother, Ludlow, Vermont, May 11, 1823

. . . Trees are now in blossom. Have some corn six inches high. Cattle live here thro' the winter without hay. We have preaching this day both from a Presbyterian and a Methodist priest. We have a Sunday School. Building a meeting house[32] and State house[33] the latter of which cost $14000.

30. See above, Pt. II, note 22. According to the court record C.F. "did make an assault" on Foote "in the peace of God and our said state of Indiana . . . and him the said Foote in a rude insolent angry and unlawful manner did touch strike beat and wound . . . to the great damage of the said Foote, contrary to the form of the statute in such case made and provided, and against the peace and dignity of the State of Indiana." The fine was $2.00. Marion County Circuit Court Complete Record, A, May term, 1823, p. 16.

31. Probably one of the many editions, including several American, of the *Reports* of the English judge Sir Edmund Saunders (d. 1683), first published in 1686, which was of particular value to pleaders; William Roberts (1767–1849), *Treatise on the Statute of Fraud* (London, 1805); and Edward Wood, *A Compleat Body of Conveyancing in Theory and Practice.*

32. The Presbyterian meetinghouse, on Pennsylvania Street half way between Market and Ohio streets. The lumber for it was obtained by subscription and it was built by volunteer labor. Indianapolis *Gazette,* March 29 and June 14, 1823; Dunn, *Indianapolis,* I, 86, 575.

33. C.F. means the Marion County Courthouse which served as the state capitol until December, 1835, when the first State House was completed. The plans for the courthouse drawn by James Paxton and John E. Baker had been accepted by the county commissioners on August 15, 1822, and Paxton and Baker won the contract to erect the two-story 60 by 40-foot building topped by a 49-foot

Clay will receive a pretty general support here for next President. Adams is here called a *Federalist.* Prejudice is strong here against the Eastern States. From what I can learn there is no man of weight, character, talant or notoriety from Vermont in Congress.

DIARY

June 1st 1823. I fear much that some business I undertook for Wm. Oliver[34] will cause me trouble—Tho' time will bring all things to pass.

Sunday June 1 1823. I have this day been looking thro' Thompsons late war.[35] In tracing the cause of the origin of our late contest with G[reat] B[ritain] I can't but be fired with indignation. It strikes up a spark of love of country which I never felt before. It causes sincere regret that I was not at an age and had an opportunity to assist in avenging the insults that was offered to our dear bo't liberty. I have commenced reading Blacks com [Blackstone's *Commentaries*]. I am determined on reading elementary law.

June 2. Raised the meeting house which was commenced on Saturday the 31st of May. Cloudy—had much rain—rather cold. Our gardins are much infested with worms except where there are hens. People have not half done planting and from the multitude of those insects which eat the stock off at the surface and the coldness of the weather there is but a poor prospect for crops of corn in this New purchase. Been cloudy thro' the day. I have set out some cabbage plants—read some in Blackstone. Brown[?] re-

---

6-inch cupola, dome, belfry, spire, and vane. It was completed by January, 1825. Dunn, *Indianapolis,* I, 61–62, 105.

34. An uncle of Mrs. Fletcher's. He was a veteran of the War of 1812 and played an important role in the lifting of the siege of Fort Wayne. He served as receiver of public money in the land office at Piqua, Ohio, and became secretary of the renowned Cincinnati Insurance Company upon its organization in 1829. B. J. Griswold, *The Pictorial History of Fort Wayne . . .* (2 volumes. Chicago: Robert O. Law, 1917), I, 206–208; Henry A. Ford and Mrs. Kate B. Ford (comps.), *History of Cincinnati Ohio . . .* ([Cincinnati:] L. A. Williams, 1881), p. 362; and information from Cincinnati city directories supplied by the Cincinnati Historical Society.

35. John Lewis Thompson, *Historical Sketches of the Late War . . .* (2d. ed. Philadelphia, 1816).

INDIANA STATE LIBRARY

First Marion County Courthouse, completed in 1825. From a drawing by Christian Schrader

turned from Vincennes, got 3 dollars. This day learned that Dr. Dunlop is about to be married.[36]

Friday June the 13th 1823. From Saturday last I have been unwell and unable to set up more than ¼ of the time. I could here recite my difficulties—dis[r]epute &c I have brought myself into by my connection with B[rackenridge]. I want 2 things to retrive my character health and perseverance. I here will withhold my description [of] my troubles. I am now comfortable compaired with my feelings days past. I have been reading Thompsons late war.

Nove. 30th 1823 (Sunday Eve.). I have just been perusing some few things noted in this manuscript. As they grow more remote from the time they were penned, they grow more agreeable. I always have had an avertion to look back upon my most recent transactions—arising I suppose, yea, I well know it from a disatisfaction of the manner in which I perform—I am half a misanthrope thro' fear. I commenced a partnership with B. F. Morris on the 12th of this month. We keep our office near the court-house square. I have made an estimate of the property we have both put into the partnership stock consisting principly of Law books. Our success is one of those matters in *embryo* whose birth I do not anticipate with only moderate pleasure.[37] I am very much pleased with Mr. Morris. I think him a man possessing a goodly quantity of human perfection. I have this day (Sunday eve) been to a Baptist meeting at Thos. Carters for the first time I have been to a meeting for 3 months. I feel some little remorse for this neglect. I find by attending meetings I familiarize myself with the countenances of people—it wears of[f] that affrighted misanthrophy which I feel more or less. I am now reading elementory law-books and attending to some practical branches of my profession. I certainly feel a thirst for improvement. I sincerely pray to him who presides over my destiny to give and grant me wisdom and knowledge that I may yet be useful to my fellow creatures and be able to answer the full designs of my maker which consists in approaching as near as posible to human perfection.

December 1st 1823. This day pleasant—streets getting tolerable

36. Dr. Dunlap married Georgiana McDougal on July 11. Indianapolis *Gazette*, July 15, 1823.

37. The partnership lasted until March, 1825. See above, Pt. II. note 75.

dry. Some Indians in with venison and bear's meat—Ven[i]son hams at twelve and one half cents a piece. Capt. John a Wyandot chief is among the number. I this morning read the life of Dr. Hutton in the Portfolio.[38] Been perusing the Statutes and read some in Blck [Blackstone] (2d vol.) com. [*Commentaries*] which I am now reading thro'. This day I got my plaid cloak which I have had made that cost me $10. Indianapolis has been tolerable lively this fall—much more business done than I expected. They are now about commencing putting the roff [roof] on to the court house which has now the appearance of a very elegant building.

Decr. 2d. Warm and pleasant. In the eve attended a debating club at Hawkin's. The subject argued—Who is the best calculated to be our next president Clay Jackson Crofford Calhoun J. Q. Adams and some few hold up Dewitt Clinton. Every candidate was thoroughly abused. The principle advocates were as follows Judge Wick for Crofford (irony) Dan Wick for Clay—A Mr. Johnson lately from Kent[ucky] for Gen. Jackson Mr. D. McGuire[39] for Clinton and Mr. Wilson for Adams. This is (the presidential election) a subject which is now the topic of the legislative bodies in each state the hobby of every newspaper and the chit chat of the counting room of the merchant the bar room of the inn the fire side of the farmer and the work-shop of the mechanic. We have formed a debating or polemic society in this place for the purpose of discussing politics and philosophic questions. The members are respectable and well informed.

Decr. 3d. This day intended to make some settlements for Mrs. Nowland with associate Judges. I have been reading Blackstone &c. Nothing particular has occurred.

Decr. 4th 1823. This day cool & clear. Read some pages in the 1st vol. of Reves History of Eng. laws[40] which contains the magna

38. Charles Hutton (1737–1823), English mathematician. A sketch of his life was given in the *Port Folio* (Philadelphia), October, 1823.

39. Douglass Maguire. Born in Fayette County, Kentucky, in 1799, he came to Indianapolis in 1823 and with Harvey Gregg, as noted earlier (above, note 8) began publication of Indianapolis' second newspaper, *Western Censor and Emigrant's Guide*, which under the partnership of Maguire and John Douglass became in 1825 *The Indiana Journal.* Maguire was a strong Whig and advocate of Henry Clay. Nowland, *Early Reminiscences of Indianapolis*, pp. 141–42.

40. John Reeves, *A History of the English Law . . .* (London, 1783–84).

charta. Mr. Blake is about to open a house of public entertainment in Co. with Saml. Henderson.[41] I do not provecy [prophesy] any very great advantage will result from the connection.

Decr. 8th. Cool. Judge Holidy[42] breakfasted with me when on his way to Corydon.

Decr. 9th. The mail arrived last night without bringing my horse which I had lent to Mr. Ray to go to Laurencburgh. This morn Snow 2 inches deep.

Decr. 13th (Saturday). Been variously engaged—making a partial settlement of Mr. Nowlands estate which has been rather imbarrassing to me as there has been some little illiberality manifested, arising from the very lowest suspicions, in the settlement of this estate tho' if our settle[me]nt answers my expectations this day I shall have triumphed ultimately. I am very busy—The prospect of law business. This eve have joined in a debating school which has been in operation for 2 eves. The question first debated was, whether it was better for the legislature to appoint electors to vote for President and vice president or that the state should be districted or we vote by general ticket. I was for a general ticket which we carried. In the debate of this question I certainly received much information. Mr. Johnson late from Kent[ucky] Mr. Greggs Partner appears to be a pretty promenant character among the members. As a lawyer I think him but poorly qualified. He's a man of very indolent habits who consults his ease on all occasions—I think not a man viciously ambitious—likes to dabble in politics will be considered a good natured fellow but a man of no force in business. At our debate last eve Dr. Mitchel President we had this question for discussion "Is the representative always bound to obey the known will of his constituents contrary to his own judgment?" I was on the negative with Hawkins, Blake and D. McGuire. Hawkins I think possesses one of the most aimiable dispositions—free from envy—friendly in his disposition and reasonable and rather interesting in debate. McGuire (Douglass) by application has a reasonable understanding of his subject—but subject to passions and insults. There is one invariable rule I would hereafter be glad to pursue—That is

41. See above, Pt. II, note 36.
42. Samuel Holliday, associate judge of Madison County.

where I speak in the opening of any subject at the bar or elsewhere, to be really candid for candour will certainly triumph—and in the answers to any thing advanced to use no personalities and pay mo[r]e att[ent]ion to the real merits of my case than to answer my opponant and if answered at all do that after advancing my arguments on the merits—and in all discussion to aim my arguments to certain points on which I calculate to rely. I have lately been made acquainted with a Mr. Ball a young man from Detroit who talks of settling in this place as a lawyer. I am certainly highly pleased with his appearance. I prophecy most favorable of his success and if I am not disappointed he is intrinsically worthy.

Decr. (Sunday) 14. This day very cold about 2 inches of snow on the ground. A number of Indians came in this eve with a great nu[m]ber of venison hams. I have spent the greater part of the day at the office. Wrote a part of a letter [to] N. P. Fletcher. Cold in the extreme.

Decr. 24. We this day have had a party of a ball at Henderson & Blakes. Mr. Foote, myself, Mr. Ralston Mr. Culberson and D. McGuire were managers. The day was clear and cold. Our party was attended by about 30 couple. Supper splendid and every thing supposingly agreeable.[43]

Decr. 25th. I visited Mr. Henderson's and Blake's in the A.M. Drank rather *too* much whiskey & Brandy & eat too much Sweet cake & came home and went to bed. The day extremely cold.

Decr. 26–7–8–9–30 & 31st. Wet—warm— & foggy atmosphere. On the 31st in the eve I visited or attended a theatrical performance had at Thos. Carters by Mr. & Mrs. Smith *perporting* to be directly from N.Y. Theater. Both not less than 50 years of age! representing *jaealous lovers!* Lord what a snow-storm in May & June! 25 cents addmintance.[44] No music at first—fiddle strings broke. Russel & Bolton were requested by our host Thos. Carter to play nothing, as he called them, but Note tunes or psalms or new tunes. I apologized

43. Maguire recalled that C.F. "was the best manager in a ballroom that he ever saw." Dunn, *Indianapolis*, I, 92.

44. The performance was advertised in the Indianapolis *Gazette*, December 30, 1823. It included "The Doctor's Courtship or Indulgent Father" and "Jealous Lovers" together with "several other entertainments." Tickets were announced at 37½ cents.

to myself for going to such a place in this way. I do not [spend] but a precious little cash unnecessarily or for any thing save what is absolutely necessary for my family's subsistance & clothing. Posibly I may improve myself thereby which is the main thing!

January First—1824. Rained all night—very foggy morning. Jim Walker out shooting all night. Got up in tolerable season. Had some serious reflection on the past year. Tho I know not what it augurs but I must say I commence this year with less fears scruples dejection and an innumerable train of imaginary evils that have heretofore troubled me, than I ever did before since my recollection. I have this day commenced a book of expenditures for the New-Year. My debts that I owe amount to about $78. and good debts which are owing me I think far exceeds that amount. Our Streets are very muddy—weather warm atmosphere foggy. I again attended another theatrical performance by the above parties at the same place upon the same principles and with about the sum totum of edification.

Jan. 2d 3d 4th and 5th 6. From the first to the fifth of Jan. wet muddy but warm. On the 2d Mr. B. F. Morris returned from Corydon with flattering reports that the legislature would move here next year which excites the feelings of our citizens to a very high pitch.[45] Some out lots will be probably sold this spring.[46] I have been diligently reading law during the above period partly from a love of the study thereof and partly from a conviction of what Wats lays down in his treatise of logick, wit, that a professional man should acquire distinct ideas of his profession and retain the same by frequent perusals of the theories thereof as well as diligence caution and reflection in his practi[c]e. Last night (the 5) it thundered and lightened, very warm. This morning the 6th snows but not very cold.

45. An act of the General Assembly, approved January 20, 1824, made Indianapolis the seat of government of the state "upon, from and after the second Monday in January" 1825. *Revised Laws of Indiana*, 1823–24, pp. 370–72.

46. By order of the General Assembly the agent of state, Bethuel F. Morris, laid off twenty lots adjoining the town on the north and south of approximately four acres each which were offered for sale to the highest bidder on January 24, 1825. The twenty outlots sold for an average of about $100 each, the highest going for $155 and the lowest $63.00. Indianapolis *Gazette*, October 26, 1824, and following issues, and Brown, "History of Indianapolis," in *Logan's Indianapolis Directory*, 1868, p. 15.

I have lately had some difficulty with Owen Batman.[47] I sent him off but his friends and brother have solicited me to take him again and have him bound to me. I have no need of him to assist in my domestic concerns neither can I make him a farmer, but I take him out of a respect to the child and his destitute situation but thro' the assistance of devine Providence I Hope to be able to cloth and instruct him so he maybe useful to his God his country and himselfe.

C.F., Connersville, to Sarah Hill Fletcher, March 30, 1824

By Mr. Bates I send you a shawl—cost four dollars—has no fringe which is now the fashion. I should not have bought it but they take treasury paper here at par. I arrived here yesterday thro' the snow. I feel uneasy about you as I left but little wood but don't freeze nor want for any thing if it takes all we have in the house to make yourself comfortable. I shall not be at home till Friday week. Take great and prudent care of your childrin. Don't forget to direct persons to Mr. Morris who call to get me to do business. . . .

47. See above, Pt. II, note 80.

Diary of a Tour of Vermont

Diary of my tour from Indianapolis to Ludlow Vermont.[48]

May the 19th [*18*]*24.* I left Indianapolis or rather my own house and while proceeding up Washington St. my neighbor Wyant hailed me & told me I had left my pocket book behind me which he brought to me, and while bringing it desired I should not proceed back to meet him, reminding me that it was ominous of ill luck to turn back after any thing forgotten when a person had started a journey. I then proceeded to Washington Hall where the mail had just arrived & got a letter from brother Elijah. Took some Egg-nog and left the town in company with Mr. Osten Bishop[49] who had started for N.Y. City messers. Ray & Blake for Ft. Wayne to locate the county seat of Allen and to lay off a state road from that place to Indianapolis.[50] Messers. Wilson, McCarty and Stephens accompanied us to Fall Ck. which we had to swim with the aid of a can[o]e. We then proceeded to William Conners.[51] His farm was

48. This diary was not bound as part of the Calvin Fletcher Diary. It is contained in two crude little notebooks, 6 by 3¾ inches, comprised of folded sheets sewed together and covered with marbleized paper. They contain a total of some seventy-six pages. The notebooks were found among the miscellaneous pieces in the Fletcher Papers.

49. Austin Bishop (1764–1833), a native of Connecticut and an Indianapolis merchant who at this time was in partnership with Isaac Stevens mentioned below. In 1827 Bishop was appointed one of the contractors to erect the Governor's Mansion on the Circle. Dunn, *Indianapolis,* I, 102, II, 1055; Indianapolis *Gazette,* September 23, 1823, and following issues.

50. Allen County was formed by an act of the Indiana General Assembly approved December 17, 1823, and James M. Ray was appointed one of the commissioners under the act to locate the seat of justice. *Revised Laws of Indiana,* 1823–24, p. 109. James Blake was named by the General Assembly as one of the commissioners to locate a road from the capital to Fort Wayne. *Laws of Indiana,* 1823–24 (special), p. 21.

51. Brother of John Conner (see above, Pt. II, note 46). Like his brother William Conner (1773–1855) was an Indian trader, scout, guide and interpreter. With Josiah F. Polk he laid out the town of Noblesville in 1823 which became the county seat of Hamilton County. That same year he also built the beautiful brick farm home on the east bank of White River known today as the Conner

beautiful with pleasing decorations of spring aided by industry. Rye had attained its full height. I mailed a letter here to Elijah. Read a description given by M[. . .] of the Nigara Falls.

Thursday morning May 20th. [MS torn] rose, fed our horses and [MS torn] to start. Mr. Wood came [MS torn] from Indianapolis and brot me a pr. of drawers which I had forgotten. We left Conners with the additional company of Mr. Woodworth,[52] Hestor[?] and W. Conner. We went by the way of Noblesvill which is laid off on the N. side of White R. in a very thickly timbered country—not a stick yet missing. We here took a little refreshment and proceeded on to Strawtown. We there called & fed our horses. I purchased a Judgment of Wood & [. . .] on Page and swopt bridles with Wood. We left Strawtown and with some difficulty swum our horses cross White River—passed Beckwith's followed up Pike [Pipe] Ck. entered a very beautiful timbered forrest. P. Ck. is about 20 yards wide. We followed up said ck. thro a beautifully timbered country of large oaks & sugar [maples] elms & a goodly proportion of ash. We campt about sundown on the E. side of sd. Ck. opsitt of a [. . .] prarie which extends up the West side of P. Ck. 8 m. off W[hite] R. N. The country we came thro this day will all admit of a good settlement. We prepared our camp & made some of the best coffee I ever drank. Our camping ground we named Smell Shot camp ground in honor of a very facetious expression of Mr. Conner. Ra[n]ge 6, T. 20, 30 m. from Indianapolis north.

[*May*] *21.* This morng about 2 were amused & rather charmed by the shrill voice of a Whipowill a little distance from our camp. This bird is rather scarce in this country. We rose about sunrise. Cloudy with a little mist of rain. After coffee we started—travelled over rather elivated land 2d rate—bout 10 we crossed thro the [. . .] of Pipe Creek—passed thro a country of good arible land of the 1st and second rate, about a north E. course. Passed in the P.M. 2 sugar camps where the Indians had this spring made sugar. About 4 we began to descend it towards the Missinwa and bout sunset camped in rather wet beechland in T23, R8 as we expected not far S. of the

---

Prairie Farm. Thompson, *Sons of the Wilderness, passim.* William Conner was one of the commissioners appointed to locate the seat of justice of Allen County.

52. Samuel D. Woodworth, Hamilton County surveyor. *Indiana Executive Proceedings,* p. 252.

Mississinewa and out of which to a [. . .] expression of Mr. Blake we chrisened our place of lodging Camp Blob. We this day travelled about 30 m.

May 22d. We this morning rose tolerable early—started a little after sun rise. Travelled 'bout 1 m. and came to the Mississinewa. We followed up the same for ½ m. We there came to an old fording place but the water was so high we could not cross. We stripped our horses and looked for a tree to make a bark canoe & While looking we herd an Indian yelp which was answered by Mr. Conner and we made towards the voice. Found 2 Indians who knew him. They advised us to follow down the Mississinewa to Gilberts[53] instead of crossing the R. We accordingly proceeded about a W. course thro good land, high & elevated banks, very large sugar trees & ash oak. Many fine Creeks put into the River. When we came with[in] ½ m. from G.'s very high banks on the S. side & bluffs both beautiful granite stone in the bottom of the R. with now & then a white cliff of the above kind of stone. G. lives at the first old Miami T. on S.W. side of the Riv. Arrived the[re] 'bout 2 P.M. Found old Mr. J. Foster got some bacon (3 cs. lb.) & some whisky. We were advised to cross the River & proceed down 5 ms. to another town before we left the R. for Ft. Wayne. We accordingly did. At G.'s we learnt that several Indians had lately been killed among themselves in consequence of the whites selling them whisky. We arrived after travelling thro a good country to one of the M[iam]i T[own]s which was burnt the last tho' Campbell[54] the Commander met with some opposition. 6 whites were killed and about the same number of Indians. We found the town rebuilt & saw a number of squaws. Found 2 or 3 white men making fence for the Indians employed by the government. Fence poor. The Indians are much imposed upon by the con-

53. Goldsmith Gilbert, who had a trading post on the Mississinewa near the line between the present Pleasant and Washington townships in Grant County. Sarah J. Line, "The Indians on the Mississinewa," in *Indiana Magazine of History*, IX (1913), 190.

54. Col. John B. Campbell, who under orders from Gen. William Henry Harrison led the attack to destroy the Miami towns on the Mississinewa in December, 1812. Logan Esarey (ed.), *Messages and Letters of William Henry Harrison* (2 volumes. Indianapolis: *Indiana Historical Collections*, VII and IX, 1922), II, 179, 211, 253–62.

tractors. We left this town & proceeded a N.E. course 'bout 5 miles & camped on good ground but poor Range and bad water. An Indian who had been to Ft. Wayne came & staid with us. Slept very comfortable. We left our camp sun 1 hour high, travelled over rather wet ground bout 5 miles to the banks of the Salomo[n]ie R., 'bout the size of White R. opposite Indianapolis. We crossed, built a fire in a rich bottom & took breakfast. We then proceeded thro a very low, muddy country to the Wabash River at an Indian village on the N. side at the mouth of Little or Portage R., 13 miles from Racoon T[own]. We crossed over at a fording place 90 yds. wide. Found a number of Indians playing cards who handled them with great dexterity on a spread blanket under a green oak. One small boy of about 10 or 12 manifested much ingenuity in the game they were playing. There were 3 white men here plowing notwithstanding it was on Sunday. We took a cold collation & prepared our horses for travelling when 5 frenchmen came up the Wabash with a peerogue loaded with furs. One perhaps the owner was dressed tolerable well, the others rather indifferent & much like Indians. At ½ after 2 P.M. we left this Indian Village and travelled 13 m. & very fast to Racoon town where we found perhaps 50 Indians worshiping or performing some ceremonies rather of a festive kind. They were certainly superbly dressed surpassing any thing in splendor that I ever beheld among them. Most of the young Indians were dressed in scarlet with large silver bands 'bout the head. When we came up they were seated on barks in a circular row smoking. We camped 'bout 200 yards from them under the hill by a spring. We soon heard them singing and dancing after the hollow sound of a large drumm. We spansilled our horses and were preparing to visit them when they broke up. A number knew Mr. Conner & appeared to be friendly. This part of the town in which these ceremonies were performed is elevated and commands a view of an extensive prarie of several thousand acres covered with very good grass. A Mr. Miller[55] from Ft. Wayne an old gent. came up and camped with us. He is an

55. Perhaps Alexander Miller, who was licensed to trade with the Indians on the Mississinewa in 1823 and 1824. *John Tipton Papers,* edited by Nellie A. Robertson and Dorothy Riker (3 volumes. *Indiana Historical Collections,* XXIV, XXV, and XXVI. Indianapolis: Indiana Historical Bureau, 1942), I, 384.

old forsaken looking gent. whom I once knew in Ohio—he now lives down the Wabash with the Indians.

Monday morning, May 24. We left our camp ground after eating up all the provisions we had and begging the bread of old Mr. Miller. We then proceeded down the hill into a low rich bottom land and shortly passed a number of Indian huts & followed the old portage road on dry oak ridges without interruption till we came to a Prarie called More de porsh[56] where we had great difficulty in crossing. The ground on which we stood shook for a number of yards 'round. We stript our horses & drove them over. I here lost my Spanish blade. We then proceeded 2 ms. and crossed the St. Maries (alias the Miami of the Lakes). Here were the first waters I ever beheld that passed into the great Lakes. My feelings were a little ex[c]ited at the tho't of the great distance they must roll over the sublime falls of Niagra and thence onward till they pass into the Atlantic at the gulf of the St. Lawrence. We arrived dirty & hungry at Ft. W. after 5 days travel in the wilderness in which time we made not far from 175 distance thro a country mostly that will admit of settlements & flourishing plantations well watered & with rich stone quarries & good timber. Our expenses were small[?] and I am fond of being in the woods. We put up at Mr. Ewings[57] where found a number of Canadian French gents. Ft. W. is situate on the S. side of the St. Maries just above the Junction of that R. with the St. Joseph's which two Rivers form the Maumee. The houses are mostly of hewn logs. The Ft. that was built in 1814 encloses about 2 acres of land. Genl. Tipton[58] the Indian agent & with whom I was before acquainted took us thro' the garrison. The soil here is rather thin & sandy—vegetation not so forward as at Indianapolis by two

56. "Marais de porche" (?), the marshy headwaters of the Wabash and Maumee rivers.

57. Alexander Ewing, whose tavern was called Washington Hall. A veteran of the War of 1812, he settled in Fort Wayne in 1822 and died there in 1827. He was the father of W. G. and G. W. Ewing, noted for their wide-ranging real estate and fur-trading businesses. Griswold, *The Pictorial History of Fort Wayne,* I, 254–55, 265; Wallace A. Brice, *History of Fort Wayne . . .* (Fort Wayne, Ind.: D. W. Jones & Son, 1868), pp. 24–25.

58. John Tipton (1786–1839), Indian fighter, sheriff of Harrison County, Indiana, state legislator, land speculator, and United States senator (1832–39). He was appointed United States Indian agent at Fort Wayne in 1823. *John Tipton Papers,* I, Introduction, pp. 3–33.

weeks. We here engage a Frenchman to carry us down to Ft. Meggs[59] in a canoe. We are to give him $4. Saw a great number of Indians & squaws who were drunk, tolerably well dressed. Rain at 8 & 9 in the eve with the prospect of a very unpleasant day before us. The French gentlemen above mentioned I learn are mostly Indian traders just returned from the woods with their furs.

Tuesday May 25th. I arose discovered there had been a heavy rain during the night. Cool. Our French man whose name is Peter Laughler informed us he was ready to start with us for Ft. Meggs. We eat breakfast and purchased of Mr. Ewing a venison ham and a few biscuit for which he charged the extravagant price of $1.12½. I mention this as a specimen of the extortionate and kitch-penny disposition of the people of Ft. Wayne. Mr. Conner, Ray & Blake accompanied us to the Canoe opposite of the fort. There we waited a long time for our man who got there & made ready to start about 10 'o the clock. Peter & his brother Solomon a lad of 18 or 19 sent their canoe forward with great rapidity keeping time with their paddles with a number of French songs they sung which were very pleasing and delightful altho' I could not understand much of the language. One sung a verse & the other repeated the same after him with much the same air and voice. The River banks on either side were covered with white oak, sycamore, poplar, ash & hickory[?]. Tolerable high banks. River 150 yards wide, deep and tolerably clear from Rocks and for 50 miles not a ck. puts in on either side. We this day descended 75 miles. Stopped about 10 at night 15 miles 'bove Ft. Defiance staid at a little cabin on the N. side of the R. The man of the house treated us very hospitably, furnished us with blankets & permitted us to sleep on the floor without any compensation.

May 26. We started a little before sun up. Very cold. Arrived at Ft. Defiance about 9 in the morn. Landed. Found Thomas Philips from Dayton in a store he had lately established there. He treated us very politely, took us out to show us the old fort built by Gen. Wayne in 93[94]. The Ft. is built in a point formed by the Oglaze [Auglaize] River which puts into the Maumy [Maumee] R. at that place. The old batteries were very commanding in all directions.

59. Fort Meigs, erected in 1813 on order of General Harrison on the south bank of the Maumee River opposite the present Maumee, Ohio, as a depot and supply base for operations against Detroit and Canada during the War of 1812.

There were some large but unpruned apple trees grown up in the Fort. At this place there is a town laid off (the county seat of Williams county).[60] The Oglaze at its junction with the Maumy is about 80 or 100 yds. wide. We left Ft. Defiance & proceeded down the River. I went to sleep & slept till ½ after one, very warm. At 5 P.M. we arrived at Prarie de Mass[?]. We called on Mr. S. Vance whom I formerly knew but he had forgotten me and I did not make myself known. We left that place & arrived at the head of what is the Rapids at dusk. Staid with a French farmer who treated us with the usual politeness common to that people.

May 27th. At sunrise we began to descend the Rapids. The water was so shallow that our waterman & boy had to get out and draw the canoe over several riffles. We passed Rush de lac[?] a little village on the right side of the R., 9 m. from Meggs. We arrived at Meggs ½ after 10. Stopped at Dr. Horatio Conant's formerly a classmate in Middlborough College with brother Elijah. Mr. Conant keeps a very good tavern on the N. side of the R. Meggs is built on both sides. The old Fort on the S. side [has] one tavern and a number of small buildings. On the N. side there are two stores and a number of other convenient houses. We here expected or at least hoped to get a passage to Buffalo or Detroit. We found one small sc[h]ooner here that is to sail on Saturday in which we shall very likely take passage. I visited the battle ground on which Dudley's[61] gallant band were cut off [in] 1813 by their own indiscreete & impetuous movements. I found many human bones among the bushes that are now growing on the place. This caused a most sad reflection. I thanked my stars that the sh[r]ill trump of war had ceased to blow, that gentle peace was now waving her olive branch over the same place that but a few years past was a scene of carnage. At 2 P.M. in company with Messrs. Lee, Gage & Bishop we visited the N. side of the R. to view the old Fort. I left my company to visit Mr. Pattersons family. I found his lady at home whom I once knew while she was a blooming romantic coquettish girl. I now found

60. Defiance became the county seat of Defiance County and Bryan of Williams County which is to the north.

61. Col. William Dudley who exceeded General Harrison's orders and along with his men was ambushed and killed at Fort Meigs when it was besieged by the British under Gen. Henry Proctor.

her the mother of one little girl, living poor and disconsolate. She did not know me at first. I spent some hours with her Mr. P. being absent. My company having recrossed the R. I visited the Fort in company with a small boy who took me round the old breast works and then to the house of a Mr. O'Neel who had collected a number of canon shot of different sizes & one bomb shell. I recrossed 'bout sun down—a very warm evening. Visited an Indian camp after tea. Mr. Bishop & the other gents except Mr. Lee made up a loo party. I conversed with Mr. Lee some time & retired to bed. It thundered & rained some before I went to sleep.

May 28th. Pleasant. Read some in the A.M. After dinner went aboard the Miami Packet which laid in the middle of the river just below the old fort loading with corn for Detroit & in which Mr. Bishop & myself contemplate going to the same place and thence to Buffalo. Eve. While on board of the Packet we fished with a line & hook with nothing upon the latter but a piece of red baize. We caught perhaps a hundred of white perch that weighed about a pound a piece. We throwed them overboard as there was no use for them although they certainly are a most delicious fish when cooked. The River here at this time is literally alive with these and other kinds of fish. The Indians catch many and the inhabitants are completely cloyed with them—air is very scented with the smell of fish. I went from the Packet to the oposite shore & again called on Mrs. P. & at her request went to Periesburgh to see her husband about a mile below the town on the same side of the river. This day 30 cows were drove thro' from Urbana to Detroit. I spent some moments in the eve very pleasantly with Mr. Conant who appears to be a very liberal & agreeable gent. I likewise was introduced to a Mr. Robins a Presbyterian preacher who is teaching a school of Indian childrin ten miles above here. The missionary society of his order have purchased about a section [of] land and have a very fine plantation opened & under good improvement. Mr. Robins & lady, Dr. Clark & lady, teachers, & Mr. Sacket husbandman. All professors belong to this family as it is called who live at the same station or farm. Mr. Robins tells me he has 27 young Indians from the age of 9 to that of 20 under his tuition & for whom the society provides in meat, drink & clothing. He likewise tells me the childrin are apt & make quite as good if not better improvement than white childrin of their age & previous opportunities.[62] I have conversed with a number of old Indians here with respect to having their childrin educated. They appear to be sensible of the importance of the measure altho' at first it is said they were hostile to the mission in their quarter. I intend visiting the station if possible before I leave. I this day saw a human skeleton that had washed out in part from the bank of the river where some person had once been buried.

May 29th. Rose in the morning found a strong easterly wind had raised water several feet high in river & a very poor prospect ahead to get out of the river till it would change.

[May] 30th, Sunday. Pleasant but the wind continued to blow from the East, very warm. I visited in company with Mr. Patterson the old B[ritish] Fort[63] 2 ms. below Meggs on the N. side of R. It was built about 50 years ago and held by the British at the time Wayne defeated the Indians in 93 [94] which was done in presents [presence] of this Fort. He threatened the commanding officer with a total distruction of the whole Fort in case he protected or admitted[?] any of the retreating Indians. It contains about 3½ or 4 acres of ground the [. . .] are formed of earth thrown up very high in a circular form with one gate way.

Monday, May 31st. I rose in the morning & to my great joy found the wind was changed. I repaired to the Maumy Packet & awoke Capt. Reed who had been dissipating on Sunday & did not feel like early rising. At 9 o'clock we set sail but had not gone 300 yds. before we were aground from unskillfulness of our commander, but after some little difficulty we got off, sailed 2 miles, stopped & took on 50 or 60 bushels of corn. We there parted with Mr. Conant & Gage & Lee. These two young gents have settled here as lawyers. They both have good natural parts but no experience in their profession. No parts of Ohio are as good for the practice of law as Indiana. We passed down the River. Mr. Patterson was on board who

62. An account of the school is given in "An Experiment in Christianity," by Dresden W. H. Howard, edited by Elizabeth Stimson Muttart, in *Northwest Ohio Quarterly*, XXI (1949), 5–17. The school, established by the Presbyterian Missionary Society of Pittsburgh about 1821, continued for some ten years.

63. Fort Miamis, occupied by the British before the Battle of Fallen Timbers and again during the War of 1812.

went down with us as far as Swan Creek 9 miles below Meggs. Portland or Swan Creek is a handsome place. The Lake forms a bay. A few miles below this we had the most delightful view. The watery prospect is expanded—at the entrance of the lake there are many small islands, to our left saw the shores of M[ichigan]. We made tolerable headway. At 4 P.M. we passed the Vermilion a sloop from Buffalo. They had a drumm & fife on board. At dusk we went to bed. It was rather cloudy. At 12 the captain cast anchor before Maulden notwithstanding there was a good wind. Our capt. was very ignorant & destitute of perseverance for as we were informed afterwards he [. . .] with a vessel of the size of his.

June 1st, 1824. The next morning by light we were up to get a view of Maulden which is situated on the East side of Detroit River which runs a S.E. direction. Opposite of that place there were many houses perhaps a hundred. I could not ascertain or form any correct opinion of their magnifficence. There was a ship which [. . .] was anchored close by the Kings warehouse which fronts the River, 60 feet long. The wind was against us & it was with great difficulty that we made any head way. There was just above us a large schooner that made a little better head way than we did. She [was from] Portland and bound to Mackinaw. At 11 we hove in site of Detroit & when within 4 miles of the place we meet 2 vessels one ½ mile distant from the other. They were going out. We haild the first the Hannah of Buffalow. She answered and informed us that she was bound for Buffalo. I asked them to come to us & take Mr. Bishop & myself 'board. They complied. We found their Capt. (Fox) a more decent man than Reed & a much better ship (70 tons burthen). I felt much shagringed that we could not have the pleasure of viewing Detroit when we were [. . .] with its prospect at only 4 miles distant. But however we were anxious to make our way for Buffalo. We slowly descended the River again. The Cannady shore was tolerable well settled & handsome orchards & a great many wind mills. At sunset we anchored just below Mauldin near the same place we had staid the night before. We here landed & visited the fort. The country back of the town is flat, an extensive common literally covered with cattle & horses. We applied to an officer or rather Mr. Bishop did to enter the fortifications. He refused. A young Irish soldier neatly dressed informed us that the

Americans were in a habit of making fun of these fortifications and other apparatus; therefore they could not permit others to have the privilege of entrance. I disavowed having any curiosity. I likewise felt disgusted at the demeanor of the officers and believed they treated perfectly right, for were I an American officer I would treat a British subject with great indifference & should illy represent the politeness of our nation. We found all the officers & soldiers Scotch & Irish, all the merchants & men in civic offices of the same description. The houses in Maulden are tolerably well built but the streets narrow. The merchants do but little business. Enterprise of no description save what relates to the fur trade is encouraged or fostered by the British government in the 2 provinces of Canada. Every American who rides into Upper Canada has to pay a duty of 15 per cent on his horse or mule & cattle (horned) the same. I believe emigrants [immigrants] to that province are exempted. I saw a great many free negroes or rather those who have escaped from the States at Maulden. Many of them are employed in making tobacco which is cultivated here to considerable amount.

Tuesday, June 2d. At 1 in the morning with a good wind we left Mauldin and entered the lake where we met with head winds and beat about among a number of Islands all day without making but little head way. We passed Put-in-Bay where was fortified by Commander Perry a small island called Gibralter from the immense rocks which front to the lake. 'Bout 2 P.M. four of us went on to a small sand island of ½ acre which was covered with gulls very similar to those which inhabit the salt waters & we gathered better than ½ bushel of eggs ⅔ the size of hen's eggs. These were all good & just laid for the place is visited every day by a wretched set of Negroes & whites who inhabit an island on the British side of the lake. At 4 P.M. we saw the light house at the entrance of Sandusky Bay. We kept in site of this till 12 at night at which time the wind changed in our favor & we made tolerable head way. This day in the morn I was very sick for a little time. But by keeping on deck I recovered but soon. Bishop kept in the cabin & being taken like myself continued very sick for the whole day. I was not but I read in the after part. I found a book called the *Universal Restoration* wrote by Elhanon Winchester which I am tolerably well pleased with & am [in] know doubt I shall become confirmed in the doctrine it holds forth.

June 3d. Fair wind in the morning. Made tolerable headway. Foggy in the morn. In site of the American shore. All vessels in the spring & summer run next that shore as winds generally at those seasons blow from that quarter & in the fall from the British side. I am informed that there are about 50 American vessels from 50 to 150 tons burthen [. . .] on Lake Erie & about 5 or 6 belonging to British.

We passed Cleavland and Grand river at the mouth of which is a town of considerable [. . .] at which the steamboat calls. About sundown rain which continued most all night, not much wind. The steamboat passed us in the night as the sailors informed us next morning.

June 4th. Cloudy in the morn—no wind of consequence. At 9 saw the town of Eri Pa. to our right. It appeared to be about the size of Mauldin. To the right of Eri is a light house. (We can see a range of mountains Extending along the shore.) There is a very safe harbor at Eri & a place of much business. Perry's fleet was built at that place & where now a no. of his ships are sunk for preservation others are made merchantment men. Mr. Bishop Capt. Fox & a Mr. Hail from Detroit are now playing cards and I have as usual been solicited to join them. My ignorance of the common games prevents my taking any part, however I spend my time quite agreeable reading & viewing the lake islands & towns on the shore. The water in lake Erie is very excellent at this time of the year—clear cerulean or sky color. Foggy till 4 P.M. The first land we discovered was near a small town called Portland in Chautauque county, one of the W. counties in the N.Y. We anchored about 8 in the eve off Dunkirk in the above county but could not enter the harbor as it was by our capt. deemed dangerous, but he, Bishop & Hail went on shore. Dunkirk is a small town containing about 30 good dwelling houses & some store buildings.

June 5th. We entered Dunkirk harbor a good wind for our passage to Buffalo. Our sailors have discharged their cargo & are now at (10) ready to leave but our capt. who is contemptably disipated has gone to a small town 3 ms. off and has not returned. My impatience to be off renders me unhappy. Went into town & having 'bout 1 P.M. heard there was to be a lawsuit at Days tavern in which there would be imploied lawyers I had a curiosity to hear it. I accordingly repaired to a hall where a justice had empanneled a jury of six men Dr. Williams Plaintiff & one Lions defendant. Mr. Gurnsey as I was informed was the counsel for the Defendant. This gent. appeared to be a man of 35 or 40 well informed & a good advocate. The Plaintiff happened to have no counsel. Gurnsey opposed introduction of the plaintiffs first and principle witness on the grounds of interest & in so doing took a very illiberal & insulting course, spoke very detractingly of the plaintiffs character as well as of his first witness a Dr. Gray a young man of handsome manners & genteel appearance. It was reported by our boats crew that I was a lawyer to a friend of the Dr. who came to me after Gurnsey had made his defense & asked me if I was a lawyer to which I answered in the affirmative. He then requested me to make a closing speech in his case to which [I] assented tho' I trembled like a leaf. However I went at it with much diffidence which I soon got over and exerted myself for an hour. It was the request of the Dr.'s friends to answer abuse with abuse which I think I did to very good effect. Gurnsey winced at my lashes & was much surprised at my appearance as an opponent. He had while the constable was making up a jury discovered me and requested the constable to place me on the panel to which I declined. The Dr. offered me $5. for my services which I refused. We left Dunkirk bout sundown. We had no wind. Another 3 passengers and Smith & wife absent.

June 6th. Rose in the morning & from report lear[n]t we had made but 25ms. head way during the night & no wind. We passed on slowly & at 8 we discovered Buffalo & Ft. Eri. We are now within 2 miles of B. I have concluded to part with Bishop & walk to the Niagra Falls in company with Mr. [blank]. B. is situated on high ground. Fort Eri on the Canadian shore is much lower than B. which is contrary to my expectation. We have at length arrived at Buffalo where there are anchored 13 sail. The wharff is crowded with spectators. We are asked by the hackneys if we want a carriage. Put up at the Eagle tavern—find Buffalo to be a place flourishing and filled with men of business. Contains 200 excellent houses mostly of brick. After dinner I designed to attend the Presbyterian church.

Went to the door after meeting had commenced & recollected that I was very likely in the land of Presbyterian aristocracy. I inquired of a gent who stood at the door if there was seats for strangers he answered in the negative. I turned on my heel & went directly to a [. . .] house where was preaching a Mr. E[. . .] a Universalist who had advanced some ways in his sermon. He was very insinuating in his address. His congregation were mostly young men—clerks, merchants doctors & lawyers. His doctrine advanced I conceived to be subversive of morality religion & education. He rediculed most the idea of giving young men a clasical education in order to prepare them for the ministry. At sundown I retired to bed being informed that the stage would start at 11 at which time we were awakened. It thundered & lightened. We set out—it rained soon very hard.

My passage from Detroit to Buffalo	[$]7.
Barber	0.6 ¼
Bill at Buffalo & stage fare [?]	3.87½
Hair dressing, Dr.	00.12½
Ex[penses] from Buff . . . to Canan [daigua]	0.87½
For hat	2.25
Bill at [ ]	0.62½

[*June* 7]. Left Buffalo June 6th at 11 o'clock at night. Took a seat in the stage with Mr. Bishop Mr. Hail and little daughter from Detroit & two other persons but it was so dark that I could not discover whom but I found one to be a very decent young man by name of Stephenson who had the charge of the stage line and other young Steffin[?] who was from Pen. & who I believe was a pick pocket. The old Lady Mrs. Day from Dunkirk & who had promised the night before to accompany us durst not start with us as it thundered & lightened. We proceeded along apparently a smooth road by the light of lamps for it was dismal & dark.

We saw a light in almost every house which I told our company was caused by loving couples who were setting sparking. 'Bout daylight a young lady got into the carriage & rode a few miles, bout sun ½ hour high we took breakfast 22 ms. from Buffalo. Found the landlady a Yankee school mistress from Vermont. I disliked our breakfast as we had no coffee. We left our place of breakfasting & proceeded over a good country, undulating. The road was cosswayed rough & muddy. We passed in the A.M. many pleasant villages Batavia.

We found the country pretty generally well settled & rich. We took in another passenger little before noon who was rather a quizical. From him I purchased a book on free masonry compiled by [. . .] of Middlebury Vt. We arrived at Canadagua about 8 in the eve. The stage stoped at the Hotel but was soon invited by an opposition tavern to cross over to them which I did. Mr. Bishop here parted with me and went on to Geneva the same night.

June 8th. I procured a transcript of a Judgment for Mr. Osborne at the Clerk's office and got their Judge (Howell) to certify the same. Canadagua is a very falourishing town containing I should say 4 or 500 hundred good houses built of brick & stone. I here purchased a hat for $2.50. There being no stage that left this place for Palmyra the nearest place on the canal, on this day I concluded to walk from there to Palmyra. I left that place 'bout 11 and by riding occasionally as I could get opportunities I got within 2 miles of Palmyra at 2. It rained & I stopped at a Mr. [. . .] who inquired if I knew Hiram & W. Bacon near Indianapolis[64] to which enquiry I was pleased to gratify them by an affirmative answer. There was a young lady who appeared to be the daughter of the old man who gave me a history of the fashions. The fashions now in use as to bonnets are colashes & Hoods which I never have seen in Indiana. She offered to make me one of each kind if I would stay till they were done. I arrived at P. 'bout sundown gave the bar tender at the stage house (St. John's) directions to forward my verlease. I there steped into a packet boat on the canal. I was tired yet I felt a peculiar sensation to think I was riding on the great, the famous Western Canal.[65] There were a number of Passengers aboard. We arrived at Newark the residence of Sister Lucy, Laura & Louisa

64. Hiram and William Bacon were brothers who came to Indiana from Williamstown, Massachusetts, about 1821. They acquired land in Washington Township, Marion County, and became successful farmers. Sulgrove, *History of Indianapolis*, pp. 625–26.

65. The Erie Canal from the Genesee River to Albany had been opened in 1823.

'bout dusk.[66] Being sensible that I was within so short a distance of them it gave me uncommon feelings. Almost eight years had passed without my seeing them. I landed & enquired for Mrs. Buttons residence which was shown me. I soon arrived at the door & entered found her husband the Dr. holding a little girl their first born 9 months old. I was compelled to resort to a subterfuge or show [?] the child. I therefore informed the Dr. I had a letter for his wife whom he said was out & would be in a short time. She came in & I told [her] I was a cousin of hers from Westford but that I left there some time ago. We talked some time together on matters & things & she asked if I did not know Calvin when he lived at Westford. I told her I [. . .] and asked her if she would not be glad to see Calvin. She said yes, but that he lived a great way off. I then asked her if she would not be surprised to learn that I was Calvin. She said it could not be possible!

After our feelings were a little regulated Lucy & Laura [Louisa] were sent for who soon came in. Lucy knew me Louisa did not, nor I her. I was much pleased with her appearance. Likewise with Mr. Miller her husband. I spent the 9th & 10th & 11 without receiving any news of my valiece & it not coming on the last day mentioned went back to Palmyra for it where I learned that it had been sent in the Packet boat Chancellor Kent on Thursday but had been carried by on the 12th. I went to Geneva with Dr. W. saw Mr. Cook Mr. Austin [Bishop] & Mrs. Coe's mother. Returned from Geneva that night to Newark.

Sunday [June] 13. Spent the day with my sisters alternatly & at sundown received my valliece again which I am determined not to leave again.

Monday June 14. I entered another packet boat. Wm. C. Bauch (named after one of the canal commissioners) Capt. Bristol . . .

June 15. Arrived at Utica.

June 16. At Albany.

[June] 17th. At Michaels.[67]

66. Lucy (b. 1792) was the wife of Dr. Richard Williams; Laura (b. 1796) was the wife of Dr. Calvin Button; and Louisa (b. 1804) was the wife of Joseph Miller. All lived in Newark, New York.

67. C.F.'s brother who then was living at Staatsburgh, New York, and who would later, in 1835, move to Indianapolis.

[June] 18th. At Miles.[68] Arrived & 19th Saturday spent the day there & Sunday 20 Did not go to church but staid at home and talked with Miles and eat cherrys.

Monday [June] 21. Spent the fore noon with Miles. Received my pocket book and started with Miles for Newburgh where we arrived. I met Mr. Prichet who once lived at Indianapolis. I called & left a letter wrote by Mr. Hults[?] to Mr. Corwin who treated me very politely. I took tea with him & left board a sloop David Porter, Capt. Bellnap for New York about sundown. Adverse winds. I lament to pass West Point in the night.

[June] 22. Arrived in N.Y. City 9 A.M. I visited their court of common pleas & Magist[rate] court both of which were not conducted with more dignity than our courts in Indiana. I visited the American museum. Left N.Y. bout 3 P.M. and arrived in Newark N.J. at 4. Found Mr. Ross. There I was happy to think I had got to the end of my journey South. I am treated very politely.

[June] 23. Spent the P.M. in the court of quarter sessions.

[June] 24th. Attended court. Felt rather discontented.

[June] 25. On Friday left Newark which is a beautiful village containing about 7000 inhabitants. A vast[?] many shoes are manufactured there & shipped for sale. The people are industrious. Coach lace & harnesses are likewise made in great quantities. I with Joseph[69] went to see 3 small women[?] who were exhibited. We arrived in the City of N.Y. about noon. I went to the State prison which certainly was a very great curiosity. The prisoners were busily engaged. We left N.Y.C. about sundown aboard of the Meridian with Mrs. Ross. Had a no. of ladies and gent.

68. C.F.'s brother who lived in Marlboro, New York.

69. Joseph M. Moore, who was eleven years old at this time and living in Newark with his mother. His uncle, James M. Ray, had sent for him to come to Indianapolis, promising to educate him and prepare him for business. Moore became a partner in J. M. Moore & Company, dealing in general merchandise, along with Ray, James Blake, and Nicholas McCarty. He served as private secretary to Governor Wallace and edited the *Spirit of '76*, a Harrison campaign newspaper published in Indianapolis in 1840. He joined in organizing Christ Church Parish, the first Episcopal congregation in Indianapolis. He later became cashier of the Madison branch of the State Bank. He died in 1858. Nowland, *Early Reminiscences of Indianapolis*, pp. 321–23; Dunn, *Indianapolis*, I, 81, 129, 389, 486, 611.

[June] 26th. Found ourselves under good head way. Run aground but soon got off. We stopped at W. Point which is a very commanding place on the W. side of the River. Ft. Putman [Putnam] is situated a little back of it. Rather in a decayed state. We likewise past Stony Point which was taken in the time of the A. revolution. Landed about 12 at Newburgh. I saw Mrs. Clinton's daughters and son Cousin or relitives of Mr. Little of Shelbyvill Ia. They treated me very politely. Likewise Mr. Cowin & [. . .] were very attentive. I left Newburgh and arrived at Miles about sundown. Next day 27th went to Michaels in a wagon. Past Poughkeepsie in company with Miles.

[June] 28th. Spent the day in conversation.

[June] 29th. Left him about sundown went aboard of the Chancellor Kent.

[June] 30. Arrived in Albany 'bout sunrise. Left Albany after making provisions for Joseph to go to Newark in a boat for White Hall. Got about 1 mile I went back after a hand box and did not get into the boat again till the next morning as I unfortunately passed it.

July 1st. Left one mile N.[?] of Waterford at the 3 locks. We about 11 A.M. passed the still water and Beamses [Bemis] Heights where the battle was fought with Burgoin in Decr. 1777. Arrived at Ft. Miller bridge about sundown. Staid over night.

July 2d. Proceeded on to Ft. Miller by the way of the River which we entered. We [arrived] at Ft. Miller town took the stage in company with Wilkerson of White Hall who came up from N.Y. in the boat we were in. This northern canal is not now navigated with only one packet boat that plys between Ft. Edwards & White Hall. This boat was the first boat built on the Western canal but it was found to small for the business then had. It is now owned by the stage line from Albany to White Hall and navigated by Capt. Cummins a very diminutive man. We entered the packet boat about 3 P.M. and just as we were about to leave two stages came up from Albany loded with Montreal gentry and heavy baggage. We proceeded on the canal about 12 miles to Ft. Ann & there changed horses. Went a little beyond that place the canal was turned into Wood Ck. which they use for six miles. We were sent forward very fast arrived at White Hall about 10. We put up in company with a Mr. Spear from Crown Point at Mr. Hains tavern where I heard a Methodist minister pray etc.

July 3d. Got up early in the morning and called Mr. Gilbert brother to Goldsmith Gilbert who lives on the Mississenwa [in] Ind. He treated very politely and found a wagon to bring me to Rutland. I called on Mr. Wright merchant of that place who came up from Troy with us. White Hall is fast growing about 10 stores notwithstanding it is situated in the mountains. The first locks from the lakes are very large. I was at the arrival of the steamboat Phoenix whose passengers left Montreal the day before—they were a mottle mess—men, women & childrin from Ireland some horses & dogs. The Irish looked poor and distressed. I could not but contrast the difference in the appearance between the passengers of this boat. We left at 10 A.M. passed thro' Fare Haven and thence to Rutland. I this day reflected with some satisfaction that I had once more set my foot upon the soil of my native land. We got to Rutland 4 P.M. I by accident was invited to tea at Mr. Ruggles.

July 4th Sunday Morning. We left Rutland in the morning about 4 o'clock—very cool. We had but one lady and little girl besides Fanny[70] and myself. I soon passed places I well knew in my early years. The country looked barren & poor corn not more than 8 inches high. When we got to Greens six miles from father['s] stopped to breakfast. I here met with Joel Wheeler an old acquaintance. I began to feel an unbounded solicitude to enter the old domicil. We at length proceeded. The distance seemed short. We stopped a few moments at Nath. P. F.[letcher's] to open the mail. I made myself known to him. At length we reached the old place which had so long occupied my thoughts. The stage drove up. My father felt surprised to see Fanny who he expected would stay till fall with her brothers & sisters. He & mother both wept at being informed I was *Calvin.* I was pleased to find them in good health & spirits and in much better circumstances than I had anticipated. After gratifying them in my answers to their many questions we took dinner and father & I went to the new meeting house to hear

70. C.F.'s eldest sister, who married Dr. Calvin Bliss, March 12, 1812. Dr. Bliss died the following year. Fanny died in Newark, New York, in 1872. Von Briesen (ed.), *Letters of Elijah Fletcher,* pp. 56n, 256n.

a Mr. Kendrick a Baptist preacher. There I beheld many new faces. All the young people were to me strangers but I could discover but little difference in the countenances of the old. But there were many strangers I knew not who have emigrated to this place since I left. Our minister attempted [to] preach something of a political sermon being the anniversary of our American independence. After church I shook a cordial hand with many whom I knew.

Monday July 5. I visited Asa Procter my old cousin & school mate. This A.M. strange as it may be I had a severe fit of the fever & ague. I felt tremendously ill out of my head & crazy to see my wife whom I tho't was the only person fit to wait upon me while sick. I vomited. In the P.M. I visited Capt. Levi Ive's. Went to Ludlow village to a training or as we in the West call it muster. I here saw many who knew me. Many questions were asked that I endeavored to answer without ostentation.

Tuesday July 6. I went in the P.M. to Cavendish with father. Called on Capt. Webber's family found that my old friend Sumner was at Litchfield Con. tending law lectures. Call[ed] on Nancy Parker now Zacheriah Bates's wife & took tea with her. Saw Jabez and John Procter's wife. Returned home about dusk.

Wednesday July 7th. Had the fever & ague again in the A.M. and in the P.M. went up to the village. Saw Dr. Walner. Did propose and start to go to the grave yard but it was rather could [cold] & I gave out. Received a letter from E[lijah] F. Returned home & in the [. . .] Asa & James Fletchers wife called and I agreed to visit Asa's on Friday.

Thursday [July] 8th. Staid at home. Walked with father in the A.M. over [to] the River. In the P.M. went with Martin Smith & Brother Stoughton[71] south to what was once called the Leman lot where I had walked many a day early in life.

July 9th. In the P.M. visited in company with Mother Capt. Asa Fletcher's. Spent a very pleasant P.M. in company with Joseph's widow and Mrs. Walner formerly my old playmate Betsy Reed.

July 10th. In the P.M. agreeable to a note I received from Nathan P. Fletcher I visited him. Spent my time only tolerable

71. C.F.'s youngest brother, born August 22, 1808. He would make his home in Indianapolis.

agreeable. He treated [me] very politely however he is considered a great hypocrit & a grinder of the faces of the poor. He urged me to keep up a correspondence with him, reminding me that any dispute which might have originated between our family and himself, ought not to sever any friendship that may exist between himself & me.

Sunday July 11th. Warm. I staid at home & wrote 2 letters one to E. and one to Sumner Webber. Father staid at home in the A.M. but went to meeting in the P.M. Father and I had a conversation on religious subjects. I was supprised to find he and I tho't much alike bothe restorationers. In the P.M. I went down as low as Dutton's village. Called on Jabez Procter returned in the eve and prepared to leave my father & mother the next morning for Indiana where I have attractions that nothing but Death can prevent its force. I have endeavored whilst with my father & mother to banish all tho'ts of wife & child however I can't help devoting some thots on them.

Monday July 12th. I rose 'bout sunup took breakfast with our family collected my things with uncommon cheerfulness and took leave of my father mother and Sister Fanny—tho' did not flatter myself with ever seeing them again. I with Stoughton in a one horse waggon was soon out of sight of the place that gave me birth. At Ludlow village I called on N. P. Fletcher but he was not at home on Joseph's widow and Asa's family. We passed on and arrived at E. Rutland about 11 where there was an exhibition of several monkies and a sea *serpent.* I here concluded to go by the way of Whitehall and have now arrived at Castleton four corners 12 miles from that place. Put up about sundown with the Widow Bishop who treated us very well, 3 miles E. of Whitehall.

July 13. Rose early in the morn and started into Whitehall where I again met with Mr. Wright Wilkerson & Gilbert. Found Sister Fanny's cloak. Left Whitehall at 8 and proceeded to Fort Ann and from thence to Sandy Hill. I[t] began to rain when we had got 10 miles from Whitehall. We stopped and staid 2 hours. I read newspapers. Started again in the rain over a bad road and arrived at Sarratoga about sundown. This is a fine looking place at this season of the year. Invalleads from all quarters are here assembled.

The country people have mostly gone but New York Albany Troy Philadelphia and other cities are now beginning to pour forth their thousands say 3000. Sarratoga village contains about 300 very good houses mostly calculated for boarding houses.

July 14. Left Saratoga and travelled over a very rough road to old M. Veeders in Glenvill six miles North of Shenectedy. This is very cloudy and disagreeable day. Stoughton & I stopped several times to eat cherries. We arrived at old Mr. V.'s about 12. They treated us with a great deal of hospitality. Stoughton appeared to be very much affected at parting with me could not eat nor drink. This made me as unpleasant as every thing that has occured since my leaving home. I rode to S[chenectady] on a waggon of old Mr. V.'s got there about 4 P.M. I soon engaged to proceed up the canal in a scow—Philips No. 3 from Salina 3 rough hands aboard. We proceeded about 20 miles this night.

July 16. Proceeded as far as Little Falls. Started the next morning went thro' [. . .] and arrived at Utica at 5 P.M. Staid a few minutes and left. Took on board a Mrs. Woods an Irish lady living at Oriscane [Oriskany] a great manufacturing village six miles from Utica. We passed on 4 miles from the latter place and my boat stopped at a Mr. Burrows where I stopped a few minutes—a vulgar hovel where I saw 2 or 3 girls with each 3 beau and besides there was a negro tumbler or jugler. Being determined to leave I made enquiries for a boat that was going to run all night. I found Mr. Richard Smith going to Montezuma. At 8 I left Burrows with him and proceeded to Rome 5 miles beyond and there fed. Started from there about 12 and by sunup we made 20 miles.

July 17th. We passed [. . .] New Boston and passed Sarycuse about sundown. This is a flourishing place containing about 100. It was crowded [with] people. A circus exhibition was going on which in some measure accounted for the concourse however the salt works at that place being most contiguous to the cities of Albany & N.Y. makes that a place of resort for many boats. They here make salt by eveverating [evaporating] the water. We passed into Gettesburgh [Geddes?] and put up till about 12.

July 18. We travelled on to Jordan where we arrived about sun 2 hours high. There fed. The packet boat passed us in which I had a good mind to take a passage but believing I could get to Millers Basin this eve I concluded to keep on with Capt. Smith. This is Sunday a very warm day. I had many things to perplex my mind last night and this day about home but I have endeavored to banish every disagreeable tho't in my power and trust to the disposer[?] of all events for the issue. Arrived at Montezuma about 12 and travelled from there to Clyde there being no boats passing. When at Clyde I found no boats coming up the canal and although tired I concluded to make heed[?] for Newark. I travelled six miles it rained and I stopped and staid over night.

July 19. Next morning I rose & travelled to Lyons and waited an hour for the packet boat to arrive so as to go to Newark. I was anxious to see my sisters [. . .] for it had offered me much pleasing anticipation that I could relate to them the prosperity of my friends I had visited. I entered the packet and dispelled my anxiety reading news till I arrived at Millers Basin. The first friend I met with was Joseph the lad I am to take on to Ind. I was sincerely rejoiced to see him. I was solicitous to see him. I found him well & glad to see him [me]. My sisters received me with smiles. I spent this day very pleasantly with my sisters who appeared to be very cheerful except Louisa.

20 July. In the morning prepared to take a waggon for Geneva and so on by the way of Ollean Point contrary to what I had anticipated when I left father's. There and all long I did expect to go by the way [of] Erie home but from inquiry I have concluded to go this way. I may perhaps regret. After receiving very satisfactory testimonials of my sisters friendship I parted with them at 10 o'clock and proceeded on to Geneva in an open waggon. I felt in some measure a mixed sensation of grief & sorrow. I had just parted with kind sisters whom I never expect much to see again yet I was consoled to think I had accomplished all my visits and had started for Indiana where I hoped to arrive soon and with [no] interruption. We got to Geneva bout 5 P.M. Saw Mr. Cook—came a heavy rain.

July 21. Left G. at 4 in company with 3 gents & one lady in the stage for Bath. Passed over rather a rough road to Penn Yang. The country on either side appeared to be rich wheat fields looked elegant. Rye ripe some cut. Arrived at Bath a very pleasant village containing about 75 or a hundred good houses two churches—one Presbyterian—very handsome and the other Methodist substantive but plain. The country round Bath appears to be very well watered & excellent for wheat.

July 22d. Left Bath at sunrise and passed over a hilly broken pine country to Angellica where we arrived about sundown put up at Dutremonts tavern. Angellica is a small town of 30 houses situated in Allegany Co. on the very highest land in the state. The water[?] from this county runs into the Chesapeake Bay St. Lawrence and Mississippi. The country is high cold and frosty. I was here treated very well by Mr. McGee stage driver.

July 23. Travelled over a very rough road poor pine country rather flat. Had one lady Mrs. Osborne who had a small child 10 months old. She was very willing I should carry it over the rough going without expressing fear or feeling any sense of gratitude. She was a Penn(?) by birth. We arrived at the far famed Olean about 6 P.M. Found it to have been truly represented by travellers. I was very unfortunate as there had been 2 men a little before who wished to get company to go down the river & had purchased a boat. I found there was no better way than to proceed down the R.Allegany in a skiff. I agreed for one at 3 dollars.

July 24. At 9 o'clock we Joseph & myself & a Mr. Jones formerly of Clermont N.H. the mail carryer between Warren, Penn. & the above place. He was something used to rowing a boat. We this day made about 34 miles passed the Seneca nation of Indians who were settled on the River as far as the N.Y. line extends. They own some very handsome land on the river. There is a vast quantity of pine on the mountains or perhaps by some may be called hills that close in upon this River. We stopped after dark and went some distance to get lodgings.

July 25. On Sunday. We started tolerable early and passed on down to Warren. We found some very good farms on each side of the River. We arrived at Warren about 3 P.M. This is a small ill shaped lonesome[?] place containing about 20 good houses. Here we parted with Jones. I proceeded down the River 13 miles & staid with a dirty Irish man only four miles from Thompsons where the 2 men who set out before lodged. We started about sunrise very foggy and found at Thompsons that the men were about 5 miles ahead. I this day being determined to ketch them rowed very hard. It was warm. The sun came down most excessively hot. Passed a no. of perogues that were from Pittsburgh managed by Indians who had [come] down after iron ware. I rowed till sundown at which time we were 8 ms. from Franklin where we learnt that the 2 men would put up that were before us. Joseph he cried was tired & afraid to go any further. I made him lay down and I managed the boat alone and arrived at 11 tired & weary at Franklin at the mouth of French Creek about 80 yds. wide at its entrance with the Allegany. It was a mere accident that I happened to land—being dark. I with difficulty found a poor dirty cabin the worst calculated to entertain of any one I ever met with. Jos' & I tumbled down on to the floor without stripping & went . . . .[72]

Rout from Cavendish Vt. to Indianapolis Ind.

To Greens	6 [miles]
from thence to Finneys, Shrewsbury	10
from thence to Golds, E. Rutland	8
to W. Rutland, Corbet	4
to Castleton, Ladds	6½
Castleton 4 Corner, Williams	1½
Farehaven, Wilmoth	3
Whitehall, Bull's	9
Saratoga	35
Schenectady	24
Utica	80
Montezuma	96
Millers Basin or Newark	26/305
Geneva Stones	14
Penn Yang	16
to Bath	30

72. The diary breaks off here. In the entry for August 21, 1838, C.F. recalled that he returned home from his visit to Vermont in 1824 "by the Alleghany & Ohio in a flat [boat] & skiff part [of] the way & brought along Joseph Moore." From the Ohio River to Indianapolis they both rode on one horse, arriving there on August 8. Nowland, *Early Reminiscences of Indianapolis*, p. 321; below, p. 131.

to Angellica 42
to Olean 32

305
124
250
679 from Ludlow to Pitt.

IV

Diary and Letters of CALVIN FLETCHER and Letters of SARAH HILL FLETCHER

December 8, 1824–December 31, 1829

Sarah Hill Fletcher, Indianapolis, to Dear Sisters,[1] *December 8, 1824*

I scarcely know how to address you as I have so long neglected to write since Mr. Fletcher returned from the East. Your several presents were safely received by your brother and but little injured by so long a journey. I shall hold them as valuable pledges of your esteem and friendship and feel sorry I can't return you something more than my acknowledgments of your friendship.

Mr. F. arrived home the Eighth of August about midnight.[2] I had been expecting him for a week and felt somewhat concerned about him. I need not tell you I was surprised as well as rejoiced to [see] him after the absence of Eighty-two days. We had so much company for a week after Mr. Fletcher returned that I scarce had an opportunity to pass a leisure moment with him. I felt sorry to find him discouraged as respects another visit for he says he never expects to make another such a visit.

About the 16th of August myself James and a little girl living with us were all taken sick. I had a severe attack of the fever and was confined nearly six weeks. The two or 3 first weeks Mr. F. entirely devoted to the attention of the family to the neglect of his professional business much to my regret as he had been absent so

1. C.F.'s sisters, Lucy Fletcher Williams, Laura Fletcher Button, and Louisa Fletcher Miller, all of Newark, New York.

2. From his trip to Vermont. See above, pp. 104–29.

much of the summer.[3] We found it very difficult to get a girl as it was generally sickly through the county for a short time. You can't immagine my gratitude to kind Providence that Mr. F. had returned.

He felt much gratified with his visit. He says the real happiness he enjoyed in company with his 3 sisters and two brothers in New York was such that he never again expects will occur unless they make a journey to see him. Yet I flatter him that we shall visit the East in Eight or ten years.

Mr. F. never injoys any thing in anticipation but imagines the next scene that will present itself will be worse than the present.

We have another son about [ ] months old.[4] It was very unhealthy at first and I had but little hopes of rasing it but it has grown of late and appears to be very healthy. We gave it no name till a short time ago. I wished Mr. F. to name him after his father or some one of his brothers. We have concluded to call him Elijah Timothy F. When we use only the first letter of the middle name, it sounds very well. James is the very picture of health. . . . He has been the cause of great uneasiness to me this fall as two of our nearest neighbors lately whilst playing round the fire have had children about his age burnt so they died. They both had on cotton dresses. One was burnt in October and the other in November. This I consider is an awful warning to parents to guard against clothing children with cotton the fall & winter. . . .

Sarah Hill Fletcher, Indianapolis, to C.F., Martinsville, September 6, 1825

. . . Sunday Eve. after you left home Father arived and started back yesterday. He would of staid till this time but it was uncertain

3. However, C.F. was gaining in his profession. At the October, 1824, and May, 1825, Madison County circuit courts he served as one of the defense lawyers in the trials of the men indicted and convicted of murdering a party of peaceful Seneca Indians on Fall Creek in Madison County in the spring of 1824. Indianapolis *Gazette*, October 12, 1824, and May 17, 1825. In the trials he was associated with such legal talent as Harvey Gregg, James Noble, Philip Sweetser, Bethuel F. Morris, Martin M. Ray, Oliver H. Smith, and James Rariden.

4. Elijah Timothy Fletcher, born August 21, 1824. In his diary on August 21, 1838, C.F. wrote: "My son E. is 14 this day. I was absent on the day of his birth.

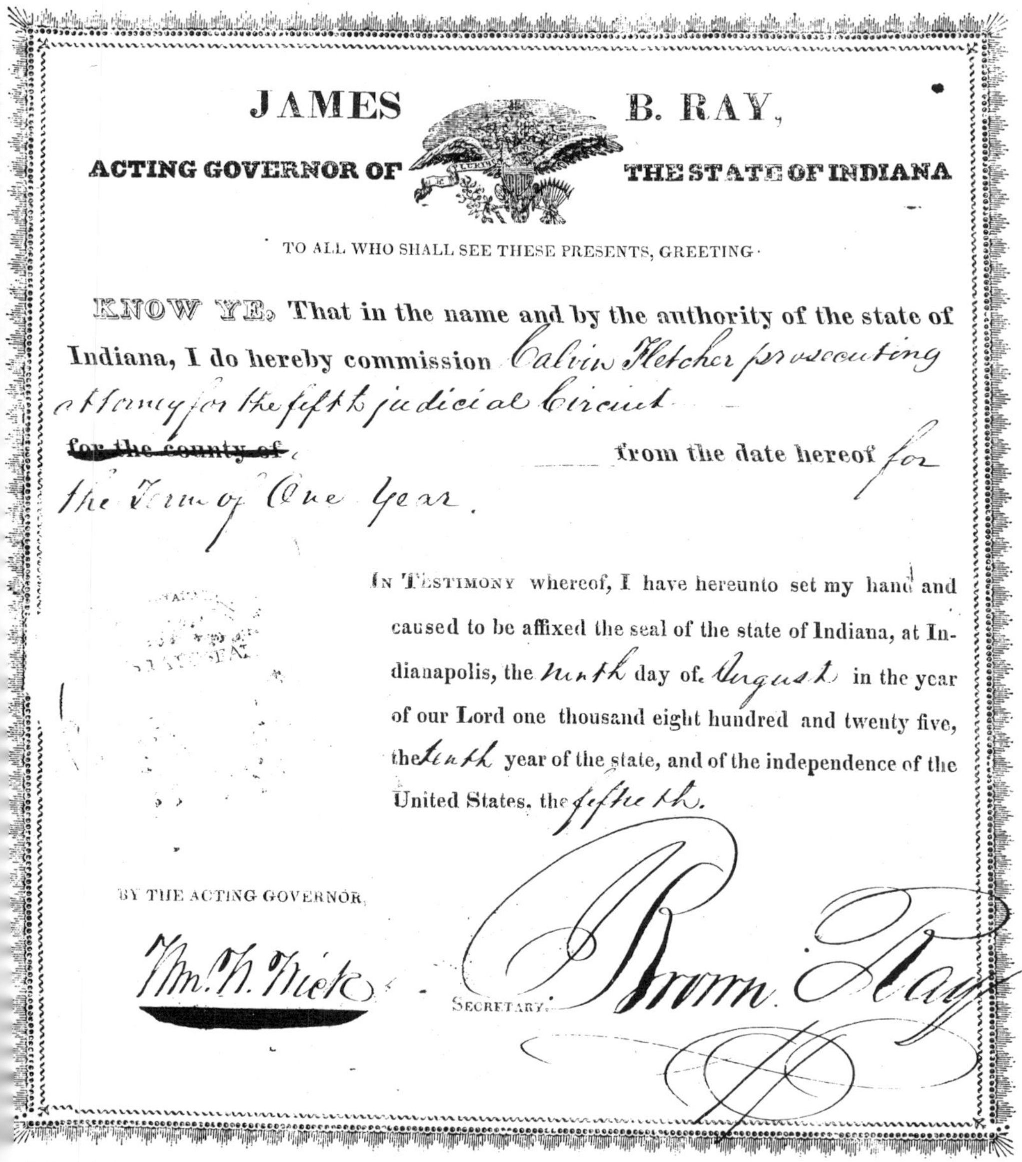

JAMES B. RAY,

ACTING GOVERNOR OF THE STATE OF INDIANA

TO ALL WHO SHALL SEE THESE PRESENTS, GREETING:

KNOW YE, That in the name and by the authority of the state of Indiana, I do hereby commission *Calvin Fletcher prosecuting attorney for the fifth judicial Circuit* ~~for the county of~~ from the date hereof *for the Term of One Year.*

IN TESTIMONY whereof, I have hereunto set my hand and caused to be affixed the seal of the state of Indiana, at Indianapolis, the *ninth* day of *August* in the year of our Lord one thousand eight hundred and twenty five, the *tenth* year of the state, and of the independence of the United States, the *fiftieth.*

BY THE ACTING GOVERNOR,

Wm. W. Wick SECRETARY.

J. Brown Ray

FLETCHER PAPERS

Calvin Fletcher's commission as Prosecuting Attorney for the Fifth Judicial Circuit, August 9, 1825

when you would return.[5] He lamented to think he could not see you after comeing so far.

James has been confined to his bed for a week past but is geting well. He has take 2 potions of calomel and 1 of antimonial wine. Do not be uneasy about him he has all the attention thats necessary.

This day week ago we had a very hard hail storm. Done considerable damage to the windows of this plase. Twelve lights were broken out of this house.

John McCormac[6] and Mrs. Colaps sister died since you started. I understand Sweet is recovering to the great sorrow of his neighbours. . . .

P.S. I shall send your tooth brush by Mr. B.

C.F., Columbus, to Sarah Hill Fletcher, September 21, 1825

. . . I have had only tolerable health since my arrival here but am in good spirits and feel well at this time. I shall start for Decatur tomorrow and shall be at Rush on Thursday where Mr. Morris or

---

I had been to attend a trial before a J.P. at the falls of Fall Crk. now Pendleton 30 miles distant the way the road then run for which I got $5. . . . I had been to Vt. that summer had expended all I was worth on that visit to my father."

5. C.F. was away on the fall circuit. On August 9, 1825, he was appointed by Acting Governor James B. Ray prosecuting attorney for the fifth judicial circuit and served for one year. *Indiana Executive Proceedings*, p. 504. This meant that in the following fall and spring he attended courts in the dozen counties comprising the circuit: Morgan, Johnson, Shelby, Bartholomew, Decatur, Rush, Henry, Madison, Marion, Hamilton, Hendricks, and Monroe. His commission as prosecuting attorney is in the Fletcher Papers.

John B. Dillon, Indiana historian and friend of C.F.'s, wrote that as prosecuting attorney C. F. "was diligent and faithful . . . but if local authenticated tradition be true, he sometimes, in very extraordinary cases, availed himself of the use of novel and irregular powers, in order to prevent the defeat of the ends of justice by the ignorance and stubborness of foolish men." Quoted by Simon Yandes in his "Recollections of Calvin Fletcher as a Lawyer," MS in Fletcher Family Papers, Indiana Historical Society Library. Prosecuting attorneys at this time were paid an annual salary of $250 plus $5.00 for each judgment on criminal prosecutions. *Revised Laws of Indiana*, 1824, p. 128.

6. John McCormick. Perhaps the first white man to settle in Indianapolis. According to Nowland he arrived February 26, 1820, and built his cabin on the east bank of White River near the present Washington Street. He opened the town's first tavern. Nowland, *Early Reminiscences of Indianapolis*, pp. 23–24.

Lilly[7] will be. I wish you to write by them and in case I have had any letters of importance arrived in the mail or other communications that I ought to see, be so good as to forward them to me. Judge Wick informs that James has been sick with the ague. Tell Ingram to keep in good heart and spirits—that I hope to be better natured on my return than when I left.

If you should get out of money there is a little assumed to be paid by Mr. Ray for Jo Reed and Basy[8] was to collect some from Seth Bacon[9] for me. Whiter [?] is owing me some on a note. If all these fail Borrow of Dr. Scudder Mr. Bradley or any other person who [will] lend. You better get what winter goods you want from McCarty—particularly sheeting. Don't suffer for nothing. I shall be home in about two weeks. . . .

Sarah Hill Fletcher, Indianapolis, to C.F., Rushville, September 27, 1825

You cant immagen my disapointment when I opened your letter of the 21st and found you had not received mine in answer to yours of the 15, In which I had enclosed a letter from Mr. Cooly on business. I thought you would wish to answer it before you came home. As soon as I recieved your letter I sent to the post office thought purhaps they had neglected puting it up, but no so. They say it has bin detained between this plase and Columbus. . . .

I got some sheeting & table linen soon after you started. Dont be uneasy I shall not suffer for want of money. I got 2 dollars from Mr. Ray & a little from Dr. Scuder and if I should want more I will call on some of those whom you mention was owing you. . . .

We have the lion tiger panther [. . .] hog and 2 monkies in

7. Judge Bethuel F. Morris and William H. Lilly, auditor of state.

8. Lismond Basye, who moved to Indianapolis from Franklin County in 1821. He served as a justice of the peace from 1822 to 1827, then moved to the northern part of the state. Nowland, *Early Reminiscences of Indianapolis*, pp. 74–76; *Indiana Executive Proceedings*, pp. 221, 382, 515n. In his Diary under date of June 12, 1865, C.F. wrote of Basye: "He was my early friend & gave me good advise when I began the practice of the law here & especially on the subject of restraining my temper & prejudices toward my adversaries."

9. Seth Bacon and Peter Negley built and operated a mill on Fall Creek near present Millersville. Sulgrove, *History of Indianapolis*, p. 633.

town. I have not room to describe them. Polly was very anxious to see them. I went this P.M. took her & the children. James says I tell papa when he comes home I see tiger and monkeys *they eat chees too.* Polly was very much frightened when the lion rord. She thinks the panther is the same catamount that used to come to the house & there is no danger now it is in such a strong cage. . . .

C.F., Rushville, to Sarah Hill Fletcher, September 27, 1825

. . . I shall be at home the latter part of next week and if ever I was anxious to get home I am now. . . . I wish Mr. Ingram would speak to old Mr. Mad Cap or his son to get the post Master at Columbus to remail my letter.

DIARY

December 25th 1825. On Sunday cool weather no snow on the ground. Went to hear Mr. Scott[10] preach with Mrs. F. and James.

January first 1826. On Sunday in the morning very cold. Snow covers the ground continued extremely cold thro' the day, in consequence of which I did not go to meeting but staid at home and read Donnald Campbells travels.[11] I now live in Dr. Scudders house which is niether comfortable situated for my business nor is it convenient for the domestic circle.[12] I have now as inmates Dr.

10. The Rev. James Scott, who had conducted the Methodist camp meeting in September, 1822 (see above, p. 68), and the following November assumed charge of the circuit which included Indianapolis and northern Marion plus Hamilton and Madison counties. Dunn, *Indianapolis,* I, 85.

11. *A Journey Overland to India . . .* (1st ed. London, 1796).

12. In a note dated October 1, 1857, at the front of the first numbered volume of the Diary, C.F. recalls that in 1826 the family was living in Dr. Scudder's house "adjoining the state bank on the avenu[e] leading to the graveyard." The house was on the south side of Kentucky Avenue south of its junction with Illinois Street. The State Bank building was erected on the adjoining lot in the point between the Avenue and Illinois Street in 1840 (lot 1, square 67). This would have been the "new graveyard," so-called to distinguish it from the "old graveyard," the town's first burying ground. The original town plat did not provide for a cemetery but the General Assembly gave to the citizens of Indianapolis a public burying ground of four acres located on the east bank of the river on the southwest edge of the town. In 1834 the "new graveyard" comprising five acres was laid out extending from the border of the old one south to Kentucky

Scudder and Mr. A. Ingraham who is with me studying law. We have two children James almost 3 years years of age and Elijah past two [one]. They afford us much pleasure and satisfaction. My professional business is good compared with the amount done here. During the past fall and summer I have not been in that state of health that would warrant much progress in my studies but I am now fast gaining and feel as anxious to acquire knowledge and make my self useful as ever and I have much more faith to believe that by persevereance that I can accomplish and attain a competance that I once had. I am confident I enjoy to the fullest extent that quantity [of] domestic happiness I ever anticipated. I wish not to be too worldy but always mindful of that *end* we must all come to. I am certainly anxious to make myself and family useful members of society.

Jan. 2d. The trial of N. W. Marks[13] commenced before the high court of impeachment the senate of the state. He suggested to the court that he was poor and unable to employ counsel. A vote was taken whether to employ counsel or not. It was decided in the affirmative and he desired that Judge Wick and Mr. Blake of Tarrehaute[14] might be emploied in his behalf which request was granted. The counsel requested the court to adjourn which they accordingly done.

Jan. 3d. Pleasant. The trial of Marks again came on—the Managers on the part of the state Messrs. Switser [Sweetser] & Howk.[15] The day was occupied in receiving the testimony and the arguments commenced about sundown. The case was opened by Mr. Switser. He made a few pertinant observations and set down—

Avenue. In 1860 Greenlawn Cemetery, a seven and a half acre tract, was laid off adjoining and to the north of the older cemeteries. *Laws of Indiana,* 1822–23, p. 28; Sulgrove, *History of Indianapolis,* p. 385.

13. Nathaniel W. Marks, sheriff of Rush County. He was convicted by the Senate of making a false certificate of the amount of revenue due the state from the county and of forging the county clerk's signature. Indiana *House Journal,* 1825–26, pp. 127–29; Indiana *Senate Journal,* 1825–26, pp. 126–29, 131–33, 134–36; *Indiana Executive Proceedings,* p. 586n.

14. Thomas H. Blake, who served as judge of the first judicial circuit, was a member of the state legislature for several sessions, and for one term a representative in Congress, 1827–29. *Indiana Executive Proceedings,* p. 70; *Indiana Election Returns,* Index.

15. Isaac Howk, representative from Clark County.

answered by Messrs. Blake and Wick rather. . . . Howk tho he is rather singular in his manner of address answered the arguments of the counsel for the prisoner with vehemence & force.

February Fourth 1826. The birthday came on Saturday. Pleasant but cloudy with two or three inches of snow that has lain on for Several days. I this day was employed to appear before Justice Basye's Court for old Wm. Coal. I at this time enjoy tolerable health and prosperity. I am about to commence the Spring circuit court. The duties to be performed by me are somewhat arduous.[16]

Sarah Hill Fletcher, Indianapolis, to Louisa Fletcher Miller, Newark, New York, January 5, 1826

. . . Your brother has not enjoyed good health this fall and has had to be absent from home from about the 20th of August until the 3d of December, he having been appointed State attorney in this district. Has to go twice a year into twelve counties. He will leave home the last of February and will not spend more than ten days at home again untill the first of June.

We are blessed with the trouble of only two children. . . . Since October I have had no girl to assist me. We have besides our own family Dr. Scudder who has boarded with us two years and a young gentleman studying with Mr. F. . . . Mr. F. is absent several months in the year and when he is at home, he does not spend an evening with me scarcely once in a month—as he spends most of his time in his office. He tries to comfort me by telling that it takes

16. Simon Yandes, who read law with C.F. and later was a law partner of his, wrote in his "Recollections of Calvin Fletcher as a Lawyer," that C.F.'s earliest practice must have been "very miscellaneous, ranging from the Justice of the Peace to the Supreme Court, including both law and chancery, civil cases and criminal, with, however, an undue proportion of criminal and tort cases, among which last slander suits were quite common. In early times there was less appeal to authority, and more to the feelings of the jury than now. In new counties the court rooms were always crowded; and often by citizens who had no business at court, but came to see and hear. The lawyers were much tempted to make speeches for the lobby in part, and it was quite an object to entertain and amuse the audience generally; and even those who like [C.F.] . . . were indisposed to encourage this abuse, occasionally gave in to it." MS in Fletcher Family Papers, Indiana Historical Society Library.

him longer to do his business than any body else. I do not visit much although we have good neighbours but I never feel happy if I leave my children at home to go a visiting and to take them with me is not always convenient. Our place is now crowded with strangers as the legislature are in session. . . .

C.F., Bloomington, to Sarah Hill Fletcher, February 9, 1826

. . . The time since I left home seems long and tedious and more I consult my feelings on the subject more determined I am to be more domestic in my life than circuit prosecuting will admit. If poverty is the inevitable consequence I shall submit with great patience if you are content but perhaps you may think that occasional absence makes me appreciate properly the sweets and comforts of home with you and my boys. . . .

You will recollect that I told you that I had purchased certain grave-stones &c.[17] A Mr. Mathews had agreed to put them up for $4. I was to send him the age of your mother and father. I am to send the inscription to be put on the marble or grave-stones. I want something humble and decent—Something that our children will not be ashamed of should they be ever so learned. . . . Should you meet with an inscription in any of your reading or can devise one write them down. . . .

. . . You better buy your sugar even at 8 cts. per lb. Make yourself happy and comfortable. . . .

C.F., Bloomington, to Sarah Hill Fletcher, March 2, 1826

. . . I advised you to get you a Canton Crepe dress. I mention in Ingrams letter that possibly you better get two but do as you think proper. Be sure and get that of the best quality or wait till that which is good comes to town. Perhaps you better b[u]y Sugar if you can get it at 6¼ cts. per pound and that of a good quality. I thought two hundred cwt. would be as much as we shall want. I understand

17. To mark the graves of Sarah's father and mother in Urbana, Ohio. Sarah's mother had died in 1816; her father died in 1836.

that it is selling for 6¼ cts. in Johnson and Shelby Counties and I presume it will not be more at Indianapolis. . . .

Sarah Hill Fletcher, Indianapolis, to Louisa Fletcher Miller, Newark, New York, March 25, 1826.

. . . Mr. F. has been absent about six weeks returned 2 days since and leaves us tomorrow morning again. If it was not for my two Boys I should be very lonesome—they divert my attention so much in Mr. F.['s] absence that they appear more interesting every time he leaves home. James will be three year's old the 15th of next month is very anxious to attend church can not be hired to stay at home unless he has ragged pantalloons. When he hears me mention Sunday he will speak very quick and say, I will go to meeting—have you mended my trowsers. . . . I am about to have my likeness taken with James and Elijah's on the same piece of canvass James on my right with a little book in one hand standing—Elijah on the left sitting in a small chair. Mr. F. will have his on a seperate piece.[18] Some people think such painting unworth the expense & trouble of procuring them and that they are vain and foolish. I should deem it a very great satisfaction if I should survive Mr. F. to have his portrait to remind me of the happy years we spent together. I presume it would be as much so to him should he survive, and should we both live to good old age, it would be pleasing to us to see how our children looked when they were young. . . . Mr. F. visited Urbana this spring for the first time since we came to this place. I have not yet been back but expect to go this summer take my two boys and stay about six weeks. Father visited us last August.

18. In his diary on October 4, 1860, C.F. wrote "At an early day I had an ivery potrait for myself taken by D. Verbrack (In 1832) & anterior to that a likeness for self & wife by Sloan. It was rude but we yet retain it—that was as early as 1826." The portraits that Mrs. Fletcher refers to must be the ones by Sloan. No record of a painter by that name has been found. However, "D. Verbrack" was probably Richard Verbrick, a miniaturist and portrait painter who worked in Cincinnati from 1825 to around 1831. *The New-York Historical Society's Dictionary of Artists in America 1564–1860*, compiled by George C. Groce and David H. Wallace (New Haven: Yale University Press, 1957), p. 648. C.F. was in Cincinnati in 1830 and likely in 1832 and he may have had a miniature on ivory painted while on one of these trips.

Sarah Hill Fletcher, Indianapolis, to C.F., Madison County, Indiana, April 8, 1826

. . . I have felt quite uneasy about you on account of the high waters the River has never bee[n] fordable since you left home, nor the ground dry enough to plow. Last Thursday night we had a storme haild for about 5 minutes very hard and rained till day the hardest I ever heard. I unders[t]ood next morning Pog[u]es Creek was four foot higher than it has been this Spring. I expect you would be glad to know something about the election.[19] Well that is a subject I can give no light on. . . .

Dr. Kenneth A. Scudder, Indianapolis, to C.F. [Noblesville], October 12, 1826

The situation of your wife is such that it is absolutely necessary that you should come home immediately. She has had one of those cold spells which are always dangerous. This is her first days sickness and should the disease increase she must inevitably die.[20]

19. The Indianapolis *Gazette* of March 28, 1826, carried the announcement that C.F. would be a candidate for the state Senate at the annual election in August to represent the newly formed district composed of Marion, Hamilton, Madison, and Hendricks counties. His opponents included John W. Redding of Marion County and Josiah F. Polk of Hamilton County. The former probably offered no great competition. Nowland wrote that Redding "was a candidate for clerk of the county at the first election in 1822, and was a standing candidate for years for any office that might be to fill by the people." *Early Reminiscences of Indianapolis*, pp. 134–35. Apparently he was never successful. The June 6 issue of the *Gazette* carried a letter from C.F. to the citizens of Hamilton County in which he promised, if elected, to work for an ad valorem form of taxation. A handbill distributed by Polk declared the writer to be in favor of an ad valorem system of taxation, opposed to a poll tax, in favor of internal improvements "of every kind to the utmost extent," and in favor of altering the United States Constitution "so as to prevent the house of representatives in Congress from making the President in any event." The handbill also touched on disposition of the public lands, election of United States senators, and the extension of jurisdiction of justices of the peace. A copy of the handbill is in the Fletcher Papers. C.F. was elected. In order to maintain the continuity of the Senate, senators of the newly formed districts drew by lot to determine the length of their terms and C.F. drew the two-year term. The regular Senate term was three years. *Indiana Election Returns*, p. 198; Indianapolis *Gazette*, April 25, 1826.

20. In a memorandum dated October 1, 1857, at the front of the first numbered volume of the diary, C.F. inserted an account of the birth of his third

C.F., Indianapolis, to Sarah Hill Fletcher, Urbana, Ohio, June 17–22, 1827

After I left you[21] and Newton on Thursday I returned as far as Jennisons[22] and spent an hour and then started and arrived at Wicks (of whom I got the horse I rode) about half after twelve. I met Genl. Noble[23] and nothing would do but I must eat dinner with him after which I returned to the house. James had gone to school,[24] Elijah was at play and all things in good order.

---

child and third son Calvin, born September 30, 1826. He noted that, "In a few days thereafter I left for Noblesvill court leaving the boy and Mrs. F. in good condition. But was sent for by Dr. Scudder who took the charge of Mrs. F. after the birth of the boy. Mrs. F. ate some water mellon which bro't on a chill & she come near dying & Dr. S. sent a line & [by] Veeken [?] then a taylors prentice. I was sleeping with H. Gregg at old Mr. Mallerys. I left at Midnight had to follow a trace thro the dark woods. Got lost & did not get home till next morn at sunrise. As I entered the door poor old Mr. Ralsten a good neighbor had been in & was just coming out of the house. I learned from him Mrs. F. was alive and better. She recovered after a severe spell."

21. Sarah Fletcher was on her way to Urbana, Ohio, to visit her old home for the first time since she left there in 1821. C.F. had escorted her out of Indianapolis. In the Fletcher Papers there is an item in C.F.'s hand headed "June 2, 1827, Memorandum—1 Trip to Urbana" which apparently is a list of instructions to his wife for her journey. It reads: "You will pay Mr. Campbell five dollars and take his receipt and to Mr. Lewis three dollars & 50 cts. You better get the grave stones [see above, p. 139] lettered and put them up while you are there if possible as it may not be attended to. Call on Mr. Rariden and deliver him the deed and letter. You will give your grand-mother a present and sisters if you desire. If you get your money changed get it in U.States paper."

22. Samuel Jennison, an early settler of Warren Township, Marion County. His farm lay in the west half of the southwest quarter of section 1, T15N, R4E. Sulgrove, *History of Indianapolis*, p. 615.

23. Noah Noble (1794–1844), who moved from Brookville to Indianapolis upon his appointment in December, 1825, as receiver in the land office which was moved from Brookville to the capital that year. He had served one term as a state representative and would serve two terms as governor, 1831–37. Dorothy Riker (ed.), *Messages and Papers Relating to the Administration of Noah Noble Governor of Indiana 1831–1837* (*Indiana Historical Collections*, XXXVIII, Indianapolis: Indiana Historical Bureau, 1958), Introduction.

24. This may be the school, called the Indianapolis Academy, presided over by Ebenezer Sharpe, held in the Presbyterian meetinghouse. Sharpe began teaching there in 1826, and in 1830 moved his school to a frame house on the corner of Ohio and Meridian streets where he continued teaching until his death in 1835. Dunn, *Indianapolis*, I, 91–92.

This morning . . . we went to class meeting and then went to the ground where Mr. Ray[25] preached last Sunday beyond Esqr. Basys where he delivered a sermon this day & sprinkled I think seven women. . . .

Tuesday June 19th. . . . I set out all your cabbage plants. We have had company most constantly and Friday the 22d old Lorenzo Dow[26] preaches and all the Quakers from Hendricks will be present. Several have sent me word that they shall call on me. Well they are my friends and I shall make them as happy as possible. . . .

Our town this day (22) was crouded with people to hear Lorenzo Dow preach but in consequence of high waters he did not get here.

Sarah Hill Fletcher, Urbana, Ohio, to C.F., Indianapolis, June 22, 1827

. . . the day you left us we traveled slow. We arived in West Liberty about sun set. My horse went dull and would not eat. Next day it was with great difficulty that I got him to Senters Ville where I left him in the care of Mr. Rariden telling him you would be at all expense. I shall always consider Mr. R. one of the kindest & best of men. He let me have an elegant horse. . . . On Saturday I was very near giving out. I did not eat more in four days than one full meal but since I have becom wrested my appetite is better. . . . The people all appear very glad to see me. . . . James I expect will come down this fall.[27] . . . I did not get to see Mathis [Matthews] till this morning. He said he would try to get larger stones. I shall have them put up before I leave. I think of visiting the Yellow Springs before I

25. Edwin Ray, a young Methodist preacher who was assigned to the Indianapolis circuit in 1826. Nowland, *Early Reminiscences of Indianapolis*, pp. 223–25.

26. An account of this eccentric itinerant preacher, who replied when asked what religious faith he adhered to, "I am a Methodist chain and Quaker filling," and his visits to Indianapolis is given in John H. B. Nowland, *Sketches of Prominent Citizens of 1876, with a Few of the Pioneers of the City and County Who Have Passed Away* (Indianapolis: Tilford & Carlon, Printers, 1877), pp. 365–67.

27. James Hill, a younger brother of Sarah Hill Fletcher who came to Indianapolis in the fall of 1827 to live.

go home. . . . Tell James & Lijah to be good boys & say their prayers. I shall be at home in the fore part of July. . . .

C.F., Indianapolis, to Sarah Hill Fletcher, Urbana, Ohio, July 2, 1827

. . . Elijah and James have enjoyed good health since I wrote. . . . Last Sunday there was a vast congregation assembled to hear Lorenzo Dow. It was a warm day. I brought Calvin home from Mrs. Basys.[28] He was highly pleased to see the children. We kept him till near night & Polly Darnold took him back. I regretted to see the little fellow sent back and would have kept him but mother Basye made particular inquiries when I took [him] at what time I would return him.

I have wrote to Mr. Rariden to provide you with a horse from Centreville home. I hope you will return his horse to him in good order. . . .

I never felt half the anxiety in my life to meet a friend than I now do you—but do not let my solicitude make you unhappy. It is my greatest desire that you should make a long satisfactory visit for as good a wife as you have been deserves great indulgence. . . .

C.F., Indianapolis, to his brother Elijah Fletcher, Lynchburg, Virginia, September 8, 1827

. . . It gives me great pleasure to learn that you are prosperous in your concerns. Your past industry and economy have no doubt made you in every particular comfortable, for no man can be happy who properly considers the uncertainty of life and who has a young family dependant upon him, unless he knows he has accumulated something that he can leave behind that will be an assurance against that abject poverty which falls to the lot of many widows and orphans. This consideration has operated as a very considerable stimulous to me and should I ever become avaricious I shall attribute its origin to sheer poverty and necessity, the mother of many inventions to which all our habits all our manners bend.

28. Wife of Lismund Basye. See note 8, above.

My family for the summer and fall thus far have enjoyed good health. I have every year untill this been subject to billious attacks but I have taken better care of myself of late than usual.

Our town & country are populating with considerable rapidity. The national road[29] has been permantly located as far as this place and the commissioner Mr. Knight has run a random line West to the state line and has just returned for the purpose of again retracing his steps West to the line dividing this state & Illinois in order to compleat the permanent location in this state during the present season.

I have received the Virginian[30] regular up to the 15th of August which I got last night. If I should measure the [. . .] feelings of your subscribers or the people of your town, by your paper, I should conclude you all felt a very considerable interest in the event of the coming Presidential election and that there must be a corresponding heat & violence opposed to your sentiments. As for myself I felt very anxious for Jackson's success at the last canvass. As a man I have always liked him better than Adams and notwithstanding he has less ability to reduce them to practice yet were his political sentiments & principles the same I should prefer him to Adams for reasons too tedious to mention. But as long as I regard the interest & welfare of my country and as long as I regard the honor and integrity of a partizan who intends not to desert his friends I cannot support any man for president who goes heart and hand with the friends of genl. Jackson; for no state in the union is more deeply interest[ed] in the success of the leading measures of the present administration than Indiana, yet with these sentiments I have never

29. The Cumberland Road or Old National Road, a Federal project, which was designed to connect the Mid-Atlantic Coast with the Mississippi. The first legislation providing for it was passed in 1806 and it was opened to traffic between the Potomac and Wheeling in 1817. In 1825 funds were appropriated for construction from Wheeling to Zanesville and for laying out the route from the latter place through the capitals of Ohio, Indiana, and Illinois, and on to the Mississippi. The road was finally opened to Vandalia, Illinois, in 1852. Buley, *The Old Northwest,* I, 446–48.

30. In 1825 Elijah Fletcher had acquired the Lynchburg *Virginian,* a Whig paper. It had a large circulation and was a profitable venture. Von Briesen, "Elijah Fletcher, a Citizen of Lynchburg," in Lynchburg Historical Society Museum, VII, No. 2 (1970).

felt the least warmth on the subject neither do I think it possible for me to be brought to feel that concern that many others of my neighbors do.[31] Two of the electors on the Jackson ticket at our last presidential election & one of our Jackson electors have wrote to him of late, demanding an unequivocal answer as to his sentiments in relation to the present system of internal improvements & informing him that on his answer being unfavorable thereto they cannot give him their support.[32]

My business gradually increases. [At this point two lines have been blotted out.] He is my successor,[33] about my age—had a good education to begin with—has no family to trouble his mind—is in easy circumstances procured by industry—is never ending in his researches—temperate—Jealous—avaricious—proud—circumspect—*professes religion* and has the art and address to make most people believe he professes and injoys to the full extent of his professions—

31. It is interesting to note that on December 6, 1827, the fourth day of the 1827–28 session of the legislature, C.F. introduced a joint resolution to instruct Indiana's senators and request her representatives in Congress "to use every means in their power to restrain the importation of hemp, and wool, and woollens; and generally to use every reasonable effort to carry into effect the *American System*," which was passed. Indiana *Senate Journal*, 1827–28, p. 33; *Laws of Indiana*, 1827–28, pp. 143–44.

32. On January 22, 1828, the Senate instructed the Governor to write to Jackson requesting his views regarding Federal appropriations for internal improvements and the tariff. Indiana *Senate Journal*, 1827–28, p. 226. Fletcher is not shown as voting on the resolution. Jackson's reply was that his sentiments were the same as they had been in 1823 and 1824 when he voted for the tariff and for appropriations for internal improvements. Dorothy Riker and Gayle Thornbrough (eds.), *Messages and Papers relating to the Administration of James Brown Ray Governor of Indiana, 1825–1831* (*Indiana Historical Collections*, XXXIV. Indianapolis: Indiana Historical Bureau, 1954), pp. 319–28, 337–41. Jackson carried Indiana in 1828, receiving 22,000 votes as opposed to 17,000 for John Quincy Adams. *Indiana Election Returns*, pp. 10–13.

33. James Whitcomb (1795–1852), who succeeded C.F. as prosecuting attorney. Like Fletcher, he was a native of Vermont. After graduating from Transylvania University he came to Indiana and began the practice of law in Bloomington. He served as prosecuting attorney until 1828 and was a member of the state Senate from 1830 to 1836 when he was appointed Commissioner of the General Land Office by President Jackson, which position he held until 1841. He served two terms as governor of Indiana, 1843–49, and was elected to the United States Senate, serving from 1849 until his death. *Biographical Directory of the American Congress*, p. 1099.

is eloquent—and in fine he [MS torn] an eminent degree that rascally virtue called pru[dence]. Our Governor Treasurer &c &c have late got into very con[MS torn] in which a number of our citizens are more less involved [MS torn] been invited to attach myself to the several sides.[34] I have declined to being any part with either, having been on the best of terms with the contending parties but more than likely their official conduct may come before our next legislature and in that event I shall be compelled to act openly and decidedly whether I rise or fall & let me act as I may—it will be used against me by one side or the other. Let the result be as it will I am determined not to form the habits or character of a violent partizan. I have thus far got along without making but few enemies. I intend to pay a strict regard to candor and to act openly & for the people when called upon in a proper manner but not for any one or any set of individuals. I have taken great pains to quell all Jealousies among my brother lawyers at this place and I have now the apparent friendship of every one. They sometime accuse me of being a peoples man—that I have ambitious views—that I want to go to

34. The Governor was James Brown Ray. A native of Kentucky, he came to Brookville, Indiana, in 1818, and was admitted to the bar. He served one term as representative from Franklin County and was a member of the Senate on January 30, 1824, when Ratliff Boon, the lieutenant governor and president of the Senate, resigned to take a seat in Congress. Ray became president pro tem, and when Governor Hendricks resigned in February, 1825, following his election to the United States Senate, Ray succeeded to the governorship. He had little formal education and was very young; some questioned whether he was yet thirty, the age required for the governorship in the Constitution. He was elected governor in August, 1825 and re-elected in 1828.

The treasurer was Samuel Merrill. Born in Vermont, he graduated from Dartmouth College and came to Indiana in 1816. He served two terms as representative from Switzerland County and was elected state treasurer by the General Assembly in 1822, serving until 1834 when he became president of the State Bank. The personal political feud between Merrill and Ray, which had been smoldering for some time, burst into the open in May and June, 1827, in the columns of the Indianapolis *Gazette*. Merrill's letters to the *Gazette* and Ray's reply and other pertinent items are in *Messages and Papers relating to the Administration of James Brown Ray*, pp. 218–26, 229–33, 339–68; see also pp. 3, 12–13. On September 11, 1829, Merrill wrote to his brother, the Rev. David Merrill of Urbana, Ohio, that Governor Ray was ill. While some believed he had been poisoned, Merrill believed that the Governor "might take arsenic with impunity." Merrill Family Papers, Indiana Historical Society Library.

Congress at the next apportionment &c &c. All this I take good naturedly. I was a little captious when I lived with you but I now have compleat controle of myself compared with some others. . . .

C.F., Indianapolis, to his father, Ludlow, Vermont, January 27, 1828

. . . Our legislature after a session of 7 weeks and 3 days adjourned on Thursday last and I have served the 2 sessions in the Senate for which I was elected. I entered upon this public duty without much confidence in myself. I had raised no ones expectations by promises which is usual for candidates in this country, to make, therefore let my performance be what it might I had not the mortification of disappointing my friends, at least, in that particular—but I must say that I surpassed my own expectations and I further think I have given no offence to any party that is willing to be satisfied with good intentions.

I have remarked to you I believe in a former communication that political life was calculated to bring upon a man cares and troubles for which he never receives any thing like an adequate compensation. It makes him less independent; but in order to keep up the public tone and good will in his favor, he must often sacrifise his own private interest. If a man is a public servant, he is bound and obliged in this country, to be very accomodating—this being the price of a political station. I think it doubtful whether I shall decline all further pretentions at present and devote myself entirely to my profession. However, I have warm solicitation from friends to present myself again as a candidate for the senate. I have not fully determined against it. It would be against my pecuniary interest should I even succeede—but pride and I may say the honor of being the choice of a majority of the freeman of 4 counties to represent them in the Senate & likewise a desire to ascertain whether my past services meet their approbation so far as to reelect me, are almost inducements sufficient to suffer myself to become a candidate once more under the conviction above stated.

We have had a very open wet winter. The ground has not been frozen more than once or twice. Immense rains have fallen since New Years day. Our rivers have been higher than ever before known. Consequently we have had no mail for several weeks. . . .

My children grow finely—the two oldest go to school. . . .

C.F., Indianapolis, to his father, Ludlow, Vermont, March [1828][35]

. . . We have just heard of the death of Dewit Clinton & Major Genl. Brown. The former once held the highest place in the esteem of the West but his late preferences for Jackson has hurt him much.

We have had an open winter but little sugar weather. Mrs. Fletcher and her brother[36] a lad that lives with me have made better than 120 lbs. of the very best domestic sugar. I have a fine sugar orchard on my place. She would take her horse every pleasant day and ride to the place where I have a very pretty improvement a good log cabin & other buildings. . . .[37]

. . . I have consented to consider myself a candidate for the senate again. I know that to continue in that station will not be to my immediate pecuniary interest. But should I be fortunate it may not do a great injury. The district in which I shall be obliged to hold a poll is composed of six counties at this time.[38] It runs back into the new settled parts of the State. It is from North to South 80 miles & from East to West 50 miles. To represent a district of country like this is some what difficult. New Counties are to be formed—

35. The top of this letter was torn off and apparently about half of the contents lost.

36. James Hill. See note 27 above.

37. Between 1826 and 1830 C.F. acquired a total of 450 acres of land about five miles northeast of the edge of the town at that time, in Sections 21 and 22, T16N, R4E. It was northeast of what became the Brightwood section. It was later intersected by the Pendleton road and the Bellefontaine (C.C.C.&I.) Railroad. In his diary for February 4, 1839, C.F. recalled that "on 4 of Feby. 1828 the day on which I was 30 Mrs. Fletcher myself and Jim Hill went to the place with 7 or 8 head of cattle waggon & sugar kettles &c a beautiful day & made on the first day 8 lbs of sugar. Staid over night in the little cabin. . . . It was the first tract of land I bo't at Congress price & 2d piece of land I ever owned. I bot it because it had a spring on it." The Marion County deed records indicate that 160 acres were purchased from James Rariden, 50 acres from Robert Kelly, and the rest from the government. James Hill lived there until 1834. C.F. then rented it to "old David Fletcher" (not a relative). For C.F.'s first land purchase see above, Pt. II. note 81.

38. The district comprised Carroll, Hamilton, Hancock, Hendricks, Madison, and Marion counties. Fletcher was unopposed in his bid for re-election.

their boundaries to be defined which often causes much heat and disatisfaction among the people. . . .

DIARY

January 1st 1829 (Thursday Eve). In former years I kept a Journal or diary of the occurrancies of life and important dai[l]y transactions. And I now most sincerely regret that I had not continued the same with regularity and care down to the present piriod, at the age of thirty one (in Feb. next). Many transactions worthy of note are now forgotton, others the recollection of which is very imperfect, and which I some times have wanted and often may hereafter want in aid of the adjustment in my own mind [of] some difficulty which had grown out of imperfect recollection of facts.

For two or three months past I have felt st[r]ongly impressed with the great importance of religion and have felt sensible of the vanity and great uncertainty of the things of the world and further feeling sensible that I am approaching what is certainly the meridian of life in this country (thirty five). I have been led to inquire into the truth of the scriptures in relation to that intelligent immortal part called the soul which partakes of no part or property of terrestial world—and as the body must return to its parent dust so must that soul return to the God who gave it. In order to satisfy myself on this subject of which at first I had some serious doubts—yes I even found myself to be almost an infidal, I appl[i]ed to a number of my friends who had professed religion (I feel greatful that I had such friends for they have been a consolation and a light which I little suspected). I found on inquiry that they were injoying treasurs of which I was intirely ignorant. I attended several class meetings of the methodist church in which I found further evidences of the good things which religious & pious people enjoy. The last week of the year or rather on Tuesday night before New Years I resolved almost within myself to go forward at the meeting of the methodist in Indianapolis on the watchnight as they called it praying and preaching the old year out and the new year in. It would take volumes to tell the doubts and fears I had in coming into a conclusion on this gr[e]at undertaking. I had for a long time clung close to the world and my affections [were] strongly rooted therein. I was a representative of a district in the senate a lawyer &c &c. All were objections. Legislature in session which all tended to frighten me. However I tremblingly advanced this morning and gave my hand and there openly to the world more st[r]ongly confirmed on my part the covenant I had made to serve God as far as in me lay during the year 1829. The Revr. Mr. Wiley[39] Presiding Elder. Edwin Ray local Preacher at Madison Indiana Preached 2 sermons beginning at 9 o'clock of the old year and preached till 12 when Mr. Armstrong[40] our local preacher gave an exortation and open the door to receive members. I at first felt my unworthyness to such an extent, I resolved not to go forward "until some more convenient season." However I went—and sensible am I now I was too unworthy to make such a profession.

I returned home after meeting, 2 o'clock in the morning, went to bed and rose about ½ hour before sunrise determined to set my house in better order than before. Our brother James Hill also a member of the methodist church performed a duty which before I had always neglected (family prayer) to have performed in my family.

I at 9 o'clock went to the senate chamber as usual. We had much discussion on the final passage of the Michegan Road bill[41]—and we adjourned for that day about 12. The day was remarkably warm and pleasant. About 2 P.M. my friend Rariden came to see me and we took a walk and had a serious conversation on the subject of religion. In the evening after dark I went to see my friend James M.

39. Rev. Allen Wiley (1789–1848). He served as presiding elder of the Indianapolis District, 1829–30 and 1833, and as a stationed preacher 1838–39. Dunn, *Indianapolis,* I, 592. A sketch of his life is given in "Methodism in Southeastern Indiana," by Allen Wiley, in *Indiana Magazine of History,* XXIII (1927), 1–2.

40. James Armstrong, the first stationed minister of the Methodists in Indianapolis. Dunn, *Indianapolis,* I, 592.

41. A land cession to provide means to construct a road from Lake Michigan to the Ohio River was obtained in the treaty concluded by the United States with the Potawatomi Indians in 1826, in which the tribe gave up a strip of land one hundred feet wide from Lake Michigan to the Wabash plus one good section of land for each mile of the proposed road. Charles J. Kappler (ed.), *Indian Affairs. Laws and Treaties* (2 volumes. Washington: U.S. Government Printing Office, 1904), II, 274. In 1827 Congress gave to Indiana the right to dispose of the land and out of the proceeds to locate and build the road. U.S. *Statutes at Large,* IV, 234–35.

Ray. He was just going to the presbyterian meeting house to attend a sunday school meeting, but none of the members attended. We went in—dark—no candles or light. He very affectionatly expressed his Joy that I had on the new years day commenced the service of the Lord. We review[ed] our whole life & proceedings since we had been residents of this place at its first settlement. We covenanted with each other to watch pray for and admonish each other—to suppress all heart burnings in and against the respective churches to which we belonged. As a friend well tried I have had none better than Mr. Ray & Mr. James Blake our absent friend who both have within the past year become the members of the Presbyterian church. The latter of whom in his conversations after I revealed my first convictions to him gave me good counsel & consolation and strength in the steps I was desireous to take. While at the meeting house my friend Ray at my request made a most pathetic and feeling prayer which to me was as the refreshing dews to the parched earth. We parted pleging to be each others friends not only in the world but in the cause of Christ.

I returned home about 8 in the eve and went to the school house & invited Mr. Benjamin Noble[42] to come and stay with me over night. He came spent about 2 hours with me—told me he had had some concern about religion and he then returned home promising to attend our general class meeting Sunday morning. I had forgot to mention that on this day I wrote a letter to Honl. Wm. Hendricks[43] on business for Mr. Skendage[?] (for a pension). Thus I have given a brief sketch of the transactions of the 1st day of January 1829 without any comment.

Jany. 2d. Rose this morning at usual hour. Weather changed—colder. Our pump[k]ins had froze in the corn fodder which had kept without rotting. Went to the senate at the usual hour. This day the bill for the sale of School sections was taken up and by Messrs. Stephen[44] & Raridon objected to and at last referred to a school com-

42. Representative from Franklin County.

43. United States Senator, formerly governor of Indiana.

44. Stephen C. Stevens, senator from Ripley and Switzerland counties and a lawyer. He first became a member of the Brookville bar, then moved to Vevay. He served as representative in the legislature for five sessions and as senator for one and was judge of the state Supreme Court from 1831 to 1836. Monks *et al.* (eds.), *Courts and Lawyers of Indiana,* I, 84; *Indiana Election Returns,* Index.

mittee. I am very anxious that a sale of these lands should be authorized—that we should be stir ourselves in bringing about a system of free schools.[45]

This P.M. I received singular communication from my friend Harvey Gregg on the subject of my joining the church which I answered immediately.[46] In the evening Mr. Armstrong came to my house took tea and we went to church where a young man quite a youth by the name of Bonner[47] preached a sermon from these words "Rejoice & be exceeding glad for great shall be your reward in heaven." This young man is the circuit rider for the fall creek circuit as it is now called. Returnd home very cold the ground white with snow. Received this day a letter from Ovid Butler[48] & one from Dr. Harrison on business. The day passed off without any further notable occurrence.

Janry. 3d 1829. Arose late this morning very cold. Went to the senat chamber at the usual hour. This day the additional apportionment bill passed in the house of Representatives. Very cold. In the Eve the Indianapolis Temperence society[49] met at which Messrs.

45. An act was passed and approved at this session of the Assembly providing for the sale of the sections 16 reserved for school purposes upon the approval of such sale by the majority of the voters of the respective Congressional townships. Money received from the sales was to be lent at 6 per cent on freehold security, the income therefrom to be applied to schools. *Laws of Indiana*, 1828–29, pp. 120–28.

46. Two letters from Gregg to C.F. dated January 2, 1829, are in the Fletcher Papers.

47. Charles Bonner. He was serving the Fall Creek Circuit which included at this time Andersontown and Noblesville. Wiley, "Methodism in Southeastern Indiana," in *Indiana Magazine of History*, XXIII, 320, 325–26.

48. At this time Ovid Butler (1801–1881) was practicing law in Shelby County. Born in Augusta, New York, he came to Indiana in 1817. In 1836, on C.F.'s invitation, he came to Indianapolis and the two lawyers formed a partnership which lasted for eleven years. Butler was a member of the Disciples of Christ Church, and the last thirty years of his life were devoted to that church and to Northwestern Christian, now Butler, University. He served as president of the University for twenty years. Dunn, *Indianapolis*, II, 1165; Nowland, *Sketches of Prominent Citizens*, pp. 523–26.

49. The Temperance Society of Marion County was organized at a meeting in the Methodist meetinghouse (see below, note 66) on October 3, 1828, with the Rev. John Strange serving as chairman and James M. Ray as secretary. It defined its objective as "to discontinue the use of ardent spirits, except as medicine, both by precept and example." Ebenezer Sharpe was made president, James Givan and Henry Bradley vice-presidents, and Ray secretary. Dunn, *Indianapolis*, I, 447.

Sharp[50] Coe & Ray delivered an address. I did not attend having other business to attend to. After Dark Messrs. Goe of Hamilton & young Pendleton[51] called at our house. This Eve I have mad[e] some very slight examination of myself in relation to my fitness to go forward on tomorrow & partake the solemn ordinancies of the Lord's Supper. In this I feel greatly & awfully deficient & doubtful.

Sunday Jay. 4th 1829. I this day went to Br. Phips in the morning to class meeting Revd. Williams class leader old Mrs. Hansan & daughter both there and a number of others. I then returned and went to hear the Revd. Mr. Ray Preach who done himself much credit. I again returned home and Mr. C. Test[52] & Morris Morris called down & spent some time with me. After dark went to meeting again. Revd. Mr. Armstrong preached a powerful sermon from 33d Ezekil 11 vs. After meeting door was opened for those who desired to come forward when old Mr. R. Patterson with his grey hairs advanced. On this day for the first time I went forward & pertook of the solemn ordinance & example set by our Lord & Savior. I had many doubts and many difficulties in coming to a conclusion as to my fitness in so important a step. I felt truly unworthy yet from prayer I satisfied myself that it was my duty to advance that I was unworthy to be called his follower untill I could & would fully confess Jesus Christ before men. This day clear & cold—Water in the well very low.

50. Ebenezer Sharpe, the schoolteacher (see note 24, above). He also served as agent of state for the sale of lots in Indianapolis from 1828 until his death in 1835. *Indiana Executive Proceedings*, p. 278. He was the father of Thomas H. Sharpe who succeeded him as agent of state. The son also served as teller, then cashier of the Indianapolis branch of the State Bank and would later engage in private banking with C.F. upon the expiration of the charter of the State Bank. Nowland, *Early Reminiscences of Indianapolis*, pp. 219–22.

51. William S. Goe, sheriff of Hamilton County, and Harry Pendleton, son of Thomas M. Pendleton, proprietor of the town of Pendleton in Fall Creek Township, Madison County. J. J. Netterville, *Centennial History of Madison County Indiana* (2 volumes. Anderson, Ind.: Historians' Association, 1925), I, 320; Samuel Harden, *The Pioneer* (Greenfield, Ind.: William Mitchell Printing Co., 1895), p. 239.

52. Charles H. Test. He served as representative from Rush County in the 1826–27 session of the General Assembly and was president judge of the sixth circuit, 1830–36.

Monday Jany. 5th. This day very pleasant. I went to the senate at the usual hour. We this day concerned in the amendment made in the house of Rept. to the Michigan Road law—so far as to take the road to Columbus but refused to concur in that part which proposed to carry it thro' Salem &c.[53] In the P.M. Ladi[e]s Misses Walpoles [. . .] Walker from Shelby &c came to the Senate.—We proceeded to the house & elicted Jeri Sulivan agent on the part of the state to convey the land donated in Ohio to this State for canal.[54] This was very pleasant day. Board of Justices met. Elected old John Johnson Treasurer over Danl. Yandes. In the eve my old friend Wm. Ray & Basy spent the eve at our house—Basy performed prayer. Basey stayed over night also old Mrs. Jackson. Basey slept with James & Elijah.

Jany. 7th 1829. On yesterday cloudy & wet. On the eve of the 6th I attended a class meeting at Br. Holidays where much friendly religious feeling was manifested a zeal for the cause of religion. Mr. Dabney[?] came home with us & Mr. Hand[55] invited me to attend a class meeting at Dr. Ross school room but my business would

53. Legislation was enacted at the 1827–28 session of the General Assembly providing further for surveying and marking the road from Lake Michigan to Indianapolis, but the location of its route from there to the river excited such strong sectional feelings that no decision in that regard could be reached. *Laws of Indiana,* 1827–28, pp. 87–89. During the 1828–29 session, as the House and Senate *Journals* show, the debate continued and no further legislation was enacted regarding the location of the road. The two houses were deadlocked—the House insisting on terminating the road at the Falls of the Ohio and the Senate adhering to its amendment which located the road to Columbus and left its route from there to the Ohio to be determined by the Michigan Road commissioners.

54. The reference is to the lands granted to Indiana by act of Congress in 1827 for the construction of a canal to connect Lake Erie with the Wabash River (the Wabash and Erie Canal). A subsequent act of Congress ceded to the State of Ohio all that part of the grant to Indiana which lay within Ohio to enable that state to construct the section of the canal that passed within her limits. Agents representing both states were to be appointed to convey the lands to Ohio and devise a convention between the two states for the operation of the canal. *Messages and Papers relating to the Administration of James Brown Ray,* pp. 377–78n, 493–96. Jeremiah Sullivan, a lawyer, settled in Madison in 1817. He served as judge of the Indiana Supreme Court from 1837 to 1846.

55. Charles J. Hand, who established a "hat manufactory" on Market Street in 1825. Dunn, *Indianapolis,* I, 95; advertisement in Indianapolis *Gazette,* November 22, 1825, and following issues.

not permit it as we had made engagements with a Mr. Tharp to carry our sons James & Elijah in a waggon to Mr. Mallerys.[56]

Jay. 8th. Rose this morning. Cloudy but not could. I rose early and went up to Harrisons[57] store to see Mr. Tharp who was to cary my 2 boys up to Mr. Mallerys. The waggon arrived at ½ past 8 o'clock. At 9 we put our babes our boys one 5½ years old the other 4½. It caused no very extraordinary sensations to part with these childrin. However I soon found that I should miss them very much & in the P.M. I felt much concerned for them as it grew cold. I felt glad that I had sent their uncle James Hill along with them to see them safe along. This being the 8th of Jany. the House & Senate both adjourned to commemorate the Battle of N. Orleans. The Jacksonions had a dinner at Mr. Buchannons.[58] Eve very cold. For the first time attempted to offer up prayers in my family.

Wrote 5 letters this day.

9 10th & 11th of Jany. Very cold a snow covered the ground. We were very much concerned fearing Jas. H[ill] would not [get] our boys up to Mr. Mallerys on the 8th as 9th was very cold & we feared that he would be compelled to travel on that day. We Waited with much impatience untill Sunday 11th a very cold day when Jas. H. returned and we were agreeably disappointed in learning

56. In the Fletcher Papers there is a note to C.F. from Curtis Mallery of Noblesville dated November 28, 1828, saying that he was setting up a school in his house and that Mrs. Mallery would board one or both of the Fletcher boys if C.F. deemed it expedient to send them. Curtis Mallery (1774–1851) had come from New York State to Hamilton County before 1821 and the Mallery family was influential in the development of that county. John F. Haines, *History of Hamilton County, Indiana* . . . (Indianapolis: B. F. Bowen & Co., 1915), p. 955.

Elijah Fletcher recalled in later years, "I could not have been more than four or five years old, when together with my eldest brother, Cooley, I was sent to Noblesville, and placed under the charge of a good old man by the name of Mallory. On the occasion of our departure I remember of mother putting new shoes on me; and of her lifting me into an open wagon, which was to convey us through the woods. . . ." "Recollections of My Mother," a manuscript bound in a notebook in the Fletcher Papers.

57. Probably Alfred Harrison who was then a clerk in the Conner and Tyner store. He became one of the most successful drygoods merchants in the city and was also in banking. Nowland, *Early Reminiscences of Indianapolis,* pp. 156–57.

58. David Buchanan, proprietor of Traveller's Hall, a tavern opened in October, 1825. Advertisement in Indianapolis *Gazette,* October 18, 1825, and following issues.

that he had taken the boys to Mr. M's. on the 8th which was a tolerable warm tho a cloudy day. We felt very much lossed by the absence of James C. & Elijah. They when at home very active & sportive about the house when not at school. Elijah only 4½ years of age I found was more a favorite that I was sensible of untill I had parted with him. He was very sickly from the time of his berth untill about 8 months old at which time he was weaned and immediately began to grow. He has not evinced thus far that aptitude to learn that James has but we discover him to be a sterling independant fellow—talks much—and asks many questions. Cooley as we call him has more art and a little more brilancy than E. but I do not think a better mind.

From the 11th to the 19th. Weather moderate—nothing very particular happening.

Monday 19th of Jay. [*—the 23d*]. Legislature met. This week we had to decide upon the canal bill[59] Bill to Sell school sections and Bill to terminate the Michigan Road. (Weather pleasant.) In the 3 foregoing measures I felt more anxiety about the Passage of the school section bill than the other 2. This Bill remained very doubtful as to its passage. It was difficult to agree on any system. However on Wedensesday we passed the bill as amended in the senate and on Wednesday passed the house. Much anxiety prevailed in both houses relative to the Michigan Road. As it relates to myself I was willing intended [to] give any vote that would terminate a question which when agitated in either branch of the legislature produced very unpleasant feelings. However I felt instructed to vote against taking the Road to the Falls & did accordingly. On Thursday we compleated the principal business of the senate and waited for bills to come from the house. On Thursday eve Genl. Clark[60] and Mr. Armstrong spent the eve with me. On Friday 23d we sat but little part of the day but done a great deal of business but in haste as usual at the close of the session. 23d a very pleasant day.

59. The action of the Assembly in regard to the Wabash and Erie Canal is covered in *Messages and Papers relating to the Administration of James Brown Ray*, pp. 379–82.

60. Marston G. Clark, senator from Washington County, veteran of the Tippecanoe campaign, and major general of the fourth division of the Indiana militia. *John Tipton Papers*, I, 134n.

We adjourned about 4 P.M. to meet at 6 next morning. I had Mr. Rariden to tea with me and in the eve visited the most of my friends.

24 Jay. 1829. Next morning I rose about 5. It was clear with a white frost but not cold. I went to the house & found most had [gone]. I as one of the enrolling Committee presented the last of bills to the Govr. and we adjourned without prayer a little after sunrise. I with sentiments of much attachment parted with my fellow members of the senate. However had some very plain conversation with our President Mr. M. Stap relative to his appointment of chairman of the committee on Indianapolis affairs.[61] I told without the least disguise my sentiments towards him. At about 9 o'clock every member of both houses except Hillis Palmer Ewing Riley & Sweetzer[62] left town. The day vastly pleasant like an April morning. I took home my papers &c and put them out of the way which concluded my legislative business. In the P.M. drew my winters per diem allowance $110.00. Paid $13. thereof to Merrill—$32 to Harrison. Next to see McCarty in the eve & promised to pay him $40. out of the $60. owe him.

In the eve Mr. Gregg called down & spent some time in conversing about our future prospects in the profession of the law which both agreed were gloomy. Mr. Crossly from Madison also called & paid me some money collected for Brownlees.

Altho' I was at home during the session yet I was pleased & even felt much relieved that it was over. During this session I had

61. Milton Stapp (1793–1869) was lieutenant governor and president of the Senate. A veteran of the War of 1812 and a lawyer, he served ten years in the General Assembly, one term as lieutenant governor, was cashier of the Madison Branch of the State Bank and mayor of Madison. He died in Texas. William Wesley Woollen, *Biographical and Historical Sketches of Early Indiana* (Indianapolis: Hammond & Co., 1883), pp. 168–72. As lieutenant governor and president of the Senate he appointed the standing committees. The committee on Indianapolis in the 1828–29 session included James Gregory from Shelby, Decatur, Johnson, and Morgan counties, who was named first and acted as chairman, C.F., Daniel C. Lane of Harrison County, James Rariden of Wayne County, and Marston G. Clark of Washington County. Indiana *Senate Journal*, 1828–29, p. 27. In the preceding two sessions Fletcher had headed this committee.

62. David Hillis and Nathan B. Palmer, representatives from Jefferson County; John Ewing, senator from Knox County; John C. Reily, representative from Knox County; and Philip Sweetser, representative from Bartholomew County.

been brot in direct contact with the interests of some of my warm & personal friends and more especially in the election of Auditor of State[63] and in the vote which I was compelled to give on the change of the Governors house to a state house which I voted against.[64]

Sunday Jay. 25th. This morning pleasant. I attended Br. Foundaries[65] class meeting held at Wattons Shop. Then went to hear the Revd. Mr. Armstrong preach a very able sermon. Returned home & feeling a little drowsy went to bed having been up late the 2 preceeding nights. In the Eve it Rained. Mr. Ingram staid at home. Mrs. F. Eliza & James H[ill] went to church. Mrs. Armstrong returned home with them to stay over night.

Jany. 26th. In the morning cloudy and wet. We have had no rains of consequence for the last six months. Water in our wells very low. This is Monday morning. I arise with some new covenants & promises to my God and myself if I am spared. I intend to commence the business of my profession under the *christian era.* I do intend to abandon that selfish peevishness that restlessness That rancor towards my adversary that exultation in victory and that remorse & private chagrin when defeated. But hereafter if God spares with health & ability to pursue the profession I intend to leave off and discourage lounging in my office as time is precious but I hope to pursue my avocation with renewed dilligence punctuality and attention—to avoid any business or law suits which are

63. The election of the auditor by joint ballot of both houses of the Assembly was held on December 4. On the third ballot Morris Morris was elected, receiving forty votes as against Benjamin I. Blythe's thirty-four and Harvey Gregg's five. Indiana *House Journal,* 1828–29, pp. 41–42.

64. A series of bills concerning the Governor's Mansion, a statehouse, and improvement of the Governor's Circle were introduced into the Senate. None of them passed. The bill for the completion of the Governor's Mansion for a statehouse was postponed indefinitely by a vote of eleven to nine, C.F. voting with the majority. Indiana *Senate Journal,* 1828–29, pp. 153–54. Construction of the Governor's Mansion on the Governor's Circle reserved in the town plat for that purpose was begun in 1827. However, both the location and plan of the mansion were so unsuited to family living that no governor ever lived there. The house was completed and occupied by various state offices and finally demolished in 1857. Rose, *The Circle,* pp. 360–63.

65. John W. Foudray, who came to Indianapolis from Champaign County, Ohio, in 1824. He was active in organizing the Methodist Church. Nowland, *Early Reminiscences of Indianapolis,* p. 175.

not strictly Just in their prosecution so far as I am able to Judge—To deal Justly with all and compell others to deal so with me. I say compell others. This I believe to be my duty, unless others are punctual with me I cannot be so to my neighbor. I have always let my law business *drive me,* I never have drove my business. This neglect has done me much serious injury. It has made me often captious & Jealous towards my professional opponants and rendered me very unhappy. To cultivate good feelings towards them I consider of the highest importance. It has been often suggested to me this winter that I could not live up to my religious professions for the want of time. I have lost much time by long stays and talks with others both at my office & other places. I hereafter intend to use plain dealing with such loungers and I have no doubt that I can gain much valuable time to devote to that cause of the greatest and most consequence to me not only this life (which I have already I believe experienced) and more especially in that eternity—vast eternity to come.

Motto
"Of all forms, reform is the best"

Wedensdy [*Jan.*] *28th.* Cloudy and cold. In the eve went to Baptist prayer meeting at the old Methodist church.[66] Mr. Smock[67] presided very lively—much appearence of a reformation. The night was dark and the snow fell six inches. This day read some law.

Thursday Morning [*Jan.*]*29th.* Snow on more than at any one time for two years past. This day I wrote several letters & received one from Genl. Tipton inclosing several resolutions relative to the appointment of Sheriff & Coroner of Cass County.[68] This eve

66. The "old Methodist church" probably meant the log structure on the south side of Maryland Street between Meridian and Illinois which served as the meetinghouse from 1825 to 1829. In the latter year a brick church, Wesley Chapel, was erected on the southwest corner of Meridian and the Circle which was used until 1846. Dunn, *Indianapolis,* I, 593.

67. The Rev. Abraham Smock, pastor of the Baptist church from 1826 to 1830. In 1829 the Baptists, too, built a brick church, located on the southwest corner of Maryland and Meridian. *Ibid.,* I, 566.

68. Cass County had been organized by act of the session of the General Assembly just adjourned. William Scott was appointed sheriff and Hugh B. McKeen coroner by the Governor on February 19, 1829, to serve until the regular annual election in August. *Indiana Executive Proceedings,* p. 379. Tipton as

visited Mr. McCartys family with Mrs. F. Spent a very pleasant eve. Mr. McCarty is a very intelligent fine friend a man whose accquaintance & friendship is worthy of much respect.

Weather cold & Cloudy. Sent several newspapers to Hendricks & Morgan Counties to announce the change of courts which commence in Hendricks next week. I have spent this week more leisurely than I should.

Friday [*Jan.*] *30th.* Snow melted but little not very cold. In the evening according to appointment & promise I visited my friend C. J. Hand where with my wife spent a very pleasant evening.

Saturday morning Jany. 31st. Rose rather late. Went to the office. Wrote a letter to Edwin Ray at Madison informing him that I would sell my block[?]. Gregg went to the office with me read a speech made by J. Noble in congress which plainly indicates that the man was in a state [of] inebreation. About 12 Govr. Ray called into my [office] to take a copy of some accounts left by Mr. Blair[69] and for the first time he & I had some conversation for the last six months. I have said many hard things against him of which I did not deny but told him from our present situation both members of the Methodist church we at least should be apparently friendly—That I had no political views—that I considered such views entirely incompatible with correct christian conduct. We parted half pledging to treat each other well and so far as it relates to myself I wish that it was in my power not to mention his name again for the next 3 years—for I cannot speak well of him to speak evil is highly improper. May I be preserved from uttering anything about the man either pro or con, for I am almost sure to do him injustice.

In the eve Mrs. Paxton Wilkins & Lady[70] visited & Mr. Ray called.

Indian agent had succeeded in having the Indian agency moved from Fort Wayne to the newly platted town of Logansport designated as the county seat of Cass County. Tipton had not only the agency business in mind with the removal, for he had acquired much land adjoining the town which he sold at handsome profit. *John Tipton Papers*, I, 20–21.

69. Perhaps James Blair, senator from Vermillion County and a brother-in-law of Governor Ray. *John Tipton Papers*, II, 60.

70. John Wilkins (1797–1889) and his wife Eleanor Bruce Wilkins. They came to Indianapolis in 1821. John Wilkins was a partner of Daniel Yandes in various enterprises, a member of the Methodist Church, and one of the first trustees of Indiana Asbury (De Pauw) University. Dunn, *Indianapolis*, II, 1034.

Sunday February 1st 1829. Rose this morning in season Mrs. F. very sick. Called on Dr. Scudder & found she had the symtons of the measles. Jas. Hill a little sick—found he was catching measles. I staid at home to nurse the sick. Read the History of the churches by John Taylor of Kentucky[71] a book wrote in very plain style yet interesting for its developement of the pious characters of the first Christians of the Western country in their early settlements also a disclosure of the many hardships the servants of God under went in these new settlements.

Tuesday [Feb.] 3. Judge Morris Wick Qua[r]les[72] and Brown[73] started for Hendricks circuit court. Ground covered with snow. It grew colder after we left home. We called about 8 miles from here and warmed. Arrived at Danville about sundown where we found Mr. Gregg.

Wedensday Feby. 4th. Very cold. This my birthday. I took this morning in a short ramble tho' very cold a retrospect of my past life. Poor court house. Many rough people attended Court from the North part of Hendrecks County. Nothing occurred this day worthy of note.

Febr. 5th & 6. Attended to a little business.

Saturday [Feb.] 7th. Mr. Qua[r]les & myself came home from Hendricks together. Weather a little modified. Got home about sundown. Found Mrs. Fletcher & James Hill very sick with Measles.

Sunday morning the 8th. My wife some better. It began to rain in the night. Mr. Quarles & myself started about 10 in the morning for Morgan county. Previous to my leaving home Mr. Ingram went & bought me an umbrella. We left while the rain poured down in torrents. Rode about 8 miles when it tourned to snowing & snowed and blew until [we] arrived about one o'clock at old [. . .]. At that time it ceased snowing & became excessively could. We left there and road to Mortinsvill that night—a colder ride I never had. At

71. John Taylor, *A History of Ten Baptist Churches of Which the Author Has Been Alternately a Member . . .* (Frankfort, Ky., 1823; 2d ed. Bloomfield, Nelson County, Ky., 1827).

72. William Quarles, who came to be regarded as one of the first criminal lawyers in the state. Sulgrove, *History of Indianapolis,* p. 241a.

73. Hiram Brown, see above, Pt. II, note 77.

Mortinsvill found bros. Hester[74] Whitcomb Gregg Brown & Judge Morris.

Monday [*Feb.*] *9th.* Very cold but little business done in court.

Tuesday [*Feb.*] *10.* A trial for a rape came on in which one of the most disgraceful scenes was devel[op]ed I ever witnessed. It was a young woman about 16 complaining of her father whom she charged with committing a rape in the presence of her mother.

Wednesday [*Feb.*] *11th.* Wick Brown & Qua[r]les & self came [home]. Gregg Morris &c went on to Monroe. This a very severe day. Arrived home about [blank] found Mrs. Fletcher in much better health almost recovered from her measles. This was an excessive cold day.

Thursday [*Feb.*] *12th.* I started with young Mr. Ricd. Conner[75] who is no[w] a clerk in Harrisons store for Hamilton County to see my boys James & Elijah at Mr. Mallorys at school. This was another very cold day. I arrived at Mr. Mallories about sundown. There I found my boys in good health. James had felt & still felt the effects of his last fall ague. Both highly pleased to see me. They were very small to be sent from home to school one 6 & the other 4. I left there the next day & came to Wm. Conners & staid over night. This was the 13th.

[*Feb.*] *14 Saturday.* Arrived at home. This night Mrs. F. taken very sick with the pleurisy.

[*Feb.*] *15th Sunday.* Mrs. Fletcher very sick with pleurisy and dangerously so.

From Monday 16th untill Saturday 21st. Very cold. Indianapolis crowded with slays. I was confined at home to nurse Mrs. Fletcher who was dangerously sick with the measles. This week received 2 letters one from Father the other from my friend Jas. Blak[e].

Saturday Febry. 21 1829. Not very cold but so much so snow did not melt. This eve the Indianapolis legislature[76] celebrated

74. Craven P. Hester. Monks *et al.* (eds.), *Courts and Lawyers of Indiana,* Index.

75. Son of William Conner.

76. In anticipation of the removal of the capital from Corydon to Indianapolis a number of young men of the town organized the Indianapolis Legis-

Washingtons birthday as the 22 came on Sunday. Messrs. McGuire[77] Bolton[78] &c delivered addresses at the court house in the Senate Chamber. Did not go in consequence of wife's sickness.

Sunday Febr. 22d. Rose late this morning and at 11 A.M. went to Methodist church to hear the revd. Mr. Richy preach. This day Sunday as it was great many people from the country in with slays. Very cold. Snow did not melt snow 8 inches deep. The Baptist Church met at the court house—2 baptised—Jeptha Bradly & a Miss Kimberly. Ice cut away at the River for the purpose. Minister the revd. Mr. Smock. I this day concluded by & with the advise & consent of Mrs. Fletcher & Ingram to visit my old father in Vt. this insuing Spring who last week writes me that he is laboring under great bodily infirmities and does not expect to live but a short time. My business which has become a little confused is not in a situation to leave. I have much important business to do as a lawyer. I have let too many precious hours escape without much account. If I go to see my father I must make somewhat of a sacrifise. My business of law has indeed been poorly attended. Mr. Ingram does everything I could ask yet as for myself I have not so closely devoted myself to study as I should have done. I hope to repair my neglect by making immediate amends. I consider it my religious duty to be industrious.

Friday the 6th of March. My well tried & faithful friend K.A. Scudder departed this life after lingering illness—died about ten minutes past 3 o'clock P.M. of a fever brought on by exposure after having the measles. Mortification shortly set in after several days fever. By will which I drew for Dr. Scudder I became his executor. Dr. Scudders remains after a funeral sermon preachd by the Revd. Mr. Armstrong was followed by large concourse of people to the grave yard on Sunday 8th of March.

---

lature in the fall of 1824. It was a discussion and debating society which lasted some ten years, meeting weekly throughout the year for the education and amusement of the community. Dunn, *Indianapolis,* I, 81.

77. Douglass Maguire, one of the proprietors of the Indianapolis *Indiana Journal.* See above, Pt. III, notes 8 and 39.

78. Nathaniel Bolton, who, with his stepfather George Smith, founded the Indianapolis *Gazette.* See above, Pt. II, note 44.

April 1st on Wedensday [*—April 4*]. My worthy friend James Paxton was taken with a fit of the billious collick. On Thursday night just as I sat down to tea Joseph Smith the boy that lives with Col. Paxton called on me & informed me that he was sick & desired to see me. I went immediatly & found him in great pain & distress. He told me that he desired me to draw his will but rather put it off till next morning hoping to be better. I sat up till about 2 o'clock in the morning with Mrs. P. & returned home & slept till sunrise at which I went again to see him & found him worse. I immediatly set about drawing his will from a memorandum I had taken the night before. He was in great pain during the day but in his right mind. In the P.M. I completed the will Read it to him which he signed. On Saturday the 3 he became more easy & entirely reconciled to die. Gave happy evidences of his acceptance with his maker & exhorted his friends to prepare to meet the awful charge. During the day Mr. [. . .] & the Revd. Mr. Moreland[79] were invited to pray with him. Rested tolerably easy during the night & on Sunday rather slept away the P.M. & expired without a groan in the P.M. about 4 o'clock.

May 1st 1829. During all the month of April cold wet & frosty weather without any signs of vegitation of consequence untill the 26–7–8–9–& 30. Peech trees mostly dead—froze to death—some few Just blossaming. May 1st a cloudy but very pleasant day—vegitation advancing rapidly trees Just begin to look green. Mrs. F. myself & 4 boys[80] (two oldest Cooley & Elijah having returned from Hamilton county on 29ult.) compose our only family which has heretofore been large. I have Just received a letter from my father by which I find he confidently expects a visit from me during the summer. I am in a great doubt what to do.

Monday May 4th. Courts Sp[Supreme] & D[istrict] of the U.S.A. both set to day but little business in either. I feel down spirited in consequence of my great doubts as to the propriety of my visiting my father this summer who is very old & frail. My business is urgent at home so I have for some days been balancing between

79. The Rev. John R. Moreland, who served as pastor of the Presbyterian Church from 1829 to 1832. Sulgrove, *History of Indianapolis*, p. 392.

80. A fourth son, Miles Johnson Fletcher, was born June 15, 1828.

duty to myself in a pecuniary point of view & my obligations to those for whom I am intrusted with business and my duty to my old father and mother. I have however this day came to the conclusion to risk all consequences of loosing business & perhaps indanger the very reputation I have already acquired for punctuality & shall if nothing unseen interposes visit my father & mother & trust to my good maker for the consequences. Peeches what few there are now just in the bloom. No planting done yet. 3 young Hitts[81] came along & staid with us that night.

Suday August 2d 1829. On the 25th of May last I started with Mrs. Paxton & Joseph Moore for Urbana Ohio (then being on my way to Vermont to visit my father). We arrived at Urbana the 29th of the same month Where I spent the 30th & 31st days with my old friends & aquaintance. On the first of June I took horse with John Hill (bro. in law, Mr. Moore having gone on in the stage) and proceded to A. S. Hunts at the crossing [of] the big Scioto where I came up with Mr. M. & the next day we proceded on our way to the lake in the stage and arrived on the 2d of June at Ft. Ball. Staid over night and next day passed upper Sandusky and fell in company with Mr. Martin Whitmond & arrived in stage at Sandusky City in the P.M. of the same day.[82]

Decr. 25th 1829. Christmass morning. At 4 o'clock called Thomas Moore a boy of about 16 years of age living with us during the winter & going to school. He rose & my 3 oldest boys. Not that usual firing of guns & parade that is usual. Temperance & Sabbath School societies have at this time in our place produced almost a calm. This morning cloudy & warm. Senate meets as usual. Have

81. Probably the children of the Rev. Thomas S. Hitt, a Methodist minister stationed in Indianapolis in 1829 and 1830.

82. No diary or journal covering this trip has been found. On August 2, 1829, Elijah Fletcher wrote from Lynchburg to his father, "Calvin arrived here Tuesday the 14th July and left us Monday morning after the 19th, staying 5 days. He seemed very impatient to get home but still, I believe, well pleased with his trip and glad that he had taken it. He said he felt better than he had for four years, had a good appetite and in good spirits. From what I could learn I expect, what with ill health, the *methodist* and the cares of his family and complicated business, he had [illegible] become much dejected and low spirited before he undertook this trip . . ." Von Briesen (ed.), *Letters of Elijah Fletcher,* p. 106.

with Brown & Cobern[83] to assist a yallow womman & 3 childrin who are claimed by her master a Virginian[?] by name of Suel.[84] Mr. Ingram with us but is to leave for Lafayette in a few days where he expects to settle permenantly. A[t] 12 o'clock went to the court house where woman & 3 childrin girls oldest about 10 years were brought forward. The house was full. Most of the members of the legislature were present. Great excitement among the people of the county. Their sympathies were alive for the woman & childrin while the members of the legislature & some few who in our own place yet countenance the horrid trafic were almost clamerous for the pretended owner. Messrs. Ungles & Linconfelter[85] witness for the man—& Hanna Stoops Govr. Ray & Johnson[86] for the woman. After evidence thro' I spoke in behalf of the woman & read law. After me Mr. Wick spoke in oposition with much severity & abuse against persons & against me—all of which I overlook in him. Mr. Brown then answered & Hannagin[87] closed for the claimant. Much prejudice was raised against several witnesses who testified in favor of the woman in consequence of some intemperate lan-

83. Law partners Hiram Brown (see above, Pt. II, note 77) and Henry P. Coburn. The latter, a native of Massachusetts and graduate of Harvard College, came to Corydon, Indiana, in 1816 and to Indianapolis in 1824. He was appointed clerk of the Supreme Court in 1820 and served until 1852 when the office was made elective under the new state constitution. Coburn, like C.F., was very active in the promotion of free public schools and a strong temperance man. He died in 1854. Dunn, *Indianapolis*, II, 1235–37.

84. This was the first case involving the fact that Indiana was a free state and the protection of Negroes in their legal rights that that fact implied. William Sewell, a Virginian emigrating from Virginia with four female slaves, was detained because of high water in Indianapolis for a few days. Someone told the woman that in Indiana, a free state, they were free and they left Sewell. He retook them and they were then brought into court on a writ of habeas corpus. Indianapolis *Indiana Journal*, December 30, 1829; Dunn, *Indianapolis*, I, 239.

85. Perhaps Wilford Ungles (see Pt. V, note 75) and Archibald Lingenfelter. A sketch of the latter is in Nowland, *Early Reminiscences of Indianapolis*, pp. 186–87.

86. Robert Hanna and James B. Ray. Stoops and Johnson have not been identified.

87. Edward A. Hannegan, lawyer of Covington. He was appointed prosecuting attorney for the first judicial circuit at the 1829–30 session of the General Assembly. *Indiana Executive Proceedings*, p. 305. He later served in the state legislature and as a congressman and United States senator.

guage used by them while giving in testimony. Trial closed about 8 o'clock at night & Judge took time 26th to give Judgment.

Decr. 26th 1829. In the morning wet & cloudy tho warm. Mrs. F. curing & making Bacon from pork bought of Thos. Beeler & brought in yesterday about 9 & 10 pound—very fat & cornfed at $2. per cwt.

Senate met at 9. Attended in the A.M. At 12 adjourned till Monday morning. At 2 P.M. Judiciory committee met. After business over I returned home. Did not attend to hear Judge Morris give his opinion in the case of the colored woman & 3 childrin but learned from Mr. Ingram that the Judge decided that a man abandoning a Slave state with his Slaves for the purpose of setling in a free state the moment, the moment that his slaves & himself reached a free state they were free. This decision will produce great excitement. Most at least a majority of the members of the legislature were of opinion from some exciting cause Just at this time not from sober reasoning from the principles contained in the constitution & laws of the country. What violence what outrages may yet be committed on the poor negroes I know not. I have discharged my duty towards them & in accordence with my own sober convictions.

This night I have written a letter to Asa Procter of Proctersvill Vt.

Decr. 31st 1829. This day the last of the year was peculiarly pleasant perhaps more so than any other for 2 months. In the legislature we passed the bill thro' the Senate for the establishing the Michigan Road as it is called.[88] In the eve went with Mrs. F. to church. Bro. Wily first preached—address followed by Mr. Ray then succeeded Br. Hitt. But few auditors. Returned home about 10—all abed.

88. Two laws concerning the road were enacted at this session. One accepted the route laid out by the commissioners going from Lake Michigan to Indianapolis and determined that south of Indianapolis the road should pass through Greensburg and terminate at Madison. The other act provided for the letting of contracts for construction. *Laws of Indiana*, 1829–30, pp. 111–14, 114–16.

V

Diary and Letters of CALVIN FLETCHER *January 1, 1830–July 4, 1834* and Journal of a Visit to Ohio of SARAH HILL FLETCHER *June 8–29, 1830*

Jany. 1st 1830. Thomas Moore & Orinderio Crombaugh[1] rose early this morning. I got up a little before daylight dressed wrote a little. Had some conversation with Mr. Ingram about our past lives for the last 9 years. The sun rose very clear—warm as an April morning. The Senate met & continued in session till about 11 A.M. then adjourned in the P.M. on a Judiciary committee. Bo't a bible & made a present of it to Mr. White from Lafayette. Paid Mr. Thomas Beeler for about 1000 wt. of pork at $2.00 per cwt. cash. In the eve with Mrs. Fletcher to Mr. John [James?] Blakes. Spent the evening &c. This new years has not been spent in our place as usual—not a gun been fired no childrin running the street calling for New Years gifts &c.

February 4th 1830. This day rather cold cloudy—snow on the ground about 3 inches. Town looks rather gloomy legislature having Just adjourned. I this day received a letter from my father & a document from Mr. Hendricks. Had some conversation with N. Noble who recommends me to prepare for political life. I feel desireous to live more independent than political life will allow. I have much business on hand some of a disagreeable nature. James

1. In the Diary under date of September 26, 1835, C.F. wrote: "Dorio Crumbaugh is this day 18 years of age & her term expires for which she was bound." She apparently lived with the family under a contract, performing household chores and receiving in return board and room.

Hill is now hauling wood for me. Mr. C. Mallery is now boarding with me—teaching school.

Sarah Hill Fletcher's Journal of a Visit to Ohio, June 8–29, 1830

Tuesday June the 8th 1830. Mr. Fletcher & myself set out on a journey from Indianapolis to Urbana with an intention of going through several Towns in Indiana. The 1st Eve. we arived at Mr. Banks about 8 o clock ten miles from town. The rode was very bad and rained on us several miles. Weddensday we set off early breck-fasted at Dr. Tracy's. Came to Rushvill staid with Mr. Pew[2] found his lady a very pleasant woman and heard of the Oliver family.

Thursday 10th we arived at Connersville half past 9 o clock put up at Mr. Claypool's.[3] I found a very great contrast between the two lanlady's Mrs. P. & Mrs. C. I there washed my riding dress, red considerable in the Western Suvenor,[4] Staid all night.

Friday we came to Brookvill about noon stoped at Mr. Noble's took breckfast. His lady did not altogether please me. Old Mother Noble has just called on me. I feel mortafied that I did not call on Mrs. Russell before I left home. Mrs. Phipps's niece called to see me.

We staid all night 4 miles east of brookville at a Mr. Vandikes. Saturday we came to Oxford took breckfast walked half mile to see Mrs. Cooly[5] dined with her. The family appear poor. We saw the collage at a distance. It is an eligant bilding. We had not time to go

2. Reu Pugh who not only had a tavern but also a grocery, tanyard, and shoemaking shop in Rushville. *History of Rush County, Indiana* (Chicago: Brant & Fuller, 1885), p. 630.

3. Newton Claypool received a license to operate a tavern in Connersville in 1819. He served six terms as representative and two as senator from Fayette County. Frederic I. Barrows (ed.), *History of Fayette County Indiana* (Indian-apolis: B. F. Bowen & Co., 1917), p. 520.

4. *The Western Souvenir, a Christmas and New Years Gift for 1829,* edited by James Hall (see Pt. VI, note 132) and published in Cincinnati in 1828 by N. and G. Guilford, and printed by W. M. Farnsworth. This little book, 3½ by 5½ inches, 324 pages, is now a collector's item. Among the contributors of the fifty-seven pieces that it contains, besides James Hall, were Timothy Flint, John B. Dillon, and Benjamin Drake. The best known piece is Morgan Neville's "The Last of the Boatmen," a tale of Mike Fink. Buley, *The Old Northwest,* II, 636–37.

5. Widow of James Cooley. He had died in Peru while serving as the United States chargé d'affaires there. See above, Pt. I, note 18.

through it and view the differant rooms. In the P.M. we road to Hamalton crossed the Miama River on the toll bridg, staid all night at Mr. Blares. Sunday morning rode to Springfield,[6] breckfasted at Mr. Stearn's tavern had the best and fullest table that I have seen on the rode. He is a notheran man & his wife a dutch woman.

We left Springfiel at 4 o clock arived at Cincinati after sun down put up at the broad way hotell. Monday morning Mr. F. bought for me a fan & reticule. Saw uncle Oliver. We could not well get over going there. In the Eve we walked down. Aunt recieved us very kindly. They were makeing preparations to visit Georgetown Ky. to see their son. I think they indulge thir childrin very much. Became acquainted with Mrs. Fletcher[7] living near to uncle O. Went to the infant school with her, and was much gratafied to see the progress such small children had made in four weeks.

Monday Eve. Mr. F. went on board of a steamboat to Lewisville. I never felt more anxiety about him in my life. Through difficulty's & danger's he returned safe thursday nite.

Tuesday Eve I visited the museum. Thursday I went to see the paper mill & took a ride on the rail road carridge. Fri. I went on a steam boat made me sick. In the Eve we set out for Urbana. Staid all night in Reding. Set off early next morning breckfasted in Lebanon. In the P.M. it rained very hard. We stoped under a shelter. Staid all night in Xenia and till after breckfast Sunday morning, then rode to the yellow springs. Took breckfast again. We walked round & looked at all the curiosities. It is a beautiful situation, white buildings, a great many large green trees, and seder groves. I saw the first high rock that I ever saw. We staid about one hour & had to pay 1 dollar. We set out from that place. A Mr. Dunlap fell in company with us. It rained very hard & we stoped under some t[r]ees. We arived in Springfield at 2 o clock stoped at Mr. Wordens staid till 9 next morning then rode to Urbana about 12 o clock. As quick as our horses were put up we had an invitation to a wedding dinner at Mrs. G. We did not attend. Mon. Eve came to Fa[t]hers. They all appeared glad to see us.

Tues. [June] 22d. Mr. F. went to town, mother & myself went

6. The name was changed to Springdale for postal reasons; it was fifteen miles north of Cincinnati, on the road to Hamilton.

7. Probably the wife of Calvin Fletcher of Cincinnati. See note 95, below.

to see Malinda Stretch. Wed. we visited aunt Caty Harbo & Mr. Arrowsmith. Thursday I called on Mother Dunlap and James Watt. Fri. I borrowed a horse, started to Urbana met Mr. F. on the bridg. He went back with me.

We drank tea with Mrs. G. staid all night arose early next morning took breckfast with Mrs. Colwell. Called on Mrs. Chaplen. About 10 o clock Mr. F. & myself walked out to old Father Hitts, returned to Mr. Pearson's and dined. Called on sister Sweet took tea with Mother Luce staid all night. Next morning, Sunday, after breckfast we went to Fathers, returned to town in the Eve. staid till Tuesday morning. We arose at 3 o clock rode to Fathers for breckfast, then left for home with glad harts. Staid all night at a farm house.

C.F., Indianapolis, to his father, Proctorsville, Vermont, August 16, 1830[8]

. . . The fore part of June Mrs. Fletcher & myself visited Ohio. We went to Cincinnati. . . . Mrs. F. spent near a week in Cincinnati while I was absent down the Ohio River.* On my return we Journeyed to Urbana, passed thro' Oxford the residence of my friend Cooley's wife who has returned from South America & we spent one day with her. We went horse back as the roads in going & coming in this state & Ohio which we travelled will not admit of Journeying with a waggon the time of year we were absent. Mrs. F. rides horse back with great ease & is very choice or rather proud of a good horse & riding dress. I took great pains to show her Steamboats, Steam engines *museams* paper mills—Sunday schools—Infant schools high life & low life. Nothing improves even a woman with good common sense more than to travel—to put up at some of the best houses & stay at some of the meanest. Let her keep a Journal

* On the margin of the first page of the letter C.F. wrote: "When I went from Cincinnati to Louisville aboard a steam boat she received a small snag in her side & almost filled before it was discovered—about one half mile from land when it was discovered—I witnessed a scene of great confusion. She was run ashore and all was saved—but we were badly alarmed.

8. This letter is in the collection of Sweet Briar College, Sweet Briar, Virginia. A photocopy was sent to the Indiana Historical Society by Martha von Briesen, director of public relations of the College.

& observe all things as women usually do & in a Journey of four hundred miles which we took she must learn many things & more especially how to be agreeable to strangers & to keep a neat house when at home.

At Urbana we met with many friends who appeared glad to see us. We returned home after an absence of 4 weeks—both in excellent health. Found our childrin well—2 oldest I left in the care of a very favorite schoolmaster who boarded with us & the 2 youngest we sent to an uncle or rather to Mrs. Fletcher's brother who lives 5 miles distant on a farm.

Our trip cost us one hundred dollars tho' I had some business two law suits to settle & arrange as Executor at Urbana which will ultimately pay my expenses.

At Urbana I had an opportunity to learn the progress of the men of my profession who were doing business there when I first went to the country & I had the conceit to think that as a business man I was equal to them.

Our season has been remarkably dry so much so as to injure the corn crops very much. Our crops of small grain were excellent & our fruit trees are breaking down with their burthens. Thousands of peaches can be had for gathering of them.

August & September are our most gloomy months in the whole year—if we get safely through them we feel safe. Our sickly season has began—great numbers of my neighbors are down & three of our children are now sick with fevers & the little girl we are raising. The diseases do not as yet discover anything of the malignant cast. In consequence of the Journey we took Mrs. F. & myself are in good health as yet.

Until their late sickness my 4 boys were growing & doing well. We have lately brought them all to eat with us at the table. The eldest is now able to water and feed my horses & I rejoice at the prospect of having my own servants or rather childrin to wait upon me. The eldest is a Fletcher in form and appearance but has an excellent good disposition—is generous & very affectionate—still afraid of specters & ghosts after dark, & notwithstanding he associates with his next brother & sleeps with him & would of course communicate all his fears to him yet none but the eldest has these slavish fears which troubled me & you in our boyish days. You told me once that you considered it constitutional & that it came from the female branch of your own family.

As to futurity & things to come you say in your last that you are in great doubt & that you do not give yourself much concern about it. My first strong impressions as to religious matters I learned from father. They were strongly impressed on my mind. You must have felt the same then or would not have had the power to communicate to me or your other childrin in so forcible manner. You since have changed your views. I believe you were once right on these matters but are now wrong or that you are now in doubt and confusion. When you had the strongest faith were the days of your happiness & greatest worldly prosperity. In this I can't be mistaken. Should I not then stand to the faith—should I not then seek for that which gave you the greatest quantity of earthly happiness? If I am wrong tell me so.

Many very poor people have emigrated from the southern to this state. They have never had the advantages of those who came from the free states. These people in the sickly seasons suffer immensly for the want of medical aid & other necessaries. I have this day visited several poor families of this kind & found them very low & our present sickness presents rather a gloomy aspect. In my next letter I may have to communicate more sad intelligence.

As for Stoughton I have been looking for a letter from him. I depend on his visiting me next summer according to agreement. I shall expect to be able to bear his expences here & back & give him a horse saddle and bridle to return with if he prefers returning on horseback. In the meantime I look to him to use every exertion to make you and mother comfortable and himself respectable. . . .

I am reasonably prosperous in my wordly concerns. I spend my money I think liberally—yet I am very industrious. I have been blessed with a Judgment to calculate well as to some investments I have made in lands which have raised much in value. I have not heard from any of our family except Miles since I wrote you last. I take E.'s paper which is also taken by two presses here. The people speak here highly of a toast E. Gave at Mr. Barber's dinner at which

E. acted as one of the Vice Presidents.[9] E. is a great and good man as a brother I like him much. "By his fruits I know him." As for Miles I know him not by his fruits for I never saw any. . . .

DIARY

Dec. 25 1830 (Saturday) [*—Dec. 27*]. The legislature adjourned on yesterday until Monday. Cloudy cold weather. I had several papers & letters which I read. Wife went to quarterly meeting. Brought home for dinner a Miss Brenton & Oneel. Mr. Ingram was here. I waited with much patience for J. Hill to bring home James Cooley who is going to school at his house.[10] I wanted him to come in to take him to a barber shop to show him a variety of pretty pictures. He did not come in Saturday. Sunday weather moderate but snow fell fast. Mr. Armstrong preached. Monday very cold & clear. The methodist Bible society met & I had the appointment of President to which I objected considering my piculiar situation—holding a devise of $300 for said society.

January 1 1831. This day very pleasant. Legislature in session. Snow on the ground about 2 inches with ice at the bottom. Many people in town. John Hill[11] came in with Mr. Butterfield.[12] I bought

9. Philip Pendleton Barbour (1783–1841), a member of Congress from Virginia was honored by citizens of Lynchburg at a public dinner on July 13, 1830. Among the several volunteer toasts which followed a speech by Barbour was one offered by Elijah Fletcher who served as third vice-president of the affair: "States Rights and United States' Rights: While we vigilantly guard the one, let the Whiskey Insurrection in Pennsylvania, the Hartford Convention, and the threats of Southern Nullifyers remind us that the other may be invaded." Lynchburg *Virginian*, July 15, 1830.

10. Since the first of December James Cooley had been boarding with his Uncle James Hill at his home on C.F.'s farm northeast of the town and attending a nearby school. James Hill had married Maria Harbour of Urbana, Ohio, on June 30, 1829. Nowland, *Sketches of Prominent Citizens*, pp. 164–65.

11. Brother of James Hill and Sarah Hill Fletcher. He was born in 1812. During the previous year he had come to Indianapolis and was living with his brother. Nowland, *Early Reminiscences of Indianapolis*, pp. 234–35.

12. John Butterfield who settled in Clay Township, Morgan County, in 1820. Noah J. Major, *The Pioneers of Morgan County* (Indiana Historical Society *Publications*, V, No. 5, Indianapolis, 1915), p. 425; Charles Blanchard (ed.), *Counties of Morgan, Monroe and Brown Indiana* (Chicago: F. A. Battey & Co., 1884), pp. 119–20. He and his son Velorous were widely known as "bee men" and for years helped C.F. gather honey.

a hat & handkerchief for John. James Hill hauling wood with horses. James Cooley was to have come in but was left behind but he absented himself towards night & arrived home about dusk. We were surprised at his appearance it being very cold & he never had travelled the road alone before in his life. His shoes were bad.

Sunday January 2d. Pleasant day. Mr. Hitt preached. People came to church with Slays. James & John Hill came in & took Cooley back with them.

3d Jany. Snow & rain all day. The earth being covered with ice before the fall of the last Snow the rain has melted the snow & left the same quantity of ice.

Jany. 4th. Very cold & slipery. Col. Jenners[13] Ch. Ewing[14] & others came to town.

Jany. 9th Sunday. Very cold. The whole earth been covered with Snow for the last 8 days—very slipery. In the fore noon went with Calvin & James to hear Mr. Hitt Preach. In the P.M. took James out to his uncles to school. Returned in the eve read some in the Diplomatic correspondence of the first Congress.

Monday Jany. 10. Cold clear morning—ice as yesterday. I fear much disagreeable discussion [in] the legislature this week. It is expected the Governor will nominate Supreme Judges.[15]

13. William M. Jenners of Lafayette. He was one of the town's first lawyers, a volunteer in the Black Hawk War, and the first cashier of the Lafayette branch of the State Bank. R. P. DeHart (ed.), *Past and Present of Tippecanoe County Indiana* (2 volumes. Indianapolis: B. F. Bowen & Co., 1909), I, 204–206, 274, 476.

14. Charles W. Ewing, of Logansport, a lawyer who served as president judge of the eighth judicial circuit from December, 1836, until his resignation in 1839. He died in Wisconsin in 1854. *Indiana Executive Proceedings*, p. 312; Monks *et al.* (eds.), *Courts and Lawyers of Indiana*, II, 584–85.

15. The battle that Governor Ray waged with the Senate over the appointment of judges of the Supreme Court is covered in *Messages and Papers relating to the Administration of James Brown Ray*, pp. 15–16, 627–34, 634–35. There was strong sentiment in favor of the reappointment of the incumbent judges, Isaac Blackford, Jesse L. Holman, and James Scott. On January 12, Ray reappointed Blackford, but dropped Holman and Scott and named Stephen C. Stevens and John T. McKinney. Blackford was unanimously confirmed immediately and after two weeks Stevens and McKinney were confirmed by votes of eleven to ten, C.F. voting for the confirmation of Stevens and against confirmation of McKinney. Indiana *Senate Journal*, 1830–31, pp. 259–61, 395–96. Ray was accused of using his appointive power to try to gain support for his efforts to win election to the United States Senate.

C.F., Indianapolis, to Joseph Hill, near Urbana, Ohio, January 30, 1831

. . . Our four boys are growing well—Elijah the second one we have sent about 24 miles distant to go to school to an old friend of ours.[16] It costs us about 50 cts week for board. He went last November. His mother has visited him once he being a little unwell. James Cooley has boarded with his uncle James since the first of December and gone to school with his uncle John. There is an excellent school about one mile from James's. John & Cooley have been almost two months & have not missed but one day. They are learning fast. John had advanced to the single rule of three. James Hill has attended at night school and kept up with John. The School Master boards with them. . . .[17]

DIARY

Febry. 4th 1831. Legislature in Session (windmills & John Ewing). The snow is about 18 inches deep upon the surface in the cleared land. The snow has laid on for about 1 month. This day very cold. Thermometer below zero. James Hill came in & staid with us on his road to Dabneys for hogs.

Sunday Decr. 25th 1831 (Christmas). Snow about 2 inches deep. Legislature adjourned yesterday at 12 for Monday. James Hill & wife came in with Slide.[18] In P.M. went to my office. Done some business. Received a letter from Ingram[19] at Covington where he

16. In his "Recollections of My Mother," in the Fletcher Papers, Elijah wrote: "The Winter of 1830–31 I spent at Mr. Mallorys. I forget whether mother carried me there or not. But I do recollect that she came to see me when I lay there dangerously sick with an ulcerated throat. She watched over me day and night until I recovered. She came up alone on horseback through the then almost unbroken forest. Indeed she was well skilled in horsemanship."

17. The school and schoolmaster have not been identified.

18. The Fletchers were now living in a house located on lot 12, square 42, on the south side of East Ohio Street between Alabama and New Jersey streets. They had moved there from the Kentucky Avenue house in the preceding spring. Diary entry for January 1, 1840. According to the Marion County deed records the lot and house were bought from Edwin Ray for $400; the deed was dated December 29, 1830.

19. Andrew Ingram had opened a law office in Lafayette and was living there.

had gone for business for a house in Phila. Yesterday bought a box of paints for James Cooley as a christmass gift. He has a desire to paint but I dout his taste. This day Sunday. Went to love feast with James Hill. He returned home on account of John's being in bad health. C[l]oudy. Israel[20] & my Brother Stoughton.[21]

Sunday January [1] 1832. This day cold snowing all day. Wrote two letters—one to Elijah & one to Asa Proctor. John & Sweet came in on foote to meeting & returned home the same night.

February 4th 1832. My birth day—34 years old. Very muddy cloudy weather.

Spent part of the day in my office. Mud so deep that I could scearcely get from street to street. Called on Noble [. . .]. Spent some hours with Messrs. M. Roberts Cravens & Hubbart at Browns tavern.[22] They were from Illinois on business. Most of the members of the legislature are gone. Waters are very high. I have heretofore concluded that I should on this day resign my seat in the senate[23]

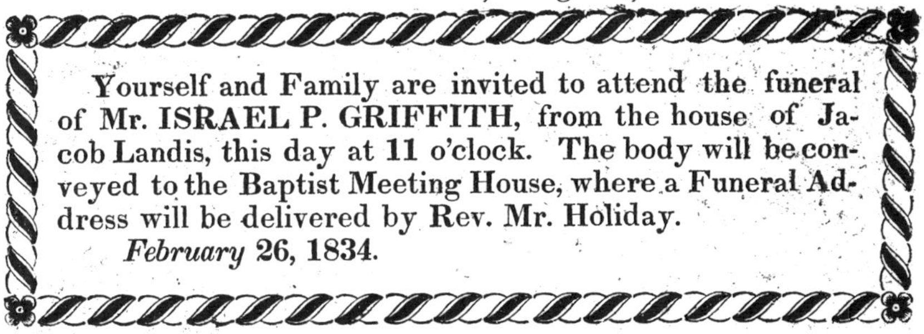

Yourself and Family are invited to attend the funeral of Mr. ISRAEL P. GRIFFITH, from the house of Jacob Landis, this day at 11 o'clock. The body will be conveyed to the Baptist Meeting House, where a Funeral Address will be delivered by Rev. Mr. Holiday.

***February* 26, 1834.**

One of a collection of printed funeral notices and invitations in the Fletcher Papers, reflecting a custom of that day.

20. Israel P. Griffith. The March 1, 1834, Indianapolis *Indiana Journal,* carried a notice of the death of Griffith on February 25, "a young man of fine promise, who enjoyed the esteem of all who knew him." See also entry for February 4, 1833, below.

21. Upon the death of Jesse Fletcher, C.F.'s father, in February, 1831, the Fletcher farm at Ludlow, Vermont, was rented and Stoughton, C.F.'s youngest brother, came to Indianapolis. He was twenty-three years old at the time.

22. In 1826–27 Basil Brown built the Union Hotel, a two-story brick on the site of John Hawkins' Eagle Tavern on the north side of Washington Street a half block east of Meridian. It became the Democratic headquarters. Sulgrove, *History of Indianapolis,* p. 269.

23. C.F. had been re-elected to the Senate in August, 1831, defeating George L. Kinnard by only eleven votes. *Indiana Election Returns,* p. 210. See below, pp. 388–89.

but it seems rather difficult to accomplish this. If Wm. Conner had consented to run I could have resigned with my own & especially that of my friends whom I was to consult. I feel it my duty to double my dilligence. My professional business has accumulated upon my hands to an undiminished degree. My collecting is to a very considerable extent increased. I feel that I have a great responsibility resting upon me—a large & helpless family. I pray that I may have wisdom to govern myself discharge all my duties to my father who art in heaven to my family & to the common country [in] whose happiness & prosperity I feel a deep interest.

Our place is increasing in wealth & prosperity. If I do not accumulate property and all event keep even with the world & have the means for the glorious privilege of being independent, I must also loose much oppertunity of doing good. I possess an uneasy & fretful disposition. I wish I could perform my duties [to] myself family to those who employ me.

Feby. 5th Sunday 1832. Attended preaching in the evening—Br. [. . .] exhorted.

Feby. 6. Waters high. No Brookvill mail & several mails turned back that started on Saturday. Illinois Gentlemen left in a carriage with Mr. Finch. Mr. Thornton left here. Been ingaged in my office. In P.M. went to see br. Strange[24] who is very feeble. Don't think he will survive many months. Appears consumptive.

C.F., Indianapolis, to his mother, Proctorsville, Vermont, January I, 1832

. . . He [C.F.'s brother Stoughton] has many new things to attract his attention—new manners & new customs of the people here have been objects of speculation and remark by him. His acquaintance with the world was very limited when he started from home but his opportunities have been & will be great to learn mankind as they really are.

S. is studying geography &c and is getting along very well. Has good sense enough to make a good schollar—if he can only acquire

24. The Rev. John Strange, Methodist minister and presiding elder of the Indianapolis circuit from 1825 to 1829 and again in 1833 until his death that year. Sulgrove, *History of Indianapolis*, p. 339; Dunn, *Indianapolis*, I, 591.

habits of reflection & study—and get rid of many of his prejudicies. He like me has a naturally peavish temper. . . . S. must learn patience & meekness. . . . He has an affectionate warm heart—is a devoted generous friend & had he now or if hereafter acquires a decent education & a government over his temper he will make a man of whom we shall be proud. . . .

We have had a cold winter & have now some two or 3 inches of snow. My wife has been very unwell for the last 2 months but is getting better. We call our 5th boy Stoughton. . . .[25]

C.F., Indianapolis, to his mother, Proctorsville, Vermont, June 10, 1832

. . . There has been for the last month much alarm on the frontiers of our neighboring state Illinois & the north part of the State in consequence of some outrages committed by a band of hostile Indians who murdered a few white people in Illinois. In consequence of which the people upon our frontiers have left their homes in great numbers & many are daily passing through this place going south. In order to quiet this alarm our governor last Monday ordered 150 mounted riflemen from this place & about 250 from this vicinity, making in all about 400 men, who assembled here on yesterday & left this morning for Chicago in Illinois on lake Michigan.[26] Stoughton was desireous to go—and apprehended no difficulty for the object of the expedition being rather to quiet the people who have settled on the frontier than anything else, I readily consented for him to go. He immediately equipped himself with a rifle—two blankets, tom hawk, knife, canteen—cap &c &c. His equipment & horse were appraised at $105. so that in case his horse should die or he should loose any of his equipment the government will pay for them. He took 20 days provision consisting of parched corn, ground and mixed with sugar. He has been exercising himself with his rifle & horse for the last week—says he can shoot as well as the best of them—& left home this morning about

25. Stoughton Alonzo Fletcher was born October 25, 1831.

26. This is the Black Hawk War, the last Indian war in the Old Northwest. Buley, *The Old Northwest*, II, 59–80.

sun rise. 3 of my little boys went to see their uncle start with the men who camped about a mile from my house. Elijah the 2d boy cried to go along, the other two were willing to stay at home. Some of our best citizens have gone & some who are perfectly acquainted with Indian warfare. Our Secretary of State[27] & Brigadier General[28] have gone as common soldiers. S. belongs to a mess of 5—Genl. Wick a lawyer & formerly a Judge of this district, a Mr. Hand a hatter & a fine man, a young merchant & a printer compose the mess. Stoughton is the only New Englander in company. . . . Had my family & business permitted it, I should not have hesitated one moment to have gone myself, & under all the circumstances as there is but little danger to be apprehended I fully believe you will not disapprobate my permitting S. to enter this short campaign.

My wife whose father lived upon the frontiers of Ohio during the last war with great willingness spent the whole week preparing S.'s equipments. S. said nobody but mother would have done more for him. . . .

The garden seeds S. brought with him have done well. The onions have began to bottom & the corn has been tassling for several days past. Our spring was not considered forward. We have had cold rains. I shall leave home Tuesday next to be gone two weeks. . . .

C.F., Indianapolis, to his mother, Proctorsville, Vermont, June 30, 1832

Before I left home for a visit to Ky. & Ohio I wrote you, giving you information that Stoughton had gone out on a short Campaign on the Northern Frontiers. On my return I rather expected to find him at home but I have received word from him & others that they have gone to the Mississippi. After they proceeded about 100 miles

27. James Morrison. He served as secretary of state from 1829 to 1835, as president judge of the fifth circuit from 1839 to 1842, and succeeded Samuel Merrill as president of the State Bank the following year. Nowland, *Early Reminiscences of Indianapolis*, pp. 212–16; Monks *et al.* (eds.), *Courts and Lawyers of Indiana*, II, 393.

28. William W. Wick, brigadier general of the seventeenth brigade.

from this place counsel was held by the officers as to their place of distination & a young friend of mine writes me that S. was very anxious that they should proceede directly to Genl. Atkinsons army near the Mississippi River, at which place I have no doubt they have arrived before this date. I do not apprehend any danger that may befall S. in the field of battle as I believe peace will be made without an ingagement. He has a good constitution & has gone into a more Northern climate than this....

C.F., Indianapolis, to Samuel Judah [*Vincennes*], *July 31, 1832*[29]

Your favor of the 20th inst. was received last week, & I can assure you that it was met in the same spirit of friendship in which it was written by you.

You are aware of my peculiar situation as a representative. My humble services are rendered in the midst of my constituents whose real wishes in relation to so important a matter as the choice of a senator, it would become me to consult. But if Genl. Tipton retires from the field and there be no Clay candidate, the contest must of course be between you & Mr. Boon. That this will be the case I have been told by others besides the confidence expressed in your letter; and in that event I cannot hesitate in saying to you, that if left to myself you would be my choice over any man of similar politics in the state speaking as I do under the belief that you are favorable to the rechartering of the U.S.B. & are a reasonable tariff and internal improvement man. It would be my pride to see elected a young man of talents & abilities, of a respec[t]able order to the U. States Senate.

As to who will or will not be candidates I cannot say. I am under no pledge to any Clay man to vote for him, and have not heard a single individual named as a candidate.

Please to drop me a line when convenient....

P.S. The foregoing & any other remarks I may hereafter make on the subject referred to, I hope will also be received as confiden-

29. This letter is in the Judah MSS, Lilly Library, Indiana University. It is of interest as the only "political" letter of C.F.'s that has been found.

tial. Such are the opinions entertained by many individuals of men & their sentiments residing at Indianapolis, that all I might say would be but a dead weight upon your prospects.[30]

C.F., Indianapolis, to his mother, Proctorsville, Vermont, October 21, 1832

. . . Stoughton I learn arrived with about ten thousand dollars worth of Indian goods for a Mr. McCarthy[31] about the 15th of September at Fort Wayne one hundred miles North of this place. He had to imploy French Boatmen to carry those goods in Perogues or canoes up the Maume River about 80 miles then procure waggons to take them about 100 miles by land and he is now at a treaty with the Potwatomi Indians on Eel River 130 or 140 miles north of this place. He landed his goods safe & to the satisfaction of his imployer whom I have seen & who I am pleased to say is well contented with S.'s perseverance. I was under great fear lest S. would make some mistake—Sink a boat or get his goods wet. For if he returns safe to this country he will get great credit for his performance. Those who have become acquainted with him look upon him as a smart young man. I have had a letter from him & he will be at home in a few weeks. His imployer has sent a horse for him. My children and wife are very anxious to see him & think S. is of great consequence.

Should Stoughton arrive home in safety that is arrive at this place, he will have seen more than any young man of my acquain-

30. Samuel Judah, of Vincennes, was a brilliant lawyer and successful attorney. He was elected six times as representative from Knox County between 1827 and 1840. In 1831 he was one of the candidates for the United States Senate in the election to fill the vacancy occasioned by the death of James Noble, in which John Tipton was successful. He was not a candidate the following year when Tipton was again successful, being elected to a full term in the Senate. *Indiana Election Returns,* Index.

31. Nicholas McCarty, one of the persons supplying goods for the treaty negotiations with the Potawatomi held on the Tippecanoe River in October. Stoughton Fletcher was employed by McCarty to oversee the transportation of the goods which he supplied from New York to the treaty grounds. *John Tipton Papers,* II, 688–90; Kappler (ed.), *Indian Affairs, Laws and Treaties,* II, 353–56, 367–70, 372–76.

tance during my whole life—for one year. He will have gone to school for about 6 months—better than a month in the army. His trip home. His return by New York Albany and Buffalo when the cholera was raging,[32] pas[sage] on the lake with ten thousand dollars worth of goods—ascending a river with them 80 miles then carrying them 135 by land and building a log house to place them in—Be present at two Indian treaties—one trip to Cincinnati with several thousand dollars to deposit in the Bank &c &c. I have no hesitation in saying that had S. had an early education he would have made a brave and persevering man—and as it is I look to see him do well. I shall spare no pains to make him respected and useful if he stays here.

My family are in good health at this time but we are looking & expecting daily to have the cholera. It is within two days ride and rapidly advancing. We may be the victims of the pestilence yet I feel under no apprehension myself. . . .[33]

DIARY

December 25th 1832. A cloudy wet morning. The legislature set as usual in the forenoon. Returned home at 12. Found Rev. Mr. Holiday[34] Pres[byterian] preacher, James Hill & wife—Mrs. F. hav-

32. The Asiatic cholera which had spread from India across Europe, England, and Ireland was carried to America by an emigrant ship which landed at Quebec in 1831. The disease moved up the St. Lawrence to Montreal, then the next year to Albany, New York, thence westward to Buffalo, Detroit, and Chicago, and southward. Stoughton wrote to C.F. from Rochester, New York, on September 1, 1832, that he had left Vermont and gone to New York, "stayed a bout one day, I then stered my course for Newark [N.Y.] . . . to morrow if I have good luck I shall reach Buffalo. The goods are a head of me. I hav not half the fears of the cholera in N.Y. that I have here. But I hope that I shall be spared to get back." Fletcher Papers.

33. The spread and ravages of the Asiatic cholera through the West in the summers of 1832 and 1833 are described in Buley, *The Old Northwest,* I, 251–52. The toll in Indiana was greater in 1833, when in Aurora and Salem one hundred out of eight hundred inhabitants were said to have died within a week, the college at Bloomington had to be closed, and Indianapolis had sixty-two deaths in a month. See C.F. to his mother, July 16, 1833, below.

34. The Rev. William A. Holliday, son of Judge Samuel Holliday. He became pastor of the First Presbyterian Church in Indianapolis in 1832 where he served for two years, then devoted his life to teaching. He conducted a school

ing made preparations for a Christmas dinner. Israel P. Griffith having left the Senate Chamber with me for that purpose. We (Mrs. F. & myself) having intended to have the company of Messrs. Ingram Griffith Richmond[35] & wife Mrs. Paxton & [her]·Sister Roda Luse and brother Stoughton who is with us. I went to the methodist church for the two latter Rev. Mr. Wiley having preached & had all the above person at dinner except Mr. Ingram. His absence was the cause of great uneasiness & still is fearing that some mishap has befallen him. His presence was looked to with much interest by our children all esteeming him as one of the family. Legislature adjourned till Wednesday.

Decr. 26th 1832. Mr. Ingram has not arrived yet. Pleasant cloudy day. Hanover College bill passed to a 3d reading.[36] Mr. Graham dined with me & Rev. Mr. Wiley (Methodist E.P.C.) supped with me. I went to court house to attend on the Judiciary committee at night. Dark & Rainy. Stoughton came for me with a lantern.

Sunday Decr. 30th. Rev. Mr. Wiley[37] from the Bloomington College preached at the court house to a very large congregation

---

for a short time on the northeast corner of Pennsylvania and New York streets, taught one year at the Marion County Seminary (1837–38), then had his own school again at various locations. Nowland, *Sketches of Prominent Citizens*, pp. 537–38; Dunn, *Indianapolis*, I, 122, 127. For the Marion County Seminary see below, Pt. VI, note 180.

35. Ansel Richmond, who served as clerk and recorder of Madison County from 1826 until he moved with his family to Indianapolis in 1831 and was associated with C.F. in his law business until his death in December, 1833. *Indiana Executive Proceedings*, pp. 507, 511; diary, August 25, 1861.

36. Hanover Academy was incorporated in 1829. By the act passed at the 1832–33 session of the legislature the name was changed to Hanover College and it was provided that students "of sufficient bodily ability" should be "exercised and instructed in some species of mechanical or agricultural labour, in addition to scientific and literary branches there taught." It was also provided that the trustees were to report annually to the legislature "the plan, progress and effects of such agricultural and mechanical exercises and instruction upon the health, studies and improvement of the students." *Laws of Indiana*, 1832–33, pp. 6–7. C.F. was interested in this act because he was considering sending James Cooley to the school. See below, note 55.

37. Andrew Wylie, Presbyterian minister and formerly president of Washington College in Pennsylvania, who had been appointed president of the newly created Indiana College at Bloomington in 1828.

against Sectarianism. A very warm day. In the evening went to the Pres. church & there heard him preach.

Monday Dec. 31st. Warm & hazy. Went in the eve to court house to hear Mr. Wiley deliver colonization address.[38] It was much admired. Was elected one of its managers. Morris Morris called on me in the eve & took tea. Very warm for time of year—no Snow on.

January 1st 1833. A very pleasant day—no snow on the ground. Legislature sit all day. Our family consisting of my wife brother Stoughton Orindorio Crombaugh Giles Isham[39] my sons James (not 9 years old as yet) Elijah, Calvin, Miles, Stoughton—all in good health. The 3 oldest went to Mr. Blakes in the P.M. after school to take 1st volume of Burns poems home. I should on this day return with gratitude, praise & thanksgiving to Him who has watched over me & mine for the last year—none missing—all are with us! ! How little do I deserve such mercies! What may not another year bring!

I have for the last year felt less ambitious for the acquisitions of the worlds goods yet I have been equally industrious to acquire them or rather to protect what I had previously acquired by paying my debts. Once my professional cares were the bane of all injoyment. My fears made me miserable. I do not look upon defeat as so ruinous [as] I once did. I have learned thank God some lessions of patience. I feel it my duty to double my dilligence—to suffer no man's business to receive an injury from my negligence. So I will try to render unto every one his due.

We are now legislating upon the State Bank a doubtful experiment to relieve our citizens against unavoidable hard times.

38. The Indiana Colonization Society was founded in Indianapolis November 4, 1829, as an auxiliary of the American Colonization Society, with the object of colonizing "the free people of colour of the United States on the coast of Africa." Officers included Jesse L. Holman, president; James Scott, Isaac Blackford, and Ebenezer Sharpe, vice-presidents; James Rariden, James Morrison, Samuel Hall, Calvin Fletcher, and Samuel Merrill, managers; Isaac Coe, treasurer; and James M. Ray, secretary. Indianapolis *Indiana Journal,* November 12, 1829.

39. A boy who lived with the Fletcher family, probably bound under a contract to perform certain chores in return for board and room.

Could we charter a bank upon such principles as would secure the object to relieve the people—to regulate exchange after the U.States Bank paper is withdrawn[40] I think a good thing, yet it is fraught with some fearful consequences. I find there are many of our most respectable citizens intending to tourn merchant so soon as a bank is established & others to inter into hazzardous business. If the Bank is secure I hope the enterprise will be incouraged.

Our Senate consists of 30 members[41] excluding the president.[42] I cannot but say that I feel more comfortably situated than [in] any former session not having much local business crowded upon me as yet. I have no wish or rather not being compelled to be on the look out for future promotion I have fe[l]t easy. I design to surrender all political honors at the close of this session.

Saturday January 5th 1833. Mr. Ingram came to see us and brougt the childrin all presents.

Sunday [Jan.] 6. Went to meeting in the A.M. P.M. read. In the eve staid at home with Mrs. F.

[Jan.] 7th. Pleasant.

January 8th. This day the Senate adjourned on motion of Mr.

40. On July 10, 1832, President Jackson vetoed the bill renewing the charter of the Bank of the United States due to expire in 1836.

41. A broadside bound in with the Diary lists the members of the Senate at this session (twenty-nine in number instead of thirty), giving their places of birth, ages, counties of their residence, occupations, and politics. There were eighteen listed for Clay, nine for Jackson, and two for John McLean. C.F. is listed as a Clay man. Eighteen were farmers, five lawyers, four merchants, one a physician, and one a painter. A similar list of the members of the House is also bound in with the Diary.

42. The lieutenant governor and president of the Senate was David Wallace (1799–1859). A native of Pennsylvania, he came with his family to Miami County, Ohio, and attended a school in Troy, Ohio, where among his fellow students was Sarah Hill, later Mrs. Calvin Fletcher. He graduated from West Point in 1821 and joined his family who had moved to Brookville, Indiana. He read law in the office of Judge Miles C. Eggleston, was admitted to the bar, served in the legislature as representative from Franklin County in the 1828–29 and 1829–30 sessions, was elected lieutenant governor in 1834, and governor in 1837. He was elected to Congress in 1843, and was elected as a delegate from Marion County to the state Constitutional Convention in 1850. Dorothy Riker (ed.), *Messages and Papers relating to the Administration of David Wallace Governor of Indiana 1837–1840* (*Indiana Historical Collections*, XLIII. Indianapolis: Indiana Historical Bureau, 1963), Introduction.

Feeny[43] to celebrate "the 8th of Jany."—Anniversary of the battle of New Orleans. An address delivered by a Mr. Slaughter[44] only passible. In the eve a party at Mr. Browns tavern. Did not attend. Growing colder at night. A little snow fell.

Wednesday [*Jan.*] *9th.* Cold & blustery. Senate in committee on the Bank question. Going to elect a Judge & prosecuter for 8th circuit, a new circuit imbracing the North part of the State.[45]

January 17th 1833. This day very cold. There was a dinner given to Genl. Henry Harrison. I did not attend—misunderstanding the invitation.[46] Very cold for the last 4 days—ground covered with snow. Mr. Ingram with us.

January 23d. A Pleasant day. Rose early examined the Bank charter under debate in the legislature. In the P.M. addressed the chairman of the committee of the whole. I deem the present charter unconstitutional so far as it proposes to make the several branches *independant corporations* believing as I do that the word Branch by our Constitution only means offices of discount & deposit—that they are synonymous terms. My friends & a majority of my constituents are desireous of having a state Bank—but I go upon the presumption that they want a Constitutional Bank.

In the evening visited Mrs. Paxton took tea with her & Mrs. Richmond & wife & I then went to Genl. Drakes[47] where I spent

43. Hugh F. Feeny, senator from Parke County.

44. William B. Slaughter of Bedford. His address is printed in the Indianapolis *Indiana Democrat,* January 12, 1833.

45. Gustavus A. Everts was elected president judge and John B. Chapman prosecuting attorney of the Eighth Judicial Circuit by the General Assembly on January 9 and 10, 1833. The circuit comprised Carroll, Cass, Miami, Wabash, Huntington, Allen, La Grange, Elkhart, St. Joseph, and La Porte counties. Indiana *House Journal,* 1832–33, pp. 345–46, 346–48, 350–51; *Laws of Indiana,* 1832–33, pp. 4–5.

46. The printed invitation is bound in the diary. An account of the affair is given in the Indianapolis *Indiana Journal,* January 19, 1833, and the speech which Harrison delivered is printed in the *Journal* of January 23.

47. James P. Drake, who came to Posey County in 1816 when nineteen years old. He was chosen a brigadier general in the militia in 1819. Upon his appointment by President Jackson as receiver of public moneys at Indianapolis in 1829 he removed there. During the Black Hawk War he was chosen captain of one of the companies raised in Marion County. Dunn, *Indianapolis,* I, 135, 139.

some time with the members. Called on Mr. Farrington[48] & returned home with Mrs. F.

Jany. 26th 1833 (Saturday). I this day rose early and prepared a resolution on the subject of electing visiters to the Indiana College. Mr. B. Dunning from Hamilton[49] called on me but Just before I left for the State-house. My friend N. McCarty called on me and requested me to absent myself from the senate at the request of some of the members of the house by which it was believed that the bill from the house to incorporate a State Bank and 9 Branches could pass the Senate. This bill proposes to make a state Bank & nine independant Branches as they are called but they sue & are sued in their seperate corporate capacity & have no Joint liability directly or indirectly except by a safety fund paid in by each in corporation to the state treasury at the rate of two per cent per ann. on the stock & on winding up no Joint loss or profit and authorizes the stockholders to make a permenant loan of five years of one half of their stock secured to be refunded semiannualy at the rate of ten per cent. I had in committee of the whole helped to sustain a motion to strike out those provisions. The circulating medium of the country being nearly destroyed or rather made very scarce by the U. States B[ank] winding up her concerns there is a great rage for Banks, State Banks—scarce a State legislature in the Union but have created within the last year a great many state Banks. The people here demand one. I have been favorable to *"a State Bank & Branches"* as provided by our constitution but could not support a charter for *ten independent Banks*—it being as I believe unconstitutional. Also I could not conceive but that it would be an infringement of that instrument to allow the Individuals authorized to become stock holders on subscribing & paying in thirty thousand dollars—to allow those stockholders to receive from the Bank or Branch on a permenant loan in consequence of their subscription

48. James Farrington, senator from the district composed of Vigo, Clay, and Sullivan counties.

49. Bethel J. Dunning, of Noblesville. He conducted one of the town's first taverns, was an active Methodist, and served as Hamilton County coroner in 1834. Augustus F. Shirts, *A History of . . . Hamilton County, Indiana . . . 1818 to the Close of the Civil War* (n.p. 1901), pp. 70, 173, 186.

for five years to be returned in semiannual payments of ten per cent.[50]

I informed my friend McCarty that the objection I had to the charter was not one going to expediency of the measure but that I had the above constitutional objections. I therefore could not leave the Senate chamber. I could not desert the state let what would insue. But knowing that a number of the members of the legislature had really attributed my opposition to the bill from motives of selfishness or to monopolize influence at this place by making a central or Mother Bank acting & eating upon the branches & they upon each other, also believing my const[it]utents a great portion of them and some of the most intelligent differed with me in opinion—to save them from the wrath of such as were about to visit my constituents with appre[hen]ssion for my acts I determined to resign & did so as will appear from the several papers & documents hereto attached.[51]

50. The section relative to banks in the Indiana Constitution of 1816 reads, "There shall not be established or incorporated . . . any Bank or Banking company or monied institution, for the purpose of issuing bills of credit, or bills payable to order or bearer; Provided that nothing herein contained shall be so construed as to prevent the General Assembly from establishing a State Bank, and branches, not exceeding one branch for any three Counties, and be established at such place, within such Counties, as the directors of the State Bank may select; provided there be subscribed and paid in specie, on the part of individuals, a sum equal to thirty thousand dollars. . . ."

51. Copies of C.F.'s letters of resignation to Governor Noble, the Secretary of State, and the President of the Senate are included in the Diary. Only in the one to the President of the Senate did he explain that he was resigning because he regarded the provisions of the bill as unconstitutional, therefore could not vote for it, and "finding that a number of the most intelligent of my Constituents differ from me in opinion and that probably a large majority of them wish me to support the bill, I can pursue no course more in accordance with the spirit of our institutions than to return to those who gave it the power which I can not in this case exercise, according to their wishes." This letter is also printed in the Indiana *Senate Journal*, 1832–33, p. 354. See also Indianapolis *Indiana Democrat*, January 30, 1833.

There was both a House and a Senate bill creating a state bank before the 1832–33 session of the General Assembly. The House bill was the one attacked by Fletcher because it provided for a principal bank and branches that were in effect separate corporations. The Senate bill would have established a bank in Indianapolis and branches out in the state all responsible to each other. The former bill was printed in the Indianapolis *Indiana Journal* of February 23, 1833, and the latter in the *Journal* of February 16. No agreement was reached on either bill and action was postponed until the following session.

I expect the love of many to wax cold. I feel conscious I have done right. I therefore am prepared for the cup that will not pass by me—probably the execrations of the multitude. I am sensible that I must redouble my dilligence to be useful. I have been in the senate of the state for seven winters in succession—have seen public excitements repeatedly. Their effects & ultimate effects have been so serious that I have lost that man fearing spirit I once possessed—I may fail to sustain myself—But I owe it [to] myself my Country & my creater to try to be useful.

February 4th 1833 Monday. This day I arose about 5 o'clock & prepared to go to the legislature who were about to adjourn *sine die.* James Cooly & I arrived there about 6 o'clock. House in session—Senate soon went into session. Sent Cooly out to tell Mr. Jas. Blake that his father was in town—having left home unobserved being old & a little out of his reason. Govr. Noble in the South West room of the court house signing the bills with a plenty of good wine, rum brandy sugar &c &c of which, temperate as the members have been during the present year not seen to drink any spirits at all, yet they partook a little at parting. I left all my old associates in the senate with expressions of good will. Very muddy—no snow on the ground. Warm pleasant day. I returned home with my papers that I had in my drawer in the legislative hall. When I arrived near my gate I was overtaken by a mail carrier who wanted me to pay a protested order on A. D. Baird Esq. atty. at Law at Crawfordsvill for $10. This young man had obtained my services as an attorney for which he promised to pay the order drawn by himself. I paid the amount as it was going to a poor man who if I had not would have had just cause to have distrusted all the profession. I then went back to take leave of the members who were mounting their horses & giving the parting hand to each other. I went to Beards[52] room & wrote a letter to Crawfordsvill to the young lawyer. I then sought John Ewing's room. Ewing Senator from Knox he and myself had not been the best of friends until the question on the State banks arose—when he became friendly. I gave him an extract from the Journals of the convention relative to the bank. He promised me to send his address to his consti[t]uents. Mr.

52. John Beard, senator from Montgomery and Clinton counties.

Farnham[53] came to my office and left directions for me to take a deposition on the 16th of the month.

Mrs. Fletcher having proposed to give me a birth day dinner (Monday as it was) (washing day) I went to Mrs. Paxtons & gave her an invitation—also invited Mr. & Mrs. Richmond and promised my sons Cooley, Elijah, Calvin, Miles, & Giles Isham to eat at the same table. I parted with Mr. Whitcomb with pledges of good will &c. Israel Griffith Hugh O Neel[54] and Cutberth Huntington[55] called on me & urged me to accept of the office of Governor to the Indianap-

53. John Hay Farnham, who was secretary of the Senate during the 1832–33 session. A native of Massachusetts and graduate of Harvard, he came to Salem, Indiana, and was admitted to the bar in 1823. He was one of the organizers of the Indiana Historical Society chartered in 1830 and was elected its first corresponding secretary. He died of the cholera in 1833.

54. In 1821, when a boy, Hugh O'Neal came to Indianapolis with his family. He served as town clerk 1833–34 and 1836–38 and as town attorney 1838–40, was admitted to the bar and began a successful practice. He went to California for awhile after gold was discovered, then returned to Indianapolis. Nowland writes that "No young man in the State bid fairer to rise to eminence and distinction" but he "fell victim to that destroying demon (intemperance)" and died in December, 1860. Sulgrove, *History of Indianapolis,* pp. 214a, 486, 487; Nowland, *Early Reminiscences of Indianapolis,* pp. 111–13.

55. In his diary entry for December 28, 1860, at the time of O'Neal's death, C.F. recalled that he and others in Indianapolis had aided in the education of these three promising young men, Griffith, O'Neal, and Huntington. In the Fletcher Papers there is a letter from Huntington to C.F. dated South Hanover, May 16, 1833. Apparently he and Hugh O'Neal were enrolled at Hanover College for the spring and summer session in 1833, and C.F., who was considering sending James Cooley there, had asked for a report on the school. Huntington described the town of Hanover as "situated one mile from the Ohio River, five from Madison, contains 25 dwelling houses and 175 inhabitants exclusive of students." He reported that the new college building was nearly completed. "In their manual labour system I have been deceived," he wrote. "I supposed that a larger farm was under cultivation . . . there are 7 or 8 acres cleared and planted with broom corn and a few acres uncultivated. They furnish the students with wood cutting in which O'Neal & myself are engaged two hours each day, but I think the exercise hardly suitable for such as us, have not been accustomed to it—to go from entire inactivity to the severest exercise is a change too sudden & violent to be holesome. We receive 40¢ per cord. There are already 160 students here principally young men, although there are several who are neither older nor larger than Jas. . . . the majority of the students are either stupid or indolent. Morality is indeed much observed, but where there are so many & such a variety of characters, there are sufficient opportunities for the indulgence of immoral habits. Messrs. Matthews, Niles, Harney & Crowe are gentlemen & scholars, well liked, Doctor Blythe is a Kentuckian and of course a great pedant . . . if you

olis legislature. I declined not without feeling very greatful to those young men.

We had our dinner as above proposed without any show or ceremony. In the P.M. I met with old Mr. Givans & explained the reasons I resigned my seat in the legislature which he appeared to receive as satisfactory. I tried to relieve Harbin Moor[56] whose horse & carriage was executed to pay a debt or rather the horse & carriage of his brother in law. John Givans would not return the property altho' it had been awarded by a Jury to the claimant. I tendered$12. to the keeper who refused to give it. Mr. McCarty called to see me & spent 1 hour. I also began reading Kents Commantories[57] 2d vol. in which it is plainly shown the impropriety of many of our Conventions adopting certain political axioms as fundamental rules in their constitutions. In the eve I returned home read the National Intelligencer of 26th of Jany. in which Mr. Calhouns speech is against the New Judiciary act. I wrote a letter to Elijah.

February 5th 1833. I this day 'rose at 5 o'clock—thought over the proceedings of the past day—eat breakfast and went to my office where I was soon visited by Messrs. Gregg[58] Govr. Noble & B.F. Morris. The fore noon I read some in the 2d vol. of Kent. In the P.M. wrote two letters &c. In the eve returned home & Miss Orinderio had 11 girls to help her quilt—two Miss Bays two Miss Win-

---

know Jas. to be willing to learn & ambitious to keep up with his class mates or pass them, you may safely send him; but if he is indolent as boys of his age often are . . . you may as well keep him away; for all the morality & religion of the institution cannot prevent him if so disposed from forming bad habits & yielding to temptation, which might be avoided with Gregg." No further information about Huntington has been found. For Gregg, see note 58, below.

The student enrollment of 160 seems exaggerated. William A. Millis, in *The History of Hanover College from 1827 to 1927* (Hanover, Ind.: Hanover College, 1927), p. 223, gives the total enrollment for 1833 (Preparatory and College departments) as 87 and for 1834 as 176.

56. Harbin H. Moore, representative from Harrison County.

57. *Commentaries on American Law* (4 volumes, 1826–30), by James Kent (1763–1847), American jurist.

58. Thomas D. Gregg. About 1830 he opened a school in a shop at the northwest corner of Delaware and Market streets which he conducted for some three years. In November, 1835, he took over the Marion County Seminary for one term. See below, Pt. VI, note 180. James Cooley and Elijah were attending Mr. Gregg's school at this time. Elijah recalled him as a "cruel tyrannical man, though an excellent teacher." "Recollections of My Mother." Fletcher Papers.

gates 2 Miss Pattersons Miss Holland Miss Margaret Hand. By no means a party from the aristocracy. Mr. Gregg school master called & spent an hour with me. I then went to Mr. Richmonds. He had retired to bed but got up and I read Mr. Clays speech upon the subject of distributing the proceeds of the public lands by giving the new states 17½ per cent to the states in which there are public lands annually out of the proceeds of sales and also an equal portion according to Federal members with the other states during the time of peace. Very pleasant weather. No snow & too open for sugar making—bees out this day &c.

Feby. 6 1833. Rose early. Pleasant weather. Wrote to Morison of N.Y. City. Went to the office done some business for McCracken of Morgan county with Yandees, Cain[59] & Brown and one Barret. At noon was invited to dine with Mrs. Paxton—her birth day. In the eve Mr. Hawkins of Shelby brought me some money from Butler $25. for self $775. for Johnsons of Cincinnati. In the eve received News of the allowance of three pensions to applicants & the return of three without allowance for defects. I read a newspaper sent by Miles. Went to bed at 10. Pleasant weather. Have concluded to send Cooley to Bloomington.[60] I fear the policy of continuing him longer at Mr. Greggs school.

C.F., Indianapolis, to his brother Elijah Fletcher [*Lynchburg, Virginia*], *February 6, 1833*

... On the 26th ult. I resigned my seat in the Senate as you will have seen by the Democrat of that date. The causes to a certain extent are there slightly hinted at but more fully explained in my communication to the president of the Senate subsequently published. Our constitution prohibits all Banking companies except a state bank and *branches* allowing individual subscribers provided they pay in at least thirty thousand dollars before commencing banking operations. This winter a bank charter was presented to

59. John Cain (1805–1867), who came to Indianapolis in 1826 where he opened the first bookshop and book bindery. A strong Jackson man, he was appointed postmaster in 1829. Nowland, *Early Reminiscences of Indianapolis,* pp. 208–11.

60. James Cooley did not go to the academy at Bloomington until a year from the following June. See C.F. to his mother, June 1, 1834, below.

both houses of our legislature to incorporate a State bank and Nine branches which were to be inderpendent corporation and not responsible for each others debts and to render seperate dividends. The State to furnish the main bank & each branch with eighty thousand dollars to be obtained on a loan & for 27 years and individuals were to subscribe eighty thousand to the bank & each branch making the whole capital stock one million six hundred thousand dollars. Individuals to pay three eights of their stock in before any issues to be made—to have a majority in directory of the bank & branches with the exclusive privilege of obtaining on a permanent loan one half of their stock subscribed for five years on refunding ten per cent sem anuly to the bank or branches for which it should be collected. I viewed this bank charter unconstitutional for two reasons one because the bank and branches were maid independent of each other. Should one fail it was to be settled as an insolvent estate—to be sure a *safety fund* of one half per cent on the capital stock was to be paid to Treasure according to Mr. Vanburens plan as an indemnity &c but our constitution requires a State bank & branches—the latter means nothing more than *offices of discount and deposit* according to the difinition of the best financiers. Again the constitution requires that thirty thousand dollars on the part of individuals to be subscribed *and paid* before banking operations should commence. The charter required this but permitted them to borrow more than that amount back on a permanent loan as above stated. I conceived the framers of the constitution intended this sum to be paid in and used for ordinary banking purposes. I would have premise[d] with the distruction of the bank of the U. States was connected another bold and I fear [. . .] which originated with van B. and his Warll street friends—that is operating the whole vally of the Miss[iss]ippie tributary to N.Y. by the aid *of British capital*. Now for my proof you are apprised that the states Alabama Louisiana Tennessee have already applied to that city within the last year for capital to commence banking upon. The Governors of both Kentucky and Ohio have both reccommended the means of State banks &c. Last year we authorized three commissioners to negotiate a lone for canal purposes.[61] They went

61. The commissioners were appointed to manage and superintend the Wabash and Erie Canal Fund (money obtained from canal lands, loans based on

to N.Y. city. They then obtained the loan on terms surprisingly good for the State. They were disclosed the whole *areana* of the monied operations of the world to them. There were presented to them in [. . .] the vast hidden resources of them States which only required banking institutions to bring them fourth, and no doubt in my mind they were initiated and taken through a most artifull and I will require [?] passing process and like the queen of the east came to the conclusion that the half had not been told them. They immediately wrote letters to a number of the members of the Legislature on the subject of a State bank. They returned home & the most showy of the three who had been marked out as the principal *usee* by the great monied men came forward to the legislator & presented the charter the outlines of which I have above set forth. Had his own name[62] inserted with the other two canal fund commissioners though not with their will & approbation as the persons suitable to negotiate the lone. Our house of Representatives largely Jacksonians easily took the bait. The bill came to the Senate where it met with oposition. My constituents were as much influenced by the large majority friendly to the measure in the house as for their own pressing pecuniary wants and there fore were anxious for a bank. When the objections as to its constitutionality came before us I attacked the charter on that ground. I was soon viewed as a chevaux de friese to its passage. The Senate ascertain by *counting noses* my determined friends would not consent to an alteration. Members applied to my constituents to request me to *be absent a few days. That* I considered an insult to my *dignity*. Instructions were got up for me to vote for it & I resign[ed]. Our member in the house[63] who forgot to urge of constitutional objections to the

future sales of land, and money received from tolls and water rights), and were authorized to contract for a loan of $200,000 at 6 per cent for construction of the canal. William C. Linton, Vigo County, Nicholas McCarty, and Jeremiah Sullivan were named commissioners. *Laws of Indiana*, 1831–32, pp. 3–8; Indiana *Senate Journal*, 1831–32, p. 272. A loan of $100,000 at 6 per cent was negotiated with J. D. Beers & Co. of New York in August, 1832, at a premium of $13,260. *Ibid.*, 1832–33, p. 42.

62. Nicholas McCarty.

63. Robert Hanna, representative from Marion County. A native of South Carolina, he came to Brookville, was a member of the Constitutional Conven-

bill but who voted against it becaus he disliked the Governor who had the appointment of part of the directory has since my resignation tried to turn the rath of sovereigns on me which rests on him.[64] I left the senate of which I have been a member 7 years I believe with the harty good will of every member and such was their abhorence of the course pursued that my resigning was assigned as the only cause of opposition by some members to the bank afterwards which bill [failed] in the senate. Of the people to whom I return my office which is rarely done under any circumstances I have no fears. But as to political life for the present I have done. . . .

DIARY

[Feb.] 7th. Mr. Peesley from Shelbyville[65] & brother here. Called in the evening on Genl. Walter Wilson[66] who has been sick

---

tion of 1816, and appointed register of the Brookville Land Office in 1820. He came to Indianapolis in 1825 when the land office was transferred there and continued as register until removed by President Jackson in 1829. He was elected brigadier general of the Indiana militia, and on August 19, 1831, was appointed by Governor Ray to the United States Senate to fill the vacancy caused by the death of Senator Noble. He served only briefly, until the election of John Tipton the following December. Hanna was elected as a representative from Marion County in 1832, 1836, 1837, and 1838, and as senator in 1840. He lived on his farm adjoining the northeast corner of the Indianapolis donation. Nowland, *Early Reminiscences of Indianapolis,* pp. 193–95; *Indiana Election Returns,* pp. 128, 134n; *Biographical Directory of the American Congress,* p. 1264.

64. The Indianapolis *Indiana Democrat,* January 26, 1833, in reporting C.F.'s resignation said that he had acted honorably and correctly in vacating his seat. The following issue (January 30), carried a letter from Hanna which said, in part, "For the honor of Mr. Fletcher and for the honor of his constituents, I hope Mr. Fletcher was actuated by more noble considerations of honor and patriotism, than to resign his seat in the Senate to permit the passage of a law in violation of that constitution which he has sworn to support. . . . I voted against the Bank Bill that passed the House of Representatives because I believed it both unsafe and unconstitutional, and I say this without intending to impute improper motives to any member who voted in support of the measure. . . ."

65. William J. Peaslee. He served as prosecuting attorney of the fifth circuit, 1839–41, and for seven years as president judge, 1842–49. He was a native of Vermont. Monks *et al.* (eds.), *Courts and Lawyers of Indiana,* II, 795.

66. Representative from the newly created counties of Cass and Carroll. Wilson (1782–1838) had served as a messenger to the Indians for Governor Harrison and was a veteran of the Tippecanoe expedition. *John Tipton Papers,* II, 69n.

at Brown's tavern since the rising of the legislature in consequence of a fall from his horse. Came home at 8 in the Eve.

Feby. 8 1833. In the morning wrote a letter to Dr. Morris[67] by Mr. Peesley. Pleasant day. Discovered that I had sent money to Cincinnati by Mr. McCarty on the 30 of Jny. last to Jones $150. or 200 but we had made no entry as to the amount. Pleasant day. Some little difficulty in relation to a suit commenced vs Br. Foudey [Foudray]. Called in the eve & settled with Alfred Harrison. Dined with McCarty by accident.

Febry. 9th 1833. A very pleasant day. Examined Kents Commentaries on the subject of [. . .]. In the P.M. attended 2 trials one for Quill Noe & Duke[68] vs a young Mr. Stag[?]—one of Conner [and] Harrison vs Josh Glover. Messrs. Cummings & Rich[69] called in to my office in the P.M. Mr. Hugh O Neel desired my advise relative to his future course. H. Bradly called to talk with me about going into business with Stoughton. Had a conversation this day with Mr. Roop Representative from Franklin on the subject of cheerfulness. He recommended as a specific that we should always recollect that we did not *make* ourselves & that we are sent here to do some good which we cannot accomplish by gloomy fo[re]bodings—& that most men are willing that they have passed through much more than they had expected.

I received a letter from D. Cumpstack Madison[70] requesting me to get a note from Sheets & collect the same on John Gardner Noah Noble &c. I take the order to Mr. Sheets[71] on whom it was drawn for

67. Sylvan B. Morris, physician and clerk of Shelby County.

68. Probably Aquellin W. Noe and Samuel Duke, whose names appear in the Marion County census for 1830. *Names of Persons Enumerated in Marion County, Indiana at the Fifth Census* (Indiana Historical Society *Publications,* IV No. 5, Indianapolis, 1908), p. 343.

69. This may be Virtulon Rich (1809–1873), of Vermont, who made a journey to the West in 1832, then apparently spent some time during the winter of 1832–33 reading law with C.F. whom he described in a "Memoir" as "a distinguished Lawyer and native of Vt." Rich practiced law first in Ohio and then in Michigan and engaged in farming. *Western Life in the Stirrups, A Sketch of a Journey to the West in the Spring & Summer of 1832 by Virtulon Rich,* edited by Dwight L. Smith (Chicago: The Caxton Club, 1965), pp. vii–xiv.

70. Daniel Comstock of Madison.

71. William Sheets, secretary of state. Upon his election to that office by

the note & I found that it had been sent to him also for collection but that the fee had been prescribed to $20. on a $1000. note. He had declined collecting on those terms. I was offered $25. in the letter & from the circumstances I also declined receiving it but wrote back to the foresaid Mr. Cumpstack.

This a very beautiful day. Mrs. Fletcher & Stoughton opened a sugar camp of 20 trees & made about 16 lbs. of sugar—S. bot 23 crocks of [. . .] to make more. Cooley went to Mr. Wilkins & made a powder horn & brot it home. Received a letter from Ingram.

Sunday the 10 Feby. 1833. Mrs. Fletcher set up late & stirred off 7 or 8 lbs. of sugar. I got up a little after 5—a very pleasant morn. I brought with Stoughton Giles & Cooley several buckets of sugar water from the lot—it having run all night. Stoughton & Mr. Richmond rode out. I went with 3 oldest boy[s] to love feast. Returned home with them and returned to meeting again. Mr. Root[72] preached a good sermon Text— "Moses smit the rod &c." Returned home from meeting & walked with my wife it being very pleasant & dry. John [Hill] called on us & I went to class meeting with him at Mr. Kettlemans.[73]

I this day strove to rid myself [of] all my worldly business or rather to banish the same from my thoughts. If I know my own heart I have not an inordinate desire to get rich yet I have business & am desireous of doing it right. I have [made] many errors in transacting the same. So much of it is performed from home it is almost impossible to keep regular books & often things are omitted to be entered. Should God spare me I hope to be dilligent in prayer & constant in business. I pray that I may have wisdom to comprehend & understand every duty that devolves upon me that I may injure no man by negligence.

In the eve went to the post office. While there the subject of

---

the General Assembly in 1832 he moved to Indianapolis. About 1838 he began operation of a successful paper mill. He was a Whig in politics and a Presbyterian. Nowland, *Early Reminiscences of Indianapolis,* pp. 269–70.

72. The Rev. Calvin W. Ruter, Methodist minister, stationed in Indianapolis at this time. Dunn, *Indianapolis,* I, 592.

73. James Kettleman, a shoemaker by trade whose shop was located on the southeast corner of Market and East streets. He was an ardent and enthusiastic Methodist. Nowland, *Early Reminiscences of Indianapolis,* pp. 85–87.

nullification & the Tariff arose between me & Alic Morrison.[74] He contended that it would not compromit the national honor by a reduction of the Tariff at this time. I tried to maintain the negative of the proposition. I went to church in the eve returned & went to bed at an early hour.

Feby. 11th 1833. Rose early and at 7 went to the office. Soon had several present—a Mr. Woods from Shelby County emploid me to bring a slander suit. Went to the probate court to try & settle Setters business with old Mills & Norths heirs. Called on Noah Noble in the P.M. In the P.M. [. . .] calld on Richmond & myself for a settlement of widow Richardsons business. A very wet day. In the [. . .] Stoughton went to see Ungles.[75] Cooley Elijah & Giles had a "family" legislature & I attended & assisted them & they done better than I could have expected.

Feby. 12th Teusday 1833. This eve Mr. Richmond at my house and Cooley James & Giles insisted on having a family legislature. So to gratify them our four oldest boys Giles Mr. Richmond & Uncle Stoughton went into an election for speaker. Cooley was elected and took his seat upon the table in a little chair and returned his acknowledgments for the honer conferred.

We proceeded then to elect other officers & then to passing laws. We passed one law fining any boy for leaving down a pair of barrs by tying the boy just as long to the barrs as he suffered them to remain down—also another fining a boy three fips for leaving a Sunday School book or abusing it & Keeping [it] down Celler one night.

Pleasant day. Snow on the ground.

Feby. 13 Wedinsday. Bradly & Ungles came to my office to

74. Alexander F. Morrison, brother of James Morrison, secretary of state. After representing Clark County in the 1829–30 session of the legislature, Alexander Morrison remained in Indianapolis where in the spring of 1830 he began publication of the weekly *Indiana Democrat* in the interest of the re-election of Andrew Jackson to the Presidency. Nowland, *Early Reminiscences of Indianapolis*, p. 218. He was elected to fill out C.F.'s term in the Senate, defeating Austin W. Morris by one vote. *Indiana Election Returns*, pp. 217, 218n.

75. Wilford Ungles. Stoughton Fletcher opened a general store in partnership with him and Henry Bradley. In a letter to his mother on March 31, 1833, C.F. wrote: "Stoughton has entered into partnership with two Gentlemen of this place & with them is going into merchandising. . . . S. put in $600." Fletcher Papers. Their store was on the south side of Washington Street east of Meridian.

advise with me relative to their preparing to go after goods immediately with Stoughton & they among them raising two thousand dollars. I rather discouraged the precipitancy. The matter remained undetermined. The evening mail brought 3 successful pension applications forwarded by Genl. Tipton.[76] I received a letter from James Noble at Charleston S.C. Mr. Richmond & myself inspected our many matters in the eve. Set up till nearly 11 for that purpose.

On Monday our youngest boy Stoughton took sick—vomiting—with a slight fever without much pain. On Teusday Miles took sick with same complaints. On Wedin[s]day Cooley & Elijah also complained & did not either of them go to school.

[Feb.] 14th Thursday morning. Rose early Stoughton Uncle having set up most of the night with the sick child. He had talked of going to Louisvill on Elijah['s] business but from the ill state of health of the childrin &c he gave it out for the present. I this morning settle with J. M. Ray $77.91 costs in the case of Jennerson v Graves in the Marion C[ircuit] C[ourt] in which I very improvidently went security. Passed the day in business in the office. In the P.M. returned home early—went for Mrs. Paxton.

16 of Feby. Saturday. Took Coburns deposition for Mr. Farnham. A Pleasant day. Sugar water run well & Mrs. F. [and] Stoughton having tapped about 40 trees they made 7 or 8 lbs. The water run all night.

[Feb.] 17. I went to hear Mr. Holiday preach. Rather misty warm day. Read a number in the N. American review on the subject of forrest trees.

Monday [Feb.] 18th. I have a large weeks work before me. I received a letter from Genl. Tipton inviting me to move out to the Tippecanoe River for what I cannot say.[77] But this I will say tho' I esteem the invitation from him as an evidence of good feelings and friendship yet I cannot think of leaving this place for any consider-

76. Tipton was now in the United States Senate, having been elected in 1831 to fill the vacancy caused by the death of James Noble and re-elected the following year. *Indiana Election Returns*, pp. 128, 219–31.

77. The letter dated January 18, 1833, is in the Fletcher Papers and printed in the *John Tipton Papers*, II, 778–79. One paragraph read simply, "what would you think of setling in the north in a year or two?"

ations. I feel no desire to be wealthy—a competence is all I want. I do not make this remark because it [I] look upon it as doubtful whether I could become so—for on the Contrary I am sensible were I to have my health I could probibly by using the same exertion that others do I could acquire property or fortune as fast as men usually do with my capital. I have at this time a very fine business in the law. However the most profitable part thereof is collecting. It keeps me and Mr. Richmond busy & then we cannot do justice to all.[78] I fear many times that I do not use that dilligence that is required of a man so highly favored. I look upon the faculties competent to acquire business & much more to perform it right a blessing from God.

There is much difficulty in the way. I [do] business with persons who have heretofore stood well who are failing in business—men to suspect whom one year ago of insolvency would have been to incurr censure & the character of illiberality. I look to see a great portion of the country merchants if not broke, very much imbarrassed. U. States B[ank] is setling up her business & withdrawing all the circulating medium thereby. One or two Banks in Ohio have already failed. When I see those who have great possessions involved in debt & imbarrassed I am reminded that a competence with entire independence is all I should covet.

Tuesday [Feb.] 19. A pleasant day. Mrs. F. and S. have made since Saturday from 40 trees 50 lbs. of sugar. Messrs. Commings & Rich Vermonters visited us.

19th Feby. 1833. We had a debating society to please the childrin. Cooley was presedent. Messrs. Comings & Rich made a speach. Subject of debate the punishment of a boy for leaving barrs down when they should come from the field. Cooley appeared to be at home in the chair & performed well for a boy at his age.

Received a letter from Cincinnati inclosing a claim on Hays at

78. Daniel D. Pratt (see below, p. 236n), who started working in C.F.'s office in the fall of 1833, remarked that C.F. had at that time "a very large collecting business which was steadily increasing. Besides he was investing largely in Government lands. He needed an assistant to keep his land books, to do scrivener work & especially to scour the state on horseback to look after his collections." Pratt to Dr. William B. Fletcher, October 6, 1873, Fletcher Family Papers, Indiana Historical Society Library.

the Bluffs. Our childrin have all been sick & Mrs. F. sent for Dr. Coe last week but all have got reasonably well except the youngest Stoughton whose teeth have not appeared except 3 at 16 months old—& he is very unwell.

Feby. 22. Bro. Stoughton left home for Louisville Ky. to settle Elijah's business with Mr. Cook &c the business is [. . .]. I hope he will succeed &c.

Feby. 23d Saturday. Mr. H. Gregg & myself left Indianapolis for the Hancock C[ircuit] C[ourt]. A little Snow on, a gloomy day. Rode to John Hagers. Arrived there about 4 P.M. Grew cold towards evening & we staid over night. In the eve went with Mr. Hager to Esq. Parkers J. P.[79] to get Judgments fer McCarty & Williams.[80] There saw two Messrs. Fees [?] of Marion county going in to White water or Ohio after sheep. Next morning after Breakfast we left for Greenfield. The snow the night we staid at Hagers having fell a few inches very bad travelling—cold. Arrived at G. a little after 12 meridian. No lawyers had arrived before us but we had for our company that P.M. a Mr. Berton a merchant of that place.

Feby. 24 Sunday. The mail brought the national Intelligencer of the 9th of Feby containing Mr. Clays Tariff bill & his speech on introducing it into the Senate. This to me [. . .] much surprise. His course was to me almost incomprehensible as well as unjustifiable yet on reading the whol *pro & con* I did & still do believe that the American people have not sustained him as they should, that it is a project of the next administration to destroy the Tariff (Genl. Js.) project but to hold out for the present in order that it will have the semblance of deliberation not preciptancy or fear.

This eve Judge Morris Wm. Brown Greggs partner lately from Ky. H. Brown & Kilgore[81] arrived and also a Mr. McCarty from Cincinnati called in with whom I got acquainted.

79. James Parker, justice of the peace for Hancock County. *Indiana Executive Proceedings*, p. 680.

80. David Williams, a cousin of Nicholas McCarty and a clerk, then a partner, in McCarty's store. The partnership was dissolved in 1836 but Williams continued as a merchant in the city with other partners. Indianapolis *Indiana Democrat*, February 2, 1836; Nowland, *Early Reminiscences of Indianapolis*, p. 160.

81. David Kilgore, lawyer of Delaware County.

25 Feby. Monday. Cold. Little business in court.

Teusday [Feb.] 26th. Still cold & dissagreeable. I roomed with Judge Morris. He informed me that he designed giving up his commission as Judge &c.

Wedensday [Feb.] 27. Attended to a little business—case of Alley assignee of Jo. Chapman was tried.

[Feb.] 28 Thursday. Very cold. Govr. Ray & myself agreed to return home together. About 12 we started but R. could not keep up with me—very rough riding—& I rode on & left him. Called at Fullens[82] where he came up. We there warmed. He electioned for congress—promised Fullen & 2 other men if he was elected he never would rest satisfied until he procured each poor man a quarter section of land.[83] It began snowing & snowed untill I arrived home where I found all well & a pleasant fire after so cold a ride.

Friday March first 1833. Unpleasant & cold day. I done but very little.

March 2d Saturday. Very cold.

March 3 Sunday. I rose early. Judge Morris Mr. Quarles & myself left for Shelby County. Road rough, yet froze so as to bear. Very cold—having the night before been one of the coldest during the winter. Went to Dobles[84] 12½[miles] & took dinner. While there Govr. Ray passed. We soon overtook him & passed in turn. Arrived at Shelbyvill little after dark. I stoped at Powels tavern. There met with Wick & Sweetser. Night very cold. Sweetser related to me his adventures at Washington &c.

[Mar.] 4. Next day I answered or prepared an answer to O. H. Smiths Certificate forwarded me by Rariden in which Smith relates somethings very disgraceful & equally false as to my acknowledg-

82. Samuel Fullen's tavern in Cumberland. Sulgrove, *History of Indianapolis,* p. 619.

83. Ray ran a very poor third in his bid for representative in Congress from the sixth district in 1833, winning only sixteen votes against the victorious George L. Kinnard's 5,412 and Judge Wick's 4,818. The district comprised Bartholomew, Boone, Cass, Hamilton, Hancock, Hendricks, Johnson, Madison, Marion, Monroe, Morgan, and Shelby counties. *Indiana Election Returns,* p. 89.

84. William Doble's tavern, in the "lost" village of Doblestown, Moral Township, Shelby County. Edward H. Chadwick, *Chadwick's History of Shelby County Indiana* (Indianapolis: B. F. Bowen & Co., 1909), p. 447.

ment to him relative to the Senatorial election last winter in which S. implicates my veracity.[85] I have given the *lie* direct to his statements. I probibly shall have trouble with him. But I have truth on my side.

[*Mar.*] 5. On Teusday Judge Morris informed the bar that he should send home his resignation as Judge to the Govr. The bar consisting of Gregg Quarles Butler Brown (Wm.) Vanpelt[86] Peaslee & Robinson[87] all signed it for my appointment. Mr. Sweetser refused & said and declared he intended to apply for it himself—threatened to visit it on the bar at Indianapils if I were appointed &c. I informed him that I had made many sacrifices already to keep peace at Indianapolis & should not therefore present any recommendation to the Govr. for my appointment & would therefor leave it to him to appoint whom he pleased. Wick & the bar generally desired Morris to hold on to his office but he seems to be determined not to try James[?] a 3d time but he appeared to have made up his mind on the subject from which he could not depart.

Thursday 7th of March. About 2 Quarles & I left for Indianapolis & rode home together. Rather muddy but it had not thawed thro'. Sweetser sent a letter by me to Govr. Noble relative to Morris appointment & Morris arrived home the next day.

Friday 8th March. I presented S-s letter to Noble & expressly told him that I did not intend to present any written application to him for the Judgeship. If I was appointed I would serve &c. I have had & still have strong doubts as to the propriety of accepting the appointment. My present business is far better than the salary of $700. per an. yet it would give me more time to spend with my family & time to study. I have no idea that I shall ever again receive

85. The election for United States senator by the General Assembly in 1832 had required nineteen ballots with votes being cast for over thirty-one persons in the course of the balloting. John Tipton was finally elected. Oliver H. Smith appeared a serious contender in the early stages. In a letter to Tipton of January 24, C.F. wrote that O. H. Smith had reported that he, C.F., had been "*bought up* by Tipton." *John Tipton Papers,* II, 787. It was contended by some of Tipton's supporters that Smith had allowed his name to be used in the election in order to draw votes away from Tipton. *Ibid.,* II, 732.

86. Mathew C. Vanpelt. Chadwick, *History of Shelby County,* p. 198.

87. Humphrey Robinson. *Ibid.,* p. 199.

an office from the people &c. Judge Morris had an interview with the Govr. on Saterday March 9th. Govr. refused to make an appointment unless there were petitions &c in favor of some body. So Morris concluded to hold on for the present.

Sunday March 10th. A very pleasant day. Went to meeting in A.M. to hear Mr. Rooter. In the eve received National Int[elligencer] of the 28th where I found that Mr. Clays Teriff bill would pass both houses of congress.

Monday March 11th. Pleasant morning but soon clouded. Mr. Peek called to alter my hogs &c. Cooley & mother boiling sugar water on the block.[88] Calvin & E. to school & Dorio keeping house. About 12 it began raining & continued to rain all the P.M. Frost coming out of the ground. Mrs. F. & Cooley been boiling sugar water —made six or 7 lbs. Mr. Smith my neighbor had his house broken open & about $50. stole. Thefts I awfully fear will become common. There not has been anything stole in Indianapolis for the last 8 years of any consequence. Called at the land office on business. There learned that Mr. Hendricks (Wm.) will be appointed commissioner of the General land office.

March 12th. Cold bad day. From the circumstance of several thefts having been committed in town within a few weeks & attempts to break into houses the first attempts of the kind were made from the first settlement of the place I was called on to patrole the

88. In 1832, according to the Marion County deed records, C.F. bought the west two thirds of lots 1, 2, and 3 of square 42 from William Lingenfelter and in 1834 bought the east one third of these lots from Richard Williams, the deeds being dated February 15, 1832, and January 20, 1834. The total paid was $220. Elijah Fletcher in "Recollections of My Mother" recalled this "piece of woodland sown in blue grass and generally used as a pasture ground for cows" which lay to the east of the Fletcher house. "In this 'block' as we called it," he wrote, "the sugar maples abounded. These with the first thaw of the opening year were 'tapped' and sugar making began. Mother was the *fac totem* in this business; but she carried it on very differently from the careless manner of most Hoosiers. Instead of sugar troughs, which were liable to stain the sap she had clean crocks placed under the spills. The sugar water when collected was carried to a half face camp and poured into kettles suspended by the side of a huge oak log. There when the boiling was going on mother stood and stirred, and tasted, and added until all was reduced to a thick syrup. This was carried to the house, reboiled & grained lest in the woods the flying pollen and early insects should ruin the unsullied whiteness of the sugar." Fletcher Papers.

street—Wiley & McGuire[89] shop was made a place of rendezvous. Capt. Wily James Smith (Tailor) a Mr. Wright[?] (Tailor) Oliver an Irishman A Mr. Tharp living with Mr. J. Givans & myself. James Smith & myself took the squares North & south of the court house. Cold night. We met every two hours at Wily shop. We [. . .] a gambling establishment opposite Givens store. Smith & myself caught one boy who proved to be innocently returning from a country sugar camp. We retired about 4 in the morning.

March 13. Mrs. F. making sugar. A pleasant day. From March 13 to first of April nothing new.

Sunday the 23 [24] of March. Wm. Brown & myself left Indianapolis at 4 o'clock in the morning for Franklin Johnson county for H. Gregg Esq. who had there been taken ill—had staid from the day we left him at court in consequence of such sickness. We had not proceeded more than 8 miles before we met Mr. G. returning in a waggon with a young man. He appeared to be very sick—informed us that from Teusday previous he had not slept any. We returned to Sangsters[?] tavern & ordered breakfast. He shortly came up. We wished him to stop but he would not—but ordered the waggon to proceede. After breakfast we rode on but did not overtake G. until after he arrived at Mr. Henderson. The 24th our court commenced. I called only in the morning & went for Dr. Coe to call until Dr. Sanders[90] could arrive from the country. He appeared to be a little flighty. On Teusday much the same. Came up to my house—

89. Capt. Alexander Wiley and Edmund McGuire, tailors. Sulgrove, *History of Indianapolis*, p. 479; Eliza G. Browning, *Lockerbie's Assessment List of Indianapolis, 1835* (Indiana Historical Society *Publications*, IV, No. 7, Indianapolis, 1909), p. 419.

90. John H. Sanders (1791–1850), a physician who came from Kentucky to New Castle, Indiana, then to Indianapolis in the winter of 1829–30. While he practiced medicine, he also speculated successfully in real estate. He built the mansion on the northwest corner of Market and Illinois streets which was purchased by the state in 1839 and used as the Governor's Mansion until 1846. His eldest daughter became the second wife of Governor Wallace. Dr. Sanders died of cholera on board a Mississippi River steamboat returning from New Orleans April 4, 1850. C.F. purchased the Wood Lawn property from Dr. Sanders in December, 1835. Nowland, *Early Reminiscences of Indianapolis*, pp. 290–91; Brown, "History of Indianapolis," in *Logan's Indianapolis Directory*, 1868, p. 41; diary, April 11, 1850; and entry for December 4, 1835, below.

out of his head. On Wedensday he was very sick & on Wedensday eve I set up with him.

March 26 1833 [—*April 4*]. I set up with Mr. G. also Mr. True.[91] He was up many times in the night—Talkes very rationally—said he wished to get out of the bustle of the world. I saw him on Sunday night. He was rational and on Monday morning I again called. He seemed to think he would get well & go to Morgan court. Wanted me to do some business for him. On Monday after noon he became worse—disease tended to the head. On Tuesday 2 Apl. remained out of his head & on that night set up with him. He remained sensless but easy. Wm. Brown set up with me. On Wedensday 3d of Apl. about 2 o'clock P.M. He died. It was announced to the court which was in Session. It shortly adjourned when the bar & court met to make preparations for the funeral. On Thursday the court adjourned at 12 to meet next day & We attended the funeral. No ceremony performed except a hymn sung at the grave. Mrs. G. was not at home having gone to Ky. No Ladies except Mrs. Henderson Blythe[92] & David Greggs widow. A tolerable pleasant day trees just begining to bud &c.

June 25 (Monday) [*Tuesday*] *1833*. I left for Cincinnati in the stage in company with Miss Eliza Wood & her little brother about 13 & a little sister about 10. It had rained the night before—the road a little muddy but our stage driver Mr. Wright drove very safely & we arrived in about 4½ hours at Hankinses in Shelby County where we breakfasted. We arrived at Nepolian at sundown. Here we met with David Bay who drives the stage from ten miles beyond Lawrenceburgh to Cincinnati. He informed us that the chollera was very bad in Cincinnati & between the two points last mentioned. I felt a little alarmed also I saw several persons who had left Aurora Dearborn County in consequence of the disease. I was some little concerned for myself & the orphan childrin with me.

June 26. We left Nepolian before daylight and proceeded throught the new town to old Lawrenceburgh where several had been attacked & died with the chollera. We arrived at the latter

91. Glidden True, town marshal. Dunn, *Indianapolis*, I, 114.

92. Wife of Benjamin I. Blythe, who served as agent of state for the sale of lots in Indianapolis from 1825 to 1828 and as state auditor 1828–29. *Indiana Executive Proceedings*, pp. 278, 288.

place about 10 A.M. where I staid about ¼ of an hour. Saw G. H. Dun[93] Esq. and young John Test.[94] Lawrenceburgh is a flourishing money making place—very dirty at this time & ill calculated to meet the scourge that prevails in the neighborhood. Our company here increased to 4 persons besides our company from Indianapolis who were going to Cincinnati. They were produce merchants & 3 out of 4 took the ardent freely. I passed in sight of the Big bottoms as they are called in the bend of the Ohio where I saw very extensive fields of corn The wheat harvest had just commenced. We crossed White water & the Miami. No bridge over either of them. It raind some & the road was very bad. The trees at each farm house were loaded with ripe cherrys. No person dare eat them as it was believed that they would induce the frightful disease. With in about 8 miles of Cincinnati we stopped to open the mail & found the post master very sick with the chollera. We arrivd at our place of Destination about sun set. Left Miss Wood at Mr. Andersons her uncle & I was dropt at the Pearl St. house, where I was recd with very suitable attention. Had two hands to help me out with about $3000 in specie which I took for Mr. Mcarty merchant & myself to deposit not being able to get paper or drafts at this place. There being no iron chest at this tavern, I deposited the money at a merchants on Pearl st.

I learned that the chollera was prevailing here to some extent.

June 27th. I done various errands but expecting to stay a day or 2 I did not comple[te] many but had agreed to call again. I found Cincinnati very dull—no country merchants in—& every 3 citizen had some badge of moarning for departed friends. Mr. Webster (Daniel) had left the house I put [up] at the week before to return to N. E[ngland] by the advice of his friends who recommended him not to pursue his Journey further west on account of the scourge abroad in the land.

About midnight I felt a little somewhat alarmed for fear I had

93. George H. Dunn, lawyer, state representative in the 1828–29, 1832–33, and 1833–34 sessions of the General Assembly, representative in Congress, 1837–39, state treasurer, 1841–44, and president of the Cincinnati and Indianapolis Railroad. *Biographical Directory of the American Congress*, p. 1108.

94. Son of John Test (see above, Pt. III, note 26) and prosecuting attorney for the third judicial district. *Indiana Executive Proceedings*, p. 307.

the premonitory simtons of the chollera. Got up & went for a candle—sensible I was only alarmed I took Bacons & Locks Essays & read till the town clock struck 1. This day I had seen two funerals & heard of several dying. The streets were clear from country people & every fourth citizen wore badges of moarning for some relative who had been carried off by the scourge. Every man was talking about the chollera—giving his prescription. On Thursday morning I rose & went to a book store & I again feared the approaching simtoms. I went immediatly where I could get the fresh air & cheerful company & soon dissipated all gloom. I this day compleated the most part of my business having taken with me about seven thousand dollars to be disposed of for various persons. I spent sometime with L. Gwynne Esq. now a lawyer in Cincinnati & formerly my pupil. Also visited Wm. Olivers family.

Friday [*June 28*]. In the morning it rained. I visited Calvin Fletcher of Cincinnati.[95] Found him engaged in his counting room —much engaged. While with him he received returns from some of his shippers from N[ew] O[rleans]. He is about 42—a man of small statu[r]e—slim but dark complected—much of a schollar & has a great taste for mechanics. He is a man of no pride lives in a very ordinary house & in plain style far below his means but in all there is a temperance philosophy that is worthy of imitation. He has a plain wife—a daughter & 3 sons—the Eldest about 16 is now a fine schollar & his father talks [of] sending him to college. I dined with him & shortly after took a passage in the Ben Franklin for Louisvill. Left Cincinnati about 5 oclock P.M. There were only five passengers —such is the fright & terror of the people of the chollera that they have abandoned this expiditious & cheap mode of conveyance. My friends at Cincinnati even recommended me not [to] go by land but

95. A distant relative of C.F.'s. C.F. first became aware of the Calvin Fletcher of Cincinnati in 1821 while he was living in Urbana. Some law books directed to C.F. fell into Fletcher's hands and he advertised that he had the books in his possession. C.F. apparently met Fletcher for the first time when he passed through Cincinnati on his return trip from Vermont in 1824. He later recalled that "from the time of the organization of our bank in 1834 our intimacy of a business character commenced & he kept the deposits of our bank till sometime in 1854 or 1855." Fletcher was a successful businessman and merchant, served as a member of the Cincinnati city council, and was active in the educational and cultural life of the city. Diary entry for November 17, 1860, with clipping of Fletcher's obituary in the Cincinnati *Gazette*.

my business required me to go to Louisvill & with a sense of my own danger relying on a good Providence I concluded to proceed. The Boat between Cincinnati & Louisvill never stoped no one haild her to get on nor were there any that wished to get *off*.

Saturday June 29. I arrived at 9 o clock at Louisville. Called on Mr. A. Cooke [?] Esq. the sheriff of the county in which Louisvill was situate to pay him some money. He invited me to his house where it would be convenient for him to give me a receipt but informed me that a negro girl & a small child of his were sick and he supposed with the chollera. I went with him—saw the child who I thought dying. Having compleated my business I visited several other gentlemen with whom I had business. And at 2 o'clock P.M. I was ready to leave. At six I took passage in the Wm. Parsons for Madison. There was not but one cabin & 2 or 3 deck passengers. Louisvill seemed to be in better health than Cincinnati but Kentucky is suffering much with the great scourge.

Sunday June 30. I was landed at Madison about 8 in the morning. Stopped at Mr. Pughs tavern where I was introd[uc]ed to Dr. Soule[96] the Methodist Bishop's son who was there on his way to the lower country. I met with Judge Eggleston.[97] He went with me to an apothecary shop where I purchased some medicine having felt a little predisposition to a diarear—one of the premonitory symtoms to the attack usually made by the chollera. I took a pill went at 11 to hear Mr. Daily[98] formerly of our place (School master) preach. He had method & matter in his sermon that was creditable but spoke in too hurried a manner.

C.F., Indianapolis, to his mother, Proctorsville, Vermont, July 16, 1833

. . . Our last winter was mild and our season very forward. Everything has yielded as if the seed fell in good ground. We had

96. Dr. Joshua Soule, Indianapolis' first dentist. He came to the town about 1833. Sulgrove, *History of Indianapolis*, p. 299.

97. Miles C. Eggleston, president judge of the third judicial district.

98. William M. Daily, who had kept a private school in Indianapolis for a brief time. He later (1853) became president of Indiana University. Wiley, "Methodism in Southeastern Indiana," in *Indiana Magazine of History*, XXIII, 419, 422–23; James Albert Woodburn, *History of Indiana University* ([Bloomington, Ind.:] Indiana University, 1940), p. 211; Dunn, *Indianapolis*, I, 92.

roasting ears from the second crop of corn which S. brought us on the 2d day of July. Our common corn is very high. . . . All have a plenty. I have not seen a beggar for a whole year. These are our good things—what are our evil ones? Last year the cholera passed up and down the Ohio River 70 miles from this place. It arrived so late as to do but little comparative damage to what it was expected. But the scourge has returned again upon us. It has not reached this place but it has spread thro' Kentucky—sweeping all before it. . . . It has recently commenced in our state—and more than likely on the advance toward this place. Every preparation of a temporal kind has been & will be made. . . . Persons scarce dare eat any vegitables or fruit. A few weeks since I passed through places where the cholera prevailed and saw trees lodded with ripe cherries of the largest and finest kinds & gardens red with ripe currans—but no one durst eat. All vegitables are considered dangerous. . . . We have prepared ourselves with medicine & most every family have done the same. We keep a lamp burning all night. It is our duty to do all we can to arrest its progress.[99]

DIARY

☛ [*No date*]. Mr. Ansel Richmond died at Pendleton the 22 day of Decr. at 9 o'clock Sunday morning.

Decr. 25 1833. This morning Cooley & Elijah arose at 4 o'clock & visited their uncle Stoughton now merchandizing with Mr. Bradly on Washington St. opposite the tavern built by J. Hawkins & their uncle John Hill who is now a clerk in the store of James Blake J. M. Ray N. McCarty & Jo. Moore trading under the firm of

99. Bound in with the Diary is a broadside "Report of the Board of Health in reference to the approach of CHOLERA," Bethuel F. Morris, chairman, James M. Ray, secretary, Indianapolis, June 19, 1833. The report of the Medical Committee to the Board which is included is signed by Drs. Isaac Coe, Samuel G. Mitchell, John L. Mothershead, Livingston Dunlap, John E. McClure, and John H. Sanders. The committee gave advice to the inhabitants of Indianapolis and Marion County in the event of a cholera epidemic in regard to diet, medicines, and care of the stricken, and pledged themselves to minister to all afflicted whether they could pay or not. The doctors also recommended that associations of five, ten, or more families be formed, pledged to care and nurse each other. See note 33 above.

Report of the Board of Health in reference to the approach of CHOLERA.

At a meeting of the Board of Health of Indianapolis, on Friday, July 19, A. D. 1833, with reference to the duties assigned them by their fellow-citizens in anticipation of the Epidemic Cholera: Dr. Coe, from the Medical Committee, made the following Report, which, after being somewhat modified, is unanimously adopted, to-wit:

The Medical Committee appointed for that purpose, respectfully report the following advice to the inhabitants of our town and county:

1st. That in anticipation that we as well others may be visited with the cholera, they would recommend at present as a preparatory preventive, a strict course of temperance and regularity in diet, drinks and exercise, the spare use of meats; vegetables and fruit, and more particularly if the bowels be in any degree disordered, avoiding especially fresh pork, spiritous liquors, green corn, cucumbers and melons, excessive fatigue, wet and night exposure; and the keeping comfortably clothed especially during sleep. Of meats they would recommend ham or bacon, chickens and mutton as best; of vegetables, good ripe potatoes, boiled onions and cooked tomatoes; of table drinks, sage tea, store tea, sweet milk, chocolate and coffee.

2d. *Should Cholera appear*, Be still more careful in observing the above directions, use no fruit, no vegetables except potatoes, onions and tomatoes as above and little or no meats, live chiefly on bread and butter, toast, crackers, rice, gruel or light soups, and the table drinks above named, and above all do not overload the stomach with any thing.

3d. Should any looseness of the bowels or sickness of the stomach occur while the disease is prevailing, consider it the commencement of a disease which may then easily be cured, but if neglected will certainly kill. Go to bed between blankets and be pretty warmly covered, and if you have lately taken a hearty meal or eaten fruit or vegetables, or if there is much sickness at the stomach, take a table spoonful of salt in half a pint of warm water, and repeat it every five minutes until it vomits, then immediately take from 20 to 30 grains of calomel, mixed with dry sugar and wash it down with water or tea, and if purging with watery and thin stools continues, repeat it every two hours, adding half a tea spoonful of laudanum to each dose, until the discharges are checked or billious ones take place, and if after this it does not operate in 6 or 8 hours, take two or three table spoonfuls of castor oil every two hours until it does, and immediately after giving the first dose of calomel, if there be fever or a strong pulse, bleed and let the drinks be warm sage or other herb teas and take no food but gruel. This course has in other places been sufficient to cure in almost all cases when early commenced.

4th. When the cholera decidedly attacks, producing frequent and copious stools resembling rice water or soap suds, and which is generally followed by spasms, take the salt and water emetic if the stomach is loaded or very much sickness is present as above directed and after it calomel, but if not, begin with the calomel and laudanum, and take from 40 to 60 grains of calomel and a teaspoon ful of laudanum every two hours until this thin purging is stopped, and the spasms, if occuring, checked, and then in six or eight hours afterwards if the medicine does not operate and bring away billious discharges from the bowels, give castor oil as before until it operates.

Apply a large mustard plaster over the stomach, and if coldness occurs, apply mustard also to the soles of the feet and inside of the thighs as hot as it can be borne; if spasms occur, rub the places well with the hands; and if the pulse is strong or there is fever, bleed as before directed, but if the pulse is weak, bleed only under the direction of a physician, and depend chiefly on calomel and laudanum; and in all cases call in a physician as soon as one can be got, not forgetting that wherever the disease has prevailed, it has generally been easily checked at the first moment of attack, but delay is dangerous and often death.

5th. Every family should be supplied with calomel in ten and twenty grain doses; an ounce or more of laudanum; a vial or bottle of castor oil, and some ground mustard, and fire and candle should at night always be ready to be lit. The above doses are for adults. For a child 8 years old, 10 grains of calomel and 5 drops of laudanum in diarrhoea, and 20 grains of calomel and 10 or 12 drops of laudanum in cholera. One year old, 5 gr. calomel and two or three drops laudanum in the diarrhoea, and 10 or 15 gr. calomel and 5 or six drops of laudanum in the cholera. And for other ages, proportionally to the age and severity of the attack, but in giving laudanum, much will depend on the child being accustomed to its use.

In conclusion, the committee would remark that after full consideration of the subject, they believe, by making due preparation our citizens will be exposed to less danger by calmly remaining, should the cholera appear, than by flying from their homes, and would recommend that families now take care to secure female and other family help who will not desert them and flee in the hour of need; and that as there are abundant funds, that the Board of Health assure all such persons acting as domestic assistants, that they shall be well attended in case of sickness from cholera, without charge.

All which is respectfully submitted.

ISAAC COE,
SAMUEL G. MITCHELL,
J. L. MOTHERSHEAD,
L. DUNLAP,
JOHN E. M'CLURE,
JOHN H. SANDERS.

In furtherance of the above suggestions, *the Board of Health pledge themselves* to every resident of this place or wayfaring person here, if the Cholera prevails, that our efforts and the liberal means furnished by the citizens shall be promptly used for their comfort and aid, which shall be extended without charge to all such as are unable to pay.

It is recommended to every family to supply themselves with the Medicines above recommended, within a week from this time: and all families in this place, unable to procure them, will be furnished by the Ward committees.

It is recommended to the citizens to form into associations of five, ten or more families, according to their own discretion, without reference to wards; who will pledge themselves to remain with, take care of, and nurse each other, in case of Cholera, under the direction of a Superintendent chosen by themselves; and that the names of those belonging to each association be furnished by its Superintendent to the Committee of the Ward in which he resides.

B. F. MORRIS, *President.*
Teste,—J. M. RAY, *Sec'y.*

FLETCHER PAPERS

Broadside issued in anticipation of a cholera epidemic, July, 1833

Jos. Moore & Co. They soon returned with numerous presents for themselves & other brothers—Miles being absent at Mr. Mallaries in Hamilton County & Calvin at his uncle James Hills where he is sent with his little sister Maria[100] to nurse her as Mrs. Fletcher is very unwell & has been for some weeks.[101] Giles left home after breakfast for Mr. Mallorys to see Miles & carry a letter & some books. This day very pleasant no snow on the ground—26–7–8–9–30 very pleasant but roads bad.

Decr. 31 1833. The grave of the year. This morning rose at 5 o'clock. Orinderio had got up at 4 o'clock with Catherine Smith who is here nursing Mrs. F. who is very feeble. The little girl & Calvin at their uncle James Hills. I wrote a letter to Wm. Brown of Jacksonvill Ill. to be conveyed by Ensley Gaudy. My little boys Cooley & Elija are ingaged in reading the life of Casper Hauser[102] likewise in drawing some & this day bo't a paint brush &c. Very cold. Mr. Southgate Noble left on my horse for Columbus on business. He is now reading with me in my office. I esteem him as a good hearted young man who has been so unfortunate as to acquire a bad reputation. I have intrusted some important business to him. I fear that his disposition to accommodate will distroy his usefulness. Since my worthy friend Richmonds discease I have thought of imploying Noble or at least trying what friendship will do for him & kindly treatment & advise. I this day have drawn the pension application of old Mr. White—Settled with Fletcher & Bradly—Done some business for M. F[. . .] in relation to rent. Wrote several letters. Alfred Harison is in my office exchanging scrip with those who came to the land office.

I also received a bank bill for the new bank[103] from Mr. Mor-

100. Maria Antoinette Crawford Fletcher, the Fletcher's sixth child and first daughter, born October 29, 1833.

101. Elijah Fletcher recalled this period in his "Recollections of My Mother": "When Maria was born . . . Mother was very sick. Maria was taken away from her and put out to nurse with Aunt Maria Hill [wife of James Hill]. When mother was recovering she attempted, as was her wont, to superintend the yearly pork packing. The brine, the salt, sausage meat &c were brought in to her in tubs; but she was too weak & brought on a relapse by her exertions." Fletcher Papers.

102. The German foundling Kaspar Hauser (1812?–1833). It was popularly believed that he was of noble birth, perhaps the Prince of Baden.

103. The bill creating a State Bank which was passed and approved Janu-

rison. Messrs. Merril & Blackford are spoken of for President of the mother bank. M[errill] called on me was a little elated at the idea of being President had seen the Governor who had flattered him a little in that particular. I had been spoken to serve as a director but I think those who first suggested it have given me up for my want of capacity or in consequence of the indifference I have manifested on the subject.[104] I doubt whether I have been sufficiently forward & attentive to make those necessary friends in order to [win] preferment. I hope I may not turn to the right or left to gain popular favor. If my doing right will not accomplish what I disire I say let me go down or remain in *statua quo*. I admit that good sense should teach every man that he should not be entirely indifferent to the good opinion of his fellow citizens. My wife is very unwell. I hope She is on the mend.

This night a meeting at the methodist church (Mr. Rooter preacher) at 8 o'clock & to continue until the new year comes in. Cooley Elijah Giles Dorio & Mrs. Smith the nurse have gone. Cooley objected on the account that he believed there would be shouting &c. I am left with Mrs. F. who is confined to her bed & says but little. Elijah [*sic*] & his little brother Stoughton are in bed asleep. I have concluded to close my naritive & write a line to Miles.

January 1st 1834. This morning rose at 5 o'clock. Elijah & Cooley & Giles were up. No snow on the ground. Not very cold. Elijah went to his uncle Stoughtons for New Years gifts. Cooley declined going not wishing to leave a comfortable fire. After Breakfast I left the house. Mrs. Fletcher having been confined to her bed

---

ary 28, 1834. Under it the state was divided into ten districts with a branch bank in each district. Additional districts with branches could be created. A head office was to be located in Indianapolis but there was to be no parent bank. The branches were to be mutually responsible for the obligation of each branch. A president was to be elected by the General Assembly and there was to be a state board consisting of a representative elected by the directors of each branch and four directors elected by the Assembly. Branch boards consisted of directors (seven to ten) elected by the stockholders plus three appointed by the state board. *Laws of Indiana*, 1833–34, pp. 12–38. At a meeting of the state board on February 13, 1834, branches were located in Indianapolis, Lawrenceburg, Richmond, Madison, New Albany, Evansville, Vincennes, Bedford, Terre Haute, and Lafayette.

104. For the election of the bank officers see below, note 125.

for 2 weeks I have Catherine Smith to nurse her. Dr. Coe the physician. She seems to be a little better to day. Soon after I arrived in my office Wm. McLaughlin[105] & old Mr. Harrison Alfreds father called to get me to write a deed for a piece of ground given by old Mr. McL. for a meeting house 1½ mile South East from Indianapolis—also a subscription paper for donations to build a house &c. At noon when I came home for dinner found Mrs. Bradly & Mrs. Forse[?] at our house. They took dinner with us. Cooley & Elijah were absent at Judge Morris on a visit. In the P.M. old Mr. Townsend called on me James Townsend from Putnamvill & paid me $100. for A. White & Co. Our family in consequence of Mrs. F. illness are not so numerous as they otherwise would have been.

I commence the New Year sensible of the great changes in the past 365 days. Several individials with whom I have had a long intimacy viz Harvey Gregg Obed Foote Mrs. James M. Ray & poor Richmond. The latter was intimately connected with me in business & in friendship. He has gone the way of all the earth. As a friend I valued & esteemed him as a citizen. There was none who had higher claims.

January 2d 1834. The Snow began to fall last night & it is this morning 2 or 3 inches deep. It is extremely cold. Ground I think had become well frozen before the Snow. It was late before I went to my office Having written a bill in chancery for Wright Smith of Cincinnati vs. J.W. Davis[106] & B. I. Blythe I done but little else. Capt. McGeorge called on me. I partially settled an old matter between the Catses & Elijah Wood. Received a letter from Genl. Howard[107] inclosing $200. for the Messrs. Griswolds collectr of

105. A native of Virginia and veteran of the War of 1812, William McLaughlin entered a quarter section of land two miles southeast of the center of Indianapolis in 1821 and settled there with his family. He was a Methodist and a camp meeting was held on his farm as early as 1826. He died in 1836. Sulgrove, *History of Indianapolis*, pp. 399–400.

106. John W. Davis (1790–1859), of Carlisle, Sullivan County. He received a degree in medicine from the University of Maryland and came to Indiana in 1823. He served as representative in the state legislature and as representative in Congress for three terms, and was one of the commissioners appointed to treat with the Miami and Potawatomi in 1832. *Biographical Directory of the American Congress*, p. 1062; Woollen, *Biographical and Historical Sketches*, pp. 233–40.

107. Tilghman A. Howard, a native of South Carolina who came to Indiana in 1830. He was a lawyer, practicing first in Bloomington then in Rockville. From

[illegible] &c also one from L. Combs of Lexington R. Cooper of Bellvill. Returned home after dark. Cooley had prepared a good quantity of wood had good fires & proposed that we should injoy a yankey winter evening eating apples cracking nuts &c description was taken from Peter Parley.[108] I indulged the desire & we spent the evening as he requested. Mrs. Fletcher better & took part in our conversation.

A very cold night. The mail was carried through from Madison to this place in 19 hours—1st time it was carried in a day.

Friday Jany. 3d. This a very cold day. Nothing occured worthy of remark. In the evening a house adjoining Browns tavern took fire. Sam'l. Patterson[109] dragged out a bea[m] in a full blaze which extinguished the fire. Many assembled on ringing the bells but all in confusion. No apperatus prepared engine or buckets & I am daily expecting some very great calamity to occur for want of some such preparations.

Saturday [Jan. 4]. Very cold. I rose early & prepared a letter for John D. &c Jones[?] & sent it [to] Ab. McCarty[110] with $95. This day Capt. McGeorge again called on me. I transacted various business by J. P.

Sunday Jany. 6 [5]th 1834. I this day rose early. Catherine Mrs. F.'s nurse went home. Myself & boys went to meeting. John Moore of Shelbyville called on me & wanted to leave $125.50 for me to pay into the loan office. S. Noble in the P.M. returned home from Columbus having received $101.87 of Washburn & [. . .] Gwin &c. Had done about as well as I could expect. Had treated my horse very

---

1833 to 1839 he served as United States district attorney for Indiana and was elected as a representative to Congress in 1839. He resigned his seat to run for governor in 1840. He was a strong contender for the United States Senate in 1838 and 1848. Woollen, *Biographical and Historical Sketches,* pp. 262–72; *Indiana Election Returns,* pp. 100, 101n, 132–33, 134.

108. Peter Parley was a pseudonym for Samuel Griswold Goodrich (1793–1860), under whose direction beginning in 1827 over a hundred Peter Parley books were written. Instructive tales told to children by a kindly old man, they were extremely popular in their day.

109. Samuel H. Patterson at this time had a wholesale grocery and liquor business in Indianapolis. He later became lessee of the Indiana State Prison at Jeffersonville. Nowland, *Early Reminiscences of Indianapolis,* pp. 294–96.

110. Abner McCarty, of Brookville, at this time receiver in the Indianapolis Land Office.

well. Stoughton came & took Dinner with me. James Hill Came in after cows that had run away. In the eve Henry Sims came up (son of John Sims[111] 14 years of age rode 30 miles without stopping to warm). This man raises his boys as they should be. I received a letter from Saml. Findly of Laport wishing me to patronize one Lacey[?] a young lawyer. Catherine Dorio Cooley Elijah & the Drs. Boy & uncle James went to church. I staid with Mrs. [F.]. She is unable to set up as yet. Snow two inches. I wrote this day to Mr. Ingram by [. . .] making a proposition for him to return & live with me if he sees proper not without. Cooley also wrote him & sent him some of his drawings.

Jany. 8th. Pleasant day much ingaged. Had a trial before Scudder[112]—[. . .] vs James W. Johnson & [. . .] was appointed to take depositions before Merrill [for] Aldrige vs Blythe. This day Richd. Johnson was to deliver an address to commemorate the battle of New Orleans. I could not attend in consequence of business. Delivered at the methodist church.[113] Dinner at B. Brown's hotel—a ball at night and a balloon was expected to be raised but was not. On this eve I went with Mr. Quarles to see our neighbor Joseph Wingate[114] who lay very sick & indeed I thought was dying. Wm. W. Laughlin was the attending physician was present & Messrs. Landus who had called as a neighbor.

9 Jany. Warm & the ground began to thaw. I was invited to take dinner with Messrs. Guard Dunn of Dearborn Fowler of Decater Evans of Fountain Hargrove of Gibson Dunning of Monroe.[115]

111. Dr. John Sims, a native of New Jersey and a physician, came to Martinsville in 1823. He carried on a successful practice, operated a general store and tanyard, and invested heavily in land. He suffered heavy financial losses following the Panic of 1837 and died in 1843. He was a representative in the 1837–38 session of the General Assembly. Major, *Pioneers of Morgan County,* pp. 433–35.

112. Caleb Scudder, justice of the peace for Marion County. See above, Pt. III, note 12.

113. The occasion is detailed in the Indianapolis *Indiana Democrat,* January 11, 1834. Richard M. Johnson, of Tennessee, was highly favored in Indiana to succeed Jackson as President.

114. A bricklayer by trade, Joseph Wingate came to Indianapolis in 1826 from Kentucky. Like Fletcher he was converted to Methodism. Nowland, *Early Reminiscences of Indianapolis,* p. 206.

115. Members of the legislature, David Guard, George H. Dunn, William Fowler, Thomas J. Evans, John Hargrove, and Paris C. Dunning.

Genl. Wilson (not a member) & several others (Palmer the speaker[116]) at Noah Nobles governor at his new residence.[117] His hospitality surpasses any mans in the state. However it may be questioned whether it be hospitality or not. He is a candidate for Govr. next summer & I question whether treats, feasts &c should be considered to come under that denomination and whether they should not be viewed in the same light that entertainment of the landlord or hosts who gets a good dinner upon the faith of a subscription list. I had a little conversation with Messrs. Guard & Dunn on the subject of the Bank. I agreed with Guard that so far as the deposites of the Genl. Govt. which are anticipated to aid the institution that it was illusory & perhaps calculated to lead the bank into difficulty—that this state could not like the Genl. Govt. calculate on the amount of the deposits from the commercial operations of any one year & that the same might be deposited or drawn for the ordinary expenses of the Govt.

I returned home with a view to attend the fune[r]al of our neighbor Wingate but it rained & I was too late. In the eve I went to Mr. Merrills to take depositions &c.

Saturday 10 [Jan. 11 and Sunday Jan. 12]. I rose early having been up late the night before preparing a bill in Chancery vs one West & Potter & went with the Sheriff in the morning to serve the writ. This day felt very unwell. Did not do much. In the P.M. it rained—I returned home early. Sent Elijah to the post office & he brought me the Octr. No. of the N. A. Review. I went to bed early. Sunday morning with Dorio went to love feast. It was very wet & the wind blew but few attended. Left love feast returned home & Cooley & I went to church. Bro. Wingates funeral sermon was preachd—Text "O Death where is thy sting O Grave where is thy victory." I read some in the North A. Re[view]. Mrs. F. in better health & spirits than she had been for some time before. Very cold —freezing.

116. Nathan B. Palmer, representative from Jefferson County and speaker of the House of Representatives.

117. The white-painted brick house with broad center hall with rooms on each side and extended wings stood on what is now East Market Street but was then in the middle of the Noble farm which was bounded by Washington, Noble, Walnut, and Arsenal streets. *Messages and Papers relating to the Administration of Governor Noble*, pp. 20–21.

Monday Jany. 12[13]th 1834. Rose 5 [o'clock]. Cold & clear.

Jany. 15th. Muddy in the extreme. Nothing worthy of notice except a large purchase of land in Laport county of Sidney Williams —1200 acres near lake Michigan for which I agreed to give $2000. I am to pay Danl. Yandees & Porter $1500. in Decr next $666 in 18 months to Williams. I made this contract upon the representation of Williams having never seen the land. I admit for my means it was no small contract.[118] I have been offered by H. Bates an equal partnership by himself if I will except it. I have concluded to run the risk, to be sure should it not be the will of God that my unprofitable life is not to be continued I may intail upon my family a great curse by this purchase but I trust that I may be able to dispose of it with[out] injury to myself and family. I hope to be able to keep it several years before my pecuniary calls will require a sale of it.

Mrs. Fletcher is fast recovering.

Jany. 16. Muddy.

[*Jan.*] *17.* Muddy warm no snow.

[*Jan.*] *18.* The Bank bill passed the lower house—Merrill Sering[119] & Genl. Howard spoken of for President. Received a letter from Tipton.[120] Handed a piece to be printed in Journal to Judge Morris to correct. Saml. Jennerson asked me to aid him in election for J. P.[121] Called at the room of Brackenridge & Battell.[122]

118. The La Porte County deed records do not show any transaction between Williams and C.F. at this time. The reference may be to the fifteen tracts of eighty acres each of Michigan Road land purchased by Williams and patented to Elijah Fletcher in 1842 as the assignee of Williams. The tracts lay in T37N, R1W, T37N, R2W, and T36N, R4W. C.F. acquired title to the tracts from his brother Elijah in 1847. La Porte County deed records, L:236; R:119. See diary entry for April 22, 1842.

119. John Sering, who became cashier of the Madison branch of the bank.

120. This letter, dated January 5, 1834, is in the Fletcher Papers and printed in the *John Tipton Papers*, III, 5. With it Tipton enclosed an article to be inserted in the Indianapolis *Indiana Journal* (referred to by Fletcher immediately below), strongly supporting Richard M. Johnson for the Presidency. The article appeared in the *Journal* of January 22, and is also printed in the *John Tipton Papers*, III, 6–9.

121. Samuel Jennison, who was commissioned justice of the peace for Marion County, March 11, 1834. *Indiana Executive Proceedings*, p. 517.

122. John A. Brackenridge, representative from Vanderburgh and Warrick counties, and Charles I. Battell, senator from Posey, Vanderburgh, and Warrick counties.

Sunday Jan. 19. Muddy. Went out to uncle James to see Calvin & his little sister. Found both well. Staid took dinner—James Hill gone to meeting to Widow [. . .].

Monday Jany. 20th 1834. Stormy disagreeable day. Bot a [. . .] old Dietz Williams. In the eve Harry Pendleton came down for advice in relation to his duties as administrator of his fathers estate.

Tuesday Jany. 21st. Snow about 4 inches deep. Went down to McGuires to take a communication written by Tipton signed voter.

Jany. 24. Mrs. Richmond and her little boy[123] was bro't down. I expect she will stay with us. Her little child is a handsome fine boy. I feel interested for them both. I hope I maybe blessed with Judgment & discretion to direct & counsel them a right so far as it may be required of me.

[*Jan.*] *25.* Sold the house formerly occupied by Mr. Richmond[124] to Sam. Smith for $400.

Feby. 1st. I was elected bank director. The vote stood as here exhibited by the Journal & Democrat. The latter sets the vote forth as it occured the latter [former] just makes the a statement of the result.[125]

February 4 1834. The Anniversary of my THIRTY SIXTH

123. Eliza Pendleton Richmond, widow of Ansel Richmond, and her son Ansel. She was the daughter of Thomas M. Pendleton and sister of Harry Pendleton. Mrs. Richmond continued to reside in Indianapolis after her husband's death. She became a schoolteacher and was a devout Methodist, "a lady of agreeable manners" whose "constant piety gave her great influence in society." Holliday, *Indiana Methodism,* p. 202; Dunn, *Indianapolis,* I, 127.

124. Ansel Richmond devised to C.F. his house and lot. He also devised to him his interest in outlot 51. C.F. completed the payment on the outlot and recorded the deed on October 3, 1835. Agent of State, Indianapolis Sale of Lots, Payments, May 1832–, in Archives Division, Indiana State Library; Marion County deed records. Ansel Richmond's will is in the Richmond-Kennedy papers in the Indiana Historical Society Library.

125. C.F. and Seton W. Norris of Indianapolis, Lucius H. Scott of Terre Haute, and Robert Morrisson of Richmond were elected by the General Assembly to the state board of the bank. Others receiving votes were David H. Maxwell of Bloomington, James Givan of Indianapolis, Christopher Harrison of Salem, and Newton Claypool of Connersville. Samuel Merrill was elected president. On the first ballot he received 33 votes, John Sering of Madison 18, and Gamaliel Taylor, also of Madison, 16, with 3 scattering. On the final ballot Merrill received 37 votes, Sering 15, and Taylor 17, with one blank. James M. Ray was elected cashier by the state board on February 14. Indiana *House Journal,* 1833–34, p. 463; Indianapolis *Indiana Democrat,* February 15, 1834.

Year of my age (36). Rose Early. Our family consists of Mrs. Richmond her little boy Ansel Onderio Crombough, Giles Isham, Elijah Calvin & Stoughton (son). James & Miles are absent from home. The former is at his uncle James Hills taking care of his little sister Maria—Miles at Mr. Mallories at school. The weather very pleasant. No Snow on the ground but the F[r]ost not so far out as to make very dissagreeable travelling as yet. Alfred Harrison in my office with me exchanging scrip. My professional business occupies all my time & much of it I fear I shall neglect. I am wonderfully blest with health & think I am more capable of doing my business correctly than ever yet I find myself imperfect & subject to make very mortifying mistakes. I pray that I may have wisdom to so discharge the various avocations of life so as to be servisable to my neghbors & country—yet regardless of that ephemeral applause in which there is but little or no merit.

The various duties to be performed in relation to the bank as a director thereof are truly difficult & delicate. My neghbors Judge Morris Isaac N. Phipps Dr. Sanders & James Morrison are all candidates for [. . .] clerk.[126] A Mr. North from the city of N.Y. is here as a representative of an association of merchants—I have letters of introduction to him from Mr. Jones[?] of Urbana Judge Lane [of] Huron County Ohio.

John Hill being sick was brot here today. Mrs. F. & myself took tea at James M. Rays with the old Lady Mrs. Coe & Mr. McChesaney.[127]

Sunday Feby. 9 1834. This day warm the frost going out of the ground. Mrs. F. has had Mr. Peek preparing for sugar making but have not opened the camp as yet. On yesterday I made some examination of the Bank charter. I discover I have assumed a fearful responsibility. Nothing but Divine aid can prepare me to discharge those arduous & delicate duties with propriety. May God give me

126. James Morrison served as clerk of the town of Indianapolis, 1834–35. Sulgrove, *History of Indianapolis*, p. 486.

127. Jacob B. McChesney, a cousin of James M. Ray and Joseph M. Moore, who had just arrived in Indianapolis. He served for nearly thirty years as secretary of the state sinking fund. Nowland, *Early Reminiscences of Indianapolis*, pp. 349–50.

wisdom. I this day went to church with Calvin Elijah & Giles. Mr. Rooter preached. On my return Mr. Peek Stoughton & John came & took dinner. Cooley returned from Uncle James where he has been staying for the last week. James pleased with him. Appears to have a good heart & an understanding that is rather more than ordinary.

I have this eve received the National Intelligencer of the 1st int. & from the resolutions introduced by Mr. Wright of the N.Y. legislature I fear that there is no remidy to be had from the Genl. Govt. on the subject of the currency. This circumstance alone admonishes me that my late election as Director of the Bank throws a fearful responsibility upon me. I have hoped that the effects produced by the removal of the public deposits[128] would only be temporary. I now view differently. I pray God that I may have wisdom to do all things so far as I am concerned to his honor glory & to the good of my country. I am called to act without much experience. The partiality of friends have thrown burthens upon me that I fear I can't sustain. Yet I feel it my duty to try.

C.F., Indianapolis, to his mother, Proctorsville, Vermont, June 1, 1834

. . . I last fall gave you some assurances that I should visit you this summer, but I have been accidentally placed in a situation that I cannot possibly leave home this summer. The public duties required of me as a state Bank director, which, when I gave you assurances of my visit, I did not in the least anticipate, that I should be called to perform—preclude the possibility of my return this season. My three associates & myself have to organize 10 state Banks this summer, & put them in operation.[129] They are the first

128. A reference to the removal of the government deposits from the United States Bank under order of President Jackson in September, 1833.

129. The election of directors of the Indianapolis branch of the bank by the stockholders on November 11, 1834, resulted in the choice of Samuel Henderson, Hervey Bates, Benjamin I. Blythe, David Williams, Alexander W. Russell, John Wilkins, Homer Brooks, and James Blake. Directors for the branch chosen by the state board were Samuel Herriott of Johnson County, Alexander Worth of Morgan County, and James Givan. Hervey Bates was elected president; the cashier

banks that have been organized in the state. The public are much interested in the immediate attention to this business. I blame you as I stated to Stoughton, who said a short time since, that I must go home, as you would be much disappointed—I told him I blamed *mother* for it all—that I once wanted to become *a tin pedlar*—yes, a happy tin pedlar, with my little cart—could have returned & seen you every year or oftener & have made you & Susan[130] some handsome presents—A fine pepper box, Tea cannester &c., but you was opposed to my following the trade & I have been compelled to seek my fortune in a distant country.

My wife is much disappointed as she expected to accompany me. But if nothing occurs to prevent more than my private interest I will come next summer....

Stoughton visited Philadelphia in March, returned in April. Will in October leave here again for the same place & will call round & see you. He is in good health & spirits. Is devoted to his business. Has a fine man for a partner—a Mr. Bradley—a Baptist and a native of Kentucky—they are doing well. S. will make money as I have for years past, if he meets with no bad luck & in one year, more than he would have in five at hard work in Vt. He has made an astonishing change in his appearance & behavior—you would scarcely know him. He is very lean & spare. Is very saving much more so than men of his business in this country. Has no idea I presume of getting married. Comes & sees us on Sundays. My wife & children are very fond of him.

My second boy Elijah T. Fletcher we have sent to school ten miles from this place to a lady a preachers wife—a Mrs. Kent born & raised in Timouth [Tinmouth?] Vt.[131] Is a celebrated instructress.

---

was Bethuel F. Morris. The State Bank and branches were proclaimed open for business by Governor Noble on November 19. Indianapolis *Indiana Journal*, November 14, 1834; Dunn, *Indianapolis*, I, 342; *Indiana Executive Proceedings*, p. 290. The Indianapolis branch included Marion, Johnson, Shelby, Hancock, Madison, Hamilton, Boone, and Hendricks counties.

130. Susan Sargent, who lived with C.F.'s mother. Timothy Fletcher, C.F.'s brother, left her the sum of one thousand dollars in his will "in consideration of her services in attending to my father and mother in their old age." She continued to live on the Fletcher farm in Vermont after the death of C.F.'s mother. Von Briesen (ed.), *Letters of Elijah Fletcher*, pp. 258–59n.

131. In his "Recollections of My Mother," Elijah wrote that after Mr. Gregg

E. has been home once—came a foot & alone, & like his uncle Elijah, when he used to return from school, brought home a certificate of his good conduct &c. James who is Eleven years old in April leaves home tomorrow for the purpose of attending an academy 60 miles distant.[132] His mother goes with him & a boy who lives with me. I make her attend to this business so if I should happen to be called off, she will have had some experience in these matters. Besides should my boys do well I want their mother to have the creadit in a great measure. Our boy Calvin will go to

---

closed his school in 1833 he was sent to an academy conducted by Mrs. Frances Kent in Greenwood, ten miles south of Indianapolis. "In the spring of 1834 mother carried me there on horseback. Charles J. Hand—since deceased—accompanied us. . . . the greater part of the way the road seemed as if hewed through the dark forest. As we picked our steps along over the rough log causeway, for which the Madison road is renowned, we saw deer and turkey tracks; and once, if I remember rightly two bucks. . . . Mother took me to the house of an aged couple 'Uncle Henry' and 'Aunt Patsy' Smock, situated a half mile east of the 'state road.' This with the exception of the 'Academy,' was the only frame building at this time in the neighborhood." Elijah recalled that he was something of a hero among his fellow students since he came from the "far distant town of Indianapolis."

A note from Mrs. Kent, dated Greenwood Academy, June 21, 1834, to C.F. is in the Fletcher Papers. It states that she has no hesitancy in saying that Elijah would meet with his father's warmest expectations. "Except in a very few instances he has been punctual in acquiring the lessons given him at the specified time." Two notes from Elijah to his parents from Greenwood, September 1 and 16, 1834, are also in the Papers.

132. In the Fletcher Papers there are seven letters from James Cooley to his parents written from Bloomington between June and September, 1834, while attending the state school. The boy lived with the Beaumont Parks family. In his first letter he reported: ". . . I went to College and Mr. Maxwell [his tutor] did not put me in a class but said I had better read a spell by myself, until I learn to parse. He makes the boys parse almost every word. After while I shall be in a class. I am going to have a copy book and write every day so as to improve my writing. This is a small letter but I think it is large enough for so young a lad as I am." On June 28 he wrote that on "Monday Doctor Wylie came home and there was a great rejoicing among the students they Illuminated the New Colege and fired the guns and rung the bells." He apparently did very well in his studies and won a good word from his instructors. James D. Maxwell wrote to C.F. on September 25, 1834, when James Cooley left Bloomington that he "has not only been obedient to his teachers in every instance, but particularly attentive to his studies for one so young. As to his advancement in study I am confident you would have been fully satisfied, if you had witnessed his examination."

Maxwell (1815–1892), son of David H. Maxwell, had graduated from Indiana College in 1833. He attended the medical school at Transylvania College,

school here with his brother Miles. Stoughton the youngest boy is a fine child, much admired by his uncle. We are all thank God, doing as well as we deserve....

DIARY

July 4th 1834. Rose this morning about sunrise—cloudy. My hay had been cut down several days previous by Mr. Peek but so wet could not get it in. Mr. Peek hauled it. Consisted of about two tun had it sold. I went & sold my sheep (10) I bot of a Mr. Baldwin, weathers middle sized two & 3 years for $1.25 a piece. Went to my office. Settled a case about to be commenced for possession of Judge Blackfords house. Received the National Intelligencer from Washington. Read the rejection of Mr. Speaker Stephensons nomination.[133] Went to the Sabbath School celebration at the Methodist chappel about 200 or 300—a union meeting of the methodist Presbyterian & Baptists Service opened by the Revd. Mr. Rooter—an address by Rev. Mr. Fisher[134] Baptist—able & by Rev. Mr. Holiday (Presb.) very good. There was a celebration of a political nature at the Court house oration by J. Morrison. I did not attend. Judge Morris & little son and daughter came home took dinner. We discussed the politics—Mr. Stephenson rejection by the senate Bank loan for the state which Judge Morris does not believe will go into operation. Very warm—walked to my block.

A celebration takes place at Shelbyvill at which an exhibition of an experiment on the rail road will take place. I should have been

---

graduated from Jefferson Medical College in 1844, and practiced medicine in Bloomington until his death. He served as secretary of the Board of Trustees of Indiana University, 1838–55, and as a trustee from 1861 until his death. Burton D. Myers, *Trustees and Officers of Indiana University* ([Bloomington, Ind.:] Indiana University, 1951), pp. 255–57.

133. President Jackson had appointed Andrew Stevenson, speaker of the United States House of Representatives, as ambassador to Great Britain, but the Senate refused to confirm the appointment. Jackson made no other appointment and two years later Stevenson was confirmed.

134. The Rev. Ezra Fisher, who served as pastor of the Baptist Church in 1834 and 1835. Dunn, *Indianapolis,* I, 567.

pleased to attend but could not well.[135] We have had an uncommon wet season. My corn is about as high as anywhere.

135. As a promotion measure to stimulate sales of stock in the Lawrenceburgh and Indianapolis Railroad, in which several citizens of Shelbyville were actively interested, an experimental section of railroad extending a mile and a quarter was constructed near Shelbyville in 1834. Judge William J. Peaslee was the leader of the project. The car, track, and roadbed were made entirely of wood, and the car was horse drawn. The railroad was first put in operation on July 4, 1834, with much festivity. The car was kept constantly full, passengers paying twenty-five cents for a round trip. Marian McFadden, *Biography of a Town, Shelbyville, Indiana 1822–1962* (Shelbyville: Tippecanoe Press, 1968), pp. 82–83; Chadwick, *History of Shelby County*, p. 260.

VI

Diary of CALVIN FLETCHER *January 1–December 31, 1835*

January first 1835. Rose Early ½ 4 o'clock—a habit practised by the family for the last 4 years. Our circle is composed of our 5 sons little daughter Orinderio Crombaugh (17 years) Mrs. Richmond & little son Ansel 18 months.[1] Mr. Ingram at our house on a visit is considered one of the family.

The weather has been very pleasant during the month of December. It has not been unseasonably warm or extremely cold. Some light snows. Roads very good. Our legislature in session. On the 30 had Messrs. Batel Amory Morgan, Long, Wallace of Davis

1. In the 1835 assessment list for Indianapolis as reported by the assessor George Lockerbie on April 15, the Fletcher household is reported as including one male between 21 and 45 years of age (C.F.), three between 10 and 21 years (James Cooley and Elijah Fletcher and perhaps Giles Isham), and four under 10 years (Calvin, Miles, and Stoughton Fletcher and Ansel Richmond), and two females between 21 and 45 years (Sarah Hill Fletcher and Mrs. Ansel [Eliza] Richmond), one between 10 and 21 (Orindorio Crumbaugh), and one under 10 years (Maria Fletcher). C.F. is listed as the sole owner of lots in the town of Indianapolis valued at $1,545 with buildings thereon valued at $550. His personal property was valued at $500. His tax totaled $9.11. Besides the lots he owned in square 42 (see Pt. V, notes 18 and 88) he is shown as owning all of square 39 which lay north of square 42 and was bounded by Ohio, Alabama, New York, and New Jersey streets. He is also shown as owning the east one third of lot 9, square 57 on the north side of East Washington Street between Delaware and Pennsylvania streets, the rest of the lot belonging to Nicholas McCarty. The entire lot was valued at $700, the building thereon at $100, and the total tax amounted to $1.37½. Browning, *Lockerbie's Assessment List . . . 1835*, pp. 411, 420.

[Daviess] Wallace President, Fowler, Boon (George) Griffith—to dine.[2] On the 31 had Messrs. Hanner, Hillis, Hamilton, Sigler[3] &c & Mr. Ingram who has been with us since the eve preceding Christmass. This morning the carrier of the Democrat broght his New Years address. I shaved myself—a late practice—from economy & convenience & went to my office about 8 now in the upper room in the brick building opposite Browns tavern where it has been located for the last 6 years.[4]

About 9' *Calvin* Rooker name sake called for a contribution. I gave a cap cost $1.12½. I gave the cap notwithstanding the liability of having 10 other applications of equal merit. Garret Seymour's son from near Lafayette called & paid me $2040 for my Wabash land.[5] I paid Yandes $1300 towards lands I bo't of Sid Williams at Laport. Settled several matters with James Hill for entering land &c.[6] Had various calls for professional advise. Received a fee of $20. in cash from Mr. Banbridge of Lafayett. Mr. Bell[?] of the house of Avery Sharpless & Co. called to settle some business. In the Eve Calvin, Cooley & Elijah went down town after New Years gifts they

2. Charles I. Battell, senator from Posey, Vanderburgh, and Warrick counties; Amaziah Morgan, senator from Rush County; Elisha Long, senator from Hancock, Henry, and Madison counties; William Wallace, senator from Daviess, Knox, and Martin counties; David Wallace, lieutenant governor and president of the Senate; William Fowler, senator from Decatur and Shelby counties; George Boon, senator from Clay, Sullivan, and Vigo counties; and Andrew C. Griffith, senator from Jackson, Jennings, and Scott counties.

3. Samuel Hanna, senator from Allen, Delaware, Elkhart, Randolph, and St. Joseph counties; David Hillis, senator from Jefferson County; John Hamilton, senator from Fountain County; and Daniel Sigler, senator from Putnam County.

4. This would have been on Washington Street about a half block east of Meridian.

5. The Tippecanoe County deed records show that C.F. conveyed to Garret Seymour on January 1, 1835, some five hundred acres of land in sections 4, 5, 8, and 9, T23N, R4E, a few miles south of Lafayette. Four hundred and eighty acres of the land, lying in sections 4, 5, and 8, had been purchased at the Crawfordsville Land Office in 1828, 1829, and 1830 for $1.25 an acre.

6. In December, 1834, James Hill entered in C.F.'s name at the Indianapolis Land Office 320 acres of land in section 7, T15N, R5E (Marion County) and six hundred acres in sections 31 and 22, T20N, R5E, sections 17 and 18, T19N, R5E, and section 14, T19N, R4E (all in Hamilton County). The Hamilton County deed records show that C.F. disposed of most of the above entries in that county by 1840 at $2.00 to $3.00 an acre. The Marion County land was sold to Nicholas McCarty. See note 44, below.

having attended Mr. Wm. Holidays[7] school thro the day. Pleasant day.

Jany. 2d 1835. Rose this morning ½ past 4 o clock—pleasant, agreeable for the season. Eat by candle light. Mr. Ingram very unwell with a bad cold caught in consequence of sitting up late. Settle with John Givan several claims placed in my hands for collection by taking a farm in Morgan County & other demands & property to the amount of $3330 &c. Settled with the executor of Ansel Richmond the Revd. Nathaniel Richmond.[8] Received several letters & documents from our members of Congress to wit from Messrs. Ewin, Kennard & Tipton.[9] Wrote a letter to the Honl. Garret Davis of Parris. Ky. & now a member of the Ky. legislature. Received a number of newspapers. Turned very cold. Mrs. F. visited Mrs. Blak[e].

My professional engagements occupy all my time & I have so much business that I do not get time to read. I have to go to Cincinnati next week & at the same time I can not well leave home in consequence of my professional concerns.

Jany. 3 Saturday. Cold. Preparing for Cincinnati. Settle with Joseph Moore. Learned that application had been made to bank directors to appoint Messrs. Cobern or Morrison attorney. Any right that [I] might be supposed to have having been supposed to be forfeited because I was a director of State Bank.[10] I view no office to be filled by he who is the most indigent but an employment to

7. "Mr. Holliday," Elijah wrote many years later, ". . . was a man whom I remember without the least degree of love or gratitude. A more cruel, hard hearted man I never knew, minister though he was. He fairly starved, and cowhided knowledge into his scholars on study days; and then on Saturdays impudently demanded their services in sawing his wood, digging his potatoes &c." Elijah went on to describe a cruel beating Holliday gave James Cooley for failing to memorize an unreasonably long Greek lesson. "Recollections of My Mother." Fletcher Papers.

8. A brother of Ansel Richmond and the first minister of the Baptist Church in Pendleton, Madison County. Netterville (comp.), *Centennial History of Madison County Indiana,* I, 165; Harden (comp.), *The Pioneer,* p. 241.

9. John Ewing of Knox County, representative in Congress from the Second District; George L. Kinnard, representative from the Sixth District which included Marion County; and United States Senator John Tipton.

10. C.F. became attorney for the Indianapolis branch. See entry for February 10, 1835, below.

be given in consequence of meritt. My business with the branch for the last 6 weeks has been upwards of $8000. which I have deposited principally from collections. I ask no favor of the kind. If I get it it must be a voluntary act.

Sunday Jany. 4 1835. Rose early. Mr. Ingram better—has talked of going to Cincinnati with me but is very unwell. He & I went to see Mr. Bradly. He has been & is very sick. Cold but pleasant. Cooley, Elijah, Calvin, Miles, Mrs. Richmond & Dorio went to Methd. church. Mr. Conwell member of the Legislature[11] preached 6 Prov. 22 v. "Train up a child in the way he shall go" &c. Read 2d Series 1st vol. Tales of My [. . .]. John Hill called. Went to the Bank after dark to get papers for Cincinnati where I am to make some arrangements for redeeming our paper carried there by the land office. Cool clear night no snow.

Monday [Jan.] 5. Rose ½ after 4. All in health. Mr. Ingram has given out going to Cincinnati. I shall probably s[tart] about 10 A.M. 12 Mr. Ingram has agreed to go with me. It is very cold. 2 P.M. we leave well prepared for a cold journey. Proceeded to Greenfi[e]ld. On our way travel with a Mr. Reynolds of Wayne co. Arrive about 1 hour after dark. Very cold. Stop at Mathews. I have with me about sixteen thousand dollars—part to be left at the Commercial Bank Cincinnati part for our merchants & $3000. to be paid to persons for whom I have collected & who reside in Cincinnati. I have been deligated with power by the Indapolis branch bank to make an arrangement for exchange with the Commercial B[ank].

At Hanco[c]k Mr. I. & myself spent some time with Mr. Mayhew & young Milroy.[12]

6 Jany. Leave after breakfast. Very cold. Take the national R[oad] as the roads that have not been much travelled are very rough. We proceede thro Knights town, with about 60 houses. National Road not yet contructed but workmen at it. Raysvill close by with 4 houses & we passed on to Milton, a Mr. Unthank a saddler in Company.

We arrived at M[ilton] about sun down. It is laid off about 1½

11. James Conwell, of Franklin County.

12. Henry A. Milroy, who opened a store in Greenfield in 1834. George J. Richman, *History of Hancock County Indiana* (Indianapolis: Federal Publishing Co., 1916), p. 123.

m. from the R[oad] about 100 houses in Wayne Co. Put up with a Mr. Lampson. Read the life of Nicias in Plutarch. Very cold night.

Wedensday [*Jan.*] *the* 7. Leave before light for Centervill where we took breakfast at Nobles Tavern.[13] Saw Rariden. Went to Richmond. Stopped visited the bank saw E. Coffin cashier.[14] Left at 12. Went to Eaton thence to Winchester 9 miles S. on the Cincinnati road. Arrived an hour after dark. Staid with a Mr. Patterson.

Thursday [*Jan.*] *the 8*. Left early & rode across to Middleton on the Miami. Very cold suffered much. Got breakfast. Called on Mr. Tytus. Done business with him. Left at 12. Weather Moderated. Rode thro' Reading & there commenced the Lebanon McCademised road. The weather being pleasant & good moon, we concluded to reach Cincinnati that night where we arrived at 7. We had supper.

Friday [*Jan.*] *9*. Deposited my money in Commercial Bank. Gave several checks for the same. Called on all those with whom I had business. Mr. Ingram crossed into Ky. There he spent the day with his old friends where he had formerly kept school. The river was not froce up but the ice run so that Boats do not pass up.

Cincinnati not very full of business but such houses as have recovered from the panic are doing well. The markets are rather slim in consequence of there being no fruit. I saw a few apples at 2 cents apiece.

At night heard a Mr. Powers[15] lecture on phrenology especially on the organ of consciousness. Was pleased with the moral & practical remarks of the speaker a man of 35 or 40.

Saturday Jany. 10. Weather much moderated. Mr. Ingram returned. Called on my clients for further orders for business. Bo't a set of silver spoons for Mrs. F. toys &c for $13.75. In the eve went

13. Thomas G. Noble opened a tavern in Centerville in 1834. Henry Clay Fox (ed.), *Memoirs of Wayne County and the City of Richmond Indiana . . .* (2 volumes. Madison, Wis.: Western Historical Association, 1912), I, 139.

14. Elijah Coffin, Richmond merchant and Quaker, who served as cashier of the Richmond branch of the State Bank from its opening until its closing in 1859. Andrew W. Young, *History of Wayne County, Indiana* (Cincinnati: Robert Clarke & Co., 1872), p. 394.

15. According to the Cincinnati *Democratic Intelligencer and Commercial Advertiser*, January 3, 6, and 20, 1835, a Dr. Powell, not Powers, was lecturing on the subjects of phrenology and geology.

with Mr. I. to the museum on corner of Pearl & Main St.[16] Very few attended.

Sunday [Jan.] 11. Went to Unitarian Church with Calvin Fletcher wife & daughter. Heard a good sermon from Mr. Pebody.[17] In P.M. went & took tea with Dr. Wilstack. At night heard Dr. Beacher *pray*[18] & Dr. Stowe preach.[19] [. . .].

Jay. 12 Monday. Rain, a prospect of the ground thawing but cannot leave. Compleated all the business I had to do, which consisted in no small degree in errands for my neighbors. But mainly I was engaged in contracting with the Commercial B[ank] as to the manner they would redeem our Ind. B. paper. In the eve went with a Mr. McCarty [to] Uncle William Oliver (Mrs. F. uncle) to tea. Spent the eve.

Tuesday Jany. 13th. Left Cincinnati with Mr. I. at 9 A.M. Rained. We took the river road to Lawrencebugh which we passed after 2 P.M. Staid at Ustales[?] 10 m. from L. Got very wet. Rain. Spent the eve with a lawyer Hopkins [and] Dr. Hardin.

Jany. 14. Leave before breakfast. Road breaking up. Ride to Napoleon. Wet & dissagreeable. Breakfast. Ride to St. Omer. Put up for night.

Thursday [Jan.] 15. Arrive home 5 in the eve wet & very cold. Found all well. Feel truly greatful that I have arrived safe. It is the first winter visit I have ever made.

Friday Jany. 16 1835. Wet dissagreeable day. Got to my office about 10 A.M. Visited by Mr. Burton of the house of Johnson Tingley & co. of Phila.[20] Made deed to Mr. Rutter for Hager land.

Saturday [Jan.] 17. Wet & disagreeable not through.

16. The Western Museum Society of Cincinnati, founded by Dr. Daniel Drake, was located here at this time.

17. Ephraim Peabody. Charles T. Greve, *Centennial History of Cincinnati* . . . (2 volumes. Biographical Publishing Co., 1904), I, 624.

18. Lyman Beecher (1775–1863), Presbyterian clergyman, father of Henry Ward Beecher and Harriet Beecher Stowe, who served as president of Lane Theological Seminary in Cincinnati from 1832 to 1852. *Dictionary of American Biography* (20 volumes. New York: Charles Scribner's Sons, 1928–37), II, 135–37.

19. Calvin Ellis Stowe (1802–1886), scholar and educator, who came to Cincinnati in 1833 as professor of Biblical literature in Lane Theological Seminary. The following year he married Harriet Beecher, author of *Uncle Tom's Cabin* (published first as a serial in 1851–52). *Ibid.*, XVIII, 115.

20. A wholesale house patronized by Indianapolis merchants.

Sunday [*Jan.*] *18*. Disagreeably muddy. Read the newspapers Clays report on the French spec[u]lations &c. Went to church. Heard Mr. Ames.[21] Has talents. Isaiah 2 & 3 vs. P.M. Mr. Peck[22] & Stoughton called.

Monday 19. Mr. Ingram left us. We feel lonesome.

Teusday [*Jan.*] *20*. Have set myself about squaring my books of accounts & have learned that this is one branch of my business that must hereafter receive my special attention.

Wedensday [*Jan.*] *21*. Wet, rainy weather. Settled with Conner & Russel.

Jany. 22d. Pleasant. Mr. Beezley whom I knew in Urbana 15 years past & with whom I boarded at a Mr. Downs' a blacksmith, dined with us. Saml. Findly called on me from Laport. Finish my settling with A. W. Russel & Co. & Conner & Harrison also with McCarty & Williams. Much difficulty grows out of my not keeping regular books & making short settlements. I intend to reform in this particular as the whole business community are improving in this particular. My collecting business at home is on the increase—abroad on the decline.

Friday [*Jan.*] *23*. Cloudy morning. Pleasant day. Messrs. Dr. Curry [and] Green from Posey Henkle & Hannaman[23] dined with us also Mrs. Paxton. Settled with J. & P. Landis & have been regulating my books & papers preparitory to the commencing an examination of my cases in court which will require a more than ordinary degree of attention as I shall have 20 or 30 chan[c]ery cases in the next Sp [Supreme] C[ourt].

21. The Rev. Edward R. Ames, Methodist minister who was stationed in Indianapolis in 1834 and 1835. He later became a bishop of the church. Dunn, *Indianapolis*, I, 592.

22. Edwin J. Peck (1806–1876), who came to Indianapolis from Connecticut in 1833 as superintendent of the masonry and brick work on the State House. He served as designer and contractor for other buildings over the state, including the charming Greek revival Second Presbyterian Church in Madison (1835), was a director of the Madison and Indianapolis Railroad, was active in promoting the Indianapolis and Terre Haute Railroad Company, of which he became president, and was president of the Union Railway Company. Nowland, *Early Reminiscences of Indianapolis*, pp. 252–54; Wilbur D. Peat, *Indiana Houses of the Nineteenth Century* (Indianapolis: Indiana Historical Society, 1962), p. 182.

23. Representatives Thomas Curry, from Clinton and Montgomery counties, George S. Green, from Posey County, Benjamin Henkle, from Tippecanoe, and Robert L. Hannaman, from Boone and Hamilton counties.

In the Eve called at the Representatives Hall for the first time in the session & heard a short discussion on the project for a system extended of internal improvement—much heat & confusion. I am desireous that the bill shall pass.

Mrs. Paxton staid with us.

Saturday Jany. 24. Rose at 5. Breakfasted. Pleasant. Rode to Danl. Smiths J. P.[24] to attend a trial State vs [blank]. Overtook Mr. Cobern who was on his way. Imploid by the complainant Miller. Arrived about 10 o'clock. A little cabin Full of County people came to see the trial. Defendant br'ot part of his neighbors to prove that they would not believe complainant under oath. Complainant prepared to show his good character—advised my client to enter into a recognizance without investigation. All spectators disappointed. I was treated cleverly—invited to attend a debating society—Question which the greatest evil the sale & use of ardent spirits or Slavery—to meet at schoolhouse near home [of] Culbersons.[25]

Returned home with Dr. Stip[26] & Cobern.

Brother Sweet arrived from South Bend.[27] Had been absent more than a year. Looked healthy &c.

Monday 26 Jany. Wet disagreeable weather. P. Patrick[28] down preparing papers for Mr. Pratt.[29]

24. Daniel R. Smith, justice of the peace in Washington Township. Sulgrove, *History of Indianapolis*, pp. 626–27.

25. Joseph Culbertson, who settled in Washington Township in 1829. *Ibid.*, p. 634.

26. Dr. George W. Stipp.

27. Alhannon Sweet. See above, Pt. II, note 85.

28. Palmer Patrick, a Pendleton merchant. Netterville (comp.), *Centennial History of Madison County*, I, 320.

29. Daniel D. Pratt (1813–1877). While this is the first mention of him in the diary, Pratt had been reading law and working in C.F.'s office since the fall of 1833. He was born in Maine and came to Indiana in 1832. He taught schools for a little over a year in Lawrenceburg and Rising Sun before coming to Indianapolis. After being admitted to the bar he moved to Logansport in 1836. He served as state representative, as representative in Congress, as United States senator, and as commissioner of internal revenue. *Biographical Directory of the American Congress*, p. 1700; Nowland, *Early Reminiscences of Indianapolis*, pp. 255–62. George H. Dunn (see Pt. V, note 93) addressed a letter to C.F., dated Lawrenceburg, September 26, 1833, introducing Pratt. Copy in Pratt Papers, Indiana Division, Indiana State Library.

Heavy rain. Frequent professional calls. Set an arbitration in case of John H. Scott[30] vs. his late wifes heirs. Messrs. Palmer & Scudder associates. Went to bed at 12.

Teusday [*Jan.*] 27. Pleasant but very muddy. Mr. Pratt set out on business for Randolph County with Mr. Aker in company with Palmer Patrick & Mr. Sweet who left for the South Bend. I lent him or rather gave him $45. He is a poor economist. Paid my instalment on $800. borrowed of Commercial B[ank]. Got a cognovit from Ingram Brown McOuat[31] & John Givan. Received a letter from Dr. Fithian in the Illinois legislature. Werth of Moorsville.[32] & Anderson of Louisvill Ky. Examined some pension papers in order to write to Kinnard. Saw Harriott[33] who has come to attend the meeting of the directors of bank. Talks [of] resigning his seat as State delegate. In the eve retired from my office & set with my family. J. H. Scott came after me to set as arbitrater &c. I spent this day without doing but little business.

Wedensday [*Jan.*] *the 28.* Wm. Hill[34] sent to old Mr. Butterfield to see to the corn & rent the Givan place. Received on account of Mr. Shaw (member[35]) from Dr. Hitt on a man in Shelby Co. Counseled St. Clear.[36] Collected $5. of J. W. Davis for house rent paid by

30. Ignatius Brown lists a John H. Scott as a speaker at the first meeting of the Whig party in Indianapolis, May 17, 1834. Other speakers were John Hobart, Hiram Brown, and William Quarles. Scott was a lawyer. He died probably in 1836. "History of Indianapolis," in *Logan's Indianapolis Directory*, 1868, p. 31. See entry for February 4, 1837.

31. Thomas McOuat, a native of Scotland and a merchant who settled in Indianapolis in 1830 although he had purchased lots in the first sale in October, 1821. He helped organize the Protestant Episcopal Church in Indianapolis. His wife was Janet Lockerbie, daughter of George Lockerbie, and a daughter, Elizabeth, became the wife of Ovid Butler. Nowland, *Early Reminiscences of Indianapolis*, pp. 229–31; Sulgrove, *History of Indianapolis*, p. 411.

32. Alexander Worth, who settled in Mooresville in 1826, opened a store, and built and operated a woolen mill. Major, *The Pioneers of Morgan County*, p. 429. He was a director of the Indianapolis branch of the State Bank.

33. Samuel Herriott, clerk of Johnson County and a director of the Indianapolis branch of the State Bank.

34. A younger brother of Sarah Hill Fletcher (born 1814), whom she invited to come to Indianapolis to live and go to school. See Sarah Hill Fletcher to her father and C.F. to same, July 14, 1834. Fletcher Papers.

35. Henry M. Shaw, representative from Knox County.

36. Arthur St. Clair, register of the Indianapolis Land Office.

Mc. & W[McCarty & Williams]. Commenced suit for Phil Harding in c[ircuit] c[ourt] vs M. Dorson. Received a note on Campbell Shank *et al* from Blachly Wells[37] &c.

Thursday [Jan.] 29–Friday 30 & Saturday 31. Cloudy dissagreeable weather.

[Jan.] 31st. N. McCarty called on me & desired me to engage more largely in the buying of land. At this time I have used all the means that I can spare without anticipating them. He proposes to borrow from $5000. (beyond our means to be vested in the purchase of land) to $10000. I have ever been opposed to borrowing money. Indeed have seldom or never borrowed. And I have my doubts as to the propriety of such a measure. Life is very uncertain & it is very rare that men leave their estates in a condition to extinguish any debts without a sacrifice & much less debts for borrowed money. However the proposition is from one who will not give but a moderate interest for money which so far as I am concerned Shall not be vested in real estate above the congressional price (1.50$) one dollar & 50 cts. per acre & this description of land must soon [be] beyond the reach of purchasers as it is nearly all taken up at this time.

Sunday February 1st 1835. Mr. Pendleton (Harry) staid with us last night & is with us to day. Very cold & dissagreeable. No snow on the ground. Mrs. Richmond Dorio & James Cooley went to hear Mr. Ames Preach. Very few attended in consequence of cold. Stoughton came up & took dinner, Mr. Pratt returned in the eve from Randolph Co. Went to Mr. Hands. His son Pike fell from the stable & dislocated shoulder. Mr. Webster sent by mail American Almanac. 8 letters on business answered. Read the intelligencer.

Monday [Feb.] 2d. Very cold. Mr. Pendleton & Jackson[38] leave for home. Took tea at N. McCarty's with Messrs. Jef. Evans Dr. Hamilton[39] & Jack Hawkins. This day Honl. Wallace from Daviess

37. Cincinnati wholesale merchants.

38. Probably Andrew Jackson, sheriff of Madison County. He later served as county treasurer, county clerk, and state senator. He was a successful farmer and miller. Harden, *The Pioneer*, p. 184.

39. Thomas J. Evans and John Hamilton, representative and senator from Fountain County.

Co.[40] who died last night was taken to his family. P[r]ocession accompanied of [by] both houses a short distance.

February 3 1835. Very cold no snow but after late rains have made the ground rough. Messrs. Bigger Ca[r]ter from Logansport & Smith (C. B.) from Connersville[41] dined with us. Messrs. Cole & Stephenson down from Hamilton County.[42] Called by my friends McCarty & Williams to witness their agreement of dissolution &c.

This eve called on by Dicken of Danville[43] and about 9 o'clock heard the melancholy news of the death of my old & once esteemed worthy friend John Hays who it is said was last night burned at Greenfield while confined in Jail for insanity. I once knew no man more honorable—none more interprising—none more kind & deserving—but dissipation & bad associates has ruined [one] of natures happiest models for real excellence.

February 4. Rose about 6 having been detained late at my office last night. Very cold ground froze no snow on. This the anniversary of my nativity—*am* 37—more than one half of my life has undoubtedly passed. There are many reason to me why life & its scenes should be strongly impressed on my mind. Yet the past seems a dream, a delusion. I have witnessed a total wilderness converted into a flourishing city an improved country—one hundred & fifty families that settled & wintered in Indianapolis in 1821 in the short space of 14 years entirely lost in the great flood of immigration. At least out of six or seven hundred families residing here at this time there are Dr. Coe, Mrs. Nowland, Henry Bradley, James Blake, J. M. Ray Mrs. Paxton Mrs. Givan, Thos. Chinns, Danl. Yandes & Saml. Henderson only left. In a new country like ours the destruction of human life is far greater than in an older country with the same natural salubrity as all local changes are illy calculated to promote health.

40. William Wallace, senator from Daviess, Knox, and Martin counties.

41. Samuel Bigger, representative from Rush County and later governor (see below, note 63); Chauncy Carter, representative from Carroll, Cass, Miami, and White counties; and Caleb Blood Smith, representative from Fayette County.

42. Either Bicknel Cole or Albert B. Cole, both of whom were justices of the peace in Hamilton County, and John D. Stephenson, clerk and recorder. *Indiana Executive Proceedings*, pp. 452, 453, 454.

43. Pemberton S. Dickens, of Danville, Hendricks County.

We have had some sickness in our family. In 1822–3 I had several severe attacks of billious fever. In 1824 & 6 Mrs. Fletcher was dangerously ill but we have been greatly blessed compared with most families.

This day made a deed to the undivided half of the 26 pieces of land I have recently entered in Marion Hancock Madison Hamilton & Boon counties to N. McCarty who advanced one half the amount[44] &c. Cole & Stevenson are yet here.

Mrs. Fletcher made a dinner anniversary dinner. Cooley. Elijah, Calvin, Miles. Stoughton, Mrs. Hill, Dorio, Mrs. Richmond were present & all in health. How ignorant & blind to the events of the next 365 days. May I rest relying on the Disposer of all events & ask & fervently pray to have grace to encounter every difficulty that may be presented.

Mrs. Paxton Mrs. & Mr. Wm. Hannerman[45] & Mrs. & Mr. Robt. Hannerman with us to tea. Cooley came to the office for me.

Teusday [Thursday, Feb.] 5. Cold. Received money of Cole of A. Paterson. Sold Morgan Co. corn 300 bushel at 25 cts. per b. Had Messrs. Jef. Evans Marshall[46] Thompson[47] of Lawrence & Liston[48] to dine.

N. McCarty left for Phila. Cold. Legislature about to adjourn. Lent Sam. Bell $50. Worked in my office till 10 o' P.M.

February 6 1835. Very cold, dry weather. Members of the legislature just returning home one by one as they may get leave of

44. The Marion County deed records show that on February 4, 1835, C.F. deeded to Nicholas McCarty land in sections 7, 8, 9, and 10, T15N, R5E, in section 5, T14N, R3E, section 33 in T15N, R3E, and in section 5, T16N, R3E. The deed was not recorded until April 4, 1859, five years after McCarty's death.

45. William Hannaman (1806–1880), a printer by trade, came to Indianapolis in 1826 and worked in the *Indiana Journal* office. In 1832 he entered into the drug business with Caleb Scudder and also engaged successfully in other business enterprises. In 1833 he married Rhoda A. Luse, a sister of Mrs. Paxton. Nowland, *Early Reminiscences of Indianapolis*, p. 430; Sulgrove, *History of Indianapolis*, pp. 162–63.

46. Joseph G. Marshall, representative from Jefferson County.

47. Richard W. Thompson (1809–1900), representative from Lawrence County, later representative in Congress, and secretary of the navy in the cabinet of President Hayes. Charles Roll, *Colonel Dick Thompson, the Persistent Whig* (*Indiana Historical Collections*, XXX, Indianapolis: Indiana Historical Bureau, 1948).

48. Jonathan A. Liston, representative from La Porte and St. Joseph counties.

Absence. Mr. Brackenridge had my horse to go to old Mr. Brentons. Wrote to Dennis Pennington.[49] Old Mr. Geo. Isham to pay the bill I advanced to Dr. Coe.

Mrs. Fletcher called by Judge Morris to go to his house which prevented her visit with Mrs. Richmond & self to Mrs. Paxtons to eat her birthday dinner—a festival I claim to have introduced among a few friends. This is the only kind of celebration I encourage. At such an event we should feel greatful to the Disposer of all events for having carried us thus far on the journey of life. At the same time we should renew our resolutions to spend the remainder better than the past.

Mrs. Richmond & myself visited Mrs. Paxton as contemplated. It is severly cold. I left the comp'y & went to my office but returned at Sundown & took tea with Mrs. & Mr. R. L. Hannerman Susan Luse. Mrs. P. Wm. Hannerman & wife. Returned about 8 o' clock. Severly cold more than at anytime before this winter. I fear that fires will break out & there is not an engine in the place. Mrs. F. returned from Judge Morris' who has a daughter second child by present wife.

Saturday 7th Feby. Very cold. Left to go to my office about ½ after 8 & discovered the court house on fire. The cry was raised—fire extinguished. Bur[n]t a hole thro the rough [roof]. Very cold day. Returned home at 12 & did not return. Saml. Collip called on me to employ me against H[. . .] estate. Very cold mercury below zero.

Very cold eve. Mr. Holiday called & bro't me two numbers of the [. . .] to read the address of John Sergeant & treatise on popular education. Spent some time in conversation & retired. Rose tolerable early.

Sunday morning the 8 Feby. So cold none of us except Dorio went to Church. Read through the Merican Almanac for 1835.

49. A Virginian, Pennington (1776–1854) was in Harrison County, Indiana, by 1804, served in the territorial General Assembly, was contractor for the courthouse at Corydon which was used as the state capitol, served several sessions in the state General Assembly, and at this time was sheriff of Harrison County. He was strongly antislavery. Sketch in *Journals of the General Assembly of Indiana Territory 1805–1815*, edited by Gayle Thornbrough and Dorothy Riker (*Indiana Historical Collections*, XXXII, Indianapolis: Indiana Historical Bureau, 1950), pp. 1002–03; *Indiana Executive Proceedings*, pp. 458, 459.

Stoughton came & dined with us. Potatoes froze in a good celler last night. Received the intelligencer—letters from G. L. Kinnard L. H. Scott now at Washington negotiating the deposits of public monies &c & from T. L. [D.] Gregg at Boston an old school master. Legislature adjourns tomorrow. Murcury still.

Feby. 9. Weather moderated, *a little moderated.* Legislature adjourned in rather confusion. I am endeavoring to prepare my business to leave for court. Mr. Ungles called from Bellville. Nothing new. Weather stil moderating. Old Mr. McDaniel died last night. Did not go to my office this night. Read the Biblical repository handed me by Mr. Holiday on popular education. I have much labor before me of a professional character.

Feby. 10th 1835. The weather much modified. Arrived at my office tolerably early & went to work. I have various calls—not very profitable. Probate court. I called on Austin W. Morris & requested him to become a candidate for Representative.[50] It is an important post to be filled & the best abilities are required at the next session in consequence of the contemplated canal.[51] James M. Ray called on me to endorse for the Steam Mill Company[52] for $4500. I took

50. Morris was elected a representative from Marion County in 1835 and 1836. He was a son of Morris Morris, a Methodist and a Whig. Upon his death of typhoid fever in 1851 C.F. recalled that he had "studied law a short time with me & manifested great aptness but was called on to attend public surveying and left the law. He & I in 1826 or 1827 went to the upper Wabash by Lafayette & camped out 2 nights together . . . were always on terms of intimacy." He served as trustee of Asbury College and of the Indianapolis Female Seminary, as deputy state auditor for his father who was auditor, and as director of the Bellefontaine Railroad Company. Nowland, *Early Reminiscences of Indianapolis,* p. 106; diary, June 20, 1851.

51. The Central Canal, projected to extend from a point on the Wabash River between Fort Wayne and Logansport down White River via Muncie and Indianapolis to the forks, thence to Evansville. This was one feature of the general system of internal improvements provided by the 1835–36 session of the General Assembly. *Laws of Indiana,* 1835–36 (general), pp. 6–21. While considerable excavation was done at various points along the line, only about seven miles extending from Broad Ripple north of Indianapolis south through the town to a point about where Kentucky Avenue crosses the river were completed.

52. The Steam Mill Company was organized and incorporated in 1828 under the leadership of Nicholas McCarty, James Blake, and James M. Ray. Its building, located on the east side of the river above Washington Street, was the largest in the town, being three stories with a gambrel roof covering two additional stories. It comprised a sawmill, grist mill, and wool-carding apparatus. It

the matter under advisement. I once determined most important matters with more pre[c]ipitancy than at present. I consulted Mrs. F. on the subject & I came to the conclusion without fear of offending to adhere to my former determination not to endorse for any man. I am now the attorney for the Bank (Indianapolis branch) also a director on the part of the state. My character for solvency should not be suspected. I am under no necessity of borrowing money & I should not place my own independence and the comfort of my family at stake without any adequate consideration. I have refused to endorse.

In the eve went to hear Mr. Merrill deliver an address to the Atheneum.[53] Retired at half past 9 o clock.

Feby. 11 Wednesday. Pleasant weather. Dined at Mr. Wilkins with Mrs. Fletcher & Richmond. In the eve received the pleasing intelligence that L. H. Scott had effected an arrangement with the government for the Deposits of the public moneys collected in this state by the sales of lands of the U. States for the use of state Bank. I feel an interest in this matter as I am a member of the state board of Directors. But the same mail that brings this intelligence also brings the sad tidings of Wm. C. Lintons death who departed this life at Phila. one of our canal fund commissioners.

Feby. 12. Having retired to bed at 12 o' I had not lain more than 2 hours before I was wakened by Mrs. Richmond stating that there was a fire on Washington St. I arose. Wm. Hill & myself went found Bazel Brown's Kitchen all in flames. A still night & by great exertion the fire was got under [control]. Clear cold still. This day a public meeting called to fence against fire at the Methodist Church. I attended. A resolution adopted instructing the corporation to raise means to cooperate with state in procuring a fire engine &c.[54] Mr.

---

was not a financial success. The machinery was sold in 1835 and the structure left vacant until 1847 when it was refitted as a woolen mill. It burned in 1853. Brown, "History of Indianapolis," in *Logan's Indianapolis Directory,* 1868, pp. 16–17.

53. The Indianapolis Lyceum or Athenaeum was organized in 1831 to promote literary culture through lectures and discussions. It was succeeded by the Young Men's Literary Society in 1835. Sulgrove, *History of Indianapolis,* p. 106.

54. The Indianapolis Fire Company had been organized in 1826. Its only apparatus was leather buckets and ladders. An act of the 1834–35 session of the General Assembly subscribed on the part of the state one half the cost of a first-

Burr Canal Commissioner[55] & Genl. Tiptons son[56] took tea with me. James Hill Just return[ed] from the South bend having been absent to enter land for McCarty.

Sunday Feby. 15 1835. Rose this morning early. It began to snow. At 8 Mr. Herrod of Columbus[57] now prosecuting attorney called to accompany me to Andersontown to attend the C[ircuit] C[ourt] for Madison Co.—We left. The snow fell faster & thicker. Mr. Quarles soon overtook us. Judge Wick could not go in consequence of ill health. It snowed incessantly. We dined at Arnets[58] arrived at Pendleton after sun down. We staid at Bostons.[59]

16 Feby. Next morning found the snow 8 inches deep. Breakfasted & left for Andersontown. Poor court house. Stopped at Jackson Sheriff—the only decent tavern in [. . .].

[*Feb.*] *17.* Several trials for lewdness. Defended Abbot &

---

rate fire engine, the people of Indianapolis to provide the other half. On February 12, 1835, at the meeting referred to by C.F., it was decided to work toward organizing a new volunteer fire company and to ask the trustees of the town to levy a tax toward the purchase of the fire engine. An engine house was constructed on the north side of the Circle west of Meridian from funds obtained from the county, and a secondhand end-brake hand engine named the Marion was bought from Merrick & Company of Philadelphia for $1,800. It arrived in September, 1835. Dunn, *Indianapolis,* I, 167; Rose, *The Circle "The Center of Our Universe,"* pp. 367–68.

55. David Burr, who had been elected one of three commissioners of the Wabash and Erie Canal by the General Assembly in 1830 and was re-elected in 1833 and 1836. *Indiana Executive Proceedings,* pp. 685, 686, 687. A native of Connecticut, he lived in Salem and Brownstown, Indiana, before moving to Wabash County where he traded with the Miami Indians and operated an inn. With Hugh Hanna he laid out the town of Wabash in 1834. *John Tipton Papers,* II, 11n.

56. Spier Spencer Tipton (1814–1847).

57. William Herod, of Columbus, who served as prosecuting attorney of the fifth circuit from 1833 to 1836. He was elected a state representative in 1829, 1830, and 1844, and state senator in 1831 and 1848, and was elected a representative in Congress upon the death of George L. Kinnard and re-elected, serving from 1837 to 1839. *Indiana Executive Proceedings,* pp. 307–308, 310, 312; *Indiana Election Returns,* Index.

58. Thomas and Samuel Arnett were early settlers in Fall Creek Township, Hamilton County. Haines, *History of Hamilton County,* p. 170.

59. Jesse Boston, tavernkeeper who opened the Madison House in Pendleton in 1835. Netterville (comp.), *Centennial History of Madison County,* I, 320–21.

Markee. La[w]yers who attended court two Messrs. Kilgores Herrod Quarles & Henderson & Anthony.[60] Very Pleasant weather.

20 Feby. Mr. Quarles & myself left at 10 o' clock. Came to Pendleton done some buseness & rode home a little after dark. Snow melting away very fast. Road from Andersontown in 6 hours. Very tired. Began to rain soon after my arrival. My fees at this court amount to about $200. including collections.

Satturday 21 Feby. Snow all gone frost coming out of ground very muddy. Our merchants preparing to go to Philadelphia. Rained all day. Very busy in my office.

Sunday Feby. 22d 1835. This is Washingtons birth day. From former celebrations when a young man I am reminded of this anniversary as well as from the reflection upon the character of so good & great a man as W.

John Hill called. I sent a letter to Mr. Moore to be conveyed to McCarty in Philadelphia. Wrote to Mr. Ingram & handed [the letter] to Mr. Pratt who called on me. I am expecting to leave in a few moments for Hancock County in company with Messrs. Morrison & Quarles. Very dissagreeable travelling. It is with regret that I leave for courts. Went to Hancock county Greenfield in company with Mr. Quarles. Put up at Mathews & Boyers. Staid in a room with Messrs. James Morrison Herrod & Quarles.

Monday Feb. 23. Emploid with Mr. Morrison to prefer charges against Thos. D. Walpole an attorney for malpractise &c.[61] Court held in the court house unfinished & open above—a disagreeable arrangement &c.

Teusday [Feb. 24]. Court met charges preferred rule to answer tomorrow. Little business. Lawyers resident Walpol[e] Mayo[62] & Hanner[?]. From Indianapolis the first named Quarles Morrison H.

60. Thomas C. Anthony or Joseph Anthony, of Muncie. G. W. H. Kemper, *A Twentieth Century History of Delaware County Indiana* . . . (2 volumes. Chicago: Lewis Publishing Company, 1908), I, 69.

61. The proceedings in the case of Thomas D. Walpole, Hancock County lawyer, are covered in Monks *et al.* (eds.), *Courts and Lawyers of Indiana,* II, 722–23. Walpole was finally admitted to practice in the presence of the full court in January, 1838.

62. Addison F. Mayo, of the Hancock County bar.

Brown. From Rush[ville] Alley & Bigger.[63] Brookville Rimond[64]—Shelbyville Butler[65]—Herrod Prosecuter. Not much business. My fees received $50. on old claim $50. new fees.

Wedesday [Feb.] 25. Argued the case vs Walpole for professional misconduct. Argued by Mr. Morrison who opened the case answered by Messrs. Brown Bigger Jas. B. Ray & responded to by myself. Court suspended Judgment until Thursday 26 1835 when they pronounced the charge in the 3d specification proved & disbared the defendant.

Thursday Feby. 26. 1835. Returned from Greenfield with Messrs. Morrison Wick Brown Quarles & Nave.[66] Very cold—suffered [. . .] from it & the roads are werse than I have seen this year. Arrived a little after dark.

Feby. 27. Very cold extremely cold. Past[u]r[e] got a fire by accident. Burned all the grass.

[Feb.] 28. Extremly cold. Miss Sergent[67] Staid with us last night. Found her an interesting woman teacher of infant school. This day bot a lot at public sale.

March 1st 1835. Sunday morning cold but clear no wind. Ground froze several inches say 8 inches.

About to start for Shelby court with Judge Wick.

Very cold. Ground froze 18 inches. Very rough. We went to

63. John Alley and Samuel Bigger. Alley was elected associate judge the following August. *Indiana Executive Proceedings,* p. 590. Bigger (1802–1846), law partner of Oliver H. Smith, served as representative from Rush County in the 1833–34 and 1834–35 sessions of the General Assembly and was elected president judge of the Sixth Judicial Circuit in 1836. He resigned as judge in March, 1840, upon being nominated for governor. He served one term as the state's chief executive, 1840–43. *Messages and Papers relating to the Administration of Samuel Bigger,* Introduction, pp. 4–5, 50.

64. John Ryman, who was admitted to the Franklin County bar in 1832. Monks *et al.* (eds.), *Courts and Lawyers of Indiana,* II, 682.

65. Ovid Butler. See above, Pt. IV, note 48.

66. Christian C. Nave, Hendricks County lawyer. He served as state representative in the 1834–35 and 1835–36 sessions of the General Assembly and was elected to the state senate in 1839 and as a delegate to the Constitutional Convention in 1850. *Indiana Election Returns,* Index.

67. Indianapolis' first kindergarten was conducted by a Miss Sargeant. It was located in the damp and disagreeable basement of the Governor's Mansion in the Circle. It is said to be the first school in the town in which objects were used to illustrate the lessons. Miles Fletcher was one of the first pupils. Dunn, *Indianapolis,* I, 122. See below, entry for May 4.

Kellers to dinner. Arrived at Shelby after dark. Stoped at Sleeths tavern. Emploid in case of Graves vs. Rhodefer—case of much excitement.

2d March. Cold & clear the same 3–4 & 5 & 6. Attorneys attending Sweetser James Brown[68] Butler Vanpelt. I agreed with Butler to go on the circuit & do my business. I have been now engaged in the practice of the law for about 14 years in this place say in all 15 years & I have concluded to confine my business at Indianapolis.

March 7 1835. This morning cold but pleasant. Ground not thawed. Roads good as in Sept. I left this morning leading a stray horse. Dined at Kellers. Arrived at home about sundown. All well. Mr. Pratt had many things to say in relation to business that had accumulated.

[*Mar.*] *8.* Sunday went to hear Mr. Havens[69] preach.

[*Mar.*] *9.* Ground yet froze. State Bank directors met.

[*Mar.*] *10.* Cold.

[*Mar.*] *11.* Mrs. Fletcher commenced opening Sugar camp. Mr. Pratt starts to the Bluffs with Gamaliel Taylor Marshall.[70] Our Bank board adjourned. We have agreed to accept the deposits of the public revenues of the State & disburse the same in Ky. Mo. Michigan & Ill. Messrs. Deming represented Ter[r]e Haute Branch —Fairman Lafayette—Snap Vincennes—Clark Bedford—Collins New Albany—Lanier Madison—Guard Lawrenceburgh—Graves Richmond—& Herriot Indianapolis.[71]

[*Mar.*] *12 13 & 14.* Gloomy disagreeable weather. Frost remains in the ground yet sugar water has not run any as yet. Mr. Pratt returned from the Bluffs.

Sunday 15. Wet dissagreeable cold day frost yet in the ground. Went with Elijah Calvin & Miles & Dorio to hear G. Tayler preach. Read several papers this day. Quarles & Wick started for Franklin

68. Perhaps James T. Brown, Dearborn County lawyer. Monks *et al.* (eds.), *Courts and Lawyers of Indiana*, III, 1140.

69. James Havens, Methodist minister stationed in Indianapolis from 1833 to 1836. Dunn, *Indianapolis*, I, 592.

70. Gamaliel Taylor, United States marshal for Indiana.

71. Demas Deming, Loyal Fairman, John F. Snapp, —— Clark, James Collins, James F. D. Lanier, David Guard, Jacob Groves, and Samuel Herriott.

court where I have been in constant attendence for the last 12 years without missing a court.

Monday [*Mar.*] *16.* Very raw cold frost yet in the ground.

Mar. 17. More pleasent. Have received 3 nos. of Halls Western magazine.[72] Sugar Water begins to run. No birds of passage yet arrived yet or striped [s]quarrels appeared as yet.

James & Elijah attended their debate before Mr. Holiday. Question who'se the greater man Bonepart or Washington. Cooley for the former & Elijah for latter.

I am preparing for Court next week. Have several chancery suits &c. It will require some effort for me to retain my business.

23 March. Our court commenced. Had but little business of importance. Lawyers James Morrison Quarles Brown Cobern J. H. Scott, Sheets—residents. Herrod States attorney & Nave from Hendricks.

I have abandoned the project of attending any court beside those of the Marion circuit Sup[reme] & Dist[rict] Court. I have entered into an agreement with Ovid Butler Esq. of Shelbyvill to attend to my business except such as I may have at this county & Shelby. I am to enjoy one half of the proceedes for 2 years, am to commence & prepare suits in the counties of Hancock Bartholomew Johnson Morgan Hendrick Boon Hamilton & Madison & he will give his immediate presence to the same.

Weather cold & dissagreeable from the 24 of March until the first of April.

1st April. Pleasant day. Ploughing my ground for corn. Provision very scarce. Corn 50 cents per Bushel.

5 April. Sunday. A cold cloudy day. Left with Mr. Quarles for Morgan Court. Vegitation backward no grass yet grown leavs not yet developed. Frosty nights. Staid [April] 6 & 7 at Martinsvill. Gave up my business to Butler & returned home.

Sunday [*April*] *12.* Went to Da[n]vill Court with Mr. Butler. Found Quarls & Brown there. Very cold.

Tusday [*April*] *14.* A snow. Wedensday a very cold day.

72. *Western Monthly Magazine,* edited by James Hall (see note 132, below) and published in Cincinnati beginning in 1833. Buley, *The Old Northwest,* II, 528–30.

Gloomy prospects. Provisions very scarce. Poor prospect for small grain. Corn & potatoes 50 cents per bushel.

Thursday [*April*] *16.* Cold as march heavy frost.

Friday [*April 17*]. Morning cold.

Saturday morning April 18. More pleasant.

Sunday [*April*] *19.* Sent my papers to Boon Court for Mr. Butler attention & am at home. Have been to hear Mr. Smith methodist preach.[73] Had a pleasant shower. The grass is coming forward, leavs develloping themselves. The blossoms on the plumb trees begin to be disclosed. Planted potatoes & sowed some. Stoughton came up & took breakfast. I am reading the 28 no. of Halls Western Monthly Mag[azine] which I now take. Our family are in good health & I have abundant reason to be greatful.

April 20. Cloudy damp day. I have taken up the 16 no. of the Waverly novels. I never read but two of the series before. I have not devoted my time to such reading indeed beyond the Scottish Chiefs Vicar [of] Wakefield, Raselas & Thadeas of Warsaw. I cannot boast of reading of British novels & the [. . .].

Teusday [*April*] *21.* Cloudy & windy. Not warm. Mr. Pratt & myself preparing to remit money to our clients. Plumb trees begin to Blossum.

Wedensday [*April*] *22.* Cold no frost. Mrs. F. has just sowed her garden. Mrs. Paxton Miss S. Luce dined with us have just finished. James is preparing to get my old files of news papers bound. Mrs. Richmond teaching our boys.

Thrusday Ap. 23. Very great frost—fear the fruit is killed. Cold windy. Grain very scarce. Corn 50 cents per bushel & it is supposed will be $1. before new corn. The engineers to examine the several routes for canals & railroads are here. It is understood four divisions will be in the field this summer. I expect much from these examinations. Others expect but very little.

Young Polk[74] from Logansport here after money for Genl.

73. The Rev. John C. Smith, Methodist minister, who was stationed in Indianapolis in 1835 and 1837. Dunn, *Indianapolis,* I, 592.

74. Perhaps Benjamin C. Polke, son of William Polke. The latter served as commissioner of the Michigan Road lands and as register of the Fort Wayne Land Office. *John Tipton Papers,* I, 468n, III, 702. See also note 147 below.

Tipton McKeen[75] & others. Wm. Conner down to enter land. Certificates for lands bot on the canal has come to hand—3–80ts [?] entered near Wabash town.

Apl. 25. Cold rainy day. Preparing for Hamilton court. Made calculations as to the quant[it]y of land I have entered in conjunction with N. McCarty since last Novr. (1834) three thousand & 76 acres which together with other real estate I have purchased for our joint benifit cost $6470. I owe about $1000. My income from my profession & other sources about $2000. *per ann.* I must decline purchasing real estate yet I deem it a profitable investment but I cannot do it without running in debt. I cannot consent to this for various reasons.

Sunday April 26 1835. Mr. Quarles & myself just ready to Start for court (Hamilton). Brown has [. . .] to go with Herod. Cool not growing weather. Have mad[e] our garden but not planted our corn.

April 27 1835. At Hamilton county Noblesville c[ircuit] c[ourt]. Present Judges Osbern & Cottingham[76] Lawyers—Morrison Herrod —Butler Quarles & Brown.

Monday very cold rainy. Cleared off at night. I visited my friend Hannerman at night. Read thro' the New England Tale. Had many civil cases—enough to occupy the court 3 or 4 days.

Tusday [April] 28. Fog this morning prevented the frost doing much injury. There is an abundant indication of a fruitful season.

Wednesday [April] 29. More pleasant. Trial of Boxleys case much difficulty in consequence of the absence of the President Judge.

Thursday 30th April. Pleasant cloudy. Vegitation rapidly advancing. Visit Mr. Mallerys family.

Friday 1st of May. The 14 anniversary of my wedded "Blessedness." Mr. Quarls & myself after the minutes of the previous day left about 9 o'clock A.M. & proceeded home—Messrs. Herrod & Butler having gone in advance. By the former I sent word to Mrs. F. to prepare *an anniversary dinner.* It was one of the most lovely

75. Hugh B. McKeen, Indian trader and merchant at Logansport. *John Tipton Papers,* I, 393n.

76. David Osborn and Joshua Cottingham, associate judges of Hamilton County. *Indiana Executive Proceedings,* p. 453.

days I ever saw except its representative 14 years past. All nature was lovely. The trees in the forests in full bloom. The plumb & cherry white with blossoms. People just preparing corn ground. Dogwood just beginning to peep out but not yet flowered. We called at Carters half way house—took a little luncheon & started. Soon met Mr. Hannerman & wife going a visiting to Noblesvill. Just at the crossing of fall creek met Mr. Colrick[77] proceeding to Ft. Wayne. He returned with Quarles. I arrived at home about 2 o'clock. All my little children were on the look out & 6 of them & Ansel Richmond the (infant) came out to meet me. They had been hard at work & were up from the field the 4 oldest boys waiting my return to eat dinner with me. I dined with the family & went down to my office & saw McCarty who had just returned from the East.

2d May. This day planted the corn. James Elijah Calvin & Miles & uncle William planted.

Sunday May 3d. One of the most lovely days I ever beheld. I feel uneasy & dissatisfied that I cannot enjoy so great a blessing & realize the same to a greater extent. I went with Mrs. Richmond to hear Dr. Wily preach at the Presbyterian church. He preached a masterly sermon in the M[orning] "cast ye up cast ye up remove the stumbling block" &c the text. In the eve I went to hear him preach on family education which was also a treat. I spent the day much to my satisfaction. Such a Sunday with such pleasure & privilege I fear will never again occur.

Monday May 4 1835. Another delightful Spring morning all nature seems to rejoice and hymn(s) are [. . .] to the father [of] all for the comforts so bountifully showered down.

Cooley Elijah & Calvin start to Mr. Holiday—Miles to Miss Sergents School. I have my business for the Supreme court to prepare.

May 5th. Cool this morning & thro' the day. Our bees work well & begin to gather outside of the hive. Mrs. F. & R. visit J. Wilkins. Mrs. F. bot her boys (2 oldest) a suit of clothes each & got

77. David H. Colerick, Fort Wayne lawyer, practicing from 1829 until 1872. He served in the General Assembly as a representative in the 1833–34 session and was elected to the Senate in 1835. *John Tipton Papers,* II, 475; Monks *et al.* (eds.), *Courts and Lawyers of Indiana,* III, 1141.

the Tailer to make their coats—the first expense of the Kind I have ever had to incur. Provisions very scarce. Corn meal 75 cents corn 50 per bush. Bacon lb. 8–9 butter 18¼ flour $3.50.

May 9. I went to Noblesville, bot the land belonging to S. Dales heirs.[78] Returned the same day—rained most the whole time. People just thro with their corn planting. Frost this night injured some of the fruit. On the night of the 9th a frost injured the plumbs on my early wild p[lum] tree. From May 10 to May 25 nothing extraordinary. Busy preparing for Sp[Supreme] court.

May 25. Sup[reme] & District Court commenced its Session—not as many lawyers as usual—Smith, Rariden, Sulivan, Perry.[79] Dewey,[80] Griffith, Huntington,[81] White[82] & Ingram & Finch.[83] Monday noon on my return at dinner found Mr. Ingram at home. Pleased to see him. His health is very delicate. Pleasant day.

[May] 26 Teusday. Nothing more than usual. Got near thro the business of Sup[reme] Court. I have my portion of business but I think there is rather a decline—or suspension—Indeed the bretherin of the profession have decreased for the last year. Mr. Ketcham[84]

78. The Indianapolis *Indiana Journal* on January 6, 1835, advertised for sale 154 acres of land on White River adjoining Noblesville which belonged to the heirs of Sydnor Dale. According to Hamilton County deed records C.F. bought from Dale's heirs 154 acres in the northwest quarter of section 31, T19N, R5E, November 9 and December 2, 1835, paying the sum of $1,610. The deeds were recorded on November 20 and December 2, 1835. C.F. sold this land on November 1, 1837, for a good profit. See below.

79. James Perry, of Liberty, who became prosecuting attorney for the sixth judicial district in 1830. *Indiana Executive Proceedings*, p. 305. In 1837 he became president judge of the district. Monks *et al.* (eds.), *Courts and Lawyers of Indiana*, Index.

80. Charles Dewey (1784–1862), first of Orange County, then of Clark County, who was appointed to the state Supreme Court by Governor Noble in 1836 and served until 1847. *Ibid.*, I, 198–201.

81. Elisha M. Huntington (1806–1862), who served as state representative, prosecuting attorney, and president judge of the seventh circuit, and as United States district judge 1842–62. *Ibid.*, II, 411–12.

82. Perhaps Joseph L. White of the Madison County bar. He served as representative in Congress from the third district 1841–43. *Ibid.*, I, 90–91.

83. Fabius M. Finch, member of the Johnson County bar and brother-in-law of Judge Wick in whose office he had studied. *Ibid.*, III, 1143.

84. John L. Ketcham (1810–1869). Born in Kentucky, he grew up in Monroe County, graduated from Indiana University, and studied law in the office of Judge Isaac Blackford. He was one of the founders of the Second Presbyterian

has been licensed & will commence business in our place—a very decent but not briliant young man.

Wedensday May 27. Early this morning Messrs. Wiggin & Fowler from Marlboro, N.Y. called on me from Miles (bro.) with a letter. They were on a visit to the far West. They informed me that Michael my oldest brother was on the road & would probibly be here in a short time. I hope [I] shall see him in a few days. He is my oldest bro' born at the first setling of Vermont soon after the revolution. From my fathers indigent circumstances did not derive the advantages that my younger brothers did.

May 31 Sunday. Went to church in A.M.—read Hall Mag[azine] for May. An excellent essay on the elevation of character by which I endeavored to measure my own sentiments & conduct. I find that I really lack ambition to make myself a useful man—that I must become devoted & attached to my profession—must endeavor to elevate my character—improve my faculties & grow a better man. I have concluded to let the pecuniary matters so far as possible hold a secondary place in my estimation.

June 1st 1835 Monday. Wet & dissagreeable weather. James Hill left with Col. Steel[85] for the Wabash to enter lands for McCarty & self on yesterday.[86] Our Supreme Court are advancing in business —not but few lawyers in attendance. District Court rather more business than Common.

Church. In 1836 he married Jane Merrill, daughter of Samuel Merrill. Dunn, *Indianapolis,* II, 1191–92.

85. Col. William Steele, veteran of the War of 1812, lawyer, and merchant, who moved from Wayne County to the new town of Wabash in 1834. He served in five sessions of the General Assembly as a representative from Wayne County and was the first clerk of Wabash County. Clarkson W. Weesner (comp.), *History of Wabash County Indiana* (2 volumes. Chicago: Lewis Publishing Co., 1914), Index.

86. During the summer of 1835 C.F. alone, C.F. and Nicholas McCarty, and C.F. and Charles J. Hand purchased about one thousand acres of Wabash and Erie Canal lands in Allen, Huntington, and Wabash counties for which C.F. received the patents (Nos. 295–307). C.F. purchased another 320 acres in Wabash County which was later assigned to McCarty and patented to him (Nos. 388–391), and C.F. and Hand purchased 160 acres in Wabash County which was later assigned and patented to James Ford (Nos. 1300–1301). The price paid for the lands is not indicated. Wabash and Erie Canal Land Office, Logansport, Report of Final Payments in the Office East of Tippecanoe River (not heretofore reported) up to 1st May, 1849, in Archives Division, Indiana State Library.

From 1st till the 7 wet dissagreeable weather.

Sunday 7th. Wet. Rains every night. The army worm is in the country.

Monday [June] 8. Rainy wet weather.

Teusday [June] 9. High waters. A Mr. Elsworth[87] from Connecticut here. Wishes to buy property. Attend a circus & Show of annimals.

Wedensday [June] 10. Wet weather—gloomy prospects for the farmers. The army worm makes its raviages. Reading the last days of Pompeii by Bulwer.

Thursday [June] 11. Simon Yandes called & informed me he desired to Study law with me. I have assented. He commences on Monday 15.[88] Visited Judge Stevens who leaves here tomorrow morning for Vevay his residence. He is a man of acquirements & great labor.

Friday [June] 12. Am reading law. Mr. Quarles has his office adjoining. I am about making preparations to adopt a course of elementary reading. Have determined to examine each section of the practise act. Have advanced with the section on bail. Make many new discoveries. Visit Judge Blackford[89] in the evening & staid till

87. Henry L. Ellsworth, U.S. Commissioner of Patents. In 1835 he began buying prairie land in Indiana and Illinois, entering 18,000 acres in the land offices of Danville, Illinois, Fort Wayne, and Crawfordsville that year. Ten thousand acres lay in Tippecanoe County and Lafayette became Ellsworth's home. He continued to buy land, becoming a great champion of prairie farming. Paul Wallace Gates, "Land Policy and Tenancy in the Prairie Counties of Indiana," in *Indiana Magazine of History*, XXXV (1939), 8–12; Henry W. Ellsworth, *Valley of the Upper Wabash, Indiana, with Hints on Its Agricultural Advantages . . .* (New York: Pratt, Robinson & Co., 1838).

88. In his "Recollections of Calvin Fletcher as a Lawyer," Simon Yandes wrote: "It was [his] . . . habit to make the acquaintance of the boys that were growing up around him, and he was inclined to take hopeful views of their prospects. No other citizen did this to the same extent. Knowing of these facts I came to read law with him. About this time Horatio J. Harris and myself took a room, in the rear of his office, and there recited to him. He was then about 36 years of age, full of life, thorough, energetic, and enthusiastic. He was an excellent teacher, always vivacious, and he enlivened recitations by anecdote, history, and personalities." MS in Fletcher Family Papers, Indiana Historical Society Library.

89. Isaac Blackford (1786–1859). Appointed by Governor Jennings to the Supreme Court in 1817, he served until 1853. He is remembered for the eight

9 or 10 o'clock. I find him a good friend & intelligent man whose society I ought to court. A Mr. Humphreys from Mr. Starrs[90] office Cincinnati called on me & by him I sent Mr. Ingrams horse who left here for Cincinnati in the Stage & wrote me that he had gone round to Lafayette in the Stage.

Saturday the 13th June. Nothing worthy of notice. The waters very high—roads bad. Study law. Read an address or law lecture delivered by Professor Greenleef & one by Mr. Starkie.

Examined several subjects of law especially the effects of special bail—original writ &c Setoff &c. Wrote to Joseph Miller.[91] Cooley, Elijah, & uncle Wm. Hill went to the river to go in Swiming—rode a pony (grey) I have just bo't of Majr. A. C. Griffith. He slipt his bridle & run off. The boys return after dark—pony not found. My corn is knee high—good color. Have green peas. Potatoes in blossom. Army worm subsiding.

Sunday morning very pleasant. No rain last night. A little cooler but yet very warm. Cooley went early this morning to Moores store to wake up Uncle Wm. H. to go after horse. Pleasant morning. Read a tale attached to the last days of Pompeie [Pompeii]. Went to church [with] Miss [Mrs.] Richmond Dorio James Miles Calvin & Stoughton. Rev. Mr. Smith preached—1st Psalms. Public collection. On our coming out of church met Dr. Sanders who informed me that James Wiley son of Capt. Wiley a lad of about 15 years of age very bad boy had just drowned himself. It appears that he was angry at his father & that he voluntary went into the river for the very purpose after having been arrested in his purpose from committing the deed, just before. Came home. Bro. S. came & took dinner with us. I then went to the office for my papers. Found a letter from a Mr. Reed from Va. who writes me that he is at Knights town on his way to Laport. Has stopped in consequence of bad roads & desires me to write him &c. I wrote a new will. Boys Cooley

---

volumes of *Reports* which he compiled, a restatement of selected cases that came before the court, published between 1830 and 1850. Monks *et al.* (eds.), *Courts and Lawyers of Indiana*, I, 187–95. In his diary on January 12, 1860, at the time of Blackford's death, C.F. wrote a brief sketch of his life and work.

90. Henry Starr, Cincinnati lawyer.

91. Husband of Louisa Fletcher Miller, C.F.'s sister.

& Elijah went to the River. Wm. not returned. Will probibly go to Brownstown for horse. The body of young Wiley not found. Very growing weather.

Monday June 15 1835. Rose at sunrise. Cool more so than for two weeks—examining the [. . .] May 1835.

Invited with others Genl. Harrison (who is on an electioneering campaign for Presidency or trying to ascertain the public pulse) to dine. He declines a public dinner & I was invited to dine with Messrs. Judge Blackford, McCarty, D. McGuire, Hurst,[92] Dr. Sanders, Mears[93] &c at Mr. Sheets. Genl. H. made himself interesting as an agriculturist. Some anecdotes while minister to Bogata. S.A. Left him at 2 o' P.M.[94] Brown Lawyer from Lafayette here.[95] Heard from my pony 8 Miles off.

June 16 1835. Cloudy morning. Cooley & Mr. Morehouse start to old Mr. Kellys for pony. Exam[in]ing the rights & duties of surviving partner relative to Milton Morries[96] estate. Pony bro't back. Cool pleasant day. Bot two lots of Alexr. Wiley for $325. Town property raised in value. Several men from Con. were here

92. Henry Hurst, clerk of the United States District Court at Indianapolis. He had served as an aide-de-camp to Harrison on the Tippecanoe campaign and was a representative from Clark County, 1837–38 and 1838–39. *History of Ohio Falls Cities and Their Counties* (2 volumes. Cleveland, Ohio: L. A. Williams & Co., 1882), II, 433; Monks *et al.* (eds.), *Courts and Lawyers of Indiana*, III, 1145.

93. George W. Mears, a physician, who came to Indianapolis in 1834. He was originally from Philadelphia and had lived some time in Vincennes. He had a large practice and in 1848 helped to organize and taught in the Indiana Central Medical College, Indianapolis' first medical school. He was one of the organizers of the first Episcopalian congregation in the town and in politics was an ardent Whig. He later was to be active with C.F. in the organization and management of the School for the Blind. Nowland, *Early Reminiscences of Indianapolis*, pp. 270–73; Dunn, *Indianapolis*, I, 546, 547, 548.

94. Harrison had visited the Tippecanoe Battleground and been feted at public dinners at Vincennes, Crawfordsville, and Lafayette. Both the Indianapolis *Journal* and *Democrat* carried a letter of appreciation and esteem addressed to him by Isaac Blackford, Nathan B. Palmer, Morris Morris, John Cain, Calvin Fletcher, Douglass Maguire, Alexander W. Russell, J. S. Barnes, George W. Mears, and Bethuel F. Morris, and Harrison's reply. See Indianapolis *Indiana Journal*, June 19, 1835.

95. Thomas B. Brown, who was elected as representative from Tippecanoe County in 1833, 1835, and 1836. *Indiana Election Returns*, pp. 217, 225, 230.

96. Milton Morris, son of Morris Morris. Nowland, *Early Reminiscences of Indianapolis*, p. 106.

on the 8th & bo't property. Merchant Tailor from Cincinnati gave very high price from [for] property. Simon Yandes recited one lesson in Black Com. [Blackstone's *Commentaries*]. Examined law of partnership for Morris Morris. Wm. returned from his hunt after horse.

June 17th. Cool clear morning. My corn about waist high. Army worms ceaseing their ravages. At 12 o'clock came home found Mr. Reed from Va. at my house from Lynchburg on his way to Laport. His family were at Buck Creek. Pleasant day. At 2 went with a man to my farm to see the same he desiring to buy a farm. Found it looking very well. Returned spent the eve with Mr. Reed.

June 18th. Rained some last night. Went with Mr. Reed to Mr. Sharps & got a horse [?] of Mr. McGuire.

Mr. Kintner from Logansport bro't money for Dr. Todd.[97] Wrote a letter to Miles. Mr. Reed returned to his family. In the eve Mr. Reed arrived in a little waggon 2 little boys & a daughter & a young woman. Cooley Elijah & James went to see them & took milk &c.

The stage arrived this eve 6 o'clock brot the unpleasant news of the arrival of the cholera at Madison. Out of 20 cases 16 deaths. Among the victims was James Wallace late a representative. This disease bro't home several workmen on the Presbyterian church at that place. This fo[r]bodes much danger to our place. There is no doubt of the dreadful maladys being contageous. We may reasonable expect it at this place in a few weeks. Our town have been fortunate—have not been visited with this scourge. I hope that the police will take some steps to mitigate i[t]s rage. I trust in God that it may pass slightly over us if not entirely go by.

19 June. Last night a very severe heavy rain with terrific thunder & lightning. The wet season is very discouraging to farmers. Mrs. Reed & husband & family visited us with a Miss Davis. Been a wet disagreeable day. Roads almost impassable.

20 June. Very cool in the morning. A little rain in the night.

97. Dr. Hiram Todd, one of the first settlers and merchants of Logansport, and one of the first associate judges of Cass County. Thomas B. Helm, *History of Cass County, Indiana* . . . (Chicago: Brant & Fuller, 1886), pp. 298, 373, 399, 458. As noted below (note 150), he was one of the proprietors of the town of La Porte.

[In the] Eve Mr. McCarty called. No news from Madison. Mail has not arrived. Very Cool—I fear a frost. Waters are very high. Grain scarce—meal $1. per bushel.

Sunday 21st June 1835. No mail from Madison on yesterday & none from the East this day. Very cool. Went to church with little boys—heard Bro. Smith preach a good sermon. Read June No. Western Mag. Went to Mr. Reeds after dark. Pleasant family. Just left Virginia to try their fortune in a new country. Stoughton & J. Hill called on us. Cooley received a letter from Mr. Ingram, giving an account of his voyage round from Cincinnati in a steam-boat.

Monday June 22d 1835. 7 child born this morning about sunrise. Son.[98] I went for Mrs. Paxton & Wilkins & Dr. Coe about 1 o'clock.

Cool night—pleasant day. Did not sleep any. Must acknowledge (tho' it is not fashionable to be the parents of many childrin) that I am more gratified than at any time heretofore on a similar occasion. In this as in the life of all my childrin I live a new life, in their several prosperity or adver[s]ity I participate. They each add a new checker to the scenes of my own life.

[June] 23. Our grass is nearly fit to cut. The wet weather has been of service to it. Corn looks tolerably well—but in the wet farms it has not nor could not be worked. We learn that the people at Madison have fled their town in consequence of the chollera. Our Bees began to work this day having suspended because of wet.

June 24 1835. Cool cloudy in the A.M.—in the P.M. rain moderatly. Town full of strangers. Reading Blackstone & doing other necessary business. Read cherrys ripe. New potatoes sent by Mrs. Hill. Ours are setting. In the eve heard S. Yandes recite. He is a young man of a good mind. Bids fair to make a useful man.

June 25. Cloudy but warm. James bro't home last night a painting representing the genealogy of the Fletchers for 200 years. Uncle Stoughton had it executed by a *daub* for $10.

26 June. Pleasant cool day. Dr. Rose[99] from Lynchburg & family

98. The child was named Ingram.

99. Dr. Gustavus A. Rose, who moved to Indiana from Virginia because of his dislike of slavery and became a successful physician in La Porte County. E. D. Daniels, *A Twentieth Century History and Biographical Record of La Porte County Indiana* (Chicago: Lewis Publishing Co., 1904), p. 272; Von Briesen (ed.), *Letters of Elijah Fletcher*, p. 139.

are here. Called on them in the evening. Col. Lemon[100] also here. Mr. Reed & family leave with Dr. R. tomorrow for Laport.

June 27. I wrote two letters to Genl. Tipton, one in behalf of Mr. Reed, the other of Dr. Rose by way of introduction. The family of Mr. R. left about 8 for Logansport. The roads are very bad—rains continue to fall & the roads are extremely bad. Our Grass is fully ripe to cut but the continued rains prevent its harvest. Corn can scarcely be worked but such necessity stares us so fully in face that no moment is neglected when the work can be accomplished. Mr. Pratt went to Franklin yesterday to buy in the Wheatly land to satisfy judgment in favor of Stapp Lanier & Co. John H. Scotts goods were sold.

Our County agricultural society met at the court house.[101] N. B. Palmer elected Prest. D. McGuire Secy. & *Self* Treasury &c.

In the eve N. McCarty returned from the Bluffs and presented a proposition from D. E. Allen to sell his property. Mc. desires me to go down & consumate the contract. I have but little doubt of the reasonableness of the price $3600. 1200. in cash account—rest in goods next Spring for 430 acres.[102] Yet I fear I am going in rather deep. The naked land without prospect of canal &c is worth the money. I hope I am not operated upon from a spirit of pure madiness & rage for speculation & not by my Judgment in these matters. Should I fail totally fail in business it may be quite as well for my childrin. Riches I do not expect will be of any service to them.

June 28 Sunday. Rained last night again—cool & pleasant. Stoughton came up. Went to church. Heard Mr. Smith preach. Returned. Stoughton dined with us. Wm. Hill sick having eat too many cu[cu]mbers. Read a review of the life of Hannah More[103] Jan-

100. John M. Lemon, receiver of public moneys at the La Porte Land Office.

101. In 1825 a Marion County Agricultural Society had been organized to encourage the cultivation of tobacco, but it did not last long. By an act of the 1834–35 General Assembly a State Board of Agriculture was created which in turn urged the formation of county agricultural societies and the holding of county fairs. In response to this the Marion County society mentioned by C.F. was organized. Dunn, *Indianapolis*, I, 98. The state board made only one report and after two or three years ceased to function. *Messages and Papers relating to the Administration of Noah Noble*, p. 432n.

102. See below, Pt. VIII, note 2 and entry for March 5, 1837.

103. English religious writer who died in 1833.

uary No. A. [North American] Review. Wrote a letter to my mother & one to Mr. Ingram.

[June] 29 Monday. Pleasant. Preparing to go with Messrs. Hand & Stansbury[104] to Ft. Wayne to celebrate 4th of July.

30 June. Mrs. F. taken very unwell. Doubt the propriety of my leaving home. She has a fever. Send for Dr. Coe who says he thinks I best go. Mr. Hand calls & says he cant leave with us—must attend to other buseness. Write to Messrs. Joe[?] & Drake & prepare to leave with [. . .]. At 9 o clock called on Col. Stansbery who boards at Mr. Hendersons. He is the chief of the Engineer corpse in this State detailed by the W[ar] dep[artment] to run several routes for Railroads, a gent. about 30 formerly imploid as a surveyor with Messrs. Moore & Shriver[105] in the survey of the Wabash & E. canal. We left at 10. Mrs. F. desires me to go but I apprehend she is liable to a severe attack. Very cool. Waters getting down. Corn about waist high in my lot. Garden corn tassling & tasseled. We proceede after an agreeable ride to Pendleton. Very cold—I fear frost. Had a fire made up for us. Called on by Messrs. Silver (who had a hay making at his farm where we passed) Shanklin Mershon & Noble.[106]

July 1st. Some frost. Very cold but no injury to vegetation. Left P. at sunrise. Rode with a [. . .] to Andersontown. Breakfasted at A. with Andrew Jackson. Great complaint of the people of A. that the feeder to W[hite] R[iver] passed North of the town on the other side of River. Left A. at 9 o proceeded up Kill buck 10 miles on the road direct to Marion. Over took Surveyors of Canal route. Passed on to Palmers on the summit level & arrived at Marion about Sundown. There found a Dr. Trask[107] from Vt. & staid with him over

104. Col. Howard Stansbury, engineer of the United States Topographical Bureau, who headed the survey for the Wabash and Erie Canal and other internal improvement projects. *Messages and Papers relating to the Administration of Noah Noble,* p. 43.

105. Col. James Shriver and his successor Col. Asa Moore were assigned by Congress to make a preliminary survey of the canal. Both fell victims of malaria. Griswold, *Pictorial History of Fort Wayne,* I, 282.

106. Thomas Silver, Andrew Shanklin, William H. Mershon, and D. S. Noble, all early settlers of Madison County. Netterville (comp.), *Centennial History of Madison County,* I, 276, 320; Harden, *The Pioneer,* pp. 240–41.

107. Dr. Ezra Stiles Trask, who came to Marion from Vermont in 1833. He

night. Could not procure grain for horses. Dr. had a pleasant family. Breakfasted.

2d July. & proceeded to Lagro on the Wabash. Cool but pleasant. No flies. Arrived at Lagro about 2 P.M. Found Mr. Findly of Richmond candidate for Congress.[108] Messrs. Burr & Hugh Hanner[109] also arrived. Here we dined & fed & at 3 oclock left for Huntingdon & overtook Genl. Tipton & we all proceeded upon the line of the canal now in progress in the construction, to within 6 miles of Huntington where we staid overnight. Mrs. Burr & Hanner with their childrin came up. Slep with Col. Stansbery.

July 3d. We left & proceeded with Genl. Tipton along the canal line to Huntington at the locks East of that place. The canal is finished to Ft. W[ayne] 25 Ms. Here we Breakfasted. Met with a millitary company commanded by Capt. Fate a Dr. residing at H. I Breakfasted at Helveys.[110] At 10 we left the lock accompanied by 2 boats beside the one we were in one loaded to the very top with Deer & fur skins. About 50 ladies & 100 gentlemen. Saml. Hanner Esq. on the part of a committee of arrangements at Ft. W. was present & accompanied us. At first the boat grounded inasmuch as the water had not been let in from above—but we soon glided along. It was with inexpressible delight to all the company (among whom were all the engineers Col. Burr &c) to glide along upon the Waters that by nature were & had been by the Great Architect from the beginning designed & used to run into the St. Lawrence now by art & science made subservient to the purposes of commerce in the great valley of the Wabash making their way to the Mississippi.

---

was Grant County's third physician. He died in 1839. *Combination Atlas Map of Grant County Indiana* ([Chicago:] Kingman Bros., 1877), p. 29.

108. John Finley. He was opposed by Jonathan McCarty and James Rariden in the fifth congressional district composed of Allen, Delaware, Fayette, Grant, Henry, Huntington, La Grange, Randolph, Union, Wabash, and Wayne counties. McCarty was the winner in the contest. *Indiana Election Returns*, pp. 91–92.

109. Brother of Samuel Hanna. He came to Fort Wayne in 1824 and in 1834, with David Burr, platted the town of Wabash where he lived until his death in 1869. Griswold, *Pictorial History of Fort Wayne*, I, 271.

110. Joel and Champion Helvey, brothers, were the first white settlers on the site of the town of Huntington. They operated the Flint Springs Hotel, a double log cabin. *History of Huntington County Indiana* (Chicago: Brant & Fuller, 1887), pp. 401–402.

We dined at Vermillias[111] 10 ms. from Ft. Wayne. Left V.'s & soon met J. Williams[112] principal Enginear who had been up for 2 nights to watch the embankments of the canal. Arrived within 5 or 6 miles of the place of destination & met several companies of Gents. from Ft. W. and within a ½ mile a company of *melish* [militia] who marched us into town the canal not being compleated within ½ m. I was invited by Mr. A. Hamilton[113] with Genl. Tipton to spend our time with him as we were all [. . .] out among the neighbors.

[*July 4*]. The morning of the 4th was ushered in by salutes. At 9 the companies of milish & all interested formed & marched to the canal where 5 boats were prepared to carry the company up to the St. Joseph feeder 6 miles accompanied with music. Cols. Spencer & Bourie were the officers of the day. At the feeder dam all debarked. Col. Burr made a speech & Genl. Tipton gave a toast &c & the boats were turned back at 12 & we arrived at Ft. W. at 2. Went to the court house. Mr. McCullock[114] delivered a good oration. After which a dinner was had and after that toasts.

July 5 Sunday morning. Left in canal boat with the company

111. Jesse Vermilyea, who came to Allen County in the early twenties and engaged in farming and Indian trading. He was one of the first directors of the Fort Wayne branch of the State Bank and conducted the Vermilyea House, a hotel on the canal fourteen miles southwest of Fort Wayne. Griswold, *Pictorial History of Fort Wayne,* I, 274.

112. Jesse L. Williams (1807–1886), who as a very young man made canal surveys in Ohio. He was appointed chief engineer for the Wabash and Erie Canal in 1835 by the Indiana General Assembly and the following year was made chief engineer for all the canals projected in the great internal improvement program of Indiana. In 1837 he became chief engineer for all roads and railroads as well. After 1842 Fort Wayne became his home but he engaged in engineering projects that took him all over the country and won him a high national reputation. *Representative Men of Indiana* (2 volumes. Cincinnati: Western Biographical Publishing Co., 1880), II, D 12, pp. 75–77.

113. Allen Hamilton, Fort Wayne merchant and Indian trader who invested in Indian lands in partnership with Tipton. He later became a banker and served in the Constitutional Convention of 1850. Griswold, *Pictorial History of Fort Wayne,* I, 259; *John Tipton Papers,* I, 607.

114. Hugh McCulloch (1808–1895), a young lawyer who became cashier of the Fort Wayne branch of the State Bank in 1835 and continued in banking, becoming president of the Bank of the State of Indiana which was chartered in 1855. In 1863 he was appointed United States comptroller of the currency and served as secretary of the treasury from 1865 to 1869. Griswold, *Pictorial History of Fort Wayne,* I, 316; *Dictionary of American Biography,* XII, 6–8.

that came up from Huntington & arrived at H. at 9 o clock P.M. Genl. Tipton & myself staid at Capt. Murrys.[115]

July 6. Left Huntington at 9 & with Genl. T. arrived at Col. [. . .] at Miamis town at Sundown.

July 7th. Arrived at Genl. T. at 9 o c[lock]. A.M. Breakfasted & went to Logansport. Done some business & left there at 3 P.M. and came to Stipps or rather Stocktons at Wild cat.[116]

8 July. Left Stocktons & came to Mich[i]gan town. Breakfasted at Mrs. Johnson. Arrived at McQuedys[117] at 2 P.M. where there was a show. Found 200 people. Mr. Quarles who rode home with me where we arrived at about dark.

July 9. Been ingaged at my office. Cool. James Hill & Wm. are at work hauling hay from old Mr. Fletchers.[118] Our bees have commenced robbing each other. Mrs. F. in better health than when I left home. Corn in the garden silked.

July 10. Cool. Moved our bees. James & Wm. Hill gone to the place to help get hay &c. Wrote McCarty at Philadelphia relative to our land. Told him we ought not to buy any land above congress price & no more than we could keep 5 years that lands in 6 miles of the W. & E. canal 2d rate better than those 1st rate 20 ms. distant that I did not wish to involve myself that I would go in $6000 if I could have 2 years to pay without that I could not go in &c.

Cool pleasant day. Did but little. Went before Reagin case of Yeager[?] on compt vs Reeds securities.

Simon Yandes came to recite.

115. Capt. Elias Murray, who settled near Huntington in 1830 and became Tipton's real estate agent. He later served three terms in the Indiana legislature, was a member of the Constitutional Convention in 1850, and superintendent of Indian Affairs for Wisconsin and Minnesota. *John Tipton Papers*, II, 345n–46n.

116. Probably in the village of Burlington, Carroll County, which was on Wildcat Creek. The town was laid out by David Stipp in 1828 and a tavern was opened in a house built by him about 1833. *History of Carroll County, Indiana . . .* (Chicago: Kingman Bros., 1882), p. 274.

117. Probably Hiram McQuiddy or McQuitty, one of the early settlers of Union Township, Boone County, and a merchant in the village of Northfield. Samuel Harden, *Early Life and Times of Boone County Indiana . . .* (Lebanon: Harden & Spahr, 1887), p. 32.

118. David Fletcher, who leased C.F.'s farm northeast of the town after James Hill moved off it. David Fletcher stayed there until 1838. See above, Pt. IV, note 37.

July 11 Saturday. Rose at 4 & started Wm. to market for a pi[e]ce of mutton. I have indulged myself more this than any previous year for the last 6. I must stake off my lethergy. My business requires my best exertions.

Cloudy. Wm. ploughing corn 4th time. 6 ft. begins to show tassel.

Visited my farm with Mr. Quarles on which old David Fletcher resides. There is about 30 acres of meadow 25 of corn—has cut 6 ton of hay—put up one stack.

Returned. Found Mr. Boxley[119] at my house who stayed over night.

Sunday morning 12 July. Cloudy but warm. Went to love feast with Mrs. Richmond. Stoughton (son) very unwell. Broke out. Went to church heard Peter Smith[120] preach. Old Mr. Givan is said to be very sick chollera morbus.

Received letter from Mr. Gregg & P. Patrick.

Read several newspapers. Proposed to my wife to hold a meeting with our childrin privately on Sunday—at least 2 hours agreed to—about their habits, religious views &c. I feel deeply concerned.

Wm. & James Hill went out to meeting to old Mr. Fletchers. Cloudy & a shower at 10 o'clock A.M.

Monday July 13 1835. Rose at Sun rise. Wrote a bill in Chancery. Cloudy. James & Wm. went to Mr. Fs. to fix barn. Went with C. J. Hand to see old Mr. Givan who is very sick. Mr. & Mrs. Holiday called to see us in the eve. Saw Mr. Stansbury & Williams. Called on Mr. Vigas[121] & lady come in from Logansport. Had conversation with Govr. Noble. Says crops of every Kind—that unless the residue of July & the month of Augt. are favorable few crop of corn will ripen—that a great scarcity must prevail another year &c.

119. George Boxley, a native of Virginia and strongly antislavery, was the first permanent resident in Adams Township, Hamilton County, settling on land which he entered north of the present site of Sheridan in 1828. He kept the first school in the township in his cabin. Haines, *History of Hamilton County,* pp. 146–51, 257–58, 973–74.

120. Not identified. Perhaps C.F. means the Rev. John C. Smith.

121. Jordan Vigus. A veteran of the War of 1812, he moved from Kentucky to Corydon in 1816 and from there to Logansport in 1828, where he became a close business associate of John Tipton. He served as commissioner of the Wabash and Erie Canal from 1829 to 1833. *John Tipton Papers,* I, 169; *Indiana Executive Proceedings,* pp. 685–86.

[July] 14. Cool. Started Mr. Hand to the Wabashtown Perue &c on business as deputy Marshall &c. Nothing very interesting—James went to Eli Wells to get a lease—Morris Morris called on me.

[July] 15. Dr. Cook[122] from Pendleton here. Bo't 5 Shares of bank stock of him. Very cool—too cool for corn to grow. Ploug[h]ing my corn 4th time. Old Mr. Fletcher making hay. Wrote T. D. Gregg Rariden. Read of the Death of Chief Justice Marshall—also the unfortunate Southgate Noble who once lived with me—throwed himself over board from a steam boat.

Wm. Oliver (Irishman) came in from the Wabash to get arms to Keep down an inserrection among the Irish which is expected.[123] Mr. Pratt leaves tomorrow for Danville.

16 July Thursday. Cool. Mr. Pratt started for Danvill. Paid this day the last of the $2000 for which I gave for 15 lots of land at Laport of Sidney Williams. I bot these lands in Feby. 1834 without seeing [any] of them. I soon after added 3 other lots making 18 which cost $2300. I fear I made poor investments but shall let these lands lay for the present. Supposing I can now sell them at $3000. I think I should Keep them until they bring $300. each.

Indianapolis July 17 1835. Cool. Getting my hay at the farm. Have a good crop. Rev. Mr. Havens called on me. Read agricutural paper printed at Albany.[124]

David Wallace Liut. Govr. took tea with us. He no doubt will be our next executive a man of agreeable temper—at this time 36 years. He is on his way to N.Y. City for goods—trading at Covington. We had conversation in relation to the Wabash & Erie canal for the commencement of which project we were early advocates while in the legislature. Govr. W. & Mrs. Fletcher were at the same School in Troy Ohio when 9 or 10 years of age. Went to her grandfather old Mr. Oliver. Mr. Pratt returned in the eve from Danville. Saw Mrs. Gregg, Harveys widow.

Saturday 18th July 1835. Cool morning but warmer than yester-

122. Probably John H. or Ward Cook, both of whom were physicians in Fall Creek Township. Harden (comp.), *The Pioneer*, pp. 29, 127–30.

123. The so-called "Irish War" a feud that developed between the northern Irish and southern Irish laborers on the Wabash and Erie Canal. Griswold, *Pictorial History of Fort Wayne*, I, 323–25.

124. Probably the *Cultivator*, published by the New York State Agricultural Society beginning in 1834.

day. Very pleasant. Mr. Esty[?] of the house of Blachly & Simpson[125] called. Paid him $100. collected. Had a meeting of agricultural society. Messrs. Palmer Morris & McGuire to report proceedings &c. This our first effort.

Mrs. Mears & Williams (Jesses wife), Miss Sergant & Bennet took tea. Had some conversation with Mr. W. in relation to internal Improvements. We fear our next Legislature will be greatly divided & distracted. We both agree that our State is so far committed that it will be a great disgrace to fail in the grand project. We think 7 million may be safely invested for the Eastern middle middle & Western canals—one rail road—&c.

Sunday July 19 1835. Warmer than for two weeks past. Learn that our old friend & neighbor James Givan died last night at 11. He was one of our first settlers has lived here 15 years—a man of more than common energy—had a regard to the rights of others as well as his own—of strong prejudices. Died of billious collic.

Attended church in the A.M. Heard a good sermon from the Revd. Mr. Smith 19 Ps. 7 v. Shower in the P.M. At 4' attended the funeral of Mr. G. at his house boys Elijah Calvin & Miles went with me the latter rode behind. Many attended. No sermon old R. Brinton made an able prayer at the grave.

Read the life of Judge Marshall in the N[ational] In[telligencer].

Went to church at candlelight to hear a sermon preached by the Revd. Mr. [. . .]. Text last C[hapter] of Hosea last verse.

I this day proposed to my childrin that on every Sunday P.M. we have a family prayer meeting. They all readily assented. At which we will have none but our own family to be spent in family prayer & examination reading the Bible & singing.

Monday July 20 1835. Pleasant morning. The first neighbor I met with informed me that Majr. John Redding[126] died on yesterday with the congestive fever. He was one of our oldest citizens a man of good neighborly feelings well disposed.

Saw Mr. Kelly who had been to Ohio to get land from [. . .]. Done some business in Bank. Preparing to go to Cincinnati on Friday. Bro. Holiday called this eve. Brot suit vs Hillis & Grader &c.

125. Wholesalers in dry goods in Cincinnati.

126. A sketch of Redding is in Nowland, *Early Reminiscences of Indianapolis*, pp. 134–35. See also above, Pt. IV, note 19.

July 21 1835. Pleasant day. James Hill went to see the Bluff property.[127] Jake Lowe made a stump speech at the court house for congress.[128] Disclosed the corruption of the times. Very cool pleasant day. Heard of the death of Judge Park[129] & Young Dr. Sanders.[130]

July 22d. Pleasant day. Preparing for Cincinnati. Warmer. Rose early & went with Wm. to old Mr. Fletchers. Found things not as well as I would wish. Killed one pa[r]tridge & squirrel.

July 23. Capt. Mury & Johnson[131] Sheriff of Huntington Co. came in with 8 irish prisoners from the Wabash canal to lodge them in a safe jail. A Mr. Monroe took tea with us. James & Wm. Hill started for the Wabash to deaden some land on the canal belonging to McCarty & myself.

Very warm. Preparing for Cincinnati. Cooley & Elijah accompany me—the first time either ever started a journey out of the state. E. never went beyond 20 ms. from home James to Bloomington.

July 24. Up at 3. Woke Dorio. Prepare for the journey—leaving family not entirely well. I am reminded of the escapes & difficulities I have passed on Journeys. I should be greatful—yet remembering that we are as safe "In the natal as in the mortal hours."

Very warm & pleasant indications of rain.

Breakfasted & ready for the journey trusting in a Good Providence. Left at 5 with Elijah & James C. for Cincinnati in the stage. Fellow passengers Messrs. A. Milroy of Delphi & Starkie merchant

127. The Morgan County deed records show that McCarty and C.F. had acquired some 125 acres of land near and adjoining the town of Port Royal, at the Bluffs above White River, on August 30, 1834, for $500, the deed being recorded January 4, 1836. They owned altogether 450 acres at the Bluffs. See entry for February 4, 1836.

128. Jacob B. Lowe of Monroe County. He was defeated in the election for representative from the Sixth Congressional District by George L. Kinnard. The district included Bartholomew, Boone, Cass, Hamilton, Hancock, Hendricks, Johnson, Madison, Marion, Miami, Monroe, Morgan, and Shelby counties. *Indiana Election Returns,* p. 92.

129. Benjamin Parke (1777–1835), soldier, lawyer, jurist. He served as a judge of Indiana Territory and as United States district judge from 1817 until his death. *Dictionary of American Biography,* XIV, 209–10.

130. Dr. William T. Sanders, who had lived in Indianapolis, but at the time of his death was a resident of Covington. Indianapolis *Indiana Democrat,* July 24, 1835.

131. Elias Murray and William G. Johnson.

from Louisville—first going to Philadelphia & the latter home. Rained in the A.M. Dined at St. Omer. Arrived at Nepolian about sundown. There met with Mr. Blythe. Went to bed early.

July 25. Started at 4. Arrived at Watson's at 8. breakfast. At 11 at Lawrenceburgh. There dined met with young John Test & wife who went to Elizebeth with us. Crops of corn only tolerable in the big bottom. Apple fruit in great abundance. Hay very good—better than any year past for the last 5. Very warm more so than for the present year. Arrived at Cincinnati about sundown. Put up at the Pearl Street House Room No. 31. Pleasant & cool as any [in] the house. But a few guests at the house Judge Hall[132] & Harrison (Genl.) absent. Very warm. James & [. . .]. City rather dull not on account of there being any dull fo[re]boding but on account of the absent of many merchants East & others visiting springs &c.

Sunday July 26. Rose at ½ past 6. After breakfast went with my boys to the Episcopalian church—one of the finest buildings in the City new. Walked from there to the Broadway house. Saw Judge Rowan former Senator of the U.S.A. from Ky. Went to the Cincinnati Hotell & saw Thos. Sharp. Showed the boys Steamboats. Went back to Pearl St. house from there to the Episcopalian church. Took seat. Saw Messrs. Caswell & Gwin. P.M. Staid at my room till about 5 & then went to Calvin Fletchers & took tea with the boys.

Monday July 27th. Went thro' Cincinnati. Done my business. Very warm. Met with McDougal Leut. in the navy wife with him on his road to Indianapolis.[133] In the eve went with boys to the theater. Play not very important—Herr Kline a tumbler very excellent. Returned at 12.

Teusday 28th. Performed my business thro' the city. Called

132. James Hall (1793–1868), author, jurist, banker, who lived from 1828 to 1833 in Illinois where he practiced law, served as a circuit prosecuting attorney and judge, and as state treasurer, and edited the Shawneetown *Illinois Gazette.* He also founded and edited the *Illinois Monthly Magazine,* the first western periodical. In 1833 he moved to Cincinnati where he edited for two years the *Western Monthly Magazine,* then became cashier of the Commercial Bank and in 1853 its president. His many writings form an important record and interpretation of pioneer life, history, and legend of the Ohio Valley. *Dictionary of American Biography,* VIII, 134–35.

133. David McDougal, brother of John McDougal. See below, note 138.

on Mr. Gwin. At eve went to theater—Brutus performed. Her[r] Kline again.

Wedensday 28 [29]. Went with boys & Calvin Fletcher on the Ky. side. Saw the Rolling mill. Boys much pleased with it. Recrossed & went up the river with Calvin & Sam[u]el F. to another rolling mill on the Ohio side. Called on Messrs. Fox & Story Caswell Morris & Starr Lawyers all.[134] Treated me kindly.

[July] 29 [30] *Thursday*. Preparing to leave the city. I have bot Mr. Pratt a summer suit of clothes at $10. all Peter Parlys works for the boys Capt. Ross Journal[135] Chittys chancery forms[136] Saunders pleading & Evidence[137] &c. Very warm. Put the boys to bed & went to theater at 8. Saw She Stoops to Conquer very well done full house very warm.

Friday 31t July. Left Cincinnati at 5 in company with a Mr. Williams I presume a preacher a nephew of Dick W. residing near this place. Pleasant & cool. Arrived at Lawrenceburgh at 11. Here took in Mr. & Mrs. McDougal & proceeded to Watsons took dinner very good & arrived at Nepolian at 6 P.M. The Indianapolis stage brot John McD.[138] hunting his brother. Stayed over night.

Augt. 1st. Left Nepolian at 4. Breakfasted at Coats at Greensburgh—dined at Shelby & arrived at home at Sun one hour high.

134. Charles Fox, Bellamy Storer, Daniel J. Caswell, William R. Morris, and Henry Starr. Ford and Ford, *History of Cincinnati, Ohio*, pp. 315–16.

135. *Narrative of a Second Voyage in Search of a North-West Passage, and a Residence in Arctic Regions during the Years 1829, 1830, 1831, 1832, 1833 . . .* (Philadelphia, 1835), by Sir John Ross (1777–1856).

136. Probably a work of Joseph Chitty (1776–1841), English lawyer and barrister who published a series of legal manuals.

137. John Simcoe Saunders, *The Law of Pleading and Evidence in Civil Actions . . .* (Philadelphia, 1829).

138. John McDougal, who came to Indianapolis from Ohio. He served as superintendent of the state prison, was with the Marion County Volunteers in the Mexican War, and then went to California where he prospered. He served briefly as governor of California, 1851–52. Dunn, *Indianapolis*, I, 136, 137, 139, 522; *Messages and Papers relating to the Administration of Samuel Bigger*, pp. 179n-80n; Hubert Howe Bancroft, *History of California* (7 volumes. San Francisco: The History Company, 1890), VI, 645n–46n. In his diary entry for July 14, 1849, C.F. wrote: "In the eve Hugh O Neel came to see me. Let me know that Col. McDougall who ran away 3 or 4 years ago went to California made his fortune came back & remarried his wife who had been divorced had persuaded him O['Neal] to go to California as a lawyer, that he had great suits in which they would engage him."

Found all well. Mr. Danl. Wise called. Stayed over night. Mr. Pratt called. Corn looks well. One litter of pigs this day 11 will loose a part of them. Very cool. No heat as to elections.

Sunday August 2d 1835. Very warm. Went to church with my boys. Read part of the Naritive of Capt. Ross. Day past off without any remarcable occurrence.

Augt. 3d. Election takes place—one Rep. for Cong. 1 for State leg. 2 Judges & Clerk & corener to be elected. Bob Hanner A.W. Morris Arch. Reed candidates. Election passed off without much apparent excitement—yet such is the injustice fraud & demagogue-ism of our great men & so easible imposed upon are the greater portion of the community by false representations that it is calculated to deter an honest man from being a candidate. Indeed under my present views I think I never shall be again.

Kennard & Lowe for congress. The former gets a majority of [. . .] votes in Marion Co. is no doubt elected.[139] A. W. Morris Rep. Adam Wright & Tom O Neel associate Judges Bob Duncan[140] clerk.

Tuesday 4 Augt. An Italian minstral came & took dinner by invitation in order that my boys might hear the organs. Bot Packers lot of Smith agent for $210.[141] B. Cole called & paid some money. Dr. Hitchock of Terre Haute called in the eve. Was on his way from N.Y. Had heard of the death of his only son. Was in great distress. Very warm pleasant day. Want rain.

Augt. 5 1835. Cloudy in the morning—Warm during the day.

[*Aug.*] *6.* A. Harrison arrived. Pleasant weather.

[*Aug.*] *7.* Took depositions in the case of Bryant vs Blythe.

[*Aug.*] *8. Saturday.* Mr. Pratt returned from Danvill. Aided in

139. The vote in the district was Kinnard 7,483; Lowe, 4,658. *Indiana Election Returns,* p. 92.

140. Robert Duncan, who came to Indianapolis in 1827 and served as deputy county clerk under James M. Ray and as clerk from 1834 to 1850. He then practiced law. He married Mary E. Sanders, daughter of Dr. John H. Sanders, in 1843. Nowland, *Sketches of Prominent Citizens,* pp. 82–83.

141. The Marion Couny deed records show that John Packer conveyed to C.F. on December 15, 1835, for the consideration of $210, lot 14, square 46, in Indianapolis, and that on May 1, 1836, C.F. conveyed this lot to a James Spencer for the consideration of $450. The lot was on the south side of West Ohio Street, the second lot east of Illinois.

procuring subscription for our agricultural society—also in procuring a recommendation for Stephen C. Stevens to be Judge District Court. Received a letter from N. McCarty. Elections are over. My friend Butler beat & suppose my friend Ingram also.[142]

I am reading Capt. Ross's Journal in the North seas 1829–0–1–2–3. Some good lessons of perseverance & moderation in the day difficult & danger.

Sunday Augt. 9. Pleasent day. Finished reading Ross naritive. Some things I condemn in it—especially a remark that in republics women are not treated with proper respect—but I forgive him for this unjustifiable stricture for the lesson of patience he has taught the world. His remark that his ships crew cultivated good feeling & courtesy towards each other & thereby affected the natives in return is excellent. John Hager clerk Hancock [Co.] called—also Gibson from Boon to stay over night. I dislike to be interrupted on Sunday.

Monday Augt. 10 1835. Pleasant. Nothing worthy of note. Visited Govr. Noble with Mrs. Fletcher. Spent the day conversing on the subject of internal improvements into which the state is about (as is hoped to enter). There are several Railroad routes surveyed by the order of the last legislature. The extension [of the] Wabash Canal to Lafayette White River canal—from Indianapolis to the Wabash certainly practicable—from here to the River Ohio not certainly so—White Water canal already surveyed but the part thro' Ohio possibly can't be used as their last legislature seem to be hostile. Railroads have charters that require [. . .] subscriptions. Now the difficulty seems to be this—If the various projects contemplated by the surveys should be attempted the present state of the country does not demand it nor will its resources warrant the undertaking. Indeed the Govr. & myself agree in this that canals are the best because the capital to be expended in their construction to be left in the country. Railroads for machinery & iron will carry the money out of the country ⅔ or ½. Canals will grow more

142. Ingram was defeated in his bid for representative from Tippecanoe County, and Ovid Butler was defeated in his bid for representative from Shelby County. *Indiana Election Returns*, p. 225; Indianapolis *Indiana Journal*, August 28, 1835.

permanant—Railroads will wear out in 10 or 15 years. We are fearful that unless all can be undertaken none will be accomplished. His next message on the subject should be penned with care.

View Govr. N. farm. Very handsome.

[*Aug.*] *11*. Dry & warm.

[*Aug.*] *12*. The same. Jesse & David Fletcher & two sons eat dinner with us. More Fletchers that are grown eat than ever before at once at my table.

[*Aug.*] *13 Thursday*. Mr. Seal & wife visited us New Englanders about to return to Massachusetts.

[*Aug.*] *14*. A little rain.

[*Aug.*] *15 Saturday*. James & Wm. Hill returned. Cleared off dry. Not sufficient rain yesterday to wet the ground thro.'

Sunday [*Aug.*] *16*. Quarterly meeting. Went to hear Bro. Havens preach. In P.M. Mrs. Richmond Sister in law &c returned home. Read Western Mo. Mag.—July number.

Monday [*Aug.*] *17*. Cool no rain. Bank directors met Messrs. Morrison Norris Scott Owen McCall Lanier Guard Herriott.[143] Norris President pro (Forman), No[thing] very important. Merrill President sick. Rode out with Messrs. Scott & Norris to see him.

Rained gently in the A.M.—very hard & at night about 12. Went to see D. Williams who is very sick.

Tuesday [*Aug.*] *18th 1835*. Things look the better for the rain. Bank in session. Appointed Jeremiah Johnson state director on part of State to fill old Mr. Givans place &c.

Wedensday 20 [*19*] *Augt*. Rain. Mr. Adison Boxley[144] left with 29 head of young cattle for home which I had advanced money for except 2 calves furnished. Young James Fletcher son of old David F. came last night to work &c.

Augt. 21. Mr. Quarles & myself left for Madison court—Staid at Arnets over night.

Sunday 22 [*23*]. Cool. Went to falls after breakfast. Called on Noble. Arrived at Anderson town 3 P.M. Kilgore & Butler arrived. Staid at old Mr. Harpools. Macy H. Brown Henderson & Aly Kil-

143. Robert Morrisson, Seton W. Norris, Lucius H. Scott, William Owens, —— McCall, J. F. D. Lanier, David Guard, and Samuel Herriott.

144. Son of George Boxley. See above, note 119.

gore Anthony were present—[145] examined for admission a young man from W. City who has settled at Munsy.

Judges Winsel & Mitchel associates[146] Wick P[resident Judge]. Some business—Horse thieves vs Danl. Wise the most interesting cases. One tried. W. beat the rascal.

[*Aug.*] 29. Returned home alone. Road from Andersontown after 12 meridian. Stopped 2 hours at Pendleton & arrived home at 11. The night air injures my lungs—will not ride hereafter so late if possible.

[*Aug.*] 30. Stoughton arrived from Philadelphia.

3 Sept. 1835 Thursday. Messrs. Alf Harrison Merrill Palmer & Alexr. Morrison left for the sales of land at Laport. Very warm. Merrill had proceeded to McQuadies 18 miles where we overtook him. Dined & went to Michigan town. Stayed over night at widow Johnsons. Met a Mr. Hobson a Virginian who had letters from Laport to me.

Sept. 4. Went to Stocktons to breakfast. Very warm. At 3 we arrived at Logansport. Staid over night.

Saturday 5 Sept. Went 12 miles to breakfast. At 2 arrived at Tippacano River. Judge Polks.[147] Dined & proceeded to Sidney Williams.[148] Got a little wet. Arrived after dark. House full.

Sunday Sept. 6. Breakfasted. Wet morning. Went [to] Clarks & dined. Wet morning—cool. Arrived at Treadways[149] sun 2 hours

145. David Macy, of New Castle; Hiram Brown, of Indianapolis; —— Henderson; John Alley, of Rushville; David Kilgore and Thomas C. Anthony or Joseph Anthony of the Delaware County bar.

146. Adam Winsell and Charles Mitchell, associate judges, Madison County. *Indiana Executive Proceedings*, pp. 510, 512.

147. William Polke, commissioner for the Michigan Road. He was a veteran of the Tippecanoe campaign, had served as judge of Knox County, as a member of the Constitutional Convention of 1816, and as state senator. In 1841 he was appointed register of the Fort Wayne Land Office. *John Tipton Papers*, I, 468n.

148. In 1836 Williams was licensed to keep a tavern at the site of the town of Argos, Marshall County. The site was first named Sidney (for Williams) who settled there in 1835. He served as associate judge of Marshall County, 1836–38, went to California in the early 1850s, but later returned east and settled in Illinois. Daniel McDonald, *A Twentieth Century History of Marshall County Indiana* (2 volumes. Chicago: The Lewis Publishing Co., 1908), I, 60, 61, 119–20.

149. Griffin Treadway, who later had a hotel in La Porte. Jasper Packard,

high. Merrill & Palmer staid over night & we Morrison Harrison & self went to Laport.[150] But few people had assembled as I had expected. Here I met with Govr. Hendricks Messrs. Hills[?] Brown of Lawrence[151] John Walker[152] &c &c. Stopped at Grovers[153]—Went [to] Mr. Reeds & stopped. James Hill was there.

Monday 7 Sept. Sales commenced. Saw Mr. Sweet. A very fine country to be brought into market but Indian floats & preemption rights cover near all the good lands that sold this day S. E. of Laport. Not more than 300 on the ground. Much of the land passed without sale.[154]

Teusday the 8. Mr. Sweet bid off 4 pi[e]ces for me 9 miles from St. Joseph. Not much sold this day. In P.M. Merrill & self went to Michigan City.[155] Much pleased with our ride. I killed a rattle snake

---

History of La Porte County Indiana . . . (La Porte: S. E. Taylor & Co., 1876), pp. 119, 414.

150. La Porte, county seat of La Porte County, was laid out in 1833 on land sold as Michigan Road land to Walter Wilson, Hiram Todd, John Walker, James Andrew, and Abram P. Andrew, Jr. *Ibid.*, pp. 100–101.

151. John Brown. He served as representative from Lawrence County in 1833. *Indiana Election Returns*, p. 216.

152. At this time a resident of Shelbyville. John Walker and his wife conveyed to the Shelby County agent the land on which the county seat was platted in 1822 and he platted later additions to the town. He also built the first flour mill and sawmill for the community. He was a contractor for clearing the Michigan Road and used the scrip which he received in payment to purchase land at South Bend and Logansport. He owned a portion of the land on which La Porte was platted and he moved to that town in 1839, where he died in 1844. McFadden, *Biography of a Town, Shelbyville*, pp. 32–34.

153. A license was granted to Grover and Williams in 1835 to operate a tavern in La Porte. Packard, *History of La Porte County*, p. 102.

154. The La Porte Land Office records show that C.F. purchased three tracts of land in St. Joseph County (400 acres) in sections 9, 18, and 26 in T36N, R1E on September 8 and on September 12 he purchased with Nicholas McCarty three other tracts in Fulton County (222 acres) in sections 20 and 21, T30N, R3E. On October 1–2 William Clark transferred to C.F. and McCarty two tracts in Porter County which he had purchased on these same days. These were in section 8, T34N, R5W (160 acres) and in section 11, T36N, R5W (80 acres). C.F. sold the land in section 8 in 1856. Clark Papers in La Porte Land Office records; Porter County deed records. During the first six days of the La Porte land sales in 1835 approximately fifty thousand acres were sold. The sale continued for several weeks.

155. Michigan City was laid out by Isaac C. Elston of Crawfordsville (see note 170 below) in 1832. In 1836 he sold the lots not yet disposed of to the Michigan City Land Company, represented by William H. Goodhue and William Teall as trustees. Packard, *History of La Porte County*, p. 96.

7 or 8 rattles. A Sloop had Just arrived in M. city. Went to the beech. 50 people were imploied in trying to unload vessel. Could not come within 300 yards in consequence of sand. Saw a bark canoe returning from Chicago loded with 11 Indians been to payment.

Sept. 9 1835. Sales continued. Returned from Michigan City.

Thursday [Sept.] 10. Went with Messrs. Palmer & Polk to the Morgan prarie.[156] Examined silver lake & several mill seats. Staid over night at an old mans by the name of Wallace 20 ms. from Laport.

Friday 11 Sept. Inspected Silver lake again & returned to Laport after dark very tired.

Saturday [Sept.] 12. Wet & cold. Prepared to leave. Mr. Palmer & myself left in the rain & went to the Tere Cope Prarie[157] staid over night at a Mr. Davises.

Sunday Sept. 13. Arrived at South bend. Took breakfast. Saw Listenn, Sweet & old Mrs. Skinners family.

Left S. B. & rode to Tabers.[158] Scarcely a house between Yellow River [and] S.B. Staid at Tabers & saw a Mr. Stanton quaker & a Mr. Boon from Washington City who was driven off in consequence of the mob.[159]

Monday [Sept.] 14. Arrived at Judge Polks on Tippacanoe. Visited Potwatmi Mills.[160] Examined the country. Returned to Judge

156. In Washington Township, Porter County, so-called after William and Isaac Morgan, the first settlers in the area. *History of La Porte County Indiana* (1912), I, 35.

157. Terre Coupee prairie, in Olive Township, in northeast St. Joseph County.

158. Samuel D. Taber, one of the contractors for the Michigan Road. He moved from Allen County into the area that was to become Marshall County in 1833. For several years he operated a country hotel on his farm. McDonald, *A Twentieth Century History of Marshall County*, II, 446.

159. Probably a reference to a race riot that swept through Washington in the summer of 1835. An angry mob, made up chiefly of gangs of boys and young men out of work set out to intimidate free Negroes and punish those who were circulating abolitionist literature. Constance McLaughlin Green, *Washington Village and Capital 1800–1878* (Princeton, N.J.: Princeton University Press, 1962), pp. 141–42.

160. One of the provisions of the 1826 treaty with the Potawatomi was that the United States would build a gristmill for the tribe on the Tippecanoe River and provide a miller. Actually the mill was built at the outlet of Lake Manitou into Mill Creek, a tributary of the Tippecanoe. By the 1834 treaty with the Potawatomi the mill site reverted to the public domain. *John Tipton Papers*,

P-s. Found Merrill. He Palmer & myself agreed to purchase mills at public sales to take place on the next day.[161]

15 Sept. Rose early. About 50 attend the sales. Discovered I had entered a piece of land wrong for S. Masters. Merrill myself & Palmer bought the Mills above alluded to—cost 55 acres about $1900. We bought several other pieces afterward my share amounting to about $1500. Helped Judge Polk clerk.

Sept. 16. Merrill & Palmer sold their interest in the P. mills to Dr. Colwell of Virginia for $200. as a bargain over the price given. I refused to sell. We left at 10 & rode to Logansport. Merrill & myself left there about sun ½ hour high. Came to Stipps 18 miles.

Sept. 17. Rose early & travelled all day without stopping but a short time & arrived home at dusk.

Sept. 18. It began raining this day & never ceased all day.

Sept. 19. Wet & cold.

Sept. 20. Went to church with my boys. Spent the day reading & conversing with Bro. S.

Sept. 21. Cold dissagreeable day. Mr. Gregg called in the eve.

Sept. 21 [22]. Sold the Givan farm in Morgan County. Mr. Pratt went to Danville.

Sept. 22d [*23d*]. The first frost this morning heavy. Killed all the vines. Cooley staid in the office with me. Called on a sick family. Sent them butter & potatoes &c coal.

Sep. 24. Frost. Mrs. F. & childrin James Elijah Calvin & Miles went to the farm. Returned with ½ of the apples about 16 bushels fine apples. The boys rode on those in the waggon bed 4 bushels and spoiled them—the rest were preserved in basement. This the first fruit of the kind we have received from the place. Trees were set out in 1828 or 1829 bo't of Aaron Aldridge.

Mr. Quarles returned from the Johnson court which I have declined attending. I attended all the courts in the circuit until this year. I have entered into a partnership with O. Butler who is to do

---

I, 749n; Kappler (ed.), *Indian Affairs, Laws and Treaties,* II, 274, 430. The mill site was then selected as part of the Michigan Road lands.

161. This was the sale of the Michigan Road lands granted by the 1826 treaty with the Potawatomi. See Pt. IV, note 41. William Polke served as commissioner to select the lands and conduct the sales.

all our business. I am to have half the profits. My business at home is sufficient to keep me ingaged.

Saturday Sept. 26. A very pleasant day. Stoughton & Mr. Bradley wish James (Cooley) to come stay with them in the store during the absence of James Bradly on a visit to Ky. James went early—is to [be] paid board & such wages as may be deemed right. This is an epoch in his life rather worthy of note.

Dorio Crumbagh is this day 18 years of age & her term expires for which she was bound. Mrs. F. gathered 2½ bushels of apples from the tree near the well *climb* the tree saves them for winter. Elijah & Miles & Calvin assist Mr. Holiday dig Sweet potatoes. Calvin & hired man (James Fletcher) took two cows to be fattened to the farm. I went [to] look [. . .] Messrs. Willet & Underhills[162] st[. . .].

Sunday [Sept.] 27. Mr. McCarty has just arrived. Cloudy & wet. Did not go to meeting. Stoughton came & took dinner. John at tea. Read several journals & papers.

Monday Sept. 28. This the 1st day of M.C.C. [Marion Co. Circuit Court]. Court commenced at 10. Do not feel very well prepared nor as much interest as in former times. Wick gave a very good charge to Grand Jury. Judges Stephens & Wright.[163] 5 young lawyers admitted Messrs. Vawness, Ketcham[164] Stagg & Pratt.[165] No other foreign lawyers but Herrod & Nave.

State vs Hensly for larceny came on—acquitted. Mr. McCarty & Myself going to send Pratt to Cincinnati. Pleasent cool weather. Not much business in court.

162. Jacob S. Willets (Willitts) and Robert R. Underhill, Quakers. They both came to Indianapolis in 1834 and started a successful iron foundry at Pennsylvania and Vermont in partnership with John Wood in 1835, making ploughs, andirons, and castings of all kinds. It was probably the earliest manufacturing concern in the town to employ a variety of laborers. Wood retired from the partnership in 1837. Dunn, *Indianapolis,* I, 344, 626; advertisement in Indianapolis *Indiana Journal,* April 29, 1837, and following issues.

163. Joshua Stevens and Adam Wright, associate judges of Marion County. Stevens later served as justice of the peace. He was a native of Vermont and brother of Thaddeus Stevens. Nowland, *Early Reminiscences of Indianapolis,* pp. 207–208.

164. Edward Van Ness and John L. Ketcham.

165. James M. Stagg and Daniel D. Pratt.

From the 28 Sept. to the 10 Octr. Marion Circuit Court in Session. Nearly 100 cases disposed of. Was ingaged in the most of them—Wick President Judge who performed his duties with great promptness & dispatch.

We have had heavy frosts cool weather but reasonably dry. On the 4th Octr. Sunday Mrs. Hill & childrin started for Ohio. Old Mr. Fletcher carried them. Mr. Pratt left for Cincinnati on business for McCarty & myself.[166]

Friday [*Oct.*] *9.* Mr. Pratt returned.

Saturday 10 Octr. Pleasant day. Making preparations to go to Ft. Wayne. Mr. Ray wishes me to go on the business of the bank. Be absent a month. This I must decline. 4 days meeting—several preachers Revds. Havens, Rooter, Aymes & others.

Sunday [*Oct.*] *11.* I this day rose expecting that I would go to Ft. Wayne but for various reasons gave it out. Went to church in the P.M. Mr. McCarty called. Mr. Dunning & wife came & Staid over night.

We have Just seen the blazing Star. It is a little N.W. of the North Star—not brilliant—rather above the ordinary size but dim or hazy over the disk[?].

Monday Octr. 12. Pleasant morning. Have good health much to do. I have borrowed money to enter land which must be paid. Have clients whose debts must be collected—my own private debts to secure & collect—the agricultural Socity of Marion County to help organize—my domestic affairs to attend to &c.

Teusday [*Oct.*] *13.* Very pleasent. Went out with two Messrs.

166. This may be the journey Pratt recalled in his letter to Dr. William B. Fletcher, C.F.'s son, October 6, 1873, in the Fletcher Family Papers, Indiana Historical Society Library. "I have said there was no Bank in those days through which remittances could be made. Most of our traders made their purchases at Cincinnati or Louisville. Your father sometimes sent me to the former city on horseback with the proceeds of his collections for distribution among the creditor merchants. In one of these years late in the fall & when the roads were so deep that it took four days to reach Cincinnati I took in my saddle bags $5000 of collections for distribution."

"It was a habit of your father," Pratt continued, "when he made a collection to promptly remit it with full explanations. It was one of the secrets of his success as a collecting lawyer, and at that time he almost monopolized the business, and it was the source of much profit. . . . in this lucrative branch of the profession he had no rival."

to see my farm they wish to buy. Ask 1800 for it & $1500 for Kelly place. Dont care whether they buy or not.

Wedensday [Oct.] *14*. Very pleasant. Streets crowded with people—movers—emigrants. Judge Demming[167] arrived from the East. Speaks of commencing a system of internal improvements. Says we are 10 years ahead of what he expected before he went East. Democrat came out this day containing two numbers on the subject written by Jesse Williams Engineer in order to prepare public mind. The Editer says we *can go* $10 million.

Thursday 15 Octr. 1835. This day Examined the subject of the liability of persons taking gravel out of the bed of the River &c.

Very pleasant. Govr. Noble called on me. Had further conversation in relation to internal improvements. He has just received a line from the Madison R. C. to procure the apperatus & assistance to survey from M. to Nepolian to intersect the Lawrenceburgh road in consequence I presume of the unexpected high estimate of the direct route. It is a favorable indication of the union of the two points. The route for a canal down White River to terminate at Evansville seems to be favorable & if the practicability of uniting the waters of Eel & the Wabash in Vigo County can be ascertained I look upon the whole project of internal improvements in this state to be the most interesting of any in the union & one that is more deserving. There will not be thirty miles in the state without a water communication or railroad.

Bro. Holiday arrived from his mothers.

Sunday 18 Octr. 1835. Pleasant. Prepared for Hendricks court. Stoughton (bro.) went to Bridgport with me. 8 miles from Danville overtook bros. Herrod Brown & Peasly from the Morgan court. Cloudy. Arrived at Danville about sundown. There met Messrs. Morrison Quarles Ray Morris & Nave. Put up at Comengoes.

Monday [Oct.] *19*. Pleasant. Performed much of my business. Cowgill from Putnam[168] arrived—a clever fellow. I am winding up my business at this court & do not expect to attend again.

Teusday [Oct.] *20*. Pleasant day. Col. Blake arrived & settled a case Blake & Ball vs Johnson. At 12 C. J. Hand asst. Marshall arrived

167. Demas Deming, associate judge of Vigo County.
168. John Cowgill, Putnam County lawyer.

on his way to Lafayette to do some business in which I was interested & was to go with him. We left Danville at 4 rode to Davises 9 or 10 ms. and staid over night.

Wedensday [*Oct.*] 21. Left Davis early. Pleasant morning. Rode to Crawfordsvill 16 miles to breakfast. Eat at Restines.[169] Saw Elston[170] who wishes a br[anch] bank established at Michigan City this winter.[171] Left Crawfordsville (which is fast improving) at 11 rode in company with an old soldier (Revolutionary) name of Gable from East part of Ky. Saw a thousand sand hill cranes between Crawfordsville & Lafayette. When we arrived within 8 or 10 miles of the latter place we met several of the preachers that had been to the annual conferance. Arrived at L. just after dusk. Could not get into the best tavern. I had not been in the place for 4 or 5 years. Improved much.

Thursday [*Oct.*] 22–[24]. Took Dr. Martin on a debt of Foster[?] & brother of Cincinnati. I tried to compromise. Ingram was at Carrol & White Courts & not expected till Saturday. I spent till 5 P.M. in fruitless efforts to compromise with Dr. M. & then went 7 miles West to the Grand Prarie to see Tommy Stretch an old Patron who [was] imploied on Mad river "to teach the young idea how to shoote" in 1817. I found his family but he had gone with his team to Chicago after salt &c. The family did not know me but when I mad[e] myself known they were much pleased to see me. The family had endured great sickness & poverty since I saw them. But what surprised me a new generation had been born & grown to man & womanhood since I saw them. The old woman said she never expected to see "Schoolmaster Fletcher" again if she ever saw the same character again it would be "lawyer F." but she recognized the same plain man "Schoolmaster F." On the 23 Friday I left & returned to Lafayette & made a partial negotiation with Dr. M. Met

169. Maj. Henry Ristine kept the first regular tavern in Crawfordsville. H. W. Beckwith, *History of Montgomery County* . . . (Chicago: H. H. Hill & N. Iddings, Publishers, 1881), Pt. 2, pp. 121–22.

170. Isaac C. Elston, Crawfordsville merchant and banker. *History of Montgomery County Indiana* . . . (2 volumes. Indianapolis: A. W. Bowen & Co., n.d.), I, 692. See note 155, above.

171. The Michigan City branch of the State Bank did not open until early 1839. Annual Report of the President of the State Bank, November 27, 1839, in Indiana *Documentary Journal*, 1839–40, House Doc. No. 6.

with a Mr. Sergent from Chester Vt. who took a letter to my mother.

On the 24 Visited the widow McGeorge an old acquaintance 8 miles East of L. Returned in the P.M. Negotiated the matter with Dr. M. thro' a lawyer Brown a very mean man (a lawyer). About 8 in the Eve Mr. Ingram returned. I spent the night with him at his office.

Sunday [Oct.] 25. Started for Boon court in company of a lawyer Petet[172]—Pleasant day. Rode to Thorntown staid at Mr. Dailies.

Monday [Oct.] 26. Left Thorntown & rode to Lebanon. A bea[u]tiful day. I have prepared to leave my business in the hands of Mr. Butler who is to take my law business in all the counties except Marion & left L. about 2 P.M. It rained. I rode a little gray Pony horse in 5 hours 26 ms. found all well.

Teusday [Oct.] 27. Commenced preparing for the first agricultural fair ever held in the county & I think in the state. It devolved on me as treasurer to raise about $200.

28 & 29 Octr. Imploied in preparing for the fair. Had the aid of Mr. D. McGuire & N. Palmer Esq.

30 Octr. 1835. Pleasant day. I have much anxiety for fear our fair would turn out a failure. If the Marion Cty. Ag. S. should fail it will prove injurious to the organization of societies in other counties.

At 10 the persons competing arrived on the court house square viz Jesse Wright[173] John Johnson[174] & others. At 12 the yard was full

172. John Pettit (1807–1877), Lafayette lawyer, who served in the 1838 session of the General Assembly, was United States district attorney, 1839–43, representative in Congress, 1843–49, United States senator, 1853–55, mayor of Lafayette, 1867–70, and judge of the state Supreme Court, 1870–77. *Biographical Directory of the American Congress*, p. 1674.

173. A native of North Carolina, who came to Decatur Township, Marion County, and purchased a farm on the northwest corner of section 29, T15N, R3E. In 1838 he moved to Iowa. Sulgrove, *History of Indianapolis*, p. 511.

174. Son of Jeremiah Johnson and brother of Thomas and Jeremiah, Jr., all of whom settled on farms just north of Indianapolis in 1821. John Johnson's farm was an eighty-acre tract on the west bank of Fall Creek where the State Fair Grounds are now located. He won first and second prize ($12.00 and $4.00) for hogs at this fair. *A Home in the Woods. Oliver Johnson's Reminiscences of Early Marion County, as related by Howard Johnson* (Indiana Historical Society *Publications*, XVI, No. 2, Indianapolis, 1951), pp. 143–44, 214–15.

First Annual Fair

OF THE

Marion County Agricultural Society,

To be held at the Court House Square in Indianapolis, on Friday and Saturday, the 30th and 31st of October, 1835.

The Board of Managers have determined on that occasion to award the following Premiums:

1. For the best Stallion,	$15 00
2. Second best do.	5 00
3. The best Mare,	13 00
4. Second best do.,	3 00
5. The best Colt, (not over three years old,)	10 00
6. Second best do.,	4 00
7. The best Jack,	10 00
8. Second best do.,	3 00
9. The best Mule,	5 00
10. Second best do.,	2 00
11. The best Bull,	5 00
12. Second best do.,	3 00
13. The best Yoke of Oxen,	12 00
14. Second best do.,	4 00
15. The best 3 years old Steer,	3 00
16. Second best do.,	1 00
17. The best Cow,	10 00
18. Second best do.,	3 00
19. The best Calf, (not more than 5 months old,)	2 00
20. Second best do.,	1 00
21. The best Five Hogs,	11 00
22. Second best do.,	1 00
23. The best Five Sheep,	7 00
24. Second best do.,	3 00
25. The best Cheese, (made in Marion county, weighing at least 16 lbs.)	5 00
26. Second best do.	3 00
27. The best Ten pounds of Butter,	2 00
28. Second best do.,	1 00
29. The best piece Mixed Jeans, (at least 10 yards,)	4 00
30. Second best do.,	2 00
31. The best Pair of Woollen Socks,	1 00
32. The best piece of Domestic Flannel, (at least 10 yards,)	3 00
33. Second best do.,	1 00
34. The best piece of Domestic Carpeting, (at least 10 yards,)	3 00
35. The best piece of Domestic Linnen, (at least 10 yards,)	3 00
36. The best Essay on the Culture of the Mulberry and Production of Silk,	2 00
37. The best Essay on Grasses, one volume of Indiana Aurora.	
38. The best Domestic Wine, (not less than one gallon,) one volume of Indiana Aurora.	

RULES OF THE FAIR.

1st. The names of all candidates for premiums, must be entered with the Secretary of the Society before 9 o'clock, A. M. of the first day of the Exhibition, and each candidate will be expected to furnish in writing, a description of the animal or article offered, where grown or manufactured; to which must be affixed his name and place of residence. If the animal be of the horse kind, its age, height, pedigree, and place where foaled, must be inserted: of all other animals, the particular stock or breed,—their age, marks, &c., as well to guide in the future selections of the best breeds, as to prevent imposition as to what particular animals have received premiums.

2d. Articles of produce or manufacture must be marked with a private mark; a duplicate description of which must be enclosed in a sealed note, containing the name of the manufacturer, and proper proof of the place where manufactured. All articles exhibited, and to which the premium has been awarded, may be sold at public sale on the ground, for which no charges will be made.

3d. All animals or articles to be exhibited for premiums, must be placed under the exclusive care and direction of the officers, or persons appointed by them, before 9 o'clock, A. M. of the day of exhibition, that they may be arranged in their proper places; and they must continue in such places until otherwise disposed of.

4th. The several Committees appointed by the Society as Judges of the Exhibition and Fair, will meet at the place of exhibition at 9 o'clock, A. M. of each day, and proceed immediately to the discharge of their respective duties.

5th. The reports of the Judges, signed by at least a majority of each, shall be handed to the Secretary of the Society at 12 o'clock, M., of the second day.

6th. The Judges may withhold premiums on articles where there is no competition, or where those offered may not be deemed worthy of reward.

7th. At 1 o'clock, on the second day of the Exhibition, the reports of the Judges will be publicly read, when the President shall declare the premiums awarded;—after which a short Address will be delivered by the President.

8th. Two assistant Secretaries shall be appointed to aid the regular Secretary in receiving entries of articles offered for competition, and furnish the Judges with a list; to take an account of such as are exhibited but not entered, and to report the same.

9th. Marshals shall be appointed to execute the directions of the officers.

10th. A majority of the Judges shall be sufficient to act,—but in case a majority be not present, the President or Vice President shall appoint members to supply the deficiency.

11th. No person will be permitted to make entries or compete for a premium, except members of the Society, or females belonging to the family of a member.

12th. The Judges shall have power to determine on the propriety of awarding certificates or diplomas, or of reporting to the Society the merits of any animal or article, other than those to which premiums may be awarded.

13th. The President and Vice President will superintend the Exhibition.

14th. Premiums awarded, and not called for in six months, will be considered as declined.

15th. Booths or stalls for the sale of spirituous liquors, or for any articles not the growth or manufacture of the United States, are expressly prohibited.

16th. Betting or gambling of any kind is expressly prohibited; and it shall be the duty of the Marshals to remove from the grounds any person transgressing against this rule.

17th. Animals, or articles of produce or manufacture to which premiums may be awarded, and which the owners may desire exposed to public sale, shall be collected at some convenient place, and sold immediately after the delivery of the address.

The following shall constitute the Judges and other Officers for the Day.

JUDGES.

Of Horses—John Thompson, John Woods, Rezin Reagin, Henry Porter, George Marquis.

Of Cattle—N. McCarty, Hiram Bacon, William Sanders, S. W. Norris, James Rains.

Of Mules and Asses—C. Fletcher, John H. Sanders, Cornelius Elson, Robert Hanna, William Reagin.

Of Hogs and Sheep—Thomas Johnson, A. C. Reed, William W. Jones, James McFarland, Adam Wright.

Of Articles of Produce or Manufacture—Noah Noble, John C. Hume, John Foster, Daniel Yandes, Joseph Beeler, Benjamin H. Canby.

Of Essays—Samuel Merrill, William Hill.

Marshals—D. L. McFarland, A. W. Russell.

Assistant Secretaries—Joseph M. Moore, James Morrison.

Auctioneer—Joseph P. Duvall.

FLETCHER PAPERS

Broadside announcing the first Marion County fair held October 30 and 31, 1835

—some fine stock but mostly of the scrub kind. Pride prevented many from competing. At 1 the Judges of the several articles commenced business. At ½ past 3 the several individuals who had live stock took it away to return it in the next morn at 9.

Nov. [*Oct.*] *31 1835*. The court house yard was again full at 11 & at ½ past 11 the awards were read in the court house, after which an address by N. B. Palmer Esq. was delivered appropriate to the occasion and after that the premiums were paid in Gold half Eagles (American).[175]

Great emulation seems to have alight up on this occasion. Col. John Owens[176] from Bloomingto[n] was present & made a member. Has subscribed 5 per cent on every hundred dollers—promises to bring his cattle here next fair. A beutiful day. This fair has cost me 1 week from my business & more money than I ought to contribute but the premiums must be paid & as Treasurer could not in the eyes of the most competiters have no excuse.

After the premiums were paid a sale of the Prize chees sold at 31 cts. per lb.—butter at 31 &c.*

Novr. 1. Sunday. Mr. Quarls & myself left for Noblesvill Court. [by] the river road. Dined at Medskers. Very pleasant day. Arrived at N. about sun down. Found at Dunnings bros. Herrod & Butler.

Monday Novr. 2d. Plasant but cloudy. Not much business.

Teusday [*Nov.*] *3d*. Some business. Pleasant cloudy day.

Wedensday [*Nov.*] *4*. Plasent. Got nearly thro' business.

* Memo made Octr. 21 1860.

This was the first fair I ever attended. I acted as treasurer. Mrs. Fletcher (my wife) compeated for the butter premium—I remember some of her competitors—Mrs. Genl. Hanner and Mrs. Beeler.

Mrs. F. took the highest premium. I had purchased a deep red cow from Isaac Stephen of Noblesvill—Large, of the native stock. From her Mrs. F. had made a pound of butter per day. She & I felt bad even to take the award as others seemed to set their hearts on it. I was glad no Ill will grew out of it as women set their hearts on what they manufacter.

---

175. The Indianapolis *Indiana Democrat*, November 4, 1835, in reporting the fair remarked, "Our friend Fletcher, the Treasurer of the Society, although somewhat partial to the United States bank, procured a sufficient quantity of Jackson money—real Benton yellow-jackets—to pay the premiums." A complete listing of the prizes is given in the *Democrat*.

176. Member of the State Board of Agriculture.

Thurs. 5 Novr. 1835. Closed our buseness at 12. It rains. Messrs. Herrod Wick & Brown leave. Mr. Quarles & I went to Strawtown. It rained while we were absent. Got back about sundown. Q. & I spent an agreeable night at Mr. Du[nnings]. Butler was out.

Friday [*Nov.*] *6.* Wet—cool. At 8 left for home with Mr. Q. overtook Wick with his little daughter near Carters where we stoped and dined. Arrived home here about 4 P.M.

Saturday [*Nov.*] *7.* Pleasant weather for time of year. Many calls on business.

Sunday [*Nov.*] *8.* Cloudy. I did not feel like going to church. Examined many letters. Wrote to Joseph Miller & Miles. Stoughton & John H. dined with us.

Monday [*Nov.*] *9.* Pleasent attended & compleated my bank buseness. Cole, Hughey[177] & Stephenson arrived.

Tuesday [*Nov.*] *10.* Intended to begin my preparations for the Supreme Court & District Court. My business in these two courts have been shamefully neglected in consequence of my other business but today my calls are too numerous to do anything with them.[178]

Wedy. [*Nov.*] *11.* Cole & Hughey entered one piece of land for McC. & myself[179] & several for R. Buchanan[?] Cincinnati.

Had a meeting of the board of Marion Cty. Seminary trustees for the first time. Messrs. Morrison Henkle Cobern Wilkins Dr. Sanders & myself present[180]—Mr. Hill had been put into the S. by

177. James Hughey, early settler of White River Township, Hamilton County. He served as county surveyor (1830–34) and as county commissioner (1831–32). Shirts, *History of Hamilton County*, pp. 74, 75, 126.

178. In his "Recollections of Calvin Fletcher as a Lawyer," Simon Yandes wrote: ". . . he undertook to do too much, for he included in his practice not only litigated business but a large collecting business, the details of which last required much of his time and vigilance." MS in Fletcher Family Papers, Indiana Historical Society Library.

179. The land entered was the west half of southwest quarter, section 13, T19N, R5E, northeast of Noblesville, purchased for $100. Indianapolis Land Office, Register of Receipts.

180. Under provision of an act of February 7, 1835, C.F., James Morrison, Moses Henkle, Henry P. Coburn, John Wilkens, Dr. John H. Sanders, and Samuel Merrill were appointed trustees of the Marion County Seminary. *Laws of Indiana*, 1834–35 (local), p. 192. Their bond is recorded in the Marion County Commissioners Record, Book 1, p. 83. The Marion County Seminary was opened September 1, 1834, in a building erected on the University Square (square 25).

Mr. Merrill last Spring. His claims with Mr. Thos. D. Gregg Hill friends refuse to give up the academy &c.[181] I will not sacrefise my own peace in a quarrel on the subject. I have my own private affairs to attend to—do not seek or desire any office & tho I feel for Mr. Gregg whose merits are well known I shall not go beyond prudence in this matter by suffering my temper to carry me away.

Hill is a man of notorious bad character. At Baltimore where he came from the board are apprised that he is suspected to have such character & if they do not investigate the matter I cannot help it. I sometimes suspect that I am guilty of the sin of indifference about public matters.

Mr. Butterfi[e]ld & lady called & staid over night. A few flakes of snow—cool this day. I condemn myself tho' could not help it that I should have done so little this day.

Thursday 12 of Novr. Cool. Up at 5. 16 Bank directors present (meet). Messrs. Law Scott Vestal Morrison Deming Leeds Jennisons Owen Norris Blythe,[182] &c.

Novr. 19. Visited Mr. Yandes in company with Mrs. Fletcher & Richmond. Were others present Mr. Hannerman & lady—Merrill & Lady—Mr. West daughters & son Mr. Holiday & lady &c.

[Nov.] 22 Sunday. Went to church Mr. Smith preached. Snowed. Returned home & [in] imitation of a merciful man housed my cattle hogs &c. Tied up two wild cows myself. Stoughton & John dined. Received letter from J. F. Wright relative to selling his land. Read Western magazine Thompson's season's &c. Snow fell 3

It was supported by the county seminary fund derived from fines for penal offenses and money paid for exemption from militia duty and by tuition. Those in charge of the Seminary were Ebenezer Dumont, 1834–35; William J. Hill, 1835; Thomas D. Gregg, 1835–36; William Sullivan, 1836–37; William A. Holliday, 1837–38; James Sprigg Kemper, 1838–45; J. P. Safford, 1845–46; and B. L. Lang, 1846–52. Dunn, *Indianapolis,* I, 121, 122. Reminiscences of the seminary may be found in an account of the reunion of the "Seminary boys," in Indianapolis *Indiana Journal,* July 18, 1878.

181. What C.F. intended to say here is not clear. William J. Hill had taken over the Marion County Seminary in January, 1835. Advertisement in Indianapolis *Indiana Journal,* January 2, 1835.

182. John Law, Vincennes; Lucius H. Scott, Terre Haute; John Vestal, Bedford; Robert Morrisson, Richmond; Demas Deming, Terre Haute; Noah Leeds, Richmond; William M. Jenners, Lafayette; William Owens, Evansville; Seton W. Norris, Indianapolis; and Benjamin I. Blythe, Indianapolis.

inches. All nature looked gloomy. 3 little pigs lost from their mother asked admittance into our yard & Calvin & Elijah permitted them to enter & shelter under the barn.

Monday [*Nov.*] *23*. Pleasantly cold. Snow remains on. Some sleighs running. Preparing for Supreme Court.

[*Nov.*] *24*. Mr. Gregg commenced his school in the Academy. Mrs. Richmond Cooley Elijah commenced with him. I fear he will not be as successful a teacher as formerly. Killed hogs this day. Old Mr. Fletcher & Mr. Wood helped James F. 6 that were only 15 months old weighed 1070¼ lbs. neat—the white breed. Cool & pleasant. Snow remains on.

Decr. 1st [*–4*] *1835*. Cool. Dist. Court & Sup. court commenced its session on the 29 inst. Judge Holeman[183] on the bench of District court Vice Judge Park diceased—who was one of the oldest jurists in the state—was an early settler say as early as 1790 at Vincennes—much respected by the bar for his aimiable temper & as a Judge had there been business adequate to his talants he would have stood first as a jurist in the West. Mr. Dewey gave notice he would call the attention of the bar to the subject of his death which was accordingly done on the 5 of Decr.[184] The Sup. court not as numerously attended as usual.

On the 4th of Decr. Joined with Mr. McCarty in the purchase of Dr. Sanders farm joining Indianapolis 264 acres for $13200.[185] This is considered an extravagant price but we design laying it off

183. Jesse L. Holman (1784–1842), who served as judge of the state Supreme Court from 1816 to 1831 and as United States district judge from 1835 until his death. Monks *et al.* (eds.), *Courts and Lawyers of Indiana*, I, 186, II, 413.

184. Charles Dewey (1784–1862) was appointed to the state Supreme Court in 1836 to succeed Stephen C. Stevens who had resigned. *Ibid.*, I, 198–201; *Indiana Executive Proceedings*, p. 311. He delivered a eulogy on Parke in Indianapolis on June 1, 1836, which was issued in pamphlet form by Bolton and Livingston, printers.

185. The Marion County deed records show that on February 4, 1836, John H. Sanders conveyed to C.F. outlots 94, 95, 96, 97, and 98. The amount paid is not given. The lots lay to the southeast of the town, east of Virginia Avenue and south of South Street. The Indianapolis *Indiana Democrat* of December 8, 1835, reported that during the past week Dr. Sanders had "sold his Wood Lawn estate adjoining Indianapolis, comprising 269 acres, at the rate of fifty dollars per acre, or $13,450. Mr. Nicholas McCarty is the purchaser." The *Democrat* described the place as being one of the "most desirable situations in the neighborhood."

into town lots soon & should not the expected French War [come] we can sell for a handsome advance in small parcels. Should this affliction be brought upon by improvident rulers the whole country must suffer exceedingly just as they are preparing to commence an extensive system of internal improvements. The people are not prepared for war & nothing but the popularity of the President can induce either branch of Congress to urge or consent to a declaration of war.

[*Dec.*] 5. Entered Orinderio Crumbaugh a girl we have raised 80 acres of land. Mr. Boxley is here. Cold pleasant weather—ground froze.

I have this day entered into partnership with O. Butler of Shelby County in the practice of law for the next 5 years. My domestic & other business is such that I cannot do justice to my professional calls. I have between forty and fifty thousand dollers worth of real estate under my charge on the management of which depends a future sustenance for myself & family. Indeed I cannot say the prospect of abundance affords me any happiness but the fear of its loss causes me much trouble. I would not recommend it to any young man to run many risks in the acquisition of property.

Mr. Pratt who has lived with me for the last two years will probibly settle somewhere in this country. If so I will try & aid him.

Decr. 6. 7. 8. 9. 10. Cold—a little snow just enough to cover the ground. On the 8 went with Mrs. Fletcher to hear Govr. Nobles message to the legislature. It was read by Mr. Ketcham. A high toned internal improvement document. Recommends the borrowing of ten million of dollers for that purpose. It was an able document.[186]

Mr. Dewey has been appointed by the bar of the Dist. & Sup. Court to deliver an eulogy on the life of Judge Park.

186. The message is printed in *Messages and Papers relating to the Administration of Noah Noble*, pp. 385–412. The legislature was meeting for the first time in the new state capitol. The building, designed and built by Ithiel Town and Andrew J. Davis, was in the form of a Doric temple with a large dome on the roof. It had quarters for the Supreme Court, offices for the secretary of state and state auditor, rooms for the state library and the law library, as well as a representatives' hall and senate chamber and committee rooms and clerks' rooms. A total of $60,000 was appropriated for the structure. Dunn, *Indianapolis*, I, 104–105.

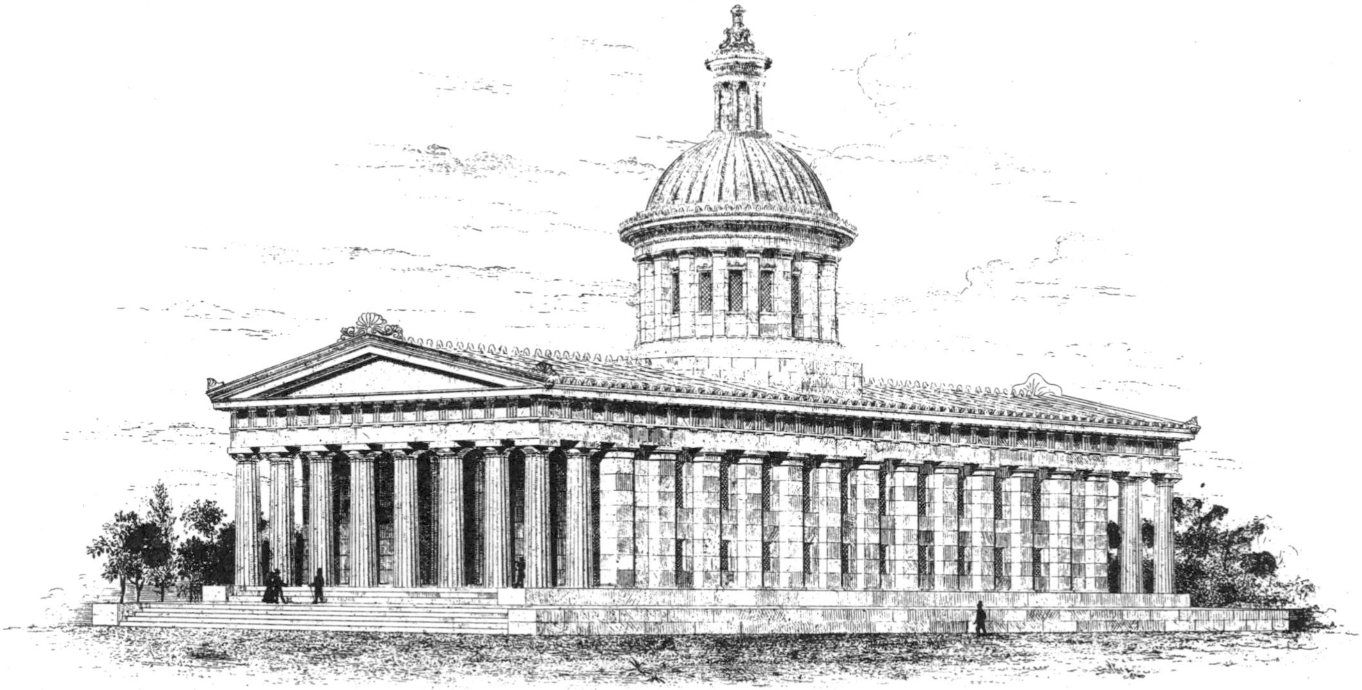

CAPITOL OF THE STATE OF INDIANA.

I. TOWN & A. J. DAVIS, ARCHITECTS.

1834

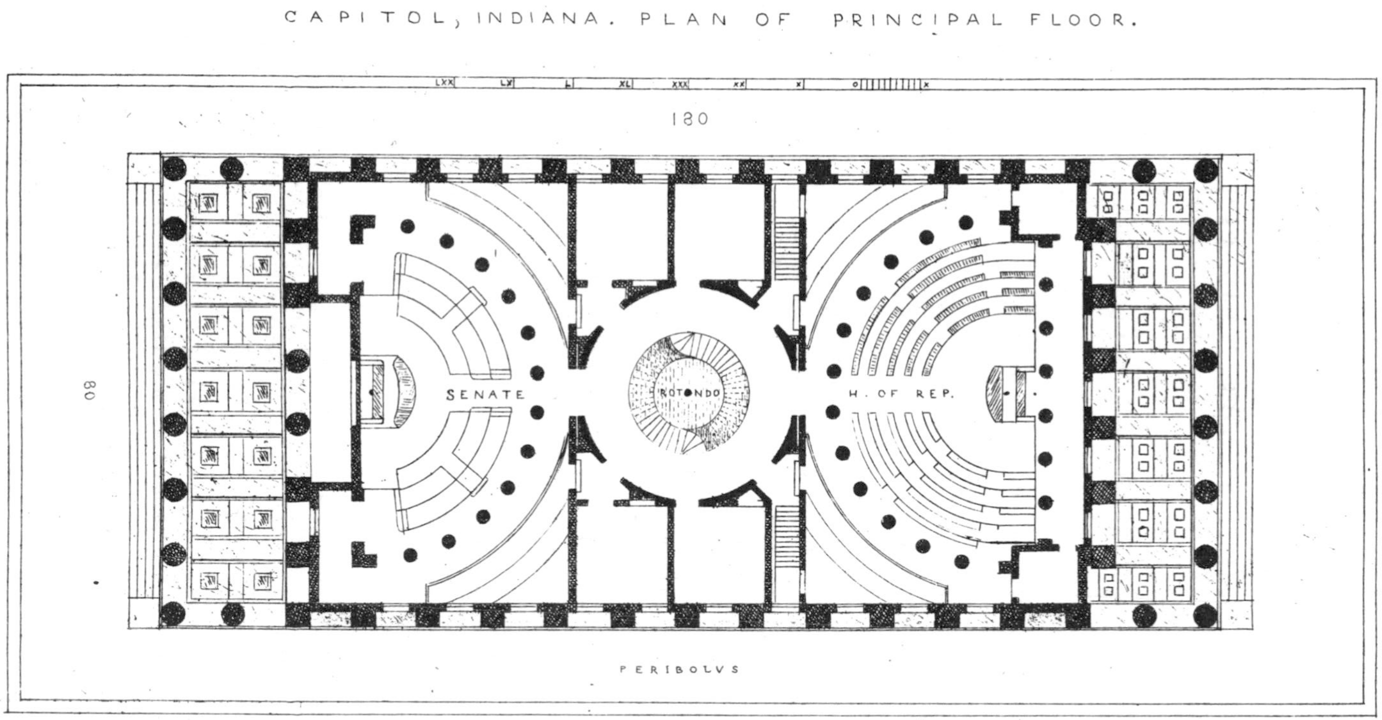

INDIANA HISTORICAL SOCIETY

Architect's drawings of Indiana's first State Capitol, completed in 1835.

Saturday Decr. 12. Mr. Ingram arrived from Lafayette. Rode to see the Sanders land. Pleasant day.

Sunday [Dec.] 13. Cool pleasant day. Went with Mrs. F. to Methodist Church. Old Mr. Conwell Senater from Franklin [County] preached. Mr. Ingram Elijah & Miles went to hear Pres't. Baldwin[187] preach—the first time he has appeared here. Have not seen him.

Monday Decr. 14. The Harrison convention has assembled here. Mr. Ingram is a delegate—A large convention. I shall not support Genl. Harrison for reasons hereafter expressed.

State Agricultural Society met at Statehouse in the eve. Not very numerously attended. I prepared some resolutions made a small speech. Cooley went with me. Messrs. Thompson & Caleb B. Smith made very pretty speeches. Mr. Dumont[188] & Judge Holman talked about raising beans &c. It is hoped another convention when the objects of this grand scheme is better known will give some light on agricultural science.

Mr. Butler arrived in the eve. Sup. court has not yet adjourned. Pleasant weather. We are waiting with impatience to see the President['s] message. Rumor says it breathes war.

Decr. 15. Pleasant morning. Old Mr. Butterfield staid with us. A pleasant morning. Went to Harrison convention a few moments.[189]

Mr. Butler has arrived.

Decr. 16. Cold. Went with Mr. Wood to show how to cut fire wood. Dined with Mrs. Fletcher & Richmond at Mr. Hannermans.

187. Perhaps Elihu Baldwin, Presbyterian minister and first president of Wabash College, who came with his family from New York to Crawfordsville in October, 1835. James I. Osborne and Theodore G. Gronert, *Wabash College, The First One Hundred Years 1832–1932* (Crawfordsville: R. E. Banta, 1932), pp. 40–41.

188. John Dumont, senator from Ripley and Switzerland counties.

189. Held in support of the nomination of William Henry Harrison for President. Marston G. Clark of Washington County was chosen president; secretaries were Albert S. White of Tippecanoe County and Austin W. Morris of Marion County. Richard W. Thompson of Lawrence County was the chief speaker, praising Harrison to his audience as having "periled his life in defending their frontiers from the inroads of the savage. . . ." Indianapolis *Indiana Journal,* December 18, 1835.

President['s] message not arrived but expected of a war like character.

Old Mr. Plummer stayed over night. Messrs. Gregg Dr. Richmond[190] & Shanklin call in the Eve.

Decr. 17 1835. Cloudy cold morning. Old Mr. Plummer staid with us. No snow on. Preparing for the argument of Bryan vs Blythe in the Sup. court & [. . .] vs Wood &c.

Dec. 18. Cloudy wet day—thawed a few inches. Argued case of [. . .] vs Stephenson—occupied the day. In the Eve took tea at Mr. Holidays with Judges Blackford & Stevens & A. Ingram Esq.

Spent eve at office. Made an arrangement to take 130 shares Logansport Bridge stock.[191]

Decr. 19. Saturday. Wet ground thawed a few inches.

19 Dec. Wet & rainy. Closed my business in Sup. court. Went to hear Jimmy Havens preach. In Eve Ith[i]el Town[192] came to my office & I draw Power of Atty. for him. President['s] Message is thought not to portend war.

Sunday 20 Decr. Clear muddy under foote. Went to love feast with Mrs. F. & Richmond. Returned home then went to church. Mr. Havens preached—very full congregation. Stoughton & J. Hill dined with me. Old Mr. Butterfield brought us a barrel of cider & 3 cheeses last eve & he & Mr. Tryon staid over night. In eve went to church with Dorio. Nat[ional] Intelligencer believes the President['s] message breaths war with France. I hope not—I do believe this grows out of a prejudice to the P.

Monday Decr. 21 1835. Rose late in the morning—Exhorted

190. Dr. John L. Richmond, a physician and clergyman who came to Indianapolis in July, 1835. He practiced medicine and also served as pastor of the First Baptist Church from 1835 to 1839. Sulgrove, *History of Indianapolis*, p. 391; Dunn, *Indianapolis*, I, 567. The Indianapolis *Indiana Democrat* on January 1, 1836, carried a notice that Dr. Richmond and Dr. George W. Mears had formed a partnership for the practice of "Physic, Surgery and Midwifery." Their office was on Washington Street a few doors west of Samuel Henderson's hotel. Dr. Richmond was a brother of Ansel Richmond and the Rev. Nathaniel Richmond. Harden, *The Pioneer*, p. 241.

191. This was an investment in the toll bridge erected by a private company over the Wabash River at Third Street in Logansport. The bridge was opened to traffic in the spring of 1838. Jehu Z. Powell, *History of Cass County Indiana* (2 volumes. Chicago: Lewis Publishing Company, 1913), I, 207.

192. See note 186, above.

Judson Benjamin[193] an orphan boy to make himself a useful man & as one means to rise early & devote every spare moments to books & especially biography. Pleasant—white frost.

Decr. 22d. Cold. Nothing new—visit the farm to make arrangements with old Mr. Fletcher & son to tend the farm next year. Old man at home. Concluded to have the N. E. corner about 30 acres on the tract he resides cleared. Young man not at home.

[*Wednesday, Dec.*] *23.* Went to the funeral of Wm. Ray brother of James M. Mr. Butler left for home. Very cold. Mr. Pratt absent for clients to Boon Cty. Very cold.

24 Decr. B. Cole down. James Elijah & Calvin going to have their first party of males & females—there assembled 45 childrin of both sex between the ages of 10 & 13 at 5 P.M. & retired home a[t] 9. The[y] spent the eve in singing & in plays. At first they were a little awk[wa]rd as it was the first time they had thus assembled. Their names are as follows [. . .].[194]

Decr. 25 1835. Wet dissagreeable day—ground is thawing a 2d time after a deep freeze. Very little parade about Ch[r]istmass. Govr. Noble has a party. Employs stages to convey the guests to his house. Mr. Pratt returned from Boon county very wet.

Spent some hours with Lanier, Farrington and A. Williams[195] appointed by state bank to obtain amounts of charter.

Decr. 26. Weather changed a little but still thaws some say 2½ of the 4 inches now thawed. I fear it will prove distructive to wheat & rye.

Sunday Decr. 27. Froze last night so as to bear a horse nearly. Read review of the 2d vol. of Websters speeches—Nat[ional] I[ntel-

193. In his diary on September 15, 1855, C.F. wrote: "Mrs. Judson Benjamin & Baby came to see us. She is the wife of a former law Student & afterward a missionary to Berma India. Benjamin is dead left her with child."

194. On December 26, 1835, C.F. wrote his mother: "Our boys . . . had their first party at which they had 45 little boys & girls between the ages of 10 and 13 & only one of whom was born in N.E. They came at 5 o'clock P.M. & left at 9. The parents of several came for them in carriages. . . . The party passed the evening in singing & playing in very good order.

"James has spent 2 months with his uncle Stoughton & partner this fall but is now going to school & will return to his uncle in 2 months from this time to live the next year. We shall board him." Fletcher Papers.

195. James F. D. Lanier, of Madison; James Farrington, of Terre Haute; and Achilles Williams, of Richmond.

ligencer] Genl. Farmer[?] 10 chaps in the bible with my childrin. Went to hear Mr. Smith preach in the A.M. Mr. Peck & Stoughton dined with us.

Decr. 28. Cool in the morning froze again hard. Went to the state house to hear Mr. Quarles' defence of Ch[r]istian C. Nave charged with having committed pirjury before the commencement of session but since his election. Acquitted on the ground that the house of Representatives of which he is a member had no Jurisdiction &c.

[Dec.] 29. Went to the house with Mr. West who with myself is appointed to negotiate the change of the Aurora Mr. Henkles to an agricultural paper &c.[196] Butler is preparing to go to Strawtown Pratt to Cincinnati & myself to Morgan.

[Dec.] 30. Cool but pleasant—froze no snow. We have just heard of the awful calamity that has just befallen N.Y. City by a conflag[r]ation that is supposed to destroy between thirty & sixty million of property & many lives. We have not heard particulers. It has been a subject of so serious import as to call the attention of congress to the relief of the sufferers.

James Hill has arrived from Laport—is sick. Mr. McCarty is also sick. Cloudy, cool weather. The legislature have under consideration the subject of internal improvements & the amendments to the bank charter. I fear the favorable result of the projects.

Decr. 31 1835. Dorio sick. Stoughton (little boy) got up at half past 3 o'clock in the morning [and] made up a fire for us.

James Hill is no better. I fear he will have a severe fit of sickness.

196. M. M. Henkle, printer, publisher, and bookseller, and secretary of the State Board of Agriculture, had begun publication of a weekly paper called the *Indiana Aurora* in August, 1835. It was "devoted to agriculture, education, and internal improvements, etc." Only one issue is known to survive today, that of December 26, 1835, in the Library of Congress. The *Aurora* apparently was discontinued in March, 1836, when the *Indiana Farmer* published by Moses Henkle under the direction of the State Board of Agriculture commenced. It was devoted almost entirely to agriculture and lasted until January, 1837. A fairly complete file is in the Indiana State Library. It in turn was succeeded by *The Indiana Farmer and Stock Register* (see Pt. VIII, note 97). The *Aurora*, along with the *Indiana Journal* and *Indiana Democrat*, was distributed to members of the General Assembly during the 1835–36 session.

Sent for Calvin to [come] home & help his mother. Am preparing my business for Cincinnati. Mr. Butler gone to Hamilton Cty. P. Patrick called & settled with me. Mr. Silver also called.

I have this day laid by correspondence & receipts for the past year. A watch night at Methodist Church. Judson Elijah & Miles went. I had to go after E. He staid to church till after 12.

VII

Diary and Letters of CALVIN FLETCHER *January 1–December 31, 1836*

January First 1836. Rose this morning a little after 5. We still continue this practise. I trust it will not be forgotten or abandoned by my childrin.

Pleasant morning just cold enough to prevent a thaw & warm enough to be comfortable. James Hill is a little better as well as Dorio.

Went to my office before 8—still kept in front of Bazel Brown Hotel over Landis Store. Mr. Pratt is now with me but expects to leave in a few months. Simon Yandes Hugh O Neel & a Mr. Harris[1] studying law with me.

I have the care of the 3 law students, my own professional business, the annual value of which I think is between $1500. & $2000. I am director of State Bank, Commissioner of sinking fund.[2]

1. See above, Pt. VI, note 88.

2. The Sinking Fund was provided for in the act creating the State Bank. It comprised all unapplied balances of loans procured on the part of the state for its stock in the bank or for the purpose of being lent to stockholders to enable them to meet installments on their bank stock; the semiannual payments of interest on state loans to stockholders and sums received in payment of said loans; and dividends paid by the bank on state stock. The principal and interest of the Sinking Fund was to be devoted to liquidating loans to the state and interest thereon obtained for the payment of the state's stock in the bank and payment of the second and third installments of the shares of other stockholders. *Laws of Indiana*, 1833–34, pp. 35–36; Dorothy Riker (ed.), *Messages and Papers relating to the Administration of David Wallace Governor of Indiana 1837–1840* (*Indiana Historical Collections*, XLIII, Indianapolis, 1963), pp. 203n–204n.

[I have] a family of 7 childrin to look to besides Mrs. Richmond son & several others whose direction I am bound to look after, the supervision of several improved farms with tenants to watch—and at this time something like 18000 acres of land, mostly wild, the one half of about 13000, belongs to N. McCarty jointly with me—my correspondence my news paper reading, miscellaneous & law reading. [I am a] member of the board of the colonization society, treasurer Marion County agricultural Society &c &c.

All occupy my time & thoughts. To more serious matters I try to give some of my time & attention. Every Sunday when at home I go to church & if possible take my childrin with me. We have a family prayer meeting on that day at which no other but the childrin my wife & self attend & what is pleasing our childrin do not look upon it as a burthen. Every morning we assemble ourselves in the winter at 6 & in the summer before sun rise to read & pray. This we should do in the eve but for the circumstance of our childrin retireing very early to bed & their mother sees that they repeat the Lords prayer & I am usually absent at my office. In the midst of the blessings of unusual health & reasonable prosperity no family should be more greatful to the Disposer of our lives.

During the last year I have invested with N. McCarty between $15000. & $20000 *on my part* in real estate. $9000 of this I have borrowed. This anticipating my means to such an extent is very hazardous & contra[r]y to the views I have usually entertained—but the circumstance of the last public lands, almost, in the state having been brought into market this season at the *minimum* of $1.25 per acre the great probibility of a system of internal improvements, have influenced my rashness on this subject but the fears, the responsibility, the accumulated cares cannot not be repaid by any reasonable success & that those who should ever read this account may not venture on such an experiment I will here mention another circumstance which alone brought me to adopt the foregoing hazard. [It] was that I had secured & paid $5000. worth of Bank stock in Indianapolis branch also brother Elijah advised me to anticipate my means investing money in real estate & that my crediters or character should not suffer should any adverse fortune occur in the undertaking otherwise highly improper. What will be the issue of this undertaking I am a[t] loss to foretell. Another year will put to the test my skill to discharge these debts. I now anticipate sales of real estate to effect this object. In this I may be totally disappointed, if so I shall be hard pressed. The accumulation of property does not make me happy—constant business & attention to the affairs of life do add something to it.

Jany. 2d 1836. This day Mr. Pratt & myself have prepared to remit $5500. to Cincinnati & Louisville—money I have collected for various individuals at a profit of 6 per cent.

James Hill very sick. I fear he will not recover. Mr. Merrill bought widow Amacks farm at $24 per acre. He called on me to talke about Mr. Ketcham who is about to marry his eldest daughter to learn something of his character.[3] I do not think highly of the man. I called at Messrs. Garder & Collets room[4] the latter sick. Called on Mr. Wallace. Stoughton dined with us. John Hill took the measels & he & James are confined in one room. Mrs. F. & myself were up several times in the night.

Our family consists of Mrs. F., 7 childrin, Orindorio & Judson Benjamin an orphan the son of a baptist missionary who died in this country in 1824. He is going to school to Mr. Holiday. A remarkable pleasant new years the 15th I have spent in Indianapolis. Received the new years address here attached.[5]

3d January 1836. Sunday morning. Rains. Mr. Pratt starts for Cincinnati with 3 or four thousand dollars for Mr. McCarty 20 thousand for the bank as well as about 5 thousand for my clients.

At 10 I left for the bluffs on my way to Martinsvill to get a ferry established at the first named place. It rained all the way. Arrived at Mr. McGrews, Allens old stand, at sundown. Mr. McGrew is now the renter of that stand from Mr. McCarty & myself. Found the family [and] a Mr. McCollock &c.

Jany. 4. Left the bluffs with Mr. McGrew & son for Martinsvill the former after a license to Keep a tavern. Arrived at Martinsvill at 1 o'clock. Performed our buseness before the board of Com-

3. See above, Pt. VI, note 84.

4. Stephen B. Gardner, representative from Vermillion County and Stephen S. Collett, senator from Vermillion and Warren counties.

5. There is no Carrier's Address attached to the diary. Among the clippings and broadsides in the Fletcher Papers, however, there is a copy of the "Address of the Carrier to the Patrons of the Indiana Democrat, January 1, 1836." In the Papers there are a few Carrier's Addresses for other New Year's days.

missioners. Mr. McG. & son returned home. I staid at Mitchels tavern[6] had a room & fire & read several papers.

Tuesday Jany. the 5 1836. Mild pleasant day frost coming out of ground. On yesterday I met with bro. Daily Methodist preacher & several hog droves.

I this day compleated my buseness got the ferry established. Examined the records office as to land at bluffs. Got two deeds recorded called on Dr. Sims family & returned alone to the Bluffs. At Mr. McG.'s met with a Mr. Gallpo[?] of Vermont getting subscribers for the [. . .].

Jany. 6. Pleasant day frost coming out of the ground. After breakfast went to Majr. Lusks & Kings—examined the place on which King lives—went over the orchard on the Allen place—went to the mill above the bluffs—rented the King place to him. Engaged the building of a ferry boat by young Tell[?] & Paul—for $1. per foote, 55 ft. Rented the whole ground to Mr. McGrew—ferry & all.

In the Eve Col. Lee & Gorman on their way to the Van Buran convention to be held on the 8th inst. also a Mr. Stout printer at Vincennes & several other gentlemen.[7] Staid at McGs. I went to Mr. Davises & spent a pleasant Eve & staid over night. Slept with Mr. H. Wright, Tailor.

Jany. 7. Rains. Leave the Bluffs with Henry Wright & overtake the Gentlemen that staid at McGs. Rains hard. Arrived at Indianapolis at home at 12. Wet & cold. Went to my office. Morris Morris called. A young Mr. Corwin called introd[uc]ed by Hiram Brown. 2 drove of stock hogs passed going East & several hundred conventioners arrived. Each tavern filled to the overflowing.

Returned home & spent the Eve with my family. Jas. & John Hill both confined in the West room (better). Calvin waits upon them. Read the Intelligencer.

Jany. 8. Cloudy frost coming out of ground. Nothing new.

6. Giles Mitchell opened a tavern in Martinsville around 1834. Blanchard (ed.), *Counties of Morgan, Monroe and Brown Indiana*, p. 84.

7. Thomas G. Lee of Bartholomew County, Willis A. Gorman of Monroe County, and Elihu Stout, publisher of the Vincennes *Western Sun* were delegates to the Democratic Republican Convention which convened in Indianapolis on January 8, 1836, in the interest of the nomination of Martin Van Buren for President and Richard M. Johnson for Vice-President. Indianapolis *Indiana Democrat*, January 8, 1836.

9 Jany. Very muddy desagreeable travelling. Nothing new. James Hill recov[er]ing slowly.

[*Jan.*] *10.* Still muddy & disagreable moving about. Election between Messrs. Burr & Long canal commissioners. Burr succeedes by 1 vote.

11 Jany. Things remain as on yesterday. Mr. R. L. Hannerman & son took tea. Son staid over night. Was introduced to a Mr. Teel of Michigan city. Muddy. Our citizens constructing tan bark walks.

12 Jany. Pleasant a little more dry than heretofore frost nearly out of the ground. Killed a fat cow one of the best we ever had. Weighed about 650 lb. 100 cwt. of tallow.

This day the great internal improvement Bill past the house of Representatives by which it is contemplated to expend about 12 million of dollars by a board of public works.[8] The principal works terminate & pass thro Indianapolis (to witt) The White River & Wabash canal the Madison railroad Lawrenceburgh railroad & the Lafayette &c. This grand project will exalt Indiana among the nations of the earth. I have a strong desire to live to see the completion of this splendid system.

I was this day emploid by Judge Everet to appear before the Judiciary Committee to examine witness on charges exhibited to impeach him for mal conduct.[9] I tried to get off having a bad

8. Known as the Mammoth Internal Improvement bill, this measure which the Governor signed on January 27, 1836, provided for construction of a canal from Lawrenceburg to Cambridge City (the Whitewater Canal); a canal from the Wabash River at some point between Fort Wayne and Logansport via Muncie and Indianapolis, down the White River to the Forks, thence to Evansville (the Central Canal); extension of the Wabash and Erie Canal to Terre Haute and a canal linking it with the Central Canal; a railroad from Madison via Columbus and Indianapolis to Lafayette; a turnpike from New Albany to Vincennes; a road or railroad linking Jeffersonville and Crawfordsville via Salem, Bedford, Bloomington, and Greencastle; removal of obstructions in the Wabash River; a canal or railroad linking the Wabash and Erie Canal near Fort Wayne to Lake Michigan. The act also authorized the Lawrenceburgh and Indianapolis Railroad Company to borrow $500,000 on the credit of the state secured by a mortgage on real estate owned by the company. *Laws of Indiana*, 1835–36 (general), pp. 6–21.

9. Gustavus A. Everts, president judge of the eighth circuit. He was charged with acting as an attorney for various persons in matters relating to land claims and with adjourning the Allen County court early in order to attend land sales at La Porte. Indiana *House Journal*, 1835–36, pp. 81, 273–77; Indiana *Senate Journal*, 1835–36, pp. 462, 483, 502, 505, 511, and Appendix. He resigned his judge-

opinion of the Judge but I could not well be excused in the estimation of the Judge. Prepare for the foregoing.

Jany. 13 1836. Ezekiel Slaughter called & paid one of the notes for Givan Morgan Cty. land.

I appeared before the Judiciary Committee composed of 7 or 8 members—M. Stapp Chairman. Went thro the examination & made the points relied upon by the Judge.

Clo[u]dy but pleasant weather. Received a letter from bro. Miles. Concluded to write him & suggest his [he] emigrate to this state. Elijah & Ingram sick with the measles. Calvin & Miles had them in 1829—rest of the family subject to them. Dorio & [I] went to hear an Indian missionary.

Jany. 14. Rose at 5. Pleasant weather—cloudy. Went to the state house. The committee on Judge Everits case sit this eve. Mr. McCarty & myself bot of Saml. Miller of Mich. City 80 acres of land laying near that place for $1000. $800. down. This lays near two other tracts we own & the only consideration moving me to this purchase was the prospect of selling the same for an advance & thereby extricate myself for part of the debt hanging over me.[10] I have promised myself to purchase no more except it is to fit & prepare some other tract we own, the better for sale. I feel somewhat alarmed at the debt that hangs over us should the internal improvement bill now hanging with some doubts in the Senate, fail—the harbor bill for Mich. City not pass this session of Cong.[11] I must be

ship the following June and was elected to the state Senate in August. *Indiana Executive Proceedings,* p. 311; *Indiana Election Returns,* p. 234.

10. The La Porte County deed records show that C.F. and McCarty purchased of Samuel Miller on January 14, 1836, the east half of the southwest quarter of section 33, T38N, R4W for $1,000. They had purchased from Alfred Harrison on October 31, 1835, the east half of the northeast quarter of section 32 and the east half of the northwest quarter of section 31 for the same price. It proved to be a profitable investment for on July 16, 1836, they disposed of one eighth of their interest in the three tracts to Alfred Harrison for $4,000; on September 3, 1836, they sold their undivided three-fourths interest in the same tracts to William Teall and David Sprague of La Porte for $16,800; and the following year C.F. sold his remaining 1/16 interest in the same land to David Castleman of Fayette County, Kentucky, for $2,500. See entries for January 12 and 16, 1837.

11. Congress appropriated $20,000 for improvement of the harbor in 1836, $30,000 in 1837, and $60,733 in 1838. *Messages and Papers relating to the Administration of Noah Noble,* p. 490n.

much prepared if not hard pushed to meet my contracts. I have promised myself to stop purchasing except as above & to extricate myself. Should both of the above circumstances eventuate [. . .] the French War would probibly blast my hopes of independence. However in this matter I have but little feeling. My great desire [is] to retain my character for punctuality & do no injustice to all with whom I have business.

A girl living with Mr. McChessney was found burned to death—had probibly a fit & fell in the fire. Had a talk with Mr. Merrill this eve. He accuses me with improper conduct in raising the price of land producing a fictitious notion of real estate &c &c. We settled the matter in friendship. I like him & have agreed not to purchase more land for the coming year than he would. His [. . .] cause of complaint is that I had publicly stated that I would not have missed voting for the bill for the expenditure of 12 millions of dollars for internal improvement for $1000. He fears that this bill will ruin our state financially & morally. I do not believe it. Time will determine [if] I am guilty of the sin Mr. Merrill alleges &c.

Jany. 15 1836. Pleasant morning—ground covered with snow. Wrote a letter to Miles & one to Miss Fellows.

Great excitement in relation to internal improvement in the senate. It is disputed whether the govr. shall have the nominating power.[12] I do not much fear the passage of the law in some shape.

The Judiciary have agreed to report against Judge Everit. Done some business for Wm. Pratt Pittsford[13] & a Mr. Wm. Blue. Old Mr. Fraze was buried a good old man who resides at the south part of our town whose son John died a few years past greatly respected who had been a merchants clerk for Phipps & McCarty & was Just entering into business with D. Yandes. Mr. Butler is absent to Shelbyville.

My house presents rather a singular aspect. In the West room James & John Hill have both laid confined for 10 days together—the former with a fiver the latter with measles who has got well &

12. The bill as passed provided for a board of internal improvement to be composed of the Wabash and Erie Canal commissioners and six members appointed by the Governor with the consent of the Senate.

13. William Pittsford, of Madison County. Harden, *The Pioneer*, p. 138.

gone to his buseness—the latter is yet confined. In Mrs. F. & my room James & Elijah are both streached upon a trundle bed thickly broke out with the measles. Dr. Richmond tends on J. Hill a little but Mrs. Fletcher is principal doctor. 3 or 4 sick persons under her care gives her new energies & she is not as like to complain under such a state of affairs as when her burthens are light. In the administration of medicine & the general care of the sick & the afflicted under her ministration no one is better adapted. Her confidence & wisdom in management increase with the importance of the difficulties presented.[14]

January 16, 1836. This day the bill adopting a system of internal improvement before alluded to in this Journal, passed both houses & became a law. It passed about 1 o'clock P.M. The Senate adjourned immediately until Monday (This day being Saturday). In the evening a splendid illumination took place. Every house in Washington St. was illumined & most off[ices on] the street my office with the rest. Calvin & Miles took some candles down & spent the eve in the streets till 8 o'[clock]. James & Elijah regretted that they were confined with the measles. Some few members got a little *drunk* to speak in plain terms on the occasion tho' I must say that temperance prevails very generally in the body. Not many strangers in town. I feel on this occasion like others of a similar character—I feel that we should be greatful to this disposer of all events for the march of intellect liberal principals & Science—that as a state Indiana by liberal & wise legislation is to be under the smiles of a kind Providence to be exalted among the nations of the

14. In his "Recollections of My Mother" Elijah Fletcher wrote: "Her knowledge of domestic remedies, and her skill in their application passed almost into a proverb. I think there was not a nurse in the whole town equal to her. In her numerous and constantly increasing family there were many aches and pain, real and imaginery to heal. Sometimes three or four of us would be down at once. At such times she seemed to possess the ubiquity of an angel; flitting from bed to bed she administered to our ills; and at the same time kept the domestic wheel turning. On these occasions she never took off her clothes, and caught the little sleep she had between the calls of the sufferers. Besides her own immediate family, she had the care of such of her relatives, or friends as were taken sick without a fathers house at hand. In this way she nursed Uncle James, and John & William; Israel Griffith, Judson Benjamin & B. B. Barker. To these names should be added that of poor Giles Isham, who lay long and dangerously ill from a fall from a horse. In the same connection might be mentioned the many girls brought up under her care." Fletcher Papers.

earth. 10 years will multiply our population. This town will progress from 8 to 12 thousand our state more than a million should these improvements progress.

Judge Everit has to have articles of impeachment referred as by order of the house.

Mr. Pratt returned from Cincinnati. In conversation with him I am not well satisfied that he is a man of as sound judgment as I could wish. I do believe his infidelity does him much harm.

Mr. Pittsford from Andersontown here to get me to do him some favor at the land office. John & James Hill yet confined. Our childrin sick with the measles.

Cloudy warm pleasant weather not so as to stay the grass.

Jany. 17 1836 Sunday. Rose at 5. Read the life Gurlys life of Ashman.[15] Went down to town to get a paper for Pittsford. Went to Methodist church. Misty damp wet weather. Stoughton dined with us had a goose &c.

Mr. Holiday rode pony to preach at Mr. Bates. Returned at night & offered to set up with our sick. Read the review of the life of Mathas [Matthias] the imposter [and] some in the old testament.

Jany. 18—Monday. In the night grew cold—ground not very wet neither much froze.

[*Jan.*] *19.* Cool Nothing new. Our childrin Cooley Elijah Stoughton & Maria sick with the measles.

[*Jan.*] 20. Preparing for Judge Everits trial of impeachment. G. H. Dunn Esq. to assist.

[*Jan.*] *21.* Snow fell last night so as to cover the ground. 21°. Cool snow remains on.

[*Jan.*] 22. Cool. Snow to cover the ground yet on. The high court of impeachment opened. Messrs. Jeff Evans Huntington Leston & Thompson[16] managers on the part of the house—Case continued till tomorrow.

Saturday [*Jan.*] 23. Cool. Mr. Dunn & myself argued the motion to quash articles against Judge Everit. I opened the cause & read the

15. Ralph Randolph Gurley, *Life of Jehudi Ashman, Late Colonial Agent in Liberia* (Washington, D.C., 1835).

16. Representatives Thomas Jefferson Evans, Fountain County; Elisha M. Huntington, Vigo County; Jonathan A. Liston, La Porte and St. Joseph counties; and Richard W. Thompson, Lawrence County.

law. Answered by Messrs. Liston & Evans. Mr. Dunn closed. Question not to be taken until Monday.

Sunday Jany. 24 1836. Very cold. James Hill remains yet sick & has a dangerous cough. His family are dialy expected.

Mrs. Richmond Dorio Calvin & Miles went to Methodist Church. Stoughton & John dine with us. Examined boys in speaking &c. Read Govr. Morleys message (Gov. of N.Y.). Messrs. Willit & Whitman[17] called to see Mr. P[. . .]s daughter.

Feby. [*Jan.*]*25 Monday* [*–Jan. 26*]. Our little girl sick—a malady consequent on the measles. A pleasant cool morning. I expect to hear the decision in Judge Evrits case to quash article. I doubt however whether it will be done. I fear external interest operating on some of the undecided Senators to wit a brother lawyer now private secretary[18] a man who is hostile to every other of the same profession in the place.

Vote was taken at 10 o'clock. Articles of Impeachment quashed. Entered one quarter section of land for Mrs. Richmond. I have now in the midst of the rage for speculation entered one 80 acre for Dorio & 2 for Mrs. R. So the widow & orphin are provided for.

Very cold day. Mr. Butler has just moved his family to town & is now ready for business. Wrote to Michael that Stoughton would leave in a few days & would bring him out. He is now about 50—has two children a son & daughter[19]—the former with Tim & Elijah, the latter with my sisters. They are about 14 & 16. He was the third child of the family. Born in the state of Vt. in Ludlow. The seasons were inclemmant & the hardships my father underwent he showed & what is more remarkable left home at 17 or 18 one of the first adventurers from his native town. His father did not encourage him to aspire above the grade of a common laberer but yet he had acquired an uncommon stock of Knowledge. Lacked in moral courage to move from the grade he was thrown into & he married an ordinary woman in Duchess County N.Y. about 25 or 30 years since.

17. Marinus Willet, representative from Rush County, and Shepherd Whitman of New Albany, representative from Floyd County.

18. John L. Ketcham, who acted as Governor Noble's private secretary.

19. Richardson and Louisa were the names of Michael Fletcher's children who came to Indiana.

He has owned a little farm has some weaknesses brought on by the sever[i]ty of treatment in early life in stead of kind admonition. Is a man of uncommon good sense & very extensive knowledge. Has become somewhat infirm & manifest a great want of that moral courage necessary to take him thro' life & of which he was made deficient in early life in consequence of the severity before spoken of. S. & myself are determined to take him under our charge & help smooth his declining years. S. will use his best endeaver to bring him on. Wrote Miles this day to prepare M. to come out with him &c.

Judge Everit gave Mr. Dunn & myself $150 for our services & left. Mr. McCarty & myself purchased a bond given by Danl. Yandes to Thos. Hogland. It was given for & on account of the following contract & sale of H. to Y. for 3 lots for which Y. gave $1000. Took a deed & gave H. a bond to pay the [. . .] differance between the present estimated price & 7 per cent compound interest at the end of 9 years to be estimated by the officers of state &c under oath. We gave $130. for the bond. Mr. McCarty says in 9 years the estimated value will not fall short of 6 thousand dollars & will probibly go as high as 9 tho[u]sand. This a great ways ahead. The parties likely mostly deceased & our town much altered. I have but little confidence in such speculations.

This day we received news that Mr. Buchannon had purchased Dr. Todds interest in 2 pieces of land amounting to 80 acres near Michigan City for $1200. We have offered Mr. B. to take one third or give him $800. for his speculation.

Very cold. Little snow on the ground. Old Mr. Fletcher broght me a load of hay with a sled &c.

P.S. I have since writing the above seen Mr. McCarty who says I misunderstood him; that he said the 3 lots at the end of 9 years will be worth at least $9000. if no calamity befalls the town or country.

Jany. 27. Cold. Am attending the Legislature in order to obtain subscriptions for an agricultural paper to be published by M. M. Henkle.[20] I succeeded in getting about 150 subscribers semi monthly at $1. per ann.

20. See above, Pt. VI, note 196.

Jany. 28. Soliciting subscribers &c. cold—a little snow. Mr. Wood hauling wood.

Jany. 29 1836. Cold disagreeable day. Roads getting smooth. James Hill getting better. Mr. McCarty & myself partially contracted for Walkers Mills in Shelbyville at about $4000.[21]

Jany. 30 Saturday [–*Jan. 31*]. Intended to visit my farm this day early in the morning but could not leave my office till 12 when I started with Mr. Butler['s] horse & arrived at Mr. F. at the farm at 1. Pleasant. I went over [to] the Cox place[22] & agreed with John Fletcher to reset the fences clear & put in grass about 12 acres &c &c. He to give ⅓ of crop & I give him $120.

I then arrived at old Mr. F. about dusk, set down wrote a lease with him & settld with him & James. Got thro' about 11 at night—was a mind to go home—grew very cold. I conclud[ed] to stay over night. I slept very cold. Rose early in the morn & started home. Horse covered with frost. I Stopped [at] Mr. Hizers & took breakfast with Mr. Woods family just settled there. Arrived home about 9 o'c. Coldest day this year. Judson sick. Mr. Wood tends to the horses. Did not go to meeting this day John dined here.

Stoughton left yesterday for Philadelphia to go as far as N.Y. for Michael. Jim Hill still better.

Wrote Elijah.

Sunday Jany. 31 1836. One of the coldest days this year—a little snow on the ground. Mr. Wood came & watered the horses.

Feby. 1 1836. Very cold. Dr. Cobb of Va. now from Laport.[23] Went to the state house to present P. Patricks name to the Govr. for

21. Mills built by John Walker, proprietor of the town of Shelbyville. See Pt. VI, note 152. According to the Shelby County deed records, on February 9, 1836, McCarty and C.F. acquired "the Jackson area" in Shelbyville, the deed being recorded the following day. In May, 1837, they purchased from John Walker additional lots in the town totaling sixty acres for $1,333.33. They continued to increase their holdings there; an 1880 town plat shows the Fletcher and McCarty addition on the north side along Big Blue River. *Atlas of Shelby County, Indiana . . .* (Chicago: J. H. Beers & Co., 1880), pp. 20–21.

22. "Cox place" refers to land comprising part of C.F.'s holdings in sections 21 and 22, T16N, R4E. See Pt. IV, note 37. A family by the name of Cox had lived there before C.F. acquired it. Diary, February 5, 1862.

23. Dr. John P. Cobbs who moved with his family to Indiana from Virginia, stopping first in La Porte then moving to Michigan City. Von Briesen (ed.), *Letters of Elijah Fletcher*, pp. 145, 146n.

nomination as Canal Commissioner. This day Messrs. E. Long Woodburn Judge Hall Dr. Maxwell & Blake of Terre Haute were nominated & appointed by the Govr. as such.[24]

Mr. Pratt called to go to Bridgeport to help commit a fellon. Called on Dr. Cobb in the eve &c.

Dr. Sanders 2d payment became due this day. Have ingaged Mjr. Skenk to help lay off town lots West of the town. Mr. Hand returned from the Wabash. Mr. Pratt concluded to go to Logansport.

Feby. 3d. Very cold dry weather. Nothing new from Washington. I fear there will be a non intercourse act as to France. Hand postponed sale of McKay land.[25] Dr. Cobb dined with us. Dr. Sanders preparing to make a deed to McCarty & myself.

Preacher Smith & Lady called in the evening. Spent some little time. Mr. Crombaugh came for the purpose of entering his land he now lives on. There is great rage to enter wild lands. I am apprehensive that there must be forced sales as so many are buying on borrowed capital.

Feby. 4. Not quite as cold as yesterday. Rose at about 5 o clock. Very cool morning, ground been froze 2 weeks—bare of snow on the commons.

The Anniversy of my birth day.

Orindorio & Judson Benjamin sick. Judson went to Mr. Butlers. Wrote a letter to Elijah by Dr. Cobb & one to Ch. Fox Esq. Bot with Merrill Judge Polks interest in a mill seat in Porter county near the supposed county seat for $700.[26] Mr. McCarty $350. I went to see Merrill in relation to the expect[ed] or rather the attempted change in the law in order to displace Judge Polk as Mich. Road Commissioner. Mr. M. talked with me relative to Mr. Ketchams going to

24. Those appointed to the Board of Internal Improvement and approved were Elisha Long, Wayne County; John Woodburn, Jefferson County; Samuel Hall, Gibson County; David H. Maxwell, Monroe County; Thomas H. Blake, Vigo County; and John G. Clendenin, Orange County. *Messages and Papers relating to the Administration of Noah Noble,* pp. 440, 441, 442.

25. The farm of the late Jesse McKay on White River in Morgan County. The sale was advertised in the Indianapolis *Indiana Journal,* January 10, 1836.

26. The Porter County deed records show that the southeast quarter of section 23, T35N, R6W (Michigan Road lands nos. 1878, 1879), purchased by Polke, John B. Niles, and Nathan B. Palmer, was patented to Niles (4/12 interest), John Matthews (5/12 interest), and C.F. (3/12 interest) on March 25, 1840.

Lafayette to do business with Mr. Ingram. I have freely disclosed my views as to the man. I do not like him.

This day Simon Yandes who has been studying law with me about 8 months & in a Little room in the same building of my office removed to my office for the purpose of doing business for me. Mr. Pratt has studied with me about 2 years is about to leave for Logansport where he is to settle. He & Mr. Harris Simons fellow student inducted S. into my office with great pomp. P. had cleaned the office out placed a chair on the table for S. to be seated & with an old rusty sword up tipped—S. placed his hat & book in the chair & P. delivered the key of the office to him with an appropriate & ludicrous speech which S. equally appropriately answered. I rather injoyed this farce. P. has acquired my good wishes. I believe he will do well. Mr. Butler & myself will furnish him with books to be added to his own library. Of Simon Y. my expectations are great.

I do not expect to devote much of my time to the law the coming year. On a Slight calculation Mr. McCarty & myself owe about 19 thousand dollars at the Banks besides a large sum to Individuals for lands. To be sure they are valuable. We now own about [. . .] acres of land & some very handsome town property to wit—In & adjoining the town of Indianapolis about 300 acres of land which I think at the lowest calculations is worth $150. per acre cash—at & near Mich. City 240 acres near Noblesvill 150 acres at the Bluffs or Port Royal 450 acres. Out of this I must raise the means of defraying our expenses another year & paying the debts above alluded to.

Should a French War come & property greatly depreciate we must suffer much. The fact is I do not feel Justified in accumulating these debts upon myself & the future alone will disclose my condition. I trust in the Providence of God that has yet protected & gave me health & if afflicted by imprudence I hope not to murmur.

I have this day looked over my life which has indeed passed like a weavers shuttle 38 years of age—Thursday. It is said I was born on Sunday in the absence of my father to the Boston (Mass.) market. Am one of 15 childrin.

In calculating 38 years to come I find should I in the Provdence of God be permitted to see that period that year will be the anniversary of a compleat century from the declaration of American Independence. I trust dead or alive it may be a glorious anniversary.

February 5 1836. Pleasant weather Nothing new. Pressed with professional business. Mr. Pratt preparing for Logansport where he is to settle & pursue his profession.

Feby. 26[6]. Legislature about to adjourn much confusion. Have passed an internal improvement Bill & authorized the borrowing of 12 million but have omitted to provide any means to pay the interest on that sum.

Feby. 27[7]. Still milder—some prospect of snow. Judson gone to Mr. Butlers to be nursed & old Mr. Fletchers daughter Martha has come to assist Mrs. F.

Mr. Bostwick from Logansport here. Legislature passed a bill for an additional bank at Logansport.[27]

Billy Polk at my office to get a deed of trust & for me to sign his bond as commissioner on Mich. Road. Went down to the house to see about the passage of Circuit Bill. Mr. Gregg called in the eve & left a long letter for me to read which I view as a great bore.

My office business kept me ingaged till 10 o'clock.

Mr. Pratt ingaged to Enroll ad vallorem bill &c.

Feby. 8 Sunday. [*Monday*]. Snow fell one inch last night. Dust & everything dry under it. Prospect for rain. Martha Fletcher got sick & left us. Dorio sick. Rose at 4. Cooley made the fire. Elijah reading Pilgrims Progress. Calvin has gone out to old Mr. F.'s Went to deliver letters to Mr. Collet & Polk &c. James Hill still with us &c.

9 Feby. Monday [*Tuesday*] *morning.* Waked by a messenger from Govr. Noble at 4 requesting me to repair to the State house without delay. In a few moments I arrived at his room which was crowded with nearly 100 bills for his approval. Mr. Ketcham his secretary present who soon withdrew & the Govr. requested my opinion as to the constitutionality of several acts of incorporation where the corporation or any individual in *qui-tem* action had a right to sue & recover a forfeiture for their use on a breach of some provision of the law therein written. He had made out his message to report them unconstitutional. I gave it as my opinion that they were not unconstitutional under that section of the Constitution giving all fines for breaches of the penal laws to the county Semi-

27. *Laws of Indiana,* 1835–36 (general), pp. 20–21. The Logansport branch bank was never established.

naries. The Govr. Signed the bill[s] except on[e] which was clearly unconstitutional.

Legislature were about meeting & I returned home before 6.

Pleasant day. Newspapers say England will mediate the difficulty between France & U.S.

Teusday [Wednesday Feb.] 10. Nothing new. Pleasant. James Hills family arrived. Wm. Hill & Joel Harber. Went to Mr. Henkles to [see] about Insurance company.[28]

11 Feby. Trying to settle my books relative to land with McCarty. Bank business.

12 Feby. Began raining. Prospect of a general break up. Arranging my land business heretofore prosecuted by Mr. McCarty & self.

[Feb.] 13. Very wet dissagreeable day. Much professional business crowding on me. Miss Bainbridge of [. . .] called in the eve.

At Sundown turned cold & froze.

Sunday 14 Feby. Cold all froze hard again. Cooley Miles & Dorio sick. Elijah [and] Self went to church. Uncle John dined with us. Reading Guy Manning[29] &c.

Feby. 15. Cold not unpleasently so. A Mr. Gentry called & wished to rent the house East of the garden for 1 year. I asked $36 per ann. but feel 'fraid to have a tenant in &c. Our State Bank meet today.

16 Feby. State Bank did not meet as I expected—postponed till Wedensday. Cloudy weather not cold ground froze.

Mr. Dennison a young lawyer late of Cincinnati called with letters from Messrs. Gwinn & Starr—formerly from Royalton Vt. E. D. John[30] cash[ier] at Lawrenceburgh called also.

Feby. 16. Prepared to go to Madison but did not get off.

Feby. 17. Went with Mr. Quarles to Hancock. Tolerable pleasant riding—only thawed a few inches on the sunny side of the road.

28. On February 8, 1836, a charter was granted to the Indianapolis Fire Insurance Company. It was capitalized at $200,000 with shares at $50.00 each. The company was organized on March 16. *Laws of Indiana,* 1835–36 (local), pp. 191–96; Dunn, *Indianapolis,* I, 360; and below, note 52.

29. Sir Walter Scott's *Guy Mannering.*

30. Enoch D. John, brother-in-law of Governor Noble and his partner in various business enterprises. *Messages and Papers relating to the Administration of Noah Noble,* Introduction, pp. 5–6. He served as cashier of the Lawrenceburg branch of the State Bank.

J. Hill moved to his house formerly owned by old Mr. Bay. We arrived at Hancock about an hour by Sun. Business tolerably lively. Staid at Hamiltons old stand. Quarles went to Harts. Cloudy not dissagreeably cold.

[*Feb.*] *18*. Left after Breakfast for home with Mr. Q. Called at Cumberland—8 or 10 houses there one tavern kept by Saml. Fullen one by Widow Smith one little Store by John Stevens. Arrived at home about 2 o'clock. Met a Mr. Atherton who returned with me to get a power of attorney given by Dr. Worthington to sell land. Went to State Bank. Found the board in session Messrs. Morrison Scott Leads Major Deming Jenners Present.[31] Done little & adjourned.

[*Feb.*] *19*. Cloudy—not unpleasantly cold. Done but very little. Vincennes Evansvill Madison New Albany Madison & Terre Haut [*sic*] not represented.[32] Agreed to accept all amendments by legislature & to discount 40000 in addition &c.

[*Feb.*] 20 *Saturday*. Rained. I left for Noblesvill Andersontown Pendleton &c. 11 miles. Called at J. [. . .]. Got to Noblesvill at 2. Stopped at Dunings. I was wet it having rained the whole way. Saw the first Robin today this Spring.

Left Noblesvill after doing some business and arrived at Strawtown after dusk wet & cold. 3 travellers & myself staid over night at Coles. Visited B. Coles store & returned to bed at 9.

[*Feb.*] *21*. Sunday rose early. Went to B. Coles store & wrote several letters for him to Merchants in Philadelphia & N.Y. where he is about to proceede to buy goods for the first time. Pleasant day—1st this month.

Left Strawtown about 9 A.M. Went with Ira Kingsberry to Kemps[33] thence to Danl. Wise & took dinner. Thereon to Andersontown where I arrived about 1 hour by sun. Staid at Harpers. Saw Jackson Sheriff about a little girl.

Feby. 22. Pleasant morning. Bot a house of Harpers Son in law

31. Robert Morrisson, Richmond; Lucius H. Scott, Terre Haute; Noah Leeds, Richmond; Daniel S. Major, Lawrenceburg; Demas Deming, Terre Haute; and William M. Jenners, Lafayette.

32. Terre Haute was represented by both Deming and Scott. Apparently there were no representatives from Bedford or Fort Wayne.

33. Gilbert Kemp, Madison County pioneer. John L. Forkner (ed.), *History of Madison County Indiana* . . . (2 volumes. Chicago: Lewis Publishing Co., 1914), II, 743.

for Porter & Harrison who are about to go to Andersontown by their clerk to sell goods—gave $400 for house & lot ½ 30 days ¼ in 9 & ¼ in 18 months.

Went on to my land near & adjoining the town.[34] Found that the canal line is to pass thro' it, that there is a lock on it near the N.W. line.[35] I have ordered 10 acres to be enclosed reserving the grove of small trees. Left A. after dinner with Jackson & rode to Abel Browns about 5 miles where I hired a young man for a year at $12 per month certain if he does well $13 per month.

Arrived at Pendleton about sundown. Staid over night at Bostons.

Mr. Irish[36] Noble Pendleton & Casswell. Very muddy to day ground thawed about 2 inches in open fild—good travelling in the timber.

Feby. 23. Leased C. W. G[. . .]s house in Pendleton to D. S. Noble for $100. Left at 10 with Harry Pendleton. Went to Hundlys and rented Carlisle & White's place. Thence to Dotys mill[37] & took down the S. East side of Fall Creek. Soon had to follow a trace—got out of the same & in searching for the road heard a cock crow—was thereby directed to the house 5 miles from any other habitation—woman directed me to find the blazed trails. Proceeded to the N.W. corner of Hancock Co. thence to Indiana [Indian] creek thence to Messrs. Thomas & Speece[38] road. Sloppy & disagreeable here. I went with Mr. Thomas to see the Wells place 1½ mile from Johnson Mill[39] and Fall Ck.[40] Returned to his house after

34. According to the Madison County deed records C.F. had acquired from Ansel Richmond in 1832 lands in the east half of the southeast quarter, section 13, T19N, R7E, paying a total of $525. The total acreage is not given. The land lay on the southwest side of the town.

35. The Central Canal, which was never completed, was projected to pass through Anderson, and with the prospects of this the town's population, which was about two hundred in 1832, was almost four hundred by 1839. Forkner (ed.), *History of Madison County*, I, 97–98.

36. A sketch of the Irish family of Fall Creek Township, Madison County, is in Harden, *The Pioneer*, pp. 223–24, 226–27.

37. In Green Township, Madison County.

38. John Thomas and Daniel Speece, who settled in Lawrence Township, Marion County, in 1828 and 1832, respectively. Sulgrove, *History of Indianapolis*, pp. 548–49.

39. The mill was on Fall Creek in Lawrence Township, Marion County. It

dark. Sent for Mr. Speece & rented the Wells place to them.

Went to bed at 10. It rained.

24 Feby. Rose a little after daylight. It snowed as fast as I ever saw it. I was bound to be at home this A.M. Had my horse brought out—would not wait for breakfast. Took directions to gain the main rode—got lost—snow filld the path. At last found the state road that led to town by Mr. Tyners.[41] The trees had been deadened in the road—the limbs loaded with snow fell on all directions. I rode in great perril & arrived home at 10. Ground was covered with 2 or 3 inches of snow.

I found Mr. Boxley at my house. A very dissagreeable day.

Majr. Griffith[42] is to be married to a Miss Wise an inmate of Govr. Nobles house where she is to be married.

Our childrin are yet unwell except Cooley who goes to school & seems to be ambitious to learn.

My friends are anxious to make arrangments for taking the stock in the insurance company about to [be] organized the first in the place. Some are opposed to it &c McCarty & Bates are favorable. I believe I shall take some stock say 100 shares. Such an institution will be wanted. Messrs. Russel Stephenson & Cole & [. . .] Smith left for Philadelphia. Stage could scarcely run.

Feby. 25. Mr. Pratt & C. J. Hand went to Morgan to sell McKay land. Snow 3 or 4 inches deep.

Mr. Boxley received $100 to buy cattle & started home with his waggon in which he brought venison hams for Mrs. F. gave 43 cents [. . .].

I settled the suit of Robert Thornton in Chancery in Sup. court. Snow began to fall about 9 o'clock. This day we have assurances of peace with France, the recharter of U. States Bank by Penn. &c.

---

was built and operated for many years by John Johnson, a native of Ireland who settled in the township in 1824. Sulgrove, *History of Indianapolis*, pp. 546–47.

40. On November 17, 1834, C.F. entered 70 acres of land in the east half of the northwest quarter, section 5, T16N, R5E, at the Indianapolis Land Office. He acquired 70 acres adjoining this to the west at a sheriff's sale for $160.56, the deed being dated July 8, 1835. He then sold the 140 acres to Daniel Speece for $800, the deed being dated August 9, 1837. Marion County deed records.

41. Harris Tyner, who settled in the northern part of Warren Township, Marion County, in 1821. Sulgrove, *History of Indianapolis*, p. 614.

42 Maj. Andrew C. Griffith, senator from Jackson County.

Feby. 26. Snow is now about [. . .] inches deep. Looks gloomy. Frost is not out of the ground. Read my newspapers in the A.M. & done some other Work. Did not go to my office till after 12. Mr. John Young dined with us—came to see me on some business for Mrs. Givan. Very bad moving about.

Done little at my office—visited Judge Blackford. He is anxious C. Dewey should be appointed Sp. Judge to fill Stevens vacancy. Returned home under a promise to meet Yandes & others at Bates to see about subscribing stock for the Insurance Company, but on my return home found Revd. Mr. Smith M. E. preacher & a young preacher of the same order going to Ill. or Osconsin & they detained me till it got too late to go down. I feel verily guilty for this disappointment & I shall hereafter I hope muster courage to dismiss company to go where duty calls me. Snow remains stationary cool but not dissagreeably cold.

[*Feby.*] 27. Books of Insurance Co. opened at 10 at Henkles book store opposite Mrs. Nowlands. Stock to the amount of 129 thousand shares taken. Some little excitement produced. It was believed that Messrs. Henkle & [. . .] had been rather sly in the organization of this institution that they had given as little publicity to it. But it is believed that our old friends have a majority. Each subscriber can under the charter vote 25 votes. Every subscriber except 3 seemed to have the elective franchise in view—subscribed just 25. The 3 went under that.

Snow 8 or 10 inches no thaw of consequence.

Mr. Pratt returned with Mr. Hand from the sale of McKay land in Morgan County bot in by Mr. P. for the [. . .] & Mr. Rariden.

I have advised Mr. P. to go to Logansport immediately where he talks of settling & that J. Hill carry him out either on a slide or horseback.

I feel that my land speculations are doubtful as to profit. The winter has been long & gloomy—yet the news of peace with France the incorporation of several banks as well as the U.S. seem to indicate good times but I much fear the result of my years operations in which I must sell real estate to the Amount of several thousand dollars—say 15 or 20 thousand. I have my cases on my mind 10 or 12 farms under my care &c. My law business tho in the hands of Mr. Butler is growing in importance and needs my whole attention which it has not had. My wish & my determination is to get rid of such incumberances as my speculations lands &c &c.

Sunday [*Feb.*] *28*. Snow remains as yesterday. Thawed a little in the day. Went to church with Mrs. R. & the 2 little girls & my two oldest boys. Revd. Mr. Smith Preached who preached vs Riches &c.

Pleasant yet cold. Mr. McCarty called. Boys reading Gil Blais & Guy Mannering. Calvin went with me & had 3 teeth pulled in order that the rest should become regular.

Feby. 29 1836. Cold in the morning with a fair prospect of Snow. I have resolved on trying to bring up my correspondence & take hold of my law business for a week before I return to preparing to sell my lands &c.

Before 12 grew warmer and thawed. Middle afternoon began raining & rained hard till after I went to bed but snow seemed to absorb &c. Dull day.

Pratt preparing to leave for Logansport.

Baz. Meek called to have suit in chancery commenced. Simon Yandes [and] I went to old Mr. Dicinger to take a statement preparatory to Chancery suit.

Mr. Pratt came to tea. Mr. Bradley came up to take acknowledgment of deeds. James Hill & wife.

1836 March 1st. Mrs. Fletchers alarm clock woke us 10 minutes before 5. This clock she had sent to us by Mr. Bond two days ago. I was called up by little Stoughton at 1 who had wakened & recalled that he went to bed without saying his prayers & demanded that mother or myself should hear him say them. I rose for that purpose & he went to sleep. James Hill arrived at 8 o clock to go with Mr. Pratt to Logensport. Cold & dissagreeable as it was they left about 9 on horseback Mr. P. taking along a few books in his saddlebags having put the residue in a box for the purpose [of] being forwarded. He has accumulated a good library for a young man under his circumstances. He is not as good a lawyer as I think he should be but I trust he will do well.

This a very dissagreeable day—cold & just froze enough to break thro. Wind rose in the after part of the day. At sundown very cold. I bought a few fish of Pense & Canine just caught out of White River—emmense schools are said to have been taken—prencipally succers.

Harry Pendleton arrived this eve. He wishes to sell me his land in Madison County & leave the country. News that New Albany have accepted the amendments to the Bank charter have arrived. There appears to be a great pressure for money. As to myself the prospect is gloomy unless I can effect some sales of town lots & other land.

March 2d. Very cold last night. I believe the snow & ice are froze hard. Got a letter last night that Mr. Town has undertaken the building the bridge at Louisville &c.—Mr. Peck wrote &c.

Harry Pendleton staid with us. Commenced suit in Chancery vs Olerman for old Mr. Dicinger. Rather a dull day. Two applications for a divorce. Staid late at my office. Sale of old Mr. Frazes property. The weather moderated a little yesterday in P.M. Mr. McCarty came to me in the eve & stated he had concluded to resign as one of the canal fund commissioners.[43] I approve of his determination.

March 3. Pleasant day. Snow yet covers the earth. Streets sloppy. Mechanics ball at Elders.[44] Mr. Bostwick from Logansport called on his return home. John Walker called to see about the mill property at Shelbyville. I have repented buying it with Mr. McC. My load of debts seem to be very great—nothing but the very best luck will save me from exposure I fear. I have had the hippo for a few days past. My business seems to multiply on my hands. I trust I may have health & discretion for as to the latter I have strong

43. McCarty submitted his resignation formally on March 24 and Isaac Coe was appointed by the Governor to succeed him. Coe's appointment was confirmed by the Senate the following December. *Indiana Executive Proceedings*, p. 688; *Messages and Papers relating to the Administration of Noah Noble*, p. 512.

44. John Elder operated the Union Inn located on Washington Street opposite the Courthouse from December, 1833, until April, 1836. The Inn was owned by Governor James Brown Ray. Elder was a builder by trade and profession. In 1836 he was contractor for the Clinton County courthouse, the first of many buildings and residences he designed and erected in the state. He drafted the plans and built the buildings for both the State Bank and the Indianapolis branch of the bank, the new Washington Hall (see below, p. 465), and the Palmer House built for Nathan B. Palmer at the corner of Illinois and Washington streets. He may have been the designer of the Indiana Institute for the Blind completed in Indianapolis in 1853, which has been attributed to Francis B. Costigan. Kenneth Loucks, "John Elder: Pioneer Builder," in *Indiana Magazine of History*, XXVI (1930), 29.

doubts in the midst of a pressure. I do say that If I escape from this enthrawlment that I do not get into it again. I trust the spirit of internal improvement will help us to sell our property.

March 4. Pleasant morning. Rose rather late. Our family are better. Mr. Wood helps us feed &c. Expect the hired man from Madison county daily &c.

Elijah & Cooley go to school to Mr. Gregg. Calvin does most of the work gets stove wood &c. Judson Benjamin has returned from a visit to his mother—is going to live with Drs. Richmond & Mears. Pleasant.

James Hill returned from carrying Mr. Pratt to Logansport & brought me a letter from him. He went from here with a light heart but in his letter shows gloom. Thinks there are too many lawyers at that place.

Saturday 5 March. Mr. Woodburn here from Madison to meet the first convention of the board of Internal Improvement under the late law. It is expected they will make a temporary loan and commence making particular estimates. This system of Improvement I trust will produce I trust a complete revolution not only in the commercial aspect but that of our agricultural affairs which are behind such a state of Internal Improvement 15 years. Consequently I fear that some of the Improvements will be commenced & completed before the agricultural condition of the country can derive but little benefit from them compared with a country which produces all or one half of the products that the soil is capable of.

Sunday March 6. Mr. Butler went to Shelby to look after the Mills bought, formerly owned by J. Walker. I fear they will be a bad concern. Cold day—ground froze so it can bear a waggon & does not thaw. Mr. McCarty called in the P.M. I went to church with Dorio Cooley & Elijah. Mr. Smith preached & read a letter (anonymous) relative to chewing & spitting tobacco & made some very severe animadversions thereon.

John Hill called in the eve. I wrote Pratt a long letter. I feel concerned about him. Mr. Gregg called in the eve & wishes to make some arrangements as to having a female department &c. Cold & a little snow.

Read Octr. No. N[orth] Am[erican] R[eview]. Poor class in Europe, Hethen Mythology &c.

Monday March 7. Mrs. Richmond called to inquire if she had best study mathematics &c. Mr. Bradley called to get Cooley to stay in the store 2 days &c. Mrs. Richmond called to see about her engaging in the academy &c. Mr. Bates wishes to prepare a ticket for directers of In[surance] Co. Met for that purpose Messrs. Merrill Bates Sharp Bradley & McCarty &c present. Ticket made out.

Board of Internal Improvement met. Messrs. Long & Blake call &c. Saw Dr. Maxwell. Jim Morrison will no doubt be appointed Secretary. Jo. M. Moore & Jac. Landis leave for Philadelphia. Send money to Cushing Vail & Hews &c.

Board of Justices meet. Called on them & left agricultural handbills &c. Harry Pendleton called in the eve to compleat purchase I am about to make of his land.[45] Mrs. Givan called at noon also Mr. Gregg & Holiday. Settled with Jim Hill—found I owed him $299 for services &c.

Cold raw day—thawed but little.

March 8. Pleasant cold morning. Messrs. Holiday & Harry Pendleton call. Mr. Butler returned in the eve from Shelby. Could rent the property bought called Walkers Mills. I induced this purchase & fear the consequence tho' my judgment approved it then & still does.

Pleasant day. News that Mr. Tyler of Va. Senator U.S. has resigned in consequence of instructions of Va. legislature. Received two letters from Mr. Ingram.

9 March. Mrs. Blythe buried. Pleasant in the A.M. Called at request on Col. Blake sitting on the Board of Internal Improvement. Letter in the Eve from Mr. Pratt by colored man who came into marry Chany.[46] I answered the letter & went with Bradley to deliver it to the same gentlemen & saw the married *couple.* Returned home at 11—cloudy & dark.

March 10 1836. Began snowing at sun rise & has continued

45. The Madison County deed records show that on March 5, 1836, C.F. acquired from H. Pendleton forty acres of land in section 9, T19N, R7E, for $500, the deed being recorded April 5, 1836.

46. According to the Marion County marriage records, Chaney Lively was married to John G. Britten on this date. She was the housekeeper for Alexander Ralston; he was a barber. Nowland, *Early Reminiscences of Indianapolis,* pp. 397–98.

snowing & blowing all day—is 4 to 6 inches deep—cold the ground froze & the Sleighs running.

Been busily engaged in my office all day. Have made $7 of Small Jobs. Saw Aaron Finch.[47] Called to see Mr. Lewis but he was not at home. Very gloomy. Mr. McCarty notified me that a $3000 & $5000 draft which by contract to be renewed at Cincinnati had been sent to this bank for collection. He has wrote. He feels determined to extricate from debt &c. Is a little gloomy.

I have been searching for a receipt among my old papers 11 years old relative to a payment made James Campbell & found one letter. Such has been the variaty of my business that a transaction of that length of time has entirely passed out of my mind.

11 March. Cold a day as any in Jany. Snow covered the ground did not thaw.

Engaged in many matters pertaining to my profession. Mr. J. L. Williams here. Had a talk as to prospects of internal improvement. He has just learned that Ohio has permitted the White Water Canal. Mr. Linsy Sheriff of Miami here. Simon Yandes & myself compaired the books of McCarty & F. in the eve.

Franklin Brown the young man I hired in Madison Cty. came. Saw him 1st at noon. He went to shucking corn. The prospect seems to be fair. Wrote Mr. Pratt. Saw Majr. Vigus.

March 12 1836 Saturday. Very cold night & morning. Rose at 5. Went to the office about 8—then to the P.O. Found a letter from Stoughton & Miles & learned that Stoughton & M[ichael] & his wife would leave Miles (Marlboro N.Y.) on 2 or 3 of M[arch]. They say the snow is very deep there—River froze 1 foote—& will have to proceede to N.Y. in Sleighs. S. requests me to send McMahan to Madison with a carriage to meet them &c. Mr. Bradley & self calculate that they are at Pitts[burgh] this day 12 M. that they will get to Madison next Friday or Saturday. I have ingaged Oliver [Van] Landingham to go for them with M. Henkle['s] carriage. Truly glad to have Michael & wife to come but I fear I cannot make them as comfortable as I would like.

Quarterly meeting commenced this day. Mr. Havens P[resid-

47. A lawyer, elected as representative from Tippecanoe County in 1831 and 1832 and senator from Carroll and Clinton counties in 1837. *Indiana Election Returns*, pp. 209, 213, 239.

ing] E[lder].—Old Mr. Plummer staid with us. The B[ranch] Bank about to buy J. M. Rays property for the erection of a banking house[48]—to give $6,000. 2 lotts on Penn. St. & a part of a lot N. of Woods livery stable.[49]

I have felt truly hyppocondrical these last 3 or 4 days—I have a number of Bank debts that will press on Mr. Mc. & myself in May & June July &c. Nothing but some fortunate sal[e] will relieve me.

Mr. Ray & McCarty fear that the basan & waterworks will be established on Dr. McClures land out of town S[outh][50]—in contemplated canal. I cannot feel so very deeply interested in the matter as they seem to feel.

Sunday the 13 day of March 1836. This morning rose about 5. It rained all night & continued till after 12 (at this time). I have written Stoughton at Madison. Went to lovefeast with Mrs. F. & Miles & Elijah. The ground is froze—the snow is melting off.

Mr. Havens preached. Thin congregation. John Hill came to dine. I am about to write Elijah & scold him a little for his indifferance in not writing or answering my letters which he has failed to do since last Spring. Very gloomy. Sacrement to be administered this eve.

Monday March 14 1836. Cool this morning. Tried to prepare a carriage for O. V[an] Landingham to go after Michael & wife. I did not like Mr. Henkles carriage which I had to take. V. L. came in & got off about 3 o'clock. I fear will not get along well in consequence of high waters. The roads are just breaking up. The coldness & severity of this winter is proverbial said to have been the most inclemmant for many years. It has not been extreme cold

48. The Indianapolis branch of the State Bank at first conducted its business in a building belonging to Hervey Bates at the corner of Pennsylvania and Washington streets. In 1840 it moved into its own building located on the point between Virginia Avenue and Pennsylvania Street. Dunn, *Indianapolis*, I, 342.

49. John Wood came to Indianapolis in 1834. He purchased land, engaged in the shipping of horses, and opened an extensive livery and sales stable. His livery business was carried on by his son Horace F. Wood. John Wood was also a partner in Robert Underhill's foundry. Sulgrove, *History of Indianapolis*, pp. 152–53; above, Pt. VI, note 162.

50. The house built by John E. McClure and later occupied by Nicholas McCarty, known as White Point, was on South Meridian Street on the rise across Pogue's Run. Sulgrove, *History of Indianapolis*, p. 50.

at any one time but a steady cold winter without intermission with but very little wind.

[. . .] Luce called yesterday on his way to Louisville. Received several letters & answered them.

Board of Internal Improvement broke up after making provision to expend 2 million.

Govr. Noble called & consented to let N. McCarty resign as canal fund commissioner & appointed Dr. Coe. Thawed in the P.M. Indications of sugar making.

Teusday 15 M[arch]. Froze a little last night—cold. Hauling wood from the Brown Block to Butler &c. James Cooley while at school yesterday fell upon the ice & cut his knee dangerously. Bro't home & Dr. Richmond came & put a plaster upon the wound & put him to bed. He is confined & must be for a week.

Old father Bay [Basye] called staid over night. He resides at Laport. Gloomy dissagreeable night—frost coming out of the ground—very muddy. Miss Merrilla Morris[51] calld to talk with Cooley about a puzle.

March 16. Wet rainy. This day held election for directors of Insurance company. Elected Messrs. C. Scudder, Wilkins, McGuire, Landis, Gregg (Schoolmaster), Henkle, Bradley, West, H. Porter.[52] Some little excitement. The election of those officers were deemed of some importance whereas they are of no consequence all the supposed good & evil expected to be gained by one party & the evil to be apprehended on the other will never be realized. Very wet dark gloomy day. Mr. Butlers connections from N. York

51. Daughter of Bethuel F. Morris. She assisted in the Marion County Seminary and married the teacher, Thomas D. Gregg. Harden, *The Pioneer*, p. 241.

52. Caleb Scudder, John Wilkins, Douglass Maguire, Jacob Landis, Thomas D. Gregg, Moses Henkle, Henry Bradley, Nathaniel West, and Henry Porter. Maguire was elected president and Gregg secretary. For Porter and West, see below, Pt. VIII, notes 7 and 24. The company had full banking powers. However, its business was never extensive and it suspended about 1860, was reorganized in 1865, did banking business as the Bank of Commerce, and finally closed in 1893. Dunn, *Indianapolis*, I, 360.

The following year (1837) the Indiana Mutual Fire Insurance Company was chartered. Its president was James Blake and its secretary Charles W. Cady. Indianapolis directors included Samuel Merrill, James M. Ray, and C.F. At first successful, it suffered heavy losses and was terminated in 1855. *Laws of Indiana*, 1836–37 (local), pp. 124–30; Dunn, *Indianapolis*, I, 360.

called on him &c. Going to Wisconsan T[erritory]. Did not go to my office in the eve. No sugar weather yet.

March 17 1836. Not very cold. Mr. Brown the young man that came to live a year is homesick—says he can't stand it to live in town. I fear he will not comply with the agreement. Mr. Blake in trouble, Burkhart & Co.[53] destroying his fences &c. Wm. C. McDougle called on me—one of our 1st settlers lives now at Natches.

Returned home in the eve & did not go to my office. I have had the glooms for the last week caused by debts hanging over me. The young man has concluded to stay &c. Frost coming out of ground. No sugar water yet.

March 18. Rose at 5 made fire & after breakfast I went with Franklin Brown to the McFarlan place.[54] Very cold. Examined the place—was well pleased. Farris[?] the tenant McF. has committed some waist. Ground froze. Returned & prepared with Col. Schenk to lay off additional lots in town &c.

Mr. Blake in great trouble with Burkhart. Negro Overhall called on me for aid to prevent the lawless aggressions of Burkhart & party. Called at Mr. Hains to see a Mr[s]. Catherine Stake. Then proceeded to my office where I spent the remainder of the Eve in business. Mr. Gregg called in the eve to talk about In[surance] Co. —wishes to be a clerk in the same or rather to get the control over it.

I am preparing to lay an additional set of lots west of the Brewery.[55]

53. David Burkhart, who kept a grocery store on the southwest corner of New York and Tennessee streets. (Tennessee Street is now Capitol Avenue.) He was described as being renowned for fighting, a "gang" leader, and was "a terror to the colored population." Nowland, *Early Reminiscences of Indianapolis,* pp. 177–80.

54. "McFarland place" probably refers to land at the northeast edge of the town acquired by C.F. from James McFarland. According to the Marion County deed records McFarland conveyed to C.F. on November 14, 1835, part of the southeast quarter of section 31, T16N, R4E. This adjoined eighty acres which, according to the deed records, C.F. had acquired from John Carr on June 29, 1831.

55. The first brewery in the town was started about 1834 by John L. Young and William Wernweg on the south side of Maryland Street between the line of the later canal and West Street. Sulgrove, *History of Indianapolis,* p. 449. C.F. acquired outlots 134, 137, and 138 lying east of South West Street and south of Maryland from Henry Bradley in 1835. The deeds were made to C.F. and Nicholas

Saturday March 19 1836. About light in the morning 1 of Overhauls' sons (a colored man) came & informed me that his father had shot a man who with Burkhart was trying to break into his house (N.W. [. . .] St. out of town) & wished me to come out immediately. I told him to go back & tell his father to maintain his position at the hazard of every man's life that might interrupt. I then ordered my hired man to prepare my rifle for action if necessary called on Andrew Smith my near neighbor (a constable[56]) who went on to Washington St. with me. He took one side & I the other & every man we met was ready on relation of the acts of the outrageous mob headed by Burkhart to turn out & see that the law should be executed. We met in a considerable number before Yandes Store from which place I have no doubt we should have marched to the scene of the riots in a few moments but we there met Dr. Richmond who had Just been to the wounded man by name of Allensworth. He thought him not mortally wounded &c.

Here Danl. Yandes & Dr. Coe came. The latter did not oppose the action of the people direct but proposed to go to Burkhart & tell him the citzens demanded his removal that they would pay him for his property the highest price &c or he might sell it & move. This was consented to.

Soon after this Overhaul's son came in, said his father was under great fear of another mob—dare not leave the house. I advised him to take a back trail & come & give himself up to the public authorities. He soon came in & gave himself up &c.

Yandes returned & reported that he had seen B. who professed to be very innocent & proposed to see Y. at my office at dusk &c.

But such was the excitement that nothing would do but to call a public meeting at 4 o clock P.M. at the court house. A very large number of the citizens of the town met. Mr. G. Lockibee made president, C. J. Hand Secy. Harrod Newland the only surviving Revolutionary Soldier residing in town [spoke]. His remarks were well received. I also added some remarks & offered a

---

McCarty on February 10, 1842. The first three payments on these outlots were made by Henry Bradley. Agent of State, Indianapolis Sale of Lots, Payments, 1832—, Archives Division, Indiana State Library.

56. Sketch in Nowland, *Early Reminiscences of Indianapolis,* pp. 124–25.

resolve that 10 Captains be appointed by the meeting & that the citzens enroll themselves to be made instruments in the hands of the Captains to aid the civil authorities &c. 10 captains appointed D. Yandes Mr. Campbell (Hatter) J. Kittleman (Shoemaker) Cox (Tinner) Andrew Smith (constable) John Wilkins (Tanner) Wernwagg (Engineer) John Woolen (Post & rail fence maker) John McMahan plasterer & Saml. Merrill President of the Bank & on further resolves several hundred enrolled themselves. Meeting adjourned. B. met Mr. Yandes at my office in the Eve but could do nothing.

This day the Ind. Insurance Co. met & choose D. McGuire President T. D. Gregg Secy.

Recd. a letter from bro. Elijah—speaking in terms that are extremely agreeable to me.[57]

Mr. Bradley received a line from Stoughton that he had got into Philadelphia with Michael & wife &c that he will have much trouble in advancing with them.

Preparing stakes to run off & mark my lots. Got a letter from Buchannan of Cincinnati &c which relieves me &c about a loan &c. Went to bed at 11. Cool dissagreeable day raw scarcely thaws. No sugar water yet &c.

Sunday March 20 1836. Cool day—not thawed a[t] 12 more than froze last night. Frost not out of the ground. Went to class meeting with Dorio & Mrs. Richmond &c to church with the same & 3 boys E. C. & M. James lame. Mrs. F. sick with bad cold. Going to write a letter to Laura.

Cool. Spent the day rather unprofitably. Did not go to church. Sugar water run a little.

Monday 21 March. Cold frozen morning. A slight Snow fell last night. Gloomy cold at 9 o'c. A.M. It is a enough to give one the *hippo* to see such a winter yet the ways of Providence are inscrutable. We know not but this is the precursor of a most fruitful year. We should submit. I feel very anxious about S. & M. while on

57. C.F.'s brother Elijah wrote from Lynchburg, Virginia, on March 7, 1836, "It gave me great satisfaction to hear by my acquaintances, who returned from a visit to your state last year, of your standing as a man, a Lawyer and of your success in business. It makes me feel happy and proud to think I have a Brother possessing and deserving so good a name." Fletcher Papers.

their journy &c. Mail Lauras letter & $5. enclosed to pay for Gennessee Farmer. This day a little excited on learning that my friend W. W. W. now Judge has given some encouragement to B. & the rioters &c. Leech the leader of B.['s] party in his absence this day arrested. This day cold. Snow fell & covered the ground. Wild geese returning from the N. to the South whither they passed a few days past.

Mr. Brown the hired man informed me that he could not stay longer than tomorrow. I could not persuade him to stay longer—tho sorry to part with him.

Very cold night—Read my 2 Intelligencers &c.

Teusday March 22 1836. Snow covers the ground. Very cold—well frozen ground. Mr. Brown left me notwithstanding I hired him for a year &c.

Just after he left my boys announced that Stoughton had arrived. He left Michal & wife at Vernon & proceeded on horseback—came 50 miles yesterday. He has been absent 50 days very cold all the time, has travelled 2000 [miles]. He is bold & adventurous. M. & wife are coming on in the waggon. Shall look for them tomorrow night or next morning.

This [day] very cold—not thawed all day. Stoughton & Bradleys goods arrived & Mr. Butler went to [at]tend a trial at Jim Johnsons[58] to try right of property. S. dined & supped with us.

A steady cold night ground froze hard. Weather settled. Cold as last of Decr. Sun goes down clear but atmosphere feels like snow.

March 23 1836. Rose at ½ after 4. Sun rose clear but very cold & has as far as we may judge from the air the appearance of Snow. Settled with Wm. Wood. Preparations for the trial of Leech one of Burkharts men. Cool. Mr. A. Cole of Noblesvill. Under great expectations of the arrival of Michael. At 3 got a horse & started for him. Went out Meridian St. & got out to Judge Morris place or a

58. Justice of the peace for Wayne Township serving from 1829 until 1840, and as representative for Marion County in the General Assembly in the 1838–39 and 1839–40 sessions. He lived on his farm on the Crawfordsville Road then about five miles west of the city, moving there in 1824. Sulgrove, *History of Indianapolis,* pp. 665–66; Nowland, *Early Reminiscences of Indianapolis,* pp. 98–99; *Indiana Executive Proceedings,* pp. 515, 517.

little beyond & the man who went for him hailed me behind. M. had come in another way & St[oughton] found I had gone for him & got the man to follow me. They arrived at my house ½ after 2. I found them & spent the eve with much pleasure. S. came up in the eve & Mr. McCarty. Went to bed about 10.

Thursday M[arch] 24. Very cool but prospect for a beautiful day. Robins singing. Wild geese went to the N. about 2 weeks ago but return last week Friday & Saturday. Old Mr. Boxley staid over night. Jane Merril married.[59]

March 25—Friday. Pleasant but cool—Michael & the boys Miles opening the sugar camp.

Pleasant day—frost not out of the ground. 3 turkeys I bo't last winter went off they were of the wild order. Bo't a mare of Quarles for $75. in notes—high price. Went with S. to see the lots Col. Shenk is laying off. Went with Michael to see S. in the eve—Procured the Pioneers from the State library[60] for C.

Good sugar day. Michael & myself went to McFarland place. Billy Herrod.

March 27 Sunday 1836. Pleasant day a little cloudy. Rose at 4 Preparing for Madison court. Made about 20 lb. of sugar. Yesterday found the Turkeys. Prepared for Andersontown court. Mr. Butler Herrod & Quarles started about 9 A.M. I waited sometime. Supposed Mr. B. would come by. Left home about 10 arrived at Arnets at 2. Found Govr. Ray Quarles Mr. Hand Herrod &c getting dinner. After that was over we proceeded to Andersontown arrived there after dark. Very muddy frost coming out of the ground—very bad travelling. Stopped at Harpoles.

Monday 28 March. Rains. Everything looks gloomy not much business. Two Kilgores, Mr. Henderson & Anthony the only lawyers from other places except Indianapolis.

Thursday [Tuesday] [March] 29. We went thro' with most of our court business. Many strangers visiting the place to buy. I have

59. To John L. Ketcham.

60. The Indiana State Library was initiated by an act of the 1825 General Assembly. The Secretary of State served as ex officio librarian until 1841 and kept the library in his office, which at this time was still in the building erected to serve as the Governor's Mansion in the Circle. Dunn, *Indianapolis,* I, 106.

made preparations to clear off 10 acres into lots. There is but one dry good store & one grocery in A. at this time.

Wedensday [*March*] 30. Pleasant but very muddy. Got thro buseness & left with Mr. Irish for Pendleton where we arrived at dusk stopped with Barton. Borrowed the Indian Wars from Mr. Noble. Judge Wick was there also.

Thursday [*March*] 31. Cloudy but not very cold. The frost which had been 15 or 20 inches deep came out of the ground to the extent of ⅔. Just holds the water & makes it as muddy as I ever saw it. I became acquainted with a Mr. Owen of Newcastle who was there & bought a pair of fat cattle from Patrick for $75. good size. I procured a boy to go to old Mrs. Walls with me 2½ miles East N.E. from Pendleton. Found the old lady with a house full of childrin & her daughter Martha about 15 was desireous of coming home with me. I entered into an article to that effect. Her brother is to bring her down the first opportunity. I left Mrs. W.'s about 10 & arrived at Arnets at 1. Got dinner & arrived at home a little after dark. Found all well.

April 1st. Very pleasant day. Michael making garden. Butler preparing for court. Mr. McGlaughlins son called on me to go out & see his mother. Went with McGuire to see the lots now laying off for Mr. McCarty & self. Also went with M. & Mr. Gentry to see the Mcfarland place. Gentry has agreed to go there to live. Mr. Boxley came.

Apl. 2d. Pleasant day. Mud begins to dry up. Town full of people. Cooley went to uncle S.'s to help in the store. I went to Mrs. McGlaughlins & to the place I got of John Givan on the Lawrenceburgh road.

Our agricultural society met & elected me to deliver an address at 4 July & reduced the premium piece of corn from 10 to 5 acres.

Mr. Boxleys started home having made a partial arrangment to get goods of Mr. McCarty. Named a town we had laid off on a piece of land bot by them for us of Masters on Cicero [Creek] Hamilton County. They wished to call it *Fletcher*. I declined the honor & had it called Boxley.[61]

61. Boxleytown or Boxley, laid out in 1836 by Addison and Dr. Thomas P. Boxley, sons of George Boxley, in Adams Township, Hamilton County. It was

Advertisements issued for sale on 28 May. Hired [. . .] Gentry the man who had rented the house East of the garden lot for 6 months at $100. He bound himself & if he makes a good crop say the best in the neighborhood I will & am to give $15. He has moved to the McFarlan place.

Sunday Ap. 3d 1836. Pleasant morning. Mud drying up. Went to meeting with Elijah, Calvin & Miles Dorio & Mrs. R. Visited Mr. McCarty who is sick. Came home. John & Stoughton eat dinner with us & Judson then Michael & myself went to the block. Spent some time in conversation about our father & mother & native country.

Monday Ap. 4. This day Michael & Mr. Wood commenced getting out manure on the block the stable stands on—the back part to be planted in corn the front in oats preparatory to sowing grass & planting trees &c. I went out to McF. place. Gentry had made a good beginning but am fraid will not hold out. Apl. Elections for center [township] tooke place—no excitement compared with former years—office is not so desirable. Deval Fergusen Mattingly & a Mr. Baker elected.[62] At a trustees election for this ward old Mr. Lockerbie was elected.

After those elections I went by the way of Gentrys then to my old place after the oxen & still found it very muddy. Mr. G. came after me & started with the oxen about dark &c. I returned horseback.

Old Mr. Fletchers family sick with measles. Met the old man on his road from Ohio. Been to move old Mr. Wood.

Apl. 5th 1836. This day very pleasant. Mr. Hundly of Madison called & sold some buckwheat flowr & Oats & I rented him the Carlisle & White place.

Mr. Patrick called & I settled with him in relation to Silvers business &c.

Apl. 6. This day A. W. Morris & a Mr. Whitcomb and myself

---

described as on the state road half way between New Castle and Lafayette. Advertisement in Indianapolis *Indiana Journal*, April 9, 1836, and following issues. Haines, *History of Hamilton County*, pp. 257–58.

62. Joseph P. Duvall, J. B. Furgason, Richard D. Mattingly, and Daniel Baker were elected constables for Center Township. Indianapolis *Indiana Journal*, April 9, 1836.

at 9 A.M. started for the Bluffs to lay off some lots. Arrived there about 2 P.M. Did not do much this day but hunt the lines &c. A very pleasant day. Portroyal looks to me as if it would ultimately make a town. Dr. Roe[?] has just settled there from Lebanon Ohio.

Aprl. 7. I settled with W. H. H. P[. . .] as to churches buseness. Went to Judge Boazs[63] looked over the farm &c. Very pleasant. A. W. Morris & myself visited Mr. Davis & family in the eve. Miss Moreland was there.

Apl. 8. Very pleasant. Rose early & help laying off about 30 lots & at 2 o'clock got started home where we arrived about sundown. Found all well. (Sent for Mr. Chins bull to Butterfield.)

Ap. 9. Cloudy dissagreeable wet day. It commenced raining in the night & this morning a multitude of fish worms are seen. Cool. I visited Ab. Harrison in the eve. Did not find him at his room. Put on a new coat—In[surance] Co. preparing to get Dr. Coe to borrow money for them in N.Y. I have concluded to go to Shelby Court to see about the Walker mill property. W. has offered to take ⅓. I have had great doubts whether to consumate the contract or not. I view it one of my most foolish bargains—not but the property is worthy the amount but there is an old mill that we can not controll. Nothing but honor urges me to fulfill the contract—the law would not & I fear it will be one of the most dragging concerns, I fear it will be a disasterous concern but I shall know how I stand when I go onto the ground. Cooley is with uncle Stoughton & has gone to a party to Mr. Hendersons.

Leave for Shelby with Messrs. Quarles Hand &c.

Sunday morning Ap. 10 1836. Cool cloudy dissagreeable—waters I fear are high. Mr. Quarles came for me to go to Shelby with him also Mr. Hand. We left about 8. Rode to Buck creek—got my feet wet. Rode pony—swim a little—dined at Keelers & arrived at Shelbyville at sundown. Put up at Mr. Bennets. Put into a room with Quarles Butler & Herrod. Slept with H.

Monday [April] 11. Met with Messrs. Brown of Decatur Sweetser M[. . .] &c. Did not accept of any fees. Talked with P[. . .] in relation to appointing dellegates to a great convention at Knox-

63. Daniel Boaz, associate judge, Johnson County. *Indiana Executive Proceedings*, pp. 253, 489.

ville Ten. For the purpose of promoting the Southern Railroad. At an expected meeting I wished him to nominate John Tipton a member of the convention.[64] Spent the eve with J. Walker, Peesly, Judge Sleeth[65] & Morgan.

Tusday [April] 12. Went to view the mill property with John Walker. On examining it I found it all I ever expected—that the Works themselves cost more than $4150. the price for which we were to pay &c. After reviewing the whole matter I determined if Mr. Mc. was willing to take the mills & give Walker a third. I may be mistaken in their value but think not.

I soon left Shelby with Mr. Hand. Cool cloudy. Dined at Keelers. There saw Mr. Tibbets & several mormonits going to Zion. Arrived home about sun 2 hours very wet. Went & agreed with Mr. McCarty to let Walker have ⅓ of the mill property & wrote to Butler accordingly.

Wrote to Mr. Buchannon enclosing two deeds for Mr. McC. & myself & 3 certificates to him &c.

It rained all the eve.

Apl. 13. Wet cloudy morning. Cool. A Mr. Coleman here from Maysvill Ky. endevering to detect frauds in our post office. Believes Banks deputy under Cain guilty.[66]

Apl. 14 1836. Cool. My own & a hired waggon hauling wood from John G. Brown block.[67] Went with Mr. Whitcomb to look at

64. On March 14 Tipton had written to C.F. that he intended to go to Knoxville to attend the convention to be held July 4, to promote the building of a railroad to connect the southern Atlantic states with the West, more particularly to run from South Carolina to Cincinnati. *John Tipton Papers*, III, 244. On June 11, at a meeting in Indianapolis presided over by Governor Noble, ten delegates from Indianapolis were appointed to attend this convention. Tipton was not among them. In all some 380 delegates from six southern states and three northern states, Indiana, Illinois, and Ohio, attended. *Messages and Papers relating to the Administration of Noah Noble*, pp. 457–58.

65. John Sleeth, associate judge of Shelby County.

66. See note 119, below.

67. "John G. Brown block" probably refers to outlot 52, bounded by Michigan, Vermont, Liberty (now Park), and East streets. It was deeded to C.F. by John G. Brown, October 3, 1835. Payments to the Agent of State for the outlot totaled $113. C.F. also owned outlots 51, 54, 57, and 58. Agent of State, Indianapolis Sale of Lots, Payments, May 1832–, in Archives Division, Indiana State Library; Marion County deed records. Brown was one of the first trustees of the town (1832–33). He conducted a mercantile business in partner-

Sanders land also to see McFarlan place. Cool day—likely for frost. Geo. Taff sold 40 acres of land for $800.[68] $50 down rest in $50 payment yearly with interest.

Friday 15 Apl. This pleasant day. Cooleys birth day. Had a dinner. No person but Uncle M. & wife. Cooley presided had raizins &c.

Saturday [April] 16. Went with a Mr. B[. . .] a Kentuckian to take deposition to Alexr. Bodkin. 4 Ms. E[ast]. Simon Yandes went to Hendricks Cty. on business. Bot a Cart at Archd. C. Reeds[69] Sale for $15. a harrow at $6. Michael & Wood worked at Gentry place. Vegetation seems to be checked—buds are swelled but blossoms on early plumbs have not yet shown themselves. I am much perplexed about my summer operations. I have much law business on hand yet I am trying to get rid of it. I shall be forced to go to Michigan City to sell property. I can scarcely sleep of nights in consequence of the debts & responsibilities resting on me.

[April] 17 Sunday. Pleasant cool. Wrote a letter to [. . .] at Columbus by H. Brown. Simon Y. returned from Hendricks & in consequence of a claim vs P. S. Dickens sent by White & Holmes I have got S. Y. to return.

Went to church. Mrs. F. went out to Mr. Gentrys with Elijah Mr. G. sick. Michael went to St[oughton's] store to write a letter.

Apl. 18 1836—Monday. Rained last night & thundered. Cool morning but cleared off about 8 A.M. Cool. Michael went to Mr. Gentry's to plant a few plumb trees taken up in the garden. Mr. Merrill returned from a tour of inspection of the branch banks.

Mr. Cole sent my watch home which he bought at Philadelphia. New silver I presume cost about $40. The first article I have had for 10 years for the express purpose of ascertaining how

---

ship with William H. Morrison as well as operating a suburban farm. He was a Whig in politics and a Presbyterian in religion. Sulgrove, *History of Indianapolis*, pp. 60, 490, 505–506.

68. The Marion County deed records indicate that on July 7, 1838, George Taffe conveyed to C.F. the west one half of the southwest quarter of section 22, T16N, R4E. The consideration recorded was $753. This adjoined C.F.'s farm northeast of Indianapolis. See Pt. IV, note 37.

69. Archibald C. Reid. He settled a half mile east of the Indianapolis Donation on Pleasant Run in 1822. Nowland, *Early Reminiscences of Indianapolis*, pp. 153–54.

time passes. I am going to try if I cannot pay the price of the watch by punctuality &c. Gold watches are in the fashion but desire nothing better than silver.

Received a bag of oats from Mr. McGrew at the Bluffs said to be English. We have not yet ploughed any yet. Michael is at work in the garden—not yet finished. Peas are coming up—plumb & early peach buds swelling to blossom. McG. also sent a few cherry & locast [trees].

Apl. 19. Frost last night—cool. Not heavy enough to injure the forward buds. Cool. Michael went to Mr. Gentrys with the cherry & locast trees received from the Bluffs. I went with an Englishman to old Mr. Fletchers to sell the farm if we can agree. I ask $15 per acre. Simon returned from an expedition to collect money of Pem Dickens. Has done well.

Apl. 20 1836. Very pleasant day. Settled with Tom Silver my old Patrick business. Sent mony to Basy & Chase[70] by young [. . .] going to Logansport.

Mr. Whitcomb commenced laying the Sanders place off into Blocks Hugh O'Neil Wm. Harris & Wm. Hill assisting. Wood began ploughing the block on which the barn stands. Michael gone to Gentrys to get out manure.

Secy. of U. States of Treasy wrote to know how much we (or State) owes. We trust the surplus revenue will be distributed.[71] Forwarded by [to] Messrs. White & Holmes $600. or $700. by A. W. Harrison. Simon Yandes went to Mrs. McGlaughlin to help appraise property.

James Cooleys legs injured. Came home from store to have his mother docter it.

Apl. 21 1836. Last night it rained very hard thundered & hailed

70. Probably Henry Chase, an attorney who moved from Delphi to Logansport in 1834. Helm, *History of Cass County* (1886), pp. 316–17.

71. By an act of Congress of June 23, 1836, it was provided that the surplus revenue in the Federal treasury on January 1, 1837, except for a reserve of five million dollars, should be "deposited" with the states in quarterly installments. While the money was to be returned should the government require it, it was generally understood that it would never be recalled. Distribution was made among the states according to the size of their electoral vote. Due to the effect of the Panic of 1837 the fourth installment was never distributed. *Dictionary of American History*, V, 209.

a little. Very cool. In the A.M. went with Alf & Ab. W. Harrison to my lots down near the River. They bot Porter house 21 ft. near the corner of Maryland[?] & West 3000 in 3.6.9 payment. Very cool all day—occasional rains—showery. Mr. Butler arrived home. Norman [. . .] came to settle law suit. Ray called on me to go & locate Branch bank at the North. I declined having an interest at Mich. City. Very cool at 9 P.M. & have covered our early plumb trees. Expect frost & fear it will hurt the fruit. Blossoms of peach & plumb just begin to show.

Apl. 22d 1836. Rose before sun rise. Frost last night pretty heavy. Hope that the fruit is not so forward as to injure it. I do not sleep as well as I use to. The summers responsibilities weigh heavy upon my mind. I endeavor to banish them as far as possible. My philosophy teaches me not to fo[r]bode evil but my habits controll. I never was made to withstand all the dangers of even reasonable expectation. I have determined Mr. McCarty consenting to sell my town property in Indianapolis the Sanders place especially.

My mare bot of Quarles run away. Sent J. Hill for her. Found her at Hardens on the Bluff road. Michael & Mr. Wood getting out manure also Mr. Gentry. Mr. Peck arrived from Madison. We have been exchanging our views as to the future growth of Madison & both agree that the rail road approved beyond Columbus in this state in the direction of Madison was a waistful expenditure of public money—that Madison left between Lawrenceburgh & Louisvill & no road south must always be a town of inferior grade compared with the two former places. We agree that there is a great danger of a *crash* engaging speculators & holders of real estate & that that it will take place in 18 months that all prudent men will prepare for it in the meantime. Mr. Butler at home preparing for court. Went with aunt Betsy[72] & Mrs. F. to S[toughton's] store. James Cooley is to live in the Store & board with us &c. I am preparing for Johnson circuit court. But for one case I should not go there that is Penny vs Taylor Marshall. I fear I shall loose it. I am right but the merits cannot come to light.

Apl. 23 1836. Pleasant—no frost. Michael to work in his garden. Mr. Wood ploughing stable lot. Preparing for the Bluffs with

72. Michael Fletcher's wife.

Quarls & Brown. We left at 1 P.M. very pleasant. Arrived at Port Royal at dusk. Everything looked well. Stayed over night at Mr. McGrews. Dr. Roe entertained us with violin flute &c.

Sunday 24 Apl. About 2 or 3 in the morning began to thunder & lighten & rained very hard till 10 in the morning. We breakfasted on fish caught in White River & left for Franklin. The farms near the bluffs beautiful. Country improved much. Only 13 years [ago] I rode from Bluff to F. & there was not a house East of Judge Boaz. Very muddy. Put up at Messrs. [?] Shaffer.[73]

Monday [April] 25. Pleasant day. I done but little business nor attempted to do it as I have declined attending the circuit &c. Lawyers present Messrs. Finch Hicks[74] Sweetser—Herrod Quarls Brown Ray Peesly & Rimond—

Teusday [April] 26. Had rain this morning & thunder from about 2 till daylight very hard.

Done some business in the A.M. At 12 Mr. Sweetser sent for. His child had died. Luce came. Mr. Quarles & myself left for home at 4 & arrived home over very bad roads at 10. All well.

Wedensday [April] 27. Very pleasant. Michael to work in garden. Messrs. Wood & Esqr. Fletcher plowing at the McF. place. Planted corn on the stable Block. Aunt Betsy Elijah Calvin Martha & Michael helped. I went to the McF. place. Returned about 12 when Cooley came up & informed me that Arnold Lashly had killed a Mr. Zacheriah Collins (collier) a young man—Lashly is (a Ky.) a carriage maker. Collins was to deliver 50 bushel of coal brought 1 load & L. objected to its quality & brought another load this day which he promised should be better. On delivering it the blacksmiths working in a shop attached to the carriage shop condemned the coal as it was full of dirt. Upon this L. ordered him to take his waggon out of the yard. C. refused. L. struck at him with a flat board to scare him as one witness thought. C. fended off with shovel—L. then threw a few coal sinders. Upon this C. leaped from the waggon & took up an ash stick 4 ft. They met. In the contest C. broke a beech board in the hands of L. & knocked L. down with

73. Nicholas Shaffer, Franklin tavernkeeper. *History of Johnson County, Indiana* . . . (Chicago: Brant & Fuller, 1888), pp. 507, 514.

74. Gilderoy Hicks, who was admitted to the Johnson County bar in 1833. Monks *et al.* (eds.), *Courts and Lawyers of Indiana*, III, 1145.

the same blow & while trying to repeat the blow the [. . .] was arrested out of the hands of C. by L.'s brother & C. retreated to the side of the gate that was open & lead[s] into the street & there took a position for fight. L. felt of his wound on his head. Said C. had cut him with the stick & jumped up & run with it & gave one blow. C. did not fall but then entered into conversation & promised to leave the yard & while putting a little coal by a man C. fainted & was taken off his horse & died in a short time. L. offered to surrender but was afterward taken up & before C. Scudder Messrs. Morrison Quarles & myself appeared at the Court house to inquire &c. Did not get thro' & adjourned L. giving a recog[nizance] of $1000. only.

Apl. 28. Very pleasant. Lashlys case under further invistigation—was ordered to be imprisoned—not a bailable case.

Apl. 29. Rose at 4. Very warm night. Plumb & peach in full bloom.

We this day planted the N. West field on the McF. place. Gentry furrowed out. Michael Mrs. F. Martha Elijah Calvin & Miles planted.[75] Lashly appointed Messrs. James & Wm. Morrison myself trustees to settle his business. I returned from Gentrys. Mrs. Fletcher rode behind me. Govr. Noble overtook us hunting a cow. I went with [him] home & bot two young cows with calves 4 year olds. Am to give $20 for one & 25 for the other. Also this day rode out to my block with Judge Wick &c.

Saturday Apl. 30. Very pleasant. Rose early. Paid Mr. Wm. Wood on contract $5. Rode out to Sanders place with Dr. Sanders. Looked over the place. Mr. Whitcomb yet laying off blocks.

In the P.M. went to the Gentry place. Michael & G. cleared the stocks with a horse rake[d] off the N.E. field preparatory for plowing. Miles Elijah & Calvin helped. Wood & Squire Fletcher ploughing the orchard piece. I fear they will not plough deep enough.

I rode Mr. Hands horse & proceeded from Gentrys to John

75. In his "Recollections of My Mother," Elijah wrote, "Father bought the McFarland place [see above, note 54]. . . . We boys were sent out occasionally to work on it. In corn planting mother always assisted, I might say, presided. She dropped most of the corn and pumpkin seeds. Uncle Michael always deferred to her judgment in these matters." Fletcher Papers.

Fletchers [and] the Cox place. I found that J. had sowed oats & clover in the orchard & also in the piece S. of the house. Was furrowing out for corn piece east of the house. Has done some work. Cooley came home. Staid over night contra[r]y to his uncles wishes.

Two Sows bo't of Farris will have pigs by Bazil Browns boar (Shaker breed) in 16 weeks from this day.

Sunday May 1 1836. Rose early—very warm pleasant weather. The two apple trees one by the Well & the one at the lower end of the garden in full bloom, the former bore last year 2½ bushel & is full of bloom now. The plumb tree (native) that came up 3 years past is now in full bloom is a week later than the plumb next to the well whose blossoms have fallen off. Our damson or large tame plumbs East of the house have blossomed very abundantly.

The oats I sowed on the Stable block just coming up & the corn in the same field planted Wedensday is sprouting. Michael & I took a walk to the pasture block & discovered the bees in the beech tree are dead.

I went with Mrs. F. Mrs. Richmond & the boys to hear Mr. Ames preach one of the best sermons 1. Ep[istle] of Jno. 5 & 10 v. After meeting John & Wm. Hill & uncle S. dined with us. This is the anniversary of our wedding day 15 years ago. Michael & I walked to the Bradley block, fenced some hogs in &c. Very pleasant growing day.

Monday May 2d. 1836. This day wrote an [. . .] for Stephen Masters & forwarded to Messrs. Carr & Kinnard Representatives in congress. Prepared my business for court. Messrs. Butler & Yandes have taken necessary steps. Two Mr. Woods [and] Esq. Fletcher went out to finish orchard fence & furrow the same one way for Gentry to plant it, Mrs. F. [and] boys to drop in P.M. Michael to pick up rubbish &c. Circuit Court commenced its session. Wick instructed the Jury in referance to Lashlys case. I should suppose the jury would not find a bill for murder &c. At 12 o clock rain began to fall. I think it has the appearance of settled rain & my teams must stop. Very few persons attending court so engaged are the farmers &c.

It continued to rain a little all the P.M. I expected that my hands would not plough but they continued. I felt a little provoked at first but now I am satisfied all is for the best. Very warm growing weather.

May 3 Teusday. I last night finished a part of a letter to D. D. Pratt in whose welfare I take a deep interest on the subject of his addresses to Miss A. M.[76] I have recommended him to ask &c.

Rose this morning later than usual. Michael up first. Mr. Gentry came in & I went to Govr. Nobles after two cows. 1 I had ingaged for $20. the other at $25 but he wanted a higher priced one so I bo't one for $25 for Gentry to Keep on the McF. place. One I am to bring home tomorrow. They are small young cows say 4 year olds such as I could have got one year ago for $12 or $15 such has been the rise in cattle. As for hogs there is none in the country. Cloudy this morning. Gentry & the little boys gone out to work. Michael got pea sticks. Mr. Ames (Preacher) dined with us. Michael took out potatoes &c & after dinner Michael Mrs. F. Martha & the boys went to plant the orchard piece at McF. place. Cloudy growing day. I find my corn planted on Wednesday last in the block coming up especially that which was planted in the A.M.

In court tried Huggins vs Nave.

Mrs. Bardwell & family here on their way to the Mississippi River—moving. B. himself yet behind &c.

I got thro court at 5 P.M. Walked with Stoughton (little). Went to office after dark & returned & spent a little time with Mrs. Bardwell & Richmond.

Wedensday May 4 1836. Cool this morning but not uncomfortable. Michael Step[hen] Wood Mrs. F. & boys preparing to plant at McF. place. They planted ½ of the orchard piece yesterday. They returned at noon & had planted the orchard piece.

Court was sitting. Mr. McCarty returned from Bluffs. I wished him to subscribe to Preachers Aid Society[77] & to sell 3 lots to Mr.

76. Pratt did not marry a "Miss A. M." In 1839 he married Sophia J. James of Rising Sun. Helm, *History of Cass County* (1886), p. 553.

77. The Preachers' Aid Society of the Indiana Conference of the Methodist Church. It had its origin in a bequest of James Paxton which was to be devoted to "extending the work of the Lord in the bounds of the state of Indiana, helping the most needy preachers belonging to that Church, whether effective or superannuated." Each of the Methodist conferences in the state had a Preachers' Aid Society which collected funds for the relief of elderly preachers and widows and orphans of deceased preachers. Holliday, *Indiana Methodism*, pp. 114, 157–58.

Ames for $1200. He thinks we should not sell under $1500. but has consented to take $1370. which will not likely be given. Allen Cole called brot money for the Ishams. Settled with the commissioner who sold Covington's land. Martin Coiner made some maps for Buchannan & Corneal land in Hamilton Cty. Went in the eve to McF. place. Gentry & S. Wood ploughing the S.E. field. Corn in N.W. field sprouted & coming up. 2 chesnut trees planted this spring growing the rest I doubt whither they will grow. Very pleasant eve. Rode Mr. Herrods horse. Mr. Malby[?] came & Staid over night. John Walker G. H. Dunn[78] here about the Lawrenceburgh rail road &c.

Thursday May 5 1836. Cool this morning. Several came to get seed corn. Very pleasant. G. H. Dunn & John Walker called a meeting at which Messrs. Henderson McCarty J. M. Ray Blake Russel Wm. Conner Govr. Noble &c were present. He proposed that the citzens of Indianapolis take the 1/5th of the five hundred thousand dollers proposed by the Charter of the Lawrenceburgh rail road company which is to be raised on the bonds of the state to be lent on mortgage & that Shelby Cty. would take the same amount & Decatur the same & Lawrenceburgh 2/5 of 5 hundred thousand & the persons taking this amount to pay the same to the company in 5 years but in order to get this many must subscribe for an equal amount of stock.

I did not wish to be forced to take the stock. We adjourned to consider of the proposition.

This day we learn that Lashly will be presented for murder of Collins.

Thursday May 5 1836. There has been several of our cases submitted to the court this day. In the A.M. I was ingaged with McCarty who is fixing for Cincinnati. I trust my business with Butler principally.

My cows run away this morning & a press for books renewed by Mrs. R.[79] & several other small crosses have put me out of

78. George H. Dunn was president of the Lawrenceburgh and Indianapolis Railroad Company, later the Cincinnati and Indianapolis.

79. The April 23, 1836, issue of the Indianapolis *Indiana Journal* contained an announcement of the spring quarter of the Marion County Seminary conducted by Thomas D. Gregg. The "Female Department" was to be taught by

humor for which I now feel sorry. I went for my letters &c to the post office now removed into Cains new brick opposite old post office.[80] I have selected box 116. I got a letter from Elijah in relation to letting Michaels son come out &c & am going to write in the morning to E. to let him come. Mrs. F. boys & M. went to plant the piece of ground on McF. place East of the orchard field &c. Did not plant much—Govr. Noble sent me a cow I bot slightly touched of the Durham &c. Gave $25. 4 year old.

May 6 Friday. Pleasant agreeable day not too warm. Mrs. F. E. & C. Martha & uncle Michael went out & planted the piece East of the orchard ground. Calvin & Elijah caught several small fish in Pouges Creek. This day Lashly was arraigned. Plead not guilty, application made to put off trial. Got letter from E. last night stating that Richardson[81] had not started but would so soon as I should say the word that it was rather his wish he should come but Timothy objected &c but if I would write he must come he should start.

Submitted the cases of Blake & St Clear vs Burkhart & others &c. McCarty started for Cincinnati. Uncle Stoughton & girls went to take tea with Mrs. Givans. 2 out of 3 of our cows returned home that run away yesterday. Nothing new from Washington.

Saturday May 7. This day court rendered judgment vs Burkhart for Mr. Blake &c $10. in each case. Lashly's case continued. Weather cool. Tried case of Colby (Tailer) vs James Smith Taylor for libel—calling the plaintiff *a dung.* Most of the causes continued until Friday next in consequence of the Morgan C[ircuit] C[ourt]. Called on Mrs. Paxton in the eve.

This night very cool—fear that there will be frost.

Mrs. E. Richmond. Perhaps the books were to be used in connection with her teaching.

80. The first post office in Indianapolis was set up in 1822 by postmaster Samuel Henderson in a house near Missouri Street and the present line of the canal. It was then moved to Henderson's tavern on the south side of Washington between Pennsylvania and Meridian. When John Cain became postmaster in 1831, he moved it to the north side of Washington half way between Illinois and Meridian. On this location Cain then erected the "Union Row," the first "block" of buildings in Indianapolis and one of these became the new post office mentioned by C.F. Sulgrove, *History of Indianapolis,* p. 254.

81. Michael Fletcher's son. He had been living and working in Lynchburg, Virginia, under the care of his uncles Elijah and Timothy Fletcher.

May 8 Sunday. No frost last night but cool. On yesterday in the P.M. Michael went to McF. farm & took the worms out of the trees. Killed a c[hic]ken also that was eating up our corn in the block.

This day preparing for church. Cooley has been to Mr. McCartys to borrow Ivenho. Turned our cows into the block the first time this year. The blue grass up about 3 inches not headed yet. Our earlyest wild plumb as large as peas.

After church M. & I went out to old Mr. Fletchers. He had never been out before. Things looked tolerable well. From there we went to the Cox place. This I offered him instead of the 1 acre lot. From there we went to Kelly[82] place. James Fletcher attends that this year. We returned to old Mr. F.'s where were assembled several of the neighbors. We staid a short time & then returned home by the Dutch settlement. Got home about sun down. Very cool. I covered my early plumb & Mrs. F. unwillingly covered a part of the beans. The girls & Jas. Hill went to church.

Monday May 9 1836. A frost came—rather slight but injured the beans & clover a little. Very cool clear dry weather. Received by Judge Polk some money from Pratt collected of Grover[83] & a letter in which he asks my advise whether he had best to *shave* &c.

I took up a renewed draft in Bank &c for $5000. (Commercial B[ank]). Went out at noon to carry dinner to Michael Elijah Calvin Miles & Stoughton. The latter never had been out before. They had just been ploughing the N.E. 6 acres piece & turned out for dinner. The corn in the N.W. piece up & in the orchard sprouted. I gave some directions & started home with Stoughton & met the Quaker for the first time who bo't the Pattingill place.[84] Stoughton got very tired & I had to carry him part of the way.

82. According to Marion County deed records C.F. had bought of Robert Kelly on August 23, 1830, fifty acres, part of the east half of the northeast quarter of section 22, T16N, R4E, for $200. He acquired an adjoining thirty acres in 1833 for $100 and sold the eighty acres to James Johnson for $620 in 1837. See entry for May 2, 1837.

83. Nicholas D. Grover, Logansport merchant. Helm, *History of Cass County* (1886), p. 510.

84. Perhaps Daniel Pattengill who entered 320 acres in Center Township, in section 32, T16N, R4E, in July, 1821. Sulgrove, *History of Indianapolis*, p. 61.

In the P.M. Simon made a deed to the lot that was devised to me by Mr. Richmond & sold to Tom Smith. Went with Bazel Brown to rent him the Pasture block. Asked him $69. for 16 weeks. Judge Polk took tea with me. Got a letter from Genl. Tipton—says there will be a bill pass for distribution of the surplus Rev[enue] but it will not become a law.[85]

Teusday May 10. Cool this morning & some frost. Michael James Hill, Mr. S. Wood went to finish planting & plowing the N.E. piece on McF. place. Mrs. F. went out to old Mr. F. to devide her wool of 14 sheep—says there was about 45 lb. The sheep are young—bot last fall.

Sent record to Mr. Pratt [of] Heaton vs Ewings & Co. in Hamilton C[ircuit] C[ourt]. Morrison & myself tried to settle a case or controversy between Mr. Young & Ramsey. Walked to the block (Bradley block)[86] with uncle Stoughton—cool but pleasant. Esqr. Casswell & Dr. Clark called on way to Cincinnati. Sent $235 J. L. Amy[?] &c

Wedensday 11 May. Cool—no frost. James Hill Uncle M. & Wood ploughing in oats on McF. place. Bot Eng. oats at Jo. Moore's Store—37½ per bush. & 7 bush. of potatoes to plant at 37½ per b. I wish to plant a good many this year say 30 or 40—for I believe another year they will be scarce at least worth 25 to 37½ per b. if the canal is made.

Warm & dry weather.

Settled with David Small *ats*[?] Higgins & Hamer.

Thursday May 12. Pleasant morning. Michael & myself went to McF. place. I drove the oxen to plough potatoe ground N.

85. This letter has not been found. However there is a letter from Tipton to C.F., May 25, 1836, in the Fletcher Papers (printed in *John Tipton Papers*, III, 282–84), in which Tipton wrote: "It is a common opinion here that some mode for distributing the surplus revenue sh'd be adopted before we adjourn. The principles of the land bill are the best for the New States, because it gives them 10 per cent. That bill however cannot become a law." The land bill refers to Henry Clay's proposal that 10 per cent of the revenue derived from the sale of the public lands should go to the states in which the lands lay, the rest to be divided among all the states in proportion to their representation in Congress.

86. Probably a reference to outlots 134, 137, and 138 acquired from Henry Bradley. See note 55, above.

orchard piece & to make a drain. Staid till 12. James Hill & Stephen Wood plowing at Sanders place. I arrived home eat my dinner & slept a short time as I was very tired it being the first time I have worked in the field for 3 years. Went to my office & about 4 we had one of the severest rains I ever witnessed mingled with Hail. It lasted only about ½ hour—first rain for 12 days. Saw Genl. Drake. Rented the pasture part of the Bradley block to old Bazel Brown 10 or 11 acres for 45 dollars to 15 of Sept.

Read Websters speech on [?] Bentons motion to pay nothing but specie at Land office.

Friday May 13 1836. This morning Mr. Gentry came in with the oxen half after 3 o'clock. Thus early he arrived in consequence of his shame for Michaels waking him one morning about sun rise. I have made up my mind that he is a trifling man. He is at one time very smart then again very lazy & trifling & I cannot depend on him. Wick (Judge) Quarles returned from Martinsville & our court commenced its session.

Pleasant day. Court permitted Lashly to be broght out & on such permission it was agreed on the part of Mr. Ketcham for the State & the counsel of Mr. Lashly to set this morning as the time for inquiry whether the offence is bailable or not. We accomplished but little in court this day. After court adjourned I walked to the McF. place, found on my way Calvin & Elijah in swimming in Pouges Ck. The corn [. . .].

Saturday May 14 1836. Gentry ploughed the corn on the Stable block. On the S. side stands well on the N. not so well.

Pleasant day. Court met at 7. Lashly brot out & trial commenced. Mr. Butler took down testimony. We advanced with harmony. Quarls Mr. Morrison & self for defendant Ketcham for deft. [State]. After a whole days investigation at sundown Court adjourned till 8 when Judge Wick delivered a long opinion & admitted the defendant to bail. House crowded to hear decision. Wick in his opinion stated that the English Judges in consequence of the light punishment for manslaughter had tried to construe everything manslaughter. But under appropriate punishment & the severity of our law it was not necessary &c. Said there was no such thing as *malice implied.* Messrs. Livingston Baz Brown Emerson & Jackson went L.'s bail.[87] Mr. Whitcomb finished surveying Sanders place.

I this day bot a breeding sow & shote of 100 lbs. of Mattingly. Gave $12—2 years ago could have bo't for $4.

Sunday 15 of May 1836. Pleasant day. M. & I went to get horses out of Bradley block. Calvin let the mare tread on his foote.

Locast trees are loaded with blossom in full bloom.

Went to Presbyterian Church. Heard a stranger preach. Mr. Lanier[88] in town. Commenced Ivenho &c.

Monday 16 May. Pleasant. Looks like rain this morning. Helped M. replant corn on stable block. Thunders a little at 10 A.M. Young turkeys. E. let the mare tread on his foote.

Went out to McF. place at 11. Got Gentry to come in & help mend fence round Bradley block. Afterwards went to old Mr. Fletchers. It rained so as to wet thro.

Mr. McCarty returned from Cincinnati. Has received some propositions to sell ½ of our town property for 25 thousand. I should be glad if we could sell for that amount but have not much hope.

May 17 Teusday. Pleasant. Locast trees in front of our house

87. John Livingston, Basil Brown, Benjamin Emison, Stephen H. Jackson, Daniel Lashley, and George Elgin (?). Bail was set at $2,000. Marion County Circuit Court Records. On May 24, James M. Ray wrote to C.F. then at Michigan City that "Lashly has run off, bag and baggage. Started I suppose last night. It is only a wonder he did not start earlier. Henry Brenton was in town yesterday, looking and speaking fierce, and with others spoke of much feeling existing in the County which unless satisfied might be mobbish or wolfish—and it resulted so far in a petition being started to the Judges to resign—for which the old man and others seem hot." Fletcher Papers. Nothing was heard of Lashley thereafter and the excitement subsided. Sulgrove, *History of Indianapolis,* pp. 122–23.

88. James F. D. Lanier (1800–1881), who moved with his family from North Carolina to Ohio, then to Madison, Indiana, in 1817. He studied law, served as assistant clerk and clerk of the State House of Representatives, and upon creation of the State Bank became president of the Madison branch and delegate to the state board of the Bank. He moved to New York City in 1848 where he joined in founding the successful firm of Winslow, Lanier & Company which specialized in railroad securities. At the opening of the Civil War Lanier lent money to Indiana to permit rapid equipment of her troops and later provided funds to carry the state through the financial crisis brought on by the failure of the legislature to pass essential appropriation bills. *Dictionary of American Biography,* X, 600–601.

especially the N. & S. trees are now the fullest in bloom I ever saw any trees. The one next to the S. tree not so full—scarcely any on it.

Michael & Gentry resetting fence at our pasture block & Harrowed the corn on the block. Sent potatoes to old Mr. Fletchers to plant.

At my office a Mr. Sergent of N.Y. City called with a Mr. Willard to buy an interest in the Bradley & Sanders property. I proposed to sell the ½ for $60000. I believe the gentleman a mere puff & looked upon the whole matter as a quiz. I am however to send a map to him to Wall St. Messrs. Dun & Tousey[89] called from Lawrenceburgh. They wish to get the additional bank stock sold. Mr. McCarty *pursuaded* me to join with 8 or 9 others to witt Messrs. Hannerman Yanders Blake Bates Williams (David) himself & others to propose to buy Hendersons property on which to erect a hotel, to give $9000. including a block of 5 or 6 acres.[90] I did what I did thro' persuasion & had I have taken one day to consider should have declined yet it may be all well. Stoughton is opposed to it.

I helped M. a little in the eve set up the harrowed corn.

Wedensday May 18 1836. Michael went to Gentrys to help harrow the N.W. field. Our State bank board met—Messrs. Ewing Vincennes, Major Lawrenceburgh, Vestal Bedford, Fitch New Al[bany] Lanier Mad[ison] Leeds Richmond, Blythe In[dianapolis] Demming Terre Haute McCulloch Fort W[ayne] Jenners Lafayette.[91]

Very Pleasant day. Our committee on business reported at 2 o clock—referred matters & adjourned at 5.

89. Isaac Dunn and Omer Tousey. The latter was director and president of the Lawrenceburg branch of the State Bank.

90. In the March 19, 1836, Indianapolis *Indiana Journal* Samuel Henderson advertised his Washington Hall for sale. In his letter to C.F. on May 24, 1836, James M. Ray added a postscript: "The Tavern (Hendersons) was bought by the Company at $13,500. As I could not feel free to be an owner in a Tavern, unless it could be conducted in such principles as I approve, I gave the Company fifty dollars, free, to help them on." Fletcher Papers.

91. John Ewing, Daniel S. Major, John Vestal, Mason C. Fitch, James F. D. Lanier, Noah Leeds, Benjamin I. Blythe, Demas Deming, Hugh McCulloch, and William M. Jenners. No representative from the Evansville branch is listed. The Fort Wayne branch, the eleventh, had been established at the November, 1835, meeting of the state board.

Friday May 20. Bank directors met. Pleasant day. Little done except declaring dividends & receiving stock in Mad[ison] Lawrenceburgh & New Al[bany] branches.

About Sundown a fine shower fell—very much needed. Vegetation never grew faster. Our plumbs on the tree near the well have almost attained full size. Pease have been in blossom several days.

Elijah says he has been elected a captain of a company of boys at Mr. Greggs school & his mother has arrayed him in military accoutrements. Mr. Harris started for Laport where I am going on Monday next if nothing unseen prevents. Michael is plowing up his lot East of my garden—Gentry helping.

Mr. Butler returned from Hendricks court.

Stoughton commenced boarding with us.

Put the Dun[n]ing Cow by mistake to Mr. Chinn's Durham bull.

Saturday May 21. Cloudy pleasant day. Yesterday discovered that a cat was catching our chickhens & Turkeys. I also got home two hogs I bought of Mattingly one sow with pig hoosier breed weghs 150 the other a barrow 100. Gave $12. for them. I have put them in pasture lot. Michael planting his lots with the orange white or yallow potatoe.

Rained in the P.M. I am preparing to go to Michigan City. McCarty & I rode out in the eve to visit St. Clears property. Stoughton handed me two pistols Miles sent.

May Sunday 22. Wet morning—but very warm. Vegitation advancing rapidly. I answered a letter written by Wm. Baldwin—also to Miles & Genl. Tipton & in the P.M. rode with Mrs. F. to Fletcher place & returned in the eve & prepared my papers for Laport.

May 23 Monday. I rose. M. went for my horse. I went to S[toughton's] Store got pair of boots Saddle blankets & about 9 left alone for Michigan City. Hugh O Neel & Mr. Palmer Treasurer of State had gone before. Cloudy gloomy day. I overtook my company, at Andrews West of White River on Michigan Road. Very cool. We travelled on to Kirks[92] where we staid over night. There

92. Nathan Kirk as early as 1830 opened a tavern at the point where the Michigan Road would intersect the road running west from New Castle. In 1837

met A. B. Strong Jerry Wright young miller &c, they returning from the North having been to the Laport District to enter land.

Tuesday [May] 24. Left Kirks & passed on to the Widow Johnsons to breakfast. Thence by a slow ride we arrived at Logansport about 4 P.M. crossed the River found the N. butment of the Bridge just going up. In our travel this day conversed with H.O'N. about Kinnards demigogical course—that he had become so great a sychophant that he dare not assist any one friend for fear of offending another &c & that he had constantly been strangling between his propensity to be popular & rich.

We met Mr. Pratt at Logan.

May 24 Tuesday 1836. This place is thronged with Strangers —A Ball in the eve at Vigus—great deal of the gay & youth displaid &c. I retired to bed under the sound of the violin.

Wedensday May 25. We left about Eleven A.M. I wrote Mr. Ewings answer in Chancery to a bill in the Hamilton Court.

Very cool this day—rained a little. We passed on rather bad roads to old Judge Polks where we arrived about sun down. Here I found old Mastin G. Clark returning from fishing. His son has just entered land & moved to Tippacanoe River. I had some conversation with him. He complained of the Bank & said if they could take more than 6 per cent interest He would publish them blow them up &c.

Thursday May 26. Cool cloudy wet day again. We left Judge Polks after Breakfast. Rode to Clarks old place stoped awhile & in good season say 4 o'clock arrived at Treadaways 10 miles this side of Laport. Put up for over night here saw a beautiful pair &c.

Went to bed about 9. Treadway did not return till after we had retired.

May 27. In the morning pleasant but cool weather. Treadway went to Laport with us. Hugh & I put up at Mr. Fletcher tavern—a discendant of Gosham Fletcher a connection distant.[93] Laport looks dull on the decline. Hugh went after compass to Dr. St. Clears & I done my business. I wrote title bonds for Treadway who sold

---

he laid out the town of Kirklin at this location. *History of Clinton County, Indiana* . . . (Chicago: Inter-State Publishing Co., 1886), pp. 661–62.

93. John A. Fletcher was licensed to keep a tavern in La Porte in 1835. Packard, *History of La Porte County*, p. 102.

several pieces of prarie land at $10. per acre not more than 5 or 8 ms. distant.

I was introduced to a Mr. Tenny & Carnehan[94] 2 Presbyterian preachers in the P.M. & attended their meeting in the eve. No meeting house—poor school room.

Saturday May 28 1836. Pleasant day. Many strangers in town to buy land some travelers &c.

H. O Neel gave up his horse to Mr. Palmer who sent his back by Treadway. We left about 10 for Michigan City. We did design going by Judge Lemons one of the Commissioners to locate Porter Cty.[95] but lost our way & would not turn back 10 mile. We met Dr. Hendricks & Mr. Rush of S. Bend & they agreed with M[r] P. & myself to descend the Kankakee. We were to meet them at Potato Ck. &c. We arrived at Michigan City about 3 P.M. Found this place somewhat improved one vessel in—unloading. Saml. Miller[96] had had a sale of 40 acres of land in lots N. of the Creek day before. Amount of sales 40 thousand dollars. Stopped at Mosses. Met Mr. John Walker & wife just as we arrived in town.

There is from 50 to 70 building[s] going up. I went with a Mr. Brown from Crawfertsville Capt. Ashton[97] &c & looked at the Miller tract of land bot by Mr. McCarty & myself last winter.[98]

I visited with Mr. Palmer & O Neel the high ground near the lake.

Sunday May 29. Mr. Harris (who had gone before with John

94. According to Packard, *History of La Porte County,* p. 419, the Rev. A. Carnahan visited the La Porte Presbyterian Church, held services for five days, but upon being offered the pastorate he declined.

95. Porter County was formed by an act of February 7, 1835, out of territory attached to St. Joseph County. *Laws of Indiana,* 1834–35 (general), p. 47. Judah Leaming of La Porte County was one of the commissioners appointed under the act of January 28, 1836, providing for the organization of the county and the location of the county seat. The other commissioners were Joel Long of Kosciusko County, Andrew Wilson of Fountain County, Matthias Dawson of La Porte County, and William L. Earl of St. Joseph County. The organization act provided that the commissioners should meet at the home of Thomas Butler in Porter County to select the county seat. *Ibid.,* 1835–36 (general), p. 51.

96. The first merchant in Michigan City. Packard, *History of La Porte County,* p. 86.

97. Capt. Eliakim Ashton, who came to Michigan City in 1834. In 1836 he joined his brother Gallatin in starting a dry goods business. *Ibid.,* pp. 85, 87.

98. See entry for January 14, 1836.

McCormick) & O Neel prepared to move on Foote to Flint or Topenaba Lake Porter County 20 miles.[99] We left after Breakfast. Mr. P. & myself loaded with saddle bags &c provision &c. Our bill for supper & breakfast lodging $2. each.

We past Waiverly a little town over half way 3 or 4 log cabins. Saw some very fine Indian horses here. We continued our course beyond there about 2 miles stopped & took a little refreshment by the way side & arrived at the lake sun about 2 hours high. Here we counted 14 boys in 2 canoes playing on the lake a beautiful scene.

We met a Mr. Jerry Bartholomew here who invited us to go home with him. I took the horses & went with him & the rest of our company went fishing. Around or near to Flint or Topenaba lake there were settled the family of Widow Hammond Bartholomew & Merrill. About sundown Mr. Palmer returned with a large string of fish in the shape & form of sun fish but much larger—weighing nearly 1 lb. each.

We fared at Batholomews rather poorly—His wife had run away & left him &c.

Monday May 30. Wet dissagreeable day. We tried to run a line in sec. 6 preparitory to laying off a town at the lak[e] on some land owned by myself Messrs. McCarty Palmer Merrill & Sheets where we intended to offer a donation for a county seat.

We had not proceeded far before we were driven in by the wet weather & Mr. P. & myself took our horses & went to the prarie about 2 miles at the place where we own a mill seat on sec. 24 where [is] another town site for county seat.[100] We passed on to

99. Flint Lake is in Center Township, three miles north of Valparaiso. It was at this site on land owned by C.F., Nicholas McCarty, Nathan B. Palmer, Samuel Merrill, and William Sheets, that C.F. proposed to lay out a town and offer it to the commissioners as the seat of justice for Porter County.

100. Upon the formation of Porter County the Portersville Land Company was organized by James F. D. Lanier, Benjamin and Enoch McCarty, John and William Walker, John Saylor, Abraham A. Hall, and James Loughlin, all residents of La Porte County except Lanier. The company laid out a town named Portersville on land owned by Benjamin McCarty in the southwest quarter of section 24, T35N, R6W, and offered to donate to the county alternate lots in the town plat plus forty acres of land in section 20 and a sum of money if the commissioners would choose their town for the county seat. The offer was accepted. The name of the town was later changed to Valparaiso. *History of Porter County Indiana* (1912), I, 192; *Counties of Porter and Lake Indiana* . . . (Chicago: F. A. Battey & Co., 1882), pp. 41–42.

Mr. Talbots town[101] where we had an interview with him & then passed on to the 20 miles prarie. We stopped by the wayside, grazed our horses & took a cold repast as we could get nothing at Mr. Talbotts—the preachers &c. We went to Mr. Turners the Clerks[102]—got there late in the P.M. & put up for night.

June 1st [May 31] Tuesday 1836. We got breakfast. Very cool —corn that is up looks yeallow.

Mr. Turner B [. . .] & Spurlocks[103] & others went with us back to where we were about to lay off the town at the lake. We passed by Mr. Brown a Virginian. Saw Mr. Tinny the preacher here.

We went to Tophenaba lake both sides. It rained. After our company left us we proceeded to Mr. Bartholomews where O Neel & Harris had staid &c. They recommended us to get Mrs. Hammonds to board us. We accordingly applied. That P.M. we run a line. Got very wet & went to Mrs. Hammonds. She is a widow lady with 2 sons & a daughter about 18—a pleasant girl. A neat little cabin 14 by 17 a good library—near the lake.

Wedensday June 2d [1st]. We went to work running out & establishing the lines &c preparitory to making a town platt. It rained & we done very little.

June 3 [2]. Thursday. Mr. Hammond assist us in running off our town. It rained & was cold. We got very wet. Messrs. Stewart & Wallace came to us tried to get us to desist from running off a town but wished us to join in the county seat at 24.

We continued to lay off till we got the blocks run out. Mr. Palmer managed the compass & [we] returned at sundown very wet.

June 4 [3] Friday. Cold wet. Mr. Palmer & myself went to the prarie & left H. [O'Neal] & Harris to go to Chicago or anywhere else they might please.

At 24 found Mr. Niles[104] & a mill right. Mr. P. & N. run a line

101. William K. Talbott laid out a town a mile and a half northwest of the site of Portersville (Valparaiso) which he called Porterville and which he hoped would be selected as the seat of justice. *History of Porter County Indiana* (1912), I, 192.

102. George B. Turner, first clerk of Porter County. *Indiana Executive Proceedings*, p. 703.

103. Cyrus Spurlock, first recorder of Porter County. *Ibid.*

104. Perhaps John B. Niles, La Porte lawyer.

with the compass. After they returned I started for Hulls mill. It rained. I arrived at Hulls having passed thro' my land adjoining about sundown about 7 miles from Michigan City. Staid over night.

June 5 [*4*] *Saturday.* I arrived at Michigan City about 10 A.M. Found Mr. Teel[105] who went out looked of my land. Town crowded with strangers.

Sunday June 6 [*5*]. Mr. Teel & myself went to Tapeneba lake. Arrived there about sundown. Found Messrs. Palmer O Neel & Harris. We all staid at Mrs. Hammonds. This a very cool day. In the eve I went to Mr. Merrills to stay over night but after I went there found that I was not an agreeable guest to the madam & returned to Mrs. Hammonds &c.

Monday June 7 [*6*]. Cold dissagreeable day. We started after breakfast for Mr. Butlers[106] where the locating commissioners were to me[e]t but Mr. P. & myself concluded to go to Mr. Stoners living on our land. We found him planting corn—very late as it was—yet most persons in the Morgan prarie had made no advances in their farming. All had turned speculater.

We arrived on the ground where the commissioners met about 10. Here I met with Judge Everit Dr. Rose Mr. Wm. O. Ross John Walker Hillis &c.

The Commissioners soon adjourned to me[e]t next morning & we returned home.

Tuesday June 8 [*7*]. Commissioners met again & we rode round Topenaba lake. Very wet & unfortunate time to exhibit our town. Dined at Mrs. Hammonds then rode with them to Mr. Talbotts town—the 3 commissioners Messrs. Lemon Earl & Dawson. We returned Mr. Palmer & self about sun down.

Wedensday morning June 9 [*8*]. Started Hugh O Neel to Michigan City to prepare for laying off some lots there. We went back to Butlers where we knew that the commissioners had determined to lay off county seat on 24. We went there. Spent the day. It was warmer this day than usual but still cool.

The commissioners determined to locate at Talbotts at 24 &

105. William Teall. See note 10, above.
106. Thomas Butler. See note 95, above.

refused to receive other propositions.[107] Judge Everit made a stump speech. We returned about sundown. Staid over night.

C.F., Topenaba [Flint Lake, Porter County], to Nicholas McCarty, Indianapolis, June 9, 1836

. . . The county seat was located yesterday on a tract adjoining our land bought of Judge Polke & near several tracts in which we have an interest. We could have had part of the town on the land we have an interest in but Sheets was absent & we did not feel disposed to act in his absence or give a donation. Town property must soon become what is said of original sin, more you have of it the worse it is. Every person is going to lay off towns & lots. I fear Michigan City will be ruined this way. I have been in company for the last 4 days with Mr. Teel the great owner of that city & I have learned many of their dirty little tricks from him. I shall lay off 80 [acres] in lots as soon as possible—shall write you next week. . . . I believe we best sell—not buy Town property unless in a very [. . .] towns must fall. . . .

DIARY

Thursday June 10 [9]. Mr. Teel & myself left for Michigan City. Mr. Harris on foote & Mr. Palmer for Laport. After Mr. Palmer had left Mrs. Hammonds I discovered he had left behind his saddlebags. I took them & thought I would overtake him at Laport. Col. Teel & myself arrived at Michigan City about 2 P.M. —I found divers letters from home all giving unfavorable accounts of the present affairs of the country &c. I found Mr. Whitcomb the survey[or] had come on by Mr. McCartys order to lay off the lots. We were like to be in want of a compass & took Mr. Palmers saddlebags & proceeded to Laport. I there staid over night at Mr. Fletchers. He & his wife treated me very kindly. Mr. P. did not arrive. I conjectured rightly that he had gone back after his saddlebags.

107. Portersville on section 24 was selected, not the town laid out by Talbott. See note 100, above.

C.F., La Porte, to Nicholas McCarty, Indianapolis, June 10, 1836

. . . There have been two sales of lots at Michigan City this week. They sold high of course. . . . I have rode and slept with Col. Teel one of the great owners of Michigan City, from whom I have I believe ascertained to a certain extent the misteries of their speculations and the cause of their high sales &c. I am sorry to tell you that the whole proceedings now are based on a species of villany that however well connected must I think in a short time produce a disgraceful disclosure such as well calculated to deceive the most scrutinizing. Every tract of land that is brought into market is owned by a large number of shareholders. The sale is advertised & the property cried in a fine ornamented room called the "auction room." Each share holder attends in person if it has not leaked out he is an owner but otherwise has a bidder. There are many honest individuals, travellers &c &c seeking to invest money. Well the bid is made by those interested with great fury. The standers by catch the fever—if not one of the by bidders will be pressed by a secret partner to take the lot off his hands that has just been bid in by a tool & will slap down the money in great haste with 300 or 400 per cent advance. Here an ignoramus or a gull will see a fortune made in 3 minutes. If the lot is struck off to a secret partner he will the next day sell it back to a tool who will give him his note for the original purchase money & 5 times as much or more to the tool who will assign the same to the known proprietor who in due season if not otherwise disposed of to a stranger will proclaim that he sees some great advantage in the property & has bought it back at a very advanced price. Now it is months before the property is publicly known to be in the hands of the original owner & in this time while those interested are selling the property to one another there are many chances to slip it into the hands of a stranger & get his money. In Chicago I have but little doubt the same process is carried on & where so many strangers arrive in both these places there is a great chance in the course of this round to draw them in & to them many *bona fide* sales are made. Col. Teel has not disclosed this process to me but parts of stories & actions speak louder than words. Samuel Miller came to me when I was in last & wished to sell me some of the lots left at his great sale. He went over his map & there were but few but had been forfeited or that some friend had left with him to resell or with his check but before he got thro' it sliped out that he was very hard pressed for money. A vessel landed a few days since a quantity of goods. The freight perhaps $1000. The money could scarcely be raised. There is no money here. If extraordinary good fortune does not occur the bubble will burst in 6 months & I fear in 3. . . .

I think you have been misled by what you have heard as relates to the real value of property here. I think it my duty to you & myself to sell out during the summer. I shall lay off one 80 acre tract into lots & while that is going on I shall try to sell the whole if I can, at ¾ to some one man who will pay the whole down or part down rest in 60 & 90 days. I fear you expect too much—2 lots cannot consistently be laid off & I shall think myself fortunate to get paid to me as above $100 per acre for the whole deducting expenses &c & if I do not do as well as that, do not be disappointed. . . .

I am pleased to learn that property is on the rise at home. The prospect of Internal improvements will keep it up—but for fear of reverses I wish to sell my interest in all altho property we own jointly especially that at the Bluffs at Noblesvill & Indianapolis. I look upon the chances of our town property falling against us after Decr next. If you can get from $8000 to $10000 sell the Bluff property. The Noblesvill at $3000. The Sanders property at $125 per acre and the Bradley and Ungles property at $300 per lot, yes $250 per lot, our lots west of the Newberry [?] property at $1200 & the lot on Washington St. at $800 if you cannot get more.

It is at your option to consider the lots you bought of Wood as our joint property or not. In either case I would give it as my opinion for you to sell at 10 per cent advance. Merrill and some of our good friends have slandered us by saying that we ask extravagant prices for our property so high as that no reasonable man will buy of us. Such a general impression is as injurious to our sales as it would be to say that we had a doubtful title. . . .

The Michigan City people wish you to visit them. The merchants want you to send your fall goods around by them. They will I believe agree to deliver them there at 1.25 per cent. If you can incourage this project I can use it to good advantage. . . .

As to my opinion of Michigan City affairs we must of course keep still. I shall look upon the announcement of the passage of the harbor bill as a propitious time to sell &c. . . .

DIARY

June 11 [*10*] *Friday.* About 10 o'clock I left Laport which looks like a graveyard. All the laboring class have left the country & gone West to the new lands. I went to Clarks [?] the surveyors after the compass. I arrived at Michigan City about sundown. It rained this P.M. very hard.

June 12 [*11*] *Saturday.* This day the boys could not in consequence of the wet get out till 10 or 11. I spent the day in examining maps &c of the place.

Sunday June 13th [*12th*]. I this day went to church. Hugh O. went to Laport for compass. I received several letters—one from my wife & 2 from Mr. McCarty. Mr. Bradley arrived in the P.M. also Mr. Sprague whom I had not before seen. This day from the news I received felt very melancholly. I had on Saturday proposed to Mr. Teel to make me a proposition to take part of 240 acres which Mr. McCarty & I owned near the place 2 tracts of 80 acres each of Messrs. Alfred Harrison & Dr. Todd 80 acres from Mr. Miller. Pleasant cool day.

Monday June 14 [*13*] *1836.* This day Mr. Bradley is trying to sell his bacon. The usual price had been & is 12½ per lb. but he could not sell for more than 10½ by the load. About 9. Mr. Teel & myself went out to look of our land & he made me a proposition to buy *himself* & Mr. Sprague ¾ of our interest for sixteen thousand Eight hundred dollars in 20 days 60. & 100 by drafts on N.Y. City. I accepted of this proposition & drew the writing accordingly. The ¼ Messrs. Teall & Sprague to sell & account for at least account for ¼.[108] I made this sale of our interest because I believed that property at Michigan City was overrated & had a fictitious value—that prices heretofore kept up by trick must fall—that I viewed the future pecuniary condition of the country equally

108. See above, note 10, and below entry for August 25, 1836.

if not surpassingly more distressing than in 1818–'20 and altho that one 80 acre tract laid within ¾ of a mile from the Lake yet I best sell it. It was estimated at $225. per acre one tract at $30 & the other at $25. per acre. They both laid some distance off. I have & still view the presant age & speculation in real estate to be more demoralizing than any gambling that ever was practised & should I be so fortunate as to get our money I shall be glad to get out of this difficulty—yet I fear now that my drafts will not be accepted yet I have no good reason to doubt. After my trade with Messrs. S. & T. I tried to help Mr. Bradley sell some bacon & for that purpose went to Mr. Scotts mill &c.

C.F., Michigan City, to Nicholas McCarty, Indianapolis, June 13, 1836

. . . We have progressed in the laying off the lots so that I presume I shall offer a few not exceeding every fourth lot in the first forty acres laying next to the lake & adjoining the present lots already laid off by the 19th inst. If you have a map of the city you can readily perceive the advantages of the tract (that is the E. ½ N.E. quart. of sect. 32). Franklin St. the main business St. runs diagonally thro' it which will cause much trouble in laying out the squares & fractional lots but as we had got under way I hope to have them all compleated in 12 days from this. The nearest lots will be within ¾th of a mile from the harbor & the lake. The buildings of the best quality are now erected within 300 yards of our line & we have about 35 acres that is high and handsome & will outlook the whole town when the timber is removed & I can now look from the Northern line up Franklin St. & see the principal Stores & both Taverns, to the lake.

I have been offered $1200 by Mr. Teel & $1000 by Mr. Burr for one acre giving them their choice on the North side but have declined . . . we have the advantage of the best street running thro our land. . . .

. . . Every man almost in this country has abandoned his business to speculate in real estate. The farmer has left his farm & omitted to put in a crop. The mechanic his shop & even the merchant his store & have vested all they had & all they could borrow in real estate. They have united with Eastern capitalists to be sure which has enabled them to Keep up a countenance. But in order to carry out the schemes they have had to effect great sales. They have sold to the innocent stranger take bad money to the lounger & rascall who had none & to one & another & all owe for the property bought. All are in market to sell & but for the policy of the pro[s]picters there would be a crash in a day—& as it is let good times even come an exposure must take place to a great extent & if evil ones follow as I sincerely believe, the scene more agrivated than in 1818–19–20 will be acted over again.

Now for instance at this place no merchant pretends to open his store & attend to it as business men should. At Laport a town lot cannot be sold and all the business men wish to leave the place or [are] about to engage in buying & selling land.

Col. Teel showed me a letter a few days since from the cashier of one of the Detroit Banks notifying him that a draft of Mr. Burr of the place had been protested at one of the N.Y.B. I learned a few days since that one of the first men were paying 1 per cent a day for money and this day John McCormick stated that since his return Mr. Miller of whom we bo't the land was paying him $5. a day for $500. They all stand here hoping and praying for the passage of the harbor bill for their relief as sincerely as ever the planter asked for rain during a six months draught & I do not belive Miller realized $1500 in his sale of $40,000. At Chicago I believe the state of affairs are no better. Hubbard only sold a few lots *here* & I believe his friends bo't them in. But everything is studiously concealed & I wish if possible to effect a sale of all our interest at least ¾ at this place. & I hope you will avail yourself of the first opportunity to sell at Indianapolis. A crash here will put property down there. Sell it in 1/4–1/3–1/5 or in any manner. I shall forward you a map of our property here so soon as it can be made & I wish you would sell out portions of our real estate at Indianapolis or here to any of your friends in Cincinnati. I differ with you as to the propriety of sacrefising or selling our lands in prefferance to town property altho no oppertunity shall escape to do either. If I effect a sale of some of the lots here high can you not sell an interest in the residue to Harrison Sheets & to our good friend Samuel Henderson? . . .

DIARY

Tuesday June 15 [*14*]. I left this morning for home. Very warm day real hot weather. I arrived in Laport about 12 staid till 2 then with Mr. Ross came to Treadways. Very warm. My horse had no water. I travelled on to where old Mr. Clark settled. Met Treadway just returning home. Also met Joe Case. Turned back young Dabny who was going to the Land office. He staid over night with me.

[*June 15–16*]. Next morning found my horse stiff a little but I started & travelled to Sid Williams to breakfast thence to Judge Polks. He was out with the Commissioners who were locating the county seat & who did on that day locate the county seat at Manchester.[109] I left Judge Polks & met McCarty Henderson & Harrison near old Mr. Martins. They were going out to see me at Mich. City. I stopped & talked with McC. an hour & then left him & overtook Mr. Chase of Logansport where we arrived about dusk. Stopped at Vigus. Found Pratt. Staid over night. Next morning found my horse badly foundered but I hated to leave her & I got on drove her thro' the River. Mr. Pratt went to Deer Creek with me & there we took breakfast with John Walker & wife. There I bled my horse & drove her before me to Mrs. Johnsons at Michigan town. Very warm day. I suffered much travelled at least 25 miles on foote. I there discovered that I could not get my horse any further. I was sorry to abandon so valuable an annimal & the first I ever foundered—but here I fortunately found a horse belonging to Judge Wright (Adam) which had been left there by his brother for dead. I done all I could for my beast but she was very bad. I looked upon [her] as ruined & regretted I had not left her at Logansport & got another but I wished to get her home where I could nurse her.

Achillis Williams also staid over night with me at Mrs. J.

109. C.F. meant Rochester, the county seat of Fulton County.

Friday June 18 [17]. I left on Judge Wrights horse & travelled to Kirks for breakfast. Made an agreement to do some law business for him. Left there came to McCurdys—fed there & arrived at home before sundown having been absent 25 days. I never was much more gratified to get home from any Journy & did & have concluded that I ought to live near Indianapolis if I wish to be happy. I have many things to endear me to the society.

Saturday June 19 [18] *1836*. Visited my friends whom I found generally well. A warm pleasant day. Went to the Gentry farm. All things looked well. Uncle Michael had tended to my business well .

Sunday June 20 [19]. A warm day. Went to church. John Hill & Stoughton dined with us. Plenty of peas & had had for 10 days beans currants & cherrys ripe & our plumb & peach trees begin to bend with their loads of fruit.

Monday June 21 [20]. Pleasant day. Michael Gentry ploughing his potatoes & the corn back of the stable a third time. Warm dry weather.

Teusday June 22 [21]. Pleasant weather went to Gentrys. Michael hoeing his potatoes. Judge Boaz sent me a shote.

Nothing new looking over my business. Mr. Butler has gone to Boon.

Wedensday June 23 [22] *1836*. Very pleasant. Michael ploughing his potato patch.

Thursday June 24 [23]. Very warm. Mrs. F. & Aunt Betsy pulled some blue grass seed. Michael went to Gentrys who is ploughing over the corn ground in the N.W. piece the 3d time. Mrs. F. & myself walked out & went to Mr. Reelys or Rives [?] the Quakers who settled on the Pattingail place.

Friday June 25 [24]. Very pleasant worked in my office.

Saturday June 26 [25]. Mr. Quarls & myself went out to the Gentry place. I worked a little this day at my business. Mr. Bradley returned brot a letter from Calvin who is with Mr. Ingram now at Lafayette. Very cool.

Sunday June 27 [26] *1836*. This day very cool. Went to church in the A.M. Messrs. Quarles Brown & Butler gone to Noblesvill Court. I intend to go with Judge Wick tomorrow. I have received the Intelligencer of the 16 by which it is shown a bill to regulate the public depositses has passed the senate.

Stoughton & John dined with us. Jim Hill & wife rode out & left their childrin with us. Billy Hill & boys went out to the Gentry place. Michael wrote to Elijah.

Monday June 28 [27] *1836.* Cool foggy morning. We have not had any rain for 2 weeks but heavy dews & cold mornings. In the middle of the day extremely hot.

Judge Wick & myself left home about 7 for Noblesvill. We rode about half way when Morrison Merrill & Mr. Bates overtook us. We rode on & arrived at Noblesvill just in time to dine. I determined not to take any hand in any suit if I could possible help it. I therefore do[d]ged around among my old clients all of whom are desirious of my attention to their cases. Noblesvill improving fast.

Teusday June 29 [28] *1836.* Cool morning as usual. I endeavored to square my business & at 12 left Noblesvill at 1 with Messrs. Bates Merrill & Morrison. We returned home on the River road. Saw Mr. Mustards[110] premium corn about 5 ft. high not tasseled. At home about sundown found all well.

June 30. Cool this morning. A Mr. Rowe here from the house of Townsend & Brothers N.Y. City. Made proposition to sell Mr. Alf Harrison ⅓ of our interest (Mr. McCartys & mine) in our land here Sanders property Bradley property & 4 lots for 21 thousand &c. Dont think he will accept. We have learned that the fund commissioners have obtained ½ million for Internal Improvement. I have made the offer to Mr. H. because I like him as a friend & wish him to share with me in the profits of the property &c.

In the Eve Stoughton & I went to Gentrys. Peck came in & I paid him $763. on Bridge stock at Logansport.

July 1 1836. Cool pleasant morning but a warm day. We have learn[ed] that the bill to distribute the public Revenue & regulate deposits have passed. Mr. Butler returned from Hamilton C[ircuit] C[ourt]. Stoughton & I bo't Michael some chairs. John

110. James Mustard. On September 13, 1834, he acquired from C.F. a total of 170 acres in section 1, T16N, R3E, paying $1,250. This was part of 190 acres which C.F. had purchased in 1833 for $990 at a sheriff's sale. Marion County deed records.

Hill bot horse for $60. of Furgeson. He is going away. Michael bot 3 sythes. He & Gentry are hoeing the last planted potatoes in North East field.

James Hill hawled 4 load of Hay from Sanders place. I went to old Mr. Fletchers—found the rye & wheat grass & corn better than I expected. Returned & made a remittance to Messrs. Combs & Vallett & Isham thro Brewster also to Kinsys of Madison thro' Lanier.

Warm a little Thunder some sign of rain. Called & heard H. O Neel read his 4th July oration. Mr. McCarty went to Greenfield. Stephen Masters called & paid off mortgage.

July 2d 1836. Gentry came in to get horse shod. John Hill preparing to travel West to look out a place to begin business.

Received a new cow from Cloud [of] Hamilton Cty. Gave $20. reasonable price. Met Messrs. Palmer Wood &c at my office relative (to) agricultural society to be held on 4th. I went with Mr. Dawson[111] to solicit subscriptions from T[. . .]. Got about $38. for Agr. S. Bot a bay horse of Quarls gave $75. cash next week. Horses are high. Bot 2 barrel of salt & a little [. . .] at Lashlys Sale for $4.25. In the eve a small shower. Michael finished hoeing his late potatoes back of the oat field on McFarland place.

Removed the Mattingly sow from the pasture to barn yard & her 7 piggs about 1 month old & took my other hogs to the pastures.

Sunday July 3. Foggy morning—sprinkles a little some prospect of rain till 9 A.M. I called down to see A. Williams just [back] from Michigan City. Went to church with Mrs. F. Miles Elijah Cooley Stoughton. Mr. Smith preached—not very full congregation. Cleared off very pleasant. John Hill [and] Stoughton dined. John Hill preparing to go West to hunt a location to commence mercantill buseness. I think a location on the Wabash between Terre Haute & Lafayette preferable. He has served 4 years lacking 1 month with J. M. Moore & Co. I have given him letters to E. J. Peck at T. H. J. Blair at Perrsyvill—A. Ingram of Lafayette—also a letter of credit to any amount required to buy or build or rent a store. Mrs. Fletcher Elijah & James Cooley rode on horseback to Fall

111. Elijah Dawson, a farmer who settled in Washington Township in 1823. Sulgrove, *History of Indianapolis*, p. 632.

Creek. I walked with Mrs. Richmond to Mr. Elders late tavern to see Mr. Patricks family. Mr. P. called in the eve.

I have to make out a report for the Marion County Agricultural Society. People commenced firing guns at 10.

July 4. Pleasant growing weather. Rose early & made out a report for the Agricultural Society. Went down town at 9. Went to hear Mr. O Neel deliver the oration at Methodist church. Mr. Cobb & lady dined with a strange woman. Agricultural S. met at 3. Mr. Merril delivered oration in which he undertook to abeuse certain individuals for cutting farms up & selling them in lots. There has been good feelings between him & me of a long standing—but from my connection with Mr. McCarty he is disposed to abeuse or hold up to view certain acts as highly immoral which are innocent in themselves & which he was the first to practise to wit buying & selling real estate. I fear his object is to keep up a mean low prejudice against me & Mr. McC. that has prevailed against such as have property not to say wealth in their hands. I believe he is too late in the day. It would have answered a better purpose 6 or 10 years past when James B. Ray was elected Governor by crying out against the rich & *aristocracy.* I hope this will all pass in quietude. I moved after the oration was delivered to have it printed. This I should not have done but for Mr. Blakes moving to have my report printed. I answered by having his oration printed.[112] After the election of members to the Agricultural S. Palmer President H. O Neel Secretary myself Treasurer—adjourned. I then called on Mr.

112. The report was printed in the Indianapolis *Indiana Journal,* July 9, 1836. The year-old society had a membership of two hundred. It was agreed at the meeting that each member should be taxed seventy-five cents for the ensuing year and that the next fair should be held the first Friday and Saturday of the following October. It was further agreed that the amount of "corn-ground" entered for competition would be five acres and that a ploughing match would be held, a plough worth nine dollars to be awarded to the winner. Merrill's oration was printed in the *Journal* of July 16. In the part alluded to by C.F. he said: "But the most alarming symptom of the times is the spirit of speculation that every where prevails. Regular business yielding its ten or twenty per cent, is deserted for the purchase of real property, and those once industrious, are no longer employed, but stand idly waiting the result. Farms are broken up to enlarge old towns or lay out new, and town lots are in market, not to *use* but to *sell.* . . . Yet those who should know better set the example, trusting that they can escape the fate of the *hindmost.* One imposition on the public makes way for another, and the fools who go ahead are followed by greater fools from behind."

Smith Methodist Preacher. We had a shower during the day. Stores shut up. A party dined on the public ground near the River.

July 5. Am preparing to go to Noblesvill Boxley Strawtown Andersontown & Pendleton with Mrs. F. Pleasant morning. We left (that is Mrs. F. & myself) at 10. horseback & proceeded [on] the River road to Mr. Beels 17 ms. There we took tea with Mrs. Dunning her son B. & her Daughter Mrs. Beel. I went thro' the cornfields of Mr. Dunning—it's about waist high. People cutting their clover. We after tea rode to Mr. Mallory's, found the old lady & genleman at home—pleased to see us. They were in trouble about their daughter who married Frybarger.

July 6. We rose early & went to Noblesville to breakfast at Mr. Dunnings. I done some business & after breakfast proceeded to Cicero town by Mr. Lemons. Cicero town has 4 or 5 cabbins[113]—2 of them little stores one kept by Ira Kingsbury. From that place to Boxley we rode in company with a Mrs. McMurtry. The roads are rather bad. We arrived at Boxley about 2 found Thomas B[oxley]. A[ddison] was at Strawtown. Mr. Boxley not having any convenience to entertain travellers we proceeded to Mr. Jones ¾ of a mile still west. We here dined & Mr. Boxley (Thos.) came & I went with him to see our prarie farm. I was pleased to find that Mr. McCarty & ourselves had 150 to 175 acres of good mowing prarie. We went to Mr. Spruces there found Mr. Wilbill[?] foundery man of this place.

We returned to Mr. Jones & where we staid over night.

July 7. Pleasant morning. After breakfast we left & proceeded thro' Cicero town to Strawtown.[114] There took dinner at Rolls. Saw Mr. Coles clerk but not Cole. After dinner very warm. We proceeded to Andersontown where we arrived just after dark. Stopped at N. Williams Clerk.[115] His mother had Just died. Andersontown is fast improving.

113. Cicero, in southeastern Jackson Township, Hamilton County, was plotted in January, 1835. Haines, *History of Hamilton County*, p. 230.

114. Strawtown was laid out by Bicknell Cole and William Conner. The former opened the first general store in the town. Haines, *History of Hamilton County*, pp. 250–51.

115. Robert N. Williams, clerk and recorder of Madison County. *Indiana Executive Proceedings*, p. 511.

July 8. Pleasant morning. After my visit to Jacksons mill[116] & inspecting certain land adjoining the town which I am getting laid off[117] we at 2 got started. We went down on the East side of the Prarie. When between Andersontown & Huntsville about 1 miles from any house there came on a sudden storm of wind & rain. The gust was furious & we were 200 yards from the open prarie. Mrs. F. good at expedients when in sudden troubles proposed to ride to the prarie. We did so & arrived thro' falling limbs & trees. Where we landed were 4 hickory sapplings on a square leaving 6 or 8 feet between. Mrs. F. spread two umbrellas in the inclosure. I took off the saddles & throwed the blankets over the tops of these bushes which bent down upon the umbrellas under which I throwed the saddles which formed a good seat for Mrs. F. All this was done in 2 minutes & before the rain fell to wet her. Under this shelter so suddenly constructed by the advise of Mrs. F. we could see the forrest trees lowered to the earth by the force of the storm which raged with uncommon fury—accompanied with heavy thunder & light[n]ing. At last the storm was hushed, & close by us the pa[r]tridge or quale from a heap of brush not 20 yards announced that the storm was over & that we could proceede. We did so & over strewed limbs & trees reached Pendleton before sundown. Stopped at Bostons. I was wet by taking off & putting on the saddles. We had a fire & dined.

July 9 Saturday. We left Pendleton in the shower this morning but it soon cleared up & we proceeded to Arnets where we dined & arrived home before sundown. Here to my great surprise found Richardson Uncle Michaels boy just from Va. unexpectedly. I was much pleased to see him. He has good sense & morals—a lad about 19—rather young looking for that age. He is going into buseness for his uncle Stoughton. I found several letters. Corn crops on my

116. Probably the gristmill built by David Williams in 1832 and later acquired by Andrew Jackson. John L. Forkner and Byron H. Dyson, *Historical Sketches and Reminiscences of Madison County, Indiana* (Anderson, 1897), pp. 607–608.

117. The "Plat of Anderson City, East Central Part," in *Atlas & Directory of Madison County Indiana* (Cleveland, Ohio: American Atlas Company, 1901), pp. 42–43, shows a section labeled Fletcher Place. Anderson also has a Fletcher Street.

journey looked very well—this article must be in great abundance if the season continues favorably.

July 10 Sunday. Pleasant day. Went to hear Mr. Holiday preach a learned sermon showing the developments of the wisdom of God in the construction of the human frame & the plantetary system. Elijah & Miles rode out on horseback to fall Creek. Michael & I went to Gentrys.

Monday July 11. Attended to my business in the office. Gentry while I was absent plowed the ground on the stable lot the 5th or 6 time & was going over the corn on his place the 5 time.

This day found Mr. & Mrs. Vorus (Engine[e]r)[118] at Mr. Browns with a sick child. She is a cousin of Mrs. F. We went down after dark & saw them. Child 4 mos. old very sick. On our return Mrs. F. sprained her foote. Very pleasent growing day.

Teusday July 12. I went down & brought up Mr. Vorus & lady with sick child. Pleasant day.

In the A.M. Mr. Quarles showed himself having been absent after Henry Banks.[119]

I hired 2 men by name of Draper at $1. per day to mow. Went with them to Gentrys. Found him plowing the orchard & Michael howing the potatos [on] N. E. piece. They look poor but I think hoeing will bring them out.

Returned & went to the office. Had a long talk with Mr. Butler in which he recommends me to look for political preferment. His recommendation grows out of his partiality to me. I convinced him I think that I was unfit & the pursuit averse to my notions. Mr. & Mrs. Vorus came to our house with sick child.

July 13d. I rose went to market. Pleasant morning. Mr. & Mrs. Vorus child very sick. She is a half cousin of Mrs. F. I this day sold the one half of our one fourth of our interest in the Michigan City land to Alfred Harrison for Four thousand dolla[r]s.[120]

118. Probably C. G. Voorhies, engineer on the southern division of the Central Canal.

119. On July 9 the Governor of Indiana made a demand upon the governors of Illinois, Missouri, and other states for the apprehension and delivery to John Cain, the agent of Indiana, of Henry Banks, charged with purloining money from the United States mail in Indiana. *Indiana Executive Proceedings,* p. 301. See above, p. 330n.

120. See note 10, above.

July 14. Warm day. Went out to Gentrys. Genl Tipton arrived in the eve. Pleasant day.

July 15. Pleasant but warm day. John Hill helped get up our hay at McFarland place I think about 6 ton—got in 4 load.

Saturday July 16. Mr. Boxley came down. I received a letter from Mr. Baldwin that Oakley had accepted the draft drawn by Teall & Sprague for $5000. A very warm day. Stoughton is preparing to go East.

I went with Mr. Boxley to the McF. place & help[ed] rake up the last of the north field of hay.

Sunday July 17 1836. Very warm. S. & I took a walk in the morning. Mr. Vorus left here on yesterday the little child very sick. I do not think it will live. I went to church in the A.M. Heard Mr. Smith preach.

We have had a great deal of company to day. I dislike to have calls on Sunday—a day I desire to rest uninterrupted. Mr. Whitcomb called (surveyer). I read some in Longs Expedition up the St. Peters.[121] Mrs. F. & myself counseled on the propriety of her going home with Stoughton. We have not determined. I took my chair & set under our apple tree in the garden platt. It has been very warm.

Monday July 18 1836. Rose this morning after sun rise. Have been uncommonly sleepy for several days past. This morning has every appearance of being followed with a very hot day. I wish to prepare for a visit to Terre Hautte by Lafayette &c. James getting up hay. The little child of Mrs. V. no better. I think it will die. Warm day. The little child died about ½ after 12. The mother wished to have it buried in our grave yard that is in our platt.[122] Accordingly the grave was dug in the N. E. corner of the square—I expect it will be again removed. Mr. Vorus the father is absent on duty as an engineer on the Evansvill route.

Received a letter stating that the draft drawn by Messrs. Teall &

121. Stephen H. Long headed an expedition to explore the St. Peter's (Minnesota) River in 1823. W. H. Keating, a member of the expedition, prepared the *Narrative of an Expedition to the Sources of the St. Peter's River . . . 1823* (2 volumes, 1824).

122. The Marion County deed records show that on February 8, 1834, Isaac Coe conveyed to C.F. lot 10 in the "new graveyard" for the consideration of $16.00. See Pt. IV, note 12.

Sprague on Mr. Oakley of N.Y. was accepted & we enclosed another Draft for $5600 payable 60 days.

Mr. Alvy Buckingham[123] of the house of Buckingham & Co. arrived from Ill. where he has been investing money in land. He for the company agreed to & did furnish drafts to the amount of $8000. to be invested by Mr. McCarty & myself. We are to divid[e] the profits any time within 5 years allowing them 6 per cent. Company liable for incidental expenses. Mr. McC. went to Greenfield to invest &c.

July 19. Teusday. We this day at 9 had a collection of friends to help bury Mrs. Vorus little child—8 carriges. Mr. McC[. . .] delivered an address. Very warm. Our family all went to the grave. This is the 2 time that death has entered our house. In 1832 Mr. Sweets little girl died & was buried at the Cox place.

July 20 1836 Wedensday. John Hill started West to look for a location for a store & Mr. Butler to Lafayette Covington Terre Haute &c. Pleasant day.

Thu[r]sday [July] 21. Pleasant day nothing new. Town in a great bustle full of strangers.

Friday [July] 22. Col. Blanding[124] from S. Carolina was introduced by H. Porter. He is right from the convention of dellegates at Knoxville Tenn. for the purpose deliberating on the best means to accomplish the great Southern railway from Cincinnati to Charleston. He has been surveying the passes thro' the mountainous parts. Is about to move to Madison with his family & relatives. I found him a very intelligent man formerly from Mass.

Saturday [July] 23d. This day pleasant. Had a little rain yesterday. Michael went to Gentrys. One of the Mr. Boxleys here after corn & bacon. Sold the Thornton lot (Wick & myself) as commissioner for about $1600.

123. Alva Buckingham (1791–1867), successful Ohio merchant and businessman. In 1851 he and R. P. Burlingame built the first grain elevator in Chicago and later extensive grain warehouses. He moved to New York City in 1865. *Biographical and Historical Memoirs of Muskingum County, Ohio* (Chicago: The Goodspeed Publishing Co., 1892), pp. 403–405.

124. Col. Abram or Abraham Blanding, of Columbia, South Carolina, a lawyer who was also interested in banking and railroads. He died of yellow fever in 1839 at the age of fifty-three. Edwin L. Green, *A History of Richland County* (Columbia, S.C.: R. L. Bryan Co., 1932), p. 610.

A Mr. Garret from Philadelphia called left a note on Decker for collection. Town full of strangers. Cooley & Elijah went to Morris Morris to a party. It began Raining. Col. Blandin[g] called this morning & gave me a number of documents of his own productions. I was invited out to Govr. Nobles with him & the Supreme [Court] Judges.

I went to bed at 9 & it began to rain soon after I retired.

Sunday [*July*] *24* [–25]. It rains. The crops have suffered much for rain.

At 8 Mr Quarles called to ride with me a piece on the way but as the mail had not come in we rode to Isaac Wilson old mill & returned by the P.O. for my papers &c then he & myself rode together as far as Rookers old place.[125] He returned & I went ahead for Andersontown for the double purpose of bying Irish's land laying near the town & to lay off a few lots in conjunction with R. N. Williams.

It was cloudy day. I arrived within 3 miles of Pendleton about sun ½ hour high when in consequence of threatened rain I stopped at C. Crosslys—took tea &c. started about dusk for P. Arrived—staid at Bostons. Mr. Bond clock pedler & a gentleman of fine estate & good talents also came in. It rained all night. Next morning went to the Fall Creek Mills owned by J. Irish to inspect a pair of gravestones to be erected at the grave of my lamented friend Ansel Richmond. Upon a proposition to Mr. Irish to buy 250 acres of land adjoining to & E. of Andersontown on which Jacksons mill stands ½ m. from A. he was to meet me there in a short time.

I rode to A. It continued to rain. Arrived there at 9. Saw Jackson & Williams relative to the intended purchase. I proposed to Williams to have a public meeting on the subject of a mail stage from Indianapolis *via* Noblesville Strawtown Andersontown Munsey Randolph county seat Greenvill to Bellfont [Bellefontaine, Ohio] to intersect the Railroad from Dayton to Sandusky. He was taken with the idea & it is agreed for me to go to Noblesville to get up a meeting. It is a gloomy wet day. I bot the Irish property at

125. William D. Rooker, who entered the west half of the southwest quarter of section 17, T16N, R4E, in Washington Township, Marion County. Sulgrove, *History of Indianapolis*, p. 631.

$2000.[126] ½ down ¼ in 1 year ¼ in 2 year—without interest. This is bought on the joint account of Buckingham & co Mr. McCarty & myself. They furnish us $8000. & we lay it out divided the profits after sale in 5 years. This I view as a safte purchase. Andersontown has a printing press 2 taverns 3 Stores &c at this time.

Mr. A. D. Bond arrived here in the eve. I agreed to start with him to Strawtown early in the morn.

Teusday July 26. Mr. Bond & I left A. at sunrise. Breakfasted at Danl. Wise. Saw a man there with a ¼ Durham Bull 6 mos. old asked $30. for him. We arrived at Strawtown at 10 o'clock. Found B. Cole & J. D. Stephenson laying off lots &c. Dined here. Disclosed the mail stage business to those gentlemen. They agreed to have a meeting called at Noblesvill on Tuesday next &c. I left S. & arrived at home at sundown. Pleasant day.

Wednesday 27 July. Our board of Directors of St. B. met. Col. Jenners Morgan Ft. W[ayne] Leeds R[ichmond] Major L. Scott & Farrington T[erre] H[aute] Ewing V[incennes] Owen Ev[ansville] Blythe In[dianapolis] Leeds & Morrison Richmond.[127] We agreed to accept the deposits under late act of Congress &c. Important session. The question & a serious one was agitated whether under the late order of the President to take nothing but gold & silver from non residents in payment for lands we should take our own paper from the Receivers &c.[128] I voted to take it &c.

126. The Madison County deed records show warranty deeds were filed on August 17, 1837, for 40 acres in section 31, T20N, R7E, and 125 acres in section 18, T19N, R8E, conveyed by James M. Irish to C.F. and McCarty for the sum of $2,000; the deeds were recorded June 8, 1838. The 125 acres lay on the east side of the town of Anderson.

127. William M. Jenners, Joseph Morgan, Noah Leeds, Daniel J. Major, Lucius H. Scott, James Farrington, John Ewing, William Owens, Benjamin I. Blythe, and Robert Morrisson.

128. A reference to the Specie Circular issued by the United States Treasury Department on July 11, 1836, providing that after August 15 only gold and silver would be accepted at the land offices in payment for public lands, except that actual settlers in the states where sales were held could use paper money until December 15, 1836. The measure checked land speculation and hastened the Panic of 1837. *Dictionary of American History*, V, 143.

On December 21, 1836, C.F. wrote John Tipton that "the full operation of the Circular has commencd—our canal hands here refuse to take any of our state paper except such as is on our branch that they can go & draw the specie—our pecuniary prospects look gloomy—I hope you will see clearly your duty

Col. Kinnard member of Congress arrived. Our approaching election produces very little heat.

Thursday July 28, 1836. Our Bank Session is yet continued. Messrs. Noble (Govr.) & Morrison (Wm.) with Mrs. Vorus, McDougal (the old lady) Mrs. Morrison Mrs. Richmond took tea. James Hill put up a stack of hay. Michael & Gentry finished putting up the oats on the Block. Pleasant day.

Friday July 29. James Hill finished putting up hay on Sanders place. Cloudy wet in the P.M. Mr. McCarty bought for him & me Dr. McClures place for $7500—$2500 down the rest in 1 & 2 years without int. I may be mistaken but think that it is only a tolerable bargain.

Saturday July 30, 1836. This day our town is crowded with people from the county to see a show of wild annimals Circus &c. From 1500 to 2000 lads & lasses—well dressed & of a far better appearance than in years past. Our population has almost changed in the last 4 years past.[129] A pleasent day H. O Neel returned from Andersontown having been up to see that my lots are rightly laid off.

I sold my interest in the ¼ of a lot bot at the sale of Thornton lot for 40 acres of land in Hamilton County. Pleasant day. Our office crowded with business. I have concluded from this time to decline all business of my profession so far as I can. In the eve I went with Car[o]line Patrick & Martha to the evening circus on lot near Norwoods Shop[130] St. West of Meridian N. of Washington. Pleasant eve at least 1500. present very warm. The horsemanship poor. Swinging on rope, tumbling &c. very good at least new. The circus is loosing its charms to me. At first I was much taken

---

to go in for restoring the old order of things in relation to the currancy. . . . you mentioned to me some time last summer that things never wd be right again until another national Bank, another monster came into existence. I now believe it." *John Tipton Papers*, III, 330–31.

129. Actually the growth of Indianapolis was rather slow. In 1827 the population was reckoned at 1,066 (525 white males, 479 white females, 34 colored males, 24 colored females). In 1835 the population had increased to 1,683 (859 white males, 743 white females, 81 colored of both sexes). By 1840 the total population was 2,662 (1,329 white males, 1,211 white females, and 122 colored). Dunn, *Indianapolis*, I, 94, 99, 100.

130. The shop of George Norwood, wagon maker, who came to Indianapolis in March, 1822. Nowland, *Early Reminiscences of Indianapolis*, pp. 152–53.

with it. We returned at 11. Mrs. F. had gone to set up with Mr. Wilkins child.

Michael & Mr. Gentry went out to D. Fletchers for Rye to sow block &c.

Sunday morning July 31 1836. Mr. Whitcomb called. I went to see Mr. Hass[?] & several from Laport at Browns tavern &c. Pleasant morning. James & Wm. Hill called. I wrote to Elijah my brother. Did not go to church. Read review of Dr. Rays political Economy & an Essay on the English Bar.[131] Mr. McCarty called. We are very much concerned about the conduct of Dr. Todd in relation to a deed to the Michigan City property—fear we shall not get a deed from him to a part. Mr. Wilkins child very sick. Mrs. F. staid there last night. Judge Hume[132] called. Election tomorrow. Pleasant day. Our Blue plumbs beginning to get ripe.

Monday Augt. 1st 1836. Cloudy morning. I have been looking over the amount of business I have to close in order to get out of my profession decently & the amount of other business to be attended to. It almost gives me *the hippo.* I visited Mr. John Wilkins family early in the morning. Found their eldest son 4 years [old] had died about 2 o'clock in the morn. The funeral hour was set at ½ after 4 P.M. I went to the grave yard. Mr. Blythe had gone before me. I called on Preacher Smith to attend. At 9 o'clock our town was crowded in consequence of the election & the circus. I saw T. J. Evans just returned from the East. Mrs. F. & Mrs. Vorus went to Mr. Blakes to dine. Took tea at John G. Browns.

At ½ 4 attended the funeral. Went to the grave yard. Rather still election. Can't say how it has resulted—But suppose A. W. Morris is elected one of the Representatives & that Hume is the Sheriff but who the other Representative I cannot tell.[133]

131. The January, 1835, number of the *North American Review* contained a review of John Rae, *Statement of Some New Principles on the Subject of Political Economy* (Boston, 1834), and the April, 1836, number a review of *The Legal Professions in England. The Sixth Report of the Common Law Commissioners on the Inns of Court* (London, 1834).

132. John C. Hume, probate judge of Marion County, 1829–36. He was a candidate for sheriff at the August, 1836, election.

133. Austin W. Morris and Robert Hanna were elected to represent Marion County in the General Assembly. Others who ran were Alexander F. Morrison, A. B. Strong, and W. Rector. Corson Vickers was elected sheriff over John C.

Went with Mrs. F. after dark to James Hills to see William who is sick. It has been a pleasant day.

Augt. 2d. Rose at 4 to assist Mrs. Vorus in taking leave for Evansvill. I saw 3 stages start one West Terre Haute—East Lawrenceburgh—& one South for Bloomington. I am to leave today for Madison County in company with Mr. Henderson. I am going to sell some lots at Andersontown.

A very pleasant cool morning. Michael & Gentry going to put in some Rye on the stable block. Cloudy in A.M. James Hill overtook Mr. H. & myself & I got him to go with us to Andersontown. We arrived at Arnets at 2 dined & went to Pendleton. Stayed over night.

Wedensday Aug. 3d. Left P. early & went to A. to breakfast. Very warm day. Sold 10 lots—av[e]raged about $33. each.

Thursday [Aug.] 4. Sold 3 lots more to Mechanics with a stipulation that if they erect a house in 6 mos. to give the 1st payment &c.

Went to Jacksons mill. Henderson went down the River to Noblesville. At 4 P.M. Hill & myself proceeded down the East side of the Prarie via Huntsvill to Pendleton. Stayed over night at Bostons.

Friday Augt. 5. We rose found it raining. Waited a while—started. It rained. Stopped at Saul Shauls.[134] Rain slacked. Went [to] Arnets. It rained & we concluded not to travel further as we must get very wet & we were unprovided with umbrellas & big coats &c. I read the Family magazine & spent the P.M. usefully & profitably.

Saturday Augt. 6. We left Arnets in the morning about 8 & proceeded homeward. Went by Danl. Smiths—arrived home about 2 P.M. Found our citzen[s] in a rage about the determination of Capt. Ogden who is superintendent on the Nat[ional] Road that he would not expend any of the appropriation of 2 hundred & fifty thousand dollars on the R. in this vicinity. I attended the meeting & was instrumental in having Col. Kinnard appointed a dellegate

---

Hume, Thomas Weaver, and Andrew Smith. Indianapolis *Indiana Journal,* August 6, 1836; *Indiana Election Returns,* p. 230.

134. One of the first settlers of Fall Creek Township, Madison County. Netterville (comp.), *Centennial History of Madison County,* I, 271–72.

to solicit Capt. O. to change his determination. I was appointed with others to address Genl. Gratiott[135] & Genl. Jackson on the subject.

Sunday Augt. 7. Rains all day. Did not go to church. John Walker & an old Mr. Thompson called to see about renting the Shelby mills. There is nothing so interrupts my happiness as to have people call on me on Sunday & I long to have the day come when such a custom will be entirely discountenanced.

Monday Augt. 8. Mr. Butler is at Shelby probate court. I have been trying to right my business in my office. Cloudy day.

Teusday Aug. 9. Pleasant. Nothing new. Our damson plumbs are getting ripe. Mrs. F. commencing making preserves &c. Wild ripe plumbs brot to market.

[*Aug.*] *10.* Left at 7 with Mr. Quarles. Left for Shelby to rent the mills to old Mr. Thompson. I dreaded this Journey for several reasons—one is I fear that I persuaded McCarty to take an interest in this property against his own judgment and on my recommendation—that we shall find it a bad bargain tho' this depends on circumstances. Shelbyvill looks bad—no public spirit—merchants are of the poorer kind. Very warm day. Met Mr. Butler at Brandywine. I arrived at S. at 2. Bargained with old Mr. Thompson to have the Mills 3 years at $500. per ann. to put $200 of improvements &c. The dam will cost us more than $500. I talked with John Walker as to the propriety laying off some new lots near the mills—I shall write to him on the subject.

Augt. 11. Left Shelby after Breakfast. Arrived home at 3 P.M. The Bank requested that a note on Col. Sigler & others of Greencastle should be collected & I sent Simon who left next morning.

Aug. 12. Nothing new. Went to Gentrys he is cutting oats with Pouge [Pogue].

Augt. 13 Saturday. I rose before light & started from [for] the Bluffs with Mr. McCarty. We arri[ve]d at McGrews at 8. We found the fruit trees breaking down. There will be 1000 of peaches. Very warm day. We are sorry to say that Mr. McGrew has not done much towards filling his contract. At 3 P.M. we left. Very warm.

135. Gen. Charles Gratiot, chief engineer of the Army.

Arrived at home at sundown. Found John Hill who had returned on Thursday violently attacked with a fever & that a young Williams an engine[e]r was about dying tho it is a general time of health. Danl. Wise calld to see about his land suits &c.

Sunday Augt. 14. Cloudy in the morning. John Hill dangerously ill—I fear his condition is critical. No methodist church today meeting house is under repair.

During the last week the Presbyterian Church has been occupied every day. Dr. Mathews a distinguished preacher has been here. Much good I believe has been done. Messrs. Blythe Merrill & others will no doubt unite with the church.

This day cloudy & warm. Stoughton Mariah & Ingram have the hooping cough. Richardson Cooley Elijah Miles went out to the Fletcher farm horseback. A shower came in their absence.

Read a review of Lord Broughams natural Theology in N.R. [North American Review] &c. Went to hear (with Michael) a stranger at Presbyterian Meeting house preach funeral address &c to the Sabbath school.

Mrs. F. & J. Hill set up with John.

Augt. Monday 15. Cloudy. John Hill seems to be better. We have killed a cat for destroying our chickhens. Brot our hogs out of the Block to commence fatting.

Aug. 16. Pleasent day. Uncle M. went to Gentrys to bind oats. Wilk Reagin Butcher & Justice of the peace one of our first setlers run off last night with his miss in a carriage leaving the Govr. & sundry citizens in trouble. He has been well known as a vulgar low bred man & those who have given him countenance are not to be pittied.

Monday Augt. 22 1836. On Teusday the 16. After dinner I walked down to my office in the hot sun & soon after that I felt the approaching attack of the billious fever & so stated it & after walking to the lower part of the town with Mr. McCarty to see the lot East of Sloan's, I returned sick & went to bed. Took medicine at 8 o'clock.

Augt. 17. Sick confined to bed. Took more medicine. Several calls on business. Got rid of them as well as possible. Among them Revs. J. Havens & Smith Mrs. Paxton McCarty Ray &c.

Augt. 18 1836. Last night very warm. Slept with window & door open. Yet sick but Dr. Richmond is getting my fever *under.* Pleasant day I believe

Our Peaches begin to ripen. We have a fine peach from those 3 trees I bo't of old Mr. J. Givans. Cooler than yesterday.

Friday Augt. 19. Better—begin to set up a little. Pleasant day. Many calls among them Mr. Quarles. Simon started yesterday for Montazuma on the Wabash.

[*Aug.*] 20 *Saturday.* Better but troubled with cold feet for the first time in my life. Read my newspapers. Judge Scott[136] of Madison stopped. Read report of the Nashvill Rail R[oad] convention.

Sunday [*Aug.*] *21.* Pleasent day. Dr. Boxley here. Wants to get goods of Mr. McCarty who is troubled with a sore hand. Dr. B. I think a clever fellow but slow & poking—no energy.

All went to church in P.M. but Mrs. F. & self & John Hill who is yet in bed—but better. Got my Intelligencer of the 13 instant. I believe no further war between Texas & Mexico this summer or year. I think Vanburans prospects good for election to the Presidency but I have determined to vote against him & go for my country. I believe the government whose principles he says he will perpetuate, is vastly corrupt.

Monday Ag. 22. Cloudy cool. I feel most too timid to go out but want to get down town today. Went down. Am a little better. Mr. Quarles called. Pleasent day—rained a little & cool. Billy Orford bro't me 2 pigs—very fat. John Mathews & Judge Mathews[137] called.

Tusday Augt. 23. Cloudy & a little wet—but pleasant. I have the hick coughs very bad for the last 2 days. Have tried various remedies. Went to the office in P.M. I feel that my business is suffering for want of attention. The Walkers came with a bill for the Shelbyvill Mills of $240. I fear this is a bad concern. Judge Polk is in. James Hill & the boys went to Gentrys after apples &c.

Wedensday Augt. 24. Pleasent morning. I am better. Must go to buseness today. I feel that my business is in great confusion. We

136. James Scott, probate judge, Madison County. *Indiana Executive Proceedings,* p. 510.

137. John Matthews and Hiram Matthews of Morgan County. A sketch of the latter is in Major, *The Pioneers of Morgan County,* p. 433.

have ripe peaches or rather unripe ones bro't to market in great abundance. Our camp meeting commences tomorrow. I have began work again—I have much to do. Mr. McCarty & myself bot lot of John Mathews for $1000. on the Lee Dater account. Simon returned from Rockvill. Had seen Genl. Howard & has given me his opinion as to what constitutes a great man—that is a rigid unostentatious discharge of every duty belonging, or attaching, to the station of the individual.

Augt. 25 [–*29*] *1836*. At our camp meeting held on the 26–7–8–9 &c there were many assembled—Revs. Messrs. Havens & brother Smith Tevis[?] Rahl[?] &c present. Great excitement & many added to the church. The camp ground N.W. of the state house in a beutiful grove on the public ground.[138] Very dry dusty &c. No rains for near a month. From the time of the commencement of our C. meeting I was on the recovery from my sickness & preparing to go with A. Harrison to Laport [and] Ill. &c to see Dr. Todd to get deed for land Mr. McC. & my self sold in June to Messrs. S. & T. [Sprague and Teall] After selling [we] learned that we had not a complete claim of title.[139]

Sept. 6 1836. Teusday. Mr. H. & myself set out cold & cloudy. Rode to Mrs. Johnsons Michigan town.

Sept. 7 Weds. Rode to Logansport. Saw Mr. Pratt Genl. Tipton &c. I delivered to Mr. Taber 12 thousand doll. Sent by our bank to canal commissioner.

Thurs. Sept. 8. Left town in company of Genl. Tipton who rode a short distance with me also Mr. Jackson (Wm. J.) [who] was on his way to Blackhawks purchase to make claims in a 1 horse waggon. I left my umbrella & coat by mistake at Logansport & he supplied me with the former & Judge Polk with the latter. It

138. The Indianapolis *Indiana Journal*, September 3, 1836, reporting on the camp meeting (which was held in what is now Military Park), said that it was estimated that between six and seven thousand were in attendance at the Sunday session and about 130 "embraced religion" during the entire meeting. Another camp meeting was held at the same time six or eight miles west of Indianapolis. In his diary on June 12, 1859, C.F. recalled that the Burkhart "chain gang" (see above, p. 323) had disturbed the meeting in Military Park. The story is told in an article written by C.F. which appeared in the Indianapolis *Indiana Journal*, June 17, 1859.

139. See note 10 and entry for June 13, 1836, above.

rained. We arrived at J. P. (Judge Polke's?) at 3 dined & rode to S. Williams.

Friday Sept. 9. Left Laport with A. W. Harrison for the Falls of the Kankake to see Dr. Todd. We went around for fear of difficulty &c. I[t] was wet cold day but no frost yet. We passed thro' the county seat of Porter 5 or 6 houses only built. We arrived at Salt River the house of Ben McCarty after dark. Staid over night.

Sunday Sept. 10 1836. Left McCartys & rode to Robinsons prarie[140] thro an unsettled country mostly prarie where we arrived at 11. Found all the people plowing & harrowing &c all infidels. First thing I had ever seen on Sunday. Left Clarks where we dined & went to Wilkinson 13 ms. where we arrived within 1½ mile of the West line of the State—dirty place to stay.

Sept. 11. Left early & crossed into Ill. where we breakfasted at the Island below the lower crossing of the Kankakee where we breakfasted at one McGibbins. But 2 or 3 houses in the vicinity land not in market nor none of the country we passed after we left McCartys.

It rained. Here we met with t[w]o Granger County men (Ohio) wishing to buy out the settlers &c a beautiful cty [country?]. At 1 we left & proceeded down the K. 12 mil[e]s S. side & crossd over to Dr. Todds. Very wet. Staid over night & much to my gratification we got him to perfect a title to the Michigan [City] land & left his right with Mr. H. to be contested[?].

Sept. 12. Left Dr. T. early in the morn proceeded up the N. side of the River to the place we breakfasted the day before. Pleasant day. After Breakfast we retraced our steps back to Clarks where we staid over night.

Sept. 13 [–14]. We left Clarks & rode to Portersvill. Here Mr. H. & I parted. I did some business & rode to Mrs. Hammonds at

140. Named for Solon Robinson who left Madison, Indiana, in 1834 with the expectation of locating on the Door Prairie in La Porte County. Finding the land there largely taken up, he entered land in the present Lake County, thirty-five miles southwest of Michigan City. He described his new location in letters to the Madison *Republican and Banner* in 1834 and 1835, which are reprinted in Herbert A. Kellar (ed.), *Solon Robinson. Pioneer and Agriculturist* (2 volumes. *Indiana Historical Collections,* XXI, XXII, Indianapolis: Indiana Historical Bureau, 1936, 1937), I, 51–64. Through his letters to agricultural periodicals in the East, Robinson attracted settlers to the prairie regions of northern Indiana.

Topeneba lake. Stayed over night & on the 14 rode to Michigan City 18 miles. Got very wet. Arrived there at 2 P.M. Stopped at Mosses. Mr. Teall absent. Met with Messrs. Sprague & Dr. Cobb from Va. &c. Staid over night—place full of Stage passengers.

Sept. 15. Friday [*Thurs.*]. After selling J. M. Rays interest in 3 acres of land for $2500. to Dr. Cobb & Mr. McCartys & my interest amounting to 30 acres in 3 tracts of land near Michigan City to Mr. Sprague conditionally to be confirmed by Mr Teall on his return for $5750. payable in 20, 60 & 100 days at N.Y. Mr. Harrison who had met me there (Alfred) we rode in the rain to Laport.

Sept. 16 1836. Mr. H. & I left for S. Bend after Breakfast. Arrived there at Sundown. Done some business. Went to bed &c. Fine crops in this vicinity. No frost yet.

Sept. 18 Sunday morning. Left after Breakfast. Pleasant in A.M. but rained in the P.M. Dined at Yallow River. There many of the Potwatme tribes passed us going to payment.

After dinner rode [to] S. Williams. Staid over night.

Sept. 19 [–20]. Started early & rode to Judge Polks. It rained very hard. Breakfasted. Thence to Logansport. Rained most of the way. Staid over night at L. & on the 20 started after breakfast & rode to Deer Ck. 10 miles on as bad a rode as ever I passed. We met many waggons movers with familes—on going out we met 50 waggons coming in & met as many on our return going out.

We dined at Stocktons & thence to Mrs. Johnsons.

Sept. 21. We left Mrs. Johnsons in the morning & arrived at Indianapolis thro' a constant rain Sun 1 hour high found all well.

Stoughton my brother arrived with his wife[141] & Michaels daughter on the day we left home.

During my absence I had most excellent health & spirits. I mention this as before I left for some days I was nearly dissolved from the hypocondria from doing business having just recovered from a sever[e] turn of sickness & much of my business pressed upon me. Apprehensions that I should be straightened in my pecuniary matters distressed me & the great likelihoods that I should meet with a great loss in consequence of Dr. Todds refusing to

141. Stoughton Fletcher married Maria Kipp, of Newark, New York, niece of his bother-in-law Joseph Miller.

make Mr. H. a deed &c agrevated my physical debility. I desire more controle over myself—a conquest that grace alone can obtain over a heart prone to evil greatly deceitful & entwined around the things of this world. In my absence I had I trust some profitable reflections on this subject & thro' the assisting mercy of God I hope some resolves I have made may place my feet on better ground.

[*Sept. 27–Oct. 1*]. Mrs. Fletcher & myself went to the Bluffs on Tuesday the 27 Sept. a very pleasant day. Dined at Mrs. Davis & returned [in] the eve. Got home late. The next & the subsequent part of the week pleasent & I was engaged in writing my address for the 2d Agricultural fair in M[arion] C[ounty] which I had been appointed to deliver on the 7 & 8th *proximo*. Mr. Butler absent at Madison court.

On the first of Octr. pleasant day. Mr. McCarty & myself went to the Bluffs to sell some lots in pursuance of a previous advertisement.[142] A pleasant [day]. We arrived there about 9 o clock. Many people assembled but we did not sell any lots at public sale in consequence of the Canal Commissioner refusing to let the section under the Bluffs.[143] We returned the same eve & I found my old friend Thos. Stretch & family on their way to Ohio.

Sunday Octr. 2d. Rainy day. Mr. Stretch & family left. I went to church. Mr. Whitcomb called.

142. The advertisement was carried in the Indianapolis *Indiana Journal*, September 10, 17, and 24, 1836. Signed by N. McCarty and C. Fletcher, it announced for sale on October 1, a number of lots at Port Royal, Morgan County. It described the town on the Bluffs above White River as "handsomely situated on that part of the Central Canal which will be placed under contract two days after the proposed sale," and well located on two state highways with a ferry across the river. The advertisement mentioned good stone quarries nearby as a source for building materials and also the good quality of the soil. The Central Canal, of course, was never completed and Port Royal never developed. When the canal was surveyed and some work actually was begun on the channel and feeder dam, the little town of Waverly became the center of action for the brief period of construction which extended from 1837 to 1839. Major, *Pioneers of Morgan County*, pp. 413–15.

143. Jesse L. Williams, canal engineer, reported to the State Board of Internal Improvement, December 13, 1836, that the line of the Central Canal at Port Royal had not been fully located. To avoid the expense of constructing a canal along the bluff it had been proposed to pass it by means of slack water formed in the river by a dam at the lower end of the bluff, and the letting of contracts for this section had been suspended until the necessary examinations in regard to this could be made. Indiana *Senate Journal*, 1836–37, p. 152.

Monday Octr. 3d. Not very pleasant. Many Strangers in town at canal letting. Snowed a little for the first [time].

4 Octr. Cannal letting [causing] much anxiety by the bidders. Most of our citizens have put in but mostly have made high bids & [blank].[144]

Oct. 5. We learn that but few of our citizens have received canal contracts. Andrew Smith & Wilson[145] have contract. The place for the canal thro' town the lock Basin water power &c designated. We have had every other day rain—a very unpropitious season to put in wheat.

6 Octr. Wet & foggy.

7 [*Octr.*] *Friday.* Pleasant. Our fair commenced & we had a very handsome display of cattle & horses & many specimens of domestic manufactures. Much interest excited at our 2d Annual fair. But we had to regret that there were not any hogs brot on except 1. But we had some very fine cattle exhibited.

Saturday Octr. 8. We [had] this day a ploughing match on the block directly N. of the capitol. John Johnson Israel Harding & a Mr. Ingold competitors—the first took the prize.[146] At one o'clock the the court house was crowded with ladies & gentlemen & after some preliminaries I delivered an address. After the premiums declared an auction was had which excited much interest. The address is to be published.[147] I do not feel particularly disgusted

144. The Indianapolis *Indiana Journal,* August 6, 1836, carried a notice signed by David H. Maxwell, president of the State Board of Internal Improvements, that proposals would be received at Indianapolis on October 4 by David Burr, commissioner, for construction of twenty-five miles of the Central Canal from the feeder dam above Indianapolis (Broad Ripple) to "the Bluffs."

145. The Indianapolis *Indiana Journal,* October 15, 1836, reported Andrew Wilson was named contractor for section 23 of the Central Canal in Indianapolis, Elder & Smith for section 19, and James Smith for section 45.

146. While the Marion County Agricultural Society had voted as a prize a plough worth $9.00 (see note 112, above), John Johnson in later years recalled that the prize was supposed to be a ten dollar gold piece. Johnson won the contest but instead of receiving the gold piece, he said that he had been given a cast plow which had been manufactured in Indianapolis and was on exhibit. He was miffed at this and gave the plow to a bystander who said he would trade it off for a coon dog. Johnson, *A Home in the Woods,* p. 216.

147. The address was published in the *Indiana Farmer* on October 15, 1836, and in the Indianapolis *Indiana Journal,* October 22, 1836. C.F. pointed out that of the 256,000 acres comprising Marion County, on July 16, 1836, fifteen

with it neither do I feel particularly flattered. I have accepted this rule of action whenever I am called upon to perform any public duty where there is no party feeling in the selection, to comply to the best of my ability & never shrink from the performance.

Sunday Octr. 9. A dissagreeable cold misty day. I went to church heard a young man preach whose name I no [know] not.

Monday Octr. 10 Introduced to Dr. Foote from Chetaque Cty. N.Y. Mr. Carlisle also from Marlboro N.Y. who came with a letter of recommendation from Miles to Stoughton. He purchased the soap & candle factery from Messrs. Mears & Willits. He returned to N.Y. to prepare to move hither. He looks like a keen enterprising man—born in Ireland.[148] He gave $700. for 2 lots. Since the prospects of the public works, there is manifested a great disposition for every mechanic to move into town. Wages are high many wish to come in to waggon &c. The prospect is fair to make our place a great town. It is believed there are about 3000 inhabitants now & that there will be 5000 in 3 & 10000 in 10 years. How this will be I cannot say. Our fall thus far makes things look gloomy.

Teusday 11 Octr. Went to Fletcher farm & bot 3 cows 1 heifer of John Fletcher cows at $11 each heifer $4½. Yearling & a 2 year old steer for $8. of Mr. Johnson. J. F. was digging the potatos. I shall have about 25. bush. I have been puzzled to know how to dispose of these 2 farms. I could get $3000 for them that is the Cox place & my other farm west of it—But have thought it advisable to keep them at present. They do not more than pay for the annual improvements. I trust they will be more useful hereafter.

Every alternate day we have rain.

---

years after the first sale of land only eighty acres remained unsold. There were 2,560 individual owners of the soil. He spoke of the recent abundance of farm produce, but chided the farmers for their wasteful habits. He observed that many farms had no barns, much of the fencing was badly constructed, and much good land lay idle. Further there was generally a lack of new and improved machinery. He said that many farmers could manufacture at home many items which they purchased abroad, and he urged the reading of instructive agricultural papers and journals. The Agricultural Society, he felt, had had and would have much beneficial influence.

148. This is John Carlisle who while he engaged in soap and candle manufacture in Indianapolis also commenced successful distillery and dairy concerns. He then went into flour milling and won a national reputation with his brands of flour. Nowland, *Sketches of Prominent Citizens*, pp. 556–58.

Friday [*Oct.*] *14.* Went with J. Hill to the Fletcher farm divided my hay with David & John Fletcher. I have about 20 Tun for my part of good hay.

Saturday 15 Octr. Tolerably pleasant in the morning but snowed before night. Road very muddy. We learn that Mr. Storer of Cincinnati Whig candidate for Congress is beat by a Mr. Duncan 4 or 500 votes—But the other elections are tolerably fair for the Whigs as far as heard from.[149]

[*Oct.*] *16 Sunday.* Cloudy raw day.

Monday the 17 Octr. Mr. & Mrs. Holiday visit us—Mrs. F. & S.'s wife preparing house to move to—moved in the eve.

Teusday [*Oct.*] *18.* Snowed—covered the ground. I am looking a little to my next C[ircuit] C[ourt] Business—preparing a mortgage for 6 shares of bank stock. A dissagreeable stormy day. No further news of Ohio elections. Received a letter from bro' Miles stating that our sister L.'s health is very bad & that she probibly will not live long. I wrote Mr. Ingram. I am a little troubled about my pecuniary affairs—I fear I am growing a little indolent—that in retiring from the practise of law I shall fail in having the necessary excitement. I believe Mr. McCarty & myself ought to sell some of our land lots &c. My private concerns are a little embarrassed. I feel yet a kind of apathy that is not commendable. My precious time glides away without a good account. I have lounged some. Michael came up & spent the eve with me. He offerds me much satisfaction. A rainy eve.

Wedensday Morn 19 Octr. A very wet morning prospect very poor. Our potatoes & corn are out but we must be patient. It is all for the best. These vicisitudes in nature keep men right—sharpens their intellects & drives them to expedients—elicits their best faculties. I am this day going to urge J. M. Ray to settle McC. & my books.

Octr. 19 Weds. I wrote a letter to J. Conrad the Secretary of Mad[ison] County Agricultural Society in answer to one notifying me of my appointment as an honorary member at their late annual

149. Alexander Duncan, a Van Buren man, defeated Bellamy Storer, a Whig, in the election in Ohio's First Congressional District. The Whigs carried eleven of the nineteen districts in Ohio. Cincinnati *Whig and Commercial Intelligencer*, October 22, 1836.

meeting. It commenced raining in the morning. I went to my office. I had some conversation with Quarles about going to Mo. next winter. He advises me not to run for Congress. I returned to dinner. It continued raining & rained all the P.M. so much so that after I read the N.Y. Ev. Star I concluded not to go to my office—I spent in reading N[orth] A[merican] R[eview].

In the eve I was very Sleepy at ½ after 7 & went to bed. This drowsyness came from eating too much supper. I intend to avoid this hereafter. Continued raining till midnight. I lay awake from 12 to 2.

Octr. 20 Thursday. Cleared off cold. Water froze in vessels out doors a little. No harvesting done yet my potatoes not dug. The streams are all up. I fear the potatoes & apples have suffered with frost. In the P.M. I done but very little that in errands. Made a mortgage to secure 6 shares of bank stock. Jo. Moore returned from Cincinnati Wilks Reagin released from jail. Received a letter from Baldwin N.Y. Mrs. Hannerman very sick—Mrs. F there. Jno. Hill has concluded not to go down the River if I can get McCartys store lately kept by Frasee. Judge Powel[150] from Shelby here & I indorsed a bill for $1000 with H. Bates &c. I bot a breeding sow of Reagin weighing about 2 cwt. for $8. white, 1 year old. Wrote to John Hamilton [of] Urbana.

Mrs. Hannerman very sick—I fear she will not get well. Uncle M. & Mrs. R. called in the eve.

Frid. 21 Octr. This day secured 6 shares of Bank stock & assigned it in trust to S. A. Fletcher. Mrs. F. & I dined at S.'s for the first time since they commenced Keeping house. Mr. Beeson called to see about his & Raridens land. It Froze so last night that it did not thaw in the shade all day. Very cool but sun shines. Set on arbitration with Cobern on Mrs. Givans business. Settled with O. Gentry &c. Read the review of Storys Eulogy on the life of Marshall (N.R.).[151]

Sat. [Oct.] 22. Rose at 5. E. made fire. Gentry called & modified

150. Erasmus Powell, who served as probate judge of Shelby County from 1829 to 1835. *Indiana Executive Proceedings*, p. 598.

151. Joseph Story's *A Discourse upon the Life, Character and Service of the Hon. John Marshall* was reviewed in the January, 1836, issue of the *North American Review*.

his contract. Sent & got the cow I lent him & calf. Cold tho' sun shines pleasant. J.P. election Weaver, Hand, Josh. Stevens[152] candidates. The rabble for the former & he [was] elected as a matter of course. Indiscriminate a Course [curse] to our country precipitating it forward to the awful precipice *anarchy, then* a military despotism to ensue, neither of which in my opinion is so far distant as is supposed by many of intelligent & observing men. I run about trying to settle old Mrs. Givans business. Received a letter [from] L. R. Cahill [?] in London on subject Pottawattemy mill property near Rochester Ia. Rev. Mr. Wiley put up with us for conferance. Cool night but weather a little moderated. Things wear rather a gloomy aspect. Simon starts on Monday for the Wabash to collect a debt of Govr. Wallace $800. from N.Y. City.

Sunday Octr. 23. Rose at 5. Calvin got up at 4. Br. Wiley preached. Rather smokey in A.M. Grows warm. In the eve heard the late Station preacher from Mad[ison]. Messrs. Quarls & Butler gone to Franklin.

Mond. [*Oct.*] *24.* Pleasant smoky day—Simon at 4 in the morn came for a horse to go with Jno. Griffith to Delphi to see David Wallace.

A circus or caravan is announced in town. I assisted Mr. Cobern in adjusting the Givan claims &c. Mr. Boxley (A.B.) came down. Old Mr. Fletcher & son & Steph. Wood killed the cow. Uncle Michail digging potatoes—got very angry for the first time to my knowledge. We learn that the Vanburan ticket in Penn. has succeeded. He will be our next President & I fear the integrity of the union.

Tusd. 25 Octr. I rose at 4. Cloudy morn but pleasant day.

Weds. [*Oct.*] *26.* Pleasant day. Conference commenced. Bro' Havens called took supper &c. Mr. Butler returned from Franklin.

Thursday [*Oct.*] 27. Genl. Howard called at the office &c.

Friday [*Oct.*] *28 1836.* John F. Wright from Cincinnati book agent put up with us. We have a full house Mrs. Prather Mr. Crumbaugh Rev. Mr. Wiley & Wright. Rev. Mr. Beck supped with us. Michael finished digging his potatoes & went with his hands out to the Gentry place. Hill with the waggon.

152. Thomas M. Weaver, Charles J. Hand, and Joshua Stevens.

In the eve Mr. Ray & I commenced making up the account of McCarty & Fletcher.

Saturday [*Oct.*] *29*. House full. Old Mr. Pavy[?] & son calld. Mr. Ray wants me to go & examine the [New] Albany & Madison & Lawrenceburg banks. I was this day called to address the Meth. Conferance on the subject of the eligibility of Indianapolis as a suitable point for a university in comparison with Greencastle, Putnamvill & Rockville.[153] I was calld unexpectedly to perform this unpleasant task & was very much disgusted with my own performance. Bishop Roberts presided.[154]

Sunday [*Oct.*]*30* Pleasant. House full—Mr. Crumbaugh Pavy[?] & Mrs. Prather leave & Mr. Jessup & another arrived. Bishop Roberts preached in the A.M. C. Ruter in the P.M. & in the eve Mr. Wright—house crowded.

Octr. 31. Monday. Pleasant. Michael & 2 hands & Jim Hill digging my potatos at Gentry place.

Called a meeting to increase Judge Morris sallary to $1200. & house rent $200.[155] Examined the mortgages taken to secure stock at Bedford with Ray. In the eve in company with Messrs. Blak[e] [and] Hannerman assisted in counting the mony at our bank. This is the first time I have attempted to look into the details. Went to bed tired.

Novr. 2d [–5]. I left home in the Stage with Br. Wright for

153. At the Indianapolis meeting of the Indiana Conference it was decided to establish a Methodist college or university. A committee was appointed to draw up a charter and the presiding elder of the Indianapolis district, James Havens, and C.F. were appointed to see to its passage through the legislature. Several towns including Indianapolis, Rockville, Putnamville, and Greencastle were competing for the location of the new school. C.F. spoke for Indianapolis, but according to a historian of De Pauw University, he "did not push his case strongly, in the belief that as large a city as Indianapolis was bound to become might not be a suitable home for the young men who would attend." Greencastle, of course, was selected and the act chartering Indiana Asbury (now De Pauw) University was passed by the Assembly and approved on January 10, 1837. George B. Manhart, *De Pauw through the Years* (2 volumes. Greencastle, Ind.: De Pauw University, 1962), I, 7–8. C.F. was listed in the act as one of twenty-five trustees. *Laws of Indiana*, 1836–37 (local), pp. 9–13.

154. Bishop Robert R. Roberts, after whom Roberts Chapel, later Roberts Park Methodist Church, was named. Dunn, *Indianapolis*, I, 595.

155. The reference is to Bethuel F. Morris, cashier of the Indianapolis branch of the State Bank, and the rent for the bank's quarters.

Madison. I started to inspect the New Albany Madison & Lawrenceburgh branch banks. I performed this duty against my own will & solely in consequence of Mr. Merrill's absence. We took passage in a long waggon—the stage could not pass in consequence of bad roads which were almost impassable. Cold day. 6 passengers. Arrived at Franklin late—dined went [to] Edinburgh after dark—dangerous crossing blue River. Very dark. Took lanterns from E. but had not done but 2 ms. before waggon broke down. Here six of us laid down in a little log cabbin 14 by 16 & the mail was carried on horse to Columbus by the boy or driver. He promised to have the Madison stage come for us & our baggage but in this he failed & [in] the morning we travelled on foote to Columbus took breakfast at Irwins & at Columbus hired a man to go for our baggage.

We spent this day the 3d of Novr. at Jones Tavern in hourly expectation we should be sent for from Madison &c. No stage came & on the 4 I procured a horse & left C. at 9 & rode with stuffed saddle bags to Madison. I never stopped to dine & did not dismount but 3 times between the points. It was very cold. I had a poor little horse badly equipped &c arrived at Madison about 9 in the eve. Put up at Pews—took supper—got warm & it was announced that the mail boat had arrived going to Louisvill. I went aboard with several others. The boat was crowded—all life & bustle on the river—Every body going to a warmer southern climate. Here I found the Southern Gentleman who had spent his summer months at the East & the adventurers going to the lower country.

I had to take the floor with divers others as all the births were filled. We arrived at L. about 2 in the morning. At 5 we left the boat for the Gault house a new & splendid Hotel. Here stages were arriving & departing. Waited till 9 for breakfast for which I paid 50 cents. After breakfast took a hack & rode to the ferry boat opposite of [New] Albany.

Novr. 5. Passed over & examined the bank. Mr. Shields Cashier & Thornton Clerk very agreeable. I got 'long as well as I could expect. Albany is growing very fast. They have laid out $60000. to improve their streets this very year[156]—I stopped at Dr. Hails.

156. C.F. may have intended to write $6,000. In 1838 the town trustees reported they had received $8,000 in taxes and had appropriated $10,011 to im-

Sunday Novr. 6. I left about 8 for Louisvill. In crossing the Ferry got acquainted with a Mr. Fleshman a german now in the Enginear department. We took a hack for L.—arrived there at 9. Here saw 22 steamboats & Sunday morning as it was all seemed to be life. The trade of this place is immense. No steamboat can pass up or down without calling. Here I took the same boat & went up to Madison. On my way got acquainted with a Mr. Roote a N.Y. broker who stopped at Madison with me.

Monday Novr. 7 1836. Presidential election took place. I went with Mr. Sullivan & offered to vote the Harrison ticket but I was refused. I commenced the examination of the bank &c. Messrs. Serring & Lee former cashier the latter clerk assisted. Pleasant damp day. Mr. Roote & myself dined with Mr. Woodburn.

Teusday Novr. 8. Continue the examination. Damp cloudy day.

Weds. [Nov.] 9. Waited all day for a boat to go up the river. Spent some time examining the pork houses &c. About dusk got aboard of a boat & proceeded up the River to Lawrenceburg. Mr. Sullivan was on board. We were landed about 3 in the Morning at Lawrenceburg. We went to Hunts tavern.

Thursday the 9 [10] Novr. [–12]. Much excitement as to the result of the Presidential election—Harrison had run beyond all expectations.[157] Cloudy wet day. I commenced the examination & continued the same till Saturday the 12 of Novr. On the 11 it rained as hard as it could. Streams all rose. Here I was anxious to get away —the stage from Cincinnati did not come & at 11 I took a horse & rode to Nepolian where arrived at 8. Here I found my old friend Jim Brown. We supped together. And about 11 the stage driver waked me up & with 2 other passengers we started for Greensburgh

---

prove the business streets, remove snags from the lower wharf, and put in sewers. A year later the tax base for the town was reported to be $1,760,735, and the tax rate 65 cents per $100, which would have brought in $10,444. Betty Lou Amster, *New Albany on the Ohio. Historical Review, 1813–1963* (New Albany Sesquicentennial Committee, 1963), p. 27. A communication to the New Albany *Gazette,* June 24, 1836, stated, "we have commenced grading the streets in the town, and, in a short time they will be beautifully McAdamized with some few exceptions."

157. Harrison carried Indiana in 1836, 41,000 to Van Buren's 33,000. *Indiana Election Returns,* pp. 21–28.

where we arrived at 2 o clock. We walked all this distance roads very bad. At G. the stage driver who was to start immediately on was not to be found & we had to go to bed.

13 Novr. We started in stage about sunrise from G. & walked for the roads would not admit of any other gait about 5 miles & we then had to foote it to St. Omer most of the way. At St. O. we arrived at 10 & here it was determined that we could not proceede by stage to Indianapolis & we mustered up saddles & started on the stage horses. I never saw the roads worse. At 2 we arrived at Shelbyvill. It was here stated we could not cross Blue River & brandywine in safety but after much debate it was concluded to take the stage horses at that stand & proceede. I mounted a blind mean horse with a short blind bridle. At Blue river I discovered that my girth had broken. I tied up & went in. My horse got into some drift fell & plunged me in up to my armpits. I got out saved my saddle bags. I was in a great peril but by a good Providence I was preserved. With great danger we got over brandy wine & at little Sugar creek my horse fell again & throwed me into the mud. At about 8 o clock arrived at Means where we stayed over night & the next day Novr. 14 arrived safe at home. In no trip in my life did I ever go thro more fatigue & danger than on this for the distance I traveled. From the 14 to the end of Novr. there was scarcely a pleasant day not sufficient dry weather to get in our corn. We had to hire &c.

[*Nov. 23–Dec. 24*]. On the 23 of Novr. our state bank held its session Messrs. Scott & Deming from Terre Haute Mitchel from Ev[ansville] Law from Vin[cennes] Brown from Bedford Hamilton from Ft. W[ayne] Leeds & Morrison from Richmond Johns from Law[renceburg].[158]

We had an important meeting. Merrill President was absent. A spirit of investigation & reform seemed to prevail. This I did not object to. It is an institution whose interests should be guarded with great care. Much difficulty occurred in consequence of the absence of the dilligates of the New Alb[any] & Mad[ison] branches.

158. Lucius H. Scott, Demas Deming, John Mitchell, John Law, John Brown, Allen Hamilton, Noah Leeds, Robert Morrisson, and Enoch D. John.

They together with the Law[renceburg] branch are the direct deposit banks of the public revenue & are bound to distribute an equal proportion to the other branches. This they had failed to do & it caused much complaint. However the matter was at last reconciled. The bank held a session of 5 days till the 29.

Sup[reme] court commenced its session on the [blank] day of Novr. I did not attend but was summoned to appear before the grand jury of the U. States. The Fed[eral] & Sup[reme] Courts sit in the capital for the 1st time. The death of Col. Kennard was announced here on the 2. He was on his way to congress from this district. He left here the day after the Presidential election went to Lawr[enceburg] & there took water & went to Evansvill & passed me when I was at Madison. On his return up the river to proceede to Washington he was scalded to death or rather died in a few days afterwards in consequence of the scald on board of the steam boat Flora.

Col. Kennard I met when on his way to this county in the Fall of 1823 while Genl. Wick & my self were going to the Lawrence circuit court then in this circuit. He was on a foundered horse between Bloomington & Bedford. In a few days we returned & I found him at Bloomington. He appeared to be a youth of about 18. He came on to Indianapolis & worked a short time at the printers business—then went on to Eagle Creek in this county to keep a little school—but that was then a wilderness. He kept school there till the Summer of 1824 when he applied to me to borrow some law books. I loaned him Blackstone's Comentaries. He read perhaps the 1st & 2d vols. He then returned them & gave me to understand he thought it an *unpopular* calling. He seemed to have determined on being a peoples man. He talked of the oppressions of the profession & the opinions the common people entertained of them & fairly gave me to understand they needed a champion &c. He remained in the county till the Summer of 1827 when he presented himself as a candidate against Morris Morris & beat him for Representative to the legislature. I was then in the senate. He was a candi[d]ate & succeeded for that office twice or 3 times. In 1831 he run against me for the senate & came near beating me. Antimasonry then prevailed in many parts of the county. I found him a dark silent man with strong prejudices & capable of exuding them in the breasts of others especially the poor against the rich. He could write well. He never talked in company much nor never gave opinions. He always took one man out after another to talk with him & was not choice as to the qualifications or character of the individual invited out. He never left him without impressing him that he was his friend & that the very inferiority of the listener was caused by some man or set of men who had conspired against his rights. He was elected to two congresses.

On hearing of his death I had concluded to become a candidate & announced myself as such to a number of my friends. This annunciation was on Thursday before the commencement of the session of the legislature. Mr. Herrod for the last 3 years prosecuting attorny of Columbus also declared his intention to become a candidate. He & I met. We both agreed if we run on the Harrison Ticket as it is calld we should be both beat. I did not find him very pertenatious however we remained as the supposd candedates for a day or two when he privately proposed that he would withdraw if it should fall to his lot to do so on *drawing*. I remarked that I would go home & reflect upon the matter & would see him in the morn. I called the next morning & in the meantime after viewing my present condition my family especially relation to crediters, to my office as State Bank director—my age—my clients the time I would have to serve if elected (not exceeding 40 days) and above all the questionable manner of determining as to which should to take the field as a candidate—I gave it out & informed him so reserving the right to run hereafter if I wished.[159]

Thursday after the commencement of session of the General Assembly O. H. Smith was elected senater—Noble beat by the con-

159. C.F. wrote to John Tipton, December 21, 1836, that Herod had presented himself as a Whig and Judge Wick as a Van Buren candidate. "Herod went & resigned his office of prosecutor—Altho much weaker in the distrct than myself yet strong enougth to beat me & himself with Wick in the field—& much to the mortification of my devoted friends I withdrew from the contest. Your friendship in the matter will not be forgotten—Peper & others of your friends were willing to do everything that was clever but I had no popularity to hazard in the contest—my judgment was that I must be beat Herrod being on the ticket." *John Tipton Papers*, III, 329.

junction of the dissatisfied or adhering Harrison-men & the Van Buran party.[160] Sheets Secretary also beat.[161] On the 14 my name with Alexr. Worths was presented as State Bank directors to the legislature. I was elected for the next 4 years on the first ballot. I did not expect it as I had not electioneered or spoken to a member in order to procure a vote & as I was somewhat identified with Govr. Noble.[162]

The fore-part of this month I heard of the death of my sister Louisa. She was my youngest sister born in 1805 & Married in 1820 or 21 to Mr. Joseph Miller of N.Y. This month has not been very cold but the roads have been extremely bad. Mr. Pratt was here at the first of the session—run for clk & Pros. Atty. & was beat for both. He read the Governor's message.

Capt. Baldwin from Cavendish came here about the 18 of Decr. Has bot land on the Solimony.

Sunday Decr. 25 1836. Christmass day. I rose at 5 o'clock. Cooley came up from his uncle Stoughtons Store bro't up some presents to the childrin—kissed his mother was in a high glee. I had to start for Noblesvill court—About 9 Messrs. Quarles Brown & myself. The day was cold the whole way was covered with ice—had to go over the bridge at West place. We dined at Carters on our way up. Arrived at N. about dark put up with Mr.

160. Balloting for United States senator by the General Assembly was held on December 8, 1836. Those receiving votes included the encumbent senator William Hendricks, Governor Noble, Oliver H. Smith, Ratliff Boon, and others. On December 21, C.F. wrote to Senator Tipton: "You have heard of the defeat of Hendricks & Noble, Sheets &c. It was found that H in no event cd be elected after there were letters exhibited by both parties showing that he had clearly given members belonging to each side pledges of support to their particular side —also his transactions with his mother in law [by which he allegedly obtained a deed unfairly] was disclosed to his disadvantage.—Both these disclosures drove his adherents to Smith's friends which elected him." *John Tipton Papers,* III, 269–70, 330; *Indiana Election Returns,* p. 131.

161. Sheets was defeated for re-election as secretary of state by William J. Brown. Indiana *House Journal,* 1836–37, p. 41.

162. C.F. was elected to succeed himself as state bank director and Alexander Worth was elected to succeed Seton W. Norris who had resigned. Each house of the Assembly voted separately. In the House the vote stood C.F., 57; Nathaniel West, 13; Frederick Goodsell, 23; blank, 3. The vote in the Senate was not recorded. Indiana *House Journal,* 1836–37, pp. 76–77; Indiana *Senate Journal,* 1836–37, pp. 90–91.

Dunning. Very cold. Here we found Mr. Herrod electionearing.

Monday Decr. 26. Pleasant but cool day. Court opened in new court house, Mr. H. made a speech. Wick arrived in the P.M. & made a speech next day.

Teusday Dec. 27. Cool. Tried Caters [?] case.

Wedensday [Dec.] 28. Sumners case.

Thursday [Dec.] 29. Barns case vs Cloud.

Friday Decr. 30 1836. Cold tho' pleasant. Wick left the court for the Falls to meet Herrod to make a speech. We took down the testimony in the case of Blackamore vs Kemp. Had some little difficulty with Brown. At Sundown I went to Mr. Mallorys having been to the Dale place[163] & rented the same to Geo. Messick who has just come from Delaware. At Mr. Mallories the Hives as they are called came out all over me for the first time in my life. I spent a pleasant evening with the old Gentleman lady & Garrick & little Henry as he is called. A more agreeable night I have not spent.

Decr. 31. Pleasant—the ground covered with ice. After breakfast old Mr. Mallory & myself went to town. I drew a lease for Messick. Sold him the rent corn 300 bushel at $25 per hundred—the Wheat at $1. per bush. At 12 we left that is Brown Quarles & myself. Our horses were well [?]. We arrived at home about sundown. I found uncle Michael sick but so as to be about with a bad cold also Stoughton was sick. I obtained my letters & papers from the office. 2 Intelligencers & N.Y. Evening Star &c. Dorio Mrs. Richmond John & Martha went to the watchnight meeting at Methodist church—Calvin & Elijah to a party of small children to Mr. Landis. This the last day of the year may be said to be a pleasant day for the time of year.

163. See Pt. VI, note 78.

FLETCHER HODGES, JR.

Sarah Hill Fletcher
by T. C. Steele, 1879,
from a water color painted c.1832
by an unknown artist

FLETCHER HODGES, JR.

Calvin Fletcher
by T. C. Steele, 1879
from a water color painted c.1832
by an unknown artist

VIII

Diary of CALVIN FLETCHER *January 1, 1837–February 4, 1838* and Diary of SARAH HILL FLETCHER *December 23, 1837–February 14, 1838*

January FIRST 1st 1837 Sunday. At one o'clock this morning the girls & John returned from church. At 5 Mrs. F. waked up the boys. At six we had prayers & then immediately breakfast. I do not feel well in consequence of the Hives. Uncle M. sick with a bad cold but is able to be up. A very cold raw day—ground almost covered with ice except in the streets. Our hay that is the stable full is about half gone—we keep 3 horses & 4 cows. Our family consists of 5 boys John & Martha Wall & Orindorio—Cooley is bound to his uncle Stoughton & Mr. Bradley for 3 years.[1]

In reviewing the last year I have abundant reason to be thankful to God for his preserving care & Kindness. We have scarcely had any sickness worth naming except that of John Hill & the little child of Mr. Vorus which died—& how many can we enumerate who have been deeply afflicted by disease & subsequent death. The destroying angel has passed over us—we are yet alive & have Just entered upon a new year. But the great afflictions & bereavements during the short period of 365 days next to ensue no one can divine—God only knows. It is well that the great mistry there rests. We are too frail to be intrusted with the ennumerable secrets to be disclosed. If we knew them it would be impossible to fill that destiny prescribed for us. May it be our chief delight "to wait the

1. C.F. fails to mention his daughter Maria.

great teacher death & God adore." If I live to the 4 of Feby., I shall enter upon the *high* meridian of life—my 40th year. If I know my own heart, my own secret desires, it is to be useful—to feel greatful, to have mercy & walk humbly before God. I pray that this new year maybe more distinguished for my carrying out those wishes & desires than in any former year. May I have assisting grace to accomplish & to fill the measure of my wishes.

During the last year I have not devoted much of my attention to my profession. I have not attended any one court through except the Hamilton court. My business has been entrusted to Mr. Butler & S. Yandes. I have been absent some portion of my time in order to sell my lands purchased in 1835—mainly to sell some town property at Michigan City.

During the last year I have effected sales & realized the money to the amount of 20800. This has all been paid to satisfy the Joint debts of Mr. McCarty & myself except $2500. we paid for Dr. McClures property.

We owe the Evansvill Bank about	$1800	
Indianapolis	4500	
D. E. Allen	1250[2]	
Dr. Sanders about	4800	
Dr. McClure	2000	
John Walker	2227	16577

Out of which we have about $14000 [*sic*] acres of land worth I think at a low estimate $100000.

My own private debts stand about as follows

For Bridge Stock at Logansport	$2500.
Washington Hall	1000
McFarlin	1000
Tyner	400
other debts	2000
	6900

All the above debts ought to be paid in one year. To be sure I am not discouraged but I am sensible that I have to use great energy

2. The Morgan County deed records show that on September 13, 1836, McCarty and C.F. acquired land from David Allen at the Bluffs on White River in sections 13 and 24, T13N, R2E and section 18, T13N, R3E. The price paid is not given. The deed was recorded March 18, 1839. See entry for March 5, 1837, below.

to get thro' with them. I should never have accumulated them had I followed my own judgment or rather had I effected sales as I should last year. I now feel as I always have felt, no pleasure in being the owner of a great property. I believe it is my duty to distribute it & I shall do it if in my power. Times are now unpropitious. But if I bring around the year with just one fourth of my present property & out of debts I shall feel better than I do now.

We had Mrs. Pendleton & Mrs. Richmond to dinner.

Jany. 2d. In the morning cool & cloudy. I expect to go to the bluffs this eve to settle with old Mr. McGrew. At 9 went to the office arranged my business with Mr. Butler so far as related to my Hamilton County trip. Went & saw my brother Stoughton who is sick—I think better. 10 went to Mr. McCartys there found old Mr. McGrew—so I postponed going to the Bluffs. Mr. Burr who is a public defalter wants me to become one of the trustees to take & settle his business &c.[3] I declined. Went to see the Phrenologist (Mr. Burns).[4] Came home took dinner. Voted for Herrod for congress.[5] Very cold. Mrs. Givan & bro. Smith dined with us. Growing very cold. Went back to office. Sold to Judge Mounts 74-34/100 acres of land on Eel River for $372.73 being $5. per acre (cost $1.62½ cents per acre) I wish to sell much of my land the present year.

After dinner went with Mr. Smith to the state house also to see the bill passed for Asbury Indiana college.

After supper called on uncle Michael who is sick—also on Stoughton who is better—& by appointment S. M. Levenworth[6]

3. David Burr, who resigned as commissioner of the Wabash and Erie Canal because of a defalcation of public funds. Daniel Yandes was appointed to replace him. *Messages and Papers relating to the Administration of Noah Noble,* p. 526. On January 17, 1836, C.F. wrote to Senator John Tipton, "Bur has failed. I was applied to help save him from exposure before the bubble burst But from what you sd & what I have seen myself I believe him to be a corrupt man." *John Tipton Papers,* III, 346.

4. K. E. Burhans. The Indianapolis *Indiana Democrat* of December 23, 1836, announced that Mr. Burhans, a "practical Phrenologist," would deliver a free lecture on phrenology that evening in the Representatives Hall.

5. In the special election held to fill the unexpired term of Congressman George L. Kinnard, William Herod defeated Judge William W. Wick 3,713 to 3,493. *Indiana Election Returns,* p. 93.

6. Seth M. Levenworth, one of the founders of the town of Leavenworth,

called to arrange a judgment who gave me his views of the future growth of Indianapolis. Very cold. Called again on the Phrenologist & heard him give his examination of H. Porter['s][7] head. Returned home at 9.

Jany. 3d. 1836 [*1837*]. Very cold morning. In A.M. attended to some business—had a call from Mr. Adams from the house of Fellows & Co. Louisvill—called on by Messrs. Hanner[8] & Burr to act as trustee to settle Burrs business as a trustee he having become a public defaulter as canal commissioner for $21000. to the state. I declined having other business in great abundance. In P.M. attended an education meeting in Representative Hall. Mr. Wiley from Bloomington here Govr. Noble in the chair.[9]

In the eve went with Mrs. Richmond & Louisa to hear Mr. Wiley deliver an address. Very cold say the coldest day this year—no snow on but much ice. John took two cows out to McFarlen place. Settled with Underhill Wood & Co.[10] Received Intelligencer & Ev[ening] Star. Took our Newspapers to be bound.

Jany. 4. Cold cloudy morning. Slight snow fell. John Hill called on me to see if I would go into business with him in merchandizing. Last fall I talked of so doing but the present pressure is such that I cannot consistently with my own Judgment engage. It strikes me that a new order of business & things must follow the late Treasury order & the great pressure in Europe as well as in America. I dare not venture to enter into trade. He reproaches me because he

---

who represented Crawford County in four sessions of the General Assembly, 1826–30. He was an early advocate of railroads and president of the Leavenworth and Bloomington Railroad Company which projected a route from the Ohio River town through Bloomington and Indianapolis to Lake Michigan. The line never materialized. H. H. Pleasants, "Crawford County," in *Indiana Magazine of History*, XVIII (1922), 154–56.

7. Henry Porter, merchant, son-in-law of Dr. Samuel G. Mitchell, and a trustee of the town of Indianapolis, 1837–38. Sulgrove, *History of Indianapolis*, pp. 275, 490.

8. Samuel Hanna, one of the commissioners of the Wabash and Erie Canal. *Indiana Executive Proceedings*, pp. 685, 687.

9. The proceedings of the "Convention of friends of Education" were printed in the Indianapolis *Indiana Journal*, January 20, 1837. See also *Messages and Papers relating to the Administration of Noah Noble*, pp. 514–24. Andrew Wylie's address was published under the title *Address on the Subject of Common School Education* (Indianapolis: Douglass & Noel, 1837).

10. See Pt. VI, note 162.

thinks he could have gone in with others. I hope however I shall be able hereafter to show him that he is mistaken. I settled with Mr. Pratt as to hay I sold him. Advised as to a deed of trust for Burrs assignees &c.

I find I must settle up my little accounts.

Jany. 5. Cool but comparitively moderated. Intend going to Bluffs to day. In A.M. settled with T. D. Gregg—calld on Mrs. Foote—received 2 notes from the Bank to collect. Underhill Wood & Co. suppressed a note protested yesterday for a small sum say $1000. The future looks gloomy to me. I cannot but view the present prices of real estate as fast depreciating. Mr. McCarty thinks differantly. I gave out going to the Bluffs this day. In P.M. snows a little very cold. Several of our neighbors are sick. I assisted Dr. Clark[11] a little as to the law to loan surplus revenue.

Jany. 6 1836 [1837]. Quarles & I going to Bluffs. Weather has moderated a little—we started at 10. Had a pleasant ride—talked on various subjects—Ph[r]enology—Wick's & Herrods canvass for congress. We stopped at Mr. Webber half way house & warmed. Madam had 2 little babes—boy & girl twins—relatives to Mr. Q. The road a great glare of ice. Arrived at bluffs at 1. Q. stopped at Paytons. I went down to settle with McGrew &c. Quarles staid a little while & went back alone. I made a partial settlement with McG. &c. Dr. Rust wants the Tavern stand where McG. now lives but I declined letting him have it. After dark I went by invitation to Mr. Davis & spent the eve. Had a good fire comfortable room—cider & apples. At 9 went to bed.

Jany. Saturday 7. Got up at 6 went out 4 ms. E. to where Mr. Ed. Boaz was keeping a grocery store to see him & a Mr. Trusler or Truslo. I did not find them (either) at the place & I rode 2 gloomy miles S. to where a Mr. T. lived. He was gathering corn on a good farm &c. I returned & found Mr. Boaz at the grocery store. This has been one of my very gloomy rides. I went to see if I could get B. & T. to take McGrews Tavern stand instead of Rust. The latter is a dissipated old man of bad habits &c but [Mc]Grew does not wish to leave without getting R. in—both I equally abhor—& I made this journy with very little hope of succeeding, but met with

11. Othniel L. Clark, senator from Tippecanoe County.

some incouragement. The multitude of business I have on hand & the prospect of pecuniary embarrassment pressed & followed me all this ride. I got back to Port Royal at 12. Saw Rust & McGrew & told them I could not let R. into the tavern &c I then went & rented the ferry to a Mr. Bradley till March for one half ferriage &c. I left for home at 1½ P.M. Got home a little before dark. Called on the Phrenologist Mr. Burhans & invited him up to examine my family. He came but could not stay but ½ hour. Mrs. Richmond & uncle Michael & J. Hill present &c. He examined Elijah first then Cooley & then Calvin & also Richardson when another ingagement called him off till Monday.

He speaks well of Elijah—good intellects &c but says he is a little cunning evasive may be a good scholar but lacks consentiveness or application. Cooley is very respectable but is in the extreme in approbativeness & amative propensities—will be fond of show &c if not checked. Both respectable in firmness but C. does not equal E. in this particular. Calvin is too timid—is in the happy mediocrity. Richardson he thinks lacks in self esteem & firmness —has not courage to go forward &c.

Mrs. Fletcher Richmond & J. Hill went to E. Porters to a singing school Elijah & Calvin to hear an address at the Representatives Hall celebration of the 8 Jany.[12] I feel tired. It has been to me a cold gloomy day.

Sunday Jany. 8. Pleasant winter morning. I went with Mrs. Fletcher H[. . .] & Mrs. Richmond to class meeting at old Mr. Browns Revs. Edy[13] & Smith present Andrew Smith & Miss Patterson. Afterwards went to church the former gentleman preached.

John Hill & Wm. dined. Went to see uncle Stoughton. Cooley came up & spent the P.M. I had a serious conversation with him as to some bad habits. He seemed to be much affected & promised to do better.

12. The anniversary of Andrew Jackson's victory over the British at New Orleans, January 8, 1815, was celebrated by a meeting featuring an address by Robert Dale Owen, who was serving as representative from Posey County, followed by a dinner in Basil Brown's Mansion House. Owen's address was printed in the Indianapolis *Indiana Democrat,* January 13, 1837.

13. Augustus M. Eddy, Methodist preacher stationed in Indianapolis in 1836. He served as presiding elder from 1837 to 1839. Dunn, *Indianapolis,* I, 592.

Monday Jany. 9. The ph[r]enologist came up & examined Miles Stoughton & Ingrams heads. He pronounced all my childrin with respectable intellects Elijah & Stoughton calculated the best for scholars &c. Mrs. F. ranks much higher than myself in her intellectual faculties. This I always knew but she fails in Hope which deprives her of much worldly happiness & counteracts her other energies. Pleasant winter day. Mathews called & paid some money.

Jany. 10. Pleasent winter day. H. O Neel has concluded to [go] South. I am to let him have $100. I view him as a young man of fine talents. Col. Teall from Michigan City is here. Mr. Mershon & wife down from Pendleton. Pleasent winter day, a little snow not too cold. Joseph Holiday stayed with us.

Jany. 11. Pleasant winter day. I went in the P.M. to help bury Mr. Roop. I made a partial sale of my 1/16 of the Michigan City property. I am to have $2875. for it in 3 payments of 6, 9, & 12 months.[14]

Jany. 12. Cool but a fine winter day. Went to Mr. Harrisons & saw Col. Teall Harrison & E[. . .] start—gave Teall a power of atty to confirm the sale of my 1/16 part of my land. Called on Mr. Burhans the phrenologist & gave him 2 letters 1 to C. Anthony Springfield & the other J. H. James Columbus Ohio. I have effected very little this day. Mrs. F. has gone to visit Stoughtons wife. I had a letter from Mr. Ingram—wrote to Jacob Mitchell of Knox county Ohio also to a Mr. Sulser of Wayne Cty. this state in answer to enquiries as to my selling them certain lands. I have offered to take $5¼ per acre. I do not know as they will take them but I intend to sell. Pleasant winter day. Mr. Herrod is elected to Congress is going to start from home in a few days. Wrote me this eve.

Jany. 13. Cold snowy day. Many slays in town, fine roads &c. I sold the N.W. quarter of my block fronting Mr. Coberns to Mr. Butler for $1000. $325. down the rest in 1 & 2 years.[15]

Jany. 14. This day received a letter from Dr. Price of Phila-

14. See Pt. VII, note 10.

15. The Marion County deed records show that on January 14, 1837, C.F. conveyed to Ovid Butler Lots 10, 11, and 12 in Square 39 for the consideration of $1,000. C.F. had acquired the entire square from the agent of state for $732, the deed being recorded October 3, 1835.

delphia that they had a copy of Whitneys[16] circular published which Mr. McCarty & I sent. I fear it will make some mischief.

I advanced $100. to H. O Neel to go South to look out a location also a letter of credit for $100. I view him a promising young man.

Sunday Jany. 15. We have 3 or 4 inches of snow most excellent slaying. I went with the boys to church. Mr. Edy preached. I read Joseph some. H. O Neel called & we had some talk as to his future prospects & his going away. Pleasant weather. Last night our sow bo't of Mr. Reagin had 7 pigs of the china breed.

Monday Jany. 16. I this morning was waited upon by a Mr. Castleman from near Lexington Ky. who had been North to buy land. He had met with Mr. Teall on his way from this place. I had a letter from him stating that Mr. C. wished to buy my interest amounting to about 15 acres in & near Michigan City—which I had authorized Mr. T. to sell for $2875. payable in 6, 9, & 12 mos. Mr. C. offered me $2500. down in U.S. paper. I accepted this sum. I owe debts & am desireous to have them paid. I must be just. I must be out of debt. I also this day sold the N. East corner of my block 39 to L. Lewis Recorder[17] for $1200. ⅓ down ⅓ in 1 & ⅓ in 2 years with 10 per cent. I have resolved on selling my property & of being less embarrassed.

16. Reuben M. Whitney, who served in Washington as agent for various banks used by the Treasury Department as banks of deposit for federal funds. It was alleged that he received handsome compensation from some banks for his services. He became the target for antiadministration elements toward the end of Jackson's second term. The Indiana Senate ordered an investigation of the relations, if any, between the State Bank, the Treasury Department, and Whitney. The committee report showed that Whitney had never been employed by the State Bank though he had sent various circulars to the bank's cashier, James M. Ray. *Messages and Papers relating to the Administration of Noah Noble,* pp. 529–30n. On January 17, 1836, C.F. wrote to Senator Tipton of the difficulty the State Bank and its branches were having in meeting demands upon them, adding "We have had the ill will of Mr. Whitney because we did not imply him & to have his ill will has been equal to having the ill will of the Treas'y. I once intimated to you that under cover of the Treasy's letters he had insinuated himself or tried to obtain the good graces of the officers of the bank–But it was done in that way that we cd not get hold of him & the officers of the bank have been afraid of him. But I think the late exposure of his circular will let the world know who R.M.W. is." *John Tipton Papers,* III, 345.

17. Lewis C. Lewis was commissioned recorder of Marion County on August 14, 1834. *Indiana Executive Proceedings,* p. 518.

This is a beautiful day—all is life. At 12 there were at least 100 sleighs in Washington Street rather rude most of them. In the P.M. Judge Cole called at my office & informed me that he & his lady were going to Hamilton Cty. Noblesvill & I proposed that he should carry Mrs. F. who started with them at 4 o clock.

H. O Neel left to day for the South. He is a young man of [. . .]. I hope he will do well. I procured $100 for him which he will return when able—also a letter of credit for $100. In the eve Mrs. Richmond & I went to see Mrs. Roop a sick woman. Dorio is going to prepare a dinner for Mr. & Mrs. P[. . .]. Quarls offered to loan me $200. & did.

Jany. 17 1837. A very pleasant day. Mr. P[. . .] Madam & Mrs. Brown Secretary's wif[e][18] dined with us. I this day paid Mr. McCarty $900. heretofore borrowed. Mr. Lewis re[ne]wed the contract for the N.E. quarter block. Old Mr. Plumer & Buterfild stayed over night. In the eve Mrs. Richmond Dorio & Louisa with Billy Hill had a slayride—Martha John & aunt Betsy in Mr. Butterfields slay. Elijah & Calvin went to Mr. Folys to a candy pulling. Beautiful day much stir in Slays.

Jany. 18. Pleasant morning. All gone to market Michael & John to sell potatoes & cabbage.

Jany. 18. Pleasant day. Mrs. F. returned from Noblesvill. Snow begins to melt. Michael James & John hauling cherry saw logs from the McF. place. Caught a cock, two Rabits &c. Richardson returned to his fathers sick.

I see Bro. Elijah['s] Printing office is burned.[19]

Jany. 19. Pleasant day. Went with Harrison opposite old Mr. Williams on bluff road to see about the canal contracters taking timber off the McClure place. Saw old Mr. McGrew. Snow disappearing fast. Mr. English called. Wanted us to sue Mr. Mitchel from Penna. Mr. Crumbaugh called. I settled taxes &c with Judge Polk.

18. Wife of William J. Brown, secretary of state. See note 38, below.

19. In 1825 Elijah acquired *The Virginian,* a Whig paper which he described to his father as having "a large circulation" and being "a profitable establishment." The plant was partially insured and Elijah purchased new equipment following the fire and continued the operation until he sold the paper in 1841. In regard to the fire he wrote to C.F. that "saving all my important [Books?] and

Two Miss Pattersons to be married—one [to] Mr. Macy & the other to Dr. Drake.[20]

Dr. Cool[21] called & stated that he had learned that I kept Mr. Butler as an underlin[g]—a creature &c. This I fear will have an improper influence on Mr. B. I know there is a great jealousy towards me from the rest of the profession and Mr. Butler has just talents sufficient to excite the envy. I trust his good sense will lead him [not] to take advantage of this imputation.

Jany. 20. This day foggy in the morning. Michael John & J. Hill & 2 young Wolvertons gone to gathering corn. I am trying [to] right up my business in the office. I paid $5. for the widow of a Mr. Baily deceased to go home to Rh. I. Cloudy day thawed a little. Went in the eve to hear Mr. Merrill colonization address. Was chosen manager for St[ate] C[olonization] S[ociety] for the next year.[22]

Jany. 21. Cool last night—a little snow. Michael & hands gone to gather corn. Hope to get thro to day. Calvin rose early & went to market to buy him a chicken cock—got one for elevenpence that suited him &c.

Snowed a little thro the day. Michael & hands got thro' with their corn. We have raised something like 1500 bushels this year & have now near 1000 at McF. place. Butterfield cow had a calf.

Sunday Jany. 22. Cool in the morning but thawed a little in town but good slaying in the country. Went to hear Mr. Edy Preach in the A.M. Read Josephus &c.

---

papers, I did not mind much the loss." Von Briesen (ed.), *Letters of Elijah Fletcher,* pp. 97–98n, 146, 288.

20. These were the daughters of Robert Patterson, probate judge of Marion County. Mary Ann married David Macy of Henry County and Eliza Jane married Dr. I. S. Drake, formerly of Ohio. Indianapolis *Indiana Journal,* January 21 and February 11, 1837.

21. Dr. Jonathan Cool who came to Indianapolis in 1821. He is said to be the first physician who preached against excessive use of calomel. He died in 1840 a victim of intemperance. Dunn, *Indianapolis,* I, 542.

22. This was the annual meeting of the Indiana Colonization Society held in the Representatives Hall. Officers chosen were Isaac Blackford, president; Andrew Wylie, Stephen C. Stevens, and Achilles Williams, vice-presidents; Samuel Merrill, Calvin Fletcher, Nathan B. Palmer, Richard J. Hubbard, James Thompson, William Sheets, and James Blake, managers; Isaac Coe, treasurer, and James M. Ray, secretary. Indianapolis *Indiana Journal,* February 11, 1837. Merrill's address was printed in the *Journal.*

Monday Jany. 23 1837. Cool cloudy morning. Went with Michael & John to get cattle from Fletcher farm. Bro't in 4 head I bot of John Fletcher & turned them into the field at the McFarlin place. I examined the calves hogs &c at that place. At the Fletcher farm there is now 52 head of horses belonging to Mr. Pratt.

Mr. Butler went to Shelbyville.

Mr. Danl. Yandes nominated & appointed canal commissioner in place of Mr. Burr. Called in the eve. to see Mr. Collins & Clark —Senators.[23]

Mrs. F. & Dorio rode out to old Mr. Wolvertons after our return from the Fletcher farm.

Learned that old Mr. McGrew had left our Bluff tavern & had put old Dr. Rust in contrary to the lease & our agreement with McGrew. I expect to have much trouble with him.

Jany. Teusday 24. Cloudy morn. About to kill our fat cow. I am progressing in reading Josephus. I hope to be able to commence settling my books with Simon to day. I have been paying out moneys collected to such as have called. I fear I shall find myself much behind. I wish to straighten my affairs & live square with the world. I stand in great need of a house but can't build until I get out of all my involvements.

Weds. [Jan.] 25. Pleasant day. I this day helped prepare some interrogatories for Mr. West[24] who has (as is supposed) had the officers of the Bank arraigned on account of allowing the fund commissioners $2. per day while they get the same from the canal fund.

Jany. 26. Got 4 hogs of Thos. McCollum 2 barrows & 2 sows weighing about 1 cwt. each on an average also 2 sucking pigs for which I gave $12.12. Got them home. Stock hogs are selling at 4 cts. per lb. Pleasant day.

Jany. 27. Cloudy morning. John & Martha have gone to visit

23. James Collins of Floyd County and Othniel L. Clark, Tippecanoe County.

24. Nathaniel West, who owned extensive lands northwest of the town of Indianapolis. About 1838 he started operation of a cotton mill where Sixteenth Street now crosses the canal and a suburb called Cottontown grew up around it. A Democrat, he was elected to the Indiana Senate in 1841 to complete the term of Robert Hanna who resigned. Dunn, *Indianapolis,* I, 434, 491; *Indiana Election Returns,* pp. 263, 264n.

their mother on Fall Creek. Snowed in the A.M. a little. A Mr. Fletcher from Springfield Ohio selling lamps. Some difficulty with the committee that are examining the bank &c. 2 loads of Lafayette merchants going East. Michael & J. Hill been out to McF. place to look for timber for barn &c. Very cold in the eve. Mrs. Richmond went to see Mrs. Wingate. Louisa went to Mr. Yandes. Elijah went after her.

Saty. [Jan.] 28. Pleasant day Michael & J. Hill getting some gums at the McFarlan place. Ground yet froze.

Sunday 29 Jany. '37. Bishop Kemper[25] preaches at Meth. Ch[urch]. Pleasant. Michael brot his pigs up out of the block. Went with Mrs. F. & boys in the A.M. to church & in the eve with Mrs. R. Reading yet the 1st vol. of Josephus.

Jany. 30. Monday. Cloudy. Thawed some. A Mr. Fletcher from Ohio here with Lamps for sale.

Teusday [Jan.] 31. Last day of Jany. Preparing to remit to N.Y. by Ed. Porter.[26] Drove 14 hogs to McF. place with Michael. Eli[jah] John [and] J. Hill went to Whites & Turners to get hogs. Michael & J. hauled rails to new clearing on Pouges run. Pleasant day.

Weds. Feby. 1 1837. Rose early & wrote 4 letters. Cool morning. Froze some last night. Frost not out of the ground. The legislature have passed a law to put one half of the Surplus Revenue in the present & new banks to be created—the other half to be loaned to the people of the counties.[27] Messrs. Butler Simon Yandes & myself are crowded with business. Obu[?] a colored man proposes

25. The Right Rev. Jackson Kemper, Episcopal missionary bishop, who spent two weeks in Indianapolis at this time, preaching in both the Methodist Church and the Presbyterian Church. Eli Lilly, *History of The Little Church on the Circle. Christ Church Parish Indianapolis, 1837–1955* (Indianapolis, 1957), pp. 36–39.

26. Edward T. Porter, an Indianapolis merchant.

27. The total amount of the surplus revenue received by Indiana in the first three installments was $860,254. The fourth installment was never paid. The act provided that one half of what was received should be distributed to the counties in proportion to the number of taxable polls to be lent to residents of the counties in amounts not exceeding $400 at 8 per cent interest. The interest was to go for the benefit of township schools. The other half was to be invested in State Bank stock. *Laws of Indiana*, 1836–37 (general), pp. 3–14; *Messages and Papers relating to the Administration of Noah Noble*, p. 487n.

to go to Africa & his friends & I have called on Messrs. Merrill & Ray for that purpose their opening a correspondence with the Parent colonization soci[e]ty. This P.M. cold. Michael & John hauling wood for Butler from the McClure place 3 cord &c. I read Tom Corwins speech on the tariff reduction.

Feby. 2d. Cool cloudy morning snow off in town. Mr. Bradley is very sick. I went to his house & drew his will. Went to the Bank & learned that a comission had been forwarded from Washington to examine our bank officers & Mr. West in relation to the corruption of the Treasury department & as to the relation of R. M. Whitney to that department.

We are busily engaged as to office buseness. Cool the ground remains froze. Michael went to McF. place. Jim & John drawing hay from Sanders place to Browning.[28] Legislature preparing to adjourn.

Feby. 3d. Pleasant day. Mrs. F. spent the day at Mr. Bradleys. He is better. We are getting along in our office—a plenty to do—preparing some business for the Bank mortgages &c.

Our legislature are winding up their business. Have disposed of the surplus revenue in the following manner ½ to be loaned to the counties agreeable to population ½ to the making not less than 3 nor more [than] 4 new branch banks.

February 4 1837. I rose this morning ½ after 4 o'clock about my usual time of rising. John Wall had made the fires & Dorio & Martha were getting breakfast. After dressing &c Michael called up & we had some conversation relative to state taxes as provided in a bill Just past assessing 15 cents for state purposes on the $100. &c.[29] M. is preparing for market—sells potatoes & cabbages—the first article for $.50 per bush the latter at 8 & 10 cents ahead. We put 300 or 400 bush. in our celler & buried as many potatoes at the McF. place but we fear the latter are ruined by frost.

28. Edmund Browning, manager of Washington Hall. See below, p. 465, and Nowland, *Early Reminiscences of Indianapolis*, p. 432.

29. The 1837 revenue act provided for the purpose of state revenue a rate of fifteen cents on every one hundred dollar valuation of real and personal property plus a fifty cent poll tax levied on all males between twenty-one and fifty years of age. *Laws of Indiana*, 1836–37 (general), p. 112.

Cloudy day. We have invited Mrs. Paxton & Hannerman to dine with us as this is the anniversary of my birth. The snow is not off in the country nor entirely from our commons.

This day I am 39 & now enter on my 40th year—*high meridian!* Yes my days more than half spent if I live to an old age. I trust I feel sensible of this advance on the short journey of life & while I pause for a moment to look back I find among the ills of life which we think made up so large an item, I have abundant reason to bless God that I have had so many undeserved blessings poured out upon me—I have uncommon health both myself & family—the 7 childrin 6 boys & a girl all alive & in good health with passible intellects & with suitable improvement bid fair with the blessing of God to be useful if they live. Besides all this I have constant imployment & am contented with what I have already acquired believing that if I owe the world nothing in dollars & cents & my daily labors will supply my daily wants—let me have ever so little laid up, I am a happier (man) than he who has thousands & is in debt or in doubt how to manage what he has acquired. I am somewhat in debt. I hope it will be my good fortune to sell what I can spare & pay those debts.

I went to the office at 7. Began the duties of the day settled with Lewis Burns as to the Givans claims. Settled Mr. Hills administration accounts in J. H. Scotts estate a deceased lawyer. Commenced a suit of attachment for Senator Chambers[30] to obtain some money from one Elliott. Gave an opinion to a man residing near the Bluffs also to the Bank relative to mortgages under their charter.

At 12 we dined & had Michael Stoughton & their wives also Mrs. Paxton Mrs. Richmond & Pendleton Louisa Richardson & Cooley & Maria Hill. James & John drawing hay from Sanders place to Browning. I rented the McClure corn ground to Mr. Got for ½ corn & he keep the stocks &c.

One of the pleasantest days this year—good sugar day. I have also this day subscribed $250. in 5 equal annual installments to the Indiana Asbury university which when paid will entitle me to a

30. Samuel Chambers, senator from Orange and Washington counties.

scholarship of 20 years. I have been appointed one of the trustees to organize this institution.

Feby. 5 Sunday [*–Feb. 11*]. Very pleasent day. Went to class meeting after which to meeting Mr. Edy preached.

From the 5 to 10 of Feby. Warm pleasant weather. Snow & ice melted & the roads very muddy. On the 8 James Hill went & bo't 20 hogs of Joe Turner for which he paid 4½ cents per lb. They cost $110. The same money 5 years past would have bot 110 hogs such has been the appreciation of property in a few years.

On the 10 warm & pleasant weather. Mr. Quarles & myself left home at 11 for Madison court by the way of Noblesville Strawtown &c to Andersontown. At Fall Ck. Mr. Quarls plunged in & swam 2 rods. I waited & went over in a canoe & swam my horse. Went on to Allisonvill. There Govr. Ray had just made his first stump speech for Congress—to 8 or 10 auditors.[31] From thence we rode to Noble[s]vill by dusk. Very muddy. Staid over night at Demoss's[32]—slept on the floor by a fire in preferance to going to a cold room. Left Noblesvill at 3 P.M. & went to Strawtown. Staid at Rolls. Also here overtook Govr. Ray. Several men from Lafayett[e] here.

Saturday [*Feb.*] *the 12* [*11*]. We left after Breakfast Strawtown & rode to Wises for dinner & to Andersont[own] by dusk. Put up at Myers—[33] had a room in Wises Store near the springs.

Sunday [*Feb.*] *13* [*12*]. Went to hear Nathl. Richmond preach. Cold windy day. Brown (Hiram) Kilgore Kenerday[34] &c came.

Monday [*Feb.*] *14* [*13*]. Very little business done. Went &

31. This was Governor Ray's fourth and last attempt to win election to Congress. His opponent was the encumbent William Herod who defeated him at the August election 9,635 to 5,888. *Indiana Election Returns*, p. 96.

32. Thomas DeMoss, early Noblesville tavernkeeper. Shirts, *History of Hamilton County*, p. 173.

33. The second tavern in Anderson was conducted in a two-story log house on the south side of the public square by "Uncle Billy" Myers. He later had the Myers Hotel on the east side of the square. Netterville, *Centennial History of Madison County*, I, 307.

34. Andrew Kennedy of Muncie, lawyer and senator from Randolph and Delaware counties, and later Congressman for three terms (1841–47). *Biographical Directory of the American Congress*, p. 1402.

agreed to let Jackson have 2½ acres of land at his mill &c of the tract bot of Irish.

Teusday [*Feb.*] *the 15* [*14*]. Nothing done but attended to a few chan[ce]ry cases.

Feby. 16 [*15*] *1837 Wedensday.* Muddy. Wick gone home. Case of Cookman vs Wyman tried before the associates.

17 [*16*] *Feby. Thursday* [*–Feb. 19*]. Began snowing in the morning & continued to snow till midnight in all fell about 13 inches—the most snow at one time since I have lived in the West which will be 20 years next summer having come to the state of Ohio in [. . .]. During this day a new trial was asked in case of Cookman vs. Wyman. Old Judge Winsel made a validictory speech having served from the organization of the county 14 years as associate Judge. I also spoke on the occasion. On Wedensday that is yesterday the Huntsvill[35] Agr[icultural] Society held their meeting at the court house at which I addressed the people on that subject & subscribed 1 set of silver spoons for 10 lb. of the best butter that may be presented at their next annual fair.[36] Here I met with some intelligent men who have recently moved to the county from Penna. Dr. Fussel & others.

On this day Thurs. the 17 [16] I left A. about 3 & rode alone to Pendleton. It snowed all the way & my horse could only walk. I arrived there at Sundown staid at Boston with Quarles & Mr. Hammond[37] who had arrived there before me. I read this night part of the life of Pompey—Having read while at A. the life of Aristides & the 2 Catos—much to my edification. I have lost much by the omission to read Plutarch more attentively.

35. A town laid out in 1830 by Eleazer Hunt and Enos Anderson a mile northeast of Pendleton. There was considerable rivalry between the two towns until the construction of the Bellefontaine Railroad brought the demise of Huntsville. Forkner and Dyson, *Historical Sketches and Reminiscences of Madison County*, p. 736.

36. According to one account the first Madison County fair was held in 1837 in Anderson—a private affair fostered by Archibald Parker and Joseph Barnes. The second fair was held in Huntsville in 1839. Netterville, *Centennial History of Madison County*, I, 108.

37. Abram Hammond, who studied law under John Ryman of Brookville and began his practice in Greenfield in 1835. He was elected lieutenant governor in 1856 and succeeded to the governorship in 1860 upon the death of Governor Willard. Woollen, *Biographical and Historical Sketches*, pp. 113–19.

At this place & in the counties of Hamilton & Madison I have been invited to run for Congress this summer. It is due to my real feelings to say that such invitations are greatful to me. I feel gratified that my countrymen should entertain such a regard for my services & but for the office I now hold to which I have recently been elected as Bank director—the unsettled & pending professional business—the amount of my real estate which I desire to dispose of & contract all my earnings into a small compass if I sacrifice half by the operation & be entirely clear of debt—& lastly & more especially but for the foregoing & the situation of my family of boys who are now just beginning to take those impressions which must last them thro' life which impressions I feel it my duty to give & direct myself to a certain extent & not leave so important a matter to the hands of the ignorant & vicious who at present compose the greater part of our teachers I would consent to serve this district in congress & with the assistance of a good Providence which has always presided over me I trust I should be in some degree useful to my countrymen in that high station. My old mother demands a visit from me next summer with whom I have only spent about 20 days in 20 years. Therefore do not expect to be a candidate.

Mr. Quarles & myself left Pendleton about 9 in the morn. Dined at Arnets where there was an infare & about 30 persons old & young. We arrived home about sundown. Saturday a pleasant day. On Sunday pleasant day. Mr. Q. & myself started for Greenfield & made to Rutters[?] Buck creek. Dined there with Judge Wick Secretary Bill Brown[38] Nave & Quarles & Butler.

Monday 20 Feby. 1837. Court opened—cloudy but snow is off in the road & very muddy. Court opened but little done. I am here solicited by the Sheriff Foster & others to run for congress. Noah Noble late Govr. & myself had some talk on Saturday. He has some idea of running & is to let me know on my return

38. Indiana secretary of state, William J. Brown (1805–1857). He came from Kentucky to Indiana in 1821 and was admitted to the Rush County bar in 1826, having read law with Charles H. Test. He was elected as representative from Rush County in 1828, 1829, and 1830, and from Marion County in 1841 and 1842, and was elected to Congress in 1843 and 1849. Monks *et al.* (eds.), *Courts and Lawyers of Indiana,* III, 1140; *Indiana Election Returns,* Index.

home. I wish him to run, if not I feel from the various solicitations that I must forego my objections.

Teusday [Feb.] 21. Johnson was tried for stealing money from Tyner. Robt. Morrison Bank Directer passed on to Indianapolis from Richmond.

Weds. [Feb.] 22. I left Greenfield at sunrise. Rode to Rutters to Breakfast & arrived at home at 12. After dinner took my seat in the Bank directery. Present Messrs. White of Lafayette Mitchell of Evansville Fitch of N. Albany, McCulloch of Ft. Wayne Lanier of Madison & Major of Lawrenceburgh Blake of Indianapolis[39] & there was in attendance about 30 delligates to get a location of some one of the 4 new branch banks we are authorized to make.[40] In the eve we invited them to appear before the board &c and an explination of our duties were pointed out & they apprised that we must first get the consent of each branch &c.

On *Thursday [Feb.] 23.* We met & commenced business. I am appointed on the new proposition of the legislature for 4 new branches as Chairman of the committee & on several other committees.

Friday [Feb.] 24. We met done some business & agreed to accept of the propositions of the legislature.

Saturday Feby. 25 '37. We finished our bank business & adjourned. Pleasant day—very muddy under foote. Michael & John repairing house for the former to move into in the McFarlin place.

Sunday Feby. 26. Pleasant day. I ought this day to go to Shelby but my business at home is crowding me & it is extremely bad riding. Mr. Butler can't leave next week & I must go to Columbus &c. I this day read the life of Paulus Aemelus to my boys. Cooley

39. James White, John Mitchell, Mason C. Fitch, Hugh McCulloch, James F. D. Lanier, Daniel S. Major, and James Blake.

40. The recent act of the General Assembly provided that not less than three nor more than four new branches of the State Bank should be established; time and place were dependent on the discretion of the state board. The provision was made, however, that no branch would open until it had the sum of eighty thousand dollars actually paid in, half by the state and half by the individual stockholders. The twelfth branch, located at South Bend, and the thirteenth at Michigan City, were authorized in 1838. No other branches were opened. *Laws of Indiana*, 1836–37 (general), p. 13.

has come home & is going to school to Mr. Ketcham. I feel very anxious he should advance in his studies & not idle away his time. He seems willing & even apt to learn but I fear he will not dig deep for the pure waters but will be satisfied with the first pool he comes to. He rode to Mr. Jones to day. The rest of the family went to church. In the eve Cooley Elijah Calvin & Miles stayed at home & Mrs. F. [and] the girls went to church. Dorio was baptised &c. Pleasant day but very muddy. Elijah & Cooley went to draw some beer & E. let the sprecket out & the gass forced the beer to the wall put the candle out & he called for me. I went & found Cooley had had the presence of mind to close the orifice with his hand. I am much pleased with the prospect of my two oldest boys—yet I have great fears that they will not hold out.

Monday Feby. 27 1837. Cloudy & snows a little. I wrote yesterday to my mother. It is gloomy weather. Michael & John gone to McFarlin place. Grew cold at noon. Tended to my ordinary business. Ground freezing—the worst travelling I ever saw. I settled with Mrs. Richmond. Cooley commenced reading lattin with Mr. Ketcham Mr. Merrill['s] Son in law. He is to board with us. Our little boy Stoughton commenced going to school to Mrs. Richmond this day for the first. We think he bids fair to be a good scholar. I wrote to a Mr. Jacob Miller offering to sell him 6 tracts of land at Laport County at $5.25 per acre.

Feby. 28 1837. This the last day of February, cold cloudy dissagreeable day. Michael going to work at McF. place &c. The ground is froze hard again.

Mar[c]h the 1 1837. This cold morning c[l]oudy. Several of our Merchants are going East & have been accommodated to an extravigant length at Bank. It has been resolved by several of us that we will put a stop to such extravigant loans. In the P.M. more pleasant but every thing looks gloomy. I bot 7 hogs of Elliott Patterson[41] for $14.

Chinns bull was put to big red cow. She will have a calf on the 1st day of Decr. next.

41. Son of Robert Patterson. Nowland, *Early Reminiscences of Indianapolis,* p. 120.

Stoughton & Mr. Bradley have concluded to sell out & settle up their business. I approbate their course. It seems merchandising cannot on such credit as is given here answer so well as other business—again all mechanical skill manifactories & agricultural products have raised to an extravigant price whereas merchandize has diminished in price & is the only article that is now sold on a credit. Consequently there is no active capital paid by the customer or in other words there is no money passing for the return trade in merchandize whereas the original buyer has paid the money for it which money he has borrowed & is paying interest for it. Now it follows when the losses by bad customers are calculated with the diminution of price or goods, compared with other business which commands money merchandizing is a bad business.

March 2. Cold dissagreeable morning with a little snow. S. & I went to Morgans brickyard & bot 19 hogs 18 of which are thrifty young shotes weighing about 50 lb. each. The old sow weighs about 200 lbs. for which I gave $40. On my return saw the first striped squirrill this year. After an inefectial attempt to sell my Hotel stock that is a company stock put in for Hendersons old tavern stand in which I subscribed last September by the urgent & pressing solicitation of N. McCarty against my own will & judgment & persuaded Stoughton & Bradley to subscribe for a like amount—one among the most foolish trades or engagements I ever made. It has already deducted $800. of my means without the least reason for so doing—or present or future expectation of securing a cent in return. It is a lesson to me never to act against my *own* judgment. In this case I did & if I help S. out of it whom I persuaded into it I shall loose several thousand dollers I fear—as the company against all expectation have gone into large expenditures &c.

After returning from the Brick yard I went out to James & David Fletchers. I entered into partnership with James to farm the Cox place for 3 years. I bot 3 cows & calf & for $35. & 32 hogs at $50. & let him have 100 bush. of corn to feed the hogs on & sold him 170 bush at .25 towards the hogs. He is to Keep 2 cows which he may milk belonging to me & 2 horses to work the place of his own to Keep the place in repair & to give me the one half the products when sold or delivered to me. There is about 40 acres under fence &c. I went to old Mr. Fletchers to leave some clover seed & made a partial agreement with him to tend the place this year.

I received a letter from Miles[42] & one from Ab. C. Neeland[43] who says he will come out & build me a barn. Miles will enter into partnership J. Hill &c. I returned & in the eve helped Cooley get his latin lesson. Michael & Betsy & John staid at McF. place. Have moved all &c.

March 3 1837. This day the sun has rose pleasently but it is very cool. A flight of snowbirds have visited us this morning. I fear falling weather. Ground froze. This is the day on which Genl. Jacksons administration terminates & Mr. Vanburans commences on to morrow. The latter cannot in the nature of things be worse but we have much to promise that it will be a better administration. Genl. J. has done more mischief in prostrating our republican institutions than any other man living could have done. He promised much in the way of reform & a confiding public with the hope common to our frailty which declares that "man never is but always to be blest" looked & expected this reform. "His Kitchen Cabinet" as they have been denominated excused his performance by alledging that his first opponents had thwarted the old Roman the Second Washington the Great & Best as he has been repeatedly called by his adulators & political [. . .], in his determination to reform &c.

Thus headed against a party the greater part of the community were daily expecting during the greater part of this administration to be tied to a political triumph & victory as signal as the battle of N. Orleans. In Indiana the weak & corrupt have filled all the federal offices & in the 4 first years the very men who controled the federal appointments in the state were turned out for corruption in office to wit Dr. Canby,[44] Bill Hurst[45]—Samuel Juda[46] &c &c Bill

42. C.F.'s brother, of Marlboro, New York. He was considering moving to Indianapolis.

43. Abner C. Kneeland, of Vermont.

44. Israel T. Canby who was the Jackson party candidate for governor in 1828 and was appointed by Jackson as receiver of the public moneys at the

Marshall[47] &c. Genl. J. was a candidate against Mr. Adams in 1824 & I voted for him. But in 1828 my judgment was better informed & tho I have not been a warm partisan I have opposed his lawless course. Mr. Van B. has not his popularity & cannot do so much mischief. Took depositions in the McDowell & Blucher case.

I got a letter from bro. Miles & one from Kneeland of Vt. who agrees to come out & build a barn for me.

March 4. Pleasent. Mr. Butler returned from Shelby &c. Several collections comes on. I am preparing to go to the Bluffs. Noble['s] cow had a calf from Chinns bull.

Sunday March 5. Pleasant morning but cool. After Breakfast left for Bluffs. Arrived there at 1 P.M. Stopped at Dr. Rusts in the house formerly owned [by] D. E. Allen & last year by Mr. McCarty & myself rented to McGrew. We bot this property 500 acres about 2 years since at 8 per acre. The farm is irregular & badly planned ½ the beech & sugar deadened. Spent some time at Mr. Davis merchant selling good for Mr. McCarty.

March 6. Very pleasant day. Rented most of the improved ground say 50 acres to King & Paul. McGrew last year failed to perform & left the ground in a very bad condition. A fine Sugar day. Went to Jesse Tulls. We examined the rock up the branches of Bluff Creek. They are of a peculiar formation—[. . .] & of vegitable matter apparently. They cover an area of one mile & a half & all seem to be of the same formation—too brittle to be of great use. The action of the frost seems to dissolve them.

At night drew several leases.

March 7[–8] 1837. When I rose this morning found it raining.

Crawfordsville Land Office. He was removed in 1832 for being in arrears in transmitting the land office receipts. He died in March, 1837. See below, entry for March 17, and *John Tipton Papers,* II, 11, 243n, 762.

45. William Henry Hurst, whom Jackson appointed receiver in the Jeffersonville Land Office. He was the son of Henry Hurst. See Pt. VI, note 92; *History of Ohio Falls Cities and Their Counties,* II, 433.

46. Samuel Judah, whom Jackson appointed United States district attorney for Indiana, replacing Charles Dewey. He resigned in 1833.

47. William Marshall, of Jackson County, who was appointed United States marshal for the District of Indiana by Jackson, serving from 1829 until 1832 when he succeeded John Tipton as Indian agent at Logansport.

After finishing two leases left for home in company of a Mr. Terry canal contractor who rode with [me] to Mrs. Parks. Arrived at home at 2. Went to the office. Hard rain till Weds. 8 on which Simon started for the Wabash by way of Danville &c.

Thurs. [*March*] *9*. Michael & John getting out clapboards for hog pen on McFarlin place. Mr. Butler & myself preparing court business. Genl. Jacksons circular stopped by act of Congress passed both houses.[48] How far this may effect matters we cannot tell. The land bill to sell to actual setlers will not pass it is said.

Friday March 10. Pleasant day. Went out to McF. place with old Mr. Butterfeld &c. Michael had the hippo. Good sugar day. Stock looks well. I returned by Govr. Nobles & he gave me a sow & I brought her home with his boar. I then went to McF. again to bring in a sow that I wish to put to him. This day I have travelled at least 10 miles & done much.

March 11 Saturday 1837. I went with Mr. Catterson to McF. place to spay sows. He commenced & spaid 12 & cut some small mail pigs. Calvin & I returned with two breeding sows to put with the Noble boar. I then went to my office & staid till 12. After dinner helped Mr. Catterson spay & cut 6 pigs. Then went with Cooley to McF. place & sowed myself a quart to the acre of clover seed on 6 acres of old meadow which I am going to have harrowed next week. The grass timothy is greatly [. . .] & cut out. I returned about sundown & after dusk spent till 9 at my office preparing for the Johnson court. The accounts of the winding up of Congress has not yet reached us but we are not looking for any particular good that can be done but what quantum of mischief.

Sunday March 12. Rose at ½ after 4. Cloudy but warm. Went out to Michaels. The spaid hogs seem to do well. Returned. It began raining. Put the chiny sow into my block. Mr. Quarles arrived & we started in the rain to Franklin court. We stopped at Nobles & dined. Just before we left home Govr. Noble wrote a line that

48. The act rescinding the treasury order (or Specie Circular) passed both houses of the Congress but was pocket vetoed by President Jackson. The Indianapolis *Indiana Journal* (March 18, 1837) reported that it was "not rescinded, repealed or superceded"; the President had merely "put it in his pocket." It described this as a gesture of "democracy with a vengeance. The will of the President has again, by a trick, triumphed over the will of the people."

he should decline running for congress & wrote & wished me to run. I promptly wrote in answer that I had made up my mind otherwise & should not be swerved from my determination. After we dined at N. we arrived at Franklin in the rain about 4. Here met Sweetser Brown Peesly Hammond &c.

Monday [March] 13. Cold dissagreeable day. I have had several new imployments.

[March] 14. Yet unpleasant.

[March] 15. More agreeable weather. Tried case of Culver vs Sells.

Thursday [March] 16. Pleasant day. Tried case of Herbert vs Case.

Friday [March 17]. A pleasant day. Left court at 9 for home. Came to J.B. Smocks[49] for dinner having heard that old Dr. Canby was dead & that Noble the tavern Keeper had gone to bury him. We met the corpse.

My sows 3 put to Govr. Nobles boar about this time.

Saturday [March] 18. Dissagreeable day. Preparing for court. Settled with Pratt for Hay on my Fletcher farm. For my part I got $137.50 the first cash I ever received from the place.

Sunday [March 19]. Cool but pleasant. Went to hear Mr. Eddy. Orindorio went to Mr. McGlaughlins to church. Stayed over night. Went to the farm with Richardson in the morning.

Monday [March] 20. Our court commenced its session. Present Messrs. Sweetser Nave Roberts Hewlit & Hammond foreigners Messrs. Brown (Hiram) Brown (Wm. J.) Quarls Ketcham Cobern & [. . .] Cloudy dissagreeable day.

March 21 Teusday. Cloudy dissagreeable. Tried old Mr. Clark & daughter for larency. Cleared—fee $50. Old Mr. Eller for usury. Cleared fee $15. The business of our court has increased some in importance if not in quantity of suits.

Weds. [March] 22. Clear cool. Michael brot in the Gentry cow with calf. Tried Andrew Smiths case with Burkhart. Lost the sow got of Govr. Noble can't find her. Genl. Tipton senator passed thro last night. Did not see him.

49. John B. Smock, whose home was two miles south of Southport in Perry Township, Marion County. He was the son of Jacob Smock who settled in the township in 1823. Sulgrove, *History of Indianapolis*, pp. 584, 588.

Thusd. 23d of March. Pleasant weather. Advancing in our court business. The President having refused to sign what is called the currancy bill the whole commercial community look gloomy. My embarrassments I fear will be considerable this summer.

I am imploid with H. Brown for several Irishmen—one of whom is indicted for murder by the name of Finch—one for theft [?] with intent to committ murder.

Friday [March] 24. Pleasant. My Mitchel sows the 2 young ones will have pigs in 16 weeks from this date by Govr. N.'s boar.

Sat. [March] 25. Pleasant day. Some are beginning to plow for oats. Cary Boatright divorced. D.L. McFarlin[50] breakfasted here &c. He came to market—sold apples at .75 per bush.

After court went out to see uncle Michael & helped take the red short horned heifer bot of John Fletcher to Nobles bull bot of John Owens of Bloomington.

Sunday [March] 26. Cloudy wet morning. Went with Richardson to see uncle Michael. Returned went to meeting. Wet drizly day.

Monday [March] 27. Cloudy cool morning. Buds have not started yet. 2d weeks court commenced—mostly appeals to be tried—Scott vs. Dawson tried—Application to continue the murder case affidavits & arguments to be heard tomorrow. Tolerable pleasant day. Cooley Elijah Calvin went to Michaels to cut corn stalks.

Teusday March 28 1837. Cool cl[o]udy morning. We have but little real spring weather yet. 2 hogs returned from McF. place. Saw first Martin to day (or house swallow). Tried case of Andrews vs Garrison & Pitts vs Lemon. Pecuniary matters look gloomy never more so. Mr. Mc. & Self owe J. Walker about $3000 due 10 Apl. Do not know where to get it. I last year had a vision of my approaching difficulties & should have heeded them but for the persuasion of others.

March 29 Weds. Mr. Boxley staid over night with us. Cool froze tolerably hard last night. Pecuniary difficulties seem not only to approach me as an individual but the whole nation are to be afflicted.

Thusd. [March] 30. Cool dissagreeable day. Fisher vs Bridges

50. Demas L. McFarland who settled in Decatur Township, Marion County in 1822. Sulgrove, *History of Indianapolis,* p. 512.

tried—verdict for B. But little else done. Peter Smith on list for divorce—not granted.

Saturday 31 March. Cold dissagreeable day some snow fell. Tried case of Tucker vs Bates &c. We have had a busy court. We have been tolerably successful. H. O Neel has returned from the South is admitted to practise law. I view him an ambitious young man will never "be at harts ease" &c.

We have the most gloomy account of the pecuniary pressure in the Eastern money market. I fear I shall be much harrassed but if God gives me health I hope to work thro'.

Apl. 1 1837. Saturday cool. Cloudy.

Apl. 2 Sunday. Left with Quarls for Morgan circuit court. Very cool dissagreeable morning. We dined at Rust at the Bluffs, Hammond, Brown & Wick all arrived. We proceeded to Martinsvill &c put [up] at Mitchills—Q. & I room together &c.

Monday the 3 of Ap. Last night about 12 inches of snow fell. Mr. Herrod & Govr. Ray at court—H. made a stump Speech. The snow partially melted off this day. Court house is uninclosed & cold. I have not attended this court for some 4 terms past & have not as much business as I otherwise would have had.

Teusday 4 Ap. Govr. Ray addressed the people for 3 hours. Warmer to day. Mr. Herrod left.

Wedensday [April] 5. Govr. Noble arrived.

Thursday [April] 6. Trying to arrange our business to return home.

Friday [April] 7. Mr. Quarles & myself at 9 rode to the Bluffs where we met with Govr. Noble Peesly & Hammond. Govr. Ray who is about to make a speech. Arrived at home about sundown a very gloomy day cold.

Saturday [April] 8. Cold dissagreeable day. The most unpleasant accounts arrive of the failures East in N.Y. The Josephs have failed. At 2 o clock Mr. Quarles & myself leave for Danvill. It snows & the road never was worse (the National). We reached Plainfield 16 miles West about sundown & staid at [. . .]. His little child was sick with the Quinsey or cramp & I advised to send for a doctor which they did but the child a fine little boy of about 2 years old died since. Plainfield now has 2 stores 2 taverns &c & about 30 houses.

Sunday Apl. 10 [9]. Went to Bellvill after breakfast in company with Dr. Moore. Stopped at Genl. Johnson's. Cold dissagreeable day. After dinner went to Danvill put up at Mr. Blakes.

Monday [*April*] *11* [*10*]. Cool but pleasant. Great deal of business in court. I am imploid for several &c.

Teusday [*April 11–15*]. Pleasant 13 pleasant 14 pleasant 15 pleasant.

Saturday [*April*] *16* [*15*]. A bea[u]tiful day. At 10 we left Danvill after a very busy court. We dined at Plainfield. Arrived home at dark.

Sunday [*April*] *17* [*16*]. Left for Lebanon Boon Cty. in company with Messrs. Quarls & Brown by the Michigan road. Cold day but clear. We dined 17 miles at McQuaddys Stand (Longs tavern) & arrived at Lebanon at sundown. Stopped at Langlys. This place has improved much for the last year & a half.

Monday [*April*] *18* [*17*]. Cold day—Messrs. Tayler Herrod Ray Angle[51] Nave &c present. Not much business.

Teusday 19 [*April 18*]. Cool. Got nearly thro.

Wed. [*April*] 20 [*19*]. Left Lebanon at 10 arrived home at 4 P.M. Just tolerable pleasant day. I found Mr. McCarty had gone to Cincinnati in order to get $5000 for us. I have not much expectation he can succeede. Things look very gloomy.

Thursday Ap. 21 [20] *1837*. Cool—frost. Michael has put in our oats & has just began to plow the corn ground. Went out to the place. Our professional business is increasing—but for this I should feel much worse but have determined to act the philosopher & fret as little as possible.

[*Friday April 21*]. Cold morning—air very cold. I bot 4 pair trees. Went out to Michaels & planted them. He had killed 176 rats & we put them under the roots of the pair trees. They have destroid a great deal of my corn. We are plowing the ground by Pouges Creek. Shall be ready to plant to morrow. Simon just returned from Putnam county. The front of the Indianapolis Hotel

51. Jacob Angle, a Boone County pioneer and attorney. He served as representative of Clinton and Montgomery counties in 1831–32 and was elected senator from Boone and Hamilton counties in 1839. Samuel Harden (comp.), *Early Life and Times in Boone County, Indiana* . . . (Lebanon, Ind.: Harden & Spahr, 1887), pp. 31, 40, 152, 156.

is being removed. Our business in our District & Sup[reme] Court increasing.

Saturday Ap. 22. Cold morning some frost. Our earliest plumb tree is swelling to blossom—the bole or bulb containing the blossom about the size of a [. . .]. shot. Elijah Miles & Calvin are cutting corn stocks at the McF. place. At 10 started for Noblesvill with Mr. Quarls for court. Very cool. Arrived at N. about 2. I helped take deposition in case of Collins vs Boxley. Very cool.

Sunday 23d of Apl. Sunday morning the earth was covered with snow. Gloomy prospects. Snow remined till 12. I went to hear a Mr. Jones a Campbellite preach at the old schoolhouse S. of the town. Read some in Plutarch, the life of Cicero & Demostenes. Mr. Herrod in company.

Monday [April] 24. Pleasent but cool—Heavy frost. I fear the fruit is killed. Held court in the new court house yet unfinished.

Ap. 25th. 1837 Teusday. Cool. We have not much business but that which was continued from last court. We tried State vs James Carter Mr. Q. & myself for Carter. He was cleared.

Wedensday [April] 26. Cool frost last night.

Thusd. [April] 27. Also very cool. I fear fruit has been ruined.

Friday Morning [April] 28. Pleasent. We finished our court & Judge Wick Quarles & myself started home at 10. We called & got some apples at Mrs. Malleries—got dinner at Carters. Mr. Quarls quite unwell—seems to be affected in the lungs. We arrived home at 4. This terminates a court of 11 weeks—I have attended all but 2 courts. It has been a dissagreeable spring. Our business has been fair. I have resumed a practise I suspended last year. I find I soon should get rusty in the practise &c.

Our collections from the East seem to be good—too large I fear—augurs bad for the future. I found Mr. McCarty had been to Cincinnati & had borrowed from the life & trust company $4000. We owe nearly $3000. of this to John Walker. We are to pay this in 4 months. I am about to bring into market our out lots on the Sanders place & must rely on them to get the money. Had no change in times occurred We could have got along. I now expect much trouble to extricate myself. Had I followed the counsels of my own view I need not nor should not have been the least involved. But as it is I have resolved not [to] act on my fears or regrets but to deal honestly let what will come—do nothing that can saver of dishonesty or impropriety or that myself or childrin will ever regret.

Ap. 29 1837. The news from the South & East in relation to pecuniary matters are desperate. One Genl. Bankruptsy must take place both in England & America. The whole vally of the Missippie must suffer & its sufferings have scarcly begun.

Pleasent day. Went out to Michaels in P.M. Devoted the fore noon to my law business which I intend to do hereafter & the P.M. to my private concerns. Michael is plowing with John & new hand the N.E. fi[e]ld. Elijah Calvin & Miles picking up cornstalks. Have planted the block No. of Mr. McOuts the fild East of Genl. Hannas.

In the P.M. visited James Fletcher & old man—they are doing very well. The Wheat sowed by the latter looks poor.

Sunday Ap. 29. Warm in the morning. Stoughton & [I] went out to see Michael—took breakfast—Returned. I went to M. Church. Jno. Holland preached. Got National Intelligencer. Gloomy accounts of failures in the East. About 2 began to grow cold—thundered a little. (Mrs. Richmond moved to Wm. Smiths house on yesterday). At sundown very cold—I fear a frost.

May 1 1837. Anniversary of our marriage. Frosty cold morning. We fear the fruit is Killed. John & James (the hired man) gone to plowing. I spent the fore noon in the office. P.M. went with Mr. Whitcomb & J. Hill to appraise the 2½ acre blocks on the Sanders place. We estimated them at $42,579. in all about 250 acres. We shall offer them at public sale if not sold before on the 29 instant. I fear we have appraised them too high.

I rented the Bradley block to Browning & Brown 15 acres for $60. & 11 for $50. Mr. Alf Harrisons son a boy of 4 years of age died this day. Mrs. F. & I went to see him in the eve.

Tusdy. 2d of May. Cloudy & cold. I have written an advertisement for sale of lots.[52] Went to the funeral of Mr. Harrisons child. Windy day. Warm in the P.M. Mr. Boxley came down. Rain in the eve. Miles, Calvin & Elijah came in from the farm. I am trying to

52. The advertisement, signed by Calvin Fletcher and Nicholas McCarty, appeared in the Indianapolis *Indiana Journal* of May 13, 1837, and following issues. It offered for sale at Brown's Mansion House on May 29 "98 blocks" each containing two and a half acres, "the whole lately occupied by Dr. John Sanders

regulate our business especially my own. I sold the Kelly place to old Jas. Johnson for $620.[53] I have likely to go to Logansport.

May 3d. Pleasant growing morning. This day another of Mr. Harrisons little childrin died. I have concluded to go to Logansport to see about my bridge stock. I unwisely took 150 shares for myself for Bradley & Fletcher—for Town & Livimore[54] & since 10 shares have been transferred to me. When I took those shares the bridge was to have been built in a short time & I understood Genl. Tipton would take part of the stock off my hands but times have changed—my stock is yet on hands—the bridge not built & a demand for pay is made. I have paid $760. already when I took them it was to have been otherwise.

Mr. Boxley & myself settled our Kimberlin business at Bank & I have endorsed at the Insurance company for him to get $250. to buy cattle. I fear he cannot buy them at this time of year & if he does they will be too high for the general prices of produce which is on the fall. Pleasent warm day. Michael is planting the N.E. field on McF. place. Genl. Hanner wishes me to send & help raise a barn &c. In the eve went with Mr. Boxley to see Michael. In the eve went with Mrs. F. Mrs. R. & Marilla M[orris] to Mrs. Harrisons &c.

[*May*] *4.* Pleasant day—warm—all nature looks beautiful. Went to help bury Mr. Harrisons child his youngest a little girl about 2 years old—died with the scarlet fever. I went out to the McF. place & started Michael & John to a raising of a barn at Genl. Hanners.

James McF. called & I paid about $25 on the land I bot of him. I filed our advertisements to sell blocks. I fear we shall not do well. I prepared an advertisement & sent it by Mr. Whitcomb to sell all our land in Hamilton & Madison.

May 5. Pleasant morning. Birds building nests—one a sparrow

---

and exhibited on Mr. Sullivan's late map." The lots were laid out with streets and alleys and pasture and woodlots were included. The map referred to was the map of Indianapolis drawn by the town's first civil engineer, William Sullivan, in 1836. A reproduction of the map is pocketed at the back of this volume.

53. See Pt. VII, note 82.

54. Ithiel Town and Jonathan Livermore, along with Edwin J. Peck, were contractors for the construction of the Wabash River bridge at Logansport. See Pt. VI, note 190.

in the plumb tree west of the well. We are doing a good quantity of collecting business. Simon just returned from Decatur.

Have discovered that our next District court is deprived of its jurisdiction &c.[55]

In the Eve a heavy storm came—blowed down a number of our sugar trees in the S. Block. I start for Logansport tomorrow.

Saturday May 6 [–7]. Cool morning after the storm. I did not sleep well—I am inclined to hyppocondria. I regret my past conduct more in not following my own judgment after imploring the blessing of that light. I have ever asked & hope ever to ask of Divine Intelligence. After this I hope I shall be able to live nearer to so great & essential principal to present & future happiness.

I left home for Logansport about 3 o'clock. Rode to Westly Smiths[56] 20 miles—horseback. Stayed over night. Sunday morning at sunrise left in company with an old man from Prebble Cty. Ohio. Rode to Kirks to Breakfast. After Breakfast rode 4 miles N. of Burlington & took dinner. I had intended to dine at Mr. Lakes but the family had gone to meeting & I called at a little cabin of a West Tenneseean at whose residence some half dozen women & childrin had assembled among the rest an old man a native of Baltimore 60 years of age who lived off the road near the Indian Reserve & had no doubt been a man of some little consequence. He lived as I was told in a cave or an excavation made by himself & a little boy.

I arrived at the Wabash about sundown—put up [at] Vigus tavern.

Monday [*May 8*]. Morning pleasant. Went to see Jordon Vigus

55. Indiana was organized as a separate federal court under an act of March 3, 1817. The act granted to the court the powers and jurisdiction of a federal circuit court as well as those of a district court. Under an act approved March 3, 1837, the court was reduced to the rank of a United States district court, the court to convene on the first Monday in May and November. By the same act Indiana was linked with Illinois, Ohio, and Michigan to form the seventh United States circuit, with the circuit court to convene in Indianapolis on the first Monday in December. Monks *et al.* (eds.), *Courts and Lawyers of Indiana*, II, 405–406; U.S. *Statutes at Large*, V, 176–78.

56. Wesley Smith settled in Union Township, Boone County, in 1826. His tavern was located near the northern boundary of the township. "Col. Smith" served as the first treasurer of Boone County. Harden (comp.), *Early Life and Times in Boone County*, pp. 9, 103, 426.

[and] Genl. Wilson & with the former went to see Genl. Tipton. He had left his house for the mill at which we found him. I tried to get him to take the Bridge stock. This he partly consented to—But I have very little faith that he will. It was partly on his account that I bot or took any of the stock myself. I dined with the General went & saw Mr. Livemore the builder—found things in rather a desperate condition. I transferred 55 shares to Fletcher & Bradley & 45 to Town [and] Peck & 4 to Genl. Tipton & after doing various things left in company with old Esq. Basy who rode 8 miles with me & arrived at Stocktons 20 miles just at dark.

May 9. Started early. Breakfasted at Mrs. Johnsons—dined at Westly Smiths & arrived home about dusk. A very windy day.

May 10th. Pleasant day. Went out to see Michael. Attending to my business. Things look gloomy.

May 11. James Hill came to look over my land certificates. Pleasant day. Finished planting part of the N.W. & middle fields at McF. place. Mr. Ab. Harrison moved in from Laport & is about to commence business here with Alfred. Stoughton started for Lafayett to see Mr. Peck. Mrs. F. & S.'s wife staid over night at Michaels as it rained.

Gentry cow sent to Govr. Nobles.

Friday May 12 1837. Pleasant day—things look well. Dunns from the East. A Mr. Jewell from Baltimore here collecting from our merchants. Simon has cleaned out Bradlys upper room & is going [to] study there. Mr. Palmer[57] is to fill his place. Simon has been ingaged for the last 18 months in active business & now designs being licensed in the Sup[reme] court at the fall term. Two fields of our corn are up. Jas. Fletcher in & I promised to send Elijah to help him &c. Received a claim on a Mr. Jordan from Townsend & Brothers N.Y. Simon goes to Greenfield tomorrow.

Saturday 13 May. Pleasant day. E. went to help Jim F. plant corn. Jas. Hill regulating titles &c.

This day at my suggestions the merchants to wit E. & T. Porter, Russel Bradly Ray Blake of the firm of Moore & Co. McCarty & Hannerman[58] met at the counting room of McC. to consult as

57. William Palmer, son of Nathan B. Palmer.

58. E. T. Porter, Alexander Russell, Henry Bradley, James M. Ray, James Blake, Nicholas McCarty, and William Hannaman.

to the general welfare of the mercantil interest here. Since the great pressure in N.Y. & Philadelphia an idea has prevailed there that there are abundant means in the West & the moment a debt is due the note is presented here or drawn for. Our merchants here all have abundant means yet they are extravigantly behind in consequence of their indulgence to their customers. The Bank has loaned them all more or less & they have extended their business without calling on their customers. These long credits have encouraged extravegance. First credits given by the B[ank] to the merchants & they to their dealers. Mischief must insue by such a course. We should live close to our earnings. Last year I was indulged by the Bank & the worst evils will insue I fear from this indulgence & I hope this will effectually cure & gard me in future.

Our merchants have privatly resolved not to do any injustice to any of their Eastern crediters but to pay them all an equal portion as it becomes due & especially to pay the Bank here as fast as any other crediter—have determined to make no nois[e] in their home collections—to resist bills drawn on them by Eastern merchants without a previous agreement so to do & to pay no one more than an equal portion of their debts to the injury of any other creditor. Mr. Boxley was here with 75 cattle. Miles went home with him. I received a line from Elijah who is about to visit Conn. with his son & Vt. He informs me that all his affairs are in a good condition. Our corn is coming up. Took tea with Mrs. Richmond. James Hills wife & Stoughtons wife there &c.

Sunday May 14 1837. Rained last night a little. It is cloudy. I am about to write to Elijah at Vt. I wrote to him & before I got thro' it was too late for meeting. Mr. Merrill called & stated that on his way from Ft. W[ayne] he had fallen [in] & travelled with Abner C. Neeland from Cavendish Vt. to whom I had written to come an[d] build a barn. He left a big coat for him.

Monday May 15. This day I am under promise to go to Shelbyville to see about renting the mills. This property I fear will be a great curse to me & McC. It is very cold dissagreeable day for the time of year. Michael is plowing the S.W. piece of ground for corn. This day our merchants at 4 o'clock had a meeting to take into consideration the presant approaching crisis. Met at Mr. McCartys counting room & agreed for the present not to pay only an equal proportion to their Eastern crediters, to sustain the Bank in case of pressure &c & to meet Every Wed. at 4 at the same time & place. I did not get off for Shelby. Mr. Kneeland arrived just at Dusk. I was pleased to see him.

Thursday May 16 1837. Rose at 4. A frost on—cool but cloudy. I left without breakfast of which I partook at Keelers 12 miles. I arrived at Shelby at 10. Found everything out of order. With much difficulty I got a Mr. Sergant to take the Mills & I left there at 5 & rode back to Keelers where I stayed over night.

May 17. Cool—some frost. I left at Sunrise in company of a Mr. Thornburgh. Arrived at home at 9, took breakfast & went to the Bank boa[r]d of State Directors which meets to day. I found Messrs. Scott Leeds Morrison Major Brown Hall Deming White McCulloch Blythe Lanier[59] &c. We all met with feelings of no ordinary concern for the institution over which we were placed. News of the failure of a deposite Bank at Buffalo—other deposit Banks at the South Mississipp & Louisiana. We were expecting others would go by the board & our Bank has 12 hundred thousand dollars in these deposit Banks out of the State & others & we have about that sum of government diposits with transfer drafts to that amount already upon us. The daily news from the Eastern cities & from Europe would indicate that the fountains of the great deep in the commercial world are about to break up. What are we to do is the enquiry from every one? In addition to these extra difficulties we have a complaint from a part of the board of the branch at Lawrenceburgh that there has been corruption by their cashier &c & require a committee which has been appointed to investigate &c. All things look gloomy both in the moral & natural world as we have had 2 or 3 successive posts. We have just learned that the Dry Dock Co. finally have failed or stopped payment with ½ of a million of public deposits & owing one of our branches 140 thousand the Tarre Haute branch. This has created much distress

59. Lucius H. Scott of Terre Haute, Noah Leeds of Richmond, Robert Morrisson of Richmond, Daniel S. Major of Lawrenceburg, John Brown of Bedford, —[?] Hall, Demas Deming of Terre Haute, James White of Lafayette, Hugh McCulloch of Fort Wayne, Benjamin I. Blythe of Indianapolis, and James F. D. Lanier of Madison.

for that branch whose concerns have been administered with credit by their officers.

May 18 1837. Our board met to day & are making regulations in relation to the transfer drafts of the U. States & appointed a committee to locate a 12th branch & to investigate the subject of buying & building a house for the Bank & Sinki[ng] fund commissioners. We adjourned at 6 to meet at nine tomorrow morning. All left the Banking room but Mr. Ray & myself when Mr. Merrill President returned with his hands full of letters he had just received by 2 messengers one from Lawrenceburgh & one from the Madison branches stating that all the Banks in the Eastern cities together with the Cincinnati banks had suspended payment—that in a few hours after the suspension in Cincinnati all the paper of our branches was bo't up & sent by runners to Lawrenceburg & to the other branches. The former prudently shut her doors against the applicants & started messengers in 4 hours afterwards. The Madison paper also reached their branch but it had closed business for the day & both dispatched messengers &c.

Our board were soon convened & by invitation the Governor & Treasurer Mr. Palmer were with us. The question presented in a solemn manner by our President was what shall the Board do—Let our specie be drawn out by Banks that owe us when they have closed their doors? It was a solemn meeting. Our Charter presented obstacles & our contract with the General Government was to be violated if we suspended. The latter obsticle was not great in my mind as she had already winked at the custom house bonds being suspended & caused a drain upon our banks. After a most solemn diliberation in which the Governor & Treasurer both took part we agreed to permit each branch to suspend if it thought best and messengers were dispatched to each branch.[60] This occurrance was sudden as it was unexpected by most. I had feared this calamity for some time yet the shape it appeared was different from what I expected. An address was prepared for the branches. We adjourned at 10 'clock at night.

60. Samuel Merrill, president of the State Bank, wrote to the Secretary of the Treasury Levi Woodbury on May 20: "The Directors of this institution being in session when information reached them of the suspension of specie payments

Friday [May] 19. Our board met again this morning with some little doubts as to what had transpired the night before but on a review all were satisfied that the best had been done & flattered themselves that it was but a temporary suspension which would not last but a few months at most. There was a slight frost last night.

A public meeting was held at 11 o clock at the court house at which Dr. Sanders presided—McGuire & Morrison (A.L.) were secretarys approving of the suspension of specie payments by our bank.[61] Also the merchants met & passed resolutions to the same effect & agreed to take the money of the Bank &c.[62]

---

by the Banks in Cincinnati and the Eastern cities generally they proceeded at once to recommend a similar course to the branches for the present. An agent will proceed in a few days to Washington to confer with you on these matters and until some other arrangement is made the deposits hereafter made on account of the Govt. will only be received *specially* for the purpose of being paid out when called on as you shall direct. This Bank may possibly lose by some of the balances in other banks but its intire solvency is unquestionable. Each of the branches has been carefully examined within a few weeks and not a single bad debt was allowed to be due from any of the individual debtors. The surplus fund set apart for losses is over $250,000, and we hope and believe that under almost [all] circumstances not even the stockholders will seriously suffer. . . ." Letter Book of the State Bank of Indiana, I, 1834–42, pp. 109–10, Archives Division, Indiana State Library.

James F. D. Lanier was dispatched to Washington where he conferred with the Secretary of the Treasury. Of all the banks then possessing government deposits the Indiana bank was the only one that offered or paid any specie. The Secretary allowed the deposits to remain until drawn in the regular course of business. Logan Esarey, *State Banking in Indiana* (*Indiana University Studies*, No. 15, Bloomington, 1912), p. 259; Buley, *The Old Northwest*, II, 285–86.

61. Samuel Merrill addressed the citizens' meeting at the Courthouse, saying in part, "Your money, fellow citizens, and the money of the state is in our vaults, and we are solemnly bound to protect it. The Banks [branches] that have suspended are *not broken*. They have been compelled to yield to circumstances not within their control." Indianapolis *Indiana Journal*, May 20, 1837. The *Journal* reported that opinion appeared to be entirely in support of the directors of the bank. There was some disapproval of suspension over the state, but Indiana notes were always quoted at par and any confidence that the bank may have lost was soon restored. Specie payment was resumed August 13, 1838, when other banks resumed. Buley, *The Old Northwest*, II, 286.

62. At the meeting of the merchants at Nicholas McCarty's counting house, McCarty serving as chairman and Joseph M. Moore as secretary, resolutions were adopted approving the action of the bank directors and expressing confidence in the bank, and the merchants further resolved to "continue to receive at par in payment of debts due us and for merchandize at the usual price, the

Saturday May 20 1837. This day pleasant. Mr. Kneeland & myself in the P.M. walked to the Fletcher farm to look for shingle timber &c. I have great doubts whether I ought to build a barn. I am sensible that I ought to commence a system of retrenchment in all my expenditures—all my business. I believe I have fortitude to accomplish so necessary an object. More disastrious news has arrived as to our national & individual pecuniary affairs. By a letter from Mr. Wm. Baldwin an old acquaintance & equal in Ohio now a very respectable merchant of N.Y. City I learn that there scarcely will be a solvent merchant in that city by the first of June. News has arrived that the Banks of Louisville & all the Ky. Banks have suspended.

My own debts to be paid this summer greatly alarm me. I have abundant means to pay but fear I cannot realize them. I am in my own mind prepared for the worst. I have no mortifications to indure by surrendering up all I have to my creditors by the reflections that I have been extravigant. We have no carriage no Turky Carpet no statly mansion to part with. On the contrary as yet we possess nothing but the necessaries of life. Besides we do & are prepared to hereafter to raise our own provision to manufacture our own butter & some part of our own clothing & I have another comfort in the reflection that if the exertion of my child is necessary to obtain a livelihood by daily labor, it will be for the best. I never worshiped the accumulated treasures of this life & on the whole I am as well prepared in my own mind to be a poor as a rich man.[63] If I can save my credit my integrity & do no one any

---

paper of each of the Branches of the State Bank of Indiana." Indianapolis *Indiana Journal,* May 20, 1837; Indianapolis *Indiana Democrat,* May 31, 1837.

The merchants also resolved that a meeting of the legislature should be called at as early a date as practicable. This brought a communication to the *Democrat* published on May 31, signed by "Many Citizens," which said that "as far as we can ascertain there is cheerful acquiescence among all the people" in the decision to suspend temporarily. However, they declared the decision to call a meeting of the legislature was premature, and might be a positive evil. Not only would it cost at least $10,000 but it could give "no effectual aid to relieve our citizens and we believe that under existing circumstances when our bank paper circulates freely at home, the proposed measure would injure our credit abroad by giving scope for exaggerated accounts of our real condition; and by impairing confidence here, would greatly aggravate the pressure and its evils."

63. Daniel D. Pratt, who read law in C.F.'s office (see Pt. VI, note 29) re-

injury by any real or supposed improvidence on my part I shall be content. What another year will produce I can not, dare not, even contemplate. But to me it seems that things cannot be much better but I think worse. In 1797 the Bank of Eng[land] suspended specie payment. In 1817 [1821] they resumed it again. We have not all the imbarrassments they had to inc[o]unter but it will take 5 years to at least to be reinstated.

Sunday May 21. Cloudy day. Mr. Kneeland & myself went to church. Mr. Edy preached. Mr. Quarles called on me after church & I walked with him. He informed me of the birth of his 3d son on that day. We walked to the grove west of the state house. I told him over my fears & my expected pecuniary imbarrassments, also my resignation & how little I believed I could do with in my family. He then stated he viewed me a happy man as I set so little estimate on what I had labored for years & my reasons why I was willing to be poor &c.

Our corn has been cut down with frost, the late plowing not up yet.

Monday May 22. Young Mr. Palmer the Treasurers son commenced business in our office this day. Simon Yandes has taken an adjoining room & is going to study law altogether. How the project will work I can't say. I have commenced an examination of my accounts—the collections I have on hand &c. Mr. Butler is preparing for Sup[reme] court.

Tusday 23 May. Pleasant day. Nothing new no mails.

Wednesday [May] 24. This day we have intelligence from the East. The Globe the Government paper contains the pro[c]lamation of the President to call a meeting of congress to assemble the Mond[ay] in Sept. next in consequence of certain commercial distress &c. The ruling party have at last made a surrender. It appears that the government have not a dollar at their command—that any

---

called C.F.'s "rigid simplicity." "He was simple in his wants and tastes. This trait pervaded all his relations and marked his whole intercourse with family, friends, the public. He lived and dressed frugally and simply. . . . There was nothing in food, furniture or surroundings calculated to instil ideas of luxury or extravagance. The house was furnished with plainest of furniture and carpets." Pratt to Dr. William B. Fletcher, October 6, 1873, Fletcher Family Papers, Indiana Historical Society Library.

deposit Bank in the union has stopped pay—that the army & navy & every other department must surrender or rather stop. No public work can move. No specie, no substitute. Treasury orders are to be issued to pay the public service. Congress is to be called for that purpose. All the safety fund Banks in N.Y. have been suspended. A general prostration of all business, of all interests in the union. The scene before me has given me the horrors & to add to this I have just learned from Govr. Wallace (now candidate for Governor) that the [New] Albany branch of the State B[ank] had 70 thousand dolls. drawn from her vaults on Friday before she learned the order of suspension.

It is a gloomy wet cloudy day—the first rain we have had for a month. I have spent it idlely. Mr. Boxley sent his teem down with sugar &c & 2 faun skins from Miles who is with him. Dorio sent a letter to him in answer to a matrimonial request. I called on Judge Wick for Mrs. Richmond to see about his daughter &c. Got some rats. Have to kill rats at the farm. Our boys picking wool. Michael & Mr. Kneeland preparing potato ground.

May 25. It rained all night. We have got the Noble sow here & 4 pigs. Put his into the block.

May 26. Pleasant day. News as to commercial distress East continues to reach us so far as relates to N.Y. which is produced [?] on the return of Eng[lish] bills.

I went with Jac Landis to McF. place to sell him some hogs. Michael Mr. Kneland & John preparing a piece for potatoes North of the old field.

27 *May Sat*. Marshall Taylor, Dumont, & Wallace candidate for governor are here.[64] Supreme court & District court sits on Monday. This is the only spring weather we have yet had. I sold an 80 acre tract of land in Hamilton Cty. for $262.50 also partially bargained for sale of a tract near Billy Orfords. Hugh Smith mer-

64. Gamaliel Taylor, David Wallace, the encumbent lieutenant governor, and John Dumont of Switzerland County who had served as both representative and senator. The Indianapolis *Indiana Democrat*, July 6, 1837, announced that Taylor was no longer a candidate; he had dropped out because his views on internal improvements were so nearly the same as Dumont's that his running would only split Wallace's opposition. The *Democrat* urged the voters to unite against Wallace. Wallace was victorious, winning 46,067 votes to Dumont's 36,915. *Indiana Election Returns*, pp. 145–47.

chant Shoemaker for whom J. W. Foud[r]ay had endorsed for $700 to In[surance] Co[mpany] made an assignment of effects to him. This I fear is the beginning of the process of insolvency in our place.

Our friend Mr. Ingram arrived in the evening. I had not seen him before for 18 months & I need not further express my joy than that I esteem him as one of my own family. Our boys went fishing in Pogues creek.

Sunday May 28. Pleasant day. Mr. Ingram & myself went to church. Mr. Eddy preached. In A.M. I reviewed the lives of the two Catoes in Plutarch. Spent an agreeable day. Banished as far as possible the doubts the difficulties the mortifications & the possible pleasures of the approaching week. Things grow fast—our garden peas in full bloom.

Monday May 29. Pleasant day. My office crowded with Cincinnati and Philadelphia Dunns. Mr. Holmes of the house of White & Holmes Mr. E[. . .] of the house of Blachly & Simpson & Mr. Miller of the house of Kilgore & Taylor are here. They are all collecting & say they have met 20 different Dunns each during the last week in this state. The scene of 1817–8–9–20 has again recurred. There was during that period scarcely a well dressed dandy looking man who passed the road but was denominated a Philadelphia Dunn. They are now visiting every village & town.

Sup[reme] Court sit to day but my office was so crowded I could not attend. Jeremiah Sullivan appointed & took his seat as Sup[reme] Judge in place of Judge McKinney deceased.[65]

Tuesday May 30. Still pleasant day. Michael harrowing the corn on the block N. of McOuits. It is about 3 inches.

Weds. May 31. Still pleasant growing weather.

Thursday June 1st. Pleasant with showers. Mr. Carlisle & lady arrived from Newburgh to settle. Sold a piece of land near Squire Bradys[66] to two Ohio men for $460 for 80 acres bot of Scott Evans for $200.

65. John T. McKinney. He served as Supreme Court judge from January 28, 1831, until his death, March 4, 1837.

66. Henry Brady, who settled in Warren Township, Marion County, in 1824. The preceding year he had entered eighty acres of land in T15N, R4E. He served as a justice of the peace from 1828 to 1831, and was elected state represen-

Friday June 2d. Pleasant day. Mr. Palmer went to Joab Woodruff in Johnson County to collect a debt for Spier & Patton. Mr. Holmes of the house of White & Holmes called & staid some time. Simon is absent to Lafayette to settle some business for the Bank against the 2 [. . .]. We have two Yankee school mistresses arrived from Geneva N.Y. to take charge of a femal academy.[67]

Received a check for Willits & Broths. N.Y. from Lafayette which are preparing to forward. The money matters have grown easier since the suspension.

Saturday June 3. Pleasant after a rain last night. Been busy all day. Mr. Ingram with us yet. Mr. Palmer returned.

We learn that the people of Boston Massa. are about to resist the order of the Post Master for the collection of the revenue of that department in specie. I regret to learn that such is the probible state of affairs in that inlightened city yet I believe they have great cause of complaint.

Sunday June 4. Went to General Class with Mr. K[n]eelan[d] & the family. Pleasant day. Heard old Mr. Havens preach.

Monday June 5. A very pleasant day. In the P.M. went with Stoughton to Michaels. James Hill preparing to visit our lands north. Kneland getting out timber for corn barn. Michael harrowing N.E. cornfield. Mr. Holiday called on me—gave the children books. Roman Catholick priest called on me to see about the Irish prisoner in jail. Our Supreme court is in session. At night I met & settled with a Mr. McDonald for attending an old Sup[reme] court case & Helped Giles Mitchel get some money out of the Bank. Mr. Gregg called on me to know if I would act as attorney for the Insurance Company. I declined & no doubt James Morrison will be appointed. Mr. Kneeland called me up to go & see about some sawing. I went to Mr. Southerlands' with him & then put him on

---

tative in 1831, 1832, 1833, 1841, and 1851, and senator in 1834 and 1837. Sulgrove, *History of Indianapolis,* pp. 66, 614; *Indiana Executive Proceedings,* pp. 515, 516n; *Indiana Election Returns,* Index.

67. In 1836 under sponsorship of a group of Presbyterians including James Blake, Isaac Coe, and James M. Ray, the Indianapolis Female Institute was chartered. It opened in June, 1837, on the second story of the Sanders' building on Washington Street near Meridian. The teachers were the Misses Mary J. and Harriet Axtell. The Seminary was conducted successfully until 1849 when the health of one of the sisters failed. Dunn, *Indianapolis,* 1, 128.

the road to Perhams mill. Mr. Ingram is about to start. James Hill about to leave. John & James brot in the 4 cattle I bot of John Fletcher & we have put into pasture over by Dr. Sanders. It is a very pleasant day but I have so many things to do I do not know which demands my attention most.

Weds. [June] 7. Mr. Butler moved & I gave out going to Noblesvill &c.

Thursday [June] 8. Mr. Butler & wife with Mr. Cole went to Hannamans. Beautiful day. Sold to Butcher cow for $18. 2 year old steer at $25. not very fat will weigh 4 cwt each. Most delightful weather. Corn grows well. Work is commenced on the Cumberland road. Mr. Palmer has gone to Bloomington to collect debt off Hemphill. Roman Catholic priest Mr. Shaw[68] called on me. He had a private room at my house to say mass. He has called to enquire about the aid necessary for a catholic in jail for murder (Finch).

Friday [June] 9. Called on Mr. Edy (M. preacher). Had a conversation with him at Mr. Phipps store. Pleasant day. Mr. Penny[?] & myself settling an old law suit—Simon Yandes assisting. Mr. Shaw the Roman Prist called & took tea. Found him an intelligent man.

Saturday [June] 10. Pleasant day. Went to farm with butcher. Sold a stack of hay. Very busy in our professional business. Attend a trial between Henderson & Miller. Bot in Emersons land for Moss &c with Jas. Morrison. Bot in Burkhart lot on judgment of Andrew Smith.[69] Mr. Smith of Philadelphia called & left some collections. This day Preachers Edy & Smith dined with us. We had the first green peas.

Sunday June 11th. Pleasant day. Got [up] early & went with

68. Probably Michael Shawe who came to America from France with Bishop Simon Bruté de Rémur of Vincennes, Indiana, in 1836. He was ordained on March 12, 1837, the first priest ordained in St. Francis Xavier Cathedral in Vincennes. Mary Salesia Godecker, *Simon Bruté de Rémur First Bishop of Vincennes* (St. Meinrad, Ind., 1931), Index.

69. The Indianapolis *Indiana Democrat* on June 7, 1837, carried a notice of the sheriff's sale of property of David Burkhart to satisfy a suit of Andrew Smith and Aaron Coppock. The Marion County deed records show that on June 17, 1837, C.F. bought from Corson Vickers, sheriff, the northwest quarter of section 5, T15N, R3E, 175 acres, for $655.35.

Elijah in swimming at the River. Michael & Kneeland came in—the latter went to church with me.

Also went [to] church in the P.M. A shower at night. Pleasant day.

Monday June 12 1837. Set up & am preparing to go to Andersontown to sell some land to meet some payments in Bank in July. I have many things to harrass my mind. I want firmness & judgment & I do try to ask for it from a higher source than man. I have many things, many responsibilities upon me & thro' the assisting Grace of God I hope I shall be enabled to get along. I have too many things resting upon me to do my duty to them before whom I must soon appear. I cant undo what I have already done—the evils must I hope & trust be beacons to guide hereafter not waits to sink me.

The business I am going on is of very doubtful issue. I started with David Williams merchant who went to see his store at Andersontown. Dined at Carters. A heavy thunder storm passed over us. Arrived at Noblesvill about sundown. Stayed at Demoss.

Tuesday morn. [June] 13. Rose before sunrise & went to Strawtown to Breakfast. At Rolls went & waked Bick Cole up. Done some little business with him & left for Andersontown at 9. A.M. Arrived at that place at 12. Took dinner at Myers. Pleasant day. Done some business. Went to bed at 10. Several travellers stopped. Mr. W[. . .] formerly Bonds Cl[oc]k Pedlar & lady Jo Howland Mr. McClung & others also stopped & boarded at the same house. Several land hunters also put up & 3 waggons from Noblesvill going to Cincinnati for goods. In the night say 11 Mr. Herrod who is now a candidat for Congress arrived from Pike Ck. where he & Govr. Ray had been making a stump speech & had several Hoosiers fight as a manifestation of the expected zeal &c.

At 12 o'clock at night the landlord called me up to Doctor my horse which was violently taken with the cholick. I called on one of the waggoners Mr. Dickson who administered some ascerfittity & he soon got relief. Very warm night.

June 14. Very pleasant day. Govr. R. & Mr. Herrod make speeches here. The main subject that heretofore engrossed the public speakers attintion on such subjects, the merits & demerits of Genl. Jackson, was not spoken of—But the currency & the present pressure is the main topic of the day. Mr. Herrod will be elected without doubt. Govr. Ray has been long since *laid aside.*

I this day intended to have made a public sale of some of my lands (wild). I altered my opinion & sold only one tract for $300. with interest at Christmass 80 acres & was offered $4 per acre for 50 acres which I declined. I sold two lots called the school house lots near Wests tan yard for $100. to [. . .]. They contained ¼ of an acre 100 yards up the hollow above the spring at Andersontown. I got thro' my business & in company with a Mr. Harris (Hatter of Indianapolis) & David Williams I proceeded to Pendleton. Stayed at Bostorns & W. and H. went to Arnets. Judge Taylor Gamaliel Taylor candidate for Governor stayed with me. I think his prospect poor. In the eve done some business with Cook & Bill Patrick &c.

[June] 15. Went to bed & rose at 3 & proceeded by Pet Simons to Noblesville where I arrived at Demoss Tavern at 10. Here I sold 160 acres of land to Cole Conner & Stephenson[70] for $480 wild & I constituted Cole my agent to sell the rest I have for sale in the county. I left with a Mr. H[. . .] a Tennesseean for home at 4. Very warm & pleasant. Wheat on my route looks very well. Corn is backward. At Bill Conners old place I met Mr. C. Mallory who had been to Indianapolis & told me my Brother Miles had come with his daughter. I arrived at home at 8, found Miles & his step daughter Anne here. I was truly glad to see him. Indeed it was the first visit I ever had from a brother or one of the family—Michael & Stoughton came to live here not to visit. This has been a pleasant day & I have done much. Mrs. F. has been called to Stoughtons house his wife is sick.

Friday [June] 16. I went to [. . .]. Pleasant day. Put up my pap[er]s & devoted my time to Miles. We dined then we rode to Michaels—thence to old Mr. Fletchers & returned to Michaels to tea. Beautiful day. Our corn at Pogues Creek knee high—that on the McF. place not yet more than 7 or 8 inches.

Saturday [June] 17. Pleasant day. Our sinking fund commissioners met and disposed of the 3d installment of the Surplus

70. Bicknell Cole, William Conner, and John D. Stephenson. Thompson, *Sons of the Wilderness*, p. 176.

Rev[enue]. I have the loaning of 30000 in Shel[by] John[son] and Morgan. 70 thousand here. Mr. Merrill goes to Lafayette Mr. Morrison [. . .].

I was this day introd[uc]ed to Rev. Mr. Bascum[71] also was asked to dine with him at Mr. Johnsons. Also the Rev. Mr. Page from Glasgo brother in law to Elijah—an Episcopalian clergyman. Went with S. to M.'s in the eve.

Sunday June 18. Went with Miles [and] Stoughton to Michaels to Breakfast.

Monday June 19. I rose early say at 3. Waked Elijah & Cooley. We had each of us horses ready to ride to Green Castle to see the corner stone of the college laid at which Mr. Bascum was to deliver an address. We soon got ready for the journey. It was a damp wet morning tho' it did not rain. We proceeded along to Bridgeport when Mr. Bascum in Mr. Youngs carriage overtook us & then we rode in company with John Hill & others to Bellville where we took breakfast. From there we proceeded in company with Rev. Mr. Daily Kelso Quarles & others to Greencastle where we arrived at 4 o'clock—A rapid journy for my boys who seemed to be but little tired. We put up with a Mr. Cooper a methodist a saddler. It rained soon after we arrived. Here we found Mr. Ingram from Lafayette & many gentlemen from various parts. Town crowded. I was much pleased with the town & county. Lands far exceede ours in natural beauty if not furtility.

Tuesday morning 20 June. I rose early. At 8 I was informed that I was to make a short address at the laying of the corner stone previous to Mr. Bascums address. This came upon me with surprise. I had not anticipated such an event—was totally unprepared. At first I was a mind to decline—But concluded at last that I would not shrink from the performance of any duty imposed upon me & returned for a few moments to collect my thoughts on the subject. But before I had been alone 15 minutes, I was notified by one of the trustees that the procession was forming & that I was wanted. I left the room & in 20 minutes thereafter was in a train of 4 or 5

71. The Rev. Henry B. Bascom, Methodist minister, formerly president of Augusta College in Kentucky and Chaplain to the United States Congress. He delivered the main address at the cornerstone laying of Indiana Asbury University at Greencastle on June 20. Manhart, *De Pauw through the Years,* I, 18.

thousand marching under the command of disorderly Militia colonels & arrived at the corner stone at 9 or ½ after. It rained—all was in confusion but a little calm ensued & on behalf of the Trustees of the college read the articles to be deposited in leaden box—then further stated that the trustees had not placed the Holy Bible of the lasted [latest] print, a statisical Report containing all the officers of the U. States of Indiana of Putnam Cty. & the town of Greencastle & the lasted coins from the mint in that indurable situation for vain show or to gratify or perpetuate the creeds of any sect or denomination, but we placed them there as an immunity or fortification against time—that when revolutions [?] in nature or necessity to extend or raise the foundation of the building should occur, we had deposited materials for posterity that might & probibly would shed a volume of light to them invaluable &c. I was to be commended for my brevity if not for my matter. We then went to a grove where we heard the address of Mr. Bascum. It occupied 2½ hours—occasional showers fell upon the audience. But all was lost in the matter & manner of the address. It will be published. After the ceremonies of the day were over the trustees of the institution met—At which were the Revs. Rooter Ames Smith Wood &c. We voted $100. for expenses to Mr. Bascum. I was appointed a committee to obtain a copy of the address. He did not decline but in his language *hesitated.* Mr. Ingram Elijah & Cooley left at 4 P.M. & rode to Stilesville. I stayed over night. Had a pleasant eve with Messrs. Nutt & Ewing Rooter Daily &c.

June 21 1837. This day rose early. Pleasant. At 8 Mr. Quarles & myself lift together. Arrived at Stilesville—stopped at Jessups. Went to Bellville—there overtook Messrs. Rooter Ames &c. Dined then returned home with Messrs. Harrison Quarles Kelso a young preacher on Brookville circuit. Arrived at home sun 1 hour high. Mr. K. staid with us.

[June] 22 Thursday. Pleasant day. Mr. Palmer birthday (Wm.).

[June] 23 Friday. Mr. Butler left for Shelby to see his wife. We asked several gentlemen & ladies to visit Miss Anne & Louisa. It commenced raining & continued for nearly all day. Messrs. Palmer ONeel & Yandes & Duncan attended the party—Misses Merrill Morris Bates &c.

Saturday [June] 24. Cool day. We are selling corn to Mr. Cheesman at 37½ per bushel at crib. I paid Jim McFarlin in full for place. Mr. Ingram left for Lafayette. Mr. McCarty returned from Chicago brings gloomy news as to the business of the North. Says Chicago is crowded but with imigrants. No business that is substantial business.

Sunday June 25. Pleasant day. Read a review by Hall of Flints Geography[72] in A.M. & went to church. Took Ansel Richmond & my boys. Old Mr. James Irish staid with me & I paid him yesterday $500. towards the land I bot of him for Mc & self for the use & profit in part of the Buckinghams.

In the P.M. read the review of the life of Frederick the Great. Went in the eve with Mrs. F. to Stoughtons & he with me went to see Mr. Quarles.

Monday June 26 1837. Cloudy—cool—gloomy. I have this morn resolved to live more prayerful more devoted to God & contemplation of his goodness to try & shut out as far as possible the gloomy prospects ahead but trust to God & his Providence. I fear I shall neglect to improve my mind & yield too much to melancholy. We expect Mr. Edy to dine with his wife. Elijah & Cooley are going to help uncle Michael disk corn. It is very backward. We have 2 pieces of 5 acres each 18 inches high—the rest 12. It is 2 weeks behind our early corn last year. Mrs. McGlaughlin daughter & son dined with us Mrs. Pendleton & Mrs. Richmond. She wanted me to advise with her son &c. I recommended law merchandising or agriculture. In the eve Mr. Mrs. Eddy, Mrs. Paxton & the same company that dined supped with us. In the eve went with Mrs. F. Mrs. R. & others to hear Mr. Hull [?] lecture on education. Rather a boar. New potatoes today.

Tusday [June] 27. Pleasant. [. . .] Mr. Page Ep. clergyman called. Wrote a letter by him to Elijah. A Mr. Philbrick formerly from Weathersfield Vt. dined with us. I transacted some Bank business & Mr. Butler returned. Mr. Boxley & another man returned with Miles. Pleasant growing weather.

[June] 28 Weds. Pleasant. Went with Mrs. R. & Louisa to Stoughtons.

72. A review by James Hall of Timothy Flint, *A Condensed Geography and History of the Western States* . . . (2 volumes. Cincinnati, 1828).

[June] 29 Thursd. Pleasant. Preparing in town for 4th of July. Attended before Esq. Stevens trial Perry vs. Ellsworth[73] for a horse said to have been sold by Perry to him. This is the first time I h[ave] appeared before a J.P. for months past. This cause presented a hardship that I felt it was my duty to attend to in person. Perry a poor but honest *colored* man who had been defrauded out of a horse by E. the son of the present commissioner of the Patent office & grandson of the 1st Chief Justice of the U. States—a young lawyer who has been living here about a year. The defendant had all the fashonables of the place on his side & the poor African dumb & ignorant. Wm. J. Brown Secy. of State for the defendant. All these things inspired me & I hope & believe I done justice to the poor African. He gained his cause.

Friday 30 June 1837. Pleasant day. Michael & Kneeland hoeing potatoes East of my house & back of Mr. Bates. John & James with two horses & two plows going over the corn on the John G. Brown Block the 3d time. Corn is about 3 feet high—corn grows very fast. We are still crowded with law business—Palmer starts tomorrow for Ladoga Putnam Cty. on business. G[. . .] of Columbus called—Mitchell of Martinsville Saml. Walker's man from Shelby & Mr. Colburn Sheriff of Hamilton. Took tea. Went in eve with S. to Mr. Carlisles.

I this day saw 20 four horse teems unloading pebbles or rock taken out of the River & creeks in Washington Street near Meridian preparitory to paving or mecademizing the former street. We have just received word that Dr. Coe has made a loan of $30,000 on 5 per ct. Bonds at 2 per ct. premium & is like to effect another loan of 200,000.[74]

73. Henry William Ellsworth (1814–1864), lawyer and diplomat, son of Henry L. Ellsworth (see above, p. 254n) and grandson of Chief Justice Oliver Ellsworth of the United States Supreme Court. *Dictionary of American Biography*, VI, 111. He was the author of *Valley of the Upper Wabash, Indiana, with Hints on Its Agricultural Advantages* (1838).

74. Isaac Coe, a member of the Board of Fund Commissioners in charge of the funds for the state internal improvement program. The Board's duties included the negotiations of loans to finance the various projects. On June 20 it negotiated a loan of $30,000, with a New York banking house and later in the year negotiated loans totaling $2,000,000 with the Morris Canal and Banking Company of Jersey City. *Messages and Papers relating to the Administration of David Wallace*, p. 85.

Saturday July 1 1837. Pleasant morning but a very warm night. Cloudy in the W. Chancey Butler[75] came for 4 young hogs. Elijah [. . .] them. Calvin went along to keep off other hogs & Chancy drove them to the McClure place. They succeeded. I have learned them to drive hogs. Cooley & myself went to the pasture with cows. A fine shower at 7.

We this day wrote 12 letters—remitted to Philadelphia and N.Y. $1400. to our clients paid 3 per ct. premium at which price I complained as they at the Bank charged only 2 for citizens. They made a distinction or rather treated us as foreigners. I have agreed to leave the matter to Mad[ison] & Lawrenceburgh branches as to this discrimination. Mr. Palmer has gone to Putnam Cty. A man drowned at the River while getting out stone for National Road.

A very pleasant day. I have labored hard during the week have abstained from sleep during the day. Old Dr. Canbys real estate set up for sale &c.

July 2 Sunday. Cool morning. Rose eat breakfast went to Michaels horsback. Returned. Went to hear Mr. McVay[76] Campbellite preach at court house. Very full house. Butler Smith[77] officiated &c. Cooley Elijah & Calvin attended with me. The M.E. preacher has gone with Mrs. R. to Camp meeting at Nightstown & others.

Elijah wrote a letter to Mr. Ingram. I read the Tragedy called Revenge—Also part of the life of Sylla in Plutarch. At sundown a very severe storm thunder rain & wind. The man drowned yesterday by name of Williams has been found. James Hill has returned from the North where he has been to sell lands for McC. and myself but I expect he has not succeeded well. Our cherrys are ripe but Robbins are taking them fast. We have green peas & potatoes.

75. Father of Ovid Butler, Chauncey Butler was the first regular pastor of the Disciples of Christ Church in Indianapolis. Sulgrove, *History of Indianapolis,* p. 175.

76. The Rev. James McVey. The Central Chapel of the Disciples of Christ was organized in June, 1833. Among its early leading members were Dr. John H. Sanders, Ovid Butler, and James Sulgrove. It built its church in the summer of 1836 on Kentucky Avenue on the southeast side, midway between Maryland and Georgia streets. *Ibid.,* p. 405.

77. A blacksmith whose shop was on Delaware Street near Ohio. He occasionally preached at Central Chapel. *Ibid.,* p. 405.

A very severe storm after dark. Much timber prostrate—corn broke.

July 3d 1837. Pleasant morn. J. Hill called. Had sold no land. Michael & Jas. Stafford came in to thin corn. John hauling plank from Mill. Kneelan making shingles. This day payment to canal hands. We are very busy. Received money from 12 persons & paid out almost to as many amounting to $2061. & also claims for collection for as much. Mr. Barns from N.Y. of the house of N. & H. Weede called & got the Givans money. Received money for Herriott collected at S. Bend 143. For 3 Mitchells of Martinsville 1500, from Fitzgibbon $30, Matlock $31, from White [of] Cincinnati for old fee $87. Harrison $2.50. Mrs. Givan $160. Free $50. Foudray $100. Terrill of Mich. city for advise fee $10. Murphy $30 &c &c. Mr. White of the house of Carlisle & White called & I settled the old business of Patrick. Several clients from the country. I called and got confessions of judgment from Nat. Davis—Ed Davis—Harris & W. Campbell. I wrote several letters on Professional business & gave counsel to several. Besides all this Mr. Butler was very busy in preparing business for court. I returned home a little before sun set believing I had done more professional business in my office than I ever performed before in one day. In the eve went to Stoughtons with Louisa.

July 4th 1837. At 3 o'clock guns commenced firing—the Marion guards were paraded. At 4 bells all rattled as old John Adams wrote to his wife they should on this day. James Stafford & John Wall staid with us but left early to merande [meander?] thro' town. I have not determined to celebrate the day as yet. My professional business & the Sinking Fund duties will no doubt prevent me. It is a pleasant morning.

I am forcibly reminded of this anniversary in 1817—20 years ago the year I came to Ohio. I was then a stranger living at a little dirty tavern [in] Urbana where the day was celebrated by a parcel of drunken soldiers 5 year men enlisted in the late war of 1812. I that day was sent by the tavern keeper to get a fiddle for the amusement of his guests. I waited on the table and dealt out half pints to the customers—half pints of whisky were dealt out in bottles or glasses in the shape of vinegar crews.

I am reminded on looking back of the many scenes I have passed & my duty and my gratitude to the Author of my existence for the last 20 years. The whole space has been filled up or rather occupied with such a variety of transitions so common to Western life that it requires a pause to make a reconing of the past in order to find where I am. I hope when more at leisure I can gratify my wishes in this particular.

At 8 between 4 & 500 childrin assembled at the Presbyterian Church being the number of Sabbath School children in the 3 schools in town. Mr. James Blake headed them. They were marched thro' several streets to the methodist church in good order teachers placed at various intervals. There Mr. Eddy made an appropriate address—several hymns were sung—one composed by Mr. John Hobert a farmer one of our first settlers from Massa.—Prayers by Revd. John Richmond & Sickels. At 11 o'clock the Marion guards paraded—Capt. Thos. Morris a cadet from W[est] P[oint] son of M. Morris our auditor of state. This new company is a revival of the dormant military spirit that has long slumbered or rather was never awakened in our place. They marched thro' town to the Methodist Church. There Joseph M. Moore delivered an excellent oriation. Thence they proceeded to the Bradley block S.W. of the town under a sugar grove & partook of a dinner. In the eve there was a ball at the Govr. circle. Judge Blackford was one of the managers. At Mr. Brownings there was what they called a military *sorie* at which the old people Messrs. Merrill Morris (cashier) also the Marion guards attended. I went. Mrs. F. was not in a condition to attend. An attempt was made to make a display of Sky Rockets on Washington St. at the corner of Meridian but it turned out a failure.

It was warm day. I did not dine at the Grove but at home. Mr. Kneeland & Michael came in but returned about 12.

July 5. This day it rained. Mr. Merrill & myself ingaged in ex[ecu]ting mortgages to loan the 3d instalment of the Surplus Revenue. I have the loaning of about one hundred thousand dolls. as one of the commissioners of the S[inking] Fund.

July 6, 1837. Very wet disagreeable day. Mr. McGuffee[78] President of Cincinnati college called with expectation to deliver an

78. William Holmes McGuffey (1800–1873), educator and compiler of the widely known *Eclectic Readers* for elementary schools. The First and Second Readers were first published in 1836 and the Third and Fourth in 1837. *Dictionary of American Biography*, XII, 57–58.

address on education but postponed it until Thursday next. He has gone to Crawfordsvill. He presented me with a series of his works &c 6 vols. school books. He is a man of talents & has & will if lives make a figure in the world. It rains very hard. Wet dissagreeable day.

Friday [*July*] 7. Rains yet. I have sold the East lot or rather one third of the N.E. quarter of Block 44 containing ⅓ of an acre to a Mr. Mendenall a lawyer from N. Carolina for $500 in U.S. pap[er] & gold. This lot has a small cabin on it—rents $30 per ann. Money down was an inducement &c. I went with Mr. Bradley to get uncle Michael and Aunt Betsy to make the deed as I had sold to them[79] & gave the Cox farm in exchange &c. We got very wet. Corn has grown fine.

Saturday July 8. Pleasant after the storm. Simon & myself examining title papers to loan Surplus &c. Mr. Palmer gone to Clinton Ver[million] Cty. Ia.

Sunday 9 July. Pleasant day. Read with my boys in the morning Mr. McGuffes Series. Went to church A.M. In P.M. read Plutarch a new philosophy & spent the time rather idly. Maria Stoughton & Miss Anne came & took tea. Mr. Kneeland came in to cradle the Rye on the Block N. of the house which is now ripe.

July 10. Pleasant morn. Mr. K. has began cradleing Rye. Boys Cooley & Elijah gone to help Michael in corn. Everything growing finely. Hired the Shearers[?] to get out & put me in a pump to my well. Mr. S. refuses. A very pleasant day. Cole & Stephenson down with a raft [. . .] the dam.

July 11 1837. Very pleasant day. Simon Yandes & myself have examined a great many mortgages for the Sinking fund—also a little law preparitory to the court next w[e]ak.

Teusday July 11. I have this day been examining Roscoes ev[idence] on criminal cause.[80] Cooley & James the hired man

79. C.F. means Block or Square 42 instead of 44. On May 11, 1836, the Marion County deed records show that C.F. conveyed to Michael Fletcher Lots 1, 2, and 3, Square 42, for the consideration of $800. The records further show that on July 7, 1837, Michael Fletcher conveyed to George C. Mendenhall the east half of the northeast quarter of Square 42 for the consideration of $500.

80. Henry Roscoe, *A Digest of the Law of Evidence in Criminal Causes* . . . (Philadelphia: P. A. Nicklin & T. Johnson, 1836).

waked me this morning. They came into Mill. Cooley crowed at my window before one of us were out of bed. Mr. Kneeland finished cradling rye.

I have not advanced as far in the examination of the criminal cause as I expected. I fear I shall not be well prepared.

Mr. Sergent from Shelby is here who rented our Walker Mills. I had a conversation with Esq. Brady our recent Senater. He says that Town people have overtraded &c that public lands will sell in one year at $1. & 75 cts. per acre &c. This I do not believe. Mr. McCarty called up this eve. He thinks it will [be] bad times yet—that lands will not sell well. This has been a hot day—I feel tired.

July 12. A very pleasant morning. We had only 4 of our childrin at home last night Martha Maria Cooley & Elijah all at the farm. I have been examining Russel on crimes[81] in refferance to the case of Thos. Finch. Went with H. Brown Esq. to examine the ground where Finch Killed Shereden. Very warm.

July 13 1837. Pleasant day very warm. I this day examined about 30 mortgages from Greencastle & about as many from Frankfort in order to get mony out of the Sinking Fund &c. John & James had some difficulty (2 hired hands) with Michael & left. In the eve went to hear an address on Education from Mr. McGuffey late a professor in Oxford College Ohio but now President of the Cincinnati College. It was very good. He is an enthusiast on the subject & I highly approve of his zeal. He presented me last week with a series of his school books which I have partially examined.

July 14. Pleasant day. Preparing myself for the criminal case State vs Finch. Rained at 2—a pleasent shower.

Mr. Ketcham called to see if I would not be the one of 20 to give him $1000. per year for 5 years to teach my childrin &c. I postponed the consideration &c.

Saturday July 15. Pleasent day. James mowed down the weeds in the street in the A.M. & in the P.M. went to Michaels to plough.

Dined with Mr. Ray (J.M.) at his house with Messrs. Guffee

81. William Oldnall Russell, *A Treatise on Crimes & Misdemeanors.* The earliest American edition was published in Boston in 1824.

McKennan[82] Tilford & two Miss Alstons.[83] In the Eve Mr. Guffee & Tilford & Mrs. Richmond & Judge Wick took tea with us under the apple tree out doors. Simon Yandes & Mr. Palmer came up also after tea.

Sunday 16. Pleasant day went to Presbyterian Ch. in A.M. to hear Mr. McGuffee & in the P.M. at 5 went to hear him at Meth. Ch. Pleasant day & feel much disturbed in consequence of Elijahs sickness the approaching court &c.

Monday July 17th 1837. Pleasant day. Very little done being the 1st day of our circuit court which is to sit 12 days next succeeding. However I have been somewhat engaged not only in court but have examined siveral mortgages for the State &c in the Sinking Fund & before night became very weary. Came home & went to bed soon after Sundown. Mrs. Paxton & Richmond both called to see me after I had gone to bed.

Teusday July 18. Pleasant day. Engaged in court & my mind as much if not more than usual, engaged in the subject of the expected trial of Thomas Finch a young Irish man who is charged with killing one Michael Sheriden in a riot at one Pendervills[?] shanty on the canal about 5 miles from town on St. Patricks day (March 17 last). With Mr. H. Brown I have been imploid to defend. The defendant Finch is a young Irishman of the common grade with great vivacity & apparent good intintion & indeed with a good character. I feel the great responsibility that rests upon me in this cause. Altho' associated with a partner capable in the law yet I feel & know of the 2 I am looked upon as the senior. The first case that has ever been brought against our bank in consequence not paying specie is now pending against our branch bank for not paying specie since the suspension.

[July] 19. Pleasant. Nothing particular done in court. This P.M. we selected a Jury to try Finch. Messrs. John Williams Hervy Bates & Col. Johnson the two first old citizens & all three respectable intelligent men of the first order of good practical sense. We examined one or 2 witnesses.

82. The Rev. James W. McKennan, pastor of the Presbyterian Church from 1836 to 1839. Dunn, *Indianapolis,* I, 580.

83. The Misses Axtell. See note 67, above.

[*July*] 20. We progressed in the trial but did not get thro' with the witnesses.

[*July*] *Friday 21*. We closed our examination & Mr. Butler commenced spoke about 1 hour when the court adjourned.

Saturday [*July*] 22. Mr. Butler concluded his speech & at 9 I addressed the Jury. As usual I was but poorly prepared. Here I would remark that the best efforts I have usually made have been upon reflection & study & I much regret that other pursuits have deprived me of the necessary time to improve myself in frorensice [forensic] addresses. In this case I had for my client a young Irishman of good countenance—a warm heart who from his friendship to his imployer while he apprehended great danger killed a man who was not at the time offending but from whom the prisoner apprehended great bodily harm.

In my remarks I succeeded nearer what I would wish & have always been ambitious to obtain than I ever did before to my recollection. I concluded my speech at ½ after 12 making about 3½ hours occupied in addressing the Jury. Then Mr. H. Brown commenced—occupied 2 or 3 hours when Mr. Quarles commenced & closed the case on the part of the prosecution. The court adjourned & after dark again assembled & Judge Wick delivered a splendid charge, but not calculated to aid the Jury much in coming to any definite conclusions. A crowded house. At 12 the Jury came down. I had returned home. Mrs. F. sit up & awaked me at ½ after 11 so that I could be present at the coming in of the Jury—For I had stuck to my client almost without fee or reward for 4 days. I took in that time no kind of stimulant whatever & eat very sparingly. I arrived stimulated on an occasion of the kind—made a failure I believe in consequence. The Jury found the defendant guilty of manslaughter & sentenced him to 5 years imprisonment in the Penitentiery.

Sunday July 24 1837. I rose this morning & went out to Michaels. I never have been much more fatigued & worn out. Went to church. Mr. Eddy Preached. Mr. Kneeland came in &c.

Monday July 25 [–29]. Pleasant day. I felt very little like doing much. I felt no disposition to tend to business. Indeed had I been highly stimulated for the last 4 days I could not have felt worse.

From this day till Saturday the 29 I done very little but advise &c. James Hill is making hay.

Sunday July 30. Pleasant day yesterday was the hottest day we have had this year. We have roasting ears &c.

Monday [July] 31. Mr. Butler started for Covington Danville Ill. Lafayette &c on business. Pleasant day.

Teusday 1 Augt. I am prepared to go to Pendleton to get Patrick to confess judgment for Vanosdall & Grey for about $1200 or 1400.

Wednesday Augt. 2. I left home at 4 o'clock. Pleasant morning. Rode to Arnets to Breakfast. Got their at 10 then rode to Pendleton. Got there at 2 done my business & returned to Arnets at ten.

Thursday 3d of Augt. Rose at ½ after 3. Warm morning. Rode home by 10 & went to business.

Friday 4 Augt. Mr. Danl. Yandes had a conversation in relation to John Hills becoming a partner of himself & his son James. Went with Stoughton to Fletcher farm found the old man had not cut more than ⅔ of the meadow. Came to conclusion to go & cut it.

John Hill has gone into equal partnership with Mr. D. Yandes & son in the store lately occupied by Smith & Yandes.

Pleasant morning. Simon started for Middletown 40 ms. East on the national road to secure a debt for Blachly & Simpson of about $1200.

Remitted several sums of mony to our clients in N.Y. Cincinnati & Louisvill.

In the P.M. Mr. Palmer left for Jamestown at 5 o clock P.M. to secure another debt of about 1200. Mr. Eddy took tea with me. Gave the history of his life to me. He is deserving of much credit for his perseverance.

Saturday Aug. 5. I this day wrote several letters. Received a demand for collection from Louisville on Fat Bill Matlock[84] of $500. Mr. Eddy called on me again. We had a conversation of ½ hour. I feel a deep interest in the man.

84. William T. Matlock of Hendricks County. He was commissioned justice of the peace in 1835 and was elected state representative in 1837 and 1844. *Indiana Executive Proceedings*, p. 464; *Indiana Election Returns*, pp. 236, 281.

John Hill has commenced business with Yandes & Son. This young man has been under my care for several years. I learned him 20 years this summer to read his letters. He then wore petticoats. He had a step mother who treated him with great rigor & he grew up till 1830 in great ignorance when he run away & came to me. He worked & went to school about 2 years & then was bound to the company store for 3 years. When his time was out he hired for one year. When that expired he expected to go into business with me. For that purpose visited Ill. to look for a suitable location. Returned with a view of settling there & while debating on the subject he took sick & came near dying—but at length recovered & in the fall visited his father. Returned late last fall & I then concluded to [. . .] him for a clothing store in Jany. When that time arrived my own affairs looked so gloomy & the general prospect so fo[r]boding of evil that I declined entering into business with him much to his disatisfaction. His knowledge & experience did not disclose or convince him of the propriety of declining the commencement of business at so critical a moment.

[*Aug.*] *6. 7. 8. 9.* Pleasant weather. Mr. Butler returned on the 8 from a trip to the Wabash Danville & Ill. Lafayett &c. Our collecting business is very good—we received something like 3 thousand a week for the last 4 or 5 weeks. On the 9 our bank directors met. We had no delligate from Vincennes & [New] Albany. We had the subject of a new branch at the North. Messrs. Scott & Blythe reported as to the advantages of South Bend Michigan City & Laport but the question on agreeing to either of these places was postponed till Novr. session.

12 Augt. On Saturday morning at 4 o'clock I left in company with Mrs. Paxton & Richmond for the camp meeting ground near the Falls of Fall creek where I was to leave them & proceede to Andersontown court. A beautiful morning. Mrs. P. & R. well mounted on good horses. This mode of riding by females has heretofore been fashinable but carriages are coming in fashion & I have no idea that one fashionable young lady in 100 will learn to ride as their mothers did before them. To my taste a female who can ride gracefully never appears better than on a fine horse. Soon after the late war I came to Urbana Ohio. Western ladies then all rode on horseback & what was peculiar from early habits riding in Indian trails or tracks, the female would as naturally fall behind her husband in the streets of a town as she would obey him when both were mounted on horseback.

We proceeded to Arnets 20 miles & took dinner. At one we arrived at the Camp Ground at Hundlys 4 miles this side of Pendleton. There were about 1000 people on the camp ground—Rather of the rough back woods order now & then sprinkled with the refinement bro't in by our late emigrants. Rev. Mr. Havens present. Other preachers except young Fletcher Truslo were st[r]angers. I heard Mr. Eddys bro' in law preach a tolerable good sermon. Left my company & rode to Pendleton with Judge Wick. Put up at Bostons. Very warm pleasant day. Messrs. Brown Quarles & Corwin & S. came at staid at the same place.

Sunday morning Augt. 13. After breakfast rode with the same gentlemen to the camp ground. Heard one sermon there & an exortation from Mr. Havens. Saw the Alter filled with morners & then returned to Bostons for dinner. Met Mr. Hammond from Greenfield who turned back with us. There came on the camp ground about 2000 thousand. After dinner our company rode to Andersontown. We put up with Myers except Judge Wick Stopped at Daggets.

Monday the 14 Augt. Pleasant day. I had some collecting to do. Andersontown is improving. Jackson Andrew [Andrew Jackson] is elected Clk over Williams (R.N.). Pleasant day.

Teusday [Aug.] 15. Heard the case of Patrick vs. James. Took 2 decrees in chancery.

Wedensday [Aug.] 16. Tried case of Jones vs Jones for a divorce for the following cause—Jones 3 years past married the widow Boston as she was supposed. Last summer the first husband returned in full life. The double bride went to see him who met her at their daughters. She was persuaded to *Stop* with him. She soon became disatisfied & soon returned to Jones who was not certain whether she was lawfully his wife or not. But the *preacher in cha[r]ge* gave it as his opinion that she was not J.'s wife. They parted. J. sues for a divorce. The court decreed the first marriage valid the latter void.

Thursday Aug. 17. After Breakfast say at 9 left Andersontown for Pendleton. There met my other brothers of the law—dined at

Bostons & at 1 left alone for Indianapolis alone—the company refusing to go further that night. I rode 5 miles when there came up a heavy shower which hindered me ¾ of an hour then I started. Calld on a Mr. T[. . .] an old scholler in Ohio who left word that I must not pass without calling to see him &c & arrived at home at 9 'o clock. Found Miles sick, had had a fever for 2 or 3 days.

Friday Augt. 18. Pleasant day. I find in my absence that Simon Y. had not returned from the Wabash on a collecting or rather securing trip—that about $4000. had come in for the same purpose in my absence.

Pleasant day. Much pressing business on me. Indeed I never have labered harder than for the last 3 months. It has not been reading but active practical business. I found that Stoughton had divided with John Givans the sheep we bo't together on Friday—gave $1.50 per head out of a drove from the E[a]st part of this State. Simon Y. returned in the P.M. Mrs. F. unwell. Dr. Richmond visited her. I returned from my office at sundown found her ill. I went for Mrs. Paxton & Mrs. Richmond & at about 4 minutes before 8 in the Eve our 8 child & 7 son was born. I was much pleased that it was a son at all events I should have been gratified even if there had been 2. I waited with out with intense anxiety to learn if it was a girl or boy—without knowing I recognized the wail of a male child. After all was over (the time was short) I went with old Dr. Richmond home to get 2 powders. He agreed to return in 1 hour himself. At the expiration of the time he returned & announced the birth of another child to wit [. . .] In the meantime I made him a present beside the usual charge of $5. gold piece.

I would here again remark that the number of childrin is a matter of differant concern to me to what it is to most persons. The generality of the world are opposed to having large families. For myself it has always been a wish of mine to have a numerous family of childrin. I am not unconscious of the great responsibility resting on me to rear them as they should be—but I have supposed the most erroneous education was given by those who have but few & equally disastrous expectations raised where the patrimony was likely to remain undivided to a single heir or a large fortune to a few. The rearing a numerous family together gives a fair trial of their tempers & prepares each member while in this little state where many interests are to be regarded by each, to be compromised, settled & surrendered admirably for the world—"its losses & crosses." I most fervently desire wisdom from that source which never fails that I may rear those gifts in the way they should go beleving fully in the promise that when they are old they will not depart from it.

We think of naming the Stranger *William Baldwin Fletcher* for my esteemed friend Wm. Baldwin when in early life my friend & comforter while suffering under the many fears so common to our nature while Just stepping upon threshold of practical life—poor, unaided by relatives with the wide world before me. While studying law at Urbana he was a clerk in a store with Messrs. Gwynnes now a merchant in the City of N.Y.

Saturday Augt. 19 1837. Pleasant day. Mrs. F. as well as could be expected—also the stranger. This is the 4th child born in the house we now occupy in Square 42 lot 12. Cooley & Elijah & Miles were born in the house owned by Mr. James Blake on Washington Street lot [12] square [67]. Calvin was born on the Kentucky Avenue lot [3] sq [67] then owned by Dr. K. A. Scudder now bot for a state Bank.[85]

Uncle Michael attempted to raise a corn barn or grainery at the McFarlan place.

Mr. Palmer started yesterday [for] Bloomington Gosport to serve claim on Duning &c.

Andrew Jackson clerk of Madison Co. here looking for a deputy. Simon preparing a temperance address. Mr. Quarles heard to day of the murder of his brother on the day of the late election by shooting at Frankfort Ky. Stoughtons wife was here & spent the day. Mr. Butler will go to Hancock to morrow. I went home with aunt Maria. Miles quite unwell.

Sunday Augt. 20. Pleasant morning. Read a late pamphlet

85. See Pt. V, notes 19 and 88. The State Bank which had its first office in the Governor's Circle, was then located on Washington Street, and in 1840 moved to its new building on the point between Illinois Street and Kentucky Avenue. Brown, "History of Indianapolis," in *Logan's Indianapolis Directory*, 1868, p. 27. The site for the building of the Indianapolis branch of the State Bank was on the point between Pennsylvania Street and Virginia Avenue.

written by Mr. Fethertenaugh the Geologist.[86] I feel a desire to acquire some information of a science of modern dissemenation.

Cooley Elijah & Miles went to church. Mrs. F.'s ill health prevented my going. Heavy shower about 12. Mr. Kneeland & Michael eat dinner with us. Our bees act as if they were about to swarm & after the rain was over large quantities of young bees seemed to assemble on the outside.

Monday morning 21 Aug. 37. This morning went with 7 hands out to help Michael & Mr. Kneeland raise the corn barn. Wet—cloudy but pleasant. Corn in roasting ears. We had 20 hands. At first Mr. Kneeland was sick but soon got up &c & went to work like a general. Mr. J. Hill killed a sheep in the morning & had a dinner at M.'s of Mutton roasting Ears corn &c. I returned at 12. Went to my office a little tired & a little impatient. I wrote Mr. Ingram & received a letter from Stephen Williams[87] informing me that he was coming on &c. Finished my letter to bro. Elijah informing him that I should draw on him for $4000 at City Bank acceptance *waived.* This aid is voluntary on his part. There never was a better brother. I cannot repay the obligations I feel under to him. Most brothers become exclusively devoted to themselves & family & forget their brothers. This has not been the case with Elijah.

In the eve went with Mrs. Richmond & Ann to hear Simon Yandes deliver a temperance address. It was his first effort of the kind. It was delivered in too low a tone of voice, but well read, well emphasised & well received. He will no doubt make one of the first men of our country. I feel a deep interest for him. He is one of the best of young men. In counsel he is old in execution sure.

Aug. 22. Mr. Boxley staid at tavern last night. Came here & breakfasted. Sold 15 2 year old steers to the butcher for $14 per head. Harry a colered man has commenced work here. He was the

86. George W. Featherstonhaugh, geologist of the United States.

87. C.F.'s nephew, son of his sister Lucy, wife of Dr. Richard Williams, Newark, New York. C.F. had suggested that Stephen might study law in Andrew Ingram's office in Lafayette and the young man wrote that he would come out to Indiana to look into the matter. The letter, dated August 8, 1837, is in the Fletcher Papers.

slave of one Webb who moved from Ky. who had sold Harry to his son in law. Harry wrote over to his old master Webb that if he would recind the contract & take him to Indiana he would work for him his life time. Webb having great confidence in the word of H. did according to his wish. He came out lived some months & the people of the neighborhood discouraged him made him dissatissified. He came to me last Spring & [I] advised him to go back & work a year. He did. He remained till about 10 days past when the overseers of the poor called on Webb to give security under a law we have compelling negros to give security for their maintanace when they come to the state. Webb alarmed at the demand called on Harry to bind himself for life to him as he must go his bail for his maintanace & support. Harry alarmed at this demand fled to me. His master followed him & after a large parly H. gave W. 4 notes of $50. each for an entire emancipation real & supposed. What is remarkable Harry admitted that as a conscientious man bound to answer at the great day he felt it his duty, as W. brought him to the county under a firm pledge that he would work for him for life to discharge in some way that pledge & trust to God for the issue. I was pleased with such integrity & believe it will be blessed.

Harry is going to make up our shoes for winter.

A Mr. Dennis called with Michael to day from Dutchess County. Has an idea of buying in this neighborhood.

Sent Boxley $120. to pay off note in Bank. Renewed note for Hotel stock. Sold two tracts of land to an old man which lay on Eel River bot of Merrill 2 year ago for $161. sold for $425.

Sent Cole a deed for two tracts he has sold to [. . .].

Last night became very cool. Cool this day. Mrs. F. is better. Butler at Hancock court. Palmer just returned from Bloomington on business.

Augt. 23–4. Pleasant. All preparing for camp meeting.[88] Mr. Mallory staid with us. John Hill preparing to go East with Alfred

88. The Indianapolis *Indiana Democrat* on August 16, 1837, announced a Methodist camp meeting for the Indianapolis station. It was to be held one mile east of Indianapolis near the National Road and to commence on the twenty-fifth.

Harrison. Mr. Havens called—told over his difficulties at Noblesville camp meeting.

I this eve settle with Mrs. Richmond as to certain moneys I had of hers & her sons. I paid them out about $425. & provided each with $200. in specie to enter 80 acres of land for each. Mr. Nathaniel Richmond is to enter the land. This will make ½ section for Mrs. R. & 160 acres for the boy.

Augt. 25. Mr. Mallery staid with us over night. Pleasant day. Mr. Butler & self been over our books of collections. Old Mr. Plummer Mrs. Oliver & son Mr. Horrace Mallery wife & uncle staid with us. Dorio cooking for camp meeting now in progress near Mr. Phipps one Mile & ¼ from this place. Mrs. F. [. . .].

Saturday Augt. 26. This day immense crowds resort to camp meeting. Mr. Butler & myself regulating our office. Rained in the P.M. Sent Pomeroy Wilson & Butler money collected of Vance.

Sunday 27 Augt. Martha, James Stafford Staid all night at camp ground. At 7 Louisa myself Calvin Miles & Stoughton went to the camp-ground. The road was full from the centre of Washington St. to the ground—at least 4 thousand on the ground altho it was cloudy. I heard two sermons & returned home. Saml. McIlvain & his father in law old Mr. Fee walkd home with me & took dinner. Mrs. F. keeps her bed yet.

Monday [Aug.] 28. Pleasant day. Stoughton's wife & Michael dined with us. Elijah wrote & read composition to Mr. Holiday—a description of his Journy to Greencastle at the laying corner stone of the Asb[ury] University. I this day seperated my obsolete letters from those on subjects not concluded. I also intered into a written contract with Jac Landis & Greer to sell them 40 hogs to be delivered fat on the 15 day of Novr. next at the average cash price, during the month of Decr. next to be ascertained by D. Yandes.

Augt. 29 1837. Camp meeting is continued. James Hill & Mr. Kneeland attend. Pleasant morning. Mrs. Oliver & son start home. Cooley & Elijah went last night to camp meeting returned at 11. I have been reviewing Rosses[89] Magnetic pole. All returned from

89. Sir James Clark Ross (1800–1862), Scottish polar explorer.

camp meeting. Mrs. Hanner Robt. Hanners wife died this day. It has been very warm. Our peaches are getting ripe. One of our trees broke down with fruit.

I have been examining my collections & correspondence. Mr. Butler is absent at Shelby Court. I received a note in Bank for Genl. Tipton & shall apply the same to the payment of my bridge stock.

Aug. 30. Pleasant & very warm day. I gave my brother Stoughton & Mr. Bradley my views as to the prevailing disposition of the merchants & professional mens sons getting their living without work—that he who never has submitted to bodily exercise can rarely submit to mental.

At 10 went to the funeral of Mrs. R. Hanner. She was buried near his residence. Mr. Reck Lutharien preacher[90] & Col. Leminouski officiating ministers. The latter was a Colonel in Bonaparts regiment of Polish lancers—was in Egypt & Rus[s]ia with him & the only individual I ever saw that was in these campaigns.

This day the Indiana Democrat in an editorial stated that a certain State Bank director had received uncommon accommodations for the purposes of town lot speculation &c &c that he followed nothing else. Some say the allusion is to my self. The charge has little truth for the statement if it is so intended—I am indebted somewhat to the Bank but trust I shall ere long be out of it. I shall bandy words with carping Editors to give them consequence when I have business of more weight & importance.[91]

At 2 o P.M. I was invited with Messrs. W[il]kins Ray Morris Landis McCarty &c to visit the Miss Axels female Academy recently established. I was much pleased with the improvement of

90. The Rev. Abraham Reck, who organized the first Lutheran church in Indianapolis, the First English Lutheran or Mt. Pisgah Lutheran Church of the General Synod, in January, 1837. The church edifice was erected the following year on the southeast corner of Ohio and Meridian streets. The Reverend Reck served this church until 1844. Dunn, *Indianapolis,* I, 613–14.

91. The editorial accused the State Bank of encouraging speculation and assisting individuals to amass large fortunes at the expense of the poorer classes. It mentioned that "at this place a state director who is engaged in no other business than speculating, has obtained large loans not only from this bank but from other branches. This is not right," said the *Democrat,* "he cannot discharge his duty as a director impartially when he is under a deep obligation to the bank."

a number of our young ladies improvement in composition &c.

Sunday the 3 day of Sept. Pleasant morning. I prepared for Columbus court. Left at ½ after 9 alone. Mr. Quarles had promised me but he was in trouble about young Obed Foote his ward who had run away &c. I proceeded alone as far as Nobles 10 ms. & there dined. Then in company with a young quaker proceeded to Edinburgh. Tavern keeper was there dying & I had to go to Thompsons to stay over night.

Monday Sept. 4. Wet morning. Went to Columbus put up at Jones S.E. corner of the Court house square. It cleared off. Full court. Resident lawyers Copper Smith[92] & Smith. Sweetser very drunk.

[Sept.] 5 Tusday. Pleasant. I prepared my pleas &c.

Wedensday [Sept.] 6. Had a trial of the case of Drybuold[?] vs Williams—pleas of Justification &c.

Thursday 7 Sept. Rained in the morning. I left at 9 rode to Franklin dined—got home about dusk.

Friday [Sept.] 8. Went to business. In my absence [. . .].

[Sept.] 9 Saturday. Preparing for Franklin court Johnson County.

Sunday [Sept.] 10. Started with Mr. Quarles & rode to Nobles to dinner. Arrived at Franklin at 3—put up at Shaffers—got a room with Q. Pleasent day cool night.

Monday [Sept.] 11. A great deal of business. A heavy docket.

Tusday [Sept.] 12. Continued 2 or 3 of our most important cases. Pleasent day.

Wedensday [Sept.] 13. Got along pretty well.

Thursday [Sept. 14]. Pleasent day. Closed business & Wick Sweetser Brown Corwin Quarles & myself started home. Dined at Nobles—arrived at home at 4 P.M.

Friday [Sept.] 14 [15]. Butler preparing to go to Fountain court. Pleasant day. Our business increasing. A Mr. Bradshaw an English Gentleman bro't a letter of introduction from Reeves & McClean of Cincinnati. Bro' of Judge McC. Mr. B. dined with me. I found him intelligent.

92. Lewis F. Coppersmith. Besides practicing law he edited the Columbus *Advocate* in the late 1830s. *History of Bartholomew County, Indiana . . .* (Chicago: Brant & Fuller, 1888), pp. 437, 586, 589.

Saturday [Sept.] 15 [–16]. Much work to do in office.

[Sept. 17–Oct. 5]. During the residue of Sept. very pleasant. Mr. Butler went to the Fountain & Montgomery courts. I remained in the office these 2 weeks. Simon Y. went to Green county left on Friday the 29. On Sunday first went with Quarles to Morgan. Very pleasant weather. Got thro our business & returned Thursday [Oct.] 5. Got home after dark.

Sunday 8 Sept. [Oct.]. Went with Messrs. Corwin Quarles & Brown to Hendricks. Put up at Blakes. Mr. Butler also came after us. I staid Monday Teusday & Wedensday when I left in consequence of attending the agricultural fair which was to come on—on the 13 & last during the 14. I got home about dark—

Thursday [Oct.] 14 [12]. With Mr. Palmer & O Neel prepared for fair.[93]

Friday [Oct.] 13. Pleasent cool day—a very general turn out to our fair. At least 50 head of blooded cattle exhibited whereas in the year 1835 at the fair there was but 3 blooded cattle. The Sinnod in session—Mr. H[. . .] of Bloomington & an old man a deacon from Clinton stay with us.

Octr. 19. John Hill was married to Miss Susan Grant[94] at Mr. Drums on Market St. Mrs. F. Stoughtons wife Mrs. Richmond, Dorio, Louisa & Elijah attended. And Miss Anne F. All Dr. Sanders family present. Altho not satisfied with this match it perhaps is suitable—matters of this kind should rarely be interfered with. I learned John to read when he was only 3 or 4 years old. I have always had care over him. I am gratified that he is doing well in his business as a merchant which he has just commenced. He was an Orphan boy & it does me good to see him advance. I expect to see

93. Nathan B. Palmer was president, Hugh O'Neal secretary, and C.F. treasurer of the Marion County Agricultural Society, sponsor of the fair. The committee on arrangements included Palmer, O'Neal, William J. Brown, Alexander F. Morrison, and C.F.; C.F. also served as one of the judges. Indianapolis *Indiana Democrat,* May 31, September 20, 1837.

94. C.F. reported the marriage to Joseph Hill, his father-in-law and the father of John Hill, in a letter dated and postmarked October 14. The wedding apparently took place on the thirteenth. C.F. described Susan Grant as "the daughter of some Majr. or Genl. Grant of Kentucky. She is a young lady of very respectable relations here—is a cousin to our Dr. Sanders whose daughter recently married our Govr. Wallace. She is poor but knows how to work." Letter in Fletcher Papers.

him one day a useful business man with a well established character.

On this day 19[95] we permitted Cooley to go to Urbana Ohio to see his grandfather & great grand mother Oliver who is yet alive & in all probibility C. will be the only one of my childrin who will ever see her. I am under many obligations to her & especially for the loan of a shirt in the summer of 1817 when I first arrived in & near Urbana O. from N.E. I had lossed & worn out all my clothes & I was so destitute that I had but one shirt. The use of one she supplied for several weeks till I fortunately obtained the pattern of one which she made for me. She was a Randolph of Va. Grandfather Oliver a Yanky or Bostonian who left his native country before the Revolution on a trading voyage to the West India isles, was ship-recked in his fortunes—returned to Va. kept school, the last resort of all N. Englanders, & married—moved to Ky. at the close of the Revolution always followed teaching school—was an eccentrick man. In 1811 or 1812 some of his childrin having moved to Ohio he also moved. He kept school at Troy Miami Cty. At which Mrs. F. also our present Govr. Wallace attended. He died in 1813–4. His sons are scattered in Ky. O. Ind. &c. One Majr. Wm. Oliver distinguished himself during the late war &c. He is now a senater from Cincinnati Ohio.

Cooley left on the 19 [12] Octr. with old Mr. Luce in a covered wagon. I gave him $13. for expenses & paid Mr. L. $5. for his passage. I sent by him $5. in gold as a present to his old Grand Mother Oliver.

95. In his letter to Joseph Hill dated and postmarked October 14, C.F. wrote: "On the 12th we started James Cooley with Mr. Luce for Urbana & he will arrive at your house I hope before this reaches you. We had been thinking of letting him come up the last of this month & therefore his mother had not prepared his clothing as she otherwise would have done. He had no mittens & she authorized him to get a pair also to get Mother Hill to make him a round about coat if she has any jeans also if she thinks best a pair of pantaloons. We wish him to stay 10 days or 2 weeks then if the weather is fair & roads good we expect him to come home. We think it best for him to get you to take him to Springfield—then he can mark his trunk by nailing a piece of past board on it & directing it to be left at Brownings tavern Indianapolis or with Calvin Fletcher. . . . He can take out a shirt or two & socks & tie them up in a handkerchief & walk home. But if Mr. Luce is coming down in a month he can leave his trunk for him to bring."

Sunday 22 [–26] *Novr.* [*Oct.*] *1837*. Went in company with Messrs. Corwin Quarles & Colrick to Noblesvill. Very beautiful weather. Dined at Carters half wayhouse. There I saw the last [. . .] peaches. Our court lasted till Thursday 25 [26] when I returned home with Messrs. Quarles & Corwin. Arrived home about sundown. Found that Mrs. F. had gone to the wedding of Mr. Gregg & Miss Marilla Morris. An invitation was left for me. I also went. The Judge resided at the Dr. Sander place. House full. I soon returned home with Mrs. Richmond Louisa & Mrs. F.

Richardson & my brother Stoughton are about entering into partnership—the latter having boght out Mr. Bradley. This I like as I wish to R. get along.

Novr. 1. Sold Mr. B. Cole the farm we bought that is Mr. McCarty & myself bought of Dales heirs near Noblesville 155 acres for the sum of $3100. in cash notes ½ due 1st Decr.—other 1st March next with ten per [cent] interest. If we get our pay without much sacrifise we shall have done well &c.[96]

Michael is making cider at old Mr. Shields.

2 Novr. Got letter (2d letter from Cooley). Says he shall start the next Sunday or Monday [Nov.] 5 or 6.

Novr. 8. Received news by letter from Cooley that he had lost his money while helping his grandfather Hill make cider & wanted me to write him &c. By this I learn that he cannot get home & his grandfather H. is so strange a man that he divises no scheme for the boy to get home. I am very much disappointed. I anticipated the pleasure of seeing C. this week. I feel more on account of the mortification he will experience for having lost his mony than on any other account. He is sensative & will feel that he will be blamed by me. This he shall not experience. I regret he is not at home & still feel more mortified that his grand father should be so stupid or weak as not to help him home without suffering him to write to me for mony. I have written to D. Luce Esq. to supply him & send him home by the stage. He has written me that he is pleased with the country & can get into business &c. This I presume grows out of his mortification at the idea of returning having lost his mony &c.

96. See above, May 9, 1835.

Saturday Novr. 11. I this day sold Saml. Henderson my two shares of Hotel stock. This stock I was induced to subscribe in the fall of 1836 by Mr. McCarty just as I was getting on to my horse to go to the lake. I urged my brother Stoughton to take a share which I promised to take off his hands if Bradley his then partner did not acqu[i]esce in it. At first there was no objection but afterwards some dissatisfaction on the part of Bradley. I then promptly took it on myself at a great sacrifise. For these two shares by improvident management I have had to borrow from the Bank $2048. I have sold it estimating it at $2100. to S. Henderson for 750 acres of land entered by him & Andrew Wilson & Noah Noble on the cross cut canal Eel River in Owen or Clay county estimated at $4. per acre. The balance $900. I am to pay in cash notes ½ in 6 & the other in 12 mos. The stock will no doubt bear a good interest but I have a strong prejudice against it & feel & shall long feel that I deserved to be punished when ever I intrust any company to go on & make expenditures for me over which I can have no controle—a professional man has no business to concern himself in such matters. As to the land I possibly may realize $4. per acre in 5 or 6 years—but it will not burn up or rot down & can be better sold on execution or at private sale than stock in such a building as the Hotel to the building of which I ought no doubt to have contributed & would have willingly done so.

Messrs. Osbern & Chamberlin have recently commenced a new Agriculteral Journal.[97] I have been invited to & have fur-

97. The Indianapolis *Indiana Democrat* of August 2, 1837, and following issues, carried an advertisement stating that J. W. Osborn & Co. (John W. Osborn and E. Chamberlain) had purchased the office of the *Indiana Farmer* from M. M. Henkle and proposed to continue publication under the title "The Indiana Farmer and Stock Register." It was followed by a recommendation signed by James Blake, Nathaniel West, Nathan B. Palmer, and Moses M. Henkle, members of the State Board of Agriculture. The advertisement stated that "while every attention will be paid to the agricultural and stock raising interests of our state, the choicest literary gems, improvements in the mechanic arts, brief articles on the subject of education, internal improvements, home and foreign markets" would be included. Apparently no numbers of the first volume of the weekly, published by J. W. Osborn & Co., have survived. The Indiana State Library has volume 2, nos. 1–26 and no. 30 (September 8, 1838–April 6, 1839, and June 15, 1839). The publishers of the second volume are listed as John W. Osborn and Jacob S. Willets.

nished 3 articles—Sheep Killing Dogs—Agriculteral fairs—*Agricultural survey.*

Sunday Novr. 11 [*12*]. Pleasant day. Michael came in the morning. Went to church fore noon. Heard Mr. Findly preach. Read Talmages speech on the subtreasury.[98]

Monday [*Nov.*] *12* [*13*]. Pleasant day. Our C[ircuit] Court commenced its session. Present as lawyers Morrison Hiram Brown Cobern Quarls Butler Wm. J. Brown Sweetser Ketcham O Neel. Foreign—Corwin from Morgan Hammond from Greenfield.

During the week till Saturday nothing occurred worthy of notice except the report of the Whig triumph in N.Y. If true a glorious victory.

Sunday 19 Novr. Rainy day. Went with my family to M.C. [Methodist Church]. Heard Mr. Smith preach.

On Wedensday last sold 40 hogs weighing 80 cwt. neat at $3. per cwt. to Earl Reed. Last year pork was worth $4.50. Produce has greatly fallen.

Monday Novr. 20. This our 2d week of court. I shall be glad when it is over. This day the case of Cader Carter against Alfred Harrison & Saml. Henderson came on. This was a suit to recover damages for refusing to receive Carters vote at the Augt. election by Harrison inspector & Henderson Judge &c. Morrison & myself & Mr. Quarles for defendants Sweetser for plaintiff. We proved that Carter was not a *white* male inhabitant within the constitution—2d that there was no malice. The Jury found for defendants.[99]

James arrived this day from a Visit to his grandfather Hills in Ohio. Came in the stage. Had been up all night as the roads were bad. The stage turned over but we were greatly thankful that he had returned a live. While absent he lost his mony & D. Luce my friend supplied him. He lost the $10. in paper by keeping his handker-

98. The speech delivered by Senator Nathaniel P. Tallmadge of New York in the Senate on September 22, 1837, against the establishment of a sub-treasury system as proposed by the President. *Congressional Globe,* 25 Congress, 1 session, Appendix, pp. 229–36.

99. Cader Carter, who had one quarter Negro ancestry, had passed as a white man and voted in several elections. However, in 1836 he became active as a Jackson man and some Whigs, who knew of his African blood, challenged him at the August election, since only white male citizens were permitted to cast ballots. Dunn, *Indianapolis,* I, 240.

chief & Pocket book in the same pocket & by pulling out the the former the latter was lost.

Tuesday [*Nov.*] *21*. Cloudy & unpleasant, cool, cloudy.

[*Nov.*] 22. *Weds.* Snowed. Our Bank directors met.

[*Nov.*] 23. Stormy disagreeable weather.

[*Nov.*] 24. *Friday.* Trial of Bradley vs Patterson.

[*Nov.*] 25. Mr. Wygant from Marlboro N.Y. arrived.

Sunday [*Nov. 26*]. Went to church with boys A.M. Read life of Themistocles. In the P.M. went over to see Stoughton [and] Mr. Wygant. I have this day determined to go home this winter by the way of Washington &c if I can get fixed.

Monday [*Nov.*] 27. Pleasent morning.

[*Nov.*] *28–29 & 30*. Wet but warm weather. On the 28 a number of persons met at the state house to take preparitory steps to celebrate the recent whig victories in N.Y. Maine &c.

Friday Decr. first. Cause of U. states vs Laurie was heard in the District Court. Wet dissagreeable day.

Saturday Dec. 2. Rains. The members of the legislature pour in. The new Washington Hall[100] Just opened & the tavern opposite just closed in consequence of the failure of Dudley the late purchaser. Mrs. Dudley buried to day. Mr. Ingram is with us. On Thursday the last day of Novr. Miss Anne my brothers step daughter was married to Wm. Wygant of N.Y. at my bro. Stoughtons by Dr. Richmond. Mrs. [F.] myself Dorio Cooley Elijah & Calvin were present also Mr. & Mrs. Bradley & J. Bradly Richardson

100. This was the hotel erected at a cost of about thirty thousand dollars by the Washington Hall Hotel Company which included Daniel Yandes, James Blake, Samuel Henderson, Nicholas McCarty, and others, in which C.F. bought stock and subsequently sold it. The new hotel was designed and built by John Elder (see above, p. 316n). It was on the site of the old Washington Hall on the south side of Washington Street east of Meridian. The main edifice, fronting on Washington Street, had four stories and there were two two-story wings extending to the rear. The hotel had eighty-seven rooms "elegantly fitted up" and the dining room measured 75 by 40 feet. The local *Democrat* declared the new Washington Hall to be the "best house west of the Alleghenies" while the *Journal* thought it might be surpassed only by the Galt House in Louisville. The manager was Edmund Browning who had come to Indianapolis the year before. The Hall was the headquarters for the Whigs. Sulgrove, *History of Indianapolis*, p. 270; Indianapolis *Indiana Democrat*, November 22, 1837; Indianapolis *Indiana Journal*, November 25, 1837; Nowland, *Early Reminiscences of Indianapolis*, p. 432.

Michael & wife Mrs. Richmond &c. My brother Miles left Miss Ann here last summer in order to prevent her marrying Mr. W. a gentleman of decent fortune & good character from Ulster Cty. N.Y. A correspondence took place between the parties & by my brother Michaels Stoughtons & my consent he married her. We could see no good cause for Miles objections.

Sunday Decr. 3. I went to church to day with my boys. I read the life of Phocion in the morning—wrote a letter to Elijah. I have concluded to go to Vt. this winter—leave here in 2 weeks. I feel it my imperious duty to go & see my mother. I cannot leave home I fear next summer & never perhaps can have a better opportunity. I cannot expect anything but a disagreeable journy yet I am bound to make it. I trust in God it may prove a blessing to me. It is a pleasant day.

Monday Decr. 4. This day the Circuit Court of the U. States set for the first time in this state before which we have 23 or 24 cases. Judge McClean[101] organized the same with Holman the District Judge of the U.S. The court went thro the docket & adopted a rule admitting all the attorneys that practise in the Sp. [Supreme] Court of this state.

Our Legislature organized this day. I paid no attention to them as my other business called me away. Indeed I have scarcely visited them for the last 4 years while in session.

Teusday Decr. 5 1837. Pleasant day. Our court [met]. We went thro' with our cases in C[ircuit] Court U.S. I am asked to spend the eve at Mr. Blakes with Judges McClean Blackford Holman Dewey Porter[102] &c. Where I met them after dark. Judge McClean related some anecdotes as to his first service in Congress. Stated that a well regulated U. States Bank would prove a blessing to the country & if the late U. S. B[ank] had been in existance the late suspension would have not taken place &c. Holman was mute on the subject.

Wedensday [Dec.] 6. Pleasant day. Judges McClean Holman Dewey Blackford & Wick & Marshall Taylor dined with us.

Thursday [Dec.] 7. Pleasant. This is our first Thanksgiving

101. John McLean. See Pt. I, note 35.
102. John R. Porter, president judge of the first circuit, 1824–38.

ever held by proclimation of the Governor.[103] U.S. Court met read the minutes—adjourned. Divine service at M.E.C. Mr. Edy preached.

John Hill & wife, James Hill & wife Stoughton & wife Mr. Wygant & wife Mr. Drum & wife, Mrs. Richmond & Pendleton Mary Sweet aunt Betsy Louisa &c Messrs. Pratt & Ingram all dined with us. At night a large and respectable meeting was held at M.E. C[hurch] for the benefit of the poor in which all the churches joined.[104] This I view as a happy day. All the stores were shut & Indianapolis was in great harmony.

Friday [Dec.] 8. Judge McClean left & we finished nearly all our buseness in U. S. C[ourt]. Pleasant day.

Saturday [Dec.] 9. Rather a wet & dissagreeable day. Election for Judges in 1st C[ircuit] Court came on. Mr. Naylor elected.[105] I have run about preparing to go East. Bot set of Shakespeare & American Almanack.

Got a letter from Elijah informing me that he had paid $4000. for me at N.Y. & wished I would [in]vest the mony at least the interest in stock for his daughter.[106]

103. See *Messages and Papers relating to the Administration of Noah Noble,* pp. 564, 565.

104. The Indianapolis Benevolent Society was formally organized in 1835 with James Blake as president. C.F. and Mrs. Fletcher were active in it from its beginning. The annual meetings were held on Thanksgiving day evenings. In his diary for November 26, 1863, C.F. recorded: "At 7 went to Roberts Chapel to attend the Benevolent socty. . . . The socity numbers 28 years yet in truth it reaches back nearly 40 years. Our early settlers had an organization under Dr. Coe & others to reli[e]ve the poor at quite an early day." See also Sulgrove, *History of Indianapolis,* p. 379.

105. Isaac Naylor of Crawfordsville who succeeded John R. Porter.

106. Elijah Fletcher's letter is interesting in the picture that it gives of financial transactions of the day: "It gives me pleasure to inform you that your Draft for $4,000 is now in my possession. By the aid of our Cashier here [Lynchburg, Virginia] Mr. Sydnor, I have made out to place Funds in N. York and received the Draft yesterday. The exchange cost $61—and had it not been for the fortuitous action of Mr. Sydnor it would have cost more than $100. He had in neither Bank here any N. York Funds and he wrote to Richmond to the Mother Bank and none could be had there. But by sending to our Branch at Danville south of this the draft on N.Y. was obtained at this small price. Exchange between N. York and Philadelphia is as high as I paid for this—and between N. York & Richmond twice as much." Elijah Fletcher to C.F., November 27, 1837, Fletcher Papers.

Sunday 10 Dec. Cold a little snow. Went with family to hear Mr. Daily preach at M.E.C. Spent the rest of day reading with my boys.

Monday [Dec.] 11 [–15]. Cold morning, I must this day begin to prepare to fix to go [on] my journy East to see my Mother. I have written to E. to meet me at Washington.

From Monday to Friday was arranging my business for the East & on this day Friday 15 the camp meeting. Father Havens staid with us.

Saturday Decr. 16. Muddy dissagreeable weather.

Sunday [Dec.] 17. Went to church. Mr. Edy preached. Dissagreeable wet day.

Monday [Dec.] 18. Old Mr. Havens left. Had some trouble about his son's marrying Eutheny McGlaflin. Revs. Messrs. Robe & B[. . .] his rivals. Went to hear Mr. Owen[107] Geologist 2d lecture. Preparing my clothes to go East. Mr. Ingram here & we spend our time very happily.

Tuesday [Dec.] 19. Simon & I have nearly finishd this day my business for the East. Mr. Owen dined with us. Examined boys specimens. Said our state was rich with mineral. That the several rocks shown by our boys were of morain origin. No stage running as yet.

Weds. [Dec.] 20. Mr. Ingram is preparing to start tomorrow. It grows colder. Mr. Owen delivered his 3 lecture on Geology.

Thursday [Dec.] 21. Snow fell last night so as to cover the ground. Mr. Ingram started.

Friday [Dec.] 22. Cold. Was introduced to Govr. Hunt from N.H. Walpole[108] Gov. appointed by Jefferson to take possession

107. David Dale Owen. He had just completed the first Indiana geological survey. Walter B. Hendrickson, *David Dale Owen Pioneer Geologist of the Middle West* (*Indiana Historical Collections*, XXII, Indianapolis: Indiana Historical Bureau, 1943), p. 34.

108. Governor Seth Hunt of Walpole, New Hampshire. The American Cannel Coal Company was incorporated by an act of the Indiana General Assembly "for the purpose of mining for stone coal at Coal Haven in the county of Perry, and elsewhere in said county. . . ." Among those listed as members of the company was Seth Hunt. *Laws of Indiana*, 1837–38 (local), pp. 216–18.

[of] Louisiania after its purchase. He is the owner of Cole mines & is here to get an act of incorporation.

I am preparing my business to start the first opportunity East. Whig celebration on Monday christmass.

Saturday Decr. 22 [23] 1837. Have been settling with Mr. Merrill Hill &c partially. I have prepared myself with a new suit of clothes. I rather dread the journey as I expect very cold weather. Shall go thro by Columbus Ohio &c.

Mr. Bobb of N.Y. of the house of Varnum Fuller & Co. arrived here &c. In the eve Dr. Clark Senater from Lafayett & Kenton from White Cty. Representative[109] called &c. I have not felt as cool as I would desire in fixing up to go [on] such a Journy. The frequent vexatious calls & demands of & from all with whom I have business gets the better of my philosophy & good intentions. I suffer small things to vex me which alone retards the progress I so much desire to make. Mr. & Mrs. Wygant dined with us.

Bot one barrel of salt to day at $1.37½ per bushel.

[*Dec. 23*]. On the 23d at 12 the stage coachman Mr. Cheeseman informed me that he was ready to leave one hour before the expected time. So I left my office & run up to my house on lot 12 in 42 N.E. of the East Market square in Indianapolis. When I arrived at my house, it was crowded with visitors to take leave of me & to get me to do errands & I was packed with a number of thousands of dollars to bear East for our merchants besides a quantity Mr. Butler & myself had to carry East.

It was a bleek cold day yet serene. I took leave at ½ after 12 & we proceeded to Greenfield where I took tea at Mr. Knights. From thence on bad roads to Knightstown with 3 horses. A Mr. Lewis was in the stage Mr. James Morrison brother in law of Baltimore. Going down a hill near K. the fore horse got loose from the tongue the chain hitting against the legs—sprang forward & drawed the driver out of the wagon who fell between the wheels & the forehorse run away. By a good Providence the wheel horses stopped. This was

109. William M. Kenton, representative from the district composed of Jasper, Pulaski, and White counties.

one very severly cold night. I had to go to bed in a cold room.

Decr. 24 Sunday. We left at 4. Cold. Called at Mr. Raridens in Centerville supped at Richmond. Here left a bundle with E. Coffin. A very cold night—rode in an open waggon to Eaton & nearly froze. Roads so we could not only go in the walk. Arrived at E. at 12 very cold.

25 Dec. Christmas morning set out at 4. Arrived in Dayton at 4 P.M. No stir in the celebration of Christmass. Bought me a fir cap for $10. In the eve went to see Honl. Joseph Crain one of the first lawyers who settled at Dayton formerly Judge & present at the court in Logan Cty. on the bench when I made my first effort at the bar & lately a member of Congress. I spent several hours with him. He is rich with knowlege & experience said if he was to live over his life again the first thing he would do would be to gain distinction in his profession & then wealth by its practise & never meddle with politics until he expected to retire for life & then with a competence. He said the profession of the law was like a Jealous wife, would not suffer you to keep mistresses.

[Dec.] 26. Went to Springfield. Rode with a gentleman by name of C[. . .] from Fairfield. At Springfield I met all the literati of Cincinnati who had been to Columbus to attend an education convention Jacob Burnet[110] Messrs. Wright Worthington & Calvin Fletchers son. Here I became acquainted with a Mr. Skenk of Dayton young lawyer also Mr. Cumings of Springfield. Called on a Mr. Fletcher at the Buckeye house having stoped at Mr. Wordons.

At 1 o'clock we left for Columbus in the mail stage. Very cold night. We arrived at Robinsons tavern at Columbus about sunrise. Here I met Dr. Masgrove of Urbana Gov. Vance Wm. Baldwin Messrs. Gwins.

Decr. 26 [27] 1837. The legislature was in Session. I staid that day. Visited Mr. Gwins & Mr. Baldwins family & on 27 dined at Levina Gwins now Mrs. Anderson.

28 Decr. Left in compay with Honl. John McClean Mr. Stod-

110. Lawyer, United States senator, and author of *Notes on the Northwest Territory,* Burnet (1770–1853) was a leading figure in intellectual and social movements in Cincinnati and Ohio. *Dictionary of American Biography,* III, 294.

dart John C. Wright & Genl. Knap Dr. D[. . .] & a Mr. P[. . .] stage agent. We went to Zanesvill.

[*Dec.*] *29*. Arrived at Wheeling where Messrs. McClean Wright Stoddart Knap & Wright made a party to cross the mountains.

[*Dec. 30, 1837–Jan. 13, 1838*]. We passed on to Cumberland. On the 1 day of January 1838 we arrived at Fredrick Maryland about 12 o clock where we staid until Jany. 2d 1838 when we proceeded in the Railroad cars the first I ever saw to Washington where we arrived at Browns hotel about 7 in the eve. I staid there until Sunday the 6 of Jany. & left & arrived in Balt[imore] the same night. Put up at the Eaton house with Mr. Stoddart of Dayton. On the 8th we looked over Baltimore rather a foggy day. Here I had business with 2 clients to whom I paid money.

On the 9 We left in the cars & arrived the same eve at Philadelphia. Put up at the U. States Hotel opposite the U.S.B[ank]. Here I staid & called on about 30 clients for whom we were collecting mony until Thursday night Jany. 11 1838 & by rail road cars proceeded to N.Y. City. It was very cold. We arrived in N.Y.C. about 10 clock Jany. 12 1838. Put up at the City Hotel on the 12 & 13. I visited about 25 clients for the most of whom I had mony collected by Western merchants.

Saturday Jany. 13 [*–14*] *1838*. This P.M. at 4 left in a steam boat for Providence R.I. and on Sunday 14 arrived at that place about 10 o'clock. Took Railroad cars & arrived at Boston Mass. about ½ after 12. Put up at Tremont house.—Went to church in the P.M.

Monday [*Jan.*] *15*–[*25*]. Took cars for Lowel. Arrived there early & took stage for Walpole N.H. Had a Mr. Skinner of Windsor & several lady passengers. Arrived at Walpole about 12 & on Teusday Jany. 16 arrived at my mothers in Ludlow Vt. about 11 A.M. I staid here until Jany. 26. Had a pleasant visit—no snow—& very little cold weather.

Jany. 26 1838 [*–Feb. 3*]. I left for Chester & Walpole where I staid over night & on the 27 Mrs. Barton & myself passed down the Connecticut River thro' Springfield to Hartfort Connecticut where we staid over night. Teusday 27 left went thro' Weatherfield Middletown to New Haven where we arrived on Saturday night. On the Sunday 28th in the morning Sidney my brother Elijahs son called on me. He is a member of the college. I went to church both in the A.M. & P.M. at the chapel. On Mond. 29 left & went to N.Y. City. Staid 2 days went to Philadelphia. Spent one day. Here found Judge Wright & Genl. Knap. We left went to Baltimore together & I proceeded to Washington where I arrived Friday eve the 2d of Feby.

On Saturday Feby. 3 visited my friends [and] our delligation.

Sunday the 4 [*Feb.*]. My birth day I dined with Honl. Richard Fletcher[111] a member of Congress, 4th cousin & supped with the Honl. I. Fletcher[112] 3 cousin. I felt solemnly impressed that I had arrived at the meridian of life was 40 years of age. It was cold dry blustering day.

As a specimen of what I felt I give the following written on a leaf of Mr. Ingrams letter as I got out of bed in the morning at Browns Hotel in Washington on Sunday morn the 4th.

"Worldly mindedness alone would lead us to establish a character for truth & honesty; therefore scarcely the advancement of one step towards being a true christian.

"The parents who brought us into the world who have done so much for us, suffered much for us, had great care in procuring foode & raiment deserve our constant attention, our constant gratitude; therefore God who made us & Christ who redeemed us are entitled to our constant gratitude & praise.

"Great & important duties of life require our best thoughts & meditation in order to prepare us for some events which will when they arrive pass off in an hour, a moment. Therefore our present relation to God in this world which so far as relates to us will pass in a day or a year, & our condition & relation to him in eternity which has no end should have our most intense thoughts & meditation morning noon & evening, should be commenced with & bear relation to every transaction in life."

The above was written Browns Hotel W[ashington] C[ity] D.C. Feby. 4th 1838 the first thing I did in the 41st year of my age.

Sunday 4th 1838. This day I am 40 years old. . . . A very cold morning ground just covered with Snow. After breakfast went to the Honorable Isaac Fletchers Room to get the family delineation

111. Representative from Massachusetts, serving one term, 1837–39.

112. Isaac Fletcher, representative from Vermont, serving two terms, 1837–41.

I had furnished him with made out by Cousin Sally Parker.[113] Did not get it as his son had not drawn it off. I then returned & shortly after went to the room of the Honorable Richard Fletcher. The first of these gentlemen is a 3d cousin—the latter a 5th. He invited me to go [to] church with him at 10 at which hour we entered the presbyterian church. A Mr. McClean of Ohio a very young man preached on foreign missions 2 Revelation "& the leaves of the tree for the healing of the nations." After sermon I went again for the deliniation at the room of the Honorable Isaac F. whose son had finished 2 copies of the same. I then again returned to R.'s room where he inspected & admired this family exposition which he had never seen before. At 2 we dined at Noah Fletchers a cousin of R. with the honorable Sampson Mason of Ohio Cushing of Massachusetts & a member from Pennsylvania. After dinner returned to Browns Hotel there met with Merenus Willit of Rush Co. Indiana now a clerk in the land office also with Mr. White member from our state (Albert S.) who accompanied me to Mr. Grahams room who joined us in a walk to the Honorable Messrs. Ewings Dunns & Herrods room & on our way met the Mr. James Whitcomb Commissioner L[and] O[ffice] & he returned & went with us some distance when he & Mr. W. went to Messrs. Raridens & Smiths room.[114] I soon left my company & went to Isaac F.'s took tea spent the eve pleasantly. At 10 returned to my room. My reflections this day on the subject of Religion are of a pleasant & agreeable hue.[115]

113. Daughter of C.F.'s aunt, Bridget Fletcher, who married Isaac Parker. Sally Parker lived in Proctorsville, Vermont.

114. Albert S. White, Lafayette lawyer, William Graham of Vallonia, John Ewing of Vincennes, George H. Dunn, lawyer of Lawrenceburg, William Herod, lawyer of Columbus, and James Rariden of the Wayne County bar, were members of the Indiana Congressional delegation at this time. The seventh member was Ratliff Boon whom C.F. does not mention. Oliver H. Smith was one of Indiana's senators; the other was John Tipton whom C.F. might have been expected to see.

115. The Diary breaks off at this point and is not resumed until June 20, 1838. C.F. arrived home about February 14.

Diary of Sarah Hill Fletcher

Saturday Dec. 23d 1837. Cold & dry this day. Mr. F. started about half after 12 o clock to visit his mother in Vermont, also Baltimore Philadelpha N.Y. & Washington Sity expects to be gone 2 months & I can not describe my feelings on account of the many dangers he will have to be exposed. The childrin all have bad colds.

Sun. [Dec.] 24th. Very pleasant. Orindora Louisa E. C. & M. all went to meeting. Mr. W. & Ann Mr. and Mr. Knowlton came home with them & took dinner went to Sun. School came back and took tea. Cooly has a gethering in his head with violent pains. About half past 8 o clock in the eve it broak & run at his ear.

Mon. [Dec.] 25. No school Christmas. Mr. K. & dory & Martha all arose at 4 o clock & went to prayer meeting. Louisa prepared brekfast. Aunt betsy sent me a turkey for dinner. Uncle M. Mr. K. James Hill and wife John's wife Mrs. Penalton & Mr[s]. R. all dined with us. C. is beter. As for myself I feel very disconsolate.

Tues. [Dec.] 26th. Louisa went out to her Father's to stay all the week. Dory washed.

Wed. [Dec.] 27. Continues pleasant. I feel the responsibility very great when left alone as it respects the instruction of my childrin, but I ask the Lord for wisdom to direct them rite. About 7 o clock in the Eve I went to Mr. Johnstone's & took tea by invitation.

Thur. [Dec.] 28th. A delightful day the sun as bright as summer to day. I made a number of call's felt very gloomy. Cooly's throat is very sore yet.

Fri. [Dec.] 29th. I called to see Mr. Halladay's child who they thought very sick. Thawing very mudy rained a little in the Eve. No school this P.M.

Sat. [Dec.] 30th. Very pleasant. E. C. & M. prepared a great quantitay of wood for new year.

Sun. [*Dec.*] *31st.* Dory Martha Louisa E. & M. all wen[t] to church. Calvin assisted me in preparing dinner. Mr. K. & his cousin dined with us. In the Eve the same Gentlemen O. & M. went to church did not return till one o clock. Stoughton insisted on being awakened at mid night to see the new Year drive out the old one. This day Mr. W. & Ann started to new York.

Mon. January 1st [*1838*]. Cloudy. All up at 5 o clock. Cooly put on his cloak went down Town and got some powder. I indulged them all in fireing a little canon at home. Calvin imploid himself the greater part of the day in puting leathe[r] straps and buckel's on scates. At 8 o clock in the Eve all retired to bed but myself. The clock strikes ten and all are raped in sleep. Martha went to the farm.

Tues. [*Jan.*] *2d.* Clowdy and muddy. Cooly started to school again, Dory washed. Stoughton has been very good to day. He has read and spelled 3 lessons heard me read with some attention. I read a letter which came from Mr. F. to Mr. Butler wrote from Columbus Ohio. In the Eve Cooly visited Charles Smith.

Wed. [*Jan.*] *3d.* It is yet warm and clowdy. In the P.M. Mrs. Johnstone and I rode out to the farm. Martha was very well satisfied. Aunt Betsy not very well. I think I shall let M. stay all winter if they want her.

Thu. [*Jan.*] *4.* Rained nerely all day. In the Eve Cooly went down Town to buy a book to studdy algebra. E. delivered a lecture on geologe done it with as much gravity as if he under stood all about it. Mr. K. staied all night with us fixed a bedstid for us. It is 10 oclock in the Eve begining to blow cold.

Fri. [*Jan.*] *5th.* Mr. K. quite sick I gave him some oil which relieved him. Today rathe(r) cool and windy.

Sat. [*Jan. 6*]. Cooly & Cordy Sharp are collecting books which were subscribed to their society. Mrs. Bates sent for me to spend the P.M. with her. After 4 o clock I took sister & the babe and staied till 8 oclock. Very lite & good walking.

Sun. [*Jan.*] *7th.* Rained all day thundered & lightened considerable. In the Eve turned cold and snowed before day.

Mon. [*Jan. 8*]. Cleare & cold. In the Eve Dory went to stay all night with Mrs. Richmond. Miles read to me about Parley's adventures. I bound a copy book for Miles.

Tues. [Jan.] 9th. I went to Stougton's store & John Hill's also and bought some clothing for myself & boys a flanlel dress & shawl for Martha. Came home about noon it was geting very cold. I read a letter today from Miles to Michal F. in which he blamed Mr. F. [for] Ann's marriage.

Wed. [Jan.] 10th. Very cold indeed. Uncle M. Killed a beef sent one half to me in the Eve. Harry cut & salted it. Cooly went to writing school, he is very ambishious & improves very fast.

Thur. [Jan. 11]. Still very cold. E. & C. commenced Viri romae. It is very hard for them to get along in it. I made a report in writing of what I had done & sent to the benevolent society. This day I have not heard Stoughton read any. After four oclock I went to Mr. Drum's & took tea. It is now near 12 oclock. Louisa is writing her composition to hand in to morrow morning.

Fri. [Jan.] 12th. Very cleare, & not quite so cold. Today I have been spining some. About four oclock I recieved a long letter from Mr. F. written in Washing(ton) City. It arived here the ninth day after it was mailed. I was much elated & a little disapointed when I read it, and found no directions where to send a letter that Mr. F. could get it.

Sat. [Jan.] 13th. Thawing. The boys prepared wood wrote to their Father in the fore noon and in the P.M. they all went to scate on the ice. They came home satisfied.

Sun. [Jan.] 14th. Rainy. Our family all went to meeting but myself & little childrin. I wrote a letter [to] Mr. Fletcher.

Mon. [Jan.] 15th. A delightful day look's like spring.

Tues. [Jan.] 16th. Pleasant. In the Eve Louisa Cooly Elijah & Miles all went to hear a lecture on chemistry & philosophy.[116] Calvin went down Town to buy a lattin book.

116. The lecturer was Dr. Luke Munsell. The Indianapolis *Indiana Journal*, January 20, 1838, stated: "We are pleased to learn that Dr. Munsell intends to deliver a course of Lectures on Chemistry and Natural Philosophy this winter. He delivered an Introductory Lecture on Tuesday evening last. . . . He will lecture again on Saturday evening at early candle lighting. . . . The Lecture room is on the second floor of the County Seminary." Dr. Munsell came to Indianapolis from Kentucky where he had served as State Engineer and published a map of that state. He also made a map of the town of Indianapolis, which he copyrighted May 30, 1836. It shows the area of the Ralston Plat and outlots and indicates the location of such features as the State House, Governor's House, Courthouse, churches, State Bank, Indianapolis branch of the bank, the Female

Wed. [Jan.] 17th. Damp & misty. Mrs. Penilton came and staid all day with us. In the Eve I wrote a 2d letter to Mr. F.

Thur. [Jan.] 18th. A little cooler. In the P.M. I attended a meeting of the benevolent society. In the Eve it turned very cold blowed & snowed. It is now after a 11 oclock all are sleeping but myself.

Fri. [Jan.] 19th. Still cold. Aunt betsy sent two turkeys in to me & one to Stoughton very nise & fat. Mrs. Penalton & Mrs. Richmond & Laura came & took dinner with us.

Sat. [Jan.] 20th. Very cold. Louisa washed in the P.M. Mr. Cobern's niece came & took tea with us.

In the Eve Cooly bought tickets for himself Elijah & Louis[a] two dollar's each & one for Mrs. Richmond five dollars to be admited at the chemical & philosophy lectures one term.

Sun. [Jan.] 21st. Ground covered with snow but pleasant. Louisa Orindora & all the boys went to meeting.

Mon. [Jan.] 22d. Cold.

Tues. [Jan.] 23d. Snow still on the ground but very pleasant. Louisa James Hill & myself went to uncle M.'s to celebrate the aniversary of Richerdsn's birth, Mrs. Curry & son were there. Aunt betsy prepared an excelant diner. We returned home before sun down.

Wed. [Jan.] 24th. Warm sun. Calvin hurt himself riding on a sled & did not go to school.

Thur. [Jan.] 25th. Clowdy & rainy in the P.M.—rained very hard, and uncle Michael halled some wood.

Fri. [Jan.] 26th. Turned cold & froze all day. Mrs. P. & John's wife helped me quilt a skirt.

Sat. [Jan.] 27th. Clowdy all day & thawing. To day the boys have had fine sport halling a large box on a sled with ropes & worked it for an ingine. Calvin & Miles have split & sawed a great deal of stove wood the two last Eves. Cooly & Elijah wrote to Mr. Ingram. Stoughton went down town and bought some sugar & [. . .].

Sun. [Jan.] 28th. The are [air] so cold & Keen that it makes a

---

Institute, County Seminary, and the old and new burying grounds. He also established the first Daguerrean gallery in Indianapolis. Dunn, *Indianapolis,* I, 52, 117.

person's hands smart when they s[t]ep out. The boys all went to church but Elijah he has a very sore throat.

Mon. [Jan.] 29th. Not quite so cold.

Tues. [Jan.] 30th. Very pleasant but muddy. I went to Stoughton's had to stay till late in the Eve in consequence of the mud.

Wed. [Jan.] 31st. Quite Cold froze all day. Mrs. Bradly made me a visit & Jame's wife came and helped me quilt.

Thu. 1st of Febuary. The coldest day we have had this winter. E. has not been to school this week.

Fri. [Feb.] 2d. Continues cold.

Sat. [Feb.] 3d. The ground is covered with snow. The boys are imploied makeing guns ornamenting them with tin.

Sun. [Feb.] 4th. Not quite so cold. All the boys went to church. Mrs. Carlile's sister came home with Louisa from sunday school & staied all night.

Mon. [Feb.] 5th. Clear & cold. C. & E. went to a party at Mr. Woods.

Tues. [Feb.] 6th. Quite a pleasant day. Dory & Mariah Hill went out to Uncle Michaels. My babe has been quite unwell all day.

Wed. [Feb.] 7th. Cloudy began to rain, the ground being froze it was soon covered with water. Snow began to fall very fast had it not been for the water it would of measured six inches. In the night it turned cold. Mr. Boxly is here.

Thur. [Feb.] 8th. Still cold I have a quilt in the frame.

Fri. [Feb.] 9th. Cleare & very cold. Mr. B. started home.

Sat. [Feb.] 10th. Not quite so cold, snowed and blowed. The boys all went to their muster. In the Eve turned very cold. I think the coldest night & morn that we have had this winter.

Sun. [Feb.] 11. Cooly has an other attact of the ear ach broke & run again. Very clear.

Mon. [Feb.] 12th. Not so cold. James Hill & Harry butcthered our hogs. I read a letter from Mr. F. written at Wa. C. he was on his way home. Snowed in the night.

Tues. [Feb.] 14th. Cloudy & very cold, snow blowing & drifting which is about six inches deep.

The Jesse Fletcher Family

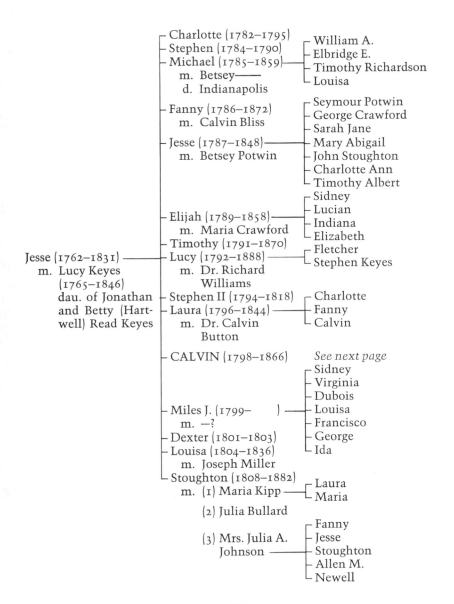

- Jesse (1762–1831) m. Lucy Keyes (1765–1846) dau. of Jonathan and Betty (Hartwell) Read Keyes
  - Charlotte (1782–1795)
  - Stephen (1784–1790)
  - Michael (1785–1859) m. Betsey—— d. Indianapolis
    - William A.
    - Elbridge E.
    - Timothy Richardson
    - Louisa
  - Fanny (1786–1872) m. Calvin Bliss
  - Jesse (1787–1848) m. Betsey Potwin
    - Seymour Potwin
    - George Crawford
    - Sarah Jane
    - Mary Abigail
    - John Stoughton
    - Charlotte Ann
    - Timothy Albert
  - Elijah (1789–1858) m. Maria Crawford
    - Sidney
    - Lucian
    - Indiana
    - Elizabeth
  - Timothy (1791–1870)
  - Lucy (1792–1888) m. Dr. Richard Williams
    - Fletcher
    - Stephen Keyes
  - Stephen II (1794–1818)
  - Laura (1796–1844) m. Dr. Calvin Button
    - Charlotte
    - Fanny
    - Calvin
  - CALVIN (1798–1866) *See next page*
  - Miles J. (1799–) m. —?
    - Sidney
    - Virginia
    - Dubois
    - Louisa
    - Francisco
    - George
    - Ida
  - Dexter (1801–1803)
  - Louisa (1804–1836) m. Joseph Miller
  - Stoughton (1808–1882) m. (1) Maria Kipp
    - Laura
    - Maria
  - (2) Julia Bullard
  - (3) Mrs. Julia A. Johnson
    - Fanny
    - Jesse
    - Stoughton
    - Allen M.
    - Newell

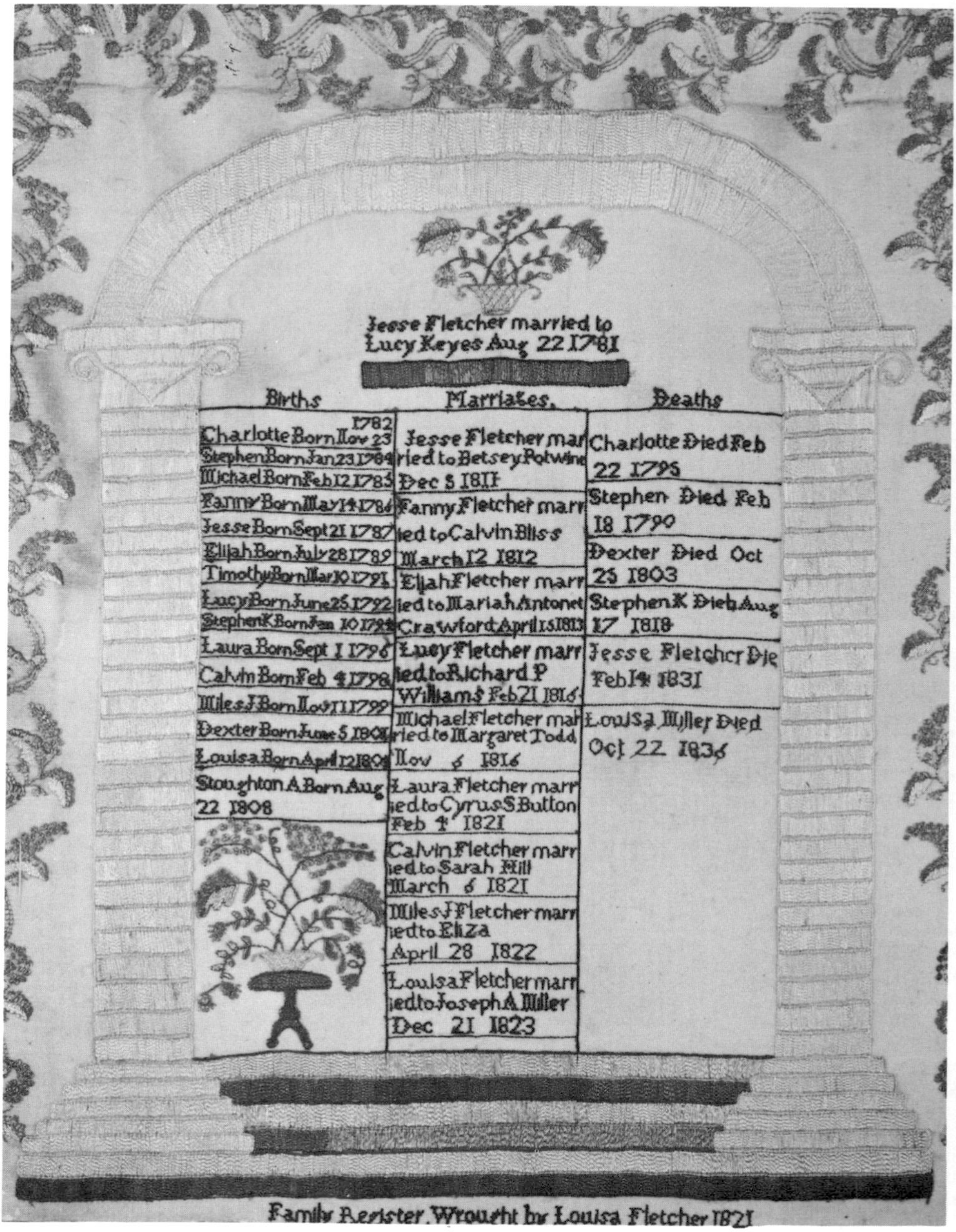

FLETCHER HODGES, JR.

Sampler showing the births, marriages, and deaths of the children of Jesse and Lucy Keyes Fletcher to 1836, made by Louisa Fletcher Miller. The record of Louisa's death, October 22, 1836, is recorded by another hand.

The Calvin Fletcher Family

Calvin Fletcher (1798–1866)
m. (1) Sarah Hill (1801–1854)
(2) Mrs. Keziah Price Lister

- James Cooley (1823–1901)
  m. (1) Henrietta Malan
  (2) Frederika Smith
  (3) Mrs. Elizabeth Curryer
- Elijah Timothy (1824–1877)
  m. (1) Eunice Allen
  (2) Mrs. Catherine Yandes Carnahan
- Calvin, Jr. (1826–1903)
  m. Emily Beeler
- Miles Johnson (1828–1862)
  m. Jane M. Hoar
- Stoughton Alonzo (1831–1895)
  m. (1) Ruth Elizabeth Barrows
  (2) Marie Louise Bright
- Maria Antoinette (1833–1860)
  m. C. C. Hines
- Ingram (1835–1903)
  m. Gertrude Newman
- William Baldwin (1837–1907)
  m. Agnes O'Brien
- Stephen Keyes (1840–1897)
  m. (1) Mary Catherine Malott
  (2) Laura Maxwell
- Lucy Keyes (1842–1918)
  m. C. C. Hines
- Albert Eliot (1846–1919)
  m. Eliza L. Sharpe

The Hill Family

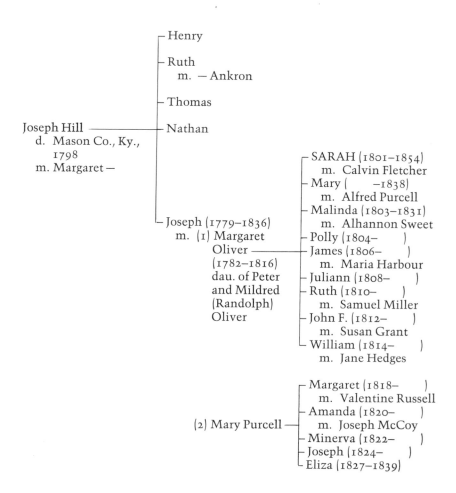

- Joseph Hill
  d. Mason Co., Ky., 1798
  m. Margaret —
  - Henry
  - Ruth
    m. — Ankron
  - Thomas
  - Nathan
  - Joseph (1779–1836)
    m. (1) Margaret Oliver (1782–1816) dau. of Peter and Mildred (Randolph) Oliver
    - SARAH (1801–1854)
      m. Calvin Fletcher
    - Mary (–1838)
      m. Alfred Purcell
    - Malinda (1803–1831)
      m. Alhannon Sweet
    - Polly (1804–)
    - James (1806–)
      m. Maria Harbour
    - Juliann (1808–)
    - Ruth (1810–)
      m. Samuel Miller
    - John F. (1812–)
      m. Susan Grant
    - William (1814–)
      m. Jane Hedges

    (2) Mary Purcell
    - Margaret (1818–)
      m. Valentine Russell
    - Amanda (1820–)
      m. Joseph McCoy
    - Minerva (1822–)
    - Joseph (1824–)
    - Eliza (1827–1839)

Index